The SAGE Encyclopedia of Industrial and Organizational Psychology

Second Edition

Editorial Board

The SAGE Encyclopedia of Industrial and Organizational Psychology

Second Edition

Editor
Steven G. Rogelberg

Volume 3

Los Angeles | London | New Delhi | Singapore | Washington DC | Melbourne

FOR INFORMATION:

SAGE Publications, Inc.
2455 Teller Road
Thousand Oaks, California 91320
E-mail: order@sagepub.com

SAGE Publications Ltd.
1 Oliver's Yard
55 City Road
London, EC1Y 1SP
United Kingdom

SAGE Publications India Pvt. Ltd.
B 1/I 1 Mohan Cooperative Industrial Area
Mathura Road, New Delhi 110 044
India

SAGE Publications Asia-Pacific Pte. Ltd.
3 Church Street
#10-04 Samsung Hub
Singapore 049483

Printed in the United States of America

Library of Congress Cataloging-in-Publication Data

Names: Rogelberg, Steven G., editor.

Title: The Sage encyclopedia of industrial and organizational psychology / edited by Steven G. Rogelberg, University of North Carolina, Charlotte.

Other titles: Encyclopedia of industrial and organizational psychology

Description: 2nd edition. | Thousand Oaks, California : Sage, [2017] |

Includes bibliographical references and index. | Earlier edition published as: Encyclopedia of industrial and organizational psychology.

Identifiers: LCCN 2016018937 | ISBN 978-1-4833-8689-8 (hardcover)

Subjects: LCSH: Psychology, Industrial—Encyclopedias. | Organizational behavior—Encyclopedias.

Classification: LCC HF5548.8 .E498 2017 | DDC 158.7—dc23 LC record available at https://lccn.loc.gov/2016018937

This book is printed on acid-free paper.

Acquisitions Editor: Maureen Adams
Developmental Editor: Sanford Robinson
Editorial Assistant: Jordan Enobakhare
Production Editor: David C. Felts
Reference Systems Manager: Leticia Gutierrez
Copy Editors: Sarah Duffy, Jim Kelly, Amy Marks, Melinda Masson
Typesetter: C&M Digitals (P) Ltd.
Proofreaders: Ellen Brink, Jeff Bryant, Talia Greenberg, Gretchen Treadwell
Indexer: Will Ragsdale
Cover Designer: Candice Harman
Marketing Manager: Leah Watson

16 17 18 19 20 10 9 8 7 6 5 4 3 2 1

Contents

List of Entries

N

Narcissism

In Greek mythology, Narcissus was a proud, attractive man who spurned others, became infatuated by his own reflection in a pool, and ultimately perished as a result of his self-absorption. In contemporary psychology, narcissism is viewed as a relatively stable personality dimension involving an exaggerated sense of self-importance, insatiable need for praise, and over-the-top expressions of superiority and entitlement. While most people hold positive self-views (i.e., believing they are above average on desirable qualities), narcissists take this bias to the extreme (i.e., believing they are better than everyone else). Their fixation on positive self-worth motivates a relentless quest to convince the world they are exceptional (e.g., wearing flashy clothes, bragging, having an exorbitant number of Facebook friends). Narcissists tend to be viewed as pompous showoffs and tiresome braggarts, and to react with strong hostility when their superiority is challenged.

Two Roads to Magnificence: Promotion and Protection

Once considered a personality disorder, narcissism is now understood as a subclinical trait ranging from adaptive levels of self-assuredness to maladaptive insecurity and consisting of several subtypes (e.g., grandiose vs. vulnerable). Current multidimensional narcissism measures include the Narcissistic Personality Inventory (NPI), Narcissistic Admiration and Rivalry Questionnaire (NARQ), Narcissistic Grandiosity Scale (NGS), Pathological Narcissism Inventory (PNI), and Five Factor Narcissism Inventory (FFNI). Reflected in all these instruments is a historical divide on how to understand a trait replete with paradoxes: socially charming yet emotionally isolated, unusually confident but easily offended, and craving praise but giving little in return. The incongruities have led to many questions. Are narcissists well adjusted or extremely vulnerable? Are they oblivious or self-aware of their conceit? Why do they spurn the people they seek to have admire them?

The NARQ framework addresses these contradictions by proposing two separate but related social pathways to gaining and maintaining feelings of grandiosity: *admiration* and *rivalry*. The model proposes narcissists sustain good feelings about themselves by (a) acquiring admiration through assertive self-promotion and (b) preventing failure through antagonistic self-protection. Further, each aspect has two sources: the self and other people. *Admiration from self* is buttressed by self-serving biases, such as overestimating capabilities, viewing the self as especially attractive and capable, and taking credit for randomly determined victories (e.g., gambling). Such biases, in turn, propel the narcissist's tremendous swagger, which draws *admiration from others*. The initial social interest makes the narcissist's ego even bigger, reinforcing subsequent self-enhancement strategies. Consequently, narcissists reinstate a grandiose self by constantly thinking and acting in ways to receive ongoing praise.

When the hollow, self-centered focus of the narcissist is revealed, others express annoyance and admiration tactics give way to narcissistic self-protection. Rather than reflect on possible shortcomings, narcissists counteract by tearing down others. *Passive rivalry* occurs by diminishing others through feeling superior to and devaluing them. Thus, narcissists believe they deserve better accommodations, discount others' opinions, and have little empathy for the people they step on. Romantic partners are trophies and employees are means to personal ends. Beyond such passive defenses, the narcissist whose ego is threatened (especially in public forums) is likely to engage in *rivalry with others* through outright aggression and hostility. Dangerous people, from playground bullies to warmongering dictators, include those holding unrealistically favorable self-views. They have an inability to take criticism, harbor feelings of ill will, and respond aggressively to derogatory comments. Hence, the rivalry component of the model explains how narcissists are able to preserve favorable self-views in the face of contradictory evidence.

Unfortunately, combining admiration and rivalry tactics leads narcissists to undermine the very goal they seek. The admiration path yields immediate interpersonal successes, where expressive and dominant self-presentations are effective (seeking admiration). This pathway explains why narcissists tend to be popular in short-term acquaintances and quickly emerge as leaders in group discussions. Over time, however, their antagonistic defenses tend to destroy otherwise beneficial alliances. Close associates are denigrated; rules are broken; relationships are ruined. Their unwillingness to consider the input and feelings of others explains why, in the long run, narcissists tend to garner conflict and negative peer evaluations. Thus, the tragedy of narcissists is that their addiction to feeling good about themselves demands that they defend themselves aggressively against an increasingly hostile social environment. In light of the two noted pathways, a cursory review is offered on research linking narcissism to job performance and leadership.

Job Performance. Narcissists' exaggerated positive self-view leads them to overrate their intelligence, creativity, and achievements, which, in the workplace, surfaces as inflated perceptions of job performance and organizational citizenship. On the upside, a narcissist's extreme confidence can engender charm, favoring approvals from others in short-term interactions (e.g., interviews, presentations). Narcissists also work harder on socially visible tasks signaling strong capabilities (e.g., oral exams, strategic initiatives, championship games), as success on such tasks is expected to serve impressions of superiority. On the downside, however, this strategy can deteriorate over time as others come to see the narcissist as in it "for the glory" rather than genuine effectiveness, evidenced by the skirting of mundane tasks (e.g., reading, daily tasks, practice sessions) and blaming coworkers or evaluators for personal failures. Because they view themselves as having no room for improvement, narcissists perform only when it provides opportunity to display self-perceived talents. If they fail, narcissists defend their self-worth by attacking or ignoring the validity of the feedback. Thus, narcissists put effort into tasks expected to attract admiration (both personally and from others) while avoiding routine tasks and remaining oblivious to signs of failure.

Narcissists also engage in more counterproductive and unethical behaviors that harm organizations and their members. Because they see themselves as uniquely "above others," they tend to feel entitled to more credit and rewards. This entitlement reflects a rejection of social norms, making narcissists more likely to ignore moral prohibitions against misconduct. Further, their self-serving mindset can lead to rationalization of bad behavior. As a result, narcissists tend to hold exaggerated expectations of what they are owed and seek to restore equity through stealing, aggression (i.e., "getting even"), and other deviant acts. Indeed, meta-analytic evidence suggests narcissism has a much stronger positive association with counterproductive work behaviors relative to Machiavellianism and psychopathy (similarly aversive characteristics).

Leadership. Positions of power are a natural draw for narcissists because the roles offer a social stage for obtaining status, material goods, and influence, all of which feed a positive self-concept. For CEOs, narcissism has been linked to (a) self-promotion, such as bigger personal portraits in annual reports and use of more personal pronouns in press releases (e.g., I, me), and (b) daring strategic initiatives, such as making multiple sizeable acquisitions and adopting discontinuous technologies. The boldness of their strategic initiatives tends to be amplified when important people (e.g., stakeholders, media) are paying attention, leading to unusually large organizational gains and losses. These findings suggest that narcissistic CEOs enjoy making visible decisions, swing big in the hope others will notice and, regardless of organizational performance, claim a greater share of organizational resources. This profile fits with the narcissist as pursuing a maximal gain strategy aimed at capitalizing on success, no matter how risky. For narcissistic CEOs, winning and status are especially powerful motivators, while maintaining the status quo offers little to affirm their sense of grandiosity. The desire for a legacy is why narcissistic leaders devote their actions to the art of impressing spectators while downplaying the possibility (or reality) of failure, all the while treating organizations and workers as tools for engaging their ego-driven desires.

Narcissism's link with leadership effectiveness depends on context and outcome. Narcissism is beneficial to organizational and team success in situations where the narcissist's personal goals (a) coincide with turbulent environments and (b) converge with follower and institutional aims. In times of strife, a narcissist's bold vision may provide the requisite force for overcoming inertia in the face of change. Their charismatic appeal and audacity to step forward help narcissists emerge as leaders, take risks, and make things happen. These actions are beneficial when narcissists identify with the organization or share team rewards; in such cases, the narcissist's need for glory is aligned with broader goals. These links allow narcissists to prove their talents to the world and, in the process, carry others along for the ride. On the other hand, narcissists' disregard for others can lead them to deliver catastrophic disasters, downplay negative consequences, and pursue their own success at their teams' expense. Indeed, presidential narcissism is positively associated with winning the popular vote and achieving consensus of greatness but at the same time carries higher risk of unethical behavior and, in extreme cases, impeachment proceedings. Hence, narcissistic leaders are mixed blessings: They can be forces of needed change and renewal but, in the long run, may blindly pursue personal agendas and callously harm others in the process.

Daniel V. Simonet

See also Machiavellianism; Personality; Self-Esteem; Trait Approach to Leadership; Workplace Incivility

Further Readings

Back, M. D., Küfner, A. C., Dufner, M., Gerlach, T. M., Rauthmann, J. F., & Denissen, J. J. (2013). Narcissistic admiration and rivalry: Disentangling the bright and dark sides of narcissism. *Journal of Personality and Social Psychology, 105,* 1013–1037.

Campbell, W. K., & Miller, J. D. (2011). *The handbook of narcissism and narcissistic personality disorder: Theoretical approaches, empirical findings, and treatments.* Hoboken, NJ: Wiley.

Chatterjee, A., & Hambrick, D. C. (2007). It's all about me: Narcissistic chief executive officers and their effects on company strategy and performance. *Administrative Science Quarterly, 52,* 351–386.

Grijalva, E., & Harms, P. (2013). Narcissism: An integrative synthesis and dominance complementarity model. *Academy of Management Perspectives, 28,* 108–127.

Morf, C. C., & Rhodewalt, F. (2001). Unraveling the paradoxes of narcissism: A dynamic self-regulatory processing model. *Psychological Inquiry, 12,* 177–196.

Wallace, H. M., & Baumeister, R. F. (2002). The performance of narcissists rises and falls with perceived opportunity for glory. *Journal of Personality and Social Psychology, 82,* 819–834.

NATIONAL INSTITUTE FOR OCCUPATIONAL SAFETY AND HEALTH/OCCUPATIONAL SAFETY AND HEALTH ADMINISTRATION

The U.S. Congress passed the Occupational Safety and Health Act of 1970, which resulted in the formation of two federal agencies: the National Institute for Occupational Safety and Health (NIOSH) and the Occupational Safety and Health Administration (OSHA). These agencies were established to reduce and prevent work-related injuries, illnesses, and deaths. Although both organizations focus on work-related health issues, they serve distinct purposes and are located in different branches of the U.S. government. Often, NIOSH and OSHA work together in an effort to protect worker health and safety.

National Institute for Occupational Safety and Health

As part of the Centers for Disease Control and Prevention in the U.S. Department of Health and Human Services, NIOSH was established to conduct research and make recommendations pertaining to work-related injury and illness prevention. Headquartered in Washington, DC, and Atlanta, Georgia, NIOSH has offices and research laboratories in Anchorage, Alaska; Cincinnati, Ohio; Denver, Colorado; Morgantown, West Virginia; Pittsburgh, Pennsylvania; and Spokane, Washington. Although all research facilities study occupational health, most of the NIOSH investigations on occupational stress are conducted by researchers in the Work Organization and Stress-Related Disorders program at the Cincinnati research laboratory. In 1996, NIOSH established the National Occupational Research Agenda (NORA) as a partnership program to encourage innovative occupational safety and health research collaborations and promote improved workplace practices.

Organizational Composition

Of NIOSH's more than 1,200 employees, many are research staff. Researchers at NIOSH work in multidisciplinary teams, representing a wide range of disciplines, such as epidemiology, industrial hygiene, occupational medicine, nursing, psychology, safety, engineering, chemistry, and statistics. The institute has eight research divisions:

- *Office of Mine Safety and Health Research:* addresses the safety and health hazards of mining (e.g., coal, metal) and disaster prevention (e.g., mine ventilation, explosives safety, detection/prevention of collapse of mine roofs)
- *Division of Applied Research and Technology:* aims to prevent occupational injury and illness, assesses intervention effectiveness, and examines ergonomic and organization of work factors (e.g., psychosocial factors) in work-related illness and injury
- *Division of Surveillance, Hazard Evaluations and Field Studies:* conducts systematic, ongoing research to examine patterns of work-related illnesses, exposures, and hazardous agents in the U.S. workforce; studies the causes of work-related diseases; and provides technical help on occupational safety and health issues to other organizations
- *Education and Information Division:* creates and disseminates information, makes recommendations to prevent occupational injuries/diseases, and develops risk assessments
- *Division of Respiratory Disease Studies:* aims to identify, evaluate, and prevent occupational respiratory diseases (e.g., asthma); administers legislatively mandated medical services for coal miners; and researches the quality of respiratory devices
- *Division of Safety Research:* takes a public health approach to occupational injury prevention (including traumatic occupational injuries) and incorporates surveillance, analytic epidemiology, safety engineering, and health communication
- *Health Effects Laboratory Division:* conducts laboratory research on causes, prevention, and control of biological health problems resulting from workplace exposure to hazardous substances; develops interventions; and designs, tests, and implements communications to control and prevent workplace safety/health problems
- *National Personal Protective Technology Laboratory:* aims to prevent and reduce occupational disease, injury, and death for workers who use personal protective technologies (e.g., respirators, chemical-resistant clothing)

The James Zadroga 9/11 Health and Compensation Act of 2010 led to the establishment of the World Trade Center Health Program. NIOSH began administering this program in 2011 to provide medical monitoring and treatment for emergency responders, recovery and cleanup workers, and volunteers who provided assistance after the September 11, 2001, terrorist attacks on the World Trade Center in New York City, on the Pentagon in Arlington, Virginia, and in Shanksville, Pennsylvania. This health program also provides health evaluations and treatment for survivors of the New York City disaster area.

Mission

The mission of NIOSH is to help ensure safe and healthful conditions for workers by providing scientific research and practical solutions to reduce risks of injury and death in industries such as agriculture, construction, and mining. NIOSH also supports research on emerging problems in the 21st century workplace and workforce. To accomplish this mission, NIOSH has three primary objectives: (1) to conduct research in an effort to reduce work-related injuries and illnesses; (2) to encourage the safety and health of workplaces through interventions, offering recommendations and building capabilities in safe work practices and conditions; and (3) to enhance workplace safety and health in the United States through collaborative partnerships.

Functions

To further its mission, NIOSH engages in both intramural and extramural programs, which are aligned to increase research in the NORA priority areas. Intramural programs include the research conducted at the eight NIOSH research divisions described previously. Extramural programs provide opportunities for researchers at other institutions to conduct quality research, receive education and training, and develop worldwide collaborations in the area of occupational safety and health. As part of its extramural research and training program, NIOSH sponsors 19 Education and Research Centers (ERCs), which offer competitive pilot grants for doctoral students and junior faculty who conduct research related to occupational health and safety. The ERCs also provide continuing education programs for practicing professionals as well as training project grants for occupational safety and health professionals and researchers.

Another major function of NIOSH is to serve as a national resource for agricultural health and safety. NIOSH established the Agricultural Safety and Health Centers to provide education, research, prevention, and intervention programs related to occupational disease and injury of agricultural workers and their families.

In addition, NIOSH runs state-based surveillance programs to enhance worker safety and health. Activities include providing grants and cooperative agreements to build competencies in state worker safety, evaluating hazards in the workplace and recommending solutions when requested, funding occupational safety and health

research at academic institutions and other organizations, and supporting occupational safety and health training programs.

The NIOSH Web site offers information on occupational health, including NIOSH publications, access to databases, and information on specific topics related to occupational safety and health. In addition, NIOSH offers occupational safety and health information in multiple languages.

Occupational Safety and Health Administration

Established in 1971, OSHA is a regulatory agency for worker safety and health protection in the U.S. Department of Labor. By providing leadership and encouragement to organizations, OSHA seeks to help them recognize and understand the value of safety and health at work. Under the Occupational Safety and Health Act of 1970, OSHA is authorized to conduct workplace inspections and investigations to assess the extent to which employers comply with the standards issued by OSHA for safe and healthy workplaces. The national office is located in Washington, DC, and there are 10 regional offices covering all 50 states as well as territories and jurisdictions under federal authority. In addition, 22 states or territories operate their own OSHA-approved state programs.

Employees and Divisions

OSHA employees include inspectors, complaint discrimination investigators, physicians, standards writers, engineers, and educators as well as other technical and support staff. The agency is organized in terms of eight directorates, one of which is administrative and the remaining seven are directly related to occupational safety and health:

- *Directorate of Construction:* works with the construction industry on engineering issues to improve safety and health awareness and reduce fatalities, injuries, and illnesses
- *Directorate of Enforcement Programs:* establishes and maintains a comprehensive occupational safety and health compliance guidance and assistance program as well as discrimination complaint investigation programs

- *Directorate of Training and Education:* offers training courses and educational programs to help workers and employers recognize, avoid, and prevent safety and health hazards in their workplaces
- *Directorate of Cooperative and State Programs:* develops, recommends, and implements policies and procedures and coordinates programs that support OSHA's cooperative efforts (e.g., compliance assistance, small business assistance)
- *Directorate of Standards and Guidance:* develops workplace standards, regulations, and guidance that are feasible; addresses significant workplace risks; and considers the potential effects of standards on the economy, affected industries, and small businesses
- *Directorate of Technical Support and Emergency Management:* provides specialized technical expertise and advice in disciplines such as industrial hygiene, safety engineering, occupational medicine, emergency preparedness and response, and technical data services
- *Directorate of Whistleblower Protection Programs:* protects workers from retaliation by employers when workers report injuries, safety concerns, or other protected activity

Mission

The mission of OSHA is to ensure the safety and health of America's workers by setting and enforcing standards; providing training, outreach, and education; establishing partnerships; and encouraging continuous improvement in workplace safety and health. These strategies are authorized by the Occupational Safety and Health Act to help organizations reduce work-related illnesses, injuries, and deaths.

Functions

The primary function of OSHA is to establish standards for protection from work-related safety and health hazards, enforce those standards, and provide consultations and technical support to employers and employees. Nearly every type of worker is included within OSHA's jurisdiction, with a few exceptions (e.g., the self-employed, miners).

The agency promotes workplace safety and health through a variety of activities in pursuit of its mission (i.e., enforcement, outreach/education, and partnerships). In terms of enforcement, OSHA develops mandatory job safety and health standards and enforces them through worksite inspections of the most hazardous workplaces, by imposing citations and/or penalties, and by providing assistance to employers. On average, OSHA conducts approximately 40,000 inspections per year. Inspections are related to safety or industrial hygiene/health. The penalty for violating an OSHA standard varies depending on the likelihood that the violation could result in serious harm to employees. In addition to conducting inspections, OSHA establishes rights and responsibilities for employers and employees to reach better safety and health conditions. Further, the agency maintains a system to report and maintain records to monitor job-related injuries and illnesses.

In terms of outreach, education, and compliance assistance, OSHA establishes training programs to increase the competence of occupational safety and health professionals and to educate employers to reduce accidents and injuries. Also, OSHA supports the development of new methods of reducing workplace hazards and encourages organizations to reduce hazardous conditions (e.g., by applying new safety and health management systems or improving existing programs). Other sources of education include OSHA's Web site (www.osha.gov), which offers publications and interactive eTools to help organizations address specific hazards and prevent injuries, a hotline for workplace safety and health information and assistance, and Spanish-language services (e.g., Web page, publications).

In addition, OSHA has cooperative programs, partnerships, and alliances to promote the safety and health of workplaces. For instance, OSHA partners with states that operate their own occupational safety and health programs, and it provides a consultation service regarding workplace safety and health issues.

Jennifer L. Geimer

See also Occupational Health Psychology

Further Readings

National Institute for Occupational Safety and Health: http://www.cdc.gov/niosh

National Institute for Occupational Safety and Health. (2013, April). *National Institute for Occupational Safety and Health fact sheet.* Retrieved from http://www.cdc.gov/niosh/docs/2013-140/pdfs/2013-140.pdf

Occupational Safety and Health Administration. (1970). *OSH Act of 1970.* Retrieved from https://www.osha.gov/pls/oshaweb/owasrch.search_form?p_doc_type=OSHACT

Occupational Safety and Health Administration. (2014). *OSHA at-a-glance.* (OSHA 3439B-12R 2014). Retrieved from https://www.osha.gov/pls/publications/publication.searchResults?pSearch=OSHA-At-A-Glance

Occupational Safety and Health Administration. (2015). *About OSHA.* Retrieved from https://www.osha.gov/about.html

Occupational Safety and Health Administration. (2015). *All about OSHA: Occupational Safety and Health Administration* (OSHA 3302-09R 2015). Retrieved from https://www.osha.gov/Publications/all_about_OSHA.pdf

NATURALISTIC OBSERVATION

Observational techniques, a cornerstone of the qualitative research paradigm, can be divided into two main categories: participant and naturalistic. *Naturalistic observation* is a method of collecting information in a setting in which the behavior of interest occurs, typically unbeknownst to the targets of observation. Naturalistic observation is often used by ethnographers examining cultural behavior, organizational development researchers, and program evaluators. The hallmark of naturalistic observation is the lack of intrusion by the researcher into the setting and behavior of interest. An example of naturalistic observation would be a training program evaluator watching the content of the training and participant observations through closed-circuit television to assess comprehensiveness of the training program. In this example, the participants are not aware of the observer and, as such, do not shift their behavior to make a favorable impression.

Participant observation is the other broad category of observational techniques and can take one of three forms:

- *Complete participant:* The researcher conceals his or her role to more fully examine the issue of interest.
- *Observer as participant:* The role of the researcher is known to those being observed.
- *Participant as observer:* The research function performed by the observer is secondary to his or her role as a participant in the actions and behaviors.

In all of these cases, the researcher's role as an observer is overt and may influence the behaviors of those being observed.

Key Elements for Conducting a Naturalistic Observation Study

As with any research design, decisions regarding the specific methods and scope of the study must be made. However, a number of decisions are unique to observational research:

1. *Level of involvement* of the researcher/observer depends on the nature and sensitivity of behaviors to be observed. Naturalistic observation is better suited to settings in which a researcher's presence might change the behavior (e.g., Western Electric employees in the Hawthorne studies). Participant observation may be more suited to those situations in which actively performing the behavior of interest lends a higher level of understanding to the researcher (e.g., understanding job content in the process of job analysis).

2. *Amount of collaboration* in the coding process depends on the setting of the observation (e.g., is it feasible to involve multiple coders?). The inclusion of two or more coders allows the research team to assess the interobserver reliability of its observations.

3. *Length of time* for observation of behaviors depends on the goal of the study. There are three general sampling frames for observational research: (a) time sampling, in which the behavior is observed for a set period of time (e.g., 3 days); (b) point sampling, in which one individual or group is observed before moving on to the next individual or group of interest (e.g., observing the training department in one

plant before moving to a different plant); and (c) event sampling, in which an event is observed every time it occurs (e.g., observing the administration of annual performance appraisals).

4. *Focus and nature of the observation* depend on the specific research question. The narrower the focus, the easier it will likely be to code the behaviors reliably and efficiently using a structured approach. Broader, unstructured context examinations (e.g., narratives) may be better suited for descriptive studies in the nascent stage of a research area.

The design of a naturalistic observation study relies on clarity in goals and measurement to target the behaviors of interest to adequately address the research questions. Because the behaviors of interest are occurring in their natural context, the researcher must be able to adeptly classify and interpret only relevant behaviors. For this reason, operationalization of behaviors is critical. The creation of a comprehensive coding sheet and training on the coding of behaviors is critical to ensure that behaviors are accurately captured.

Depending on the type of data collected during the observation period, analysis remains qualitative or turns to a more quantitative approach. If structured observation was used with behavioral checklists, descriptive statistical information may be compiled (e.g., frequencies). If the focus was broader and unstructured, narrative reviews may tell the story of the behavior in context.

Reliability and Validity of Naturalistic Observation

Interobserver reliability is the only way to assess the consistency of behavioral coding in a naturalistic observation study. For this reason, it is critical to include multiple coders in an effort to demonstrate a lack of observer bias. However, calculation of interobserver reliability is feasible only when using structured and systematic observation. If an unstructured method is used, demonstration of consistency in observation is very difficult.

In terms of validity, naturalistic observation sacrifices internal for ecological validity. Because the behaviors observed occur in context with no interference from researchers, the extent to which the behaviors observed in this naturalistic setting mimic the "real world" is very high. However, because the observer does not interact with or participate in the context of behavior, there is no control of potentially influencing variables. To link internal and ecological validity, an observational study may be used to replicate and/or extend findings from a laboratory study on the same topic.

Advantages and Disadvantages of Naturalistic Observation

The benefits of naturalistic observation research are numerous. Specifically, naturalistic observation allows researchers to examine behaviors directly in context without interference, thus providing a foundation for understanding the environmental conditions associated with the issues of interest. This is especially true when the topic under investigation is very sensitive or the presence of the researcher would likely influence behavior.

Beyond the time commitment required to conduct this type of research, the disadvantages of naturalistic observation center on three main issues: reliability, validity, and ethics. Because observation is an inherently perceptual process, bias can be introduced in the coding and interpretation of observational results in a number of ways (e.g., coding the behavior, interpreting results). Therefore, some question the accuracy of observation records (e.g., checklists, narrative reviews) and disregard their value as contextual markers.

As previously discussed, because the observer does not influence the situation, the influence of extraneous variables on the behaviors of interest cannot be assessed (e.g., no internal validity). The real-world aspect of the data may be high, but without the knowledge and/or control of influential variables affecting these behaviors, the value of the research may be limited.

Because of the unobtrusiveness of the researcher in naturalistic observation, informed consent cannot be given by participants. Under American Psychological Association guidelines, informed consent procedures do not need to be initiated when there is no expectation of harm to the participant as a result of the research. However, the application of this standard has been controversial (e.g., R. D. Middlemist and colleagues' study of personal space invasions in the lavatory). Institutional review boards should provide guidance in the interpretation of waived informed consent for naturalistic studies.

Jennifer P. Bott

See also Qualitative Research Approach

Further Readings

Creswell, J. W. (1994). *Research design: Qualitative and quantitative approaches*. Thousand Oaks, CA: Sage.

Denzin, N. K., & Lincoln, Y. S. (2000). *Handbook of qualitative research* (2nd ed.). Thousand Oaks, CA: Sage.

Middlemist, R. D., Knowles, E. S., & Matter, C. F. (1977). Personal space invasions in the lavatory: Suggestive evidence for arousal. *Journal of Personality and Social Psychology, 35*(2), 122–124.

Patton, M. Q. (2002). *Qualitative research and evaluation methods* (3rd ed.). Thousand Oaks, CA: Sage.

NEED THEORIES OF WORK MOTIVATION

Among the best-known theories of work motivation in both academic and applied settings are models predicated on the assumption that, at root, humans are need-driven creatures, most of whose behavior can best be understood by examining their need states and identifying the goals or goal states they seek to satisfy their needs.

What Is a Need?

A variety of definitions of *need* have been offered, but the one favored by the author is attributable to Henry A. Murray. In his 1938 book *Explorations in Personality*, Murray wrote, first, that need is a hypothetical construct, not a physical entity: We cannot assess it directly or determine its color. It has no physical mass, density, or specific gravity. Second, Murray's definition also implies that a person in a state of need feels a force that activates and helps to direct him or her. Third, according to Murray, needs can be aroused by characteristics of

the environment. A fourth feature of Murray's definition is that it helps us understand approach behaviors as well as avoidance behaviors. Needs are also tightly connected with emotions, although whether there are one-to-one connections between particular needs and specific emotions is still being examined by psychologists.

Needs and Behavior

Perhaps the most important point in Murray's definition has to do with the connection between needs and behavior. A number of points need elaboration here. First, not all need-driven, goal-oriented behavior is successful in reaching the goals sought. The result is defined as frustration, and sometimes fantasy must suffice to quell the force generated by a need. Nevertheless, observing behavior as a means to infer a person's needs can be a tricky proposition. One reason for this difficulty is that most needs, except for the most basic biological ones, are said to be overdetermined— that is, instigated and directed by more than one motive. Hence, any behavior, such as quitting a job, may be motivated by the frustration of many needs, as well as by the attraction of an alternative job that may help to satisfy those frustrated needs and even satisfy other needs. Moreover, different people may seek the satisfaction of a common need through different behaviors. Jon may seek a leadership position in his union to satisfy power and affiliation needs, whereas Marie may coach junior hockey to satisfy her needs for power and affiliation. In short, there is a complex relationship between needs and behavior, and we frequently project our own need state or behavior state onto others, assuming that others behave the same way(s) we do when in need.

Consider the difficulty involved in making inferences about the needs that determine a person's behavior. First, as previously mentioned, most motivated behavior is said to be *overdetermined,* meaning that deliberately or inadvertently, behavior is driven by the force to satisfy more than one need.

For example, an employee might seek a promotion for the sake of meeting several needs (although the person may be more conscious of the importance of some of them than others). The same need may be satisfied by any of a variety of acts. So our upwardly aspiring employee may in part be seeking greater satisfaction of esteem needs. Notice that gaining a promotion is one way—but only one way—to meet esteem needs. Volunteer service after hours or becoming president of the employees' union are alternative behaviors that might be employed. In short, there is no one-to-one relationship between the force of a particular need and the type of behavior observed. To complicate matters, there is a common tendency for people to *project* their own need-behavior styles into their interpretations of the behavior. (For example, one might conclude that a friend accepted a position at the grocery store rather than a flower shop because it is closer to his or her house. Here, the mistake would be attributing to the friend a preference for short commutes to work, mostly because the person making the attribution hates to commute long distances to work!)

Need Satisfaction

Need satisfaction is usually thought of as the feeling of relief or reduced tension that occurs after a goal has been attained or an act has been accomplished (e.g., a funny stomach following a favorite meal). In the case of certain needs, however, satisfaction may consist more of the experience one has while in the process of reducing the tension. Continuing our example, satisfaction consists of both the joy of eating and the state of having eaten. Moreover, greater satisfaction can occur when more tension is reduced, so people may be motivated to deprive themselves of gratification (within safe limits) so that they can experience greater subsequent satisfaction from the process of need fulfillment. Sexual foreplay illustrates this principle, as does the notion of not eating lunch to ensure that one has a strong appetite for a special dinner.

Typologies of Needs

Much of the modern work on need theory has been devoted to making categories of needs. David McClelland, a student of Murray, spent much of his career pursuing the measurement and behavioral significance of three particular needs: power, affiliation, and achievement. Early work in

this tradition suffered from problems of measurement, inasmuch as it relied heavily on the use of projective techniques to assess the strength of these needs in individuals. Nevertheless, the tradition started by McClelland and his colleagues has revealed considerable insight into the power–need profiles of effective and ineffective leaders and managers. McClelland and D. G. Winter even demonstrated in 1969 how the levels of achievement orientation in a society relate to its prosperity, and they had some success in developing achievement motivation in Third World countries, resulting in increased levels of entrepreneurial behavior in those countries.

Hierarchical Theories

McClelland never suggested any relationships among his need categories, whereas another famous American psychologist, Abraham Maslow, did. His 1943 hierarchical theory of human motivation is among the most paradoxical approaches to work motivation. On the one hand, it is one of the most familiar theories among academics and practitioners, as noted by J. B. Miner in 2003. On the other hand, it is likely the most misunderstood and most frequently oversimplified and misrepresented. For decades after it was proposed, the theory enjoyed only mixed and poor evidence of scientific validity. But it has remained popular nevertheless.

Maslow's theory holds that there are basically five categories of human needs and that these needs account for much or most of human behavior. The needs vary in their relative *prepotency*, or urgency for the survival of the individual, arranging themselves in a hierarchical order of importance. As the most prepotent needs become reasonably satisfied, the less prepotent ones (the higher order needs) become increasingly important for causing behavior.

The most prepotent needs in the theory are physiological in nature. They function in a homeostatic fashion, such that imbalances or deficiencies in certain physiological substances instigate behavior aimed at restoring the balance by filling the deficiencies. Hunger, sex, and thirst are three examples of such needs. Next come the physiological needs, or so-called security needs. When unfulfilled, they possess the same sort of potential for dominating a person's behavior as the physiological needs do when they are not being met. Later versions of this model have often combined these two categories into one set, arguing that need frustration or a threat is equally powerful in instigating and directing behavior, whether posed at the physiological or security level.

The *love needs* are next in importance; that is, they take on comparatively more influence in behavior as the physiological and safety needs are reasonably satisfied. The individual desires relations with other people, and he or she will feel more compelled than before to achieve such relations. Feelings of loneliness, ostracism, rejection, and friendlessness will become more acute. Maslow claimed in 1954 that the thwarting of the love needs is at the root of many cases of maladjustment. The theory claims that people need both to give and to receive love, and that social interactions need not be cordial to satisfy these needs.

The *esteem needs* are the next most prepotent category in the hierarchy. Maslow groups them into two sets: one includes desires for strength, achievement, adequacy, mastery and competence, independence, freedom, and a fundamental confidence in facing the world. The second set consists of needs for prestige and reputation—the esteem of others. It motivates people to seek recognition, praise, dominance, glory, and the attention of other people.

The esteem needs are seen as less prepotent than the highest set of needs on the hierarchy—the so-called *need for self-actualization*. In his various writings, Maslow provided differing interpretations of the meaning of this need, but the clearest and most widely accepted view is that it consists of a requirement for individuals to fulfill their potentials, to become that which they are capable of becoming. An important feature of self-actualization needs is that they express themselves in different behaviors in different people. Moreover, the satisfaction of self-actualization needs tends to *increase* their importance rather than reduce it—they become somewhat addictive. This difference between self-actualization and the other needs in the hierarchy makes it the most unusual. These are the primary elements of Maslow's theory. More detailed descriptions and

interpretations of the research into the theory were given by C. C. Pinder in 1998.

Existence, Relatedness, and Growth

About the time Maslow completed his writings about human needs, in 1972, Harold Alderfer generated and tested an alternative to Maslow's model, the theory of *existence, relatedness, and growth*. This model has its roots in Maslow's work, as well as in the theory and research of a number of other psychologists before Maslow who had been concerned with human motivation.

The theory posits three general categories of human needs, categories similar to, and partly derived from, those in Maslow's model. All of the needs are seen as primary, meaning they are innate to human nature, rather than learned, although learning increases their strength.

The first set in the model is referred to as the *existence* needs. They correspond closely to the physiological and security needs Maslow associated with species survival. Research by Alderfer and others justifies combining them into a single category.

Similarly, the goals typically sought by people to satisfy what Maslow calls *love needs* are fundamentally the same as those that are necessary to provide for the need for prestige or the esteem of others, as well as for the interpersonal-security needs included in the second level of Maslow's hierarchy. Successful satisfaction of each of the needs identified by Maslow requires interaction with other human beings and the development of meaningful relationships with others. Moreover, each of these three varieties of social needs, on a logical level at least, seem equally important, or prepotent. Therefore, these specific Maslovian needs are combined by Alderfer as the *relatedness* needs. Alderfer's third category roughly combines Maslow's concepts of self-esteem and self-actualization into a category he calls the *growth* needs.

Current Assessment of Need Theories of Work Motivation

As mentioned, decades of research following the publication of Maslow's work were not very encouraging. It took a while even to establish the distinctiveness of the categories. Cross-cultural work by Simcha Ronen in 1994 established at least a two-level hierarchy, with evidence that the physiological and security needs do form a coherent set, whereas the other needs may be essentially of equal importance among themselves. As in the case of so many theories of work motivation, it may be that the need theories of work motivation are more valid than social scientists are capable of demonstrating, given the practical problems of measurement, manipulation (for experimentation), and generalization, not to mention the ethics of conducting internally valid research into this subject on human beings.

Craig C. Pinder

See also Motivational Traits; Work Motivation

Further Readings

Alderfer, C. P. (1972). *Existence, relatedness, and growth.* New York: Free Press.

Latham, G. P., & Pinder, C. C. (2005). Work motivation theory and research at the dawn of the 21st century. *Annual Review of Psychology, 56,* 485–516.

Maslow, A. H. (1954). *Motivation and personality.* New York: Harper & Row.

McClelland, D. C., & Winter, D. G. (1969). *Motivating economic achievement.* New York: Free Press.

Miner, J. B. (2003). The rated importance, scientific validity, and practical usefulness of organizational behavior theories: A quantitative review. *Academy of Management Learning and Education, 2,* 250–268.

Murray, H. (1938). *Explorations in personality.* New York: Oxford University Press.

Pinder, C. C. (1998). *Work motivation in organizational behavior.* Upper Saddle River, NJ: Prentice Hall.

Pinder, C. C. (in press). *Work motivation in organizational behavior* (2nd ed.). Mahwah, NJ: Erlbaum.

Ronen, S. (1994). An underlying structure of motivational need taxonomies: A cross-cultural confirmation. In M. D. Dunnette & L. M. Hough (Eds.), *Handbook of industrial and organizational psychology* (Vol. 4, pp. 241–269). Palo Alto, CA: Consulting Psychologists Press.

NEGOTIATION

See Negotiation, Mediation, and Arbitration

NEGOTIATION, MEDIATION, AND ARBITRATION

The term *negotiation* conjures a variety of images in people's minds, many of which involve haggling over a sale price or a starting salary. In reality, negotiation is far more pervasive, involving more than just haggling over a price. New recruits may indeed negotiate their starting salaries, but they also negotiate job assignments, budgets, schedules, supplier contracts, joint ventures, and the resolution of conflicts with coworkers. Whether applied to crafting deals or resolving disputes, negotiation refers to a joint decision-making process in which two or more parties, whose interests conflict, attempt to reach an agreement. When negotiations become difficult or impossible, and when the costs of disagreement are high, others often intervene. These third parties typically act as mediators or arbitrators as they assist negotiators in reaching agreement.

Negotiation, mediation, and arbitration are therefore distinct but related processes. An important difference among them, however, is in the degree of control individuals have over the process (i.e., *how* they come to agreement) and over the outcome (i.e., *what* agreement they reach). In negotiation, parties generally have a high degree of control over both process and outcome. For example, job candidates and recruiters work together through discussion and exchange of offers in an attempt to craft an agreement that is mutually acceptable.

When third parties become involved, however, negotiators (or disputants) relinquish some control for the sake of reaching agreement. In mediation, they give up control over the process, and in arbitration they give up control over the outcome. In other words, mediators work with the parties to help them develop and endorse an agreement, whereas arbitrators listen to the parties and impose a decision.

The study of negotiation and third-party processes has a long and somewhat fragmented history. In part, this complicated past arises from differences in the nature of the processes themselves and their objectives as well as differences in their intellectual traditions. Not surprisingly, each has its distinct challenges; together, though, they promote processes designed to help individuals with diverse preferences work together to enhance individual and organizational effectiveness.

Negotiation

Because of its link to deal making, negotiation is often conceptualized primarily in economic terms. Economists, some of the first scholars to study the topic, tend to adopt a prescriptive approach; that is, they analyze the outcomes that should result assuming that negotiators act rationally. From this perspective, negotiators are often believed to be *Olympian,* meaning that they are fully informed, having perfect information about their preferences, their counterparts' preferences, the possible outcomes, and the expected utility or value associated with those outcomes. They are also believed to be motivated exclusively by self-interest, striving to make choices that maximize their individual outcomes.

Psychologically oriented researchers have challenged this perspective, pointing out that it fails to capture the experiences of negotiators and the complexity of their motivation. In reality, negotiators rarely know their counterpart's preferences and sometimes are even unsure about their own preferences, which may shift during the course of a negotiation. Moreover, negotiators are often concerned about the other party's outcomes as well as their own, suggesting that self-interest is not the only motivation.

Other perspectives have emerged, most notably cognitive and behavioral perspectives that are primarily descriptive and emphasize negotiator aspirations, perceptions, and behavior. Unlike the traditional economic approach, these perspectives focus on conflict situations as they are understood by actual negotiators who often have incomplete and perhaps biased information, limited cognitive capacity to remember facts and imagine possible alternatives, and multiple (often conflicting) motives. Psychological approaches analyze negotiation from a negotiator's point of view and identify the main tasks of negotiation.

Cognitive and Behavioral Perspectives

To analyze negotiation from a negotiator's point of view, two important questions need to be asked. First, what is the best alternative to a negotiated agreement (BATNA)? Figuring out the BATNA places a boundary on the negotiation and establishes a *reservation point,* which is the point at which a negotiator is indifferent between settlement and impasse. Because negotiators are unlikely to accept offers that are less attractive than their best alternatives, it is important to know the parties' reservation points.

Second, what are their interests? That is, what are the reasons behind the positions negotiators take in negotiations? Imagine a job candidate asks a recruiter for a $10,000 increase in starting salary, because of a desire to pay down education loans. The candidate's interest is in paying down the loans, and his or her position is for a $10,000 increase in starting salary. Additionally, the candidate indicates that starting date is relatively unimportant in comparison to financial issues. This difference in the relative importance of issues suggests certain tradeoffs or concessions the candidate might make during the negotiation.

Taken together, the assessment of negotiators' BATNAs and interests create the structure or psychological context of the negotiation. Within this structure or context, negotiators attempt to craft mutually acceptable agreements.

The Two Tasks of Negotiation

Within this psychological context, negotiators face two primary tasks: distribution and integration. *Distribution* refers to the division of existing value or resources. When managers haggle over the size of their budgets, they are negotiating the division of a fixed resource or "pie." To reach a mutually agreeable settlement, negotiators generally engage in give-and-take processes and settle on a compromise. Because of the nature of the distribution task, tough bargaining tactics are commonplace, including misrepresentation, bluffing, silence, extreme positions, and threats to walk away. Distribution represents the competitive or win–lose aspect of negotiation.

Integration contrasts sharply with distribution and refers to the creation of additional value or resources. By discovering tradeoffs that meet both parties' needs, for example, negotiators increase the resource pie and create more value by cooperating and working together. In general, when a negotiation involves multiple issues, which are valued differently by the parties, there is potential for integration. For example, when organizations subsidize employee health club memberships, they are attempting to increase employee health and well-being as well as increase employee productivity, a tradeoff that is intended to create value. In general, integrative agreements created out of complementary interests tend to support and even strengthen long-term relationships between parties.

Although desirable, integration is not an easy task. To create integrative agreements, negotiators need to know each other's interests and be motivated to work creatively to meet each other's needs. Not surprisingly, integrative negotiations are often referred to as *joint problem solving*. Because of the nature of the integration task, cooperative bargaining tactics, including honesty, openness, information sharing, and trust, are commonplace. Integration reflects the cooperative aspect of negotiation.

Negotiations that involve both integration and distribution are called *mixed-motive* negotiations, primarily because they include both cooperative and competitive aspects. In general, most negotiations are mixed-motive. Even a negotiation such as buying an automobile, which may seem to be a purely distributive task, typically involves integration as well as distribution. For example, at some point in the negotiation, one of the parties may begin to expand the set of issues beyond price to include such things are financing, new tires, floor mats, sound system upgrades, extended warranty, and other issues that may be valued differently by the two parties. By adding issues to the negotiation, the resource pie increases; however, these added resources still need to be divided between the buyer and seller.

Perhaps one of the greatest challenges for disputants is to realize the integrative potential in their negotiations and to create mutually beneficial agreements. Many disputants feel uneasy about sharing information about their interests, which is an important part of identifying complementary interests and creating integrative agreements. In cases of protracted union–management negotiations, for example, the low level of trust between the parties may cripple integrative bargaining.

There are several cognitive biases that hamper effective integrative bargaining, most notably the *mythical fixed pie perception*. According to this perceptual bias, negotiators assume from the start that their interests and those of their counterparts necessarily and directly conflict. This initial win–lose bias, along with its associated tough tactics, heightens the competitive aspect of negotiation and hampers a problem-solving approach. For example, because of the mythical fixed pie perception, negotiators often misperceive common interests to be conflicting, leading them to overlook areas of mutual benefit.

When Others Intervene: Mediation and Arbitration

When two parties run into trouble and can no longer manage their negotiation, they often turn to third parties for help. Negotiations may become tense and difficult, for example, creating frustration, anger, and distrust, or they may stall because parties lose momentum or direction, or find themselves at an impasse on critical issues. Sometimes third-party intervention is an informal process, such as when two employees turn to a coworker or to a manager for help in resolving a dispute. Other times it is part of an organization's formal dispute resolution system, in which case it may be either voluntary or required.

In general, third-party intervention is designed to get negotiations back on track and to a resolution. At a minimum, it brings negotiators back to the table and provides a cooling-off process for highly emotional negotiations. It also can reestablish and refocus communication on the substantive issues and impose or reinforce deadlines designed to keep negotiation moving forward.

Neutral third parties may also help negotiators resolve the substance of their conflicts. Mediators, who take control of the *process*, work with the parties both to repair strained relationships and to help them develop and endorse an agreement; in mediation, the parties engage in dialogue—talking and listening to each other—and take charge of their solutions. Mediators meet with parties individually, gaining an understanding of the various issues and perspectives, and identify—and help the parties develop—possible agreements. In its purist form, mediation is a participatory process involving interest-based bargaining and joint problem solving, placing a premium on party self-determination.

Arbitrators, who take control of the *outcome*, help negotiators primarily by providing a timely solution, avoiding litigation. The goal of arbitration is to design settlements. In general, the arbitrator hears each party's case and then decides the outcome. There are several forms of arbitration. In binding arbitration, the parties agree beforehand that they will accept any resulting settlement an arbitrator designs. In final-offer arbitration, parties submit their preferred agreements, one of which is selected by the arbitrator.

Mediation and arbitration may also be combined to create hybrid processes. In some organizational dispute resolution systems, mediation is a preliminary step leading to arbitration if an agreement is not reached. The reasoning behind this "med–arb" procedure is that if the parties cannot craft a solution themselves with the help of a mediator, then the dispute automatically goes to arbitration (i.e., the mediator becomes an arbitrator) and is resolved for them.

Another hybrid process is "arb–med," which consists of three phases. In the first phase, the third party begins with an arbitration hearing and places the decision in a sealed envelope. This phase is followed by mediation, during which the arbitrator's envelope (i.e., decision) is prominently displayed. If mediation fails, the envelope is opened, revealing the arbitrated decision. When comparing these two hybrid processes, arb–med tends to result in more mediated settlements and in settlements of greater joint benefit.

Like negotiation, mediation and arbitration can be extremely effective ways of resolving disputes. As mentioned above, when negotiations are tense and emotional, or if the parties reach an impasse and cannot themselves figure out a solution, it may be wise to involve a neutral third party. It can also offer the parties a way to save face by allowing them to make concessions during mediation without appearing weak or letting them blame an arbitrator if the settlement is unsatisfactory to a party's constituents. Research shows that it is best to involve third parties only after negotiators have made a serious effort to resolve their own conflict and when they realize that they can no longer manage their negotiation. The use of third parties is particularly helpful for managing conflicts in ongoing work relationships.

There are important challenges, however. Turning to third parties, especially to arbitrators, usually signals that the negotiation process has failed and that the parties could not settle their differences themselves. In the case of ongoing work relationships, this failure can be problematic. Organizations generally prefer that workers become skilled in managing their relationships, even strengthening them to benefit the organization.

Additionally, because arbitration involves imposing a settlement on the parties, there may be less commitment to the settlement than if the parties crafted an agreement themselves. The process may also inadvertently create systemic problems. For example, merely anticipating arbitration may inhibit serious negotiation, especially when both parties feel strongly about their positions and believe that a neutral third party will side with them. Such overconfidence may undermine the negotiation process and needlessly escalate conflict. It may also jeopardize the parties' acceptance of the arbitrated decision.

The legal context of arbitration also creates challenges. Arbitration is intended to be expedient and final. By design, judicial review of arbitrated settlements is limited, encouraging the process to stand firm as a mechanism for conflict resolution and discouraging litigation. The likelihood of an award being vacated, for example, is traditionally low, in part because the statutory grounds for judicial review are quite narrow. For this and other reasons, there are concerns about ethical misconduct by participants (disputants and arbitrators alike) and how it is handled. Because arbitration is distinct from adjudication and does not have the full force of criminal law, parties potentially suffer the vagaries of the process, including arbitrator discretion and inadequate knowledge, expertise, and judgment. Finding a solution—and ending the dispute—may take priority over finding the best solution.

But what if the arbitrated solution is far from optimal and one or both parties feel it is unfair? One solution is litigation. Although the goal of arbitration is to design settlements and *avoid* litigation, parties have been turning to the courts recently as a "second forum" for resolving disputes. The purpose is to have the arbitrator's decision vacated. Even though the success rate is relatively low, a recent study found that 30% of the time the arbitration award was vacated. In light of the intended purpose of arbitration, this trend is troubling and poses a serious challenge for arbitration.

One proposed solution, intended to improve arbitration process and outcomes, is to close "ethical loopholes" by bringing criminal law to bear on arbitration (e.g., including binding arbitration in the definition of official proceedings). This proposal may be viewed by some as making arbitration more like adjudication and blurring the distinctiveness of these approaches to dispute resolution. Other solutions, however, draw on insights from psychological research. It is well documented that people intentionally or unintentionally violate ethical rules and that subtle cognitive, linguistic, or environmental changes can have powerful effects on ethical behavior. For example, merely providing self-justification for an act (e.g., reasoning that ending a conflict is more important than crafting the best solution) may perpetuate ethical misconduct in the absence of any feelings of remorse. Perhaps placing greater emphasis on decision quality, rather than expediency, might prove useful.

Challenges also exist for mediation. When parties bring representatives with them, for example, core values of mediation may be compromised as advocacy comes to dominate the process. The shift away from the ideals of mediation has concerned scholars and practitioners alike. In fact, one scholar contends that mediation "stands at the crossroads" and asks: "If arbitration is now becoming the 'new litigation' and legal mediation is the 'new arbitration,' what will replace mediation?" (Nolan-Haley, 2012, p. 92).

For both mediation and arbitration, one of the biggest challenges for all third parties is being perceived as neutral by both sides. To be effective, third parties need to be acceptable to both parties and perceived to be unbiased. This may be very difficult to achieve. For example, mediators require discretion: Even when feeling strongly about one party's proposal, they risk undermining the process by appearing to side with one party. If one party begins to dominate, mediators must reestablish a balance, doing so without seeming to take sides. They must be careful not to systematically favor one side or they may compromise their image of fairness and impartiality.

Summary

Negotiation and third-party processes are part of everyday life in organizations. Work group members negotiate task assignments and days off, and prospective employees negotiate the terms of their new jobs. When negotiation stalls, third parties often step in and assist. Mediators take control of the process, attempting to help the parties find a mutually acceptable agreement. Arbitrators, who take control of the outcome, listen to the parties and then decide on a settlement, designed to be final. Negotiation, as well as third-party processes, has shortcomings. However, despite these challenges, these processes helps individuals with diverse preferences work together to enhance individual and organizational effectiveness.

Susan E. Brodt

See also Conflict Management; Judgment and Decision-Making Process

Further Readings

Babcock, L., & Laschever, S. (2004). *Women don't ask: Negotiation and the gender divide.* Princeton, NJ: Princeton University Press.

Babcock, L., & Laschever, S. (2008). *Ask for it: How women can use the power of negotiation to get what they really want.* New York, NY: Bantam Books.

Bazerman, M., & Tenbrunsel, A. (2011). *Blind spots: Why we fail to do what's right and what to do about it.* Princeton, NJ: Princeton University Press.

Beer, J., Packard, C., & Steif, E. (2012). *The mediator's handbook.* Vancouver, BC, Canada: New Society.

Blankley, K. (2014). Advancements in arbitral immunity and judicial review of arbitral awards create ethical loopholes in arbitration. In B. H. Bornstein & R. L. Wiener (Eds.), *Justice, conflict and wellbeing* (pp. 237–288). New York, NY: Springer Science+Business Media.

Brett, J. (2014). *Negotiating globally: How to negotiate deals, resolve disputes, and make decisions across cultural boundaries* (3rd ed.). San Francisco, CA: Jossey-Bass.

Brodt, S., & Dietz, L. (1999). Shared information and information sharing: Understanding negotiation as collective construal. *Research in Negotiation in Organizations, 7,* 263–283.

Brodt, S., & Thompson, L. (2001). Negotiating teams: A levels of analysis framework. *Group Dynamics, 5,* 208–219.

Friedman, R. A. (2000). *Front stage, back stage.* Cambridge, MA: MIT Press.

LaVan, H., Jedel, M., & Perkovich, R. (2012). Vacating of arbitration awards as diminishment of conflict resolution. *Negotiation and Conflict Management Research, 5*(1), 29–48.

Lewicki, R., Saunders, D., & Barry, B. (2014). *Negotiation* (7th ed.) Boston, MA: McGraw-Hill/Irwin.

Nolan-Haley, J. (2012). Meditation: The "new arbitration." *Harvard Negotiation Law Review,* 17(61), 61–95.

Shalvi, S., Gino, F., Barkan, R., & Ayal, S. (2015) Self-serving justifications: Doing wrong and feeling moral. *Current Directions in Psychological Science, 24*(2), 125–130.

Tinsley, C., & Brodt, S. (2004). Conflict management in Asia: A dynamic framework and future directions. In K. Leung & S. White (Eds.), *Handbook of Asian management* (pp. 439–458). New York, NY: Kluwer Academic.

Walton, R. E., & McKersie, R. (1991). *A behavioral theory of labor negotiations* (2nd ed.). Ithaca, NY: ILR Press.

NEPOTISM

The practice of nepotism has a long history, arguably existing in a variety of domains (political, business, religious, etc.) since the beginnings of society. Pope Callixtus III, B. C. Forbes, John Kennedy, Rupert Murdoch, and Sam Walton have all practiced nepotism—all used their positions to show favoritism to their kin, elevating them to positions of power and authority. The term originates from the Latin term *nepos,* or "nephew," and was frequently practiced in the Catholic Church when celibate religious officials elevated nephews to leadership positions. Nepotism is not, of course, limited to childless members of the clergy. The practice goes much further back to the earliest monarchies and dynasties in history. Nepotism today, however, may look much different than a familial passing of the torch. Nepotism is a practice that elicits both positive and negative responses at both the individual and the organizational levels but has received limited research attention over the years.

The changing nature of nepotism is especially relevant in 21st century organizations. Mentioning nepotism in an organizational setting will likely result in a wide array of responses. It may also conjure images of a variety of different types of organizations, ranging from a small neighborhood convenience store to a large family-controlled corporation. Nepotism is still a contentious topic that, while widely practiced, has considerable opposition. The practice is particularly undesirable in western societies, because it is viewed as fundamentally undermining the principles of fairness, egalitarianism, and self-reliance. Although nepotism has critics, proponents argue that the phenomenon has practical benefits, outweighing its social undesirability. Nonetheless, it is a comparatively understudied phenomenon in the organizational literature.

Recent writing on the topic has focused on two broad perspectives. First, definitions of *traditional nepotism* describe scenarios where there is preferential treatment (e.g., hiring, promotions) based solely on family membership regardless of merit. Much of the literature related to this perspective examines the myriad consequences of nepotism disasters (e.g., employee dissatisfaction, public family disagreements, contentious litigation). Second, *new nepotism* describes the flipside of preferential treatment: Family members learn skills and are socialized throughout their lives, leaving them highly qualified for advancement within the company. This entry presents an overview of the theory and research related primarily to these two perspectives of nepotism and offers directions for further study.

Nepotism Theory

Although the field of industrial and organizational (I-O) psychology has applied a few wide-ranging schemas to nepotism, there is currently no unifying theory. These models either describe the underlying mechanisms of nepotism or examine its effects. The first explanatory lens is an evolutionary one. Humans, generally, are predisposed to aid those who share their genetic material out of self-interest. Evolutionary theory would argue that this predisposition extends to favoritism and helping behaviors in organizational settings. Broader organizational studies have typically captured nepotism using the umbrellas of ingroup/outgroup, social exchange, and leader–member exchange theories. While these theories help explain the mechanisms behind the preferential treatment associated with nepotism, much of the research in I-O psychology has focused on the effects of nepotism. The following section expounds on the effects that nepotism has on non–family member attitudes and describes the relative pros and cons of formal anti-nepotism policies in organizations.

Non-Family Member Attitudes

The empirical literature has traditionally focused on the impact nepotistic practices have on non–family members, or non-nepots. The general consensus is that true nepotism, on its own, can lead to greater dissatisfaction, more distrust, and lower perceived procedural justice for non-nepots. However, research on new nepotism, wherein a nepot may be as competent as his or her non-nepot peers, has resulted in disparate findings. Increasingly, the literature suggests the aforementioned negative attitudinal effects may be minimized when the nepotistic decision is merit-based. In other words, non-nepots tend to react less negatively when the hired or promoted family member is perceived as highly qualified. However, because those qualifications can be attributed to family connections, employees may view nepots as less skilled compared with non–family members (i.e., a "silver spoon" backlash). Although the literature on nepotism attitudes is expanding, further research is needed to understand how these beliefs develop over time and how they impact the performance of employees within organizations.

Formal Anti-Nepotism Policies

In western societies, the practice of nepotism often raises legal concerns. In the United States, studies have shown between 10% and 40% of U.S. companies have formal policies prohibiting the practice. Those who advocate in favor of these policies often point to the attitudinal literature, arguing that the use of nepotism has the potential to alienate non-nepots, resulting in lower satisfaction, commitment, and perceptions of justice. Further, unqualified nepots may reduce organizational performance by taking the role of an otherwise better qualified non–family member. Central to this argument is the idea that we should support our best practices in selection and hiring, rather than giving preference due to the social connectedness

of applicants or employees. In doing so, many who advocate for formalized anti-nepotism policies seemingly equate nepotism with the hiring of individuals whose only qualification is relatedness. That is to say that they see these policies through the traditional nepotism lens.

Contesting from the new nepotism perspective, advocates espouse the possible advantages of the practice, arguing against formal policies. One dominant argument has been that I-O psychologists must continue to develop and adhere to best practices when it comes to selection and appraisal. It is the job of the executive and leadership teams to be transparent about employee advancement, which helps mitigate the negative effects of nepotism. Taken together, it is clear that there is simply much that I-O psychologists do not know about the effects of nepotism. Current research paints a picture that essentially says "it depends" in regard to the effect of nepotism (and, in turn, whether I-O psychologists should support formalized anti-nepotism policies).

Future Directions and Conclusions

Nepotism, as a field of study, is in its relative infancy in terms of research progress, despite its prevalence in organizations. Currently, much of the work in the I-O domain has focused on hiring and appraisal situations as they relate to non-nepot attitudes and formalized anti-nepotism policies. Little is known about how nepotism relates to other I-O constructs of interest (e.g., job stress, burnout, financial performance) and what factors may moderate its effect (e.g., organizational or national culture). While largely ignored in the I-O literature, nepotism is at the core of much of the family-owned business literature. There has been little dialogue between the I-O research and those who specialize in this area. While this literature rarely addresses the effects of nepotism, it does focus on areas such as succession planning, knowledge management, and the financial performance of family-run firms. It is a robust literature worth consulting when beginning future research into this topic. In conclusion, nepotism can result in success if used appropriately or disaster if performed with little consideration to the possible contingencies. Tackling the huge elephant in the office will require that I-O psychologists invest more energy in this field of organizational research.

Benjamin J. Biermeier-Hanson and Matthew S. Christensen

See also Employee Selection; Family Business; Groups; Leader–Member Exchange Theory; Social Exchange Theory

Further Readings

Bellow, A. (2003). In praise of nepotism. *Atlantic Monthly, 292*(1), 98–105.

Jones, R. G. (Ed.). (2012). *Nepotism in organizations.* New York, NY: Routledge Taylor & Francis. doi:10.4324/9780203805886

Jones, R. G., & Stout, T. (2015). Policing nepotism and cronyism without losing the value of social connection. *Industrial and Organizational Psychology, 8*(1), 2–12. doi:10.1017/iop.2014.3

Padgett, M. Y., Padgett, R. J., & Morris, K. A. (2014). Perceptions of nepotism beneficiaries: The hidden price of using a family connection to obtain a job. *Journal of Business and Psychology, 30*, 283–298. doi:10.1007/s10869-014-9354-9

Spranger, J. L., Colarelli, S. M., Dimotakis, N., Jacob, A. C., & Arvey, R. D. (2012). Effects of kin density within family-owned businesses. *Organizational Behavior and Human Decision Processes, 119*(2), 151–162. doi:10.1016/j.obhdp.2012.07.001

NETWORKING

Networking refers to the development, maintenance, or use of social or professional contacts for the purpose of exchanging information, resources, or services. Networking typically occurs between two individuals but can be examined as an interaction between groups, companies, or institutions. Networking is an active and continuous process and networking relationships can be envisioned along on a continuum of quality and usefulness.

Overview

Industrial and organizational psychologists have been concerned primarily with how networking affects *individual* employment status and career mobility. For instance, in the context of job search, networking refers to contacting social and professional acquaintances, or other persons to whom the job seeker has been referred, for the purposes of gaining information, leads, or advice related to obtaining a job. Research suggests that as many as 60% to 90% of individuals find jobs by networking, as opposed to traditional job search methods, such as sending out lead inquiry résumés or responding to want ads. Similarly, networking is also used by individuals for the purposes of seeking promotion, gaining visibility, or seeking out career advice or mentoring (i.e., for the purpose of upward career mobility). In fact, research suggests that individual career mobility may be equally or more influenced by informal social relationships than by formal organizational policies and infrastructure.

Both the degree to which people engage in networking and the types of people with whom they network seem to play an important role in determining career outcomes. Although there has been relatively little research on networking behavior (e.g., the intensity with which one engages in networking), a fair amount of research (in particular, from the sociology literature) has examined the structural characteristics of individuals' current social and professional networks as predictors of career outcomes. A social or professional network can be thought of as a web or series of interconnected webs, whereby links or ties exist between focal individuals and the individuals or entities with whom they share a connection or relationship. Structural characteristics of networks include things such as the size of one's network, the strength of ties that exist between focal individuals and other individuals or entities in the network, and the diversity that exists among and between the various individuals or entities in one's network. In addition, the power and influence held by individuals in one's network may play a particularly important role in whether networking will lead to upward career mobility.

Networking Behavior

Conceptual Frameworks

Various conceptual frameworks have been used to understand networking behavior since the inception of the construct in organizational research. However, this research is relatively sparse and spreads across a wide array of disciplines, including management, psychology, sociology, and others. Thus, to date, the construct of networking is not centrally defined. Nevertheless, several themes emerge from the research on networking behavior, which help us understand the construct.

First, individuals may network both inside and outside of the organization, with each leading to different outcomes. Internal networking may improve job performance or intra-organizational teamwork, while external networking may serve to enhance extra-organizational relationships or create opportunities for new employment. Second, characteristics of the job and organizational culture may serve to facilitate or inhibit networking. For example, effective networking may be a critical requirement for jobs in sales at a leading national firm, while it is not as valuable, or is nearly impossible, for a toll booth operator. Third, networking typically involves some exchange of affect, information, benefits, or influence. Researchers have traditionally sought to distinguish social networking from other social relationships. However, while some researchers employ social exchange theory, contending that networking is primarily a utilitarian or tit-for-tat behavior, others argue that it may be done without the expectation of transaction or reciprocation at all. That is, some individuals may engage in building social relationships simply because they enjoy building relationships even when they have no expectation for gain. For instance, elements of mentoring relationships may involve networking for which the mentor provides a mentee with helpful information or opportunities for visibility without expecting anything in return.

Process for Networking

Many behaviors may be used to build or maintain networks, including calling, writing or socializing with people, attending social events, providing assistance or favors, mentoring, having informal conversations, or passing along gossip. During the past decade, the explosion of social media has boosted the role of online networking for building and maintaining professional relationships. Social networking websites provide avenues for individuals to search and join groups of like-minded individuals or individuals who share similar interests or goals. Among these, professional networking communities such as LinkedIn provide individuals and companies with an alternative to the traditional methods of maintaining professional relationships, by face-to-face, phone, or e-mail contact. Unlike cold calling, or creating small talk at networking events, online platforms may facilitate networking among individuals who otherwise prefer not to invest emotional energy in face-to-face interactions with individuals whom they do not already know well. Despite these changes in the way networking is done, to date, very little research has examined individual or organizational outcomes from online networking.

Individual Differences in Networking Behavior

Research on networking suggests that not all individuals engage in networking to the same extent. In one of first studies examining individual differences in networking behavior, Connie Wanberg and her colleagues found that individuals' reported *comfort with networking* is positively related to *networking intensity* (defined as an individual action directed toward contacting friends, acquaintances, and referrals to get job information, leads, or advice) and, further, that the Big Five personality characteristics are all related to *networking comfort* and *networking intensity*. With the exception of neuroticism, which was negatively related, all traits (extroversion, openness to experience, conscientiousness, and agreeableness) were positively related to both comfort and intensity, with conscientiousness and extroversion being the strongest predictors of intensity. Similarly, proactive personality trait (the dispositional tendency toward proactive behavior across situations) appears to be positively related to networking intensity. Several other individual characteristics may influence networking intensity, including education, job level, political skill, impression management, hours worked, and self-esteem, which have all been positively linked with networking behavior. Research on gender is still mixed, but there is some indication that women and men network differently and experience different outcomes from networking.

Structural Network Characteristics

Size of Network

Among structural characteristics of individual networks, the size of one's network is thought to affect access to information and leads. However, several qualifications about network size should be made. Namely, the strength of connections or ties, the diversity of contacts, and the status of contacts in one's network may have a bigger impact than network size alone.

Strength of Ties

Despite the size of one's network, dyadic relationship characteristics such as the strength of ties between individuals and their network contacts seem to be important predictors of information exchange. In a seminal piece on network ties, Mark Granovetter explored the degree to which weak versus strong network ties would lead to information exchange. The idea set forth by Granovetter was that because individuals who share close or strong relationship ties (e.g., friends, family members) often share access to the same information, focal individuals can benefit more from maintaining weak ties with multiple individuals (e.g., acquaintances) who do not share common information with them. This argument, called the *strength of weak ties,* led to a series of studies examining the structure of networks, or *network analysis,* as a means of determining the relationship between network characteristics and career-related outcomes. The conclusion of the resulting body of literature on network ties is that both weak and strong network ties can be beneficial to career outcomes.

Diversity Among Contacts

The diversity among contacts in one's network has also been examined as a predictor of information exchange and positive career outcomes. Work by Ronald Burt suggested that the extent to which one's network contacts know one another will determine the amount of overlapping and redundant information they offer. Thus, diversity among and between one's contacts will provide greater opportunities to access unique and different information.

Power and Influence of Contacts

Last, but certainly not least, the power and influence held by individuals in one's network may be one of the most important factors influencing the utility of networking for career success. In particular, the occupational status of one's contacts (e.g., a high-ranking manager versus a low-ranking nonmanager) may determine their ability to exert influence on one's career outcomes (e.g., hiring or suggesting that one be hired, exposing one to challenging projects that help one gain visibility in the organization) as well as the quality of information they have and are able to exchange (e.g., access to important leads, reliable and accurate career advice).

Tracy Lambert Griggs

See also: Career Success; Career Transitions; Job Search; LinkedIn; Political Skill; Social Exchange Theory; Social Media: Implications for Organizations

Further Readings

Burt, R. S. (1992). *Structural holes.* Cambridge, MA: Harvard University Press.

Gibson, C. Hardy, J. H., III, & Buckley, M. R. (2014). Understanding the role of networking in organizations. *Career Development International, 19*(2), 146–161. doi:10.1108/CDI-09-2013-0111

Granovetter, M. S. (1973). The strength of weak ties. *American Journal of Sociology, 78,* 1360–1380. doi:10.1086/2F225469

Wanberg, C. R., Kanfer, R., & Banas, J. T. (2000). Predictors and outcomes of networking intensity among unemployed job seekers. *Journal of Applied Psychology, 85,* 491–503. doi:10.1037//0021-9010.85.4.401

NEW EMPLOYEE ORIENTATION

New employee orientation occurs in almost every type of organization: schools, colleges, work organizations, government agencies, social/religious/volunteer organizations, the military, and prisons. The common objective is to help newcomers make a smooth transition from outside to inside the organization.

Despite the widespread use of newcomer orientation, very little research has been conducted about it when compared with other types of staffing activities, such as interviewing, testing, recruitment methods, and sources of recruits. Although most organizations have common objectives for newcomer orientation, the methods used vary considerably both by organization type (e.g., military versus voluntary organizations) and even within a particular type of organization (e.g., work organizations).

This entry begins with a definition of *newcomer orientation* by comparing it with organizational socialization. Following this comparison, seven recommended principles for conducting newcomer orientation are presented.

Definition

A definition of *newcomer orientation* should address four questions: (1) Who is involved? (2) When does it occur? (3) What is learned? (4) How is the orientation conducted? First, newcomer orientation concerns only those who are new members of an organization. It does not concern those who have been rehired, or those who move internally, such as when a student changes his or her college major from music to business. Second, there is a loose consensus among writers that orientation almost always occurs on the first day, but there is less agreement as to how long it lasts. Most would agree that it probably does not go too much beyond the first week, as asserted John Wanous in 1992. Third, what is learned in orientation varies with both the amount of time devoted to it and the objectives to be achieved. A minimal orientation might include just the filling out of forms related to one's employment (e.g., income tax withholding, medical benefits), or it could be a tour of the organization. A typical newcomer orientation session is often limited to the presentation of factual information. Fourth, because presenting factual information is so common, the typical orientation methods and the media used are lecturing, videos, and brochures.

Another approach to defining *newcomer orientation* is to compare it with organizational socialization. This is because some writers do not separate them, therefore asserting that orientation is nothing more than the beginning of socialization. A different position is taken here. Newcomer orientation is not the same as organizational socialization, for a number of reasons discussed next.

First, orientation concerns a much shorter time period. Socialization continues well after the initial entry period. Socialization can occur years after entry, because it becomes relevant during internal transitions, such as a promotion or a move to a different functional area within the organization, as pointed out by E. H. Schein in 1971. Second, socialization typically involves a far greater number of organization members than does orientation. For example, coworkers usually are not involved in orientation. Third, the content of an orientation program is quite limited compared with socialization. Orientation concerns issues typically faced by newcomers, whereas socialization concerns all facets of one's experience in an organization. Many issues of concern in socialization do not occur until years later—learning and accepting organizational values, learning how to cope with organizational politics, understanding the performance expectations for one's own job, and so on. Fourth, the available research evidence shows that newcomers are under considerable stress resulting from organizational entry but that this stress decreases fairly rapidly. As a result, newcomer orientation should concern how to cope with these particular entry stressors. Finally, orientation can be viewed as a specific event or program that is limited by both time and content, whereas socialization is considered to be a long-term process. Thus, it is much easier to conduct research on orientation than on socialization.

Design of Newcomer Orientation Programs

Because there was no consensus about how to conduct newcomer orientation, John Wanous proposed in 1992 a new approach called Realistic Orientation Programs for new Employee Stress (ROPES). This approach was based on the idea that newcomers "need to learn the ropes" to be both effective and satisfied in a new organization. A key assumption of ROPES is that newcomers experience very high stress during their first few days. In 2000, Arnon Reichers joined with Wanous to update the ROPES model. In 2008 Wanous and Jinyan Fan renamed it

Realistic Orientation Programs for Entry Stress because it is a more comprehensive term. For example, students go through similar entry stress, but they are not considered "employees." Further, Fan and Wanous studied the entry of international graduate students who experience two distinctive types of entry stress: cultural and organizational.

The ROPES approach to newcomer orientation incorporates ideas from three areas of previously existing research: (1) both of the primary ways to cope with stress, (2) some of the principles for training developed by Arnold Goldstein and Melvin Sorcher, and (3) the stress-inoculation method described by Irving Janis and Leon Mann. With these three research areas as the foundation for ROPES, seven implementation principles were derived. Each is described below.

First, one of the two basic approaches for coping with stress has been called the *problem-focused* approach because it concerns actions that a person can take to reduce stress by addressing its sources. Thus, newcomers need realistic information about the most likely causes of stress experienced by the typical newcomer. After being provided with realistic information about the most common, important stressors, newcomers are also told about specific actions that can reduce stress. Bruce Meglino, Angelo DeNisi, Stuart Youngblood, and Kevin Williams provided an excellent example of this approach for those entering basic training with the U.S. Army. New recruits anxious about meeting new people are told that getting to know one new person is specific, effective, and relatively easy to implement.

Second, the other basic approach for coping with stress has been called the *emotion-focused* method because it concerns thoughts, feelings, and moods. This is an intra-psychic approach, and it is best used when taking action to reduce stress is futile. Raymond Novaco, Thomas Cook, and Irwin Sarason provided an excellent example of this approach being used for U.S. Marines entering basic training. One aspect of emotion-focused coping is to provide emotional support through statements such as "Everyone feels the same pressure to perform well in rifle training. You can help yourself by focusing on the specific task at hand." Emotional support can also be more specific: "If you can make it through the first 2 weeks, you can make it through basic training."

Whereas the first two principles are drawn from the stress–coping research literature, the next three are drawn from advice on training adults to master specific types of interpersonal skills, developed by Goldstein and Sorcher, such as how to give praise to an average-performing employee. Thus, the third principle for newcomer orientation is to use role models as examples of how to handle stressful situations. For example, consider the experiences of international graduate students in U.S. universities. Many such students, particularly those from Asian countries, are uncomfortable with asking questions or making comments in the classroom. Showing a short video of a student doing this successfully is the first step toward helping them overcome this fear and also demonstrates how to participate in class successfully.

The fourth principle follows directly from the third. It is to discuss what the role model did. In the example of international students, this is important so that newcomers can learn all of the specific actions necessary to speak successfully in class. The fifth principle is to have newcomers rehearse the actions that were shown by the role model. Learning is unlikely to result from just observing a role model, as is obvious to all novice golf and tennis players.

Principle six is to teach newcomers how to control their own thoughts *and* feelings, as demonstrated in research by Marie Waung. This is a technique that was initially developed to help patients cope with the stress of going to the dentist or undergoing an invasive or obnoxious medical procedure. As applied to newcomer orientation in the military, such advice might be to "listen to what your drill instructor is saying, and try to ignore the shouting that goes with it."

Principle seven is to target certain specific stressors to particular newcomers, as originally suggested decades ago by Earl Gomersall and Scott Myers. In any group of newcomers, it is likely that they will be dispersed throughout the organization, thus reporting to different bosses. To the extent that certain specific characteristics of different bosses can be identified, the idea is to provide newcomers with the most relevant information for their own new bosses. For example, one newcomer might be told: "Richard may appear to be unfriendly, but that is just his shyness. So be sure to start a conversation on something you might have in common. His hobbies are . . ." A different newcomer in the same orientation session, but with a different boss, might be told: "Your new boss, Susan, prefers to have you check in with her before taking a break from work."

John P. Wanous

See also Organizational Socialization; Organizational Socialization Tactics; Realistic Job Preview; Training

Further Readings

Fan, J., Buckley, R. M., & Litchfield, R. C. (2012). Orientation programs that may facilitate newcomer adjustment: A literature review and future research agenda. In J. J. Martocchio, A. Joshi, & H. Liao (Eds.), *Research in personnel and human resource management* (Vol. 31, pp. 91–148). Greenwich, CT: JAI Press.

Fan, J., & Wanous, J. P. (2008). Organizational and cultural entry: A new type of orientation program for multiple boundary crossings. *Journal of Applied Psychology, 93,* 1390–1400.

Goldstein, A. P., & Sorcher, M. (1974). *Changing supervisor behavior.* New York, NY: Pergamon.

Gomersall, E. R., & Myers, M. S. (1966, July–August). Breakthrough in on-the-job training. *Harvard Business Review,* pp. 62–72.

Janis, I. L., & Mann, L. (1977). *Decision-making: A psychological analysis of conflict, choice, and commitment.* New York, NY: Plenum Press.

Meglino, B. M., DeNisi, A. S., Youngblood, S. A., & Williams, K. J. (1988). Effects of realistic job previews: A comparison using an "enhancement" and a "reduction" preview. *Journal of Applied Psychology, 73,* 259–266.

Novaco, R. W., Cook, T. M., & Sarason, I. G. (1983). Military recruit training: An arena for stress-coping skills. In D. Meichenbaum & M. E. Jaremko (Eds.), *Stress reduction and prevention* (pp. 377–418). New York, NY: Plenum Press.

Schein, E. H. (1971). The individual, the organization, and the career: A conceptual scheme. *Journal of Applied Behavioral Science, 7,* 401–426.

Wanous, J. P. (1992). *Organizational entry: Recruitment, selection, orientation, and socialization* (2nd ed.). Reading, MA: Addison-Wesley.

Wanous, J. P., & Reichers, A. E. (2000). New employee orientation programs. *Human Resource Management Review, 10,* 435–451.

Waung, M. (1995). The effects of self-regulatory coping orientation on newcomer adjustment and job survival. *Personnel Psychology, 48,* 633–650.

NOMOLOGICAL NETWORKS

The *nomological network* is a tool for construct validation (i.e., gathering evidence about the meaning) of psychological measures. For example, construct validation of job performance ratings by supervisors should indicate what the ratings really mean or how accurately they reflect actual performance levels. The goal is to link observable measurements to unobservable theoretical constructs.

In 1955, Lee Cronbach and Paul Meehl described the nomological network as a system of intertwined laws that make up a theory and stated that the laws in the network should generate testable predictions. Laws could relate measurements to each other (e.g., linking job performance ratings to scores on ability or personality measures), theoretical constructs to observed measurements (e.g., linking a rating of some aspect of job performance, such as effort, to the construct of effort), or constructs to other constructs (e.g., linking the construct of job effort to the personality construct of conscientiousness). Building a nomological network involves thinking about what construct is— or should be—measured by an instrument, what other constructs should be related to that construct, and what other measures should be related to the instrument of interest.

Psychological constructs are generally not directly observable, so it is not usually possible to directly determine how well a measure reflects the intended construct. Research based on a nomological network can provide indirect evidence of validity by demonstrating how well the measure correlates with other measures it should theoretically relate to. Confirmation of relationships predicted by the network supports the construct validity of a measure, whereas failure to confirm predictions leads to doubt about construct validity. (Note: A complication with failures of confirmation is that they could result from poor validity of the measure or from incorrect theory in the nomological network, or both.) In addition to evaluating the construct validity of a measure, nomological networks can also play an important role in theory development.

An example of a nomological network involves job performance. In recent years, industrial and organizational psychologists have theorized and researched a distinction between performance on required, job-specific tasks (task performance) and performance of behaviors that are less likely to be required and not specific to particular jobs (e.g., helping coworkers, doing things that need to be done but are not assigned to particular workers); this latter type of behavior has been referred to as *organizational citizenship* or citizenship performance. If supervisors are asked to evaluate workers on both their task performance and citizenship, we might ask whether the ratings really adequately distinguish between the two performance constructs (i.e., we might question the ratings' construct validity); alternatively, ratings might be subject to a *halo effect,* in which a general impression of a worker forms the basis for each (supposedly) separate evaluation.

Testing predictions based on a nomological network could help determine the construct validity of the job performance ratings. The research question concerns a link between observed measures of performance and their constructs. This question can be addressed indirectly by examining links between the performance measures and measures of theoretically related constructs. It has been theorized that the task performance construct should relate more strongly to ability constructs, and the citizenship construct should relate more to personality (e.g., conscientiousness) and job satisfaction. There exist measures of ability, personality, and job satisfaction that have been linked to their theoretical constructs. These measures can be used to test predictions from the nomological network. Research has provided some but not overwhelming support for these links, which raises questions about the validity of the performance ratings and/or the theory. For examples of how nomological networks can be applied to personnel selection measures and to theory development, see the entries in the Further Readings by Binning and Barrett as well as by Newman, Hitchcock, and Newman.

Jim Conway

See also Construct; Criterion Theory; Job Performance Models; Validation Strategies

Further Readings

Barrett, G. V. (1992). Clarifying construct validity: Definitions, processes, and models. *Human Performance, 5,* 13–58. doi:10.1080/08959285.1992.9667923

Binning, J. F., & Barrett, G. V. (1989). Validity of personnel decisions: A conceptual analysis of the inferential and evidential bases. *Journal of Applied Psychology, 74,* 476–494. doi:10.1037/0021-9010.74.3.478

Cronbach, L. J., & Meehl, P. E. (1955). Construct validity in psychological tests. *Psychological Bulletin, 52,* 281–302. doi:10.1037/h0040957

Newman, I., Hitchcock, J. H., & Newman, D. (2015). The use of research syntheses and nomological networks to develop HRD theory. *Advances in Developing Human Resources, 17,* 117–134. doi:10.1177/1523422314559810

Ones, D. S., & Dilchert, S. (2013). Counterproductive work behaviors: Concepts, measurement, and nomological network. In K. F. Geisinger, B. A. Bracken, J. F. Carlson, J. C. Hansen, N. R. Kuncel, S. P. Reise, & M. C. Rodriguez (Eds.), *APA handbook of testing and assessment in psychology, Vol. 1: Test theory and testing and assessment in industrial and organizational psychology* (pp. 643–659). Washington, DC: American Psychological Association. doi:10.1037/14047-035

NONEXPERIMENTAL DESIGNS

The most frequently used experimental design type for research in industrial and organizational psychology and a number of allied fields is the *nonexperiment.* This design type differs from that of both the randomized experiment and the quasi-experiment in several important respects. The entry on experimental designs in this volume considers basic issues associated with (a) the validity of inferences stemming from empirical research and (b) the settings in which research takes place. Thus, the same set of issues is not addressed in this entry.

Attributes of Nonexperimental Designs

Nonexperimental designs differ from both quasi-experimental designs and randomized experimental designs in several important respects. Overall, these differences lead research using nonexperimental designs to be far weaker than that using alternative designs, in terms of internal validity and several other criteria.

Measurement of Assumed Causes

In nonexperimental research, variables that are assumed causes are measured as opposed to being manipulated. For example, a researcher interested in testing the relation between organizational commitment (an assumed cause) and worker productivity (an assumed effect) would have to measure the levels of these variables. Because of the fact that commitment levels were measured, the study would have little if any internal validity. Note, moreover, that the internal validity of such research would not be at all improved by a host of data analytic strategies (e.g., path analysis, structural equation modeling) that purport to allow for inferences about causal connections between and among variables (Stone-Romero, 2002; Stone-Romero & Rosopa, 2004).

Nonrandom Assignment of Participants and Absence of Conditions

In nonexperiments, there are typically no explicitly defined research conditions. For example, a researcher interested in assessing the relation between job satisfaction (an assumed cause) and organizational commitment (an assumed effect) would simply measure the level of both such variables. Because participants were not randomly assigned to conditions in which the level of job satisfaction was manipulated, the researcher would be left in the uncomfortable position of not having information about the many variables that were confounded with job satisfaction. Thus, the internal validity of the study would be a major concern. Moreover, even if the study involved the comparison of scores on one or more dependent variables across existing conditions over which the researcher had no control, the researcher would have no control over the assignment of participants to the conditions. For example, a researcher investigating the assumed effects of incentive systems on firm productivity in several manufacturing firms would have no control over the attributes of such systems. Again, this would greatly diminish the internal validity of the study.

Measurement of Assumed Dependent Variables

In nonexperimental research, assumed dependent variables are measured. Note that the same is true of both randomized experiments and quasi-experiments. However, there are very important differences among the three experimental design types that warrant attention. More specifically, in the case of well-conducted randomized experiments, the researcher can be highly confident that the scores on the dependent variable(s) were a function of the study's manipulations. Moreover, in quasi-experiments with appropriate design features, the investigator can be fairly confident that the study's manipulations were responsible for observed differences on the dependent variable(s). However, in nonexperimental studies, the researcher is placed in the uncomfortable position of having to assume that what he or she views as dependent variables are indeed effects. Regrettably, in virtually all nonexperimental research, this assumption rests on a very shaky foundation. Thus, for example, in a study of the assumed effect of job satisfaction on intentions to quit a job, what the researcher assumes to be the effect may in fact be the cause. That is, individuals who have decided to quit for reasons that were not based on job satisfaction could, in the interest of cognitive consistency, view their jobs as not being satisfying.

Control Over Extraneous or Confounding Variables

Because of the fact that nonexperimental research does not benefit from the controls (e.g., random assignment to conditions) that are common to studies using randomized experimental designs, there is relatively little potential to control extraneous variables. As a result, the results of nonexperimental research tend to have little, if any, internal validity. For instance, assume that a researcher did a nonexperimental study of the assumed causal relation between negative affectivity and job-related strain and found these variables to be positively related. It would be inappropriate to conclude that these variables were causally related. At least one important reason for this is that the measures of these constructs have common items. Thus, any detected relation between them could well be spurious, as noted by Eugene F. Stone-Romero in 2005.

In hopes of bolstering causal inference, researchers who do nonexperimental studies often measure variables that are assumed to be confounds and then use such procedures as hierarchical multiple regression, path analysis, and structural equation modeling to control them. Regrettably, such procedures have little potential to control confounds. There are at least four reasons for this. First, researchers are seldom aware of all of the relevant confounds. Second, even if all of them were known, it is seldom possible to measure more than a few of them in any given study and use them as controls. Third, to the degree that the measures of confounds are unreliable, procedures such as multiple regression will fail to fully control for the effects of measured confounds. Fourth, and finally, because a large number of causal models may be consistent with a given set of covariances among a set of variables, statistical procedures are incapable of providing compelling evidence about the superiority of any given model over alternative models.

Eugene F. Stone-Romero

See also Experimental Designs; Quasi-experimental Designs

Further Readings

Cook, T. D., & Campbell, D. T. (1979). *Quasi-experimentation: Design and analysis issues for field settings.* Boston, MA: Houghton Mifflin.

Shadish, W. R., Cook, T. D., & Campbell, D. T. (2002). *Experimental and quasi-experimental designs for generalized causal inference.* Boston, MA: Houghton Mifflin.

Stone-Romero, E. F. (2002). The relative validity and usefulness of various empirical research designs. In S. G. Rogelberg (Ed.), *Handbook of research methods in industrial and organizational psychology* (pp. 77–98). Malden, MA: Blackwell.

Stone-Romero, E. F. (2005). Personality-based stigmas and unfair discrimination in work organizations. In R. L. Dipboye & A. Colella (Eds.), *Discrimination at work: The psychological and organizational bases* (pp. 255–280). Mahwah, NJ: Erlbaum.

Stone-Romero, E. F., & Rosopa, P. (2004). Inference problems with hierarchical multiple regression-based tests of mediating effects. *Research in Personnel and Human Resources Management, 23,* 249–290.

NONPARAMETRIC TESTS

Nonparametric or "distribution-free" statistics are a set of statistical methods that make limited assumptions about the population distribution from which the analyzed sample is drawn. These nonparametric statistics contrast with traditional parametric methods that assume the underlying population is characterized by the normal distribution and defined by population parameters (e.g., mean, standard deviation). The nonparametric family of statistics includes both descriptive and inferential statistics, such as the Mann-Whitney U, Spearman's rho, and Chi-square statistics. Many of the commonly used parametric techniques have nonparametric equivalents, allowing for convenient use and application to traditional experimental and nonexperimental research designs and studies. Because nonparametric methods require less stringent distributional assumptions, these techniques provide statistical tests for analyzing data in conditions failing to satisfy the assumption of a normal distribution or with unknown distribution characteristics.

Benefits and Limitations of Nonparametric Methods

Nonparametric statistics provide several advantages compared to parametric statistics. First, nonparametric statistics do not rely on the assumption of normality of variables. As a result, nonparametric statistics may be used under a broader range of conditions than corresponding parametric methods. The population distribution refers to the characterized probability of each possible outcome in a sampled population. Common types of probability distributions include the normal (or Gaussian), uniform, and logistic distributions. Parametric statistics (e.g., t, F, Pearson's r) belong to the general liner model (GLM) family of statistics and are bound by the assumptions of GLM. One key assumption of GLM is that variables are normally distributed in the population. Deviations from this normality assumption will produce dramatic effects on both Type I and Type II error rates of statistical tests if parametric methods are used. An increase in Type I error rate results in the increased likelihood of incorrectly stating statistical significance (i.e., a false positive). Conversely, an increase in Type II error rate results in the reduced likelihood of correctly stating statistical significance if a real difference exists (i.e., a false negative). Departures from normality can result in marked reductions in the statistical power (the inverse of Type II error rate; the ability to detect an effect if a real effect exists) of parametric tests. For example, simulations indicate that a small departure can decrease the statistical power of an independent samples t test from .96 to .28, meaning a change from a 4% chance to a 72% chance of making a Type II error. Because nonparametric tests do not make distributional assumptions, they are more appropriate and statistically powerful when data are non-normal or the underlying distribution is unclear or unknown.

Second, nonparametric statistics can be used for a wider variety of measurement scales than parametric methods. The use of parametric statistics is restricted to interval or ratio dependent measures. Nonparametric methods are appropriate not only for interval or ratio measures but also for ordinal (ranked) or nominal (categorical) data. For example, responses along a 7-point scale of employee satisfaction can be examined using either parametric or nonparametric methods. However, a categorical outcome (e.g., employment status, employed versus unemployed) cannot be analyzed as a dependent measure using traditional parametric statistics (e.g., t or F statistics). In contrast, nonparametric tests such as the Fisher's exact test or chi-square test may be used to analyze these data to provide a measure of statistical significance.

Although there are advantages to using nonparametric methods, there are also several limitations. An important consideration when using nonparametric statistics is that distribution-free does not mean assumption-free. Although nonparametric statistics do not make distributional assumptions (e.g., normal distribution of variables), these tests still make several assumptions similar to those made for parametric techniques. For example, nonparametric methods assume that random sampling is used when drawing the study sample. Similarly, observations are assumed to be independent and from a representative sample. Ignoring the necessary assumption checks when conducting nonparametric statistical tests can result in compromised outcomes and inflated Type I and Type II error rates just as when these checks are ignored for parametric statistics.

The interpretation of nonparametric tests may be less intuitive than the interpretation of parametric tests. The null hypothesis used for parametric tests is based on population parameters such as that the means of two groups are equal. Rejection of the null hypothesis indicates that the mean of the two groups may differ and provides a quantitative comparison of these group means for interpretation and description purposes. In contrast, the null hypothesis used when conducting nonparametric tests is a more general statement of population one and two belonging to the same population. Although this more general null hypothesis allows testing by ranks (as discussed below), it also makes the interpretation of significant results more ambiguous and less specific. Indeed, as the name nonparametric suggests, nonparametric statistics do not include parameters to describe the population data making quantitative comparisons more difficult.

Using Nonparametric Methods

The most popular nonparametric techniques are based on the idea that values can be ranked and statistical tests performed on the ranked, rather than raw, values. The Mann-Whitney U test (also known as the Wilcoxon rank-sum test) provides a case example of how this nonparametric ranking method works. For instance, if a researcher wanted to compare the effects of two different workplace interventions (e.g., Intervention A and Intervention B) on job satisfaction, he or she could use the Mann-Whitney U test for comparing independent samples. In this test, all values are first ranked without regard to which group the observation belongs. Second, the ranks for each group are summed and averaged to compute a mean rank for each group. If the mean rank for Intervention A was 100 and Intervention B was 30, this would suggest that Intervention A was associated with higher ranks and, thus, higher ratings of satisfaction. Finally, the mean ranks are compared for statistical significance and a p value computed. In this and other nonparametric tests, the null hypothesis is that the distribution of ranks is random and a statement of statistical significance suggests that the two populations are different. For example, a significant *p* value would suggest that the workplace interventions differentially influenced job satisfaction. Because nonparametric methods rely on ranked rather than raw values, these techniques do not assume a particular population distribution and perform well under conditions of non-normality.

A number of nonparametric procedures that are parallel to standard parametric methods have been developed. These analogous procedures allow for the easy application of nonparametric methods to standard research protocols. For example, if a researcher wanted to compare the effects of two different workplace environments on employee satisfaction, he or she would typically use an independent samples *t*-test. However, if these data did not meet the condition of normality, the Mann-Whitney U test is a simple nonparametric alternative. Similarly, a researcher examining the effects of three different interview methods would traditionally use the one-way analysis of variance (ANOVA). Once again, a simple nonparametric analogue (i.e., Kruskal-Wallis Test) exists for this experimental design.

A short list of nonparametric alternatives for the traditional parametric tests is provided below, including examples of research designs (in parentheses) that might use these procedures. Note that this is not an exhaustive list, but instead provides case examples of analogous parametric and nonparametric techniques:

- Independent samples t-test (parametric) = Mann-Whitney U test (nonparametric; Wilcoxon rank-sum test); the effects of a workplace exercise intervention (e.g., exercise versus sedentary) on job satisfaction
- Paired t-test (parametric) = Wilcoxon matched pairs signed rank test (nonparametric); the pre-workshop versus post-workshop change in job skills following a novel workshop for job skills training
- Pearson correlation coefficient (parametric) = Spearman rank correlation coefficient (nonparametric; rho); the correlation between job performance and measures of trait consciousness
- One-way ANOVA (parametric) = Kruskal-Wallis ANOVA by ranks (nonparametric); the effect of an applicant's most recent job status (i.e., unemployed, part-time, full-time) on interview performance

- Two-way ANOVA (parametric) = Friedman two-way ANOVA (nonparametric); the interaction between applicant gender and education achievement on interview performance

Justin C. Strickland

See also Confidence Intervals/Hypothesis Testing/Effect Sizes; Descriptive Statistics; Inferential Statistics; Measurement Scales; Sampling Techniques; Statistical Power

Further Readings

Conover, W. J., & Iman, R. L. (1981). Rank transformations as a bridge between parametric and nonparametric statistics. *The American Statistician, 35*, 124–129. doi:10.1080/00031305.1981.10479327

Gibbons, J. D., & Chakraborti, S. (2011). *Nonparametric statistical inference* (5th ed.). Boca Raton, FL: Taylor and Francis.

Mirosevich, V. M., & Erceg-Hurn, D. M. (2008). Modern robust statistical methods: An easy way to maximize the accuracy and power of your research. *American Psychologist, 63*, 591–601. doi:10.1037/0003-066X.63.7.591

Siegel, S., & Castellan, N. J., Jr. (1988). *Nonparametric statistics for the behavioral sciences* (2nd ed.). New York, NY: McGraw-Hill.

Wilcox, R. R. (1998). How many discoveries have been lost by ignoring modern statistical methods. *American Psychologist, 3*, 300–314. doi:10.1037/0003-066X.53.3.300

NONVERBAL COMMUNICATION

Nonverbal behavior and communication influences all human interactions, including those occurring in the workplace. While most advances in understanding nonverbal behavior have taken place in fields such as communication, social psychology, gender studies, and anthropology, organizational scholars have acknowledged that nonverbal behavior influences a number of organizational processes. Such processes include the interview, performance appraisals, and negotiation, to name a few. Nonverbal behaviors are also an important component in instances of aggression, perceptions of interpersonal (in)justice, and discrimination. Finally, scholars have recognized the relevance of nonverbal behaviors in theories of transformational leadership, emotional labor, and emotional intelligence.

Defining Nonverbal Behavior and Nonverbal Communication

Intuitively, people define nonverbal communication as communication that does not rely on words, a defining characteristic of verbal communication. However, this definition is overly simplistic. Nonverbal communication is *not* linguistic, while verbal communication is linguistic, even in instances when it does not rely on the physical voice apparatus (e.g., American Sign Language). Moreover, both verbal and nonverbal communication have vocal characteristics, known as vocalics. *Verbal vocalic* refers to message content, and *nonverbal vocalic* to how the message is conveyed (e.g., voice tone, accent, pitch). Combining these aforementioned characteristics allows for the generally accepted definition of *nonverbal communication* as the exchange of thoughts and feelings through nonverbal behavior.

Despite their differences, nonverbal and verbal communication are related. The former can *repeat* the latter (e.g., a nod to show agreement), *substitute* it (e.g., an eye roll instead of a statement of contempt), *complement* it (e.g., reddening while talking to an intimidating person), *accent* it (e.g., a slap on the back following a joke), or *contradict* it (e.g., wiping tears away while asserting that one is fine). In organizations, nonverbal behavior will often, if not almost always, accompany verbal content and lead to complex communication interactions.

Codes

Nonverbal communication is typically broken down in a series of codes that form the basis of encoding, transmission, perception, and decoding. These codes are grouped in three larger categories: (1) body codes, (2) sensory and contact codes, and (3) spatiotemporal codes, each of which subsumes a series of smaller codes.

First, body codes encompass communication through body movement (called kinesics), physical appearance, and eye movements (called oculesics). *Kinesics,* the communication through body movement, includes gestures, posture, gait, and facial expressions. Much research in nonverbal behavior has focused on kinesics and broken them down into further categories. Specifically, *adaptors* refer to self-touch (e.g., touching one's hair or face); *emblems* are gestures that have a socially understood meaning (e.g., a thumbs-up); *regulators* help maintain the flow of the conversation (e.g., nods); *affect displays* refer to facial expressiveness; and finally, *illustrators* are gestures that accompany verbal messages. Among illustrators are *batons* (using hands to emphasize a point), *ideographs* (sketching the relationship or the direction of movement in the air), *pointers/deictic movements* (pointing to an entity or object), *spatials* (depicting the distance or size), *rhythmic movements* (using part of the body to convey a tempo or rhythm), *kinetographics* (mimicking human or nonhuman action), and *pictographs* (drawing a picture or shape). Emblems and, to a lesser extent, illustrators are culturally specific. Also part of body codes is *physical appearance.* This category ranges from characteristics such as height, weight, skin, eye and hair color, to style of clothing and accessories, body art, and grooming. As such, it encompasses both characteristics that range from difficult to alter (e.g., skin tone) to easily changeable (e.g., hairstyle). Finally, *oculesics* is concerned with ocular expression, eye gaze, and eye contact. Micro-movements such as blinking and pupil dilation are also considered part of oculesics.

A second broad category is sensory and contact codes, which encompass touch, voice, and smell. *Haptics* is the formal name for communication through touch. The location of touch as well as the intensity and type of touch (e.g., a stroke, a pat, a slap) convey different meanings. *Vocalics* or paralanguage refers to how a message is conveyed. For example, an orator's pitch, range, volume, accent, and pronunciation, among other markers, influence discourse perception. Similarly, fluency and dysfluency, such as excessive pauses or segregates (e.g., "hmm"), also convey nonverbal meaning. Finally, *olfactics* is the term assigned to communication through scent and smell. Scent plays a role in social functioning—pleasant scents serve to attract, and unpleasant ones to deter, others. Admittedly, this code is likely the least studied in industrial and organizational psychology. Yet it is still relevant to organizational life, as illustrated by "scent-free" organizational policies, for example.

The third broad category is composed of spatiotemporal codes, which include personal space, the environment, and time. Proxemics refers to the use of personal space to communicate. Both culture and the relationship between two individuals influence personal space. North Americans, for example, prefer public interactions to occur at greater than 8 feet apart, professional interactions to occur between 4 and 8 feet apart, friendly interactions to occur between 1.5 and 4 feet, and intimate interactions to occur closer. The environment and its artifacts are also sometimes included within the construct space of nonverbal communication. The type of environment that is built (e.g., architecture and physical layout of an office space) or fabricated through design elements (e.g., décor, lighting) conveys meaning. The communication of organizational culture through artifacts and creations is illustrated in this code. Finally, *chronemics* is the communication through time, and it includes walking speed, work speed, promptness, and punctuality.

Is Nonverbal Behavior Controllable?

A debate in the field of nonverbal communication is the extent to which nonverbal behavior is controllable and learned, versus spontaneous and innate. As with most social psychological processes, the evidence supports both perspectives. Some nonverbal behaviors are the product of adaptations and, as such, show substantial cross-cultural similarity. This is the case, for example, in the display of basic emotions (happiness, sadness, fear, anger, disgust, and surprise), which is quite similar across cultures and is also present in individuals who are visually impaired from birth. Behaviors linked to an evolutionary basis contain a physiological component that renders them more difficult to suppress or control. At the same time, many nonverbal behaviors are controllable. Gait, posture, visual contact, physical appearance, and other characteristics are alterable. Many behaviors are also learned and therefore differ across cultures. For example, expatriates are often trained in the meaning of local emblematic gestures to facilitate their interaction with local business partners. Still, even when we can control some aspects of our nonverbal behaviors and emotional expressions, we often experience *leakage* in the form of subtle micro-expressions that reveal our "true selves."

The existence of gender differences in nonverbal behavior supports both the innate and learned explanations. For example, compared with men, women tend to smile more, be more expressive in their face and body movements, prefer less physical distance, have higher pitched and softer voices, and use fewer speech dysfluencies. Women are often better at making sense of nonverbal cues, except when detecting dominance. These differences have organizational implications in terms of communication training.

Workplace Processes

Nonverbal behaviors serve several social functions that are relevant for understanding workplace processes, such as displaying personal attributes and emotions to others, exercising social control and establishing hierarchy, promoting social functioning and followership, and fostering high-quality relationships. The role of nonverbal behavior has been noted in several areas of organizational research.

For example, the influence of nonverbal behavior has been identified in research on interviews and performance appraisals. Using a "thin slice" study design (i.e., short clips of a person's nonverbal behavior), researchers have established that people make relatively quick judgments of others based solely on their nonverbal behavior. Furthermore, these judgments are often accurate, although accuracy ultimately depends on the specific attributes being inferred. For example, people tend to be more accurate when relying on nonverbal behaviors to assess another's social skills than to assess one's work motivation. Nonverbal behaviors can also play a role in impression management. However, nonverbal behaviors are generally considered a less impactful tactic compared to verbal impression management tactics. Even in structured interviews, nonverbal cues will have at least some degree of influence on an interviewer's assessment and hiring decision.

Power and negotiation is another broad area of organizational research that has acknowledged the influence of nonverbal behaviors. Nonverbal behaviors associated with power include talking time and interruption, eye contact, facial appearance, posture, and physical size. Nonverbal behaviors related to power can have potent intrapsychic effects. For example, people who simply display power through their posture (characterized by an expansive stance) experience a psychological sense of power and will often behave as though they are actually afforded power through their social role. When interacting, people often display complementary power-related nonverbal cues; one person enacts a high-power stance while the other enacts a low-power stance. Power-related nonverbal cues, such as facial width-to-height ratio, predict negotiation and leader performance.

Aggression and discrimination research has also alluded to the use of nonverbal behavior to debase and exclude others. Aggression can include menacing sustained stares, the invasion of space, or a threatening tone used to convey a seemingly innocuous statement. Ostracism, a specific form of mistreatment in which a person is excluded from the social circle, includes the avoidance of eye contact. Relatedly, modern-day sexism and racism tend to be covert and accomplished through subtle hostile nonverbal cues, referred to as microaggressions (or, relatedly, selective incivility). Subtle hostile nonverbal behaviors can create a self-fulfilling prophecy because the targets exhibit unfavorable nonverbal behaviors in response.

Reflected in a number of leadership training programs, transformational leadership also has a nonverbal component. A host of nonverbal behaviors, including eye contact, verbal fluency, facial and body expressions, and vocal tone and variety, are associated with transformational leadership. When used effectively, nonverbal behaviors positively impact *message delivery* and perceptions of competence. In general, a strong delivery coupled with a weak verbal message (i.e., message content) produces more favorable outcomes than a weak delivery coupled with a strong verbal message. Transformational leaders also tend to engage in interactive nonverbal behaviors that are known to enhance interpersonal relationships, including immediacy (i.e., behaviors that convey liking and approach) and mimicry (i.e., the automatic imitation of others' nonverbal cues).

Finally, research on emotional labor and emotional intelligence implicitly incorporate nonverbal behavior. Emotional labor includes the controlled or constrained display of certain emotional cues. Relatedly, emotional intelligence captures accurately understanding and responding to others' emotional cues. People are often better at genuinely displaying certain emotions if they engage in at least some degree of deep-level emotional labor (i.e., change their felt emotions along with displayed emotions). Employees who can accurately read and respond to others' emotions tend to perform better and have stronger relationships with their colleagues. However, reading too much into others emotions can cause interpersonal problems.

While this list of organizational research topics is not exhaustive, it indicates that some areas of organizational research have considered the role of nonverbal behavior. These areas, along with others, are ripe for further scholarly exploration.

Jane O'Reilly and Silvia Bonaccio

See also Charismatic Leadership Theory; Emotional Intelligence; Emotional Labor; Employment Interview; Interpersonal Communication; Interpersonal Communication Styles; Transformational and Transactional Leadership; Workplace Incivility

Further Readings

Ambady, N., & Weisbuch, M. (2010). Nonverbal behavior. In S. T. Fiske, D. T. Gilbert, & G. Lindzey (Eds.), *Handbook of social psychology* (pp. 464–497). Hoboken, NJ: Wiley.

Burgoon, J. K., Guerrero, L. K., & Manusov, V. (2011). Nonverbal signals. In M. L. Knapp & J. Daly (Eds.), *The SAGE handbook of interpersonal communication* (pp. 239–280). Thousand Oaks, CA: Sage.

Gray, H. M., & Ambady, N. (2006). Methods for the study of nonverbal communication. In V. Manusov & M. L. Patterson (Eds.), *The SAGE handbook of nonverbal communication* (pp. 41–58). Thousand Oaks, CA: Sage.

Harrigan, J. A., Rosenthal, R., & Scherer, K. R. (2008). *The new handbook of methods in nonverbal behavior research*. New York, NY: Oxford University Press.

Manusov, V. (2005). *The sourcebook of nonverbal measures: Going beyond words.* Mahwah, NJ: Erlbaum.

Manusov, V., & Patterson, M. L. (Eds.). (2006). *The SAGE handbook of nonverbal communication.* Thousand Oaks, CA: Sage.

NORMATIVE MODELS OF DECISION MAKING AND LEADERSHIP

Psychologists who have advanced normative theories of management have typically advocated highly participative processes for making decisions. The principal basis for such prescriptions is the motivational benefit that results from a leader involving group members in decision making. In spite of this advocacy, reviews of the literature suggest a much more mixed picture of the consequences of participation.

One way of reconciling the inconsistent evidence is to attempt to identify the moderating variables that regulate these different effects. Such moderating variables could then be incorporated into a contingency theory to guide managers in selecting the degree of participation appropriate to each situation. In the early 1970s, Victor Vroom, working with a graduate student, Philip Yetton, formulated a normative model of leadership style that had that objective. Expressed as a decision tree, the model distinguished five degrees of participation and eight situational factors believed to interact with participation in determining its effectiveness. The Vroom–Yetton model inspired many studies aimed at determining its validity as well as its usefulness in

leadership training. The validity data, summarized 15 years later by Vroom and Jago, showed that the incidence of successful decisions was about twice as high when the decision process used was consistent with the model as when it was inconsistent. Clearly the model had promise, but the research suggested that there was much room for improvement.

In the three decades since its original publication, the Vroom–Yetton model has been substantially revised, first by Vroom and Arthur Jago in 1988 and in 2000 by Vroom. Its current structure is shown as a balance scale in Figure 1.

The five decision processes have undergone significant modification from the Vroom–Yetton model, as have the eight situational factors, which have been expanded to 11. The factors at the left-hand side drive the recommended process toward the more autocratic end of the spectrum, whereas those at the right favor a more participative approach. Finally, the two in the center, *decision significance* and *likelihood of disagreement,* interact with those at the left or right to determine the sensitivity of the scale. For example, when a highly significant decision is combined with factors at the left, the recommended process is shifted further toward autocratic methods. When it is combined with factors at the right, it will shift further toward participation.

Figure 1   Scale Diagram

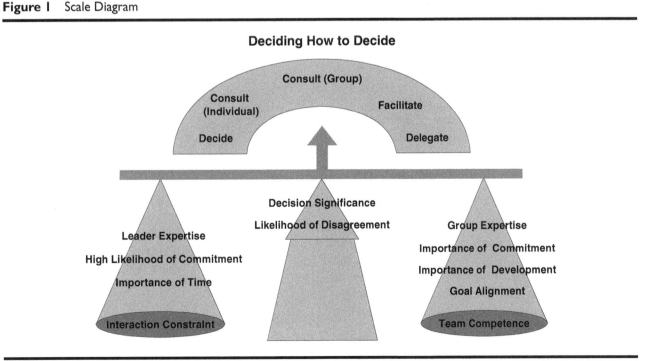

Of course, the scale is only a metaphor for the actual model, which is driven by a set of equations. To use the model, a manager, faced with a specific problem to solve or decision to make, is asked for judgments (typically on a five-point scale) concerning each of the 11 factors. These judgments are entered into four equations that estimate the effects of each of the five processes on the quality of the decision, its likely implementation, the time consumed in making it, and the developmental benefits resulting from the process. Finally these four consequences (quality, implementation, time, and development) receive differential weights corresponding to the manager's judgments of their importance in that problem.

Using the model sounds complicated but can be accomplished in less than one minute using a computer program called Expert System. Once the judgments are entered, the manager sees not a single recommended process (as in the Vroom–Yetton model) but a bar graph showing the relative estimated effectiveness of each of the five processes.

Scientific Implications

It has been said that a theory should be evaluated not only in terms of its validity but also in terms of the questions it raises and the quality of research it stimulates. Jago has recently compiled a list of more than 100 studies in scientific journals and more than 40 doctoral dissertations dealing directly with the Vroom–Yetton–Jago models. The models have also stimulated the development of a novel measure of leadership style that has proven useful both in research and in leadership development. The measure uses a set of 30 real or realistic cases, each depicting a manager faced with a decision to make that would affect his or her team. For each case, the manager chooses from the five alternative decision processes the one that he or she would select. The cases are not selected randomly, but rather on the basis of a multifactorial experimental design in which eight principal situational factors are varied independently of one another. This property makes it possible to systematically determine how managers change their intended behavior as elements of the situation are changed.

With the advent of the Internet, it is now possible for a manager to view and respond to the cases online in one of several available languages. As an inducement to enter their choices, managers can choose two groups from a list, varying in organizational level, nationality, and industry, with whom they would like to be compared. Finally, the manager downloads a 12-page individualized report comparing his or her style with the model and with the chosen comparison groups.

The data obtained from this measure has taught us a lot about the correlates of leadership style including the influence of nationality, gender, functional specialty, and hierarchical position. Managers do vary their behavior over situations in a manner not unlike that shown in the previous figure. However, they differ from one another in two respects. The most obvious is a preference for one side of the scale or another. This is similar to what is meant by describing mangers as *autocratic* or *participative*. But it should not be thought of as a general trait, because it accounts for only 10% of the total variance in behavior. Using the metaphor of the balance scale, it can be thought of as an extra weight added to one side of the scale or the other.

The other respect in which managers differ is the specific situational factors that govern their choices among the five styles. Although the pattern shown in the figure is a reasonable approximation of that of a manager choosing the modal response on each of the 30 cases, each individual manager displays a different pattern, ignoring factors or sometimes responding to them in a manner opposite to that prescribed by the normative model.

Practical Implications

Apart from the impact that the Vroom–Yetton–Jago models and derivative tools have had in the science of leadership, it is safe to say that they have had an even greater impact on the practice of leadership. About 200,000 managers around the world have now been trained in the models. Invariably, such training has included feedback on responses to sets of cases showing managers how they compare with their peers, with occupants of positions to which they aspire, and with the model. In effect, managers can compare their model of decision making and leadership with those of other groups and with the normative model.

Victor H. Vroom

See also Judgment and Decision-Making Process; Leadership and Supervision

Further Reading

Vroom, V. H. (2000). Decision making and the leadership process. *Organizational Dynamics, 28*(4), 82–94.

Vroom, V. H. (2003). Educating managers in decision making and leadership. *Management Decision, 41*(10), 968–978.

Vroom, V. H., & Jago, A. (1988). *The new leadership: Managing participation in organizations.* Englewood Cliffs, NJ: Prentice Hall.

Vroom, V. H., & Yetton, P. W. (1973). *Leadership and decision making.* Pittsburgh, PA: University of Pittsburgh Press.

NORMATIVE VERSUS IPSATIVE MEASUREMENT

When you type "ipsative" in Microsoft Word, it may be flagged as a potential misspell. This goes to show how widely or well it is known. But actually, ipsative measurement is very useful in some circumstances. Ipsative personality measurement is simply an alternative format for presenting option sets in personality or attitudinal questionnaires. Ipsative personality measurement is not as famous as the popular normative measurement. Therefore, in this entry the characteristics of normative measures are introduced first then the ipsative measures follow.

Normative measures provide inter-individual differences assessment, whereas ipsative measures provide intra-individual differences assessment. Normative measurement is very popular and prominent in the United States, but ipsative measurement is getting wider use in Europe and Asia.

Normative Measurement

Normative measurement usually presents one statement at a time and allows respondents using a 5-point Likert scale to indicate the level of agreement they feel about that particular statement. For example:

"I keep my spirits up despite setbacks."

1	2	3	4	5
Strongly disagree	Disagree	Neutral	Agree	Strongly agree

Such a rating scale allows quantification of individuals' feelings/perceptions on certain topics. Scoring of normative scales is fairly straightforward. Positively phrased items get a 5 when marked as *strongly agree,* while negatively phrased items need to be recoded accordingly, which means that you get a 5 when responding to a negatively phrased item as *strongly disagree.* Despite occasional debates on the ordinal versus interval nature of such normative scales, scores of similar items are usually combined into a scale score and used to calculate means and standard deviations, so norms can be established to facilitate interpersonal comparisons. The normative scores are aggregated across large sample sizes, and they are usually accepted as interval-level measurements.

The advantage of using normative personality measures is that normative measures present the personality items one at a time. This single-item presentation makes it clear and easy for respondents to choose their answers. The disadvantages of using normative personality measures are that research has shown that respondents have the ability to intentionally distort the answers to fit their own purposes.

Ipsative Measurement

Ipsative measurement presents an alternative format that has been around since the 1950s. Ipsative measures are also referred to as *forced-choice* techniques. An ipsative measurement format presents respondents with options that are equally positive or equally negative, thus the responses are less likely to be confounded by social desirability. Respondents are forced to choose one option that is "most true" of them and choose another one that is "least true" of them. A major underlying assumption is that when respondents are forced to choose among four equally desirable options, the one option that is most true of them will tend to be perceived as most positive. Similarly, when forced to choose one that is least true of them, those to whom one of the options is least applicable will tend to perceive it as least positive. For example:

"I am the sort of person who . . .

    a. prefers to keep active at work

    b. establishes good compromises

    c. appreciates literature

    d. keeps my spirits up despite setbacks

These four options are all positive statements. Respondents are asked to designate one "most true" and one "least true" response out of the four options.

The scoring of an ipsative scale is not as intuitive as a normative scale. There are four options in each item. Each option in the above example belongs to a specific scale (i.e., diligence, social confidence, introversion, or optimism). Each option chosen as "most true" earns two points for the scale to which it belongs; "least true," zero points; and the two unchosen ones each receive one point.

Assume that Mary chose "prefers to keep active at work" as the "most true" of her and "appreciates literature" as the least true of her. The scores for this item were as follows:

    a. prefers to keep   2 (diligence scale)
       active at work

    b. establishes good   1 (social confidence
       compromises   scale)

    c. appreciates literature 0 (introversion scale)

    d. keeps my spirits up   1 (optimism scale)
       despite setbacks

The same scoring system applies to all ipsative items. When there are 100 items on an ipsative personality questionnaire, the total score is 400. The scale that receives the greatest number of "most true" responses receives the highest score. The scale that receives the greatest number of "least true" responses receives the lowest score. High scores reflect relative preferences/strengths within the person among different scales; therefore, scores reflect intrapersonal comparisons.

In an ipsative questionnaire, the sum across all items adds to the total score, which is always a constant for every respondent. This makes the total score of ipsative personality measures completely useless and does not provide any information. This also creates a "measurement dependency" problem. The total score for every participant always adds up to be 400. Since the sum adds to a constant, the degree of freedom for a set of k scales is (k − 1), where k is the number of scales in the questionnaire. As long as the scores on k − 1 scales are known, the score on the kth scale is determined. The measurement dependency violates one of the basic assumptions of classical test theory, independence of error variance, which has implications for the statistical analysis of ipsative scores as well as for their interpretations.

The problem with having the total ipsative scores add to a constant could be solved by avoiding use of total scores. The measurement dependency problem is valid when the number of scales (k) in the questionnaire is small. However, the problem becomes less severe as the number of scales increases. In an ipsative personality questionnaire with large number of scales, researchers can choose a smaller number of scales that are particularly relevant to their research purposes to avoid the measurement dependency problem.

The advantage of using ipsative personality measures is that ipsative measures present the personality items with equally positive or equally negative options at the same time, so responses are less likely to be confounded by social desirability. This characteristic is especially important when measuring personality constructs in a culture where socially desirable responses are prevalent. The disadvantages of using ipsative personality measures are that the complexity of responses, the scoring of the responses, and the measurement dependency problems all require careful planning to resolve the potential problems.

Readers who are interested in the reliability, validity, and comparability of normative versus ipsative measurements might study the following Further Readings.

Chieh-Chen Bowen

See also Individual Differences; Integrity Testing; Personality Assessment

Further Readings

Baron, H. (1996). Strengths and limitations of ipsative measurement. *Journal of Occupational and Organizational Psychology, 69,* 49–56. doi:10.1111/j.2044-8325.1996.tb00599.x

Bowen, C.-C., Martin, B. A., & Hunt, S. T. (2002). A comparison of ipsative and normative approaches for ability to control faking in personality questionnaires. *International Journal of Organizational Analysis, 10,* 240–259. doi:10.1108/eb028952

Gordon, L. V. (1951). Validities of the forced-choice and questionnaire methods of personality measurement. *Journal of Applied Psychology, 35,* 407–412. doi:10.1037/h0058853

Hicks, L. E. (1970). Some properties of ipsative, normative and forced-choice normative measures. *Psychological Bulletin, 74,* 167–184. doi:10.1037/h0029780

NORMS

See Benchmarking

O

Occupational Health Psychology

According to the Bureau of Labor Statistics, 4,405 workplace fatalities and more than 3 million injuries occurred in the United States in 2013. Estimates from the World Health Organization (WHO) show that occupational injuries are a concern throughout the world. The WHO reports that there are approximately 268 million nonfatal workplace accidents each year, causing more than 3 days of lost work, and roughly 160 million new cases of work-related illness. These occupational illnesses include but are not limited to musculoskeletal, respiratory, and circulatory diseases. In addition to occupational illness and injuries, occupational stress has been and still is a major concern throughout the world. This concern was evident when the 1970 Occupational Safety and Health Act specifically voiced the need to research occupational safety and health (OSH), including the study of psychological factors and job stresses on potential for illness, disease, or loss of functional capacity in aging adults. According to the Bureau of Labor Statistics, in 2013, the concern about stress remained justified. Stress-related events and exposures showed higher percentages of long-term work loss. For instance, approximately 61.6% of exposures to traumatic or stressful events resulted in 31 days or more away from work. The median days away from work for these events was 33, whereas it was 8 for nonfatal injuries and illnesses in general.

Since 1990, concerns of human and financial losses associated with the aforementioned health issues have driven the development of a new discipline, occupational health psychology (OHP). Although the development of OHP may seem fairly recent, its roots can be traced back to the development of industrial and organizational (I-O) psychology. This common history will be reviewed in the sections that follow. It should be noted that OHP and I-O psychology share a common history. Even today, the Society for Industrial and Organizational Psychology (SIOP) notes that quality of work life is a major concern encountered by I-O psychologists in their professional work.

In his presidential address to SIOP in 1988, D. R. Ilgen voiced the aforementioned concern and reminded I-O psychologists that occupational health is a timeless concern for obvious humanitarian and utilitarian reasons. Workers' health, either physical or psychological, has an immense impact on their families, colleagues, organizations, communities, and society as a whole. The challenges associated with occupational health can provide I-O psychologists with invaluable opportunities and internal rewards while investigating the etiology of illness, injuries, behavioral maladjustment or deficiency, burnout, or psychological disorders occurring at work. Ilgen later raised a second concern from an economic perspective. He argued that an unhealthy workforce can lead to decreases in organizational productivity and individual performance, as well as increases in health care costs. Empirical research has supported this statement, demonstrating that job design can affect worker well-being and that changes in job design made to improve worker health are associated with reductions in health care costs.

Historical Roots of OHP

The term *occupational health psychology* was first mentioned by J. S. Raymond, D. W. Wood, and W. K. Patrick in *American Psychologist* in 1990. Although OHP has been embedded within other disciplines, psychologists such as R. L. Kahn, Arthur Konhauser, Joseph Tiffin, and Morris Viteles have taken an active role in promoting workers' psychological and physical well-being for almost a century. The beginnings of this can be traced to events in the early 1900s in the fields of I-O and human factors psychology. For example, Hugo Munsterberg (1898 president of the American Psychological Association [APA] as well as one of the "fathers" of I-O psychology) studied accident prevention and safety promotion as early as 1913. Henry Elkind applied the concept of *preventive management* in 1931 to workers in organizations in an effort to help workers improve their mental health.

Although the previously mentioned cases suggest a long history of psychologists' concern for workers' well-being, most psychologists have focused primarily on healthy lifestyles and health promotion in the general population, not the working population specifically. Given that people spend a large portion of their lives at work, and that work often has a tremendous impact on their personal as well as family lives, it seems obvious and logical for psychologists in general and I-O psychologists in particular to use their unique strengths to assist workers and management to build healthy workplaces in which people use their talents toward maximum performance and satisfaction.

What Is OHP?

According to the Society for Occupational Health Psychology, OHP is an interdisciplinary specialty that blends psychology and occupational health sciences, such as public health and preventive medicine. The ultimate goal for occupational health psychologists at this new frontier is to improve the quality of work life by developing an array of primary, secondary, and tertiary prevention programs and strategies to reduce work stress and strain; promote safe and healthy work behavior; prevent accidents, illnesses, and injuries; and enhance work and family life.

The aims of primary prevention are to identify and eliminate individual and organizational health risks. For example, organizations can redesign jobs to eliminate unsafe practices, individuals can learn how to manage time to reduce feelings of time pressure, and organizations can provide day care or elder care for their employees so that workers experience less family–work conflict. When primary interventions fail, secondary interventions can be used, such as establishing social support networks at work, altering organizational structures, providing organizational and individual stress management, or developing family policies. Although primary and secondary interventions are preferred and tend to fall into the realm of I-O psychologists' specialties, tertiary preventions might also be needed to help employees cope with psychological or physical distress resulting from negative feedback from an assessment, layoff, job loss, or injury.

Although emerging from a blend of behavioral and social sciences and occupational health disciplines, the domains falling within OHP are not yet agreed on by researchers and practitioners. Regardless of what these domains might be in the future, OHP is intended to be inclusive and interdisciplinary in nature. OHP applies knowledge and methodology from areas such as occupational and environmental health, organizational behavior, human factors, sociology, industrial engineering, ergonomics, and economics. Possible OHP domains or topics can be reviewed in the *Handbook of Occupational Health Psychology*, *Work and Wellbeing*, and *Workplace Well-Being: How to Build Psychologically Healthy Workplaces*.

Survey of Research and Practices in OHP

There has been progressive advancement in OHP literature involving the investigation of plausible antecedents and determinants of occupational health and its consequences. These investigations have focused on one or more of the following:

- dispositional factors, such as Type A personality, negative affectivity, and optimism;

- societal and environmental factors, including workers' compensation and public health policies;
- organizational factors, such as job design, organizational structure and climate, work arrangement, and compensation systems;
- management factors, including leadership and communication;
- family issues, such as variables associated with the interface between work and family; and
- interactions among these variables.

This trend has encouraged psychologists to take a proactive role in preventing occupational illness and injury and workplace aggression, reducing work stress, strengthening the work–family relationship, and improving physical as well as psychological well-being.

Many of the issues in OHP are considered to be *soft* issues, such as work–family conflict, stress, or health, which might be viewed as less important in organizations, compared with bottom-line issues, including productivity and turnover. Because soft criteria, although they occur often at work, are bound to be deemphasized because they lack the clear financial implications of *hard* criteria such as productivity and turnover, it is important for I-O psychologists to develop empirically supported applications to promote healthy workplaces and demonstrate that these soft applications affect organizations' bottom lines. A few exemplary applications have been documented and are briefly presented in the following text.

In the late 1990s, J. A. Adkins described the promising economic gains, such as workers' compensation costs, health care utilization rates, and mortality rates, of an organizational health center in the U.S. Air Force. The ultimate goal of the program was to develop a healthy workplace through promoting physical, behavioral, and organizational health so that organizational productivity could be maximized and workers' potential could be optimized. Similarly, Quick documented the culture of Chaparral Steel Company, which valued workers as resources rather than costs, and management made efforts to engage the minds and spirits of their workers. The economic gains in productivity—man-hours per ton of steel, sales, accidents, and turnover—were phenomenal.

OHP Training Programs in North America and Europe

An Institute of Medicine report in 2000, *Safe Work in the 21st Century*, voiced the urgency in training qualified OSH professionals while facing the challenges of a rapidly changing workforce in the 21st century. The report further pointed out the core disciplines in which OSH professionals should be trained. These core disciplines include occupational safety, industrial hygiene, occupational medicine, ergonomics, employee assistance, and OHP. Compared with the more established disciplines mentioned earlier, OHP has been relatively less developed.

Beginning in the 1990s, several universities in North America and Europe have developed training in OHP. As the result of a needs assessment survey from human resources management programs and schools of public health, the APA and National Institute for Occupational Safety and Health (NIOSH) conducted a pilot program for postdoctoral training between 1994 and 1998 at three universities. The main objective was to broaden the knowledge and skills of postdoctoral professionals in a range of OHP-related disciplines. Similar to the nature of the aforementioned pilot programs, postgraduate OHP programs were also developed in Sweden and the Netherlands. In addition to postdoctoral and graduate studies programs, several universities in the United States and England have developed graduate-level OHP training programs. It should be noted that most of the graduate training programs in the United States have received funding from NIOSH and have been sponsored by the APA.

Although the previously mentioned programs have different emphases on OHP training, they all share at least one common characteristic: interdisciplinary training. More specifically, it is evident when looking at these programs that diverse faculty members from psychology (e.g., I-O psychology, clinical and counseling psychology, health psychology, social psychology, human factors) and other disciplines (e.g., communications, epidemiology, ergonomics, industrial engineering, management, medicine, labor relations) play important roles in OHP training. The interdisciplinary training model is critical because discipline-specific training models as well as subdiscipline-specific training models tend to use a myopic approach that fails to capture the complexity and multilevel nature of occupational health issues. For example, fatal or nonfatal work accidents are multilevel, complex, and dynamic phenomena, which can likely be attributed to a combination of cultural, societal, environmental, economic, organizational, ergonomic, management, psychological, and family factors.

Future Challenges in OHP

Similar to any relatively new specialty, the development of OHP is dependent on continuous advancement in research and practice. The inherent nature of OHP complicates the developmental process and makes for a number of future challenges for the field. Foremost, traditional training in psychology tends to be discipline specific; OHP, however, is a blend of psychology and other occupational health sciences. Hence, I-O psychologists must step outside their comfort zones to incorporate findings and best practices from a variety of disciplines and diverse topics, such as integration of ergonomic principles, organizational support, and attitude change to promote healthy behaviors among office workers. Second, many criteria within the OHP realm present problems for research and practice. For example, if accidents, injuries, and illnesses are of interest to I-O psychologists, we must advance methodology to address issues such as low base rate, problems associated with reporting these incidents, and the delayed onset of many occupationally related illnesses. Third, it is important to point out that occupational health is more than merely the absence of injuries and illnesses at work. Hence, the traditional disease or management models (i.e., fixing symptoms or problems) are not the best models to follow when I-O psychologists attempt to develop a healthy workplace. An alternative model such as Total Worker Health, introduced by NIOSH in 2011, incorporates a more complete definition of health emphasizing not only the reduction of injuries and illnesses but also the promotion of workers' well-being. Although the introduction of this model is encouraging, there is still little research exploring interventions that integrate OSH and more general health promotion. Finally, among the many goals to be achieved by organizations, occupational health is likely a long-term goal. This presents a problem for gaining access to organizations, which is particularly critical for advancing OHP research and practice. Given the intense competition in the business world, short-term goals will likely capture management's immediate attention, and occupational health might not be considered its first priority. As a result, I-O psychologists who are trying to gain access to organizations must seriously consider the short-term gains of occupational health interventions and, specifically, consider such things as the economic gains associated with these interventions to gain attention.

Sarah DeArmond,
Peter Y. Chen, and
Yueng-hsiang Huang

See also Quality of Work Life

Further Readings

Chen, P. Y., & Cooper, C. L. (Eds.). (2014). *Wellbeing: A complete reference guide.* Chichester, UK: Wiley-Blackwell.

Day, A., Kelloway, E. K., & Hurrell, J. J. (2014). *Workplace well-being: How to build psychologically healthy workplaces.* Chichester, UK: Wiley-Blackwell.

Elkind, H. B. (Ed.). (1931). *Preventive management: Mental hygiene in industry.* New York: B. C. Forbes.

Ilgen, D. R. (1990). Health issues at work: Opportunities for industrial/organizational psychology. *American Psychologist, 45*(2), 273–283. doi:10.1037/0003-066X.45.2.273

National Institute for Occupational Safety and Health. (2015). What is Total Worker Health? http://www.cdc.gov/niosh/twh/totalhealth.html

Quick, J. C. (1999). Occupational health psychology: The convergence of health and clinical psychology with public health and preventive medicine in an organizational context. *Professional Psychology: Research and Practice, 30*(2), 123–128. doi:10.1037/0735-7028.30.2.123

Quick, J. C., & Tetrick, L. E. (2011). *Handbook of occupational health psychology* (2nd ed.). Washington, DC: American Psychological Association.

Raymond, J. S., Wood, D. W., & Patrick, W. K. (1990). Psychology doctoral training in work and health. *American Psychologist, 45*(10), 1159–1161. doi:10.1037/0003-066X.45.10.1159

Society for Industrial and Organizational Psychology. (2015). Brief description of the specialty. http://www.siop.org/history/crsppp.aspx
Society for Occupational Health Psychology. (2015). Field of OHP. http://www.sohp-online.org/field.htm

Occupational Information Network (O*NET)

The Occupational Information Network (O*NET) is the database of worker and occupational attributes that succeeds the U.S. Department of Labor's (DOL) *Dictionary of Occupational Titles* (DOT) as the primary source of information on occupations in the U.S. economy. Although the *DOT* had held this distinction for many years, numerous events—including the explosion of new occupations that accompanied the Internet and technology age, the decline in blue-collar industrial and manufacturing occupations, the dynamic nature of many of today's jobs, and theoretical and methodological advances in our understanding of work and job analysis—necessitated a new system for collecting and disseminating occupational information. The DOL responded by sponsoring the development of a computerized repository of occupational information that would permit rapid revision of the data, as well as easy access by the many individuals who wished to use the data therein.

With a strong theoretical framework, a procedure for updating content on a regular basis, an online viewer, associated career exploration tools, and links to current labor market data, O*NET offers current, diverse data on key occupations in the U.S. economy. Although no occupational information or classification system can be optimal for every purpose, O*NET provides many users with many ways of exploring the world of work.

O*NET Content

Occupations

The occupational taxonomy included in O*NET products and tools differs from that used in the *DOT* so as to reflect the changing world of work. First, job analysts aggregated the more than 12,000 *DOT* occupations into a more manageable number of occupational units (OUs). The initial aggregation yielded 1,172 OUs, which have been further refined to the approximately 950 occupations that now constitute the Standard Occupational Classification (SOC) system (SOC). Some *DOT* occupations were not aggregated and stand as SOC occupations today, whereas other SOC occupations comprise hundreds of *DOT* occupations. Consistent with the dynamic nature of today's world of work, new occupations continue to be added, whereas others are removed. Also contained by O*NET are crosswalks of SOC occupations to other classification systems such as the *DOT* and the Military Occupational Classification.

Descriptors

Second, O*NET describes occupations using an expansive set of variables drawn from a *content model*. The content model is a theoretical framework that specifies 21 types of occupational descriptors:

1. Abilities
2. Occupational interests
3. Work values
4. Work styles
5. Basic skills
6. Cross-functional skills
7. Knowledge
8. Education
9. Experience and training
10. Basic skills—entry requirement
11. Cross-functional skills—entry requirement
12. Licensing
13. Tasks
14. Tools and technology
15. Labor market information
16. Occupational outlook
17. Generalized work activities
18. Intermediate work activities
19. Detailed work activities

20. Organizational context

21. Work context

These 21 classes of occupational information, in turn, can be placed into one of six broad categories:

1. Worker characteristics such as abilities and interests

2. Worker requirements, including skills and education

3. Experience requirements such as training and licensing

4. Occupational requirements, including work activities and organizational context

5. Workforce characteristics such as labor market information and occupational outlook

6. Occupation-specific information, including tasks and tools/technology

The variables of the content model can also be categorized according to whether they are *worker oriented* or *job oriented* and whether they apply to a specific occupation (*within occupation*) or many occupations (*cross-occupation*). Worker-oriented variables that cross occupations include skills, abilities, and interests; those applicable within occupations include occupational skills and knowledge. Job-oriented variables that cross occupations include generalized work activities and organizational context; those applicable within occupations include tasks and machines, tools, and equipment.

Each of the 21 classes of occupational descriptors defined by the content model comprises multiple variables on which each occupation receives ratings on appropriate scales such as importance, level, and frequency or extent. In all, the O*NET database describes each occupation using more than 275 variables. For example, there are 52 abilities that span the cognitive (oral comprehension, number facility), physical (gross body equilibrium, stamina), psychomotor (finger dexterity, speed of limb movement), and sensory (far vision, speech recognition) domains. Similarly, the 35 skills span six domains, including basic skills (mathematics, writing), social skills, (negotiation, instructing), and systems skills (systems analysis, judgment and decision making).

Each occupation receives ratings of importance, level, and frequency or extent on each of these variables. A sample ability rating scale is given in Figure 1.

Figure 1   Sample Ability Rating Scale

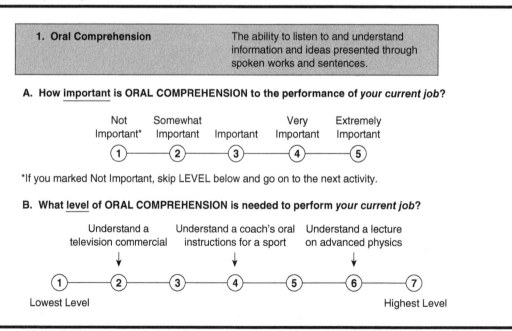

Initially, trained job analysts provided ratings of each O*NET occupation, but the National Center for O*NET Development is leading an effort to augment the O*NET database with ratings from job incumbents. Occupational experts are also used for occupations having few incumbents or for which incumbents are difficult to locate, and job analysts continue to provide abilities ratings for all occupations. Incumbent data currently are added for approximately 200 occupations annually. Collectively, these data provide a rich, common language that can be used to describe occupations in the U.S. labor force.

The O*NET System

The O*NET database is part of the O*NET System, which also includes the O*NET OnLine viewer, O*NET career exploration tools, and My Next Move.

O*NET OnLine

O*NET OnLine is a viewer that is available on the Internet. Hosted by the National Center for O*NET Development, the viewer affords O*NET users several options for using information provided in the O*NET database. For example, the viewer permits individuals to search for occupations via keywords or occupational codes, explore various job families, find occupations that match their skill profiles, or crosswalk occupations from other job classification systems to their counterpart SOC occupations.

Career Exploration Tools

DOL offers several vocational assessment tools that can be linked to the occupational information in the O*NET database. With an eye toward whole-person assessment, the O*NET career exploration tools (provided in both paper-and-pencil and computerized versions) allow individuals to determine their standing on abilities (Ability Profiler), vocational interests (Interest Profiler), and work values (computerized Work Importance Profiler, paper-and-pencil Work Importance Locator).

My Next Move

My Next Move is an online resource for exploring which careers one might wish to pursue (https://www.mynextmove.org). Developed by the National Center for O*NET Development, it allows users to explore careers via a keyword search, by exploring different industries (e.g., mining, oil, and gas; service), or by completing a vocational interest inventory (specifically, the O*NET Interest Profiler, which comprises 60 questions and is based on Holland's theory of career choice). It highlights occupations with key characteristics (careers forecasted to have rapid growth or to have large numbers of openings, careers affected by the green economy, careers with registered apprenticeships, and careers grouped by requisite levels of education and training). The site also offers veterans help finding civilian careers that would resemble the jobs they performed while in the armed forces. A Spanish version of the Web site (Mi Próximo Paso) is also available.

Rodney A. McCloy

See also *Dictionary of Occupational Titles*; Job Analysis; Person–Vocation Fit; Work Values

Further Readings

Dierdorff, E., Norton, J., Drewes, D., Kroustalis, C., Rivkin, D., & Lewis, P. (2009). *Greening of the world of work: Implications for O*NET-SOC and new and emerging occupations*. Raleigh, NC: National Center for O*NET Development.

Donsbach, J., Tsacoumis, S., Sager, C., & Updegraff, J. (2003). *O*NET analyst occupational abilities ratings: Procedures* (FR-03-22). Alexandria, VA: Human Resources Research Organization.

Levine, J., Nottingham, J., Paige, B., & Lewis, P. (2000). *Transitioning O*NET to the Standard Occupational Classification*. Raleigh, NC: National Center for O*NET Development.

McCloy, R., Campbell, J., Oswald, F., Lewis, P., & Rivkin, D. (1999). *Linking client assessment profiles to O*NET occupational profiles*. Raleigh, NC: National Center for O*NET Development.

National Center for O*NET Development. (2010). *Updating the O*NET-SOC taxonomy: Incorporating the 2010 SOC structure*. Raleigh, NC: Author.

National Center for O*NET Development. (2011). *O*NET products at work*. Raleigh, NC: Author.

Peterson, N., Mumford, M., Borman, W., Jeanneret, P., & Fleishman, E. (1999). *An occupational information system for the 21st century: The development of O*NET*. Washington, DC: American Psychological Association.

U.S. Department of Labor. (1991). *Dictionary of occupational titles* (rev. 4th ed.). Washington, DC: U.S. Government Printing Office.

OLDER WORKER ISSUES

Older workers constitute a growing segment of the workforce and must contend with a variety of distinctive concerns as they navigate their careers. These include physical, cognitive, and emotional changes that accompany the aging process; unique sources of work stress; age discrimination in employment opportunities; late-career and skill maintenance concerns; and decisions about when and how to retire from active employment. Psychologists can use information about challenges that confront older workers to develop recruitment and retention strategies and work designs that allow older workers to maintain their performance effectiveness and to see work as a satisfying and rewarding experience.

Age and Workforce Demographics

The point at which the term *older worker* is applied in studies of workforce demographics may be as early as 40 years of age or as late as 65 years of age. Nonetheless, studies of workforce demographics all come to similar conclusions: The proportion of older adults who continue to engage in paid employment well into their 60s and 70s is growing, and the proportion of our workforce that can be classified as "older" will continue to expand throughout the next decade.

Labor force participation rates generally tend to drop off beginning at about age 55, primarily because of early and "normal" retirements. However, labor force participation rates among those who are 55 and older are on the rise, with a projected labor force participation rate of 43%

among those 55 and older by 2020. Among those aged 55 to 64, participation rates are expected to exceed 68%, and participation rates among those aged 65 and older are expected to exceed 22%. In fact, it is projected that "over 55" workers will constitute approximately 25% of the total civilian labor force in the United States by 2020. This trend of increases in labor force participation for the 55 and older age group is expected to continue through 2050. The growth of this segment of the workforce represents the convergence of several forces, including improved health and longer life span, economic policies that encourage prolonged working (e.g., increases in the "standard" retirement age that qualifies an individual for full Social Security benefits), national and global economic uncertainty, and elimination of mandatory retirement policies from most civilian occupations in the United States.

Changes That Accompany Aging

Several aspects of physical work capacity, such as aerobic capacity, strength and endurance, tolerance for heat and cold, and ability to adapt to shifts in waking and sleeping cycles, systematically decline with age. Sensory skills such as visual acuity and auditory sensitivity, and some psychomotor abilities, including manual dexterity and finger dexterity, begin to decline once workers move into their 40s and beyond. Of course, the extent to which such decrements are likely to be associated with performance problems depends substantially on the nature of physical job requirements.

The most consistent finding in studies of cognitive abilities across the life span is a general slowing of response to information-processing demands as adults age, particularly as they move into their 60s and beyond. In addition, recall and working memory both decline with age. However, there are multiple types of cognitive abilities, and decline is not universal or uniform. In fact, cognitive functioning can remain stable or even improve across time for many older adults. For example, those aspects of cognitive functioning that rely on expert knowledge (or *wisdom*) continue to increase or remain stable well into the 70s. The rate of decline is slowed when cognitive skills, such as inductive reasoning and number abilities, are used regularly—"use it or lose it" seems to be an apt phrase in this case. In this regard, intellectually demanding jobs may protect against cognitive declines. Also, the manner in which learners prefer to acquire new skills differs between younger and older learners, with older learners preferring more active, experiential learning approaches and preferring to learn at a somewhat slower pace.

Although most personality traits are believed to be quite stable throughout the life course, characteristics that are helpful in the work context, such as conscientiousness, can be learned and emerge over time. Furthermore, job characteristics that are aligned with existing personality traits will foster continued development of those traits. Even so, a general dampening of emotional responsiveness accompanies the aging process. There are also age-related shifts in the kinds of coping strategies adults use to manage stressful experiences and increased skill in using such strategies.

Normal aging is accompanied by increased frequency and severity of health concerns. Clinically assessed indicators of physical health (e.g., blood pressure, cholesterol levels, and body mass index) may indicate a decline in health with age; however, self-reports of physical health may not. This indicates that even though health may have declined, the decline may be so gradual as to not be noticeable, or adjustments have been made to behaviors so that the decline does not prevent functioning. Many older workers function with a variety of chronic health conditions, such as arthritis and chronic back pain, which also prompt them to carry out work duties while coping with some degree of pain or mobility impairment. These have implications for physical stamina and the ability to sustain physically and mentally demanding work.

With all of these changes in mind, it is important to point out two other sets of findings regarding age-related changes and characteristics. First, from life span studies, we know that the rate and extent of age-related change differ considerably among adults. This is a recurring theme of findings regarding cognitive and physical abilities, health status, and most other characteristics relevant to work functioning. Thus, generalities regarding characteristics of older workers will frequently be incorrect for a particular individual worker.

Second, it is a common misconception that the changes accompanying aging will inevitably be associated with systematic declines in motivation, work attitudes, and job performance. Although it is certainly true that changes in physical and cognitive functioning that accompany the aging process provide the *potential* for reduced performance in some kinds of jobs, evidence of performance declines with aging tends to be the exception rather than the rule. In fact, there are many work-related outcomes from older workers that are beneficial to employers. There is little evidence that levels of motivation differ as a function of worker age, and studies of the relationship between age and work performance have shown no systematic relationship between the two. Absenteeism rates are generally low among older workers, and the frequency of accidents is actually lower among older workers than it is among younger workers. Attitudes such as job satisfaction are somewhat more positive among older workers than they are among younger workers. Furthermore, older workers can contribute to the work group as a whole by sharing expertise and fostering a supportive and less stressful work climate.

Sources of Work Stress

Workers experience occupational stress when there is a mismatch between the demands of the job and workers' capabilities and resources. The changes that accompany aging provide some guidance regarding the conditions under which older workers are most likely to experience stress and the strains that accompany prolonged stress, such as performance decrements, injuries, negative work attitudes, and mental and physical health symptoms.

For example, jobs that require heavy lifting and tasks that involve external pacing and substantial time pressure produce chronic demands that may be of particular significance to older workers. Likewise, hot and cold work environments may be physically more taxing to older workers than they are to younger workers, and work schedules that require night work will be more demanding for older workers than they will be for younger workers.

Other features of job design, such as the widespread incorporation of technology in the workplace, may produce both threats and opportunities for older workers. On one hand, technological innovations (e.g., adjustable illumination and font sizes on computer displays and ergonomically designed chairs and workstations) can be used as a way of redesigning work to accommodate needs of older workers, thus reducing some sources of work-related stress. On the other hand, new technologies often require skill sets that many older workers have not developed. The threat of obsolescence that this raises can serve as a stressor that is particularly salient to older workers.

Older workers are also at risk from organizational sources of stress associated with their work roles. For example, time pressures and work "overload" have become a way of life on many jobs. The long-term nature of their exposure to the constant pressure of too much to do and insufficient time to accomplish it increases the likelihood that older workers will experience negative consequences, including "burnout" and reduced health and well-being.

Distinct from work design, the social environment in which work takes place exerts a variety of pressures on older workers that may be experienced as stressful or that may reduce their ability to cope effectively with work demands. These include subtle or overt forms of age discrimination, hints about what older workers "can" and "should" do, and organizational cultures that devalue experience and "wisdom."

Age Discrimination

Although evidence regarding the relationship between worker age and work performance suggests that worker age is a singularly poor predictor of work performance, older workers encounter a variety of barriers to employment opportunities that reflect discrimination on the basis of age. Studies have documented age discrimination in many occupations with respect to hiring, promotions, salaries, and access to development opportunities. Sometimes the discrimination is fairly blatant, other times it represents more subtle (and often unintentional) differences in the way older workers and younger workers are treated at work.

One of the most common explanations for age discrimination is that managers and other decision makers are influenced by stereotypes that depict older workers as less capable, less energetic, less creative, more rigid, and less willing to learn than younger workers. This has the potential to put older job candidates at an unfair disadvantage when competing against younger applicants for jobs, promotions, and development opportunities. An additional unfortunate consequence of age discrimination is that it creates an environment in which older workers sometimes feel threats to their job security and, quite reasonably, experience anxiety about becoming reemployed should they lose their jobs.

To combat age discrimination in the United States, legal protections are afforded to older workers by the Age Discrimination in Employment Act. This legislation protects employees 40 years of age and older from discrimination on the basis of age in hiring, promotion, discharge, wages, and conditions of employment. Legal protections from age discrimination exist in many other English-speaking countries as well, often in the form of protections for younger workers as well as older workers.

Career and Work–Life Issues

Workplace norms and expectations about appropriate career trajectories (e.g., the sense that an individual is "stalled" with respect to career advancement) cause considerable distress and distraction for many older workers. As organizational structures continue to "flatten," the problem of career plateaus has become more widespread because there are fewer opportunities to continue upward movement.

Training and retraining are an important means of ensuring that older workers can continue to perform their jobs effectively and that they can move into new jobs and career paths later in their careers. However, fewer older workers participate in trainings compared with younger workers. Unrestricted opportunities for new skill development, support for participation in training, and training program design that incorporates the learning styles and preferences of older workers are all important to ensuring that late career workers can continue to be effective in their work. Training on technology use should incorporate confidence building into skill development.

Among their work–life concerns, many older workers are likely to have significant responsibilities for the care of elderly adults, financial responsibility for college students, and concerns about coordinating their own plans for retirement or continued work with those of spouses or partners. To be responsive to the work–life needs of older workers, employers need to take these kinds of concerns into account when they develop programs aimed at providing workers with options for balancing their work and personal lives.

Retirement Decisions

As they move into their 50s and 60s, most workers devote considerable time and energy to wrestling with decisions about if and when to retire. Retirement decision making is a complex process that includes consideration of the *timing* of retirement (Retire at age 55? Sixty-five? Seventy-five? Never?), the *completeness* of retirement (e.g., complete, permanent withdrawal from the paid workforce vs. alternative work arrangements such as part-time work or so-called bridge employment), and the *voluntariness* of retirement (e.g., feeling "pushed" out of one's job or retiring for health reasons vs. retiring to spend more time with one's family and other personal pursuits).

Personal preferences, health, and economic and social pressures to continue working or discontinue working as one nears "normal" retirement age all play important roles in this process. At the macro level, for example, changes in stock markets may result in losses to retirement savings. At the meso level, early retirement packages offered by many organizations as a way of reducing their workforces provide opportunities for some workers to leave the workforce early or to shift to new careers. At the micro level, chronic health problems may speed retirement or may lead to the decision to delay retirement in order to maintain access to health care benefits. In addition, personal preferences for continued work and the financial pressures of elder care and family education lead many older workers to continue some form of paid employment well past the age of 65, although it may not be in the form of traditional full-time employment. For some, retirement may mean a transition to pursue new career interests that provide continued growth and development.

As a result, the reality of retirement is that many workers will move into and out of the workforce several times during their later years, and organizations can make best use of the talents of these workers if they design flexible work arrangements that can accommodate this kind of movement.

Janet L. Barnes-Farrell
and Gretchen A. Petery

See also Careers; Retirement; Stereotyping

Further Readings

Adams, G. A., & Beehr, T. A. (Eds.). (2003). *Retirement: Reasons, processes and results*. New York: Springer.

Barnes-Farrell, J. L. (2004). Older workers. In J. Barling, K. Kelloway, & M. Frone (Eds.), *Handbook of work stress* (pp. 431–454). Thousand Oaks, CA: Sage.

Bowen, C. E., Noack, M. G., & Staudinger, U. M. (2011). Aging in the work context. In K. W. Schaie & S. L. Willis (Eds.), *Handbook of the psychology of aging* (7th ed. pp. 263–277). San Diego, CA: Academic Press.

Farr, J., & Ringseis, E. (2002). The older worker in organizational context: Beyond the individual. In C. Cooper & I. Robertson (Eds.), *International review of industrial and organizational psychology* (Vol. 17, pp. 31–75). New York: John Wiley.

Finkelstein, L., Truxillo, D., Fraccaroli, F., & Kanfer, R. (Eds.). (2015). *Facing the challenges of a multi-age workforce*. New York: Routledge.

Hansson, R., DeKoekkoek, P. D., Neece, W. M., & Patterson, D. (1997). Successful aging at work: Annual review, 1992–1996: The older worker and transitions to retirement. *Journal of Vocational Behavior, 51*, 202–233.

McEvoy, G., & Cascio, W. (1989). Cumulative evidence of the relationship between employee age and job performance. *Journal of Applied Psychology, 74*, 11–17.

Ng, T. W. H., & Feldman, D. C. (2013). Employee age and health. *Journal of Vocational Behavior, 83*, 336–345. doi:10.1016/j.jvb.2013.06.004

Posthuma, R. A., & Campion, M. A. (2009). Age stereotypes in the workplace: Common stereotypes, moderators, and future research directions. *Journal of Management, 35*, 158–188. doi:10.1177/01492063 08318617

Schaie, K. W. (1990). The optimization of cognitive functioning in old age: Predictions based on cohort-sequential and longitudinal data. In P. B. Baltes &

M. M. Baltes (Eds.), *Successful aging: Perspectives from the behavioral sciences* (pp. 94–117). Cambridge, UK: Cambridge University Press.

Sterns, H., & Huyck, M. H. (2001). The role of work in midlife. In M. Lachman (Ed.), *Handbook of midlife development* (pp. 447–486). New York: John Wiley.

Szinovacz, M. E., Davey, A., & Martin, L. (2014). Did the great recession influence retirement plans? *Research on Aging*, 37, 275–305. doi:10.1177/0164 027514530171

Toossi, M. (2012, January). Employment outlook: 2010–2020. Labor force projections to 2020: A more slowly growing workforce. *Monthly Labor Review*, 135, 43–64.

Wang, M., & Shi, J. (2014). Psychological research on retirement. *Annual Review of Psychology*, 65, 209–233. doi:10.1146/annurv-psych-010213-115131

ONLINE ASSESSMENT

Online assessment refers to the administration of tests or evaluative measures of knowledge, skills, abilities, or other characteristics of job applicants and employees through the use of technology and the Internet. In the early 2000s, organizations began to favor the administration of tests over the Internet rather than in person; most of these early online assessments mimicked the format of traditional paper-and-pencil tests in a computer format. As technology advanced, however, more sophisticated features such as adaptive logic, high-fidelity virtual environments and simulations, and gaming components became available and have since been incorporated in assessments.

There are many advantages of online assessment. Organizations are able to reach large, diverse global applicant pools, reduce labor costs, save time, and improve efficiency. Prior to online assessment, organizations were required to bring applicants on site to administer tests; this was quite costly in terms of travel and labor. Assessing applicants online removes the labor associated with scheduling, administration, scoring, and reporting. It also improves the time lapse from initial application to final hiring decision, allowing organizations to fill open positions as quickly as possible. Online assessment also allows the opportunity to capture unobtrusive measures, such as the time an applicant spends on each question, which can be a valuable source of information.

Despite these advantages, there are also disadvantages and significant controversies regarding the use of online assessment. One primary concern is that many tests delivered online are unproctored. Traditionally, organizational staff members or third-party test administrators have supervised (i.e., proctored) the administration of tests. Control over test conditions is diminished when tests are delivered online. Other issues include measurement nonequivalence, increased cheating, concern about the ethical use of tests, and adverse impact. These are discussed below. First, various types of online assessments are introduced.

Types of Online Assessments

Self-Report Assessments

Self-report assessments are tests that ask individuals to report on behavioral tendencies, interests, values, or other noncognitive characteristics. Questions on these tests do not have definitive right or wrong answers. Personality, occupational interests, culture fit, and integrity are a few examples of noncognitive constructs assessed in online formats for the purposes of personnel selection.

Cognitive Assessments

Other online tests are designed to measure the intellectual functioning of individuals. These tests have a correct answer for each question. Examples of these types of tests include general mental ability assessments and tests of specific abilities such as verbal ability, quantitative ability, and spatial ability.

Situational Judgment Tests

Situational judgment tests assess individuals' judgments about realistic situations that may be encountered in the workplace. The test taker is presented with a scenario in which he or she must make some type of judgment or decision, given a list of possible options, and is then asked to choose the most appropriate one. These tests are often tailored to specific jobs and have predetermined scoring structures. Situational judgment tests can measure a variety of constructs, such as knowledge and skills, applied social skills, personality, and a combination of multiple constructs. Online versions are presented to test takers in on-screen text format, video scenarios, or immersive virtual environments.

Work Samples and Simulations

A work sample or simulation is a test that closely resembles the work an applicant would perform on the job. This type of assessment allows test developers to capture the many types of skills, knowledge, and abilities that are required to complete a task successfully. Simulations can take many forms. For example, gamification is an emerging trend; it involves transformation of a work simulation into a game with fun and entertaining components such as rewards, challenges, and competition that also apply to relevant job objectives.

Assessment Centers

Assessment centers are collections of tests that present applicants with a variety of activities and exercises that assess different types of knowledge, skills, and abilities. Traditional assessment centers are conducted in person and require leaders to participate in role-playing tasks, leaderless group projects, or in-basket (or inbox) assignments. Online versions of assessment centers attempt to replicate these activities in a more modern or realistic form; applicants are asked to answer e-mails and conduct other tasks on the computer, or might engage in virtual communication or collaboration tasks.

Development and Administration of Online Assessments

The use of technology and the Internet in testing has drastically changed the development and administration of assessments. Psychologists must ensure that measurement properties are equivalent between traditional assessments and online assessments, appropriate methods of detecting and handling cheating are in place, systems and organizations can ensure security and confidentiality of data, and decisions regarding the features of technology are made properly.

Equivalence and Measurement Concerns

Psychologists have an ethical responsibility to provide information about the validity, reliability, and fairness of each assessment. These requirements do not change when assessments are administered online. Test developers must provide evidence that online assessments are equivalent to assessments traditionally administered in paper-and-pencil formats. Measures are determined to be equivalent if the correlation between scores on the online assessment and the paper assessment is close to perfect (i.e., 1), the two tests have comparable average scores and standard deviations, and the tests have the same relationships with outcomes of interest, such as job performance. Online assessments may be susceptible to reliability threats, because they are not administered in standardized environments (an important requirement to establish reliability); applicants can take tests whenever or wherever they choose, which introduces more variability into the environment.

There is conflicting evidence regarding whether measurement is equivalent in online assessments. A large majority of research has found equivalence between online versions and paper-and-pencil versions of noncognitive assessments. However, some evidence does exist to suggest that there may be differences across modes. Research evaluating the effectiveness of online assessments of cognitive ability has been mixed. For instance, research has indicated that measuring cognitive ability online may change the nature of the test. More research is needed to make definitive conclusions. Issues of measurement equivalence are discussed in more detail below.

Test Security

Cheating and piracy are major issues that need to be addressed with regard to the security of online assessment. Unproctored testing situations increase the potential for cheating (e.g., using prohibited resources, obtaining help) and also increase the likelihood of piracy (i.e., stealing test materials). Test publishers must determine how to detect, prevent, and handle test security in these test-taking environments.

Prevention of Cheating and Piracy

A number of approaches are available to prevent cheating and piracy, including warnings, strict enforcement of copyright laws, Web patrols to find test content being shared publicly, and the development of multiple equivalent versions of the test. It is also possible to proctor online assessments remotely by using a webcam or other surveillance device. Another alternative is the "semiproctored" approach, in which an organization places kiosks on company property. Experts in the field have pointed out that proctoring is not necessarily the gold standard for preventing cheating, as it is not perfect.

Adaptive testing is another way to mitigate cheating. Adaptive testing refers to the practice of determining which items to present to a test taker on the basis of his or her previous answers. Consequently, the test is tailored to each individual test taker, and not every test taker will receive the same questions. Thus, the exposure of items can be controlled, and the likelihood that two different test takers will see the same items is reduced. This approach requires large numbers of test takers and a very large item pool and may not be appropriate for any but the largest scale assessments.

Detection of Cheating and Piracy

There are a variety of ways to detect cheating and piracy. Technologies such as fingerprint or retina scans can be used in unproctored Internet testing situations to verify the identities of test takers. Test developers can also develop complex algorithms to detect unusual response patterns that indicate cheating. However, unique patterns of response could be due to variations in health, practice, or high motivation. To detect piracy, some testing organizations employ staff members to investigate different Web sites on which individuals may share or sell testing information.

Punitive Actions in Test Security

When suspicion of cheating or piracy occurs, organizations must determine how to handle the situation. Accusing or raising questions about an individual's integrity can have serious consequences; detection needs to be extremely accurate before discussing with the applicant. The organization needs to make decisions about whether it will let the individual retest, if it will invalidate the results, or if it will report or sue the individual for stealing materials. The Association of Test Publishers and the International Test Commission both provide best practices organizations can follow for handling test security.

Data Analytics

Scoring, analysis, and reporting of assessments are much easier when computers are used; test answers are captured in electronic form, and algorithms can be developed to check errors routinely, automatically score tests, and develop instant reports. Computing power has increased sufficiently to allow organizations to analyze and score enormous amounts of data efficiently. Big data analytics can apply real-time utilizations of data that are collected from multiple sources.

It is possible to develop dynamic reports or tailored information of each applicant's results. Reports can suggest potential weaknesses each applicant may have and considerations or suggestions for how the applicant would have to be managed if hired. Organizations can combine reports across the span of someone's career to create comprehensive profiles and reports from each assessment to use for development, layoffs, or succession planning.

Organizations have also begun tracking scores and developing large databases to create norms. Normative data can help organizations compare data across organizations in a similar industry and create benchmarks. These large databases also help organizations analyze data across occupations, languages, and geographic areas, which aids in tailoring future tests.

Technological Considerations

Other issues surrounding administration of tests online include technological issues (e.g., connection speed), variability in user interface, and applicant reactions to technology. Several technical considerations that affect the measurement or reactions of users must be made when using online assessments. The degree to which an online assessment is user friendly can affect recruitment and selection outcomes. Research has shown that applicants are more likely to complete an application when a Web site is easy to use. The specifics of the interface can also affect the reliability and validity of the assessment. If test takers have problems reading items or determining how to navigate an assessment, it may affect their overall performance.

Mobile Devices

Candidates can use mobile devices, such as smartphones or tablet, to complete online assessment from wherever they are, whether they are riding the bus across town or hanging out in a park. Given that mobile devices are less expensive than computers, it is possible that mobile-friendly assessments reach a wider applicant pool. According to the Pew Research Center, approximately 20% of adults in the United States (and more so globally) rely exclusively on smartphones to access the Internet. This likely opens access to individuals in differing socioeconomic status, age, and income groups, creating a more diverse applicant pool.

There are also disadvantages to mobile assessment. Candidates may be taking tests under conditions that are not ideal. Screens on mobile devices are often smaller and may reduce visibility and thereby create more difficult test-taking conditions. Initial research has found that mean test scores for cognitive ability tests are lower for mobile versions compared with nonmobile versions. Potential reasons for the lower scores include increased scrolling time, lack of a mobile-specific application of the test, difficult interface, or more time required to read the smaller text.

Applicant Reactions

Understanding applicant reactions to online assessment can have important implications for organizations. They can influence whether an applicant accepts a job offer, becomes or remains a consumer of the organization, or recommends the organization to other qualified applicants. Negative reactions to online assessment may also lead applicants to withdraw or challenge the fairness and legality of the selection procedures.

Individuals vary in their comfort and willingness to use technology. Organizations can offer multiple different types of assessments and a choice of method to ensure that the relevant populations of job applicants are all able to apply; the process should not favor any one group over another.

Reactions to privacy threats are of increasing concern to organizations. Applicants are specifically concerned with sharing their personal and sensitive information online, as millions of organizational records have been breached in the past. Applicants are worried that organizations may provide inadequate data security, unauthorized release of their data, or the use of invalid data for hiring purposes. Organizations assessing individuals online need to ensure that the data being collected remain confidential. As this problem becomes more widespread, the government has begun to implement laws and guidelines regarding the necessary requirements for maintaining reasonable security, which organizations can consult.

Implementation Considerations of Online Assessment in Selection Systems

Introducing online assessments into the selection process is often a large-scale undertaking that requires effective change management tactics. Organizations must ensure that users such as recruiters and hiring managers adopt the new technology and that they understand how to deliver the assessment and interpret scoring.

For any selection system to be successful, test developers must involve key stakeholders. The involvement of stakeholders can aid in the technological management of the system and adoption of the system. Key stakeholders include staff members from various departments, including human resources, information technology, operations, and finance. Test developers must understand the resources, capabilities, and constraints within the organization. Most important, the existing selection process and how the new assessment will be integrated must be understood in detail.

Researchers and practitioners have observed that managers are often reluctant to use the technical information from online assessments; rather, they prefer to use their intuitive judgment. Training managers on the development and use of online assessments can increase the likelihood that managers use scores appropriately to make hiring decisions.

Adverse Impact

The exclusive use of online assessment may have unintended consequences, such as the potential for adverse (disparate) impact. Adverse impact occurs when members of a protected class are systematically excluded from the applicant pool. Not all individuals have equal access to the

Internet. Furthermore, those individuals with access to the Internet do not all have equal access to high-quality connections. Organizations must also determine how to make their assessments available to those with disabilities (e.g., blindness). The possibility that individuals have differential access, comfort levels, or technological skills increases the chances that organizations may encounter legal consequences.

Ethical Concerns

Some psychologists consider administering unproctored assessments online a violation of ethical principles because they believe it is not possible to accurately depict the reliability and validity inferences in an unproctored setting. To support this argument, they cite sections of the American Psychological Association's *Ethical Principles of Psychologists and Code of Conduct*. To demonstrate validity evidence, there needs to be a standardized process, including standardization of the test environment. Also, it is not possible to interpret an individual's test score to a normative database if the extent of cheating in the unproctored environment is not understood. The notion that unproctored online assessment creates the opportunity for cheating, which is immoral, also leads psychologists to conclude that it is unethical. Others who disagree that using unproctored online assessment explain that the *Ethical Principles* details that is an acceptable practice as long as they have explained the potential effects after efforts they made to support reliability and validity.

Conclusion

Online assessment is the norm for assessment in organizations. However, there are still many unknowns. Although benefits seem plentiful, there are still large risks, including decreasing validity of assessment scores, an increase in cheating, increased potential for security breaches, fairness, and ethical concerns with using online assessments. Research needs to continue to investigate matters discussed in this entry and do so in a manner that generalizes across modes and time. It is no longer practical to simply compare modes (e.g., paper-and-pencil vs. video situational judgment tests), as technology

rapidly changes and there is likely more variance within modes than across modes. To truly understand the effects of technology and online settings, researchers must develop a framework with which to compare different modes of assessment. Denise Potosky has proposed a framework with which to understand the effects of technological factors on outcomes in the communication process during assessment. This framework is made up of four attributes of technology media: transparency (i.e., unobtrusiveness of medium), social bandwidth (i.e., the number of social cues exchanged), interactivity (i.e., the pace of the interaction), and surveillance (real and perceived privacy). This framework is sufficient for understanding assessment that involves two-party interactions (e.g., interviews), but in the future it should be expanded.

Tara S. Behrend and Nikki Blacksmith

See also Employee Selection; Online Survey Data Collection Methods: Leveraging Qualtrics and SurveyMonkey; Validity

Further Readings

Anderson, N. (2003). Applicant and recruiter reactions to new technology in selection: A critical review and agenda for future research. *International Journal of Selection and Assessment, 11,* 121–136. doi:10.1111/1468-2389.00235

Potosky, D., & Bobko, P. (2004). Selection testing via the Internet: Practical considerations and exploratory empirical findings. *Personnel Psychology, 57,* 1003–1034. doi:10.1111/j.1744-6570.2004.00013.x

Reynolds, D. H., & Weiner, J. A. (2009). *Online recruiting and selection: Innovations in talent acquisition.* Hoboken, NJ: John Wiley.

Reynolds, D. H., & Rupp, D. E. (2010). Advances in technology-facilitated assessment. In J. C. Scott & D. H. Reynolds (Eds.), *Handbook of workplace assessment: Evidence-based practices for selecting and developing organizational talent* (pp. 609–641). San Francisco, CA: Jossey-Bass.

Tippins, N.T. (2015). Technology and assessment in selection. *Annual Review of Organizational Psychology and Organizational Behavior, 2,* 5.1–5.32. doi:10.1146/annurev-orgpsych-031413-091317

Tippins, N. T., & Adler, S. (2011). *Technology-enhanced assessment of talent* (Vol. 30). Hoboken, NJ: John Wiley. doi:10.1002/9781118256022

ONLINE QUALITATIVE METHODS

Online qualitative methods are a mode of inquiry used in disciplines such as sociology, psychology, and management studies to research human behavior on the Internet. These methods aim at the on-site collection of rich, in-depth empirical material of a limited scope, such as interviews, observation, or visual data. Such material informs research about how the Internet functions as a mediator of communication in daily organizational life but also how novel and independent cultures, known as online communities, exist on the Internet. Online qualitative methods focus on sources such as social media, blogs, chats, discussion forums, wikis, and virtual worlds. By focusing on the "hows" and "whys" of Internet-mediated communication and interaction, online qualitative methods offer researchers tools to understand how digital technology affects areas such as group behavior, organizational culture, and change management. Online qualitative methods can be used to pursue independent research, such as case studies or ethnographies, or can be used as prestudies for establishing proper conditions for further experiential or quantitative studies.

Scope and Development

Interest in online qualitative methods arose as a response to the emergence of digital technology as a mediator of human interaction. Starting in the 1980s, researchers used such methods to understand how early Internet technologies, such as e-mail and Usenet news groups, influenced how people communicated. Those early studies typically focused on what is called paucity, that is, how online technologies inhibit natural communication because of the lack of many elements of direct face-to-face meetings such as tone and facial gestures. Some of these studies remain topical and can help to understand why, for example, it is difficult to manage teamwork using e-mail. Toward the end of the 1990s, the focus of research shifted. The Internet was evolving and could no longer be understood merely in terms of paucity. Driven by ethnographic studies of online user groups, it was now understood that the Internet nested and fostered its own, indigenous forms of culture. Thus, focus turned toward the study of online communities. This implied seeing the Internet as something that both enables and enriches human interaction. With the constant evolution and adaption of new Internet applications such as social media, online marketplaces, and persistent online game worlds, the scope of social phenomena on the Internet keeps expanding. This also applies to how people interface with the Internet, which in recent years has expanded to devices such as smart phones, tablet computers and sports watches.

Using Online Qualitative Methods

Broadly, online qualitative methods can be used to research two types of questions: how the Internet functions as a mediating technology in human interaction or, alternatively, how to understand online communities enabled by the Internet as independent sites. This choice of focus, the Internet as a mediator or the Internet as an enabler, will influence the actual research design that is adopted. If the Internet is studied from the perspective of computer-mediated communication between, for example, virtual teams located in different countries or in different time zones, then interest is in the activity of actual, natural persons. This implies gathering data on solutions such as e-mail, voice-over-Internet protocol, chat rooms, bulletin boards, virtual service tickets, and cloud computing as they are actually used in normal, daily routines. This allows researchers to, for example, understand the effects of distance, time, and sociocultural phenomena in virtual project teams working on the development of software code in two different countries. Such research often involves interviews, informant diaries, documents, or physical observation. Alternatively, if the focus is on understanding the indigenous culture and knowledge of online communities, then the subject of study is not the behavior of actual, natural persons. Rather, research focuses on studying the online behavior of representations such as chat room nicknames or online game avatars. Although real people guide these, they are studied as naturally occurring members of specific online communities. This kind of research means either active or passive involvement by the researcher in the online community being studied and thus typically draws on ethnographic fieldwork either as observation or participant observation. Such methods can be used to study a number of diverse group behaviors, such as the development of online wikis, open-source software development, virtual game worlds, and online communities dealing with sensitive social issues such as sexual minorities. Central to these research designs is that they seek to understand online communities on the Internet as independent sites, and the actual identities of the participants are a secondary concern. Although online qualitative methods imply distinct research designs with regard to data gathering and fieldwork, the analytical work in such designs typically follows established qualitative practices, such as grounded analysis, textual or discourse analysis, or ethnographic write-up.

There are many specific methods through which the Internet can be studied using qualitative methods. In all cases, such methods are adaptions of time-tested and tried qualitative methods that have been adapted to the specific considerations imposed by the Internet. Interviews can be conducted either textually across platforms such as chats or online worlds or as talk over applications such as voice-over-Internet protocol. Such interviews are particularly valuable for researchers, because they often make possible research designs that would not otherwise be feasible because of time or monetary constraints. The Internet can be researched as a source of textual material by searching for and recording bulletin boards, blogs, and social media entries. There are instances, such as the listing of some open-source software features and change logs, in which these might in fact be the only sources of information available. By studying online communities, the Internet can also support ethnographic observation or participant observation suitable for long-term, immersive research designs. Increasingly the Internet also functions as a source of visual data in the form of screenshots or recordings.

Ethical Considerations

Online qualitative methods offer many possibilities for conducting research on the Internet but are associated with a range of unique challenges. It can often be difficult to reliably determine

who our informants are, and indeed, often informants do not wish to be identified, even by researchers. This is especially true when we are researching sensitive online communities. This can weaken the value of the data. At the same time, exceptional care must be taken in the anonymization not only of informant names, real or physical, but also of excerpts presented in data, as they are increasingly easy to trace. Qualitative online methods also offer researchers unusual possibilities for conducting covert research by simply not disclosing the data-gathering nature of research activity, but it is important to realize that this implies substantial ethical ramifications that need to be cleared with research regulating bodies in advance.

Mikko Vesa

See also Case Study Method; Ethnography; Human–Computer Interaction; Organizational Culture; Qualitative Research Approach; Social Media: Implications for Organizations; Virtual Organizations

Further Readings

Boellstorff, T., Nardi, B., Pearce, C. & Taylor, T. L. (2012). *Ethnography and virtual worlds: A handbook of method*. Princeton, NJ: Princeton University Press.

Fielding, N. G., Lee, R. M., & Blank, G. (2008). *The SAGE handbook of online research methods*. London: Sage Ltd.

Hine, C. (2005). *Virtual methods: Issues in social research on the Internet*. New York: Berg.

Kozinets, R. (2009). *Netnography: Doing ethnographic research online*. London: Sage Ltd.

ONLINE SUPPORT

People are increasingly turning to computer-mediated platforms to seek support from others. Online social support, therefore, is the process by which individuals who are experiencing challenges receive comforting words or gestures from others on the Internet. The goal of social support is to uplift someone in need and reduce his or her stress. Research has shown that in addition to aiding in recovery from diseases and addiction, online social support can also have a positive impact on a person's quality of life as a whole.

Types of Online Social Support

The two main types of online social support are informational support and socioemotional support. Informational support is focused on offering specific, helpful ideas or suggestions that pertain to particular situations. An example of informational support is when a person shares a recipe for a shake that helps reduce weight in a weight-loss online forum. Socioemotional support is focused on offering words or gestures that are aimed at comforting a person's emotional, physical, or mental hardship. For example, validating someone's feelings of loneliness after a breakup and allowing him or her to vent in a chat room is a type of socioemotional support. Results from research studies suggest that people join specialized online groups or virtual communities to seek informational support at first but stay and become active members after having received socioemotional support.

Theoretical Approaches to Online Social Support

The theory of online social support was developed by Sheryl P. LaCoursiere. This theory describes the events that initiate support-seeking behavior, mediating factors, and consequent qualitative and quantitative outcomes. Online social support can also be examined through the framework of Joseph Walther's social information processing theory, which explains how online relationships are formed through verbal communication and nonverbal features that are enabled by particular virtual environments (such as "liking" someone's post).

Types of Social Media

There are multiple ways in which social media can enable the process of online social support. Previous research, however, has mainly focused on social networking sites and online groups or virtual communities when examining how social support can occur in online spaces. For example, research on social networking sites has looked at how replies to Facebook posts and Twitter tweets can help reduce people's stress. Additionally, research on online groups that are created to supplement groups that interact offline has shown that social support can occur in online spaces. Finally, virtual communities, which are entities that exist on their own merits, are hubs for online social support because they offer virtual spaces for people to visit and learn new information or receive support from others who are going through similar challenges.

Benefits of Online Social Support

Just like offline social support, there are physical health benefits to online social support. Research on online groups has found that social support can improve the well-being of patients with cancer, recovering addicts, people with suicidal ideation, and people with fertility hardships. Moreover, virtual communities can help streamline professional development support by offering a one-stop shop for individuals who are interested in learning more about how to survive and thrive in a certain profession. For example, the GradCafe Forums are designed to help future and current graduate students gain information about graduate school programs and share experiences about certain aspects of graduate school that are taboo to talk about with strangers in offline or professional settings.

Another benefit of online social support (which is not congruous to offline, face-to-face social support) is the fact that online posts are visible and beneficial to anyone who has access to a site, not just to people who are directly giving or receiving the social support. Therefore, online social support may have a greater impact than offline social support in the sense that the online environment allows the support to reach a wider audience. Additionally, the online support process can occur asynchronously, which can be more convenient for people who are not colocated but are still connected by a similar challenge. Last but not least, online social support can occur anonymously, enabling people to share their challenges freely.

Online Social Support at the Workplace

Online and face-to-face social support function similarly at the workplace, except that online social support is expressed and received through a computer-mediated platform. Workplace online social support can manifest in many forms, such as career support, supervisor support, coworker support, and organizational support. For example, a supervisor can provide socioemotional support via e-mail by congratulating an employee for a job well done or showing compassion if an employee has reached a challenging situation on a task. Another example of workplace online social support is when someone "endorses" his or her coworker's skills on LinkedIn, which can serve as both socioemotional support (i.e., the endorsement serves as a reinforcement that the coworker is competent) and informational support (i.e., others who might need help in the areas of the coworker's skills will know that he or she is an expert on the topic). Last but not least, professional social media sites such as ResearchGate enable researchers to connect with one another even though they do not work together face to face and provide informational support for those in their network.

Shahar Gur

See also Social Support; Stress and Physiological Indicators; Stress Management Interventions; Stress, consequences; Stress, Coping, and Management; Stress, Models and Theories

Further Readings

Bambina, A. (2007). *Online social support: The interplay of social networks and computer-mediated communication.* Youngstown, NY: Cambria.

Krause N. (1986). Social support, stress, and well-being. *Journal of Gerontology, 41*(4), 512–519.

LaCoursiere, S. P. (2001). A theory of online social support. *Advances in Nursing Science, 24*(1), 60–77.

Lin, C. P., & Bhattacherjee, A. (2009). Understanding online social support and its antecedents: A socio-cognitive model. *Social Science Journal, 46*(4), 724–737.

Walen, H. R., & Lachman, M. E. (2000). Social support and strain from partner, family, and friends: Costs and benefits for men and women in adulthood. *Journal of Social and Personal Relationships, 17*(1), 5–30.

Walther, J. B. (1992). Interpersonal effects in computer-mediated interaction a relational perspective. *Communication Research, 19*(1), 52–90.

Walther, J. B., & Boyd, S. (2002). Attraction to computer-mediated social support. In C. A. Lin & D. Atkin (Eds.), 2002. *Communication technology and society: Audience adoption and uses* (pp. 153–188). Cresskill, NJ: Hampton.

Welbourne, J. L., Blanchard, A. L., & Wadsworth, M. B. (2013). Motivations in virtual health communities and their relationship to community, connectedness and stress. *Computers in Human Behavior, 29*(1), 129–139.

Wright, K. (2000). Computer-mediated social support, older adults, and coping. *Journal of Communication, 50*(3), 100–118.

ONLINE SURVEY DATA COLLECTION METHODS: LEVERAGING QUALTRICS AND SURVEYMONKEY

Increased computer literacy and access to the Internet have allowed organizations and researchers to shift away from paper-and-pencil surveys to online data collection methods. Online survey methods are advantageous over traditional paper-and-pencil methods for many reasons. First, researchers and organizations can obtain data from geographically diverse sets of people. For example, organizations that operate in multiple countries can systematically collect information from all of their employees. Second, participants may take surveys from wherever the Internet is accessible, including their own homes. This flexibility can increase the number of people willing to take surveys and reduces the costs associated with bringing participants into a laboratory or copying and/or mailing physical surveys. Third, online survey methods expedite data analysis. Survey results are typically automatically acquired and stored, eliminating the need to enter data by hand. Finally, survey takers often have more positive reactions to online data collection methods than traditional paper-and-pencil methods.

There are also some disadvantages to online survey data collection methods. First, participants may respond carelessly to online surveys or quit the surveys prematurely because there is little accountability without physical oversight from researchers or organizations. Second, it is possible that a single participant could take a survey multiple times. Third, samples of participants may be inherently biased toward people who have access to computers and who feel comfortable using them, which may affect the results of a survey. Fourth, participants may be concerned about the anonymity of their responses with online surveys; the data are stored on the Internet, which makes them easily shared with others or vulnerable to cyberattacks. Finally, technological malfunctions are possible when using online data collection methods, and the data could be lost entirely.

Using SurveyMonkey and Qualtrics

SurveyMonkey and Qualtrics are the two most popular online survey administration platforms. Both platforms offer free accounts with limited features (e.g., limited number of questions, limited number of responses). For unrestricted access, both platforms also offer paid subscriptions. Paid accounts vary in price depending on whether they are for individuals or for groups (multiple users within a university, a department, or an organization). SurveyMonkey and Qualtrics are commonly used in research data collection. Qualtrics offers additional products that are tailored more for organizational needs, such as employee engagement surveys and 360-degree employee assessments (allowing performance ratings from multiple people, such as supervisors, coworkers, and direct reports). SurveyMonkey and Qualtrics are user friendly and can be leveraged in each step of the survey process. The following sections outline how these platforms facilitate (a) survey design, (b) survey administration, and (c) analysis of the results.

Designing the Survey

SurveyMonkey and Qualtrics can help streamline the process of designing an online survey. First, both platforms allow users to choose from a list of different types of questions that can be used for various research and organizational needs. For example, multiple-choice questions can capture demographic information, and matrix questions are appropriate for questions with Likert response scales (e.g., asking respondents to rate the extent to which they agree with a statement from

predetermined response choices). Such closed-ended questions are useful for quantitative methods. SurveyMonkey and Qualtrics also have text-entry questions that allow respondents to answer questions in an open-ended manner, such as for qualitative designs. Users can embed media, such as videos, into surveys to provide instructions or to get reactions to the videos from respondents. Qualtrics offers more variety in the types of questions than does SurveyMonkey.

Second, both platforms allow users to customize the logic of the survey, or the order in which questions appear. Survey logic can be used to automatically assign participants to one of two conditions in experimental or quasi-experimental designs or to counterbalance the order in which scales appear. Survey logic can be used with questions that are contingent on the response of a previous question. For example, a question asking about the host country of an expatriate assignment would be displayed only if the respondent answered that he or she was an expatriate earlier in the survey. Furthermore, survey logic can be used to screen respondents out of a survey on the basis of specified criteria. For instance, if a researcher is interested only in expatriates' experiences, survey logic can redirect participants who indicate that they are not expatriates to the end of the survey. Similar logic can be used with consent forms for informational or ethics purposes; if a participant does not agree to participate, he or she will be redirected to the end of the survey. Qualtrics offers more flexibility with survey logic than SurveyMonkey, but more advanced logic requires a fair amount of technical knowledge.

Finally, SurveyMonkey and Qualtrics allow users to customize the look and feel of a survey. Users can pick from a set of existing themes, or they can fully customize the background and font colors to match their branding needs. Users can also embed a logo that appears at the top of each page of the survey. In addition, question text can be bolded, underlined, or italicized or set in different colors and sizes to emphasize certain words or distinguish some information items from others. Finally, there are also options for a progress bar (allowing participants to see how much of the survey they have left to complete) and a back button (for participants to go back to review and/or change answers). Both SurveyMonkey and Qualtrics offer the option for mobile-friendly surveys, which can facilitate experience-sampling methodologies in which participants respond to the survey multiple times in a day, week, or month.

Administering the Survey

SurveyMonkey and Qualtrics can also facilitate the administration of a survey. Each survey has its own unique address, which can be included as a link in an e-mail or printed on a flier to recruit participants. In addition, both survey platforms include a feature that allows users to organize e-mail addresses and send e-mail invitations to participate in the survey. Users can track the number of responses that have been completed and calculate the response rate. The survey can also be exported and printed if all participants do not have access to the Internet (answers would need to be manually entered in this case). Both platforms also offer services that aid in recruiting samples of participants. The cost of the panels of participants is based on the specified criteria of the sample (e.g., working Hispanics over the age of 18) and the sample size. SurveyMonkey and Qualtrics will administer and monitor surveys until all responses are collected.

Analyzing and Reporting Survey Results

After all necessary responses have been collected, SurveyMonkey and Qualtrics offer features to simplify data analysis and reporting. With regard to data analysis, users can download survey results directly into file formats that are compatible with most data analysis software (e.g., .csv and SPSS files). Items will be prelabeled (these labels can be edited during the design phase) to make preparation for data analysis easier. Qualtrics also offers options to reverse-score items (for negatively worded items) and to create composite scores for groups of items before downloading results. In terms of reporting, both Qualtrics and SurveyMonkey offer the option to download results into a preformatted report (in Microsoft Word or PDF format) that shows basic, descriptive statistics of each item, such as the average score. Qualtrics also allows users to customize the basic statistics and visualizations of the data (tables, charts, and graphs) that appear on each page.

In conclusion, online survey platforms such as SurveyMonkey and Qualtrics can facilitate data collection in a number of ways, including the design, administration, analysis, and reporting of surveys. Although online methods can make data collection easier and quicker, there are certain risks to using such methods, such as issues with anonymity, data quality, and the possibility of technological malfunctions.

Haley M. Woznyj

See also Online Assessment; Online Qualitative Methods; Organizational Surveys; Quantitative Research Approach; Survey Approach

Further Readings

Alessi, E. J., & Martin, J. I. (2010). Conducting an Internet-based survey: Benefits, pitfalls, and lessons learned. *Social Work Research*, 34(2), 122–128.

Naus, M. J., Philipp, L. M., & Samsi, M. (2009). From paper to pixels: A comparison of paper and computer formats in psychological assessment. *Computers in Human Behavior*, 25(1), 1–7. doi:10.1016/j.chb.2008.05.012

Qualtrics. (2015). http://www.qualtrics.com

Stanton, J. M., & Rogelberg, S. G. (2001). Using Internet/intranet Web pages to collect organizational research data. *Organizational Research Methods*, 4(3), 200–217. doi:10.1177/109442810143002

SurveyMonkey. (2015). http://www.surveymonkey.com

OPEN SYSTEMS THEORY

Open systems theory is commonly traced to the work of biologist Ludwig von Bertalanffy, who influentially articulated the concept in a series of books and papers published from the late 1920s through the early 1970s. The core proposition is that living systems are not "closed," in the sense of having no external inputs or outputs, but rather are "open" to the environments in which they exist, exchanging inputs and outputs with those environments. Additionally, as articulated by von Bertalanffy and other like-minded theorists of his era, open systems comprise multiple interconnected subsystems, which must be in alignment for a living entity to function effectively and adaptively in its environment. Although the aligned subsystems themselves are important, in open systems theory, the unity of the whole and its ability to adapt to and "fit" its environment are central. In harmony with older core principles of Gestalt psychology, the whole, while made up of its parts, is greater than and different from the sum of those parts; wholes have unique, emergent properties, derived from the arrangement of and relationships among the parts. Thus, open systems theory is a holistic approach to its subject matter, emphasizing synthesis over analysis or reductionism.

Applications to Organizational Science

Open systems thinking has been applied widely across an extremely broad range of disciplines. For our purposes, it has been especially visible and influential in the organizational sciences, spanning psychology, sociology, and other branches of social science that deal with the organizational world. The targeted application of open systems theory to organizations is attributed largely to the groundbreaking work of Daniel Katz and Robert Kahn, explicated in their well-known book *The Social Psychology of Organizations*, published in the 1960s. As they and other researchers noted, for many years previously, models of the organization were predominantly mechanistic ones, articulated by prominent and influential early organizational theorists such as Max Weber, Henri Fayol, and Frederick W. Taylor. The organization was viewed more as a logical, linear, mechanical set of elements for producing products and services. Employees were commonly seen as parts, or extensions of the organizational "machine." Improvements focused mainly on making internal adjustments to the putatively closed system (at least relatively so), to enhance operating efficiency; relatively little attention was paid to the interconnectedness of the elements making up the organization or to the external environment in which the organization existed.

Such mechanistic conceptions of the organization, commonly collectively called "machine theory," were predicated on the notion that work tasks were and should be for the most part routine and repetitive, and environments, if considered at all, were relatively stable. The assembly line exemplifies such thinking, and organizations of all types, not just industrial and manufacturing organizations, operated to a significant extent as assembly lines. With the work of Katz and Kahn, though, the "great machine" metaphor was replaced with a "living organism" metaphor. Instead of seeing the organization as a kind of giant clock, it was now viewed more as a living (super)organism in an ecosystem. Thus conceptualized as dynamic living entities, organizations, if they are to be successful, have to be agile, nimble, flexible, and adaptive, in environments that are changing, even turbulent and largely unpredictable. They cannot be built in a rigid, hardwired way, to run like clockwork. As animate open systems, they take in materials in any of a number of forms (information, people, raw materials, energy, and other resources) from the environment, convert or transform such inputs into outputs, and send those outputs (products, services, information) into the environment. The role of the turbulent environment, as the source of inputs to the system and as the receiver of the system's outputs, must be considered.

Key concepts that are central to open systems theory as applied to organizations include the following:

- *Negative entropy*. Organizations to survive and thrive must take in more energy than they expend in outputs. They must be "negentropic." Otherwise, entropy eventually sets in, and they die.
- *Feedback*. Organizational systems (and subsystems) are sensitive to their effects. Thus, outputs are fed back into the system as information inputs, on the basis of which input or throughput (conversion) adjustments may be made.
- *Homeostasis*. Organizations must read and react to changes in the environment, and make adaptive internal changes, in order to continually adjust and align subsystems, to maintain internal equilibrium.
- *Equifinality*. Contrary to Taylorism, there is no "one best way"; instead, a number of different paths may lead to the same result.

Critical subsystems of the open system organization include at least the following:

- Production subsystems: for transforming inputs into outputs
- Maintenance subsystems: maintaining a positive work environment (e.g., some human resources functions, such as those related to salary and benefits, and training and development)
- Adaptive subsystems: scanning the environment to identify threats and opportunities
- Supportive subsystems: securing resources from the environment and distributing products or services into the environment
- Managerial subsystems: exerting control over the other subsystems

Open Systems Theory as Foundational to Other Models in Organizational Science

Although it is not easy to disentangle the multiple streams of influence on various conceptual approaches in organizational science, the open systems theory is visibly foundational to several such prominent models. Thus, the sociotechnical approach sees work as inherently both social and technical in nature and emphasizes that balance must be struck between both social and technical aspects if work is to be designed for optimal outcomes. The traditional mechanistic approach focused on the technical aspects of work, virtually to the exclusion of the social. As the sociotechnical systems approach was first being developed at the Tavistock Institute in the 1940s, researchers became aware of von Bertalanffy's work and introduced open systems thinking into the nascent sociotechnical approach. Such open systems principles as equifinality (first stated by von Bertalanffy) are also identified as core principles of the sociotechnical approach. In general, open systems theory, entirely compatible with the developing approach of the Tavistock group, became an essential philosophical underpinning of sociotechnical systems thinking.

Similarly, the popular concept of the high-performance organization relies on systems thinking at its foundation. The high-performance organization embraces both performance outcomes (such as long-term business success and high employee quality of work life) and the operating principles and characteristics that are predictive of such outcomes (teams, employee involvement,

open sharing of business information, focus on the customer). It is widely acknowledged in the relevant literature that high-performance organizations, focusing on the importance of alignment of internal subsystems and adaptability of the whole to changing environmental conditions, operate according to open systems principles.

Open systems thinking is also central to the concept of the learning organization, which has inspired much organizational research and practice since the early 1990s. Researchers and theorists in this area widely and explicitly endorse the open systems view of the knowledge-acquiring and knowledge-managing organization.

Possible Limitations of Open Systems Theory

Criticisms of the open systems approach in organizational science center on a few main themes: (a) The concept of a system is vague or nonspecific. Entities ranging from single cells to the universe, and everything in between, are commonly identified as "systems." (b) The theory is commonly taken as a truism and applied in such a wholesale way that it may restrict further thinking about organizational issues. Thus, there is a suggestion in some recent literature that "complexity theory," although it bears many similarities to open systems theory, may provide a clearer guide for future organizational research. (c) Although organizations are indeed social systems comprising biological human entities, they are explicitly designed, contrived systems, not natural biological ones. As intentionally designed purposive entities, they might not fully follow the rules of a natural biological system. Mere survival and reproduction are not the goals of the organization. (d) Open systems theory can be taken to imply that closed versus open is a dichotomy. On the contrary, researchers and theorists generally emphasize a continuum from completely closed to completely open, with gradations in between the two extremes.

Current and Future Status of the Theory

Despite such cautions about the usefulness or universal applicability of the theory, none of the potential limitations has proved to be telling. Indeed, so great has been the impact of open systems theory in the field of organizational science since the first applications that current sources commonly identify the open systems approach as *the* predominant organizational theory, inspiring and underlying research and practice in organizational science. Enthusiasm for the open systems view continues unabated.

John E. Kello

See also High-Performance Organization Model; Learning Organizations; Sociotechnical Approach

Further Readings

Kast, F. E., & Rosenzweig, J. E. (1972). General systems theory: Applications for organization and management. *Academy of Management Journal*, *15*(4), 447–465.

Katz, D., & Kahn, R. L. (1966). *The social psychology of organizations*. New York: John Wiley.

Mele, C., Pels, J., & Polese, F. (2010). A brief review of systems theories and their managerial applications. *Service Science*, *2*(1–2), 126–135.

Olmstead, J. A. (2002). *Creating the functionally competent organization: An open systems approach.* Westport, CT: Greenwood.

von Bertalanffy, L. (1950). The theory of open systems in physics and biology. *Science*, *111*, 23–29.

OPTIMISM AND PESSIMISM

The terms *optimism* and *pessimism* refer to the tendencies of people to expect that good things will happen and to expect that bad things will happen, respectively. Persons who believe that their goals can be achieved despite difficulties they might encounter are said to hold an optimistic view. They are predisposed to think that they will be able to manage and resolve any of these challenges. Pessimism is the general tendency to expect negative outcomes. Pessimists are predisposed to think about the potential negative outcomes of whatever problems, setbacks, challenges, or difficulties are placed in their way.

To date, optimistic and pessimistic expectations have been found to predict success. Regardless of job or level in an organization, individuals encounter many "curveballs," changes, obstacles, difficulties, and adversities on the job. Whether dealing with a sudden change in procedures; an irate customer, coworker, or boss; or an accidentally deleted important e-mail, it is estimated that the average employee can face up to 23 adversities in a single day. How well an employee handles these job challenges will then affect how productive that employee is and his or her ability to learn, adapt, overcome future obstacles, meet goals, and even lead others. In sum, how successfully employees are able to deal with adverse situations affects their success as well as the organization's success. Thus, optimism and pessimism can have important ramifications for organizations in the selection, training, motivation, and work lives of their employees and leaders.

Background and Key Issues

Within the past 40 years, there has been renewed interest among psychologists in understanding the constructs of optimism and pessimism and their effects on individuals' lives. Michael Scheier and Charles Carver were the pioneers of this research stream, based on their studies examining generalized outcome expectancies. Martin Seligman's work on learned helplessness and, more recently, positive psychology has also provided a strong influence for sparking additional research. There continues to be an explosion of studies examining the effects of optimism and pessimism on health, physical, and mental well-being and psychological adjustment. Generally, those who tend toward an optimistic perspective experience fewer physical symptoms of stress, cope more effectively with stressful events, and adjust better to life transitions. The positive effects of optimism tend to be explained by the types of coping strategies typically embraced by those with an optimistic perspective. Optimism is related to an individual's use of adaptive, engaging coping strategies that include rational problem solving, cognitive restructuring, expressing emotions, and seeking social support during stressful times. Conversely, pessimism is related to an individual's use of maladaptive, disengaging coping strategies that include avoiding problems, impulsive and careless problem solving, being self-critical, and socially withdrawing from stressful situations.

Given the potential value of optimism and pessimism, a growing number of studies have examined optimism and pessimism in an organizational context. Nonetheless, more research is needed. Before reviewing what is known about the role of optimism and pessimism in the workplace, key issues in the literature center on the measurement, dimensionality, antecedents, and relationship (or potential redundancy) of optimism and pessimism with conceptually similar and other well-established personality constructs. It is important to understand the complexity of optimism and pessimism.

Measurement of Optimism and Pessimism

A number of instruments have been developed to assess optimism and pessimism. The distinctions among the instruments stem mainly from the different theoretical perspectives held by researchers. As a consequence, it can be challenging to compare and contrast findings across studies that have used different measures. It is crucial that one become familiar with the measures in order to understand the research.

The Life Orientation Test (LOT) is probably the most popular measure and is based on the notion that optimism and pessimism are generalized outcome expectancies. An example item is "Rarely do I expect good things to happen." The LOT was revised, resulting in the Revised Life Orientation Test (RLOT). One debated issue in the literature deals with the dimensionality of optimism and pessimism. Whereas the LOT and RLOT were intended to be unidimensional measures of dispositional optimism, there is evidence suggesting that the LOT is bidimensional. The Extended Life Orientation Test (ELOT) has added to this evidence by demonstrating that a two-factor model provided the best fit, resulting in separate scores for optimism and pessimism. Regardless, the LOT, RLOT, and ELOT tend to provide the most direct assessments of optimism and pessimism.

The Attributional Style Questionnaire (ASQ) is also a popular measure and is based on an individual's tendency to explain or make attributions for positive and negative events. As a more indirect measure, respondents are given a negative or positive event and asked to indicate one major cause for the event and to rate the internality, stability, and globality of the cause. Those who are labeled as having a pessimistic explanatory style believe that bad things happen to them because it has something to do with them (internal), happens frequently (stable), and across all situations (global). Individuals with an optimistic explanatory style believe that positive things happen to them because of internal, stable, and global factors. The Expanded Attributional Style Questionnaire, a revision to the ASQ, is composed of 24 negative events only. Another technique to assess explanatory style, the Content Analysis of Verbatim Explanations, has also been developed. Other measures of optimism and pessimism include the Optimism-Pessimism Instrument, the Defensive Pessimism Questionnaire, the Workplace Explanations Survey, and the Hope Scale. Many researchers have encouraged the development of new optimism and pessimism scales.

Dimensionality of Optimism and Pessimism

Optimism and pessimism have traditionally been considered as polar opposites on a continuum. From this perspective, one would be either optimistic or pessimistic but could not hold optimistic and pessimistic perspectives concurrently. This singular way of thinking is limiting because it could be argued that overly optimistic beliefs are not always advantageous. Consider, for example, the disastrous outcome for an individual who decided to spend her forthcoming winnings after merely buying a lottery ticket, because she felt so optimistic that she would win and thus neglected to think about the dismal odds. Consequently, more recent thinking along with supportive evidence has shown that people can hold some of both aspects, and therefore, optimism and pessimism are believed to represent two independent or partially independent constructs. Notably, when treating optimism and pessimism as separate constructs, distinct results have been obtained. Specific terms have also been coined to reflect this separateness, such as *realistic optimism*, *unrealistic optimism*, *flexible optimism*, *defensive pessimism*, *cautious optimism*, and *strategic optimism*.

In addition, whereas research has predominantly focused on the dispositional nature of optimism and pessimism, current studies have found evidence that optimism can predict various organizational outcomes (e.g., burnout, job satisfaction, performance) to a greater extent than trait optimism. These findings suggest that it may be important to examine optimism as a malleable construct that can be developed (state optimism), in addition to the general trait construct.

Antecedents and Relationship With Other Constructs

Researchers have focused on other constructs that may be related to optimism and pessimism and antecedents of these constructs. There is evidence of some possible genetic aspect to optimism. Heritability estimates indicating approximately 30% have been reported. The role of the environment, such as early childhood experiences, parental modeling, and the media, is also being examined. Continued research on the neurobiology of optimism and pessimism would be beneficial.

With regard to relationships with other constructs, meta-analytic evidence suggests that optimism and hope are correlated but distinguishable constructs, relating differently to some indices of well-being and the five-factor model of personality. Using multiple measures of optimism, it was found that dispositional optimism was related to four of the five main factors of personality (all but openness). Optimism has not been found to be redundant with pessimism, and not redundant with neuroticism. There is some evidence of empirical overlap, though, with resilience and self-esteem or self-efficacy. Is optimism a subdimension of resilience? Do optimism and self-esteem have a reciprocal relationship? What role does positive and negative affectivity play? In general, research must be conducted to gain a better understanding of the complexities of optimism and pessimism, particularly in relation to other constructs.

Optimism and Pessimism in the Work Setting

Optimism and pessimism have been examined with regard to academic performance and retention among college freshman and career planning and exploration among high school students. In addition, their effects on stress, coping, and effort at work have been topics of study. In general, optimism buffered against the occupational and life stress of university teachers and burnout among information technology professionals and led to increased effort intentions of salespeople.

A few studies have examined the effects of optimism and pessimism on job performance. These studies have generally used different measures of optimism, pessimism, and job performance and have also used employees in different jobs. For example, using the ASQ, life insurance agents with optimistic explanatory styles sold more life insurance and reported a lower likelihood of quitting than did agents with pessimistic styles. In another study using a single overall LOT score, pessimistic call center employees reported higher levels of self-reported performance and satisfaction and lower turnover intent than optimists. Optimists, however, perceived lower levels of job stress and work–nonwork conflict than did the pessimists. In a third study, the effects of separate measures of optimism and pessimism using the ELOT found both optimism and pessimism to be related to supervisor ratings of overall job performance for production employees in a manufacturing plant. Pessimism, however, was found to remain a significant predictor after controlling for variance accounted for by selection measures such as a personality test and work skills inventory. These findings demonstrate the importance of assessing optimism and pessimism separately.

These three studies also vividly demonstrate the challenge of comparing across results in which different measures of optimism and pessimism are used. The establishment of a psychometrically sound measure is imperative. There is some work being conducted on developing measures. Smith, Caputi, and Crittenden in 2013 developed a work-related explanatory style measure to be used in organizational settings, which requires more investigation; a generalized expectancy measure of optimism and pessimism should also be explored. Although some progress is being made, this area could benefit greatly from more systematic research that clearly addresses the measurement, dimensionality, and antecedents of optimism and pessimism. Taking a slightly different approach to applying positive psychology to the workplace, Luthans and colleagues combined resiliency, confidence (or self-efficacy), hope, and optimism to form a higher order core factor they labeled "psychological capital," or "PsyCap." Studies on this overall factor that includes optimism may also shed light on the role of optimism in the workplace.

Given the power of optimism and pessimism on people's lives in general and the role of such positive and negative thinking in work situations, a number of important questions about optimism and pessimism await further research. There is relatively little work on the selection, training, and job performance of individuals in work settings. It will also be interesting to explore what those who hold optimistic and pessimistic perspectives do when encountering threatening, challenging, and novel situations. More specifically, what mechanisms result in divergent outcomes for optimists and pessimists in these situations? Although research has not tended to find gender difference with regard to optimism and pessimism, some cultural differences have been noted and should be further explored.

Additionally, given some evidence that optimism may be developed, work on evaluating the extent to which interventions or strategies can influence one's level of optimism in the workplace should be conducted. Online interventions may also show promise and need to be investigated. For example, Happify (www.happify.com) uses online technology (e.g., Web site, app) to deliver activities and games based on more than 10 years of scientific research in positive psychology and neuroscience such that individuals can train their brains and build skills to be more happy (and optimistic).

One must wonder, though, whether there could be a "dark side" to optimism. The evidence available to date seems to suggest that although there are instances in which optimism may be a disadvantage, those instances are relatively rare. From an optimistic perspective, the opportunities are endless for research, but from a pessimistic perspective, the construct issues of measurement and dimensionality of optimism and pessimism must be faced so that research in this area can advance.

Therese Macan

See also Hardiness; Individual Differences; Personality; Self-Esteem

Further Readings

Carver, C. S., & Scheier, M. F. (2014). Dispositional optimism. *Trends in Cognitive Sciences*, 18, 269–330.

Forgeard, M. J. C., & Seligman, M. E. P. (2012). Seeing the glass half full: A review of the causes and consequences of optimism. *Pratiques Psychologiques*, 18, 107–120.

Kluemper, D. H., Little, L. M., & DeGroot, T. (2009). State or trait: Effect of state optimism on job-related outcomes. *Journal of Organizational Behavior*, 30, 209–231.

Luthans, F., Youssef-Morgan, C. M., & Avolio, B. J. (2015). *Psychological capital and beyond*. New York: Oxford University Press.

Smith, P., Caputi, P., & Crittenden, N. (2013). Measuring optimism in organizations: Development of a workplace explanatory style questionnaire. *Journal of Happiness Studies*, 14, 415–432.

ORGANIZATIONAL ATTRACTION

Concept and Measurement

Organizational attraction has emerged as a topic of great interest to both practitioners and academics. Different definitions of organizational attraction have been formulated, all referring to individuals' affective and attitudinal thoughts about particular organizations as potential places for employment. Implicitly, if not explicitly, definitions of organizational attraction stress job seekers' perceptions of organizations as desirable, positive places to work. Organizational attraction has been measured in both direct and indirect ways. Examples of direct measures of organizational attraction include behavior-based measures, such as one's recommendation of an organization to others, one's ultimate choice of an organization, and even actual application behavior. Typically, however, organizational attraction is measured indirectly through the use of a single item or a scale with three to five items. Although the difference is subtle, some items seem to operationalize organizational attraction in more general terms than others. Some items, for instance, reflect job seekers' and applicants' *general appreciation* of organizations ("[Company X] is one of the best employers to work for."). Other items capture specific intentions or the extent to which job seekers and applicants feel personally attracted to work for a particular organization ("How much do you like to work for [Company X]?").

Recent decades have witnessed exponential growth in studies of organizational attraction. One reason is that organizational attraction seems to be a critical component to the success of organizations. Its importance relates to the effect of organizational attraction on factors that affect the overall productivity of organizations, such as the attraction and selection of highly competent and productive employees. Hence, organizational attraction is a vital theme in many companies' human resources management, particularly in recruitment and selection practices. Not surprisingly, much attention has gone to job seekers' affective and attitudinal thoughts about organizations they want to initiate relationships with, in order to optimize organizations' reputations and recruitment practices.

Criticism, however, has been expressed regarding the lack of construct clarity. As illustrated, organizational attraction has been defined in a rather broad way. Several concepts are related to the notion of organizational attraction and even used intertwined, among which *applicant attraction*, *job attraction*, *person–organization (P-O) fit*, *person–job (P-J) fit*, *organizational reputation*, *organizational image*, and *job pursuit intentions*. Below is a description of how these notions relate to organizational attraction.

Applicant attraction involves applicants' overall evaluation of the attractiveness of work opportunities, including many job and organizational characteristics. Hence, in recent meta-analyses, organizational attraction has been considered an index of applicants' attraction but has also been used as a substitute for applicant attraction because of their relatively high intercorrelations (in the range of .60 to .70). Job attraction, on the other hand, is one's overall evaluation of the attractiveness of a particular job and its characteristics ("How attractive is this job to you?"). Because jobs are typically performed within an organizational setting, recent meta-analyses have considered job attraction as an index of organizational attraction.

P-O fit covers an individual's perceived or actual congruence with an organization. For instance, an individual's personal characteristics might complement or supplement an organization's system, structures, values, and culture ("The values of this organization are similar to my own values."). Similarly, P-J fit reflects the perceived or actual congruence of a person's characteristics with a particular job ("To what extent do your knowledge, skills, and abilities 'match' or fit the requirements of the job?"). Both P-J fit and P-O fit are determinants of organizational attraction, with empirical studies showing perceived or subjective and actual or objective P-O fit to be a somewhat stronger correlate of organizational attraction (in the range of .40 to .60) than perceived and actual P-J fit measures (in the range of .40 to .50).

Organizational reputation comprises a collection of individual impressions regarding an organization's relative standing externally (with clients and other external stakeholders) and internally (with employees and internal stakeholders) in the organization's business environment. Knowledge of an organizational reputation is expected to affect organizational attraction and hence is considered a determinant of organizational attraction. Correlations between organizational attraction and reputation or prestige measures ("This is a reputable company to work for.") are typically moderate to high (around .40).

Relatedly, one of the most important correlates of organizational attraction is the organization's image (in the range of .40 to .50). In line with the instrumental-symbolic framework, as adopted from marketing research, organizational image involves both instrumental and symbolic attributes of an organization as determinants of its attractiveness. *Instrumental attributes* entail individuals' perceptions of tangible, concrete job and organizational characteristics, including job security, advancement opportunities, pay, task demands, and organizational location ("People who work for [Company X] have a solid job."). *Symbolic attributes* are more abstract, intangible characteristics that people infer from how they experience organizations. Symbolic attributes are typically measured with a list of adjectives and refer to an organization's personality: "If I were to consider [Company X] as a person, I would describe it as [adjective]." Examples of trait inferences are innovative, competent, and tough.

Finally, organizational attraction has been used as a surrogate measure of job pursuit intentions, which entail whether one intends to pursue an application to an organization ("If this company invited me for a second job interview, I would go."). Empirical studies have evidenced high intercorrelations but still conceptual differences between organizational attractiveness and job pursuit intentions (in the range of .60 to .80). From a conceptual point of view and in line with the theory of planned behavior, organizational pursuit intentions are considered an outcome variable of organizational attraction, which in turn has been conceptualized as its attitudinal antecedent.

Theoretical Perspectives

Besides the need for construct clarity, the organization attraction literature has also been criticized for its atheoretical nature. Since the mid-2000s, however, systematic efforts have been made to investigate the theoretical underpinnings of individuals' attraction to organizations. Three clusters of well-known psychological theories (i.e., metatheoretical explanations) have been put forward to explain mechanisms of individuals' attraction to organizations.

A first group of theories discusses how individuals process information about their environment, which in turn affects their attraction to organizations (*environment processing metatheory*). An example is signaling theory, which states that applicants process information about an organization as signals of organizational characteristics that affect attraction. For instance, recruiters' warmth may be perceived as a signal of a considerate and warm workplace, hence increasing applicants' attraction to that organization. A second group of theories proposes that individuals evaluate fit between their own personal characteristics (such as personal needs and values) and those from the environment (*interactionist processing metatheory*). An example is the attraction-selection-attrition theory, which states that individuals will be attracted to organizations that have certain characteristics they feel a "match" with but will leave organizations if they feel "no match" anymore. Finally, a third group of theories discusses how information about the self (such as self-esteem) moderates perceived P-O fit and individuals' perceived organizational attractiveness (*self-processing metatheory*). According to the consistency theory, for instance, individuals

with high self-esteem would prefer organizations that fit their needs and correspond to their self-images.

Some recently formulated models build upon assumptions expressed by these three metatheories, hence showing the complex and multifaceted nature of organizational attraction. For instance, the theory of symbolic attraction suggests that symbolic inferences mediate companies' market signals (such as company rankings) and applicants' attraction to organizations (environment processing metatheory) but that any effect of symbolic inferences on organizational attraction also depends on applicants' social identity concerns (interactionist and self-processing metatheories).

Researchers have started validating these mechanisms of organizational attraction. Remarkably, most theoretical models and studies are rather "static" in nature, considering organizational attraction at a single point in time. However, applicants' evaluation of organizational attributes might change throughout the recruitment process (e.g., as a function of recruitment stage) and throughout individual careers (e.g., as a function of professional experiences and personal developments). Future research, therefore, could approach organizational attraction in more dynamic ways by investigating mechanisms of change as well as conditions under which perceptions of organizational attraction would be revised or modified.

Antecedents and Consequences

The literature on organizational attraction has grown fast, and empirical research has investigated job seekers' and applicants' reactions toward a plethora of job and organizational characteristics. Although it is beyond the scope of this entry to review all of the literature, presented below are some key conclusions regarding antecedents and consequences of organizational attraction in the workplace. Antecedents of organizational attraction have received a lot of research attention in the past decades and are rooted in both the organization and the individual, as discussed next.

Organizational Determinants

Many organizational characteristics have been documented as desirable to applicants, including an organization's structure (such as a company's degree of decentralization) and policies (from workplace romance policies to the implementation of diversity programs). As mentioned, one of the strongest determinants seems to be an organization's image, including its instrumental and symbolic attributes. Other types of image concepts relate to product image and corporate social responsibility (CSR; an organization's community involvement and pro-environmental practices). In general, applicants feel more attracted to organizations that help employees and society realize their (personal) goals, show high concern for others, and display organizational fairness.

In addition, a lot of research attention has gone to recruitment-related sources and selection practices. Recruiters' warmth and professionalism, for instance, seem to strongly affect applicants' organizational attraction. On the contrary, unfairness (such as discriminatory interview questions) and privacy-invasiveness (such as screening applicants' social networking involvement) negatively affect organizational attraction. Types of recruitment media have also been considered. In general, applicants prefer organizations that make use of modern, technology-driven tools. Hence, effects of technological developments such as e-recruitment (e.g., Web sites, recruitment games) are a topic of great interest. Interestingly, less technology-driven or sophisticated tools such as word-of-mouth communication seem also to work, particularly if the source of employment information is perceived as credible. Finally, job attributes and working conditions (such as individual-based pay) and career paths that organizations offer (such as flexible career paths) have been demonstrated to positively affect organizational attraction.

Taken together, organizational policies and human resources practices that stress investment in people and society (such as training and development and CSR) are most favorably regarded. Symbolic attributes (such as trait inferences) further account for incremental variance over concrete job and organizational attributes in predicting organizational attraction. In terms of the relative strength, a recent meta-analysis further showed organizational characteristics (such as image and reputation) to be stronger determinants than job characteristics (such as benefits), followed by a group of determinants that appeared to be equally strong determinants, including recruiter characteristics and characteristics of the recruitment process (all medium-sized effects). Importantly, some determinants, such as job characteristics, seemed to have stronger effects in field than in laboratory settings, whereas the reverse was found for characteristics of the recruiter and the recruitment process.

Individual, Person-Based Determinants

Whether organizational characteristics are considered desirable seems, however, contingent on the degree of fit with applicant characteristics, which corroborates interactionist perspectives on organizational attraction. Indeed, recent meta-analyses support this assumption, given that perceived fit (P-O and P-J fit) seemed the strongest correlate of applicant attraction (with large effects) compared with organizational characteristics (medium-sized effects). Among individual characteristics that have been investigated are individuals' values and needs (such as need for materialism or a warm environment), demographic characteristics (such as ethnicity), personality characteristics (such as conscientiousness and openness to experience), and several other individual difference factors (such as one's social identity concerns and self-esteem). For instance, the degree to which individual-based pay affects organizational attraction seems to depend on individuals' standing on materialism. Organizations offering flextime are more appealing to those with high role conflict, and the effects of CSR on organizational attraction seem to be moderated by applicants' levels of Machiavellianism. Interestingly, these examples do not measure actual P-O fit but validate correlations between perceived P-O fit and organizational attraction measures.

Consequences

Finally, organizational attraction seems to have important consequences for both organizations and individuals. Specifically, organizational attraction has been related positively to several behavioral and attitudinal outcome variables, including applicants' job pursuit intentions, job acceptance intentions ("If you were offered the job, would you accept it?"), job choice (operationalized as actual job acceptance, i.e., whether one accepts a real job offered by a company), and individuals' affective commitment to organizations ("I feel emotionally attached to [Company X]."). Although empirical evidence is limited, organizational attraction is even suggested to add competitive value by increasing employee and customer satisfaction. Companies, therefore, could engage in a thorough auditing and marketing of their organizational images and reputations. Building further on the fit idea, then, other practical implications include the use of targeted recruitment practices to attract particular groups of applicants.

Conclusion

Lately, a lot of research attention has gone to organization attraction given its importance in organizations. In this entry, we provide a description of organizational attraction and related notions, the way attraction has been measured, theoretical viewpoints of underlying mechanisms, and its correlates as being reported in the research literature over the past two decades. Overall, study findings highlight the complex, subjective, and multifaceted nature of organizational attraction. Future research could investigate ways to improve organization attraction and might benefit from employing a more dynamic perspective.

Eva Derous and Lien Wille

See also Job Choice; Organizational Image; Person–Job Fit; Person–Organization Fit; Recruitment; Recruitment Sources

Further Readings

Chapman, D. S., Uggerslev, K. L., Carroll, S. A., Piasentin, K. A., & Jones, D. A. (2005). Applicant attraction to organizations and job choice: A meta-analytic review of the correlates of recruiting outcomes. *Journal of Applied Psychology, 90*, 928–944. doi:10.1037/0021-9010.90.5.928

Ehrhart, K. H., & Ziegert, J. C. (2005). Why are individuals attracted to organizations? *Journal of Management, 31*, 901–919. doi:10.1177/014920630 5279759

Highhouse, S., Lievens, F., & Sinar, E. F. (2003). Measuring attraction to organizations. *Educational & Psychological Measurement, 63*, 986–1001. doi:10.1177/0013164403258403

Lievens, F., & Highhouse, S. (2003). The relation of instrumental and symbolic attributes to a company's attractiveness as an employer. *Personnel Psychology, 56*, 75–102. doi:10.1111/j.1744-6570.2003.tb00144.x

Schreurs, B., Derous, E., Van Hooft, E.A.J., Proost, K., & De Witte, K. (2009). Predicting applicants' job pursuit behavior from their selection expectations: The mediating role of the theory of planned behavior. *Journal of Organizational Behavior, 30*, 761–783. doi:10.1002/job.570

Uggerslev, K. L., Fassina, N. E., & Kraichy, D. (2012). Recruiting through the stages: A meta-analytic test of predictors of applicant attraction at different stages of the recruiting process. *Personnel Psychology, 65*, 579–660. doi:10.1111/j.1744-6570.2012.01254.x

Walker, H. J., Feild, H. S., Giles, W. F., Armenakis, A. A., & Bernerth, J. B. (2009). Displaying employee testimonials on recruitment web sites: Effects of communication media, employee race, and job seeker race on organizational attraction and information credibility. *Journal of Applied Psychology, 94*, 1354–1364. doi:10.1037/a0014964

Yu, K. Y. T. (2014). Person-organization fit effects on organizational attraction: A test of an expectations-based model. *Organizational Behavior and Human Decision Processes, 124*, 75–94. doi:10.1016/j.obhdp.2013.12.005

ORGANIZATIONAL BEHAVIOR

Organizational behavior (OB) can be defined as the study of human behavior in the workplace. More specifically, investigators employ the principles of the scientific method to help them understand, predict, and manage employee behavior. The knowledge that follows rigorous, systematic study is used to enhance the productivity of organizations and the quality of work life for its employees.

History

The field of organizational behavior can trace its roots back to the late 19th and early 20th centuries when many industrial efficiency experts were attempting to discover how to get people to do more work in less time. These investigations in the workplace, conducted by management forerunners such as Frederick Taylor, Frank and Lillian Gilbreth, Henri Fayol, and Max Weber, to name a few, focused mainly on the hierarchical structure of the organization, division of labor, and the management functions of planning and controlling. Then in 1924 Elton Mayo led the human relations movement by focusing on the importance of human social processes in work settings. He and his colleagues helped conduct the landmark Hawthorne studies at the Western Electric's Hawthorne Works just outside of Chicago. The Hawthorne studies investigated such issues as the effects of illumination, length of workday, rest breaks, method of payment, and group dynamics on employee behavior. Despite methodological flaws present in the Hawthorne studies, an important implication of these studies followed. That is, paying special attention to the human component of an organization can affect employee behavior. Because of this focus on the social side of human behavior in the organization (i.e., rather than just investigating the physical side as was seen in the earlier efficiency studies mentioned), it is generally recognized that the Hawthorne studies served as the catalyst to propel OB as a modern field of study.

The Subfields of Organizational Behavior

The investigation of human behavior can occur at three levels of analysis within the organization: the individual, groups and teams of individuals, and the organization itself as a whole. As a result, there have been a plethora of diverse contributors to the academic discipline of OB. The original goal of researchers in this newly created field was to construct a uniform comprehensive body of organizational research. However, because of the different perspectives held by the contributors from the various areas of the social sciences (e.g., psychology, economics, sociology, political science, communication, and anthropology), the result was three somewhat distinct subfields of OB. These subfields mirrored the three levels of analysis of human behavior. Micro-OB mainly concerns itself with investigating the behavior of individuals within the organization. Meso-OB focuses on the behavior of groups and teams in the workplace. Finally, researchers in Macro-OB conduct investigations at the organizational level of analysis.

Current Topics of Interest in OB

Some research topics of interest within the Micro-OB subfield deal with selecting and training employees, employee motivation, evaluating performance of individual employees, decision making, and employee satisfaction and stress. Areas of investigation within Meso-OB include group dynamics, team effectiveness, job design, and leadership, to name a few. Some main areas of investigation at the Macro-OB level are organizational culture and climate, organizational change and development, employee socialization, power and politics within the organization, conflict management and negotiation, and the interaction of the organization with its environment.

Robert D. Yonker

See also Human Resource Management; Organizational Development

Further Readings

Fayol, H. (1949). *General and industrial management.* London: Pittman.

Mayo, E. (1933). *The human problems of an industrial civilization.* London: Macmillan.

Taylor, F. W. (1947). *Scientific management.* New York: Harper & Row.

Weber, M. (1921). *Theory of social and economic organization* (A. M. Henderson & T. Parsons, Trans.). London: Oxford University Press.

Organizational Behavior Management

Organizational behavior management (OBM) takes the principles of B. F. Skinner's reinforcement theory and applies them in organizations. Its guiding philosophy is that our behavior is shaped and maintained by the environment, especially its performance consequences. Rarely are efforts made to change workers' attitudes or personalities. Instead most interventions or efforts to improve performance involve rearranging the situation so that favorable consequences—a thumbs-up, scores posted on a graph, the way paved to a coveted promotion—consistently occur when workers perform as desired. This intervention, referred to as positive reinforcement, is the most prevalent in OBM.

Embodying the Scientist–Practitioner Model

Psychologists are encouraged to apply psychological principles, while at the same time checking to see if evidence supports their application. The same scientist–practitioner model is extolled in OBM. Behavior analysts typically evaluate treatment programs—whether they be strictly positive reinforcement or positive reinforcement coupled with directives—for their effectiveness. Testimonials or opinions, no matter how raving or expert, are no substitute for data. So strong is this belief in rigorous assessment that the primary journal in the field, the *Journal of Organizational Behavior Management*, was started at Behavioral Systems, Inc., by former quarterback Fran Tarkenton and clinical psychologist Aubrey Daniels—strong testimony indeed to the scientist–practitioner model.

Continuing this tradition at professional meetings, academics and nonacademics alike present papers and have extensive and sometimes heated discussions about the results of their interventions. In the major professional organization, the Association for Behavior Analysis International, one quarter of members conduct research, whereas fully half indicate that their primary activity is in practice. Similarly, in the Organizational Behavior Management Network, 40% of whose members are students, the remaining 60% are roughly split among professors, consultants, and managers or administrators who work for organizations serving individuals with disabilities, state governments, and companies. In the leading industrial and organizational psychology journal, the *Journal of Applied Psychology*, fewer than 15% of the affiliations of authors are outside universities. In contrast, in the *Journal of Organizational Behavior Management*, professionals in human service settings as well as members of behaviorally oriented consulting firms contribute approximately one fourth of the articles.

A Behavioral Approach to Motivating Members of Organizations

Stimulating workers to improve and maintain their performance over extended periods of time remains a formidable challenge.

Five Steps Are Integral

To implement a positive reinforcement program, behavior analysts typically take five courses of action:

1. First, they analyze the situation, looking at the ways in which workers are evaluated, compensated, and promoted to see what, if anything, happens when employees perform as desired. If employees are being appraised fairly and accurately for their performance and recognized and promoted on the basis of these assessments of their performance, then minor modifications may be made, but the personnel practices are left more or less intact. If, however, few if any positive consequences occur when workers are performing as preferred, behavior analysts often attempt to rearrange the reinforcement contingencies.

2. To do this, they specify desired performance, defining work practices (e.g., lifting properly) until the definitions meet the test of interrater reliability, in which two raters independently collect data, check for agreements, and obtain agreement scores of 90% or better.

3. Analysts then measure desired performance, going regularly to the site, recording the level or rate of performance, and conducting interrater reliability checks.

4. They also provide frequent, positive consequences, such as posting scores on a graph to permit workers and their leaders to see how their scores compare with their previous record.

5. Last, analysts evaluate the effectiveness of the program by using a research design (often the within-group reversal or multiple-baseline approach), permitting the drawing of conclusions about causality with confidence, to see if the program caused the changes.

Five Steps Used to Improve Preventive Maintenance of Heavy Equipment in the U.S. Marine Corps

Costly equipment breakdowns and replacements led Marine Corps officers to be concerned about the preventive maintenance (PM) of equipment involving the adjusting, oiling, and replacement of suspiciously worn parts. Previous attempts, using a quality-circle approach, had not been successful. Judith L. Komaki (1998), who had successfully prevented accidents by ensuring a safe working environment and positively reinforcing workers for their safe performance, was asked by officers if a similar approach might work.

1. First, Komaki analyzed the situation. Only a paperwork trail existed. More than one Marine, however, admitted to filling out PM logs without so much as lifting the hood of a jeep, referring to this behavior as "pencil whipping" and impugning the accuracy of the reports, calling them "paper PMs." Because of the questionable veracity of the reports, it was difficult to tell if PM had actually been done, which meant that few if any positive consequences could be provided for desired performance. As a result, Komaki set up a positive reinforcement program in which Marines would receive feedback every week about what they actually did regarding PM. Table 1 outlines the steps taken.

2. The first step was to specify desired performance. On the basis of the importance of getting not merely reports of equipment deficiencies but correct reports, the first target was accurately detecting deficiencies, and the second was follow-through.

3. Komaki then measured desired performance. Deficiencies detected were operationalized as a percentage score: deficiencies reported on PM logs divided by deficiencies verified by second-echelon mechanics. Once the deficiencies were reported, it was important to follow through and take timely and appropriate actions, defined as making the repair, ordering the needed part, and/or processing the paperwork for the next level of repair.

4. Next, Komaki provided frequent positive consequences. Graphs of deficiencies detected and follow-through were updated and posted weekly at battalion headquarters.

5. Last, she evaluated effectiveness. A multiple-baseline design across groups—ordnance and motor transport—was used. Results for follow-through are shown in Table 1. When improvements occurred after and not before the intervention in both groups, it could be confidently concluded

that positive reinforcement in the form of feedback posted weekly was successful in improving the Marines' performance.

A Necessary Prerequisite to Positive Reinforcement: Successfully Measuring Desired Performance

Making positive consequences contingent on desired performance is easier said than done. It is not sufficient to wish, assume, or declare that reinforcement will occur. The management adage holds: "We treasure what we measure." What is essential to any successful positive reinforcement program is a fair and accurate appraisal of what one would like employees to do. In Komaki's case, measuring PM was a challenge. Not only was it intangible—inspecting a truck leaves few if any traces—but it also had few immediate outcomes. Failing to inspect a truck, for example, did not suddenly affect its operation; the truck essentially looked and operated the same. A year of field testing took place before Komaki figured out how to accurately gauge PM performance. Komaki fell prey to expedience, counting what could be easily counted, the time spent in contact with the equipment, rather than spending 10-fold the time to reliably assess the accuracy with which deficiencies were detected.

SURF & C

As a result of the initial mistakes made in measuring PM, Komaki identified five criteria to help counterbalance these ever ready temptations. The substance of what is measured is as important as how the data are collected. Given as the mnemonic, SURF & C, the criteria of U and C are concerned with what is measured and the criteria of S, R, and F with how the information is collected. The criteria are as follows:

- The target or dependent variable is sampled (S) directly rather than using a filtered or secondary source; that is, workers or the products of their work are observed firsthand instead of relying on their own or someone else's reports.
- The target is primarily under (U) the workers' control, responsive to their efforts, and minimally affected by extraneous factors.

Table 1   Steps Taken to Improve Preventive Maintenance in Ordnance and Motor Transport Groups at Marine Corps Base

Specify desired performance	Measure desired performance	Provide frequent positive consequences
Detected deficiencies: Accurately reporting deficiencies on PM logs.	deficiencies (# deficiencies reported on PM logs/# verified by mechanics).	Feedback graph (below) posted weekly at battalion headquarters.
Follow through: Taking appropriate, timely actions (e.g., ordering part) on reported deficiency.	follow through: (# actions taken/# reported deficiencies).	
Evaluate effectiveness of feedback intervention		

- Interrater reliability (R) scores of 90% or better are obtained during the formal data collection period. Observers or raters go independently to sample workers' performance or behaviors, terms used interchangeably, rating use of the same scoring system and checking to see if they agree. They continue practicing and, in some cases, revamping the coding system or retraining the coders until they can obtain scores of 90% or better.
- The target is assessed frequently (F)—often and regularly—at least 20 and ideally 30 times during the intervention period.
- Evidence is provided showing that the target is indeed "critical" (C) to the desired result,

otherwise referred to as valid. The evidence can be a significant correlation between the measure (e.g., a safety index) and the ultimate criterion (e.g., accidents).

Using SURF & C to Recognize Teachers for High-Quality Teaching

Behaviorally based interventions are often used in treating autism and developmental disabilities. Among their special features are the expert guidance provided by teachers. The ultimate outcome, that of improving the skills of the clients, is clear. To achieve this result, however, it is not sufficient to focus on only the client. Instead, it is necessary to identify and then assess what staff members should do to enable client improvements. For teachers of the developmentally disabled, Dennis R. Reid and his colleagues pinpointed (a) giving instructions, often verbal; (b) guiding the student physically through the steps; and (c) delivering rewards that are timely and contingent. To see whether these behaviors were valid, they looked to see if there was a relationship between the behaviors of students and teachers. What they found was that as the appropriate use of teaching techniques increased, so did the skills of the students, indicating that the practices were critical (C). Their measure also met the S, R, and F criteria. The observers conducted interrater reliability (R) checks on one fifth of the observations; scores ranged between 74% and 97%. Last, Reid and his colleagues directly sampled (S) the teachers' implementation of the techniques, collecting data frequently (F), at least daily.

Using SURF & C to Positively Reinforce Workers for Performing Safely

Preventing workplace accidents is a venerable topic in industrial and organizational psychology. The focus is typically on the accidents. Unfortunately, this concentration on accidents creates problems. The base rate for accidents is low; hundreds of unsafe acts occur before a worker has an accident, making it difficult to craft a successful intervention reinforcing workers for engaging in preferred actions. Second, because of threats about losing one's job, accidents are severely underreported; a phenomenon called "bloody pockets" was coined to describe an injured worker who returns to work and places his blood-smeared hand in his pocket.

As a result, behavior analysts pioneered a new approach to accident reduction. Instead of accidents, emphasis was placed on safety. Robert A. Reber and Jerry A. Wallin examined injury reports to determine which actions would help prevent injuries; lifting properly was identified as the safe action required to avoid incurring back injuries. Care was taken to specify lifting properly and to ensure that these practices were under (U) workers' control. Validity was ensured as well. To see if their safety index was valid, Reber and Wallin collected data in different departments in a factory, evaluating the relationship between

injuries and the safety index. The lower the injuries per department, the higher the safety practices, Reber and Wallin found, indicating that their safety index was critical (C). At the same time, Reber and Wallin met the S, R, and F criteria. Trained observers went to the site and directly sampled (S) work practices. They collected information frequently (F), often at least weekly. Last, interrater reliability (R) checks were done in which two observers independently recorded identified agreements between raters, and then calculated a percentage agreement score (number of agreements/number of agreements plus disagreements). Checklist revisions continued until agreement was reached on the scoring of checklist items almost all the time. Only when this criterion was achieved were the terms considered to be acceptably defined. Reliability checks were also used in training; trainees were not considered trained until they could pass the interrater reliability test. Raters were then regularly checked to see whether they were becoming stricter or more lenient during the formal data collection. Data from the safety index enabled the providing of positive consequences, which ultimately reduced costly, tragic injuries.

Proactive Stance Plays a Key Role in the Direction of OBM

Fueled by Skinner's vision of a utopian community in *Walden Two*, the use of reinforcement for prosocial purposes took root in the 1960s. People who had been diagnosed as autistic and were destined to spend the remainder of their lives within the drab walls of institutions began to communicate and help themselves when their behaviors were reinforced. Teachers using a combination of positive reinforcement and extinction helped first graders in a disadvantaged neighborhood to learn skills critical to their further achievement. The evening news touted the results of a token economy program for soldiers in boot camp in the U.S. Army at Fort Ord, California. In 1968, in the first issue of the *Journal of Applied Behavior Analysis*, pioneers in the field—Donald Baer, Montrose Wolf, and Todd Risley—predicted that researching "socially important behaviors, such as mental retardation, crime, mental illness, or education . . . will lead to a better state of society." During that era in the

United States, dramatic societal changes were occurring: the passage of landmark civil rights legislation, the ending of the Vietnam War. Hence, it was not surprising that behavior analysts aimed the five-step behavioral process at facilitating social aims.

This desire to make a difference has made a difference. The most popular target area, accounting for one fifth of OBM studies according to a 30-year review of the literature (Komaki, Coombs, Redding, & Schepman, 2000), is patient and client care and instructional and teaching technique (e.g., Reid and his colleagues' fostering the teaching of individuals with learning disabilities). Productivity (e.g., sorting and loading packages, processing student applications, conducting building code inspections) and attendance and punctuality have been the topics of 18% and 14% of the studies, respectively. An area of concern for both management and workers, safety and health, accounts for 13% of the studies (e.g., Reber and Wallin on promoting safety).

An Ambitious Effort by a Public University to Boost Its Graduation Rate

Not limited to a single behavior or a single group, the behavioral approach can be used to tackle socially important issues affected by multiple behaviors of multiple constituencies. In higher education, a major problem is students' failing to graduate within 6 years. Facilitating student success is not only the right thing to do; it has become critical in developing budgets, particularly for public universities. Nine of 10 metrics Florida uses to fund its universities involve undergraduate education. As a result, the provost charged Douglas Robertson, the undergraduate dean, to lead the effort at Florida International University (FIU). The aim was to ensure the timely graduation of FIU's 40,000 undergraduates, 87% of whom are underrepresented and 61% Hispanic. A daunting task, it requires shaping the behavior of FIU students, advisers, faculty members, academic departments, and support offices up through the president and the board of trustees, as well as courting grant sponsors. Table 2 outlines the steps taken (and under discussion) to rearrange reinforcement contingencies: specifying and measuring target behaviors, which in turn

enable the frequent, timely delivery of positive consequences.

FIU's graduation rate had steadily declined to a historic low of 41%, in contrast to the average for public research institutions of 54%. Once FIU students were in majors, however, the graduation rate rose to 77%. Hence, Phase 1 of the Graduation Success Initiative focused on helping students identify appropriate majors early, providing a clear path, and giving immediate feedback as to whether students were on or off the path. As shown in Table 2, *desired performance* was specified for students and their advisers. Students began by consulting sophisticated but user-friendly online tools, MyMajor and My MajorMatch, to help them select majors in line with their abilities and interests. Students could then consult with advisers as well as the online tool My_eAdvisor, which displayed milestones students had attained toward graduation as well as their advisers' availability and up-to-date registration information. To *measure performance*, Robertson assessed the number of unique visitors to the online tools, the percentage of students who declared majors, the percentage of students on track, and those at risk. Favorable *consequences* occurred naturally: Students learned how their interests aligned with possible majors and, after declaring majors, students joined communities of their peers. The metrics from My_eAdvisor enabled further consequences. Students straying off track received automatic alerts. But even more important, advisers could celebrate with students as they were making progress, with the students responding in kind, providing naturally happening *positive consequences*. To motivate the advisers, the same steps are being implemented. Desired performance—proactively managing the progress of students—has been specified. To measure performance, plans are under way to track the records of students in each adviser's caseload (their students' grade point averages, retention, and graduation rate). The consistency and appropriateness of adviser notes to students as well as the accumulated interactions with all advisers are under consideration as another measure of advisers' performance. Supervisors could then use the quality of adviser–student interactions to positively review advisers. These student- and adviser-driven measures of

Table 2 Steps Taken (and Under Discussion) to Improve the On-Time Graduation of Primarily Minority Students at a Public University

		Specify desired performance	*Measure desired performance*	*Provide frequent positive consequences*
Individuals/ groups		Students choose major in keeping with interests as early as possible and follow curriculum every semester		
Students		Consult online tool helping to identify interests, majors, and what majors entail.	# of unique visitors including time spent and # of pages viewed.	Learn/confirm interests in line with major. Remove from "things to do" list.
		Declare appropriate major at admission.	% of students picking a major.	Join de facto student cohorts.
		Keep on-track, following curriculum articulated by the faculty for every semester.	% of students on-track (as per major map with milestones attained and registration information).	See progress toward graduation. Are praised by advisor. Get automatic alerts for off-track actions.
			% of students at risk.	Are contacted by adviser.
Advisers		Proactively manage progress of students assigned at admission, i.e., their student caseload.	(Planned: caseload GPA, grad rate.) (Under discussion: Quality of interactions — adviser notes.)	Celebrate progress with students. Given advising awards. Reviewed by supervisor/asst. dean.
Groups		Remove barriers (Choke-point courses chronically impeding student progress) and provide supports on path		
Faculty		Improve teaching of gateway courses.	(Indirect measure: percentage of students who passed course.) (Under discussion: learning metrics.)	(Under discussion: Recognition how and by whom.)
Learn. assts				
Departments				
Individuals/ groups		Retain commitment of stakeholders (president, board of trustees) and grantors		
Stakeholders		Take neccessary actions in support of student graduation success.	$ savings produced by retention and on-time graduation rates.	$ savings annually.
Granting agencies			(Planned: Dashboards with early alert systems for every gateway course.)	$ (Planned: Ongoing feedback.)
Evaluate effectiveness of the graduation success initiative				

FTIC 6-Year Graduation Rate

Pre-GSI | Post-GSI

Projected

Graduation Success Initiative

performance enable positive reinforcement contingencies.

Confronting another aspect of student success, Phase 2 aims to remove a major barrier, that of students' failing gateway courses, and to provide students educational supports on their paths to graduation. A total of 17 high-enrollment, high-failure, and high-impact courses (e.g., College Algebra, Writing and Rhetoric, Introduction to Psychology) were found, totaling more than 41,000 enrollments. To reach these goals, Robertson aims to improve the teaching of these choke-point courses. If instruction could be upgraded, more students would be likely to learn the required material and pass the courses. Robertson proposes a variety of avenues: from helping incumbent faculty members raise the quality of their teaching and (possibly) hiring highly developed full-time instructors and expanding the number and quality of learning assistants to providing computer- and peer-assisted instructional techniques and setting up discipline-specific learning environments. Desired performance is currently defined as improving the teaching of gateway courses. To date, however, the measure of performance used does not track the quality of pedagogy or the learning of students, although the latter is currently under discussion. Instead, what is evaluated is the percentage of students passing the course. An increase in the pass rate may reflect instructors' enhancing teaching and students' learning more. But it may not. Instructors whose reputations are at stake may have simply "dumbed down" courses and/or graded more leniently with students learning less. Highly recommended is a direct sampling of the quality of pedagogy exhibited by the faculty members, learning assistants, and departments, as was done in Phase 1 with students and their advisers. Given such direct measures, contingent consequences can then be provided for these integral groups.

Undergirding this massive effort is a hidden but indispensable labyrinth of online tools and support offices. FIU's newly opened Office of Retention and Graduation Success, for instance, identifies students at risk and passes this information on to advisers who contact students at risk and provide guidance and support. Online tools play an integral role. My_eAdvisor, for example, enables students to see if they are on track and to adjust accordingly. Advisers can use the information as the basis for interactions with students. Supervisors can base their reviews with advisers using these measures, confirming the adage "We treasure what we measure." MyMajor, MyMajor Match, and My_eAdvisor were developed at considerable cost by an internal FIU group that does nothing but develop customized applications. The initial build of My_eAdvisor alone cost about $450,000.

Further enabling the work is the largess of such granting agencies as Walmart and the Bill and Melinda Gates Foundation. Moreover, Robertson builds and makes available ongoing metrics (e.g., the savings produced by improved retention and on-time graduation rates). Planned are dashboards with early alert systems for every gateway course. Every individual at every level—from the president and the board of trustees to students and their advisers, and across functional areas, from the academic units to support offices, as well as granting agencies—knows the graduation rate and how much has been saved. The rationale is to motivate these key stakeholders to take necessary actions in support of student graduation success.

The Graduation Success Initiative remains a work in progress. The result, however, has been encouraging. As shown in Table 2, FIU's graduation rate has risen by 12% in just 3 years to a historic high of 53%. Robertson describes "a long-term, comprehensive, university-wide system of innovations that fundamentally changes the way in which the undergraduate curriculum is administered and re-orients it to student success." Baer, Wolf, and Risley would no doubt be pleased to see how the consistent and regular rearrangement of reinforcement contingencies is leading "to a better state of society."

Judith L. Komaki

See also Reinforcement Theory of Work Motivation

Further Readings

Austin, J., & Carr, J. E. (Eds.) (2000). *Handbook of applied behavior analysis*. Reno, NV: Context.

Baer, D. M., Wolf, M. M., & Risley, T. R. (1968). Some current dimensions of applied behavior analysis. *Journal of Applied Behavior Analysis, 1*, 91–97.

Daniels, A. C. (2000). *Bringing out the best in people.* New York: McGraw-Hill.

Foster, S. L., & Cone, J. D. (1986). Design and use of direct observation procedures. In A. R. Ciminero, K. S. Calhoun, & H. E. Adams (Eds.), *Handbook of behavioral assessment* (2nd ed., pp. 253–324). New York: Wiley-Interscience.

Frederikson, L. W. (Ed.). (1982). *Handbook of organizational behavior management.* New York: John Wiley.

Johnson, C. M., Redmon, W. K., & Mawhinney, T. C. (Eds.). (2001). *Handbook of organizational performance: Behavior analysis and management.* New York: Haworth.

Kissel, R. C., Whitman, T. L., & Reid, D. R. (1983). An institutional staff training and self-management program for developing multiple self-care skills in severely/profoundly retarded individuals. *Journal of Applied Behavior Analysis, 16,* 395–415.

Komaki, J. L. (1998). When performance improvement is the goal: A new set of criteria for criteria. *Journal of Applied Behavior Analysis, 31,* 263–280.

Komaki, J. L. (2003). Reinforcement theory at work: Enhancing and explaining what employees do. In L. W. Porter, G. A. Bigley, & R. M. Steers (Eds.), *Motivation and work behavior* (7th ed., pp. 95–112). New York: McGraw-Hill.

Komaki, J. L., Coombs, T., Redding, T. P., Jr., & Schepman, S. (2000). A rich and rigorous examination of applied behavior analysis research in the world of work. In C. L. Cooper & I. T. Robertson (Eds.), *International review of industrial and organizational psychology 2000* (pp. 265–267). Chichester, UK: Wiley.

O'Brien, R. M., Dickinson, A. M., & Rosow, M. P. (Eds.). (1982). *Industrial behavior modification: A management handbook.* New York: Pergamon.

Reber, R. A., & Wallin, J. A. (1983). Validation of a behavioral measure of occupational safety. *Journal of Organizational Behavior Management, 5*(2), 69–77.

Skinner, B. F. (1983). *A matter of consequences: Part 3 of an autobiography.* New York: Random House.

Websites

Association for Behavior Analysis: www.abainternational.org

Florida International University's Graduation Success Initiative: undergrad.fiu.edu/gsi/gsi-news.html

Organizational Behavior Management Network: www.obmnetwork.com

ORGANIZATIONAL CHANGE

Change has been considered the most reliable constant within organizations. Change as an organizational phenomenon has been recognized as important for years, given the proliferation of research, applied models, and books advising on change. Yet organizational change is one of the least understood aspects of organization life, evidenced by unmet expectations and failed initiatives. Despite the books and articles written about managing change, perhaps the paradox between prevalence and failure lies in the difficulty organizations have in getting a handle on change itself.

Simply put, change is the process by which an organism goes from relative stability through a period of relative instability and then back to relative stability. This is commonly represented by Kurt Lewin's three-stage model of change. The first stage is *unfreezing.* This initial stage includes the willingness of individuals to abandon the old and adopt the new and is best understood through the study of motivation. The second stage is the *change* itself, when the new is put into place. This stage is associated with new routines requiring knowledge and skill acquisition. The third stage is called *refreezing,* which focuses on normalizing the new or moving from compliance to commitment. Although attention is generally placed on the second and third stages, many believe that most changes fail because the *unfreeze* stage is ineffective.

Because organizational change is fundamental to many important topics for organizational effectiveness, it has not received the attention sufficient to provide adequate understanding and practice. That is, change is endemic to innovation (implementing new and novel ideas); transformational leadership (taking people from Point A to Point B); Total Quality Management (continuous improvement); organizational development (preparing employees to identify and implement change); and, according to Peter Drucker, the basic purpose of the business enterprise itself (constantly changing to meet customers' demands).

Addressing three aspects of organizational change should prove helpful to improve understanding this complex organizational phenomenon. First is the emerging issue of levels of analysis.

Second are the major themes typically associated with the study of organizational change. Third is explicating new ways change can be viewed.

Levels of Analysis

Although organizational change has typically been viewed nominally (e.g., mergers, policy change, new technology), there is an emerging view of change as cascading events beginning with the organization's external environment, down to the organizational level, to the work group level, and finally to the individual level. As such, change is characterized by different dimensions of the organization changing at different levels.

The environment consists of changes in the market, in government regulations, or in prevailing economic conditions. Organizational-level change generally deals with modifications to some combination of strategy, culture, or structure. Although work groups also have structure and culture, generally this level focuses on goals, leadership, and work processes. Finally, individual-level change typically involves the jobs and proximal working conditions of employees. Therefore, understanding organizational change involves understanding how dimensions at each level affect performance at the corresponding level and then how these dimensions affect change and performance at all the various levels.

Additionally, an overlooked insight about change is that different work groups and different individuals within work groups do not experience a given organizational change in the same way. This is illustrated in the case of a jewelry company that expanded its product line to include high-end jewelry, causing a reorganization of its sales staff, a renovation of the showroom, and new skills for some employees. Thus, a typical comment of employees participating in a change is "in the broad scheme of things, these were just minor adjustments to the company, but to those of us in the department, the changes were significant." Failure to recognize change in this comprehensive way results in the oversimplification of important nuances or fragmented conclusions lacking broad application.

Traditionally, levels of analysis focuses on intra-organizational change stimulated by external factors. An emerging trend is to consider change from an interorganizational perspective. That is, how does one organization actually influence change in another? This may apply to buyer changing supplier but can be even more important in reverse. When sales can be seen as a behavioral change phenomenon, the likelihood of a sale can increase. Abandoning traditional sales approaches for a behavioral change approach has been shown to be significantly more effective because the "unfreezing" stage takes the sales focus off less influential motivational factors, such as the valence of one's products and services, and places it on the more salient factors of change, such as risk perceptions.

The Themes of Organizational Change

A review of studies of organizational change conducted in the 1990s revealed four major themes. These were content (the *what* of change), context (the *what else* of change), process (the *how* of change), and outcome (the *so what* of change).

The content of change includes variables of change such as dimensions at levels of analysis (mentioned earlier), as well as the *sign* and magnitude of change. For example, the full description of a specific *reorganization* may be expressed as an entirely new (magnitude) structure (dimension) of top management (level), which will create more opportunity for growth (favorable). Thus, two different *reorganizations* should be considered different organizational changes when one or more of these four characteristics of *what changed* vary.

The context of change includes variables associated with *what else* is going on relative to the change that is outside the change itself but influences its outcome. One aspect of context deals with forces or factors that contribute to the reason for change or create significant barriers to change. Generally, these are external events of environmental influences on the organization, such as competition, government regulation, economic shifts, or geopolitical events. Another aspect of context deals with internal variables that may moderate how change is handled or experienced in the organization. This would include organizational characteristics such as climate for change, leadership style, and cultural barriers to change. A third aspect of context is the characteristics of individuals affected by organizational change. These characteristics range from distal traits, such as personality and age, to midrange states, such as general change efficacy or commitment to the organization, to change-specific individual differences in readiness for change and coping resources.

The process of change has typically been the major focus of organizational change. That is, how something is done is ultimately more important than what is done. Traditionally, *change management* has involved stage models or the proper steps to successful implementation. However, more recently change process has been viewed qualitatively. In this case, the *how* is usually characterized by the notion of procedural justice. That is, when change agents of an organization include the change participants in the process, give advanced notice and provide adequate explanations of changes, and offer an acceptable rationale for the change, those affected by the change respond more positively to the change. The process can also be characterized by the support management gives to the change. Support comes in the form of top management commitment to the change and a desire to provide adequate resources necessary for successful implementation of the change.

More recently, research conducted by Yi Liu has investigated the interaction between context and process. The key findings suggest that the nature of broad leadership (transactional vs. transformational) reduces the need for specific change management processes of justice. Conversely, the lack of transformational leadership in general does not seem to be important to change success when specific change management practices are justice oriented.

Finally, the outcomes of change are essentially attitudes, behavior, and performance assessed at various levels. When outcome is evaluated at the organizational or group level, typically the interest is in how the normal performance measures were affected (e.g., sales, profit, productivity). However, when individuals are the focus, there is a broad array of outcomes of interest. These outcomes could be either directly associated with the change itself, such as readiness for the change, or a residual effect on the individual, such as stress, change in person–environment fit, job satisfaction, and organizational commitment.

Attitude toward change has been one individual outcome of interest. It is important to note that recent research on attitude toward change has explored its multidimensional nature and the differences between it and other related constructs. Sandy Piderit posited that attitude toward change is composed of three components: cognition, affect, and behavioral intent, which do not move in concert regarding a particular change. That is, behavioral intent to support the change would typically be more positive than beliefs about the change and emotional response to the change. This is evidenced by employees affected by a change who say "Complaining is at an all-time high, yet work continues to be put out at an amazing pace." Distinction has also been made between acceptance and resistance. These are considered two different constructs rather than opposite ends of one continuum. That is, low acceptance is the absence of support, and high resistance is the presence of negatively directed effort.

The Nature of Organizational Change

In many areas of organizational behavior study, there are two different ways to approach a topic. One approach is to simply name a change phenomenon and build a body of knowledge around it. However, as mentioned earlier, this fragments understanding and restricts generalization. The other approach is to describe the phenomenon along one or more dimensions. That is, instead of studying *reorganizations* or *entering new markets* separately, it is possible to investigate amount of change in culture or structure occurring in either nominal change.

Pace, sequence, and linearity of change are another way to view an organizational change. Pace deals with whether there is early rapid change to overcome inertia or late rapid change following periods of *softening up* the organization or whether change is gradual, building trust as change progresses. Sequence deals with order of importance or what needs to be changed before anything else can be changed. Linearity recognizes that change may be nonlinear because of oscillations and delays caused by uncertainty and resistance.

Another issue regarding the nature of change has to do with whether change is episodic. Traditionally, change is viewed as a break in the status quo. This approach treats change as if it is a *single* disruption in an otherwise stable setting.

A contrarian perspective views change more as simultaneous and cumulative, sometimes referred to as *turbulence*. This perspective posits that change does not occur in isolation of other changes, and in fact, organizations are basically in a state of flux in which change is a natural state and managing change is a continual process. The success an organization ultimately has with managing change may depend on which of these two views of change applies.

Finally, an aspect that shapes how organizations view and approach change is the notion of the asymmetry of change. This involves the assumption that the motivation for and benefit of change is greater for the organization than for the individual. Although it is important for change to be a win–win experience, management cannot forget that the reality of rationale and valence of change is skewed to the organization.

Steven D. Caldwell

See also Customer Satisfaction and Service; Downsizing; Emergent Leadership; Employee Participation and Voice; Groupthink; Innovation; Leadership Circumplex

Further Readings

Amis, J., Slack, T., & Hinings, C. R. (2004). The pace, sequence, and linearity of radical change. *Academy of Management Journal*, 47, 15–39.

Burke, W. (2002). *Organization change: Theory and practice*. Thousand Oaks, CA: Sage.

Caldwell, S. D. (2013). Are change readiness strategies overrated? A commentary on boundary conditions. *Journal of Change Management*, 13(1), 19–35.

Herold, D. M., & Fedor, D. B. (2008). *Change the way you lead change*. Stanford, CA: Stanford Business.

Oreg, S., Michel, A., & Todnem, R. (2013). *The psychology of organizational change*. Cambridge, UK: Cambridge University Press.

Organizational Change, Resistance to

Each decade seems to bring an increase to the pace of business. As customer expectations continue to increase, business cycle times respond by decreasing. Therefore a business's ability to rapidly adjust becomes critical not just for thriving but now for simply surviving. As competitors and the economy make unexpected shifts, it is mission critical for leaders to be able to implement the appropriate changes in the most friction-free way. It is imperative for leaders to understand and anticipate the natural resistance to change in the ecosystem that they want to influence.

Underlying Reasons for Resistance to Change

Organizational change can affect individuals in a number of ways. From potential job loss to increased job opportunities, the costs and benefits of organizational changes to employees are often unpredictable. Resistance to change is typically rooted in the perceived negative consequences an employee fears as a possible outcome from the change. Some of the common reasons why employees may resist organizational change include the following:

- not understanding why the changes are occurring,
- not understanding what the changes entail,
- not knowing how they will be affected,
- fearing that their skills may become obsolete,
- rewards' not being aligned to the changes desired outcomes, and
- a culture of mistrust exists prior to the change.

These are just a sample of reasons underlying potential resistance to organizational change. At a deeper level, resistance can be brought about by feelings of fear regarding what the change may bring and lack of control of the process of change. To be clear, employees' perceptions do not have to be grounded in reality to seem "real" to them and thus trigger their direct and/or indirect resistance to the change. Consequently, to effectively address resistance to organizational change, it is important to understand how those affected might interpret the consequences of the proposed changes.

Models of Reactions to Change

A variety of process models describing employees' reactions to change exist. Typically, these models have been developed in a pragmatic context and have not been based on rigorous empirical research. One of the most widely used change models that looks at the transitions individuals go through was developed by William Bridges. This model proposes the following three stages:

Ending, losing, and letting go. During this stage, people are dealing with letting go of the way things were before the change. The general thrust is that before beginning something new, people need to let go of what had been before. The emotional reactions often resemble a grief process.

The neutral zone. This is the phase when the old ways have ended, but the change is not complete. The new ways of doing things are neither fully implemented nor understood. This can be a difficult time for employees because they are unsure about what is required of them, and they are caught between the two, often conflicting, ways of doing things. The emotional reactions can be frustration and confusion. Guiding people through the neutral zone is a primary target of change management activities.

The new beginning. This is the final phase of the transition process, when people engage with the new ways of doing things. There is a new sense of clarity and purpose that the change has brought about. The emotional reactions often include relief and guarded excitement.

Indicators of Resistance to Change

As a leader of a change effort, it is important to stay attuned to signs of underlying resistance. Leaders need to understand the reactions of people in their organizations to have targeted change management approaches. When individuals resist change, the indicators can range from subtle to overt; following are some of the things that may signal resistance:

- not following through on commitments,
- openly criticizing the change,
- reinforcing organizational barriers that must be overcome to be successful,
- not engaging in discussion of solutions,
- holding on to previous ways of doing things, and
- lack of public advocacy for the change.

Suggestions for Addressing Resistance to Change

The management literature provides a variety of suggestions of how to manage change. Whether based on theoretical models or on practical experience, several categories of suggestions are common:

Define a Communication Strategy

- Communicate *why* the change is occurring. The purpose of the change must be clear for employees to fully accept the change.
- Include a clear vision of the future state. This can help address fear of the unknown and inspire commitment.
- Detail the benefits to the organization and to employees. When done with regard to the future state, this can help in gaining the personal *buy-in* of employees. They need to know what is in it for them.
- Include a feedback loop in the communication plan. This helps test for alignment between what is communicated out and what is being heard and understood.

Have a Plan for Engaging Key Stakeholders

- Identify key stakeholders. Who has the critical knowledge to define the approach? Who has influence in leading the change? Who has ground-level responsibility for implementing the change?
- Know where they stand on the change. It may be helpful to rate their degrees of commitment (e.g., active resistance, passive resistance, neutral, supportive, actively supportive).
- Have a plan for engaging stakeholders. Define actions, including categories such as communications, training, role modeling, and incentivizing.
- Periodically revisit the stakeholder plan and adapt as needed to ensure that stakeholders are on board.

Communicate in a Timely, Clear, and Consistent Fashion

- Inform employees as soon as possible of the change. Once it is clear what will happen, it is better that employees find out directly from management rather than from outside sources, such as public media, or from rumors inside the organization.

- Consider the needs of the audience when communicating. Target the message at their key concerns and adapt the communication style that is used.
- Be consistent in the messages that are delivered. Keeping the message simple can help with consistency over time and across communications.
- Communicate honestly. Even if something is unknown about the change, it is better to share this fact directly with employees than to attempt a contrived answer.

Encourage Employee Input and Discuss Employee Reactions

- Whenever possible, involve employees in decisions that affect them. Involving employees enhances their feelings of control and reduces resistance.
- Allow opportunities for employees to share their reactions to the change, good and bad. By allowing employees to express their feelings in an appropriate context, everyone can move on toward acceptance.

Provide Training and Support for the Change

- When employees' skills may be affected, provide the necessary development support. Employees may resist changes that make their skills obsolete. Training employees to meet new job requirements reduces resistance. Some employees may see the change as an opportunity to enhance their skills.
- Ensure that reward and recognition systems are aligned to support the change. Visibly reward behaviors that are in line with the goals of the change efforts.

Track Progress, Maintain Momentum, and Celebrate Success

- Report on progress of the change relative to the plan. Where key milestones are met, recognize the relevant teams. Where key milestones are missed, ensure there are plans to address underlying issues.

- Key stakeholders need to continue to reinforce the reasons for change. It is typical to lose focus as implementation begins, and it is critical for key leaders to remain engaged. Ensure that leaders continue to actively listen to what employees are understanding and what they are experiencing with the change.
- Do not forget to celebrate success. Even recognition of small wins can help propel the organization forward.

*Robert A. Schmieder
and David L. Gartenberg*

See also Downsizing; Morale; Organizational Change; Organizational Climate; Organizational Culture; Organizational Cynicism; Organizational Development; Organizational Retaliatory Behavior; Survivor Syndrome

Further Readings

Bridges, W. (2009). *Managing transitions* (3rd ed.). Cambridge, MA: Da Capo.

McAllaster, C. (2004). The 5 Ps of change: Leading change by effectively using leverage points within an organization. *Organizational Dynamics, 33,* 318–328.

Piderit, S. K. (2000). Rethinking resistance and recognizing ambivalence: A multidimensional view of attitudes toward an organizational change. *Academy of Management Review, 25,* 783–794.

ORGANIZATIONAL CLIMATE

The term *organizational climate* has been used in many different ways to refer to a wide variety of constructs. In recent years some consensus about what precisely should be included in the construct, and what should not, has begun to emerge. Research interest in climate has remained high, despite the variety of conceptualizations of the construct, because climate is generally seen as related to a variety of important organizational outcomes, including productivity (both individual and organizational), satisfaction, and turnover. More recently, climate has come to be seen as predictive of specific organizational outcomes, depending on what aspect of climate is being assessed. Overall, research has indicated that positively viewed climates tend to be associated with higher levels of positive attitudes. Thus, climate continues to be seen as organizationally important, but the specific outcomes of interest seen to be affected by climate have shifted over time.

Initially, researchers used *climate* to refer to individual employees' perceptions of more immediate aspects of their work environment (e.g., supervision, work group characteristics, job or task characteristics), and the climate measures that were developed and widely used reflected this orientation. However, general measures of climate began to incorporate aspects of leadership, group interaction and cohesion, job satisfaction, and other constructs, leading to questions of the uniqueness and utility of the climate construct. To counteract this tendency, researchers strategically focused the climate construct on those particular types of climates that may emerge in each particular organization. A more targeted approach has become dominant in the past several years, as evidenced by the recent research focus on facet-specific climates and the corresponding facet-specific outcomes.

Benjamin Schneider has long been one of the primary researchers in the area of organizational climate, and variations of the operational definition he has used are the dominant in the literature today. Specifically, Schneider has argued that organizational climate should be defined as the policies, practices, and procedures that are rewarded, supported, and expected in an organization with regard to a specific organizational domain, such as safety, innovation, customer service, and ethics. This basic definition has come to be the most commonly used conceptualization of the climate construct.

There are two critical implications of this definition. First, by focusing on policies, practices, and procedures that are rewarded, supported, and expected, the definition implies that organizational climate is a shared perspective among organization members, rather than an individual perception. This focus on within-unit agreement places organizational climate in the category of compositional models that David Chan (1998) would call *direct consensus models*, in that the meaning of the group-level construct is based on the agreement (or consensus) among the individual units (group members or employees). This

agreement is often assessed using referent shift measures, in which individuals respond to items referring to the group's attributes that are then aggregated to the appropriate level. Second, by focusing on specific organizational domains, the definition implies that an organization may have multiple climates operating simultaneously and may have climates that are more active in one area of the organization than in another; for example, a climate for innovation may be most salient in a research and development division, whereas a climate for customer service may be most salient in a sales division within a single organization.

This definition is also useful because it helps clarify what organizational climate is not. Organizational climate does not refer to the *personal values* that are held by members of an organization, or shared by organization members; in general, shared values are under the umbrella of organizational culture (see the entry "Organizational Culture"). *Organizational climate* also does not refer to individual and idiosyncratic perceptions of life within an organization; in general, these perceptions fall under the umbrella of psychological climate.

In the remainder of this entry, we first focus briefly on four examples of specific types of climates: climate for service, climate for safety, ethical climate, and climates for various organizational processes. We then discuss the issue of degree of agreement about climate perceptions, which is known as *climate strength*; this leads to a discussion of when it is possible to say that a climate does or does not exist.

Climate for Service

Research on organizational climate for service has flourished and considers both employee and customer perceptions of an organization's policies, practices, and procedures that are rewarded, supported, and expected for quality service in the organization. For employees, climate for service represents their experiences of the organization's emphasis on service quality. For customers, climate for service is the perceived amount of excellent service received from the organization. Research on climate for service has found links between these dual perceptions of employees' climate for service and customers' satisfaction and evaluations of the quality of service. This research is an example of linkage research because customer service perceptions are linked with important organizational outcomes, such as customer retention.

Climate for service research builds from the theory that employees emphasize service behavior to the degree that it is rewarded, supported, and expected by their employing organization. Customers of organizations that have positive or high climates for service come to have higher satisfaction with the service they receive from the organizations because of their contact and interaction with various employees, who provide consistently high levels of service. Research on the boundary conditions of this effect has begun, and findings suggest that higher frequency of contact between employees and customers is related to a stronger relationship between service climate and customer satisfaction. Another moderator of the climate for service and customer satisfaction relationship is the proximity of the organizational target, such as bank branches versus the bank as a whole, to customers. Higher levels of service climate relate not only to more customer satisfaction but also stronger subsequent financial performance. Research has indicated that service climate is stronger when the product is more intangible and when there are higher levels of service employee interdependence.

Climate for Safety

Climate for safety has also received considerable research attention. This aspect of climate refers to employee perceptions of an organization's policies, practices, and procedures regarding safety that are rewarded, supported, and expected from employees. Several researchers have documented a consistent relationship between a positive safety climate and reduced injury rates. Zohar, a leading theorist in this area of research, has stressed the need to consider perceptions of actual safety practices as opposed to the safety policies and practices espoused by supervisors and top management, because the behaviors that are said to be expected and rewarded are often not the behaviors that are actually expected and rewarded. Interestingly, transformational or constructive leadership is shown to relate to lower injury rate, and this

relationship is moderated by safety climate, conceptualized as perceptions of actual safety practices rather than more formalized safety policies. It has been suggested that the relationship between safety climate and accidents is reciprocal and that in poor safety climates, underreporting is more prevalent. Suggested antecedents of safety climate include management–employee relations and organizational support and resources, while suggested outcomes include individual-level safety motivation and safety behavior (which predicts accident rates).

Ethical Climate

Given the many well-publicized corporate scandals of the past several years, it is hardly surprising to see that there is a sizable stream of research examining organizational ethics and ethical behavior from within an organizational climate framework. From this perspective (to use Bart Victor and John Cullen's seminal definition), ethical climate can be thought of as shared perceptions among group members regarding what constitutes ethically correct behavior and how ethical issues should be handled within an organization. This definition highlights the fact that ethical climate is not focused on what is right or wrong but is instead focused on the things that organization members perceive the organization to see as ethical. Thus employees might agree that when confronted with an ethical issue at work, they would be rewarded and supported by the organization if they engaged in behavior they personally believed to be unethical.

Although ethical climate is a relatively new research area, researchers have identified several antecedents of ethical climate. Among other things, ethical climate has been shown to be affected by gender, age, ethical education, personality traits, and stage of organizational career. Victor and Cullen (1987), who are largely responsible for starting the research focus in this area, hypothesized that social norms, organizational form, and various firm-specific factors would be the dominant antecedents. Marcus Dickson, D. Brent Smith, Michael Grojean, and Mark Ehrhart addressed the literature on each of these points rather extensively. To date, there is more theory than data about the degree to which a strong organizational ethical climate is associated with individual and organizational ethical behavior and decision making.

Climates for Organizational Processes

Recent research has begun to focus on climates for processes (e.g., procedural justice and diversity), compared with strategic outcomes (e.g., accident prevention). Climate for organizational justice normally involves employees' perceptions of how fairly they are treated, which can be divided into subcategories: distributive justice (perceptions of the outcomes of organizational decisions), procedural justice (perceptions of the fairness of organization decision making), and interactional justice (perceptions of interpersonal treatment related to procedures). Results from a recent meta-analysis identified that climate for organizational justice relates to team effectiveness.

Climate for diversity has also begun to emerge as a construct of interest. Diversity climate involves employees' shared perceptions of their organization's use of fair employment policies and procedures that assist in socially integrating underrepresented employees into the work setting. Perceived diversity climate by both subordinates and managers relates to higher unit sales, which is elevated when both perceptions are more consistent with each other. Diversity climate has also been related to customer satisfaction, smaller gaps in performance between racial/ethnic groups, and organizational performance.

Many other organizational climate facets have been investigated in the literature, including climates for behavioral guidance (e.g., political activity, justice, and ethics), involvement (e.g., participation, support, group affect, cooperation, and empowerment), development (e.g., innovation, creativity, and training), and core operations (e.g., service and safety). Of course, the climate construct could be applied to an almost unlimited range of organizational topics for which shared perceptions by group members are important.

Climate Strength

Recently, researchers have begun to focus on the importance of climate strength, which has been operationally defined as the within-group variability in member perceptions of the climate.

When agreement is high, climate is strong. (Climate strength can also be conceptualized as variability in within-group perceptions, with greater variability indicating lesser strength.) Weaker climates could result from inconsistencies in policies or procedures. Although not a lot of research to date has explicitly addressed climate strength, much published research has found that climate strength moderates the effects of climate itself on various outcomes of interest. It is generally assumed that the relationship between a climate and the outcomes of interest will be stronger when climate strength is high. For example, Jason Colquitt and colleagues found that procedural justice climate in teams predicted team effectiveness and that the effect was greater in teams with stronger climates. Dickson and colleagues found that strong climates were more likely to be found in organizations with clearly distinct climates (e.g., highly mechanistic or highly organic), and that strength was typically much lower in organizations in which the climate was more ambiguous. Climates tend to be stronger when units are smaller, less diverse, or more cohesive; when there is more communication and interdependence; and when leaders provide more, and more clear, information. We expect to see research in this area continue to grow, because the moderating effect of climate strength will be useful in better understanding the direct effects (or lack thereof) of climate itself. Additionally, Schneider and colleagues have pointed out that there are clear implications for leadership to be found here in terms of the importance of consistent behavior in a positive direction to create maximal benefit from organizational climate. Leadership has begun to emerge as a predictor of climate. Transformational leadership in particular has been indicated as an antecedent of safety climate, service climate, and climate for procedural justice.

When Does Climate Exist?

One debate in the study of organizational climate is whether there are times when there is *no climate* or whether there is always a climate, even if it is weak. This is much the same argument as that occurring in the literature on organizational culture; but given the more quantitative orientation of the climate literature over time (compared with the culture literature), the issue can become especially critical here.

Some researchers argue that unless there is some predetermined level of agreement or variability among group members, there is no climate because there is little or no evidence of a shared perspective among organizational members. This argument can be couched in terms from Chan's framework of composition models, mentioned earlier, because climate has most typically been conceptualized as a direct consensus model. In such a model, climate is considered to be the typical, or most common, response from the members of a group, provided that there is some level of within-group agreement to justify treating the mean as a group-level variable. In other words, if there is insufficient agreement (assessed statistically), then there is no *sharedness* in the perceptions and thus no climate. Researchers taking this approach have sometimes used a criterion of an r_{wg} of .70 or greater (or some other statistical cutoff point), although as Harrison Trice and Janice Beyer noted regarding culture strength, there is no clear answer on how to determine whether or not a climate exists. Because there is no clear point at which climate can be said to exist, other researchers have taken the perspective that climate is always present but may in many cases be weak.

This question is of practical importance when determining how to classify the units within a data set. For example, suppose that a researcher is investigating safety climate and has data from 100 organizations, including 10 organizations with r_{wg} results on the climate measure of less than .70. From one perspective, the 10 organizations showing little agreement on the safety climate measure would be dropped from the sample as having no climate, and of the remaining 90 organizations, the ones with r_{wg} results close to .70, would be considered to have a weak climate. From the alternative perspective, all 100 organizations would remain in the sample, and those with the lowest levels of agreement would be considered to have the weakest climates. At present, consensus on this issue has yet to clearly emerge. However, the approach of limiting the sample to only those organizations with a predetermined level of within-unit agreement is the more conservative approach, because that limitation serves to restrict the range on the strength variable.

Conclusion

Organizations tend to have as many specific climates as strategic directions, which makes organizational climate a relevant concept for organizations to consider. As Schneider noted in 1990, once a strategic direction or focus is identified for an organization, the organizational climate regarding that strategic focus can be assessed via employees. Employees' assessment of the organization's relevant policies, practices, and procedures that support the strategic focus in the organization may serve as a measure of alignment. The strategic focus of the organization needs to be clearly and consistently represented in the organization's policies, practices, and procedures. Should an assessment of the organizational climate reveal that a strategic direction of interest is not perceived in organizational practices, then policies, practices, and procedures in the organization may need to be redesigned to better align with the strategy of interest.

Marcus W. Dickson,
Michelle W. Mullins, and
Jacqueline K. Deuling

See also Organizational Culture

Further Readings

Ashkanasy, N. M., Wilderom, C.P.M., & Peterson, M. F. (Eds.). (2000). *Handbook of organizational culture and climate.* Thousand Oaks, CA: Sage.

Carr, J. Z., Schmidt, A. M., Ford, J. K., & DeShon, R. P. (2003). Climate perceptions matter: A meta-analytic path analysis relating molar climate, cognitive and affective states, and individual level work outcomes. *Journal of Applied Psychology, 88,* 605–619.

Chan, D. (1998). Functional relations among constructs in the same content domain at different levels of analysis: A typology of composition models. *Journal of Applied Psychology, 83,* 234–246.

Dickson, M. W., Resick, C. J., & Hanges, P. J. (2006). When organizational climate is unambiguous, it is also strong. *Journal of Applied Psychology, 91,* 351–364.

Dickson, M. W., Smith, D. B., Grojean, M., & Ehrhart, M. (2001). An organizational climate regarding ethics: The outcome of leader values and the practices that reflect them. *Leadership Quarterly, 12,* 197–217.

Kuenzi, M., & Schminke, M. (2009). Assembling fragments into a lens: A review, critique, and proposed research agenda for the organizational work climate literature. *Journal of Management, 35*(3), 634–717. doi:10.1177/0149206308330559

Schneider, B. (Ed.). (1990). *Organizational climate and culture.* San Francisco, CA: Jossey-Bass.

Schneider, B., & Barbera, K. M. (Eds.). (2014). *The Oxford handbook of organizational climate and culture.* New York: Oxford University Press. doi:0.1093/oxfordhb/9780199860715.001.0001

Schulte, M., Ostroff, C., Shmulyian, S., & Kinicki, A. (2009). Organizational climate configurations: relationships to collective attitudes, customer satisfaction, and financial performance. *Journal of Applied Psychology, 94*(3), 618–634. doi:10.1037/a0014365

Victor, B., & Cullen, J. (1987). A theory and measure of ethical climate in organizations. In W. C. Frederick (Ed.), *Research in corporate social performance and policy: Empirical studies of business ethics and values* (pp. 51–71). Greenwich, CT: JAI.

Whitman, D. S., Caleo, S., Carpenter, N. C., Horner, M. T., & Bernerth, J. B. (2012). Fairness at the collective level: A meta-analytic examination of the consequences and boundary conditions of organizational justice climate. *Journal of Applied Psychology, 97*(4), 776–791. doi:10.1037/a0028021

Zohar, D. (2003). Safety climate: Conceptual and measurement issues. In J. Campbell Quick & L. E. Tetrick (Eds.), *Handbook of occupational health psychology.* Washington, DC: American Psychological Association.

Zohar, D. (2010). Thirty years of safety climate research: Reflections and future directions. *Accident Analysis and Prevention, 42*(5), 1517–1522. doi:10.1016/j.aap.2009.12.019

ORGANIZATIONAL COMMITMENT

Industrial and organizational (I-O) psychologists are interested in understanding employees' psychological reactions to their workplaces. Not surprisingly, much of this interest focuses on employees' commitment to the organizations for which they work. Among the several work attitude variables studied by I-O psychologists, only job satisfaction has received more attention than organizational commitment (OC).

Conceptualizing Organizational Commitment

Early definitions of OC varied considerably. Nonetheless, most scholars view OC as a psychological state characterizing an employee's relationship with an organization. This relationship influences the employee's intention to maintain a particular course of action, in this case, staying with the organization.

Beyond this, however, early OC researchers had varied views about the nature of OC and how it should be measured. For some early researchers, OC was an emotional attachment to an organization; for others, it was identification with an organization and what it represented. Some researchers described OC in terms of a reluctance to endure sacrifices, or incur costs, that voluntarily leaving an organization would entail. Still others described commitment in terms of a moral obligation to remain with an organization.

From these early one-dimensional views has emerged fairly wide, though not universal, acceptance of OC as a multidimensional construct. Thus most current models propose that OC has at least two psychological bases, or components, each of which should be measured separately. Of these models, the three-component model (TCM) proposed in the 1990s has received the most theoretical and empirical attention, and it is from this perspective that the development and consequences of OC are described here.

The TCM proposes that OC has three distinct components (also referred to as "mindsets"), each of which develops via somewhat different processes and on the basis of different experiences that the employee has at work. *Affective commitment* refers to an employee's emotional attachment to an organization, characterized by enjoyment of the organization and a desire to stay. Employees with strong affective commitment remain with an organization because they want to do so. *Continuance commitment* refers to the extent to which an employee perceives that leaving an organization would be costly. Employees with strong continuance commitment remain because they feel that they have to do so. *Normative commitment* refers to an employee's feelings of obligation to an organization and the belief that staying with it is the right thing to do. Employees with strong normative commitment remain because they feel that they ought to do so.

According to the TCM, an employee's commitment is characterized not in terms of just one of the three components but as a profile made up of all three. Furthermore, the model proposes that the three components have interactive effects on employee behavior.

Measuring Organizational Commitment

Researchers and practitioners usually assess OC using multiple-item questionnaires administered directly to employees. Typically, employees respond anonymously, thus increasing the candidness of responses. As with any such measures, it is critical that items reflect the construct they are intended to assess. Especially in early research, this was accomplished with varying degrees of success. Of particular note, however, is the 15-item Organizational Commitment Questionnaire (OCQ). Developed in the 1970s to assess identification with, involvement in, and emotional attachment to organizations, the OCQ is a psychometrically sound measure of desire-based (affective) commitment. It has been used in hundreds of studies, contributing greatly to our understanding of the affective component of OC.

To evaluate the multidimensional model of OC outlined earlier, TCM researchers developed parallel measures of the three proposed OC components. Since then, the Affective Commitment Scale, Continuance Commitment Scale, and Normative Commitment Scale have received considerable psychometric scrutiny and have been used extensively in research conducted in dozens of organizational and cultural contexts and with members of various occupations. Overall, the evidence shows that the measures are reliable, assess three distinct constructs, and correlate with other variables in general accordance with TCM propositions. Perhaps not surprisingly, researchers have extended the TCM model beyond the organization to other focal aspects of working life, including the occupation or profession, work groups, and teams.

Development of Organizational Commitment

Although OC might be expected to develop on the basis of both person and work experience factors, the latter play the more important role.

Some person variables (e.g., age, locus of control) are modestly related to OC, but it is what people experience at work that seems to have the most influence on OC development. With respect to affective commitment, quantitative review (or meta-analysis) suggests several work experiences that seem particularly important. Affective commitment is stronger among employees who feel that they have been supported by their organizations and who have experienced procedural, distributive, and interactional justice in the workplace. Affective commitment is also stronger among employees who experience minimal role ambiguity and role conflict at work and have leaders who adopt transformational leadership styles.

The TCM proposes that normative commitment develops on the basis of cultural and organizational experiences that highlight expectations of mutual obligation between employees and organizations and make the reciprocity norm salient to employees. These ideas have received relatively little empirical assessment. Meta-analytic results show that some of the same variables (e.g., organizational support, role ambiguity, justice) that seem to influence affective commitment are related to normative commitment, but relations are much weaker. There is also some evidence that the impact of work experiences on normative commitment depends on employees' cultural values, such as individualism versus collectivism.

Consistent with the TCM model, continuance commitment is more strongly related than are the other two components to two sets of variables: perceived alternatives and perceived investments. Specifically, continuance commitment is stronger among employees who believe that they would have few, rather than several, viable sources of employment if they left their organizations. Presumably, the costs of leaving their current organizations would be quite high for such employees. Continuance commitment is also stronger among employees who believe that they made significant investments developing their skills and acquiring education that would not transfer readily to other organizations. In comparison with employees who have easily transferable skills, such employees would incur greater costs if they left their organizations.

Finally, cultural differences in the way organizations interact with their employees may also influence the nature of an employee's commitment to his or her organization. Interestingly, results of a recent large-scale (meta-analytic) study involving data from more than 50 countries suggested that cultural practices and values may be most influential in shaping normative commitment, and to a lesser degree, affective commitment. In contrast, cultural variation seems unrelated to levels of continuance commitment.

Consequences of Organizational Commitment

As previously mentioned, it is most consistent with theory to examine the consequences of OC in terms of the commitment profile (or interactions between components). Some researchers have taken this approach, but most studies have involved the examination of potential OC consequences on a component-by-component, rather than profile, basis. Outcomes that have been emphasized include employee retention, work performance, and employee well-being.

The links between OC components and employee retention are fairly straightforward. Affective, normative, and continuance commitment are all negatively related to employee intention to leave the organization voluntarily. Both affective commitment and normative commitment, but not continuance commitment, have been shown to predict actual turnover.

Just as important as retention, however, is how employees behave at work. Here the distinction between the three components of commitment becomes especially critical. Beyond their demonstrated link with turnover intention, affective, continuance, and normative commitment are considered, and have been shown, to have somewhat different implications for behavior.

Affective commitment is linked to several key performance indicators. Employees with stronger affective commitment are less likely to be absent from work, and this effect is stronger for absence that is under the employees' control than for involuntary absence, such as that caused by illness and emergencies. Affective commitment also predicts the job performance. Across a wide variety of jobs, both self-report ratings and supervisory ratings of required (or nondiscretionary) work performance are higher among those with stronger affective commitment. Such employees are also more likely to engage in discretionary organizational citizenship behavior (e.g., exerting extraordinary effort, helping coworkers, championing the organization) than those with weak affective commitment and, in so doing, help create a more productive and positive workplace.

Normative commitment is unrelated to employee absence. Its relations with other performance indicators, however, are positive, but effects are more modest than for affective commitment. Interestingly, meta-analytic evidence shows that relations between normative commitment and both job performance and organizational citizenship behavior are stronger in studies conducted outside North America, suggesting that cultural factors might play an important role in the behavioral expression of this component of commitment. Finally, although this has not yet been tested, it has been argued that normative commitment might influence the tone with which employees carry out their work, particularly if they also have weak to moderate levels of affective commitment. The idea here is that strong feelings of obligation to stay, in the absence of strong desire to stay, might create feelings of resentment, prompting such employees to carry out their duties in a competent, but more grudging, manner.

Continuance commitment is unrelated to employee absence. In contrast to affective and normative commitment, however, it is also unrelated to organizational citizenship behavior; those with strong continuance commitment are neither more nor less likely to go the extra mile. Of particular note, however, is the strong negative relation, found in meta-analytic research, between continuance commitment and required aspects of job performance. The fact that employees with strong (vs. weak) continuance commitment perform more poorly has critical implications for those organizations that develop retention strategies around what employees will lose if they resign. Such organizations might well increase retention but do so at the cost of employee performance. This will be especially so if employees are given little reason to develop affective commitment to their organizations and, as a consequence, feel trapped within them. For this reason it is especially important to consider the employee's affective-continuance-normative commitment profile.

Finally, researchers are beginning to examine whether OC has implications for employee well-being. Presumably, most people prefer workplaces about which they feel positively. It has been argued, however, that strong affective OC might reduce well-being by causing employees to focus too much attention on their work. Thus far there is little evidence of this latter view. Instead, meta-analytic research suggests that strong affective commitment is related to reduced stress and exhaustion and greater quality of life. In contrast, however, continuance commitment is related to poorer quality of life and greater stress levels.

Further Research Directions

Despite extensive OC research, there remain many challenging issues for commitment researchers to pursue. One issue involves how best to examine various employee commitment profiles (e.g., high affective–low continuance–low normative) and to link these profiles to their hypothesized consequences (i.e., employee behaviors, personal outcomes). Methodological advances that take a person-centered approach to the examination of profiles appear to have much to offer in this regard. A related challenge involves the idea that employees feel multidimensional commitment not only to their organizations but, as mentioned earlier, to numerous work-related domains or foci. These include foci within an organization (e.g., department, supervisor, team) and beyond it (e.g., occupation, union). Although complex, a comprehensive understanding of commitment in the workplace will come only through considering, in concert, the multiple components of commitment that employees feel toward these various interconnected aspects of their workplace.

Other challenges are presented by the changing workplace. For example, researchers are just beginning to examine the effects that alternate work arrangements, such as part-time employment, temporary and contract-based work, and outsourcing, have on the development and consequences of OC. Within many workplaces, greater emphasis is being placed on the interplay (or balance) between work and nonwork or family; it will be important to examine how policies and practices associated with this issue will influence the development of OC. Finally, likely driven by the increasing cultural diversity in the workforce, the challenges of globalization, and the growing international researcher base, it not surprising that increased attention is being focused on the role that cultural factors may play in shaping the structure, development, and consequences of OC.

Natalie J. Allen

See also Job Satisfaction; Organizational Justice; Withdrawal Behaviors, Turnover

Further Readings

Allen, N. J., & Meyer, J. P. (1990). The measurement and antecedents of affective, continuance, and normative commitment to the organization. *Journal of Occupational Psychology, 63,* 1–18.

Klein, H. J., Becker, T. E., & Meyer, J. P. (2009). *Commitment in organizations: Accumulated wisdom and new directions.* Routledge: New York.

Meyer, J. P., & Allen, N. J. (1997). *Commitment in the workplace: Theory, research, and application.* Thousand Oaks, CA: Sage.

Meyer, J. P., Stanley, D. J., Herscovitch, L., & Topolnytsky, L. (2002). Affective, continuance, and normative commitment to the organization: A meta-analysis of antecedents, correlates, and consequences. *Journal of Vocational Behavior, 61,* 20–52.

Meyer, J. P., Stanley, D. J., Jackson, T. A., McInnis, K. J., Maltin, E. R., & Sheppard, L. (2012). Affective, normative, and continuance commitment levels across cultures: A meta-analysis. *Journal of Vocational Behavior, 80,* 225–245.

Meyer, J. P., Stanley, L. J., & Vandenberg, R.J. (2013). A person-centered approach to the study of commitment. *Human Resource Management Review, 23,* 190–202.

ORGANIZATIONAL COMMUNICATION, DISCIPLINE OF

Organizational communication is a subfield of the larger discipline of communication studies. Organizational communication is the consideration, analysis, and criticism of the role of communication in organizational contexts. It is a major component of effective management in a workplace environment and provides crucial insight into the activities, processes, relationships, and structures of both individuals and the collective group operating in an organization. Organizational communication, as a discipline, examines all types of institutions in which "work" gets done, including nonprofits, nongovernmental organizations, corporations, bluecollar industries, and so on.

Charles Redding is often credited as being the "father of organizational communication," having led the charge in developing it into a distinct discipline at universities in the early 1950s. In this postwar era, managers, academics, and military officials were in a unique situation: They were, for the first time, communicating with one another about the future of workplaces. At that time, the field of interest was becoming known as "business/speech communication" and "industrial communication." Departments at schools such as Northwestern University, The Ohio State University, the University of Southern California, and Purdue University were developing their departments in industrial communication. Redding believed that the academic development of the field was a result of things such as a NASA-sponsored conference on organizational communication and the development of the Organizational Communication Division of the International Communication Association. Through Charles's perspective, communication is the focus of the message exchange process that defines characteristics of organizational communication as a practice and discipline.

Early and Modern Assumptions

As organizational communication emerged as a distinct field of study, there were several early assumptions about the discipline. These have since evolved into the more modern understanding of what this discipline is all about. But initially, there was the notion that humans act rationally. In fact, a metaphor was developed to illustrate this notion. This metaphor, referred to as the container metaphor, assumes that organizations exist independently of communication and serve as containers that influence communication behavior. For example, organizational structures, such as hierarchies, are assumed to exist independently and to influence the content and directional flow of communication. In this way, communication is primarily a mechanical process, in which a message is constructed and encoded by a sender, transmitted through some channel, and then received and decoded by a receiver. Distortion, represented as any differences or misinterpretation between the original and the received messages, can and ought to be identified and reduced or eliminated. No consideration was given to the environment or to the nonverbal elements of communication.

These early assumptions were later challenged, and a different approach to the study of organizational communication was considered. First, Herbert Simon challenged the early assumption that humans act rationally with his concept of *bounded rationality*. Simon believed that most people are really only partly rational. The rest of the time, humans are irrational with regard to their actions. Thus, the concept of bounded rationality revises the earlier rationality assumption to account for the fact that perfectly rational decisions are often not feasible because of the finite computational resources available for making them.

In the early 1990s, Peter Senge developed new theories of organizational communication. First, *systems theory* is the process of understanding how systems influence one another within a larger system. In nature, systems thinking examples include ecosystems in which various elements such as air, water, movement, plants, and animals work together to survive or perish. In organizations, systems consist of people, structures, and processes that work together to make an organization "healthy" or "unhealthy." Central to how a system sustains itself and remains healthy is communication. The role of communication in a systems thinking approach reveals that in an effective system, people communicate not just top down, with information being disseminated by those in power, but rather in a multidirectional fashion. Thus, systems thinking suggests that the richest understanding of organizational systems can be obtained by closely observing communication in specific organizational contexts. Additionally, one can learn how to remedy an unhealthy system by observing how organizations grapple with specific issues. Senge's second theory, that of a *learning organization*, applies when people continually expand their capacity to create the results they really desire, when new and expansive patterns of thinking are nurtured, when collective goals are set in motion, and when people are continually learning to see the whole together. Senge has said that although all people have the capacity to learn, the structures in which they must function are often not conducive to reflection and engagement. Furthermore, people may lack the tools and guiding ideas to make sense of the situations they face. Organizations that are continually expanding their capacity to create their futures require a fundamental shift of mind among their members. For organizational members to learn, they need to achieve personal mastery, construct mental models, build a shared vision, and engage in team learning.

Networks are another modern assumption in organizational communication and relate specifically to the direction and flow of communication. Communication patterns, or networks, influence groups in several important ways. Communication networks may affect a group's completion of an assigned task, the position of the de facto leader in the group, or the group members' satisfaction from occupying certain positions in the network. Although these findings are based on laboratory experiments, they have important implications for the dynamics of communication in organizations. There are several patterns of communication that can be observed in daily interactions, including the chain, wheel, star, circle, and all-channel networks.

Last, one of the more pervasive modern assumptions in organizational communication is culture. Many researchers have begun espousing a cultural assumption in the discipline, for four reasons. First, cultures offer an interpretation of an institution's history that members can use to decipher how they will be expected to behave in the future. Second, cultures can generate commitment to corporate values or management philosophy so that employees feel they are working for something they believe in. Third, cultures serve as organizational control mechanisms, informally approving or prohibiting some patterns of behavior or communicative actions. Last, some cultures are associated with greater organizational productivity and profitability. Thus, organizational culture is not just another piece of the puzzle; it is the puzzle. From a modern communication standpoint, culture is not something an organization has but something an organization is.

Approaches

Organizational communication also has a variety of approaches with regard to structure, including both formal and informal structures. In a formal organizational structure, there are two types of communication: upward and top-down communication. In an upward organization, the transmission of messages moves from lower to higher levels of the organization (such as communication initiated by subordinates with their superiors). These types of messages include performance; job-related problems; fellow employees and their problems; and subordinates' perceptions of organizational policies, tasks, and procedures. In a top-down approach to communication, upper management communicates down to the lower levels. This is used to implement policies, guidelines, and so on. In this type of organizational communication, distortion of the actual information occurs but could be remedied by effective feedback systems. Types of messages include job instructions, job rationales, procedures, feedback, and indoctrination.

Informal organizational communication structures generally get associated with interpersonal, horizontal communication whereby the flow of messages moves across functional areas at a given level of an organization. This used to be seen as a potential hindrance to effective organizational performance, but that is no longer the case. Informal communication has become vitally important to ensuring the effective conduct of work in modern organizations. The types of messages associated with informal communication are problem solving, information sharing across different work groups, and task coordination between departments and project teams. This is also where the term *grapevine* emerged, because of the social and personal interests of employees rather than formal requirements of the organization. Informal communication is inherent and a necessary aspect of organizational life.

The last approach is neither formal nor informal. The "communication as constitutive of organizations" approach takes a more nuanced view of communication. This approach identifies four constitutive flows of communication, which become interrelated to constitute organizing: organizational self-structuring, membership negotiation, activity coordination, and institutional positioning.

Research Methodologies

Historically, organizational communication was driven by quantitative research methodologies relying on statistical analyses, including surveys, text indexing, network mapping, and behavior modeling. However, in the early 1980s, the interpretive revolution took hold, with communication scholars Linda Putnam and Michael Pacanowsky arguing for opening up the methodological space by emphasizing the use of qualitative approaches including narrative analysis, participant observation, interviewing, rhetoric, and textual approaches. In the 1980s and 1990s, critical organizational scholarship began to gain prominence, with a focus on gender, race, class, and power in workplaces. Research included an examination of sexual harassment policies (or lack thereof), hierarchies, and top-down communication, as well as the marginalized "other" in the workplace (i.e., women and minorities). In its current state, the study of organizational communication is open, methodologically, with research stemming from postpositive, interpretive, critical, postmodern, and discursive paradigms. Organizational communication scholarship appears in a number of communication journals (and some outside the discipline) including, but not limited to, *Management Communication Quarterly*, the *Journal of Applied Communication Research*, *Communication Monographs*, the *International Journal of Business Communication*, the *Academy of Management Journal*, and *Communication Studies*.

Current Areas of Study and Research

In some circles, the field of organizational communication has moved from acceptance of mechanistic models (e.g., information moving from a sender to a receiver) to a study of the persistent, hegemonic, and taken-for-granted ways in which communication is used to accomplish certain tasks within organizational settings (e.g., public speaking) and also how the organizations affect their participants. The areas of study within organizational communication are still largely divided between classic areas of study and more contemporary areas of study.

Classic Areas of Study

First, leadership is an area of communication inquiry that has garnered much attention over the past several decades. From a communication perspective, leadership has been investigated primarily as the art of inducing compliance via symbols and persuasion as well as a process and an emerging effect of interaction. With regard to inducing compliance and creating influence, research has focused on communication-based strategies such as rational arguments, seeking consultation and collaboration from team members, and the effect of inspirational appeals on different audiences. Additionally, the leader–member exchange (LMX) theory has received much attention as a process of emerging effect of interactions. LMX theory posits a link between leader and member relationship quality (particularly the quality and amount of exchanges) and positive organizational and personal outcomes. In essence, this theory suggests that leaders who develop "in-group" relationships through communication with all members of the group reap a host of positive outcomes, including more productive and committed group members.

Like leadership, conflict management is also a classic area of organizational communication research, having now been examined over several decades. For many years, communication scholars, like scholars from other disciplines, examined styles of conflict management, including competition, compromise, avoidance, accommodation, and collaboration. These researchers often relied on Blake and Mouton's managerial grid as a way of exploring the styles and strategies people use when engaged in conflict. The difference between one's level of concern for oneself and concern for others would indicate what style one would apply in a given conflict situation (i.e., high concern for self and low concern for other would indicate a competitive style). More recently, however, communication scholars have looked beyond this general style approach to conflict and have begun to pay more specific attention to details concerning the style of the message and also the perceptions of the individuals in each conflict episode. For example, Jeffrey Kassing investigated how employees choose to voice dissent in the workplace and, more specifically, to whom they voice that dissent, as well as the factors that influence how likely they are to speak up about a conflict. Dissent has become a specific type of organizational conflict from a communication perspective.

One last classic approach to organizational communication is decision making. Although decision making has been examined across a variety of disciplines, the role of communication in decision making is unique to this field. Typically, decision making from an organizational communication perspective is examined at the group level. The vast majority of decisions in any organizational setting are made by standing committees, self-managed work teams, or groups of colleagues standing around the water cooler. Several communicative patterns have been observed in these small group settings when making decisions, including groupthink, functional theory, and group decision support systems (GDSSs). More recently, the *bona fide groups perspective*, advanced by communication scholars Linda Putnam and Cynthia Stohl, proposes that factors such as shifting membership, permeable group boundaries, and interdependence within the organizational context influence decision making in workplaces. Additionally, this theory emphasizes the importance of "backstage" communication and how these informal conversations between coworkers in hallways are just as important as formal group meetings when it comes to decision making.

Contemporary Areas of Study

With regard to more contemporary areas of study, many organizational communication scholars have shifted their focus to relationships at work. Although this has been examined for several decades, these discussions tended to center on superior–subordinate relationships, group–team relationships, and customer–client relationships. In recent years, peer friendships and romantic relationships have become salient. With regard to friendships, research has pointed to their having several positive outcomes and being integral to organizational functioning. These relationships can also result in negative outcomes, including conflict. Workplace romantic relationships have enjoyed recent study, particularly concerning how

coworkers perceive these relationships and the effects of these perceptions. Communication scholar Sean Horan found that there are fewer negative perceptions of peers engaging in these relationships than of those dating superiors. Communication research has also focused on how these relationships are disclosed to coworkers. When these relationships are revealed through personal disclosures, more positive reactions from coworkers can result.

Another contemporary area of research in organizational communication is technology. The range of technologies now used in the modern workplace is considerable. From e-mail to videoconferencing to GDSSs, the uses of technology in the workplace are endless. As a result, several communication theories have been advanced to improve understanding of the choices organizational members make about communication technology. The *media richness model* is a framework that illustrates how managers choose one communication medium over others depending on the level of ambiguity involved in the task. For example, letting staff members know about an upcoming meeting might be best served by a lean form of media, such as an e-mail or an automated calendar update, given that it is a relatively unambiguous message. But if a manager were faced with resolving an interpersonal conflict between two subordinates, a richer form of media, such as face-to-face communication, might be required given the highly ambiguous nature of the task. This theory, and many like it, has been the focus of recent attention by communication scholars, especially as it relates to the patterns of communication within organizations. Findings have revealed that new technologies in the workplace augment existing technologies rather than just replace them. Because of this, organizations that adopt new technologies face an overall increase in the amount of communication in the workplace. One serious consequence of this is "data smog," whereby employees can feel as though they are drowning in messages and data. However, the pervasiveness of social networks such as LinkedIn, Facebook, and Twitter has allowed employees to better connect with one another about a wide range of work-related issues.

A last contemporary area of research is work–life balance. The relationship between work and life continues to be an important area of inquiry spanning decades of research in organizational communication. What had begun as a narrow research area focused on dual-career families and working mothers has now evolved into a sprawling domain of study including an examination of rules and resources used by employees to achieve work–life accommodations, maternity leave, "family-friendly" work policies, and flexibility in terms of telecommuting. Most notably, however, is the role boundaries play with regard to work and personal lives. Several organizational communication scholars have proposed that boundaries should be regarded as a continuous process of management, rather than static entities. From this perspective, communication researchers concern themselves less with the situations and content in each sphere and more with the way people move and transition between and among the spheres and how meaning gets enacted and communicated as people move through the domains. Communication scholar Erica Kirby researches linguistic choices and discursive crossovers (i.e., using dominant language from one sphere in another sphere) among work and life domains. Language that has typically been reserved for describing work environments is also helping individuals manage their home lives. For instance, the term *micromanagement*, typically used in or associated with the workplace, is often used to describe how individuals run their household activities. Similarly, the language of spirituality and intimacy, two concepts typically reserved for the private or home sphere, is being used as a way to promote productivity and commitment at work, including beginning meetings with prayers and company-wide spiritual retreats.

Jaime E. Bochantin
and Renee L. Cowan

See also Content Analysis; Organizational Communication, Formal; Organizational communication, Informal; Online Qualitative Methods; Qualitative Research Approach

Further Readings

Cowan, R. L., & Horan, S. M. (2014). Love at the office? Understanding workplace romance disclosures and reactions from the coworker perspective. *Western Journal of Communication*, 78, 238–253. doi:10.1080/10570314.2013.866688

Hackman, M. Z., & Johnson, C. E. (2009). *Leadership: A communication perspective* (5th ed.). Chicago: Waveland.

May, S., & Mumby, D. (2005). *Engaging organizational communication theory and research*. Thousand Oaks, CA: Sage.

Miller, K. (2014). *Organizational communication: Approaches and processes* (6th ed.). Boston, MA: Cengage Learning.

Redding, C. (1985). Stumbling toward identity: The emergence of organizational communication as a field of study. In R. D. McPhee & P. K. Tompkins (Eds.), *Organizational communication: Traditional themes and new directions*. Thousand Oaks, CA: Sage.

Senge, P. (1994) *The fifth discipline fieldbook: Strategies and tools for building a learning organization*. New York: Doubleday.

ORGANIZATIONAL COMMUNICATION, FORMAL

Formal organizational communication is not an easily defined term. Because of the nature of communication, organizational communication is a complicated phenomenon that has no clear boundaries. Several definitions attempt to conceptualize the abstract nature of organizational communication. The study of organizational communication involves the intersection of two complex and dynamic concepts: organizations and communication. An organization has three primary characteristics:

1. Social collectivity (a group of people)

2. Coordinated activities (structure)

3. Goal-oriented activities (both individual and collective)

In defining communication, most scholars agree that communication is a process that is transactional (involving two or more people interacting in context) and symbolic (placing meaning and abstractions on things). To formalize organizational communication means to understand how the context of the organization influences communication processes and how the symbolic nature of communication differentiates it from other forms of organizational behavior.

Studying Formal Organizational Communication

Eric Eisenberg and Harold Goodall (2004) offered a broad but usable definition of organizational communication. They suggested that there are four ways to conceptualize and study formal organizational communication:

1. Communication as information transfer

2. Communication as transactional process

3. Communication as strategic control

4. Communication as balancing creativity and constraint

Communication as Information Transfer

The traditional approach to study communication has followed the linear model of communication, also known as the *transmission model*, the *information engineering approach*, or the *model of information transfer*. The information transfer approach views communication as a tool people use to accomplish goals and objectives. Clear, one-way communication is emphasized as a means of impressing and influencing others. The information transfer or linear model suggests that communication flows one way or linearly from the sender of the message to the receiver of the message. This model suggests that communication is a process whereby messages are transmitted and distributed in space for the control of distance and people.

Some scholars have suggested that communication operates in a predictable fashion; hence the information engineering approach. The information engineering approach advanced the SMCR model. This model posits that communication occurs when a sender (S) transmits a message (M) through a channel (C) to a receiver (R). The sender *encodes* an intended meaning into words, and the receiver *decodes* the message when it is received. The communication as information transfer model is similar to both the linear model of communication and the information engineering approach in that communication is framed metaphorically as a pipeline through which information is transferred from one person to another. Within the organizational context, managers transfer information or directives to subordinates

and subordinates do the same in their peer and superordinate interactions.

Communication theories in the information transfer approach are based on the following assumptions of transmission:

- Language transfers thoughts and feelings from one person to another person.
- Speakers and writers put thoughts and feelings into words.
- Words contain those thoughts and feelings.
- Listeners or readers extract those thoughts and feelings from the words.

There are several problems associated with the information transfer method as an approach to the study of formal organizational communication. *Information overload* occurs when the receiver of a message becomes inundated with information that needs to be processed. Information overload is made up of the amount of information, the rate at which the information is received, and the complexity of the information.

Another problem with the information transfer model is with communication distortion. Distortion is the processing noise that distracts the receiver from fully processing information. Communication distortion can be semantic (different meanings for sender and receiver), physical (sound distractions), or contextual (sender and receiver have different positions or perspectives that lead to miscommunication).

Ambiguity offers the third problem with the information transfer model. Ambiguity occurs when multiple interpretations of a message distort or misdirect the sender's intended meaning. Differing meanings and interpretations, based on one's worldviews, backgrounds, context of communication, and experiences, along with abstract language, may lead to ambiguity.

Communication as a Transactional Process

A second approach in the study of formal organizational communication is communication as a transactional process. Communication as transactional process asserts that in actual communication situations, clear distinctions are not made between senders and receivers of messages. This assumption contrasts with the information transfer model.

Instead, in the transactional process, both communicators play both roles of encoding and decoding messages simultaneously. This model emphasizes the importance of *feedback* in communication. This model also highlights the importance of nonverbal communication, which is missing in the information transfer approach. Organizational communication as a transactional process suggests that nonverbal feedback may accompany or substitute for verbal messages. Finally, the transactional process model suggests that meanings are in people, not words, as the information transfer model assumes. How an individual receives a message and how the receiver constructs the meaning of that message is the focus of the transactional process model.

The transactional process influences contemporary leadership studies. Effective and successful leaders using this approach are better able to mobilize the meanings that followers have for what leaders say or do. This creates a transactional and fluid process between leaders and followers in organizations.

The approach of studying formal organizational communication through the transactional process approach may be problematic in its emphasis on creating shared meaning through communication. By focusing on shared meaning by means of clarity, openness, and understanding, communication as a transactional process minimizes the complexities of the human condition whereas ambiguity, vagueness, and instrumental objectives are central in some forms of formal communication in organizations.

Communication as Strategic Control

Communication as strategic control views communication as a tool for controlling the organizational environment. This approach acknowledges that clarity, openness, and understanding are not always the primary goals in interpersonal and organizational interactions caused by personal, relational, social, and political factors. Communication as strategic control assumes communicators have multiple goals or agendas in organizational situations. These agendas play out in performance evaluations, delivering or accepting bad news, asking for a promotion or raise, or in various other situations in which the individual or organizational interests are at stake.

The strategic control approach to formal organizational communication suggests that individuals should not be expected to communicate in a rational or objective manner. Communication rules, clarity, and honesty may be broken or compromised when it is in the communicators' best interests to do so. Generally, strategic communicators are competent communicators. Communication competence refers to the appropriateness and effectiveness of a message. The communicating party must be *rhetorically sensitive* in that he or she must be able to recognize the constraints of the situation and adapt to the multiple goals of all parties simultaneously.

Strategic ambiguity is a common form of strategic control. Strategic ambiguity describes the ways people deliberately communicate ambiguously to accomplish their goals.

Strategic ambiguity seeks to accomplish specific goals. First, strategic ambiguity promotes unified diversity by taking advantage of the multiple meanings different people may give the same message. For example, if a supervisor directs employees to *work more as a family*, there are multiple interpretations on how this should occur.

Second, strategic ambiguity is deniable because the words may seem to mean one thing, yet under pressure, these same words can seem to mean something else. For example, if an organization has announced a merger, organizational leaders are careful when discussing job loss because of duplication of processes, so that when job loss occurs later, their words at that time appear more abstract and less definitive.

Finally, strategic ambiguity facilitates organizational change by allowing people the interpretive room to change their activities while appearing to keep those activities consistent.

The strategic control model of formal organizational communication opposes the idea of shared meaning. The primary goal of communication in this approach is organized action. Organized action minimizes the importance of understanding and clarity and highlights working and acting in mutually satisfying ways to fulfill each party's self-interest.

Many scholars have criticized the strategic control approach for several reasons. First, this approach minimizes the importance of ethics. Although strategic ambiguity is widespread in organizations, it may be used to elude the truth and escape blame.

It is also problematic because it places all responsibility on individuals without much thought about the community implications. This model implicitly suggests that individuals are concerned only with accomplishing their individual goals, often at the expense of the organizational community or the community at large.

Additional Approaches to Formal Organizational Communication

There are other approaches to studying formal organizational communication. These approaches include the functional approach and the meaning-centered approach.

Functional Approach

The functional approach is a way of understanding organizational communication by describing what messages do and *how these messages move* through organizations. The functional approach conceptualizes communication as a complex organizational process that serves *messaging*, *organizing*, *relationship*, and *change* functions. This approach suggests that that communication transmits rules, regulations, and information throughout the organization.

Message Function

In formalizing organizational communication, it is important to recognize how communication contributes to the overall function of the organization. Messages act as a communication function for production, maintenance, adaptation, management communication, regulative, integrative, innovative, informative, task, persuasion, command, and instruction.

Organizing Function

The organizing function of formal organizational communication guides, directs, and controls organizational activity. Communication functions to organize rules and regulate the environment. These regulative and organizing functions are found in employee handbooks, policy manuals, training, newsletters, memos, and so on.

The organizing function establishes what is expected at work and how individuals are required to accomplish these expectations.

Relationship Function

The relationship function of organizational communication focuses on how human interaction makes organizational functioning possible. The relationship function helps individuals define their roles and measure the compatibility of individual, group, and organizational goals. This function is particularly important because it contributes to employee morale, role in the organization, and organizational self-esteem. The relationship function establishes relationships with peers, superiors, subordinates, and customers, and it further clarifies these roles.

The relationship function is accomplished by verbal and nonverbal communication. Scholars have suggested that the informal organization, often characterized by the relational function, is more powerful than the formal organization. Relational communication ranges from the informal conversations in a break room to one's job title, office space, or cubicle to how an individual is greeted on meeting.

Change Function

The final function of formal organizational communication is its change function. The change function helps an organization adapt what it does and how it does it. This adaptation occurs in decision making, internal and external changes in the environment, organizational repositioning, and other change functions. The effectiveness of the change function of organizational communication is associated with the survival of the organization and its ability to adapt to the changing environment. Change communication is necessary for innovation and adaptation and is the process through which organizations obtain existing and new information and how they process this information in light of the current situation and emerging trends.

Meaning-Centered Approach

The meaning-centered approach is a way of understanding organizational communication by understanding how organizational reality is constructed through human interaction. This approach describes organizational communication as a process of organizing, decision making, sense making, influence, and culture. Pamela Shockley-Zalabak (2002) offered key assumptions of the meaning-centered approach:

- *All ongoing human interaction is communication in one form or another.* A major theme in the communication discipline is that an individual "cannot not communicate." This is due in part to verbal and nonverbal cues.
- *Organizations exist through human interaction; structures and technologies result from the information to which individuals react.* This idea suggests that organizations cannot exist separate from human activity. An organization relies solely on individuals' enactment of organizing and structuring. Karl Weick (1979) offered insight to these ideas by suggesting that organizations do not exist per se but are a culmination of the ongoing human interaction surrounding events that are continually created and shaped by these interactions. The meaning-centered approach to formal organizational communication describes communicating and organizing as a parallel process.
- *Organizing and decision making are essentially communication.* This is the process of choosing from among numerous alternatives to direct behaviors and resources toward organizational goals.
- *Identification, socialization, communication rules, and power all are communication processes that reflect how organizational influence occurs.* The meaning-centered approach proposes that influence is a necessary process for creating and changing organizational events. Influence plays a role in understanding how individuals identify with their organizations, how organizations attempt to socialize members, how communication rules direct behavior, and how individuals use communication to exert power.
- *Organizing, decision making, and influence processes describe the cultures of organizations by describing how organizations do things and how they talk about how they do things.*

Organizational culture reflects the shared realities and practices in organizations and how shared realities create and shape organizational events. The culture varies from organization to organization depending on the individuals' engagement with one another and the organization's goals. Culture describes the unique sense of the organization, its practices, and how the organization describes itself.

Shawn D. Long

See also Organizational Communication, Informal

Further Readings

Eisenberg, E. (1984). Ambiguity as strategy in organizational communication. *Communication Monographs, 51,* 227–242.

Eisenberg, E. M., & Goodall, H. L., Jr. (2004). *Organizational communication: Balancing creativity and constraint* (4th ed.). Boston: Bedford/St. Martin's.

Jablin, F. M. (2001). Organizational entry, assimilation, and disengagement/exit. In F. M. Jablin & L. L. Putnam (Eds.), *The new handbook of organizational communication: Advances in theory, research, and methods* (pp. 732–818). Thousand Oaks, CA: Sage.

Redding, W. C. (1972). *Communication within the organization.* New York: Industrial Communication Council.

Shockley-Zalabak, P. (2002). *Fundamentals of organizational communication: Knowledge, sensitivity, skills, values* (5th ed.). Boston: Allyn & Bacon.

Weick, K. (1979). *The social psychology of organizing* (2nd ed.). Reading, MA: Addison-Wesley.

ORGANIZATIONAL COMMUNICATION, INFORMAL

Some scholars argue that the informal organization is more powerful than the formal organization. Scholars also suggest that a great deal of communication in organizations is informal communication. Elton Mayo and his famous Hawthorne studies found that informal communication influenced the development and reinforcement of performance standards, member expectations, and values at the work group level. Informal organizational communication consists of episodes of interaction that do not reflect formally designated channels of communication. P. H. Tompkins wrote that informal organizational communication is not *rationally specified*. An organization may be formally structured with specific communication rules and patterns, such as chain of command; however, that does not mean that all activities and interactions strictly conform to the original formalized organization. A great deal of time and effort is devoted to creating an organization driven by control and predictability through formal means such as employee handbooks, rules, regulations, and procedures and standard means of practices. However, an elaborate setup of organizational mechanisms and contingencies cannot fully predict and control the dynamic and complex nature of human beings and their interactions with other individuals and the environment.

Scholars posit that in every formal organization emerges an informal organization, primarily through communication. Various groups develop their own values, norms, and practices in relation to their peers, subordinates, and supervisors. These practices construct context-specific ways of working beyond the scope of the formal organization. Rules are important in formal organizations, particularly in organizations highly characterized by hierarchy and bureaucracy. Max Weber suggested that the functioning of formal organizations is made possible by five primary characteristics:

1. There is the principle of fixed and official jurisdictional areas, which are generally ordered by rules, laws, or administrative regulations.

2. The principles of organizational hierarchy and of levels of graded authority mean a firmly ordered system of superordination and subordination in which there is a supervision of the lower offices by the higher ones.

3. The management of the formal organization is based on written documents, which are preserved in their original forms.

4. When the organization is fully formalized, official activity demands the full working capacity and attention of management.

5. Management follows general rules, which are more or less stable, are more or less exhaustive, and can be learned.

The last characteristic suggests that rules should be general to have enough scope to cover a multitude of situations or contingencies. However, not all contingencies can be imagined and prepared for, and informal communication provides a solution to this problem.

Formal Versus Informal Organizational Communication

The distinction between formal and informal organizational communication is unclear. Historically, scholars have made interesting theoretical and empirical distinctions between formal and informal communication. Scholars link formal communication with the organizational chart and formalized messages. Researchers also link informal organizational communication with the grapevine (addressed later) and communications not considered on the formal organizational chart. Scholars have attempted to distinguish formal and informal communication, but the lines are not clearly drawn. Conceptually, however, formal communication is viewed as *expected* communication patterns that are written, centralized, vertical, planned, imposed, and mandated. Formal communication is viewed as legitimate communication given authority by the organization. However, informal communication is viewed as *actual* communication patterns that are oral, decentralized, horizontal, unplanned and not imposed, and not mandated.

There have been several attempts to link formal organizational structure to organizational behavior. However, these attempts have produced inconclusive findings. Because of this lack of evidence, scholars have suggested that studying informal communication will contribute to our understanding of organizational behavior.

Why Study Informal Communication?

Informal communication in organizations is an important area of inquiry in organizational theory and behavior. It is particularly useful when studying the role of informal communication in decision making, productivity, and organizational change.

There are three primary reasons informal organizational communication continues to thrive. First, decision making does not operate in a vacuum, and many times decisions must be made that fall outside the purview of the formal organizational design. Reacting in the moment allows immediate and flexible solutions that may not wait on a formalized process that may take a considerable amount of time to implement.

Second, unofficial norms may develop to regulate performance and productivity. For example, systematic soldering resulted from rate busting in the early Industrial Revolution era, when a group of workers would pressure each other to keep productivity at a steady pace by not working too hard and fast or too slowly, to keep the rate of piecework pay the same. This pressure was placed on all workers by their peers through informal policing of productivity.

Finally, as the complex nature of social relations and informal status structures emerge, organizational change provides an important backdrop for promoting informal organizational communication. Informal organizational communication develops in response to opportunities and problems posed by the environment, whereas formal organizational communication is a response to the immediate environment of the groups within it.

Organizations are influenced by factors other than the traditional organizational chart. Informal factors such as background, demographic characteristics, workers' abilities, workers' willingness to help others, and workers' degree of conformity to group norms all shape informal organizational communication.

Traditional Formal Communication

Traditional scholars of organizational communication made no allowances for the role of informal communication in organizational functions and its influence on the organization. This was in part because of a reliance on the idea that all organizational messages should always exhibit the two characteristics of intelligibility and persuasion. Intelligible messages mean that the message should be clear and concise. Persuasive messages indicate that the average human needs coaxing to perform tasks in the interests of the organization. To better motivate and control workers in the interest of an organization, the

task goals should be communicated in such a way that they appear to serve the interest of workers.

Informal Communication Perspectives

There are two predominant views on informal communication. Some scholars argue that informal communication arises when information transmitted through the formal organization is either insufficient or ambiguous. In this sense, informal communication is used for clarity. Other scholars suggest that informal communication is much more than a surrogate from an incomplete formal system. Instead, informal communication is an inherent and even necessary aspect of organizational life. Most organizational communication researchers agree that some informal communication is inevitable in organizational life, regardless of the form the organization may take.

Grapevine Communication

A great deal of the research on informal organizational communication centers on the study of grapevine communication. Grapevine communication is a metaphor for a communication system that began in the 1860s during the Civil War in America as a description for telegraph lines that were strung through trees, resembling grapevines. This early system was neither stable nor reliable, so the term was coined for any form of communication outside the purview of formalized organizational communication.

The flow of information in grapevine communication can be complex. Some organizational members who participate in the grapevine act only as receivers of the message. These participants do not relay information to other organizational members. However, there are certain organizational members who serve as both senders and receivers of a message to other organizational members.

There are five areas of study of grapevine communication:

1. *The function and extent of grapevine communication.* The grapevine emerges from the social and personal interests of employees rather than from formalized organizational communication. This approach is more people oriented than task oriented.

2. *Participants in grapevine communication.* This studies the participants and their roles in grapevine communication. Secretaries and liaisons play critical roles in grapevine communication. Managers and other organizational members play a role in informal communication.

3. *Patterns and media of grapevine communication.* Grapevine communication is generally oral and presented in interpersonal and group contexts. The communication may begin, flow, and end anywhere in the organization.

4. *Volume, speed, and reliability of information.* The diffusion of grapevine information is rapid and the information is more accurate than inaccurate. However, most grapevine communication is incomplete.

5. *Role in rumor transmission.* Three types of rumors are spread through the grapevine: anxiety rumors (associated with perceived negative change such as layoffs), wish-fulfillment rumors (associated with salary increase or promotions), and wedge-driving rumors (once a rumor is assigned credibility, events are altered to fit in with and support the rumor).

Research on grapevine communication suggests that a great deal of organizational communication occurs through the grapevine. The grapevine serves as a rumor mill; however, only a small portion of the communication consists of rumors. There are no demographic (male vs. female) or status (managers vs. employees) differences among grapevine participants.

Current Research in Informal Organizational Communication

Research in the area of informal organizational communication has splintered from the traditional views of informal communication of examining grapevine communication to situating informal communication in various organizational structures. For example, the increased use of computer-mediated technology and communication systems has created research lines that compare the traditional organizational structure driven by formal communication with informal or emergent communication created by mediated

communication. J. D. Eveland and Tora Bikson (1987) found that e-mail served to augment, and in some cases complement, formal structures. Other scholars have shown that informal organizational communication that naturally emerges from communication technology in a sense is becoming more formalized as organizations attempt to extend control beyond time and spatial constraints characteristic of formal organizational communication.

Other streams of research include Pamela Hinds and Sara Kiesler's (1995) work that found that communication technologies were used as a tool for lateral communication across formal organizational boundaries. In another study, R. E. Rice (1994) found that electronic communication structures closely resembled formal organizational structures initially, but these similarities diminished over time. In sum, the current literature focuses on the advantages of informal communication to individuals and organizations.

Shawn D. Long

See also Organizational Communication, Formal

Further Readings

Daniels, T. D., Spiker, B. K., & Papa, M. J. (1997). *Perspectives on organizational communication* (4th ed.). Boston: McGraw-Hill.

Eveland, J. D., & Bikson, T. K. (1987). Evolving electronic communication networks: An empirical assessment. *Office: Technology and People, 3,* 103–128.

Hinds, P., & Kiesler, S. (1995). Communication across boundaries: Work, structure, and use of communication technologies in a large organization. *Organization Science, 6,* 373–393.

Jablin, F. M., & Putnam, L. L. (Eds.). (2001). *The new handbook of organizational communication: Advances in theory, research, and methods.* Thousand Oaks, CA: Sage.

Miller, K. (1999). *Organizational communication: Approaches and processes* (2nd ed.). Belmont, CA: Wadsworth.

Monge, P. R., & Contractor, N. S. (2001). Emergence of communication networks. In F. L. Jablin & L. L. Putnam (Eds.), *The new handbook of organizational communication: Advances in theory, research, and methods* (pp. 440–502). Thousand Oaks, CA: Sage.

Rice, R. E. (1994). Relating electronic mail use and network structure to R&D work networks and performance. *Journal of Management Information Systems*, 11(1), 9–20.

Tompkins, P. H. (1967). Organizational communication: A state of the art review. In G. Richetto (Ed.), *Conference on organizational communication*. Huntsville, AL: NASA, George C. Marshall Space Flight Center.

Weber, M. (1947). *Max Weber: The theory of social and economic organization* (T. Parsons & A. M. Henderson, Eds. & Trans.). New York: Free Press.

ORGANIZATIONAL CULTURE

Although there is no universally accepted definition of organizational culture, researchers generally agree that the term refers to the shared meaning, interpretations, and understanding of various organizational events among organizational members. Organizational culture serves as a guide to members to behave in ways shown to be effective over time; adds a sense of predictability and order to uncertainties in the environment; and provides a general understanding of how, when, and why members behave in certain ways.

Researchers generally agree that organizational culture is best represented as different layers along a continuum of accessibility. Denise Rousseau's description of culture suggests that the most observable layer of organizational culture is the material artifacts, such as organizational logos and office layout, found in an organization. The next layer is the behavioral patterns in which members engage. These are the routinized activities members perform, which build coordination among members. The third layer is formed by the behavioral norms that provide predictability among members and identify acceptable and unacceptable behavior. The fourth, and less readily accessible, layer is made up of the values and beliefs of organizational members. These values and beliefs represent preferences for various outcomes or behaviors and are generally conscious or espoused by organizational members. The deepest, and therefore least accessible, layer of culture is the basic, fundamental assumptions shared by organizational members. These assumptions exist outside of conscious awareness, and as such, members are typically unaware of their content or influence.

Edgar Schein's highly influential definition of culture focused primarily on the deeper levels of culture, in that he defined organizational culture as a pattern of basic, largely unconscious assumptions organizational members share. These basic assumptions are learned over time as those behaviors effective at solving organizational issues with adapting to the external environment or with resolving internal conflicts that have come to be internalized as the right way to do things here. Because these behaviors were effective in the past, new organizational members are socialized to these behavioral responses as the correct way to perceive, think, and feel with regard to external and internal issues. Ben Schneider's arguments about attraction, selection, and attrition leading to a homogeneous workforce suggest that because similar types of people enter an organization in the first place, it is often relatively easy for organization members to internalize the basic assumptions that form the organization's culture.

According to Schein's definition, true organizational culture exists primarily at the level of these basic assumptions. Although his model also includes *artifacts*, the visible structures, norms, and processes of an organization, and *espoused values*, the cognitively available and articulated strategies, goals, and philosophies of an organization, these are considered manifestations of the true, deeper culture. Other culture researchers (such as Rousseau, described previously) view all these layers as various aspects of organizational culture.

Measurement of Organizational Culture

Generally speaking, there are two distinct ways to measure organizational culture, each with advantages and disadvantages. One approach is more anthropological in nature and emphasizes the investigators' immersion in the organizational culture. When embedded in an organization, an investigator can better interpret the basic assumptions made by the organizational members. The second approach uses more quantitative methods to assess organizational culture. Through surveys of organizational members, investigators can quantify an organization's culture, which provides a means to compare organizations or branches of an organization on predetermined cultural factors.

The more qualitative approach to the assessment of organizational culture is advocated strongly by Schein and by the organizational anthropological community. Schein argues that the more efficient and accurate way to truly understand an organization's culture is to plunge into the organization. This vantage point provides an opportunity, with the help of motivated insiders, to better decipher the organizational members' basic assumptions and truly understand the culture. Specific methods used thus far in the literature include ethnographic techniques such as observation, interviews, structured focus groups, and large group meetings with organizational members designed to examine artifacts, espoused values, and basic assumptions. Schein even goes so far as to argue that a quantitative assessment of organizational culture is unethical, in that it fails to describe the unique ways in which various beliefs and assumptions are manifested in a given organization.

The qualitative assessment of culture depends on an iterative clinical approach, or a continual revising of cultural assessment as new information is made available. With this method, an investigator enters an organization and directly experiences the organizational culture. This entails both active and systematic observation as well as passively encountering situations that are different from what the investigator expected and attempting to understand these observations and encounters. An important step in this approach is to find a motivated insider who can help decipher the investigator's observations and interpretations. This motivated insider must have the mental capacity to think analytically to be helpful in this important process, as well as have a vested interest in understanding the cultural issue that has initiated the organizational culture study.

With the help of the motivated insider, the investigator attempts to identify the underlying shared assumptions and continually recalibrates these assumptions to further understand the true organizational culture. This method is more inductive in nature, and the end product in a qualitative investigation of culture is a formal description of the organization's culture. This description is in no way static but a perpetual work in progress, because organizational culture is dynamic and new information may reveal more basic assumptions or revisions to the prior basic assumptions.

The ability to converse with insiders of an organization is essential to fully understand the culture, for two reasons. First, an investigator can easily misinterpret events and observations and needs an insider to help correct these misinterpretations. Second, the insider is usually unaware of the basic assumptions in the organization, because these assumptions have dropped from conscious awareness and are taken for granted. It is the goal of the investigator to help bring these basic assumptions to a conscious level.

These qualitative methods, although thorough and comprehensive, have many disadvantages. In some situations, it is not financially feasible to conduct one or two large-group meetings at numerous organizations in many different countries. The time burden of this endeavor would cause too much time to pass for an equal comparison across organizations or countries. Furthermore, the results of this type of research do not allow necessary comparisons, because statistical analysis of qualitative data would be difficult, if not impossible.

Using Rousseau's five-level typology of culture as a framework, quantitative measures of culture vary from the more behavioral level to values and beliefs. Because quantitative measures of culture are limited to the more observable and measurable aspects of organizational culture, these self-report measures are necessarily limited to the shallower levels of the typology. However, it has been argued that when the organizational culture is strong, the material artifacts, behavioral patterns and norms, espoused values, and basic assumptions may all be in alignment. When this is the case, a quantitative measure of culture may effectively tap the deeper levels of organizational culture.

The quantitative approach to assessing organizational culture is through self-report surveys. A number of survey measures have been created and were classified by Neal Ashkanasy as either typing or profile surveys. Typing surveys classify organizations into mutually exclusive taxonomies or types. Once an organization is classified into a particular type, a description of behaviors and values typical of the type is provided. Through these types, organizations can be compared and organizational culture change can be monitored over time. Profile surveys assess an organization on predetermined cultural dimensions. High or low scores on the various dimensions of norms, behaviors, values, and beliefs provide a profile of the culture of an organization. These profiles can also be compared with those of other organizations, and changes can be tracked over time.

Assessing organizational culture using a quantitative measure provides a standardized means of understanding an organization's culture. This standardization of measurement is more conducive to comparing cultures of different organizations as well as different branches of the same organization. The ability to use statistical techniques is also a benefit of standardized, quantitative measures of organizational culture. Another advantage is that organizational members may be more likely to take part in later organizational change efforts because they were included in the cultural assessment. This commitment to the process could prove valuable later on.

There are a number of disadvantages to using the quantitative approach to cultural assessment. Self-report measures of organizational culture assume the respondent is aware of and can report the various aspects of an organization's culture. This approach assumes that everyone surveyed is motivated and mentally capable of reporting on the behaviors, values, and beliefs of the organization as a whole. Furthermore, quantitative measures are incapable of assessing all dimensions of culture identified to date. Using quantitative measures alone could miss those dimensions that are idiosyncratic, yet vitally important, to the functioning of a specific organization.

Quantitative measures are useful in assessing the more shallow layers of culture and may approach the deeper levels when the culture is strong. Although using qualitative measures may aid in the understanding of basic assumptions, quantitative measures provide information that is replicable and generalizable and that can reap the many benefits of statistical analysis. Because of the various advantages and disadvantages presented here, whether to use quantitative and qualitative measures should be considered carefully. A multimethod approach is recommended whenever feasible to avoid missing any vital level of information about organizational culture. In general, quantitative measures can be an efficient and valid measure of the more shallow

levels of culture, and the use of qualitative measures can be considered for deeper layers of culture such as basic assumptions.

Role of Leadership in Organizational Culture

The general assumption that is inherent in much organizational research on the relationship between leadership and culture is that leaders create cultures. This seems intuitive, in that organizational founders are seen as the people who create the initial culture of the organization, and in many organizations the founder's impact continues to be felt for years or decades after the founder has left the organization or died. Schein in particular emphasized the importance of the founder in shaping the organization's culture. Early research (e.g., Kurt Lewin, Ronald Lippitt, and Ralph White's 1939 study) and writing (e.g., Douglas McGregor's classic *The Human Side of Enterprise*) in this area focused largely on how managerial beliefs about employees affect the behavior of those employees. Research has demonstrated that the personality traits of the CEO may be related to certain aspects of an organization's structure, and Tomas Giberson and colleagues have shown congruence between CEO personality and values and the personalities and values of subordinates within the organization. CEO values of self-direction, security, and benevolence have been shown to relate to cultures of innovation, bureaucracy, and support, respectively, as well as subsequent sales growth and efficiency. Recent studies have begun to evaluate the mediating role of organizational culture between leadership and performance, indicating that leaders' impact on performance can be mediated by culture. The strength of leadership and strength of culture tend to be related. Clearly, leadership plays a role in the creation of organizational culture.

However, other perspectives emphasize the role culture plays in allowing people to emerge as leaders (or preventing them from doing so). For example, Robert Lord and colleagues focused on an information-processing approach to culture and suggested that the shared values and shared ways of conceptualizing and solving problems within an organization lead to evaluations of organizational members as being good or bad leaders, when a more accurate appraisal might be that a person is consistent with the type of person who has been successful as a leader in the past here. They thus argue that leadership itself may simply be an artifact of culture. The punctuated equilibrium model leads to similar conclusions: During times of calm, the people who rise to leadership positions tend to be those who do things in the same ways as the people who came before. They are likely to share the same values and perspectives, and it is only during times of crisis, when the shared values of an organization may be threatened or crumbling, that people with different leadership styles may come to be seen as leaders.

In short, leaders create cultures, and cultures yield leaders. The dynamics of this reciprocal process vary from organization to organization, from industry to industry, and from society to society. To believe that the causal arrow points in only one direction, however, is to be too simplistic in the conceptualization of organizational functioning.

Role of Societal Culture in Organizational Culture

Although it seems intuitively obvious that the culture of the society in which an organization emerges would affect the culture of the organization itself, until recently there few data have been available with which to assess this question. The Global Leadership and Organizational Behavior Effectiveness (GLOBE) project's analyses of this question have provided evidence suggesting that there is in fact some degree of congruence between aspects of a societal culture and of the culture of the average organization within that society. Speculating about the mechanisms by which this impact occurs, GLOBE researchers propose several possible avenues, including normative isomorphic pressures (e.g., organizations that structure themselves in certain ways and value certain things are seen as good within a given societal context) and cultural immersion (e.g., when an organization's founders have lived in an uncertainty-avoiding society, they are likely to have internalized that value and would thus be more likely to create organizations that manifest uncertainty avoidance). Although related, societal culture does not determine organizational culture; within societies

and nations, variability in individual values remains, though data from the GLOBE project suggest that variability within a society may center on the societal mean on related aspects of culture.

What remains unknown to date is whether the organizations in a society that are most effective are those that most closely represent the dominant values of the society or those that diverge from those values in some distinct way. Additionally, the role of the industry here is unknown. For example, it seems plausible that in a conservative, risk-averse society, a bank with a culture of risk aversion could be seen as trustworthy and good, whereas a pharmaceutical or high-tech firm with strong risk aversion could be seen as less appropriate. Research on these issues will be critical for better understanding the origins and effects of organizational culture in different societies and industries.

Organizational Effectiveness

Difficulties in evaluating organizational performance revolve around problems deciding what cultural level to focus on (e.g., artifacts, behaviors), the unit of analysis (e.g. teams, departments, the organization as a whole), and the content dimensions of the outcomes (e.g. satisfaction, sales). Using an assortment of measures, organizational culture has been related to a variety of outcomes, such as financial success, customer satisfaction, and goal achievement. In a recent meta-analysis of organizational performance, Hartnell and colleagues in 2011 used the competing values framework, which uses two bipolar dimensions (flexibility vs. stability and internal vs. external focus) to categorize culture. Using these dimensions, a 2 × 2 framework is created whose cells contain competing values of what is important to an organization, how these values are manifested, and the likelihood of success in different domains of organizational effectiveness. This framework suggests that there are associations among conceptually similar variables across different levels, which was supported by the meta-analytic result.

Organizational Culture Versus Organizational Climate

Elsewhere in this volume, we describe the construct of *organizational climate*. Although the constructs of climate and culture are clearly related, they have evolved in different ways and have come to be seen as representing different aspects of organizational functioning. Arnon Reichers and Ben Schneider, in Schneider's *Organizational Climate and Culture*, provide an extensive description of the historical evolution of the two constructs to that point, showing how the conceptualization of organizational climate followed almost a direct linear path from the early work of Kurt Lewin, with his focus on the practicality of good theory, whereas the organizational culture construct evolved more from a history rooted in anthropology. Reichers and Schneider point out the research emphasis on climate as a predictor of organizational effectiveness in some domain (which links cleanly to Lewinian practical theory), and the emphasis in culture research on descriptive, rather than prescriptive, approaches to organizational culture assessment (which links cleanly to a more anthropological, value-neutral, descriptive approach), but clearly there has been increased emphasis in recent years on the value of certain types of organizational cultures over others.

In the *Handbook of Organizational Culture and Climate*, both Schneider and Schein weigh in with their perspectives on climate and culture. Schneider argues that climate is the shared perception of the setting in which people work, the way things are around here, and that culture is the attributions made about why the setting is the way it is. Schein emphasizes the importance of attending to an organization's culture both as something that is a static property and as something that is a natural, constant process of building collective meaning. Both authors note the overlap between climate and culture, emphasize the separateness of the two constructs, and emphasize the value for researchers and practitioners of attending to both. More recently, several scholars in the *Oxford Handbook of Organizational Climate and Culture* have addressed these and related issues.

Conclusion

Several recent books, both popular and academic, have focused on the importance of organizational culture. Books such as *Work Rules! Insights From Inside Google That Will Transform How You Live and Lead*, *Creativity, Inc.: Overcoming the Unseen Forces That Stand in the Way of True Inspiration*, *Good to Great*, and *Built to Last: Successful Habits of Visionary Companies* focus on actual companies, either single companies or types of companies, used as exemplars of how to create effective, productive, successful cultures. The persistent popularity of *Who Moved My Cheese?* in its several editions, with its fanciful story of mice needing to find a new way to succeed, shows the strong desire for simple ways to understand cultural ideas. Others have noted the importance of culture match in mergers and acquisitions and joint ventures (e.g., Yaakov Weber's work), though there have been questions about this, as well, such as those raised by Lauren Rivera in the *New York Times* about hiring for culture fit ("Guess Who Doesn't Fit at Work?" May 30, 2015). The difficult but critical issue of organizational culture change when faced with an organizational crisis remains unresolved, as well. Clearly, culture matters; it matters for the organization in its quest for effectiveness, it matters for shareholders who want to see resources put to good use and not diverted by people problems, and it matters for employees who live within a system of shared values that affects their day-to-day functioning. We hope that consideration of the issues described in this entry illustrates both the utility and the complexity of organizational culture.

Marcus W. Dickson,
Michelle W. Mullins, and
Jacqueline K. Deuling

See also Attraction–Selection–Attrition Model; Global Leadership and Organizational Behavior Effectiveness Project; Organizational Climate

Further Readings

Ashkanasy, N. M., Wilderom, C.P.M., & Peterson, M. F. (Eds.). (2000). *Handbook of organizational culture and climate*. Thousand Oaks, CA: Sage.

Bezrukova, K., Thatcher, S.M.B., Jehn, K. A., & Spell, C. S. (2012). The effects of alignments: Examining group faultlines, organizational cultures, and performance. *Journal of Applied Psychology*, 97(1), 77–92. doi:10.1037/a0023684

Deal, T. E., & Kennedy, A. A. (1982). *Corporate cultures: The rites and rituals of corporate life*. Reading, MA: Addison-Wesley.

Denison, D. R. (1990). *Corporate culture and organizational effectiveness*. Ann Arbor, MI: Aviat.

Hartnell, C. A., Ou, A. Y., & Kinicki, A. (2011). Organizational culture and organizational effectiveness: a meta-analytic investigation of the competing values framework's theoretical suppositions. *Journal of Applied Psychology, 96*(4), 677–694. doi:10.1037/a0021987

Schein, E. (1992). *Organizational culture and leadership* (2nd ed.). San Francisco, CA: Jossey-Bass.

Schneider, B. (Ed.). (1990). *Organizational climate and culture*. San Francisco, CA: Jossey-Bass.

Schneider, B., & Barbera, K. M. (Eds.). (2014). *The Oxford handbook of organizational climate and culture*. New York: Oxford University Press. doi:0.1093/oxfordhb/9780199860715.001.0001

Trice, H. M., & Beyer, J. M. (1993). *The cultures of work organizations*. Englewood Cliffs, NJ: Prentice Hall.

ORGANIZATIONAL CYNICISM

At some point in our working lives, most of us feel that things at work would be fine if only we were in charge. Some people feel that way most of the time. They believe that the problems they and their coworkers encounter at work could be avoided or surmounted if someone competent were in control. This tendency to find fault with the management of the workplace and criticize the efforts of others who strive for excellence, while doubting their motives, is called *organizational cynicism* by psychologists.

Origin and Definition

The term *cynicism* originally referred to the beliefs of the Cynics, a small but influential school of ancient Greek philosophers who stressed self-control and individualism as the path to virtue. In their pursuit of virtue, the Cynics believed that rejection of social mores was preferable to material wealth and social acceptance because antisocial behaviors such as incivility, rude manners, and criticizing others freed one from society's bonds and restrictions. Rejection of social norms compels the individual to be self-reliant, and through self-reliance the individual attains a state of virtuous righteousness. In pursuing this ideal, the Cynics often took to scornful faultfinding in others.

It is this sense of the word *cynic* that has come down to present-day use.

The idea that cynics direct their negativity toward past, present, and future events neatly captures the approach that many modern-day researchers bring to the study of organizational cynicism. An *organizational cynic* may be defined as someone who believes that workplace problems are solvable and improvements are possible but that change and improvement efforts are futile because of the failings of others and the inherent incompetence of the system.

As the pace at which companies reinvented themselves quickened during the later years of the 20th century, their employees became increasingly skeptical of yet another flavor-of-the-month change initiative. This is an ongoing theme of the popular cartoon strip *Dilbert*. Organizational researchers recognize that many of these initiatives (including quality circles, continuous quality improvement, Six Sigma, process reengineering, customer focus, etc.) require acceptance and support from employees to succeed. Indeed, employee resistance to change could doom these initiatives to failure; the belief that failure is inevitable becomes a self-fulfilling prophecy that gives smug cynics a perverse "I told you so" satisfaction.

Research on Cynicism

Researchers adopt a number of conceptually distinct approaches to the study of cynicism. One school of study regards cynicism as a personality trait. Usually labeled *cynical hostility*, in this view cynicism is dysfunctional primarily in the realm of interpersonal relations. Studies indicate that cynics tend to be especially sensitive to social stress and, because of this, are likely to keep their cynical views to themselves. Even their spouses may not realize how cynical they are. Cynics have more job dissatisfaction, more job stress, and greater difficulties with the social and interpersonal environment at work than their noncynical coworkers.

Perhaps the best known treatment of cynicism as a dispositional characteristic is that of Donald Kanter and Philip Mirvis. In 1989, they conducted a national survey of cynicism among American adults. In their view cynicism develops from three key ingredients:

1. Unrealistically high expectations of self or others

2. Disappointment and frustration with outcomes and accomplishments

3. Disillusionment and a sense of having been let down, deceived, or betrayed by others

They classified cynics into types, such as *command cynics*, *squeezed cynics*, and *hard-bitten cynics*, with each type having implications for how someone expresses a personal cynical worldview. In addition to negative evaluations of attempts by others to make improvements, cynicism breeds suspicion of the motives of change agents and antipathy toward those efforts. Their findings indicated that cynicism is related to distrust of management and coworkers, job dissatisfaction, and dissatisfaction with the employer. Other researchers who used the Kanter and Mirvis survey instrument found that cynics tend to have low self-esteem, but cynicism is unrelated to other personality traits, such as introversion, extroversion, and anxiety.

Some researchers approach the study of cynicism from a perspective of work and occupations. Arthur Niederhoffer pioneered the study of occupational cynicism by looking specifically at cynicism among police officers. In his view, cynicism is an adaptive reaction for officers who must maintain an adversarial role toward the public they serve. Cynicism is thus a coping mechanism for dealing with frustration, which is learned through direct experience with duplicitous criminals and reinforced by a culture of cynical coworkers and supervisors.

Other researchers who followed the work of Niederhoffer identified specific targets of police cynicism, including the following:

- *Organizational cynicism.* Problems will not be solved because of the bureaucratic way decisions are made.
- *Work cynicism.* Problems cannot be solved, because of the nature of things; for example, human nature will always produce criminals.
- *Cynicism toward management.* Superiors are incompetent.
- *Cynicism about rules and regulations.* Bureaucracy stymies effective action.
- *Cynicism about the legal system.* Criminals go free on legal technicalities.

- *Cynicism about fellow citizens.* People try to get away with whatever they can.

Findings showed that cynicism about specific targets relates differently to aspects of work performance, including relations with coworkers, encounters with citizens, and number of arrests made. Implications of this work are that a person can be more cynical with respect to some targets than others and that social influences (from peers, coworkers, etc.) identify acceptable targets of blame, which can vary across situations.

In this era (from the 1980s to the early 21st century) of mergers, acquisitions, downsizing, restructuring, and bankruptcies, management assurances about the future of a company fall by the wayside with the next episode of corporate drama, leaving workers with ever greater levels of distress, uncertainty, betrayal, and cynicism. Another approach to the study of organizational cynicism uses a contract violation framework to argue that cynicism develops from frustration and disappointment when management breaks implicit and explicit promises to employees. Unmet expectations are the culprit, particularly when these expectations are encouraged by executives and managers who tout each flavor-of-the-month change initiative as the new best path to success.

What Is Organizational Cynicism?

These various approaches to the study of cynicism contribute essential insights into its role in the psychology of the individual and as a dimension of social processes at work.

- There is a dispositional aspect to cynicism. Some people are generally more pessimistic than others, their general negative affectivity giving them a tendency to see the glass as half empty rather than half full. When they encounter frustration and duplicity, they are more likely than optimists to become cynical, expecting more of the same. It is probably negative affect that contributes to cynics' difficulties in interpersonal relations.

- Although pessimists are likely to become cynical about a broader range of issues than optimists, cynicism nevertheless requires specific targets. If people are cynical, they have to be cynical about something. Pessimists may have many more targets of their cynicism than optimists, but given particular circumstances everyone is capable of becoming cynical about something.

- Cynicism serves a purpose. It is a psychological defense against disappointment and frustration that follows from naive credulity. Not only are cynics not as disappointed when promised benefits fail to appear, they are righteously reassured to know that their doubts were well founded.

- Cynicism is learned through direct experience and through group socialization. It is fair to say that most people begin their working lives eager to put skills acquired at school to use, learn new skills, earn a living, establish an identity, make new friends, and so on. From the outset their more experienced coworkers may try to convince newcomers that management cannot be trusted ("Listen to us if you want to know how things really work around here"), particularly in cases in which the work group itself is highly cynical. Indeed, some organizations develop cynical cultures that exacerbate the cynicism of employees and work groups. However, it probably takes at least a few personal encounters with broken promises and misplaced priorities before the eager anticipation of a novice employee turns to dejected cynicism. With experience comes wisdom and also, for many, cynicism.

- Cynicism implies behavior or, perhaps, lack of behavior. If you expect that the latest improvement program at work will fail, just like its predecessors, why bother to get involved? (Better to keep your head down until it passes.) There is some evidence, however, that cynics will become proactive if they believe their efforts can really make a difference. Cynics have been found to write more comments on employee opinion surveys than noncynics, and although the comments they wrote were negative in tone, they were also more specific about problem areas and more likely to suggest solutions than comments provided by noncynics.

Organizational Change and Cynicism

If you find yourself rolling your eyes in exasperation every time your employer announces another improvement initiative, you may be an organizational cynic. And you may be right. Research has not addressed the question of whether cynicism about workplace conditions is justified. It is known, however, that successfully implementing new processes and systems within large organizations is difficult. Most change initiatives require the support and cooperation of employees to succeed. Too often, these efforts fail to live up to expectations. Sometimes they fail entirely, wasting resources and ultimately doing the company more harm than good. When they succeed, it can take years for the benefits of new approaches to become apparent.

Executives preparing to launch the next quality improvement or process reengineering program should not be surprised if they seem to be the only ones who are truly excited about it. To them, the need for change is obvious. Their company's rapidly changing external environment forces the issue (via changing markets, technologies, resource costs, customer demands and expectations, etc.). Only through constant change can their company remain competitive.

To most people, however, change is unsettling and stressful. The known is comfortable, the unknown is threatening. Change is therefore resisted, and promises of benefits of change are met with cynicism. In reality, of course, change occurs continually. It is perhaps not surprising that researchers have paid increasing attention to cynical workers in recent years. Published studies now encompass samples representing a broad array of industries (e.g., construction, education, energy, health care, law enforcement, manufacturing, military, retail) and occupations (e.g., police officers, corrections officers, firefighters, teachers, students, army officers, national guard soldiers, physicians, nurses, home health care aides, transportation operators, entrepreneurs). The ongoing challenge for organizational researchers is to increase their understanding of organizational cynicism and to develop change management strategies that are both effective and acceptable to those who make them succeed or fail.

Robert J. Vance

See also Emotional Burnout; Organizational Change; Organizational Change, Resistance to

Further Readings

Chiaburu, D. S., Peng, A. C., Oh, I., Banks, G. C., & Lomeli, L. C. (2013). Antecedents and consequences of employee organizational cynicism: A meta-analysis. *Journal of Vocational Behavior, 83,* 181–197. doi:10.1016/j.jvb.2013.03.007

Dean, J. W., Jr., Brandes, P., & Dharwadkar, R. (1998). Organizational cynicism. *Academy of Management Review, 23,* 341–352. doi:10.5465/AMR.1998.533230

DeCelles, K. A., Tesluk, P. E., & Taxman, F. S. (2013). A field investigation of multilevel cynicism toward change. *Organization Science, 24,* 154–171. doi:10.1287/orsc.1110.0735

Kanter, D. L., & Mirvis, P. H. (1989). *The cynical Americans: Living and working in an age of discontent and disillusion.* San Francisco, CA: Jossey-Bass.

Niederhoffer, A. (1967). *Behind the shield: The police in urban society.* Garden City, NY: Doubleday.

Organizational Development

Organizational development (OD) is a field of professional practice focused on facilitating organizational change and improvement. The theory and practice of OD are grounded in both the social and behavioral sciences. The field originated in the social and political milieu of the 1960s and has been evolving ever since. This evolution has been influenced by a wide range of disciplines, including social psychology, group dynamics, industrial and organizational (I-O) psychology, participative management theory, organization behavior, the sociology of organizations, and even clinical psychology.

As a result, the application of OD tools and methodologies (of which there are many) is carried out by a wide range of professionals. For example, although some I-O psychologists also consider themselves OD practitioners, there are many others practicing OD with for-profit and nonprofit client organizations with educational backgrounds as diverse as education, philosophy, training, the military, and human resources. In part, this level of diversity of backgrounds is because of an initial lack of agreement and formal training when the field first emerged regarding its

nature and boundaries. Today, however, formal training in the field does exist, in doctoral and master's-level programs as well as professional development curricula, including formal certification groups and training firms. In any case, the value of the field of OD to continually embrace new perspectives, practitioners, and approaches is one of its defining characteristics; however, it is remains a continued source of discussion among those currently practicing in and writing about the field. For example, although some authors have introduced new evolutionary areas of theory and practice in recent years, such as dialogic OD, which focuses on organizations as socially constructed realities with an emphasis on narratives and conversations, other practitioners have made clear demarcations between OD and the practice of talent management, which emphasizes the assessment and differentiation of individual potential for accelerated development and succession. The content area of diversity and inclusion is another that has received considerable discussion in the field as being both in and out of scope for OD.

Regardless of these ongoing discussions, and the debate over the past few decades as to what is and is not included under the definition of OD, many practitioners agree that the following definition captures the essence of the field: OD is a planned process for driving humanistically oriented, system-based change in organizations through the use of social science theory and behaviorally based data collection and feedback techniques. This definition clearly reflects a number of specific assumptions. These include the importance of data and feedback to OD efforts, the notion of having a social systems perspective, and the humanistically oriented, values-based nature of the field. Each assumption is described in more detail in the following text.

Data Driven

First, it is important to understand that OD is fundamentally a data-driven approach to organizational change. Although the source of those data can be quantitative or qualitative in nature, the information gathered and fed back to clients is an integral part of the core OD consulting process.

Unlike other types of consulting models, the OD approach is generally not prescriptive. In other words, there is no single model, technique, or solution that is consistently provided by OD practitioners. Rather, OD consulting projects are based on a participative approach. This approach is known as *action research*.

Conceptualized by Kurt Lewin, a social psychologist who specialized in studying group dynamics in the 1940s and 1950s, action research consists of the following stages:

- Systematically gathering data (of whatever form and using any number of tools and techniques) on the nature of an organizational problem or situation
- Analyzing that information to find key themes, patterns, and insights that tell a compelling story about the problem or situation in question
- Feeding back that analysis in a summary form of the results while engaging with the client to ensure ownership of the diagnosis of the problem
- Determining the appropriate intervention together on the basis of a shared understanding of the issues
- Taking action to drive positive change in the organization or social system

Given this framework, it is easy to understand how OD practitioners can use many different types of diagnostic tools and interventions to produce helpful insights and feedback. Common examples of data collection methods used include surveys, interviews, group discussions, conversations and storytelling, leadership programs, appreciative inquiry, process observations, and 360-degree feedback. Many of the same methods are also used by other types of social scientists and practitioners. The key difference when using these methodologies in an OD context is that the interpretation of the results and the determination of the intervention required is a shared process between practitioner and client, and the emphasis is on organizational improvement. Regardless of the methodology, the basic notion of using data-based feedback to move clients from their comfort zones and create a need for change is common to most OD efforts.

Systems Perspective

The second major assumption inherent in the definition of OD is that the field is firmly grounded in social systems theory. From this perspective, each organization is conceptualized as a system of interdependent subsystems and components (e.g., people and systems related) that both influence each other and are influenced by the external environment in which they exist. This means that OD interventions are designed and implemented with a thorough understanding of the interplay between different factors in the organization that can either help or hinder the success of the change effort. The ideal intervention set is one in which multiple subsystems of an organization (e.g., mission and vision, rewards, leadership behaviors, communications) are aligned and/or engaged at the same time to drive the change effort. This is the framework that underpins the majority of the OD approaches in the field today and reflects its origins in the social and behavioral sciences.

Although the recent concept of dialogic OD takes a somewhat different approach by focusing efforts at the more organic level of individual exchanges and conversations, when applied to larger change initiatives there is link to integrated social networks that reflects similar thinking but from a person-centric (not organization-centric) point of view. Furthermore, proponents of dialogic OD also support the need to fully integrate interventions throughout the system versus driving a top-down or mandated change approach, which is common with other types of non-OD consulting efforts.

Although there are a number of different OD models reflecting systems theory, the Burke-Litwin model of organizational performance and change is one of the more comprehensive. Reflecting a systems thinking perspective, it outlines 12 distinct factors of organizations that need to be considered when designing and implementing any large-scale change effort. These factors reflect both transformational and transactional areas.

Transformational factors are those that are likely to be influenced by the external environment. When these factors are the focus of an OD-related change effort, new thinking and behaviors are typically required on the part of the individuals in that social system. These factors include the external environment, the mission and strategy of the organization, the senior leaders and what they represent, and the nature of the organizational culture. Changes in these factors (or a lack of alignment and integration among any of these during a change effort) tend to be more strategic and long term in nature and eventually create a ripple effect that drives change in other parts of the organization.

Transactional factors, in comparison, are those that are more day to day and short term focused. These include elements such as the behaviors of middle management, the formal structure reflecting how managers and employees are organized, the systems and processes that reinforce the right types of behaviors (e.g., the performance appraisal process), work group climate, level of motivation, needs and values of employees, and finally the fit between employees and the jobs they are in.

All these factors and their interaction with one another ultimately influence individual, group, and organizational performance. As with most systems models, performance also has a subsequent impact on the external environment of that organization (e.g., competitors, industry regulations, economic trends, technology trends), which in turn affects the organization itself. In other words, the systems approach to OD work reflects a constant feedback loop.

In sum, the systems approach is a unique aspect of OD that helps differentiate it from some of the more narrowly focused theory and practice areas of I-O psychology, human resource management, and organizational behavior. It also reflects a broader perspective for facilitating organizational change than many management consulting approaches, such as those of firms that focus only on structure, technology or business strategy.

Values Based

The third defining characteristic of the field of OD, which is shared with I-O psychology, is the notion of a normative view to working with people and organizations. This means that the field and practice of OD are values based in nature. OD practitioners evaluate their efforts, including the choices of the clients they work with and the interventions they engage in, against a normative filter. In short, they ask this question of themselves: Will

this effort result in a positive outcome for the organization and its employees?

Unlike some types of organizational consulting approaches that can be financially driven or very senior management focused, such as downsizing efforts or mergers and acquisitions, OD practitioners are particularly focused on the human relations component of their work. This means that for many, if the nature of the project will result in negative outcomes for a given set of employees, the OD practitioner is likely to turn down the project. Although counterintuitive from a business model perspective, this is one of the hallmarks of the OD profession and one of the key reasons why OD work is appealing to some people.

This emphasis on positivistic change is evident in areas such as the international OD code of ethics, sponsored by the International Society for Organization Development and Change, formerly known as the Organization Development Institute, and described in many articles and books in the field. Although an area of debate for some, research over the past 20 years has consistently shown that the majority of practitioners would endorse such OD values as improving the state of human dignity, democracy, honesty, integrity, and empowerment in organizations.

Overall, this normative filter helps OD practitioners balance the need for increasing organizational productivity and effectiveness (which is one of the most common reasons why an external or internal consultant would be engaged in the first place) with a humanistic values focus on helping improve the satisfaction and development of individuals in an organization.

OD Consulting Approach

Although it is important to understand the underpinnings of the field from a philosophical perspective, it is equally important to have a firm grasp of the tactical side of the OD profession. One of the best ways to do this is to understand the OD consulting model. There are seven phases to the OD consulting approach:

1. entry,

2. contracting,

3. data collection,

4. data analysis,

5. data feedback,

6. intervention, and

7. evaluation.

This seven-phase model is particularly relevant for OD because it

- reinforces the centrality of data or information as a key component for driving change,
- shows where and when data should be used to inform decision making, and
- reflects a systems approach to thinking about issues and interventions.

Each of these phases of the OD consulting approach is described in the following text.

Entry

Entry represents the first meeting between an OD practitioner and a client. If an external consulting engagement, this is usually the first exposure to the overall social system and as a result represents an important first step in the consulting relationship. During this phase, the OD practitioner and client determine their ability to work together collaboratively and get a shared understanding of the issues or problems at hand. The quality of the relationship established during entry will determine whether the OD effort will occur.

Contracting

Contracting is the phase in which roles, expectations, and anticipated outcomes are agreed on between the OD practitioner and his or her client. Typically, this is when individual capabilities are reviewed and difficult questions are tested. For example, most OD consultants will discuss with their clients the difference between a symptom, such as the problem at hand that resulted in their being contacted, and a root cause, including the real reason and best place for an intervention to occur.

Data Collection

Once entry and contracting are done, the OD practitioner next needs to determine a data-gathering strategy. The focus here is on determining

the best method, tool, or technique for gaining new insights into the issue or problem at hand. The collected data can be either quantitative or qualitative in nature, or some combination of both. Some of the most common OD-related methodologies include the following:

- Multisource or 360-degree feedback
- Organizational surveys
- Personality assessments
- Individual observations
- Interviews with key individuals
- Focus groups
- Process consultation during meetings
- Large-group interventions
- Appreciative inquiry

Data Analysis

Once the data are collected, they need to be analyzed. The nature of the analysis and the techniques applied will depend on

- the type of data collected,
- the analysis skills and experience of the OD practitioner, and
- the receptivity and sophistication of the client.

Analysis techniques can range from reporting simple averages or content code summaries of comments or observations to sophisticated statistical modeling of relationships among key predictors, such as leadership behaviors and employee engagement, as well as outcome variables including regional sales, plant safety incidents, and executive turnover. Whatever the approach used, the outcome is the same. OD practitioners are focused on determining the best analysis method to produce the most useful and actionable insights to share with their clients. Although the rise of big data methodologies holds significant promise for organizational change applications, some OD practitioners and even I-O psychologists have raised concerns over the current state of capability in the field to take full and ethically safe advantage of this new higher level of data-based insights.

Data Feedback

The next phase in the process is delivering the insights gleaned from the data collection and analysis to the client. From an OD perspective, it is important to work with the client during the feedback stage to help gain a shared understanding of the diagnosis rather than simply delivering the answer. As a result, one of the critical skills needed to be successful in the field of OD is the ability to tell a meaningful story with data. Although not delivering the answer per se, the OD practitioner does need to be able to convey the key findings from the data in a manner that brings the client along. This represents one of the unique aspects of the OD approach compared with other consulting models, in which the answer is clearly recommended during the feedback process. OD practitioners are much more likely to suggest ideas and work together with their clients through the issues as a part of the feedback process. The focus here is on delivering a compelling story that creates a need for change and a direction for that change. The discussion during the feedback stage is what leads to the selection of the appropriate intervention.

Intervention

The intervention phase of the model involves determining together with the client the appropriate solution on the basis of the data fed back and a shared understanding of its implications. The important point to remember here is that regardless of what intervention is chosen, the determination should be based on the issues identified in the data and what the practitioner and client think will result in the most impact. This shared approach drives client ownership and commitment, which is critical to ensuring the success of the OD change effort. This is where many consulting firms specializing in certain techniques can be faced with the dilemma of not having the right capability and tools in house that are needed for a specific situation requiring additional resources or expertise.

Evaluation

The last stage of an OD effort is a formal evaluation process. Although often overlooked by many consultants, it is a crucial step for both the client and the practitioner. From the client's perspective, it is helpful toward quantifying the successful outcome of the effort. From the OD practitioner's perspective, it represents both a measure of success and a key source of learning and development. Given an increasing emphasis on the return on investment of interventions in organizations today, the presence or absence or an evaluation strategy (and related results) can have a lasting impact on the viability of future change initiatives in those same organizations as well.

Summary

In sum, the theory and practice of OD represent a data-driven, systemic thinking, and values-based approach to helping improve organizations and the people who work in them. Fundamentally, the OD consulting model is collaborative in nature and grounded in data-based information.

Allan Church

See also Human Resource Management; Organizational Behavior

Further Readings

Burke, W. W. (2011). *Organization change: Theory and practice* (3rd ed.). Thousand Oaks, CA: Sage.

Burke, W. W., & Litwin, G. H. (1992). A causal model of organizational performance and change. *Journal of Management, 18,* 523–545.

Church A. H. (2013). Engagement is in the eye of the beholder: Understanding differences in the OD vs. talent management mindset. *OD Practitioner, 45*(2), 42–48.

Church, A. H., Rotolo, C. T., Shull, A. C., & Tuller, M. D. (2014). Inclusive organization development: An integration of two disciplines. In B. M. Ferdman & B. Deane (Eds.), *Diversity at work: The practice of inclusion* (pp. 260–295). San Francisco, CA: Jossey-Bass.

Cummings, T. G., & Worley, C. G. (2015). *Organization development and change* (10th ed.). Stamford, CT: Cengage Learning.

Shull, A. C., Church, A. H., & Burke, W. W. (2014). Something old, something new: Research findings on the practice and values of OD. *OD Practitioner, 46*(4), 23–30.

Waclawski, J., & Church, A. H. (Eds.). (2002). *Organization development: A data-driven approach to organizational change.* San Francisco, CA: Jossey-Bass.

ORGANIZATIONAL IDENTIFICATION

Organizational identification represents the extent to which individuals consider their membership within an organization as a meaningful part of who they are. Popularized by the work of Blake Ashforth and Fred Mael, organizational identification has been studied largely from a social identity perspective, which posits that one's awareness of membership in a particular, salient social group embodies an important part of one's self-concept. Employees understandably develop a sense of attachment to their organizations, given the financial importance of employment and the fact that organizations are inherent social systems in which individuals spend a large amount of time and effort in their lives. This attachment serves as a fundamental basis of organizational identification in that individuals can value their organizational membership to such a degree that this organizational membership becomes closely connected to their overall personal identities. In other words, employees with high levels of organizational identification have integrated the fact that they work for a particular organization into a meaningful part of their self-concepts. Because of this integration, employees with high degrees of organizational identification experience a sense of similarity and oneness with the organization as a whole; this concept is comparable with how individuals can feel attached to other salient social groups of which they are members (e.g., race, religion, national culture).

Researchers predominately implement one of two self-report questionnaires to measure organizational identification: a 25-item scale developed by George Cheney or the more commonly used 10-item scale developed by Fred Mael and Lois Tetrick. Other researchers have developed single-item and graphical rating scales to assess organizational identification, but the usefulness of these scales is unclear given the limited number of studies that have implemented them and the modest correlations with the two more established scales just mentioned.

Antecedents and Outcomes of Organizational Identification

Antecedents

Because of organizational identification's integration within one's self-concept, the most commonly studied antecedents of organizational identification include factors that affect one's overall self-concept. For example, employees' sense of organizational prestige (i.e., the extent to which employees feel that their organization is viewed positively by others) increases organizational identification because of individuals' desire to connect this positive aspect of the organization as a part of their own self-concept. In other words, employees of an organization that is viewed positively by others tend to experience increased organizational identification, so that this prestige transfers over to their own selves via this integration of organizational membership into their personal identities.

Another commonly studied antecedent involves leadership and its influence on employees' self-concepts. Most prominently, transformational leadership—a style in which leaders actively support and guide their followers through their goals, challenges, and needs—results in increases in organizational identification because these leadership behaviors signal thoughtfulness, appreciation, and care. These experiences help foster a sense of attachment to an organization because there is clear evidence that others view the focal employee as someone who belongs.

Perceived support from multiple areas of the organization also embodies antecedents of organizational identification. Perceived organizational, supervisory, and coworker support have all been demonstrated to directly influence organizational identification. Understandably, feeling that one's well-being and needs are valued and considered by others signifies the very likely notion that these others consider the employee in question as a meaningful member of the organization. Organizational identification increases as a result of this experienced inclusion.

Organizational structures and policies, along with employees' reactions to them, also affect organizational identification. Hierarchical structures with downward communication styles (i.e., supervisors' direct orders to subordinates without question) negatively affect organizational identification, because this communication style implies status differences that undermine the possibility of feeling that the focal employee and organization are one and the same. Relatedly, perceived organizational injustice influences organizational identification in a similarly negative manner. Feeling wronged and mistreated leads to decreases in organizational identification because these experiences imply that the focal employee is not truly one and the same as everyone else. In these cases, individuals find it difficult to identify with the organization because of the lack of oneness they feel with it.

The impacts of demographic and personality-based differences on organizational identification have received little attention in the literature relative to those of job attitudes and performance. Meta-analytic work points to no significant relationships between organizational identification and age, organizational tenure, gender, and education, but significant heterogeneity (i.e., variability) exists in the effect sizes reported in different studies, which implicates the role of unexamined moderating variables. Of note, job level has consistently been shown to positively relate to organizational identification, although only a small number of studies have documented this relationship.

Research examining the role of personality in determining organizational identification is scarce. Mostly examined via the five-factor model, moderate positive relationships between organizational identification and agreeableness, extroversion, and emotional stability have been documented, along with very weak positive relationships with conscientiousness and openness to new experience. Although the positive relationships between organizational identification and agreeableness and extroversion make sense given their social aspects (i.e., organizational identification embodies identification with a social category), the strengths and directions of the relationships between organizational identification and the other personality traits require more theoretical and empirical work to understand fully.

Very recent meta-analytic work has underscored the role of national culture in determining individuals' level of organizational identification. Researchers commonly conceptualize national culture via distinct social values that show meaningful variation across cultures. With regard to organizational identification, individualism—the extent to which cultures prioritize individual goals over collective ones—seems to have an impact; individuals in countries with higher degrees of individualism tend to experience less organizational identification. This finding aligns with the notion that organizational identification represents a degree of attachment to a collective social group, which conflicts with the idea of individualistic values. In terms of other cultural values, extant research suggests a null relationship between organizational identification and uncertainty avoidance (i.e., the degree of coping with anxiety by minimizing ambiguity) and long-term orientation (i.e., a focus on the future instead of the present), while the effects of other cultural values on organizational identification remain largely unclear.

Outcomes

The outcomes of organizational identification established in the literature mostly involve various job attitudes and work-related behavior. Of the job attitudes, affective organizational commitment—the degree to which employees are emotionally attached and desire to remain organizational members—has received the most attention and has a strong positive relationship with organizational identification. Other commonly studied job attitudes that result from organizational identification include decreased turnover intention and increased job involvement (i.e., the degree to which employees feel cognitively connected to their jobs) and job satisfaction (i.e., the extent to which employees are content with their jobs). Meta-analytic work has shown that organizational identification is not merely a component of general work-related attitudes such as job satisfaction, job involvement, and affective organizational commitment; instead, more evidence suggests that organizational identification serves as a causal basis from which these job attitudes stem, underscoring the importance of this construct.

In relation to work behavior, most research implicates organizational identification's key role in predicting both task and extra-role performance. Although meta-analytic findings suggest that job attitudes, such as job satisfaction, mediate organizational identification–performance (both task and extra-role) relationships, direct effects between organizational identification and both performance outcomes still exist, although the direct effect of organizational identification on performance is weaker than its effect on attitudes.

1114 Organizational Identification

Conceptual and Empirical Overlap With Related Constructs

Having explored the antecedents and outcomes of organizational identification, the issue regarding the considerable overlap between organizational identification and related constructs warrants discussion. Of primary concern to researchers is the distinction among organizational identification, organizational commitment, and organizational trust. Importantly, confusion regarding these variables exists at both the conceptual and empirical levels. Conceptually, the definitions of these constructs seem quite similar; a commonly accepted definition for organizational commitment, for example, explicitly incorporates a degree of identification with the organization. Empirically, meta-analytic evidence demonstrates an extremely high correlation between organizational commitment and organizational identification, suggesting possible empirical redundancy (i.e., they tend to be indistinguishable from each other statistically). Although empirical redundancy exists with other pairs of job attitudes, for example job satisfaction and organizational commitment, these other pairs at least have conceptual distinctness, pointing to the notion that these problems exist in how the constructs are measured. In the case of organizational identification, organizational commitment, and organizational trust, however, the conceptual distinctions are less clear.

Motivated by these issues, researchers have attempted to rectify these conceptual and empirical overlaps. Central to organizational identification, organizational commitment, and organizational trust is the idea of attachment to the organization. However, contemporary researchers differentiate these constructs on the basis of how this attachment to the organization operates and manifests itself. Organizational identification involves attachment that has implications for one's self-concept, whereas the other two constructs do not implicate the self. Empirically, researchers have begun to examine the incremental validity of organizational identification, organizational commitment, and organizational trust in predicting job attitudes and behavior. Most notably, evidence suggests that organizational identification has the highest incremental validity of these three constructs in predicting job satisfaction, turnover intention, task performance, and extra-role performance.

Future Research Directions

Many possible routes for researchers interested in organizational identification exist that would greatly inform knowledge about this construct. In addition to further understanding the differences between organizational identification, commitment, and trust, researchers are beginning to investigate the role of organizational identification in predicting negative behavior. For example, can individuals who identify strongly with organizations that implement unethical practices behave in ways that reinforce these practices (e.g., by not whistleblowing)? Relatedly, can high organizational identification coexist with high levels of identification in other domains, such as one's family? If so, what role does organizational identification play when these individuals experience role conflict between work and family demands? These interactions between different forms of identification would greatly assist in understanding how individuals decide to expend their time and effort in certain domains rather than in others.

Because of the important role of the self-concept in defining organizational identification, future research should investigate how organizational identification coexists with and affects other components of the self. In addition to the need to examine organizational identification in the context of well-established personality models (e.g., the five-factor model), investigating the influence of narrower personality facets and individual differences can promote understanding of how it manifests itself among particular individuals. For example, emerging research suggests that highly narcissistic individuals view themselves as core features of organizations; this stands counter to the traditional view of the organization as a core feature of the self.

Future research should also examine the possibility that organizational identification may not exist as a singular, unidimensional construct but actually contains narrower, distinct facets that combine to create an overall sense of organizational identification. Although several studies have proposed and found evidence for the existence of distinct facets of organizational identification, more research is necessary to bolster this view. Knowledge that organizational identification is composed of smaller facets would have implications for its measurement, especially for single-item and graphical rating scales.

The possibility that identification with a particular organization may still exist despite an employee's departure represents another avenue for future research. Because of the integration of organizational membership into one's self-concept, individuals may feel that they are subjectively still attached to the organization and continue to draw from their past membership within it as part of who they are. The manner in which these individuals left their organizations may also be relevant (e.g., voluntary or involuntary turnover) to this notion. Relatedly, future researchers may wish to examine the longitudinal impacts of these "lingering" feelings of organizational identification to pinpoint when and how identification with the prior organization ceases to exist. In other words, perhaps employment-related experiences (e.g., getting hired by another organization) or a certain amount of time must pass before this occurs.

Peter P. Yu

See also Attitudes and Beliefs; Identity; Organizational Commitment; Self-Concept Theory of Work Motivation

Further Readings

Ashforth, B. E., & Mael, F. (1989). Social identity theory and the organization. *Academy of Management Review*, 14, 20–39. doi:10.5465/AMR.1989.4278999

He, H., & Brown, A. D. (2013). Organizational identity and organizational identification: A review of the literature and suggestions for future research. *Group & Organization Management*, 38, 3–35. doi:10.1177/1059601112473815

Lee, E. S., Park, T. Y., & Koo, B. (in press). Identifying organizational identification as a basis for attitudes and behaviors: A meta-analytic review. *Psychological Bulletin*, 141(5), 1049–1080. doi:10.1037/bul0000012

Mael, F. A., & Tetrick, L. E. (1992). Identifying organizational identification. *Educational and Psychological Measurement*, 52, 813–824. doi:10.1177/0013164492052004002

Ng, T. W. (2015). The incremental validity of organizational commitment, organizational trust, and organizational identification. *Journal of Vocational Behavior*, 88, 154–163. doi:10.1016/j.jvb.2015.03.003

Riketta, M. (2005). Organizational identification: A meta-analysis. *Journal of Vocational Behavior*, 66, 358–384. doi:10.1016/j.jvb.2004.05.005

van Knippenberg, D., & Schie, E. (2000). Foci and correlates of organizational identification. *Journal of Occupational and Organizational Psychology*, 73, 137–147. doi:10.1348/096317900166949

ORGANIZATIONAL IMAGE

Definition

Organizational image refers to people's global impressions of an organization and is defined as people's loose structures of knowledge and beliefs about an organization. Organizational image represents the net cognitive reactions and associations of customers, investors, employees, and applicants to an organization's name. Accordingly, it serves as a template to categorize, store, and recall organization-related information.

It should be noted that there is no such thing as "the" organization's image, because an organization typically has multiple images. These multiple images result from various groups (also known as stakeholders or corporate audiences) holding different images of the same organization. At least, one might distinguish among the following organizational images. First, investors and executives hold an image of an organization as an economic performer ("company financial image"). These investors typically rely on factual economic figures as a basis of their beliefs about the organization. Second, there is the image of an organization as a social performer in the general society (also known as "corporate social performance"), which can be further broken down into an organization's involvement in the community and its pro-environmental practices. Third, customers or clients hold an image of an organization as a provider of goods and services ("product image or service image"). Fourth, each organization has an image as an employer among current employees and (potential) applicants (also known as company employment image or employer image). This is the image that is assessed in rankings such as

Fortune's "The 100 Best Companies to Work For" or "a great place to work." These multiple organizational images might not always coincide. For instance, a firm's image as an employer as held by either employees or job seekers might be different from its image as a provider of goods and services in the minds of customers or clients.

Organizational images typically develop over longer periods of time. They result from, among other things, media coverage, individual or group sensemaking, and communication on the part of the organization (as reflected in an organization's advertising, sponsorships, and publicity). However, it should be clear that organizational images are not static. Specifically, organizations often audit their images. In these image audits, the aim is to carefully determine which factors make up the image among various stakeholders. Next, organizations aim to strategically modify the image held by these stakeholders. For instance, this might be done by increasing an organizations exposure or by highlighting specific attributes in advertising campaigns.

Components of Image

The above definition of organizational image reflects a holistic view of organizational image. It is also possible to focus on specific attributes that people associate with employer image (employer image dimensions). In this elementalistic view, two broad components can be distinguished in an organization's image. First, people typically associate some objective attributes with an organization. These attributes might vary from factual or historical aspects of organizations to organizational procedures and policies. For example, in terms of a company's image as an employer, research has confirmed that applicants might have some knowledge about the attributes of the organization and the jobs they might consider applying for. Examples include size, location, level of centralization, pay, benefits, type of work to be performed, advancement opportunities, and career programs. Many of these attributes (e.g., pay, advancement) are also referred to as instrumental attributes because they have functional or utilitarian value in that they enable maximum benefits and rewards.

A second part of people's general impressions of an organization refers to more symbolic aspects,

also known as trait-related inferences. Trait inferences about organizations are different from the aforementioned objective company-related information for two reasons. First, trait inferences describe the organization in terms of subjective, abstract, and intangible attributes. Second, they convey symbolic company information in the form of imagery that people assign to organizations. For example, people refer to some employing organizations as trendy, whereas other employing organizations are seen as prestigious. People associate themselves with organizations with these symbolic aspects because they want to express their own values or impress others.

Consequences of Organizational Image

An organization's image plays a central role because what various stakeholders know about an organization influences considerably how they respond to the organization. In fact, an organization's image might have various potentially favorable consequences for the organization and its main stakeholders.

First, there might be effects on investment decisions. Specifically, firms with good images might have competitive leverage in terms of attracting and keeping new investors. Second, it has been found that an organization's image exerts effects on consumers' product choices. In this context, an organization's image might serve as a signal of product quality and might enable an organization to distinguish itself from its main competitors. Third, an organization's image seems to affect people's attraction to an organization as a place to work. This is especially the case in early recruitment stages as (potential) applicants have only a rudimentary knowledge of the key job and organizational attributes. Hence, (potential) applicants mainly rely on their general impressions of the firm (i.e., image) when deciding to apply for a job. The general effect that has been found is that employer image influences the quantity and quality of the applicant pool of an organization in that organizations with good images are able to attract more and better applicants. Apart from these general effects on applicant quantity and quality, applicants' view of the image of an employer has also long-lasting effects on other recruitment stages. Specifically, impressions of an organization as an employer measured in early recruitment stages are strong predictors of applicants' attraction measured in later recruitment stages (e.g., after a campus interview), which in turn is related to applicants' final job acceptance decisions. A fourth group of studies has examined the consequences of organizational image on employees' attitudes and behaviors toward their organizations. For instance, an employee also uses an organization's image as a mirror of how others are judging them. Moreover, an organization's image has been found to be important to employees' sense of self. If one holds the company in low regard, one has lower job satisfaction and a higher probability of leaving the organization. Conversely, if the company is held in high regard by oneself and others, job satisfaction is higher and turnover intention is lower. In this case, an employee also wants to be associated with the positive image of the organization and feels proud to belong to that organization. Finally, there is evidence that firms on the best 100 list enjoy organizational performance advantages over the broad market and a matched sample of firms. In other words, organizational image seems to enhance the competitive ability of the firm.

Related Constructs

Organizational image is closely related to other constructs, such as organizational reputation and organizational identity. However, there are also some differences. In particular, *organizational reputation* refers to people's beliefs about the general public's affective evaluation of the organization. Organizational reputation differs from organizational image in that reputation entails an affective component (a loose set of feelings associated with an organization), whereas image is mainly cognitively oriented (a loose set of knowledge and beliefs about an organization). Another difference is that reputation refers to more stable shared perceptions of how the general public feels about the organization, whereas image deals with a person's own more transient beliefs.

Another related construct is an organization's perceived identity. The key difference between an organization's identity and an organization's image is that an organization's identity is what insiders in the organization (employees) perceive

to be the organization's central, enduring, and distinctive characteristics. Conversely, image and reputation deal with outsiders' (applicants, customers) views and feelings.

Finally, in the practitioner literature, the term *employer brand* has also been used. The employer brand is the perceived package of attributes (see the image components mentioned previously) that makes an employer attractive and distinctive in the minds of both job seekers and current employees. A further distinction is often made between the external employer brand and the internal employer brand. Whereas the external employer brand converges with the organization's image as an employer as seen by outsiders, the internal brand mirrors the construct of an organization's perceived identity.

Filip Lievens

See also Assessing Organizational Culture; Dirty Work, Organizational Attraction; Organizational Climate, Organizational Justice; Organizational Structure, Recruitment

Further Readings

Barber, A. E. (1998). *Recruiting employees: Individual and organizational perspectives*. Thousand Oaks, CA: Sage.

Breaugh, J. A. (2013). Employee recruitment. *Annual Review of Psychology, 64*, 389–416.

Cable, D. M., & Turban, D. B. (2001). Establishing the dimensions, sources and value of job seekers' employer knowledge during recruitment. In G. R. Ferris (Ed.) *Research in personnel and human resources management* (pp. 115–163). New York: Elsevier.

Collins, C. J., & Han, J. (2004). Exploring applicant pool quantity and quality: The effects of early recruitment practices, corporate advertising, and firm reputation. *Personnel Psychology, 57*, 685–717.

Dutton, J. E., Dukerich, J. M., & Harquail, C.V. (1994). Organizational images and member identification. *Administrative Science Quarterly, 39*, 239–263.

Fulmer, I. S., Gerhart, B., & Scott, K. S. (2003). Are the 100 best better? An empirical investigation of the relationship between being a "great place to work" and firm performance. *Personnel Psychology, 56*, 965–993.

Highhouse, S., Brooks, M. E., & Greguras, G. (2009). An organizational impression management perspective on the formation of corporate reputations. *Journal of Management, 35*, 1481–1493.

Highhouse, S., Thornbury, E., & Little, I. (2007). Social-identity functions of attraction to organizations. *Organizational Behavior and Human Decision Processes, 103*, 134–146.

Lievens F., & Highhouse, S. (2003). The relation of instrumental and symbolic attributes to a company's attractiveness as an employer. *Personnel Psychology, 56*, 75–102.

Lievens, F., & Slaughter, J. E. (in press). Employer image and employer branding: What we know and don't know yet. *Annual Review of Organizational Psychology and Organizational Behavior.*

Slaughter, J. E., Zickar, M. J., Highhouse, S., & Mohr, D. C. (2004). Personality trait inferences about organizations: Development of a measure and assessment of construct validity. *Journal of Applied Psychology, 89*, 85–103.

Yu, K. Y. T., & Cable, D. M. (2014). *Oxford handbook of recruitment.* New York: Oxford University Press.

ORGANIZATIONAL JUSTICE

Organizational justice refers to individual or collective judgments of fairness or ethical propriety. Investigations of organizational justice tend to take a descriptive approach. As such, an event is treated as *fair* or *unfair* to the extent that one believes it to be so. This belief in fairness comes from the comparison of a particular occurrence with a set of evaluative criteria, or justice rules. If the occurrence violates the rule, it is viewed as *unfair*. Justice research is concerned with identifying the antecedents that influence fairness judgments, as well as the organizational consequences once such an evaluation has been made. Notice that this descriptive approach does not tell organizations what really is fair, only what people believe to be just. This empirical perspective complements the normative frameworks beneficially used by philosophers, whose prescriptive approach typically attempts to ascertain what is objectively right or wrong by using reasoned analysis.

This sense of justice has a strong impact on workers' behavior and attitudes. For example, perceived fairness promotes such benefits as organizational commitment, effective job performance, and increased organizational citizenship behavior. Justice also helps alleviate many of the ill effects of dysfunctional work environments. For example, perceived fairness reduces workplace stress, vindictive retaliation, employee withdrawal, and sabotage.

Different Types of Justice

Generally speaking, judgments of fairness, and associated rules, can be said to have at least three categories. Interactional justice is often considered to have two subcategories, although some researchers consider a four-factor model of justice that threatens the subcategories of interactional as unique constructs. The three categories are as follows:

1. Distributive justice
2. Procedural justice
3. Interactional justice
   a. Interpersonal justice
   b. Informational justice

Distributive Justice

Research suggests that distributive justice is distinct from outcome favorability. Although these two variables are correlated, the latter is an appraisal of personal benefit, whereas the former concerns moral appropriateness. Individuals decide whether a given allocation decision is fair by examining the actual result in light of some idealized standard. Three standards or allocation rules have been most widely discussed: equity (allocations based on contributions or performance), equality (equivalent allocations for all), and need (allocation based on demonstrable hardship). Each of these rules may engender a sense of distributive fairness for some people under some circumstances. For example, an equity allocation rule is more likely to be seen as appropriate when the participants are North Americans, when the goal is to maximize performance, and when the divided benefit is economic. An equality allocation rule, however, is more likely seen as appropriate when the participants are East Asian, when the goal is to maximize group harmony, and when the benefit that is being divided is socioemotional.

An interesting line of research suggests that equity and equality allocation rules can engender distinct organizational climates. For example, when resources are divided on the basis of individual performance, there is a greater disparity between the top and bottom income brackets and a relative lack of cooperation. When resources are divided on the basis of equality, there is obviously less income disparity: Along with this comes greater social harmony and more intergroup cooperation.

To use each allocation rule, an individual needs to evaluate the relative gains (or losses) of at least two individuals. These cognitive operations are facilitated by the existence of a *referent other* that can serve as a sort of baseline standard. For example, someone seeking equality can expect uniform earnings among everyone in a group. This correspondence can best be ascertained with knowledge of others' profits. Equity is even more cognitively complex, so it is necessary to calculate earnings relative to contributions and to compare this ratio with the ratio of the referent. The intriguing result of these cognitive operations is that distributive justice may not be absolute. If a referent changes, a person's distributive fairness judgments may also change, even when the actual allocation remains constant. For example, when female workers are underpaid relative to their male counterparts, they may see this as distributively unfair when the more highly paid men are their referent. However, if they use other underpaid women as their referent, they may sometimes perceive less injustice.

Procedural Justice

Especially important to the study of organizational fairness is work on procedural justice. Procedural justice researchers argue that workers are interested in the outcomes they receive (i.e., in distributive justice). However, they add that employees also attend to the process by which these outcomes are assigned. Procedural justice is a strong predictor of such outcomes as organizational citizenship behavior, organizational commitment, trust, and so on. Generally speaking, processes are likely to be judged as fair on the basis of the following criteria: the consistency rule, the bias-suppression rule, the accuracy rule, the correctability rule, the representativeness rule (of which voice is a part), and the ethicality rule. Other research suggests that just procedures

should provide advance notice and not violate privacy concerns.

A large body of research has investigated the design of human resources systems in light of procedural justice considerations. This work has examined personnel procedures pertaining to performance evaluation, affirmative action programs, workplace drug testing, staffing, family-leave procedures, layoff policies, compensation decisions, conflict resolution procedures, and so on. Generally speaking, this work suggests that just procedures can bring benefits to organizations, in the form of more effective job behaviors and more positive work attitudes.

Interactional Justice

In addition to the outcome they receive and the process by which they receive it, people seem to be concerned with the way they are treated by others. Although identified more recently than distributive or procedural justice, interactional justices well established as an important workplace variable in its own right. Interactional justice predicts such outcomes as supervisory commitment, citizenship behavior, and job performance ratings. In addition, individuals are much more accepting of misfortunes such as downsizing when the process is implemented in an interactionally fair fashion. Given this practical value, attempts have been made to train decision makers to show more interactional justice. Such efforts have shown some success, and evidence suggests that training in interpersonal fairness can create a more effective work unit.

The rules associated with this interactional form of justice are now commonly broken into two categories: interpersonal and informational. Some researchers consider these to be subcategories of one justice construct, whereas others treat them as part of a four-factor model. In recent years, empirical evidence supporting the four-factor model has grown.

Interpersonal

Interpersonal justice is concerned with the dignity that people receive. Interpersonally fair treatment is respectful, honest, and considerate of others' feelings. A racist remark during a job interview would likely be seen as interpersonally unfair.

Informational

Informational justice is based on the presence or absence of explanations and social accounts. More broadly, informational justice involves communication: candor, thorough explanations, timeliness, and communication that is tailored to the needs of the recipient. A transparent promotion decision would likely be seen as informationally fair.

Studying Justice: Main Effects and Interactions

The different types of justice can be studied in terms of either their main effects or their interactions. Main effect studies compare the impact of one type of justice beyond the effect of another. Interaction studies explore how different types of justice work together to influence employee attitudes and behaviors.

Main Effects of Justice

Studies of the four-factor model of justice—distributive, procedural, interpersonal, and informational—suggest that all four dimensions have relevance for organizations. When tested together, each dimension was found to have a main effect on task performance, organizational citizenship behaviors, and counterproductive work behaviors.

Interactions Among Justice Types

Scholars have also examined the interactions between different types of justice. Generally speaking, individuals appear to be reasonably tolerant of a distributive injustice if the allocation procedures are viewed as fair. Likewise, they seem reasonably tolerant of a procedural injustice if the outcome is deemed to be appropriate. However, when the outcome and the process are simultaneously unjust, worker reactions are especially negative. Put differently, distributive justice strongly predicts work-relevant attitudes and behaviors when the procedure is unfair; it is a weaker predictor of attitudes and behaviors when the procedure is fair. Research has also documented a similar two-way interaction between distributive and interactional justice. Specifically, individuals can accept a poor outcome if it is assigned via a fair interaction. Conversely, they can accept a poor interaction if it yields fair outcomes. However, employees become distressed when both things go poorly at once.

Research has begun to consider the interaction among all three types of justice together. Investigations of the resulting three-way interaction have been quite promising. This line of inquiry finds that the aforementioned two-way interaction between distributive and procedural justice is significant only when interactional justice is low. To state the matter in a different way, reactions are most negative when individuals experience all three types of injustice at the same time. Only a few studies have been conducted, but so far all have supported the existence of this three-way interaction.

Why People Care About Justice

It is not intuitively obvious why workers would care about justice, as opposed to their pecuniary benefits. Several models have been proposed and tested, but it is important to recognize these are not mutually exclusive. Most experts believe that employee responses to injustice are influenced by multiple considerations. Here we will consider the best known accounts, including economic self-interest, the control model, the relational models, social exchange theory, and deontic justice. Traditionally, it was believed that people cared about justice primarily for self-interest and control. Recent research, however, suggests that more emphasis should be placed on justice for the sake of group standing and morality.

Economic Self-Interest

One early and still influential proposition is that the concern for justice is motivated by a sense of economic self-interest. The *fairest* system, according to this framework, is the one that maximizes long-term benefits. Even if a single decision is not personally beneficial, long-term payouts are apt to be greater if the individual can rely on fair distribution systems and procedurally just policies. There is evidence in favor of this self-interest model. For example, high performers tend to prefer equity allocations (presumably because their payment will be higher when based on contribution), whereas lower performers tend to prefer equality allocations (presumably because their payment will be higher when everyone earns equivalent amounts). Despite such evidence, self-interest does not seem to be the only motive for justice. For example, if a process is fair, individuals tend not to derogate decision makers, even when their outcomes are less than favorable.

The Control Model

Another early framework for understanding justice is the control model. According to the control model, justice matters because it provides people with some means of influencing decisions. This control could be exercised at the decision stage (somewhat akin to distributive justice) or at the process stage (somewhat akin to procedural justice and especially voice). On this basis, research has found that individuals will report some measure of fairness if either decision or process controls are present. When they lose both forms of control, of course, people tend to report less fairness. The control model was originally formulated within the context of legal proceedings. It has been especially influential in research pertaining to conflict management, plea bargaining, and employee involvement in decision making.

Relational Models

Relational models of justice (the *group-value model*, *relational model of authority*, and *group engagement model*) provide well-supported explanations as to why people care about justice. According to relational models, individuals are concerned with their social status or standing within important social groups. Injustice in this respect is perceived as a lack of respect on the part of authority figures, and an individual does not feel like an esteemed member of the organization or community. Justice, especially procedural justice, is desirable because it signals that a person is valued by the group and is unlikely to be excluded or exploited. This model makes intuitive sense and evidence supports it. For example, research suggests that procedural justice is a better predictor when it comes from groups with whom individuals closely identify, and it is a less efficacious predictor when it comes from groups not identified

with as closely. This is consistent with relational models, because standing should be of greater consequence within an important group and of less consequence within an unimportant one.

Social Exchange Theory

Social exchange theory provides an interpersonally oriented understanding of justice but does so in a somewhat different fashion than the relational models. According to this framework, employees often have economic exchange relationships with their employers and coworkers. These relationships are quid pro quo, with clearly delineated responsibilities for each party. Fair treatment, especially procedural and interactional justice, can create social exchange relationships. These higher quality relationships tend to involve emotional attachments, a sense of obligation and open-ended responsibilities to the other party. Justice, therefore, improves performance. Furthermore, it engenders citizenship behavior by improving the quality of the relationships among employees, between employees and their supervisor, and between employees and the organization as a whole. There is also solid evidence supporting this model. For example, the impact of procedural and interactional justice on work behavior seems to be at least partially mediated by the quality of interpersonal relationships.

Social exchange theory also provides a context for understanding the target similarity (sometimes called "multifoci") model in justice research. This perspective recognizes that judgments of fairness are made about a variety of sources and parties. Sources range from the organization as a whole, to individual people in a group (managers and coworkers), to external parties (such as suppliers). The target similarity model has important implications for justice research. As a more nuanced model of justice sources is developed, research can focus on the interpersonal dynamics between employees and others and the behaviors that result from focused fairness judgments.

Although the relational model and social exchange theory both highlight the importance of relationships, they emphasize somewhat different mechanisms. Notice that relational models maintain that justice is based on fear of exclusion from a desirable social group, as well as worries about exploitation from powerful decision makers. Social exchange theory, however, is based on a sense of obligation and a desire to help the other party.

Deontic Justice

An interesting feature of both the economic approach and the relational models is the assumption that justice ultimately reduces to self-interest; it is less clear whether the control model and social exchange theory make this same assumption. For clarity, we define a self-interest concern as one based on achieving a personal benefit or benefits. These benefits may be financial (as in the case of economic self-interest) or social (as in the case of the relational models). The deontic model of justice breaks with this tradition by proposing that justice matters for its own sake. This approach emphasizes the importance that at least some people tend to place on their moral duty to do the right thing.

The deontic model is unique in proposing that individuals care about justice even when there are no concerns with financial gain and group status, and there is evidence for this. For example, studies suggest that individuals will forgo money to punish an act of injustice. Research has also shown that participants will sometimes sacrifice earnings even without material benefits for doing so. Findings such as these suggest that neither economic gain nor social standing provides a full account of organizational justice. Research on deontic justice is important for another reason as well. By emphasizing moral duty, it builds bridges between empirical work on fair perceptions and normative work on business ethics.

Conclusion

As illustrated, organizational justice refers to perceptions of fairness in terms of outcomes, processes, and interactions. Research to date has concerned itself with identifying the antecedents and influences of these perceptions and the resulting attitudes and behaviors once these judgments have been made. However, it is important to keep in mind that these perceptions are subject to change, especially with a change in referent, the standard, by which fairness is assessed. Considering what each possible framework has to offer can develop a more complete sense of the dynamics

involved in any study of organizational justice and its effects.

Russell Cropanzano,
Jessica Kirk, and
Sharon Discorfano

See also Abusive Supervision; Adverse Impact/Disparate Treatment/Discrimination at Work; Applicant/Test-Taker Reactions; Attitudes and Beliefs; Bullying at Work; Corporate Social Responsibility; Cyberloafing at Work; Diversity Climate; Employee Performance Recognition; Equity Theory; Illegitimate Tasks; Justice in Teams; Negotiation; Mediation; and Arbitration; Organizational Climate; Organizational Retaliatory Behavior

Further Readings

Brockner, J. (2011). *A contemporary look at organizational justice: Multiplying insult times injury.* New York: Routledge.

Colquitt, J. A., Scott, B. A., Rodell, J. B., Long, D. M., Zapata, C. P., Conlon, D. E., & Wesson, M. J. (2013). Justice at the millennium, a decade later: A meta-analytic test of social exchange and affect-based perspectives. *Journal of Applied Psychology, 98,* 199–236.

Cropanzano, R., & Ambrose, M. A. (in press). *Oxford handbook of justice in work organizations.* Oxford, UK: Oxford University Press.

Cropanzano, R., Stein, J. H., & Nadisic, T. (2011). *Social justice and the experience of human emotion.* New York: Taylor & Francis.

Rupp, D. E., Shao, R., Jones, K. S., & Liao, H. (2014). The utility of a multifoci approach to the study of organizational justice: A meta-analytic investigation into the consideration of normative rules, moral accountability, bandwidth-fidelity, and social exchange. *Organizational Behavior and Human Decision Processes, 123,* 159–185.

ORGANIZATIONAL POLITICS

The term *organizational politics* refers to the informal ways people try to exercise influence in organizations through the management of shared meaning. As such, politics should not be viewed as an inherently bad or good phenomenon but rather one to be observed, analyzed, and comprehended to gain a more informed understanding of organizations and how they operate. Theory and research on organizational politics have fallen into essentially three categories. One area concerns itself with the nature of actual political behavior, types of tactics and strategies, and their consequences. A second category focuses on *perceptions* of politics in work environments by individual employees, the antecedents of such perceptions, and their consequences. The third, and most recent, category of research on organizational politics emphasizes the construct of political skill and demonstrates the role it plays in organizational behavior.

Political Behavior

Research in the domain of political behavior has been widespread and largely disconnected, being categorized in a number of distinct ways. Some of these include influence tactics, impression management, power, and social influence. Essentially, no matter the categorization, all of these behaviors reflect attempts to influence someone or some outcome. These behaviors are generally considered to be self-serving in nature and used to achieve some benefit for the influencer. The success of the influencing attempt depends on a multitude of factors, including the appropriateness and uniqueness of the attempt, the readiness of targets, the personal characteristics of both influencer and target, and the context. Influencing tactics have been studied singularly and in combinations or strategies of tactics, such as ingratiation as a single tactic or shotgun as a combination of many tactics.

Researchers have examined political behaviors as antecedents, outcomes, and moderators of myriad organizational phenomena. Furthermore, both the antecedents and consequences of political behaviors have been studied. Although there have been numerous studies of work-related outcomes of influence attempts, many have found mixed results. The specific attempts of ingratiation and rationality have demonstrated the strongest relationships with work outcomes. Nonetheless, these mixed results suggest a need to examine whether the influence tactics are successful or unsuccessful.

Perceptions of Organizational Politics

Although the study of actual political behavior is important, many researchers consider the perception of organizational politics of equal importance. It can be argued that individuals' perceptions of organizational politics may be just as influential on individual and organizational outcomes as the actual political behaviors occurring in the organization. People react to their perceptions of reality. Because people cannot see into the minds of others to determine the motive (e.g., self-serving or not) behind influencing attempts, they must rely on their perceptions of the attempts. The investigation of these perceptions is important, even if they differ from the actual reality of the organization.

Perceptions of organizational politics are individuals' subjective attributions of the extent to which behaviors occurring in the organization are of self-serving intent. There are three broad categories, which may influence individuals' perceptions of politics: personal influences such as personality factors, job environment influences such as autonomy and variety, and organizational influences such as organizational structure.

Several reactions to perceptions of politics have been investigated in the literature. Individuals perceiving a political environment could withdraw from the environment or have decreased job satisfaction, increased job anxiety, and even increased job involvement. With few exceptions, politics perceptions have been related to negative individual and organizational outcomes, such as decreased job satisfaction and increased actual turnover. Furthermore, researchers have found that perceptions of politics can be viewed as a stressor, causing strain reactions such as job anxiety.

However, these negative outcomes may not always occur. Specifically, there may be personal and environmental moderators of the perception–outcome relation. For example, if both supervisors and subordinates are striving toward the same goals, the impact of politics perceptions on important work outcomes is lessened. Furthermore, control and an understanding of the work environment lessens the extent to which organizational politics affects important work outcomes. Individual differences also affect the relationships between politics perceptions and negative outcomes, with some individuals working quite effectively in political environments.

Political Skill

It is commonly held that organizations are inherently political. However, despite the negative consequences of politics perceptions, some individuals seem to manage or even thrive in these environments. Political skill, which encompasses a skill set individuals use to understand the environment, choose the appropriate political behaviors, and act them out in ways that appear earnest, might explain how some individuals not only endure but are able to succeed in political environments. It accounts for individual influencing style. Political skill is seen as partly dispositional and partly learned.

Recent work has identified four dimensions of political skill:

1. Social astuteness

2. Interpersonal influence

3. Networking ability

4. Apparent sincerity

Social astuteness is an understanding of the environment and the actors involved in the environment. Interpersonal influence enables politically skilled individuals to choose and implement the correct influencing behaviors for a given situation. Networking ability is politically skilled individuals' abilities to garner and use social networks of people to their advantage. Finally, apparent sincerity involves coming across as honest and without ulterior motives. Political skill is different from other social variables, such as social skill, and has been shown to be an important coping mechanism in stressful and political environments.

Research has shown political skill to ameliorate the negative impacts of organizational stressors such as role stressors and perceptions of politics. Furthermore, politically skilled individuals choose influence tactics more effectively and use them more successfully. The politically skilled are seen as effective leaders, with greater levels of intrinsic and extrinsic career success.

Summary

In conclusion, organizational politics is a vast area of organizational study that spans many literatures and many decades of research. Several conclusions can be drawn through this brief introduction to the politics literature. It is important to examine not only political behavior but also individual subjective evaluations of organizational environments. Furthermore, when examining political behaviors, it is necessary to account for the style of the influencing technique as well as the success of the technique. This information will help bring consistency to the findings of political behavior studies.

Although organizational politics and perceptions of organizational politics largely have been related to negative personal and organizational outcomes, this negative relationship is avoidable. Political skill, although partly inherent, can be taught to train individuals to thrive in organizational environments they deem political. Furthermore, a number of very recent efforts have been made to characterize the positive side of politics, as conditions of influence in organizations that can be useful and effective, without necessarily being seen as negative.

Gerald R. Ferris and Robyn L. Brouer

See also Person–Environment Fit

Further Readings

Ferris, G. R., Adams, G., Kolodinsky, R. W., Hochwarter, W. A., & Ammeter, A. P. (2002). Perceptions of organizational politics: Theory and research directions. In F. J. Yammarino & F. Dansereau (Eds.), *Research in multi-level issues, Vol. 1: The many faces of multi-level issues* (pp. 179–254). Oxford, UK: JAI/Elsevier Science.

Ferris, G. R., & Hochwarter, W. A. (2011). Organizational politics. In S. Zedeck (Ed.), *APA handbook of industrial and organizational psychology* (Vol. 3, pp. 435–459). Washington, D.C.: American Psychological Association.

Ferris, G. R., Hochwarter, W. A., Douglas, C., Blass, R., Kolodinsky, R. W., & Treadway, D. C. (2002). Social influence processes in organizations and human resources systems. In G. R. Ferris & J. J. Martocchio (Eds.), *Research in personnel and human resources management* (Vol. 21, pp. 65–127). Oxford, UK: JAI/Elsevier Science.

Ferris, G. R., & Treadway, D. C. (2012). Organizational politics: History, construct specification, and research directions. In G. R. Ferris & D. C. Treadway (Eds.), *Politics in organizations: Theory and research considerations* (pp. 3–26). New York: Routledge/Taylor & Francis.

Ferris, G. R., & Treadway, D. C. (Eds.). (2012). *Politics in organizations: Theory and research considerations.* New York: Routledge/Taylor & Francis.

Ferris, G. R., Treadway, D. C., & Brouer, R. L., & Munyon, T. P. (2012). Political skill in the organizational sciences. In G. R. Ferris & D. C. Treadway (Eds.), *Politics in organizations: Theory and research considerations* (pp. 487–528). New York: Routledge/Taylor & Francis.

Ferris, G. R., Treadway, D. C., Kolodinsky, R. W., Hochwarter, W. A., Kacmar, C. J., Douglas, C., &

Frink, D. D. (2005). Development and validation of the political skill inventory. *Journal of Management, 31*, 126–152. doi:10.1177/0149206304271386

Hochwarter, W.A. (2012). The positive side of organizational politics. In G. R. Ferris & D. C. Treadway (Eds.), *Politics in organizations: Theory and research considerations* (pp. 27–65). New York: Routledge/Taylor & Francis.

Kacmar, K. M., & Baron, R. A. (1999). Organizational politics: The state of the field, links to related processes, and an agenda for future research. In G. R. Ferris (Ed.), *Research in personnel and human resources management* (Vol. 17, pp. 1–39). Stamford, CT: JAI.

Witt, L. A. (1998). Enhancing organizational goal congruence: A solution to organizational politics. *Journal of Applied Psychology, 83*, 666–674.

Organizational Retaliatory Behavior

Organizational retaliatory behavior refers to actions taken by disgruntled employees in response to perceived injustice at work. Organizational retaliatory behavior can take many forms, including withholding effort or citizenship behaviors, intentionally performing tasks incorrectly, purposely damaging equipment, taking supplies or materials, taking longer breaks than allowed, calling in "sick," spreading rumors about people at work, refusing to help others at work, failing to report problems so that they get worse, attending to personal matters while at work, purposely wasting time, sabotaging projects, and ignoring or verbally abusing people at work.

Although many behaviors that are classified as organizational retaliatory behavior may also be called counterproductive work behavior, workplace aggression, or employee deviance, organizational retaliatory behavior is distinct in at least two ways. First, organizational retaliatory behavior places a stronger emphasis on the situational context in which the behavior occurs as the main catalyst. In contrast, employee deviance implies an underlying dispositional tendency to engage in negative behaviors at work. *Employee deviance* also refers to behavior that violates organizational norms regarding what is proper and acceptable behavior. Therefore, to the extent that retaliation is common and accepted behavior in the workplace, it may or may not be considered deviant.

Second, *organizational retaliatory behavior* refers specifically to behaviors that are provoked by unfair treatment at work and implies a singular motive—to restore justice or equity—whereas counterproductive work behavior and workplace aggression take a broader perspective regarding the motives or intentions driving the behavior. For example, counterproductive work behavior is defined as behavior that has the potential to harm an organization or individuals at work, and although it may be driven by malicious intent, employees may perform counterproductive work behavior as a means of coping with job stress, as a reaction to unfairness, or out of ignorance or boredom. Workplace aggression, on the other hand, refers to behavior by employees that intends to harm, and the general aggression literature has identified two primary motives behind aggression. Aggression can be either reactive, or "hot," (e.g., an angry employee yells at a coworker) or proactive, or "cold," (e.g., an employee spreads damaging rumors about a coworker in order to better his or her own chance of receiving a promotion). Thus, although all organizational retaliatory behavior would be considered workplace aggression and all workplace aggression would be considered counterproductive work behavior, not all counterproductive work behavior or workplace aggression would be considered organizational retaliatory behavior.

Organizational retaliatory behavior can be understood using justice theory and social exchange theory. Each of these frameworks is briefly discussed below.

Justice Theory

Justice theory is the theoretical framework most commonly associated with organizational retaliatory behaviors. *Organizational justice* refers to the perceived fairness of interactions between individuals and organizations. Researchers have discussed justice in terms of its three forms: the perceived fairness of outcomes received from an employer (distributive justice), the perceived fairness of the processes and decisions that determine organizational outcomes independent of the fairness of the actual outcomes received (procedural justice), and the quality of interpersonal treatment received during the enactment of organizational procedures (interactional justice). Additionally, retributive justice is a newer form of justice in which victims or observers know the responsible party of an injustice and are motivated to reprimand the offender. According to justice theory, when employees experience some form of injustice or inequity, they will be motivated to restore justice. Any effort to balance the justice equation would be considered a retaliatory behavior.

All forms of justice have been shown to independently contribute to employee retaliation. However, procedural and interactional justice may be more important determinants of retaliatory behavior than distributive justice. Studies have shown that the negative effects of low distributive justice can be mitigated by the presence of high levels of either procedural or interactional justice. In other words, employees are less likely to retaliate for receiving fewer rewards if the procedures that determine those rewards are fair and/or if they are treated with dignity and respect throughout the reward distribution process. Employees, therefore, appear to place greater emphasis on the fairness of the procedures and how well they are treated as individuals than on the absolute level of outcomes received when deciding to retaliate. Research evaluating retributive justice found that there is also a component of core roles, whereby third-party employees will be more likely to retaliate on behalf of core team members with core roles against the perpetrator of injustice.

Because organizational retaliatory behaviors are assumed to be motivated by an employee's desire to restore justice, retaliatory behavior is more easily legitimized in the eyes of the performer: "I had to do something. I couldn't let him just get away with treating me like that." Hence a valuable contribution of this construct is the recognition that employees may perform these behaviors out of a desire to punish the offender and correct some wrong. This is outlined in the agent-system model, in which individuals generally direct their responses toward the perceived source of fair or unfair treatment. For example, individuals who are unjustly treated by their supervisor are more inclined to retaliate against the supervisor as opposed to the organization and vice versa. Also, unlike counterproductive work behavior, workplace aggression, or employee deviance, for which it is assumed that the consequences of these behaviors are negative, no such assumption is made regarding the outcome of retaliatory behavior. In fact, it is possible that retaliation may lead to positive outcomes because there are two ways to balance the justice equation. For example, if employees feel that their supervisor is not treating them fairly, they can balance the equation by treating their supervisor unfairly in return (e.g., delaying actions on projects that are important to that supervisor), or they may balance the equation by demanding fairer treatment from their supervisor by confronting the supervisor directly or by complaining to a higher level manager. Although both actions result in a more balanced justice equation, the former case has negative implications for the supervisor and organization, and possibly for the employee to the extent that his or her job performance is affected, whereas the latter case may lead to positive outcomes if the supervisor changes his or her behavior to treat the employee more fairly. Therefore, an important contribution of the organizational retaliatory behavior construct is that it recognizes the possibility that seemingly negative behaviors may be performed as a means to a more productive or prosocial end.

Social Exchange Theory

Organizational retaliatory behavior can also be understood within the framework of social exchange theory. According to social exchange theory, employees define their relationships with their organizations and their supervisors in terms of social exchange using the norm of reciprocity. Thus, employees engage in retaliatory behaviors to reciprocate unfavorable treatment received from the supervisor or organization. For example, research shows that abusive supervision is positively related to employee deviance, where individuals react more strongly when they have greater reciprocity beliefs. If employees believe the organization is looking out for their best interests or is fairly providing them with valued rewards, they will respond in kind by performing positive actions such as organizational citizenship behaviors. However, if employees believe the organization or the supervisor is withholding rewards or punishing them unfairly, they will reciprocate by reducing actions that benefit the organization or by performing actions that directly injure the organization.

A related theory, leader-member exchange theory, is also useful for understanding employee retaliatory behavior particularly when that behavior is directed toward a leader. According to leader-member exchange theory, individual, group, and organizational outcomes are affected by the quality of the relationships that employees have with their leaders. Employees who have a high-quality relationship with their leaders are more trusted by their leaders and are given more autonomy and decision-making input. Those employees are more likely to be high performers and to exhibit more citizenship behaviors as well. However, employees who have low-quality exchange relationships with their leaders are managed more closely and provided with less support from their leaders, and they are more likely to perform retaliatory behaviors in return. Additionally, when an organization's management style is ambiguous and has high situational uncertainty, employees are more apt to respond to abusive supervision in the form of both supervisor and organizationally directed deviance equally.

Although justice theory and social exchange theory take slightly different approaches to understanding retaliation, both emphasize the importance of the relationship that employees have with their organization and the people in them as antecedents to the performance of retaliatory behaviors.

Prevention

Because organizational retaliatory behaviors refer specifically to actions taken by employees in response to some perceived injustice or inequity, to prevent retaliatory behaviors, organizations should identify ways that they can increase employee perceptions of fairness at work. According to both justice and social exchange theories, the quality of employees' relationships with their supervisors is an important determinant of retaliatory behavior, so organizations should carefully select managers and screen out those who have histories of interpersonal conflict or other unethical behavior. Furthermore, organizations should make managers aware of the importance of treating all employees fairly and provide training to managers to equip them with the knowledge and skills necessary to provide employees with fair

and just treatment, including suppressing personal biases, basing decisions on accurate information, administering policies consistently, giving employees a voice in the decision-making process, allowing corrections to be made, behaving ethically, being truthful and honest with employees, and interacting with employees in a respectful manner. Additionally, organizational policies and procedures should be reviewed and revised if necessary so that they reflect the organization's commitment to fair treatment of all employees. If employees have confidence in their ability to redress a perceived injustice using formal channels, they may feel a lesser need to perform retaliatory behaviors or otherwise take matters into their own hands.

On the employee side, there is some evidence suggesting that individual differences in personality are related to the performance of retaliatory behaviors. At least one study found that individuals high in negative affectivity or low on agreeableness were more likely to perform retaliatory behaviors when they experienced low justice. Another study found that an external, opposed to internal, locus of control enhanced perceived aggression and was associated with more destructive retaliations. A look into the work on mindfulness has identified mindfulness as a trainable regulatory factor that mitigates retaliation via reducing ruminative thoughts and negative emotions associated with injustice. Overall, organizations should modify their selections and screening processes to identify individuals who have a greater propensity to perform retaliatory behaviors or who have histories of performing retaliatory behaviors in past jobs and also offer mindfulness training.

Cody J. Bok and Lisa M. Penney

See also Counterproductive Work Behaviors; Leader–Member Exchange Theory; Organizational Justice

Further Readings

Bies, R. J., & Moag, J. S. (1986). Interactional justice: Communication criteria of fairness. *Research on Negotiation in Organizations, 1,* 43–55.

Folger, R., & Skarlicki, D. P. (2004). Beyond counterproductive work behavior: Moral emotions and deontic retaliation versus reconciliation. In

P. E. Spector & S. Fox (Eds.), *Counterproductive work behavior: Investigations of actors and targets.* Washington, DC: American Psychological Association.

Greenberg, J. (1990). Employee theft as a reaction to underpayment inequity: The hidden cost of pay cuts. *Journal of Applied Psychology, 75,* 561–568.

Greenberg, J. (1993). Stealing in the name of justice: Informational and interpersonal moderators of theft reactions to underpayment inequity. *Organizational Behavior and Human Decision Processes, 54,* 81–103.

Jones, D. A. (2009). Getting even with one's supervisor and one's organization: Relationships among types of injustice, desires for revenge, and counterproductive work behaviors. *Journal of Organizational Behavior, 30*(4), 525–542.

Leventhal, G. S., Karuza, J., & Fry, W. R. (1980). Beyond fairness: A theory of allocation preferences. In G. Mikula (Ed.), *Justice and social interaction.* New York: Plenum.

Long, E. C., & Christian, M. S. (in press). Mindfulness buffers retaliatory responses to injustice: A regulatory approach. *Journal of Applied Psychology.*

Mitchell, M. S., & Ambrose, M. L. (2007). Abusive supervision and workplace deviance and the moderating effects of negative reciprocity beliefs. *Journal of Applied Psychology, 92*(4), 1159–1168.

Mitchell, M. S., & Ambrose, M. L. (2012). Employees' behavioral reactions to supervisor aggression: An examination of individual and situational factors. *Journal of Applied Psychology, 97*(6), 1148–1170.

Siegel Christian, J., Christian, M. S., Garza, A. S., & Ellis, A. P. (2012). Examining retaliatory responses to justice violations and recovery attempts in teams. *Journal of Applied Psychology, 97*(6), 1218–1232.

Skarlicki, D. P., & Folger, R. (1997). Retaliation in the workplace: The roles of distributive, procedural, and interactional justice. *Journal of Applied Psychology, 82,* 434–443

Skarlicki, D. P., & Latham, G. P. (1996). Increasing citizenship behavior within a labor union: A test of organizational justice theory. *Journal of Applied Psychology, 81*(2), 161–169.

Thau, S., Bennett, R. J., Mitchell, M. S., & Marrs, M. B. (2009). How management style moderates the relationship between abusive supervision and workplace deviance: An uncertainty management theory perspective. *Organizational Behavior and Human Decision Processes, 108*(1), 79–92.

Townsend, J., Phillips, J. S., & Elkins, T. J. (2000). Employee retaliation: The neglected consequence of poor leader-member exchange relations. *Journal of Occupational Health Psychology, 5*(4), 457–463.

ORGANIZATIONAL SENSEMAKING

Central to the concept of organizational sensemaking is the notion that explanations of issues cannot be found in any form of structure or system but in how organizational actors see and attribute meaning to things. From this perspective, strategies, plans, rules, and goals are not things that exist in an objective sense within (or external to) an organization. Rather, their source is people's way of thinking. Moreover, from a sensemaking perspective, the issue of whether one's view of the world is "correct" is not meaningful, and the correctness of a decision is contingent on the point of view that is being used to evaluate it.

The basic idea of sensemaking is that reality is an ongoing accomplishment that emerges from the efforts of organizational members to create order and understanding from their inherently complex environments. This becomes particularly important when the environment is changing rapidly and presenting unfamiliar issues and situations. Here sensemaking allows people to deal with uncertainty and ambiguity by creating their own rational accounts of the world that then enable them to take action.

Organizational sensemaking is not an established body of knowledge. It is a developing set of ideas drawn from a range of disciplines (e.g., cognitive psychology, social psychology, communication studies, and cultural analysis) concerning a particular way to approach organization studies. Following from this, it is unsurprising that various definitions of organizational sensemaking have been presented. For some, sensemaking is an interpretive process; for others, it is a metaphor for interpretation. Some define it as interpretation coupled with action. Others divide perception into noticing and sensemaking, whereby noticing must come before sensemaking so that there is something available to be made sense of. Still others define it as structuring the unknown or as a recurring cycle that uses retrospective accounts to explain surprises. The introduction of a sensemaking perspective into organization studies comes largely from the work of Karl E. Weick, who defined sensemaking, at its simplest, quite literally as "the making of sense." By this Weick meant that organizational actors not only come to an understanding of their environments but also create those same environments. The term *enactment* is used to capture the active role that organizational members play in creating such environments. By way of example, it is on the basis of their subjective perceptions of their occupational environment (their job roles, their managers, their employment conditions, etc.) that employees will take action and make a range of decisions, such as whether to come to work in the morning and, if so, whether they will do so on time, the decision as to what degree of effort and enthusiasm to invest, and ultimately the decision whether to leave an organization. To differing degrees, each of these decisions will influence individual, team, department, and organizational performance and productivity. Hence, how these individuals come to understand their environments provides the basis for action, ultimately shaping this same environment (at least in part). For top managers, sensemaking activities such as environmental scanning and issue interpretation are critical tasks that significantly influence organizational decisions and strategic change.

Seven Properties of Organizational Sensemaking

Organizational sensemaking is inherently complex (described by some as semi-inscrutable). Weick, however, attempted to systematically organize and explain this multifaceted concept by distilling seven key properties most often mentioned in the sensemaking literature:

1. *Retrospective.* All sensemaking processes involve some variation on the theme of retrospection or reflection on experience, which provides rationality and clarity to any outcome. This supports the notion that organizational strategic planning often involves the ability to write the story that fits recent history. Of note, although there is a consensus of opinion that it is primarily by examining history that we make sense, some scholars conclude that sensemaking is also prospective and that it is the act of envisioning the future that supplies the impetus for action.

2. *Plausible rather than accurate.* Meanings are constructed on the basis of reasonable explanations rather than through scientific discovery.

Although filtered information will almost certainly be less "accurate," it will undoubtedly be more understandable.

3. *Focused on and extracted by cues.* In organizational life, we attend to and extract certain elements, which form the material of the sensemaking process. However, whereas only partial knowledge is extracted from a mass of complex information, sense will be made of the whole on the basis of this subset. What is actually extracted and how it is made sense of are complex and dependent on a variety of issues, including context and goals.

4. *Enactive of sensible environments.* By taking action, organizations create (enact) their own environments (i.e., by doing something that produces some kind of outcome, constraints are then placed upon what that person or organization does next).

5. *A social process.* Sense is made in organizations through conversations, communications, and the exchange of ideas, and it is influenced by the actual, implied, or imagined presence of others. That is how sense becomes organizational.

6. *Ongoing.* Sensemaking is an ongoing, constantly negotiated process. The implication of this insight for organizational sensemaking is that organizations are always in the middle of complex situations, which they try to disentangle by making, then revising, provisional assumptions. Viewed as systems of sensemaking, a key organizational goal is to create and identify events that recur in order to stabilize their environments and make them more predictable.

7. *Grounded in identity construction.* The process of figuring out what is going on is a product of and a process based on who the sensemaker is and is becoming. In other words, how an organization (individual or group) identifies itself (who the sensemaker is) will define what it sees "out there." Simultaneously, this will influence identity (who the sensemaker is becoming).

The Process of Organizational Sensemaking

There is no formal model for organizational sensemaking, but the basic process is found in Weick's sensemaking "recipe." This is a sequence of enactment, selection and retention.

- In enactment, people actively construct the environments, which they attend to (by bracketing, rearranging, and labeling portions of the experience), thereby converting raw data from the environment into equivocal data to be interpreted.
- In selection, people choose meanings that can be imposed on the equivocal data by overlaying past interpretations as templates to the current experience. Selection produces an enacted environment that is meaningful in providing a cause-effect explanation of what is taking place.
- In retention, the organization stores the products of (what it sees as) successful sensemaking (enacted or meaningful interpretations) so that they may be retrieved in the future.

Because one property of sensemaking is that it is an ongoing process, there is no beginning point or end to this sequence.

Some view sensemaking as always being a conscious process, coming into play at times of shock or surprise or other particular occasions, for example, in times of perceived environmental uncertainty or turbulence. Others believe that although much of organizational life is routine and unsurprising and, as such, does not demand our attention, we nonetheless make sense in those habitual situations via the assimilation of subtle cues over time.

Organizational sensemaking can be driven by beliefs or by actions. In belief-driven processes, people start from an initial set of beliefs that are sufficiently clear and plausible and use them as nodes to connect more and more information into larger structures of meaning. People may use beliefs as expectations to guide the choice of plausible interpretations, or they may argue about beliefs and their relevancy to current experience, especially when beliefs and cues are contradictory. In action-driven processes, people start from their actions and grow their structures of meaning around them, by modifying the structures in order to give significance to those actions. People may create meaning in order to justify actions that are visible or irreversible.

Research in Organizational Sensemaking

A considerable amount of research in organizational sensemaking has focused on strategic issue processing and making sense of the competition. Some researchers have concluded that strategic competition is essentially a product of the tendency of competitors to construct some shared interpretation of a competitive arena within which strategic thinking and action become meaningful. Such studies have not only provided invaluable insight into the identification of industry competitors and the bases on which they complete but why competitive industry structures in industries and markets come to develop in the first place. This is exemplified by the early work carried out by Joseph F. Porac and his colleagues in the Scottish knitwear industry.

The sensemaking approach has also facilitated an understanding of organizational process, action, and structure in a range of contexts. Notable early studies include those of Jane E. Dutton and her colleagues regarding issue and agenda formation, and how stakeholders preserve their organization's image, and the work of Dennis A. Gioia and his associates, who investigated various aspects of change management, including top management teams' perceptions of identity and image under conditions of change. Key recent contributions have also been located in the context of change management. Additional contexts include technology diffusion and various aspects of organizational socialization and organizational crisis.

Weick's concept of sensemaking has been further formulated by researchers who have coined the term *sensegiving* to describe the process by which managers attempt to influence sensemaking and meaning construction of others toward a preferred definition of organization reality.

Gail P. Clarkson

See also Assessing Organizational Culture; Organizational Climate; Organizational Communication, Formal; Organizational Communication, Informal; Organizational Image; Organizational Structure

Further Readings

Kumar, P., & Singhal, M. (2012). Reducing change management complexity: Aligning change recipient sensemaking to change agent sensegiving.

International Journal of Learning and Change, 6(3/4), 138–155. doi:10.1504/IJLC.2012.050855

Maitlis, S. (2005). The social processes of organizational sensemaking. *Academy of Management Journal*, 48, 21–49. doi:10.5465/AMJ.2005.15993111

Porac, J. F., Thomas, H., & Baden-Fuller, C. (1989). Competitive groups as cognitive communities: The case of Scottish knitwear manufacturers. *Journal of Management Studies*, 26, 397–416.

Porac, J. F., Thomas, H., Wilson, F., Paton, D., & Kanfer, A. (1995). Rivalry and the industry model of Scottish knitwear producers. *Administrative Science Quarterly*, 40, 203–227.

Thurlow, A., & Mills, J. (2009). Change, talk and sensemaking. *Journal of Organizational Change Management*, 22(5), 459–579. doi:10.1108/09534 810910983442

Weick, K. E. (1979). *The social psychology of organizing*. 2nd ed. New York: McGraw-Hill.

Weick, K. E. (1995). *Sensemaking in organizations*. Thousand Oaks, CA: Sage.

Weick, K. E. (2001). *Making sense of the organization* (Vol. 1). Oxford, UK: Blackwell Business.

Weick, K. E. (2009). *Making sense of the organization* (Vol. 2). Oxford, UK: Blackwell Business.

Weick, K., Sutcliffe, K. M., & Obstfeld, D. (2005). Organizing and the process of sensemaking. *Organization Science*, 16(4), 409–421. doi:10.1287/orsc.1050.0133

ORGANIZATIONAL SOCIALIZATION

Organizational socialization (OS) is the process through which a newcomer to an organization transitions from outsider to integrated and effective insider. Also termed *newcomer adjustment* or *onboarding*, OS includes the acquisition or adjustment of shared values, attitudes, skills, knowledge, abilities, behaviors, and workplace relationships. OS occurs whenever an employee crosses an organizational boundary, internal or external. Nonetheless, OS research focuses, in the main, on transitions into organizations rather than functional or hierarchical transitions (e.g., lateral moves, promotion) within an organization.

Process Approaches to Organizational Socialization

Organizational Actions

Van Maanen and Schein developed a model of OS tactics on the basis of the premise that newcomer learning is dependent on the process as much as the content. They outlined six tactics organizations use to influence newcomers to adopt certain role orientations. The six tactics, each of which is bipolar, are collective–individual, formal–informal, sequential–random, fixed–variable, serial–disjunctive, and investiture–divestiture. These tactics have also been categorized as institutionalized (collective, formal, sequential, fixed, serial, and investiture) or individualized (their opposites). Institutionalized tactics are associated with a range of positive outcomes, including lower anxiety, role ambiguity, role conflict, and intent to quit, yet also lower role innovation, and higher levels of task mastery, job satisfaction, and organizational commitment. Recently, socialization resources theory has been proposed as an alternative means of understanding how organizations facilitate OS, focusing on specific practices such as providing job resources, supervisor support, and information.

Pre-Entry Organization Socialization

Pre-entry or "anticipatory" OS occurs during recruitment and selection when applicants meet employees from the hiring organization, in particular assessors, but also line managers and potential future colleagues. This allows applicants to develop more realistic expectations of working life in the organization. Realistic job previews have been proposed as one formal method by which to effectively achieve pre-entry OS.

Newcomer Proactive Behavior

Although anticipatory OS helps prepare newcomers, they are still likely to experience some surprises when their expectations do not match reality. Moreover, newcomers may encounter individualized OS tactics by the organization, which is effectively a lack of structured socialization. Hence newcomers may need to rely on their own proactive behaviors to achieve a better fit with their new work environment; these behaviors have been divided into three categories. The first category is change self, in which newcomers may ask questions or seek feedback to adapt themselves to better fit the environment. The second is mutual development, including behaviors such as networking and exchanging resources, through which newcomers aim to modify both themselves and the environment to achieve socialization. The third category is change role or environment, whereby newcomers may redefine the job or change work procedures, thus aiming to realize a better fit for themselves. In general, newcomers who behave more proactively report more positive outcomes, including greater learning and role clarity and lower intent to quit.

Research has also investigated proactive outcomes, that is, whether a proactive behavior achieved its intended goal. As an example, if a newcomer sought feedback on his performance (proactive behavior), to what extent did he actually obtain performance feedback (proactive outcome)? Proactive outcomes both mediate and moderate the relationships of proactive behaviors with outcomes, such as social integration and job satisfaction. Thus, alongside proactive behaviors, proactive outcomes also facilitate socialization.

Actions by Socialization Agents

Agents of OS, including managers, peers, mentors, buddies, and clients, can influence newcomers in both positive and negative ways. In terms of positives, insiders may facilitate adjustment by providing information, feedback, role models, social relationships, and support, as well as access to broader networks and other work-relevant resources. More recent research has indicated that colleagues can behave destructively toward newcomers; for example, abusive supervision has enduring detrimental effects on newcomers. Despite potential drawbacks, newcomers regard insiders as more useful sources of knowledge and support than formal orientation programs.

In recent years, this utility of socialization agents has been understood through models that identify the different types of capital that newcomers accrue. Key among these is social capital, acknowledging that resources, such as information, are embedded in social relationships. Hence, newcomers need to access (make connections with agents) and mobilize (motivate agents to help them) useful resources. Institutionalized OS

tactics from the organization, as well as proactive behaviors by newcomers, help newcomers accrue social capital, in turn facilitating learning, social integration, and successful performance. More recently, the capital model has been expanded to include psychological capital (positive motivational tendencies), human capital (knowledge, skills, and experience), and cultural capital (knowledge, skills, and experience that confer status in that society).

Content Approaches to Organizational Socialization

Newcomer Learning

Learning is the key element underlying OS, being antecedent to other outcomes such as task mastery, performance, and job satisfaction. To date, five information-based models of OS content have been developed, with associated measures. The domains identified have included task, role (or performance), group processes (also defined as a social or people domain), organization (sometimes broken down further into aspects including history and language), interpersonal resources (or coworker support), training, and future prospects.

Proximal Outcomes

A number of outcomes, either proximal or distal (or both), have been proposed as reflecting OS success. In the past decade, researchers have focused increasingly on proximal outcomes that more directly reflect socialization itself, rather than its longer term effects. Proximal outcomes include various types of knowledge (see "Newcomer Learning"), task mastery, role clarity, social integration, and performance. Of these, newcomer performance is critical for the newcomer and the organization as it determines whether the newcomer will be retained, yet for many roles, performance relies on other aspects of the OS process, such as learning that enables the newcomer to know what is considered good performance and social integration that gives the newcomer access to intangible resources such as advice.

Distal Outcomes

Attitudinal outcomes have been the traditional, distal indicators of OS success, including greater job satisfaction, organizational commitment, and more recently work engagement, as well as a lower intention of leaving and lower turnover. Newcomer well-being has been considered also, with OS success indicated by newcomers' increased well-being and reduced anxiety and stress, after the initial demands of organizational entry. Despite these developments, there remains no universally agreed point at which it could be claimed that a newcomer has been fully socialized, nor is there general agreement over how long OS lasts in different circumstances.

Individual Differences Affecting Organizational Socialization

Because newcomers play an active role in OS, the individual differences they bring to the new role are important as the other "side" of any OS equation. In terms of sociodemographic variables, work experience has mixed effects, although past transition experience positively predicts the rate of newcomer performance improvement; female newcomers report lower self-efficacy, higher self-punishing behavior, and poorer treatment by colleagues relative to male newcomers; those who differ in education and gender from their work groups tend to behave less proactively, whereas those who differ in terms of age behave more proactively.

Turning to personality variables, newcomers with high self-efficacy and behavioral self-management tend to use more independent strategies and have better OS outcomes. Furthermore, extroversion, openness to experience, and curiosity are associated with higher levels of proactive behavior, such as information seeking, feedback seeking, and relationship building, and proactive personality leads to more positive proximal outcomes, such as task mastery and social integration. Newcomers with better objective value fit show quicker and better adjustment outcomes.

Helena D. Cooper-Thomas
and Neil Anderson

See also Career Transitions; Feedback Seeking; Mentoring; New Employee Orientation; Organizational Socialization Tactics; Organizational Sociology; Person-Organization Fit; Proactive Personality; Realistic Job Preview; Social Norms and Conformity; Socialization; Employee Proactive Behaviors; Recruitment

Further Readings

Bauer, T. N., & Erdogan, B. (2014). Delineating and reviewing the role of newcomer capital in organizational socialization. *Annual Review of Organizational Psychology & Organizational Behavior*, 1, 439–457. doi:10.1146/annurev-orgpsych-031413-091251

Chao, G. T. (2012). Organizational socialization: Background, basics, and a blueprint for adjustment at work. In S. W. J. Kozlowski (Ed.), *The Oxford handbook of organizational psychology* (pp. 579–614), Oxford, UK: Oxford University Press,.

Cooper-Thomas, H. D., Paterson, N. L., Stadler, M. J., & Saks, A. M. (2014). The relative importance of proactive behaviors and outcomes for predicting newcomer learning, well-being, and work engagement. *Journal of Vocational Behavior*, 84, 318–331. doi:10.1016/j.jvb.2014.02.007

Cooper-Thomas, H. D., & Wright, S. (2013). Person-environment misfit: The neglected role of social context. *Journal of Managerial Psychology*, 28(1), 21–37. doi:10.1108/02683941311298841

Fang, R., Duffy, M. K., & Shaw, J. D. (2011). The organizational socialization process: Review and development of a social capital model. *Journal of Management*, 37(1), 127–152. doi:0.1177/014920 6310384630

Kammeyer-Mueller, J. D., Wanberg, C. R., Rubenstein, A., & Song, Z. (2013). Support, undermining, and newcomer socialization: Fitting in during the first 90 days. *Academy of Management Journal*, 56(4), 1104–1124. doi:10.5465/amj.2010.0791

Saks, A. M., & Gruman, J. A. (2012). Getting newcomers on-board: A review of socialization practices and introduction to socialization resources theory. In C. R. Wanberg (Ed.), *The Oxford handbook of organizational socialization* (pp. 27–55). Oxford, UK: Oxford University Press.

Van Maanen, J., & Schein, E. H. (1979). Toward a theory of organizational socialization. In B. M. Staw (Ed.), *Research in organizational behavior* (Vol. 1, pp. 209–264). Greenwich, CT: JAI.

ORGANIZATIONAL SOCIALIZATION TACTICS

Organizational socialization refers to the process whereby new employees move from being organizational *outsiders* to becoming functioning organizational *insiders*. Socialization has been called the process of *learning the ropes* of being an effective employee. Organizational socialization tactics are the ways organizations socialize new employees. These tactics vary on a number of dimensions that range from formal to informal in nature.

Successful socialization should lead to an effective employee who feels confident, has limited role conflict and role ambiguity, feels accepted by his or her coworkers, and understands the organization's culture. These positive *accommodation* (or adjustment) factors then lead to enhanced job satisfaction, organizational commitment, job performance, decreased stress, enhanced job and organizational fit, and lowered turnover. Unsuccessful socialization can be identified by poor performance, poor fit, and more rapid turnover. Research generally supports these relationships.

More specifically, research has shown that the process of socialization is not caused solely by the actions of newcomers, nor is it based solely on the attempts of organizational insiders to socialize new employees. Rather, the process of socialization involves the intersection of both of these forces acting on each other.

Socialization includes learning about four important factors of organizational life:

1. *Task information.* "How do I do this job well?"

2. *Confidence information.* "Do I have what it takes to do this job well?"

3. *Social information.* "Do I fit in with my coworkers and feel accepted?"

4. *Cultural information.* "Do I understand the norms and expectations of this organization?"

Research has shown that significant changes take place for newcomers at a number of delineations, such as prior to entry (typically referred to as the anticipatory socialization stage), after 3 months on the job to about 6 months on the job (typically referred to as the accommodation stage), and after 9 months on the job (typically referred to as the role management stage). After this point, newcomers and *old-timers* seem more similar than not. Longitudinal research that follows newcomers across time has found that early indicators of socialization are predictive of later outcomes. Outcomes include adjustment variables (acceptance by the group, learning the task, forming psychological contracts) and more distal outcomes such as stress, performance, organizational commitment, job satisfaction, turnover intentions, turnover, and person–job fit.

Much work on organizational socialization tactics stems from the work of John Van Maanen and Edgar Schein (1979), who delineated six tactics that vary on a number of dimensions:

1. Level of interaction with other newcomers (ranging from formal to informal)

2. Number of newcomers within a given cohort (ranging from collective to individual)

3. Order in which socialization takes place (ranging from sequential to random)

4. Identification of whether there is a specific time frame for socialization (ranging from fixed to variable)

5. Identification of how newcomers are trained (ranging from serial to disjunctive)

6. Identification of whether newcomers are stripped of their old identities or not (ranging from investiture to divestiture)

Subsequent research has shown that these organizational socialization tactic dimensions developed by Van Maanen and Schein can be thought of as representing a continuum that ranges from highly institutionalized approaches to socialization (e.g., new army recruits going through boot camp) to more individualized approaches (e.g., a new college professor during the first term). To illustrate the differences between these two types of tactics, think first of a new recruit in boot camp in the army. This individual is in a collective situation with other recruits, undergoing a sequential process of physical demands, following a strict timetable of events, learning tasks serially, and being stripped of any individual identity during the process in favor of a collective identity with the army. However, a new college professor might be the only or one of a few new hires in a given year; undergoing a random sequence of learning things independently; undergoing no set time frame for socialization other than tenure, which is some years away; learning tasks in a disjunctive fashion; and valued for expertise and training at the individual level. The recruit is undergoing a classic case of institutionalized organizational socialization tactics with a high degree of routinization, and the college professor is undergoing a classic case of individualized organizational socialization tactics with a relatively loose structure and indoctrination. This may be because of the norms that are indoctrinated in professors as they earn their doctoral degrees, so that less direction is needed once they begin in the profession.

Tactics that are highly institutional tend to be preferred by new employees, perhaps because the definite nature of these tactics helps orient new employees and decrease ambiguity about what they should be doing. However, the potential downside of these tactics is a decrease in innovation and creativity. This is a dilemma organizations need to approach carefully.

Organizations vary hugely in terms of how they use these tactics. Research has shown that institutionalized tactics are negatively related to self-efficacy but positively related to organizational commitment, job satisfaction, and intentions to remain. Since that time, research on organizational socialization tactics has continued and has been associated with diverse outcomes.

For example, research studying psychological contract breach for newcomers found that those who perceived breaches were more likely to experience an informal socialization process. Additionally, newcomers' perceptions of fit are related to tactics that are fixed and serial. Researchers also found that institutionalized tactics were significantly related to newcomers' relations with organizational insiders as well as negatively related to role conflict and that serial and investiture tactics were negatively related to subsequent turnover for newcomers working at large financial services organizations.

In addition to organizational tactics, organizational insiders also influence new employee socialization. Two categories of these insiders exist: supervisors or leaders who oversee newcomers and coworkers or peers who work with new employees. A major goal of organizational socialization is to understand one's role in relation to these organizational insiders as well as to feel accepted by them. Newcomers who are able to do this are much more likely to become successfully socialized and integrated into their new organization. Research has also shown that newcomer personality interacts with leadership to affect adjustment and relate to turnover. A study that examined new executives across 4 years found that those who were introverted and formed strong leadership ties were less likely to turn over than those introverts who did not form these ties. For extroverts, leadership relationships made no difference.

As mentioned earlier, newcomers also use tactics to learn about their new jobs, coworkers, and organizations. These tactics usually revolve around information and feedback acquisition. Newcomers vary on many dimensions, but a key dimension is proactive personality. Those who are very proactive will seek out information, ask for feedback, and initiate ways to learn about the job, coworkers, and organization. Their less proactive colleagues will be less likely to engage in these behaviors and therefore will be more susceptible to the organization's influence.

Information seeking is related to the outcomes of socialization, by increasing knowledge regarding role expectations and by increasing confidence to accomplish personal goals. In other words, information seeking should be positively related to self-efficacy and negatively related to role ambiguity. Furthermore, by voicing questions and seeking information and feedback, individuals deal with conflicting information coming from different sources, leading to reduced role conflict. Finally, information seeking may facilitate social interactions and signal to others that an individual is motivated to do a good job, leading to acceptance by peers.

Several studies have found that information seeking plays an important role in newcomer socialization. Seeking and acquiring information is key to understanding one's roles, the norms of the group and organization, and the expectations and interconnections among colleagues and functional areas. However, seeking too much information can be costly to newcomers, who might come across as "not getting it." Timing may be the key to understanding when newcomers should seek information as well as understanding how to do it and from whom. Furthermore, information seeking has been shown to relate to distal outcomes such as satisfaction, job performance, and intentions to remain, depending on the type and source of information obtained.

Another factor that should matter in new employee socialization is personality. Some newcomers are proactive in terms of their personalities, and these individuals should approach the socialization process differently than newcomers who are not as proactive. Similarly, newcomers who are introverted need to establish strong interpersonal relationships to help them navigate the organization, whereas more extroverted newcomers are able to learn from multiple sources.

In summary, organizational socialization tactics seem to matter for newcomer organizational socialization. What remains to be seen is the relative impact they will have on the process and whether outcomes mediate the relationship between tactics and more distant outcomes.

Talya N. Bauer

See also New Employee Orientation; Socialization, Employee Proactive Behaviors; Training

Further Readings

Ashforth, B. E., Sluss, D. M., & Saks, A. M. (2007). Socialization tactics, proactive behaviors, and newcomer learning: Integrating socialization models. *Journal of Vocational Behavior, 70*, 447–462. doi:10.1016/j.jvb.2007.02.001

Bauer, T. N., Bodner, T., Erdogan, B., Truxillo, D. M., & Tucker, J. S. (2007). Newcomer adjustment during organizational socialization: A meta-analytic review of antecedents, outcomes, and methods. *Journal of Applied Psychology, 92*, 707–721. doi:10.1037/0021-9010.92.3.707

Bauer, T., Morrison, E. W., & Callister, R. (1998). Organizational socialization: A review and directions for future research. In G. R. Ferris (Ed.), *Research in personnel and human resources management* (Vol. 16, pp. 149–214). Greenwich, CT: JAI.

Fisher, C. D. (1986). Organizational socialization: An integrative review. In K. M. Rowland & G. R. Ferris (Eds.), *Research in personnel and human resources management* (Vol. 4, pp. 101–145). Greenwich, CT: JAI.

Kammeyer-Mueller, J., Wanberg, C., Rubenstein, A., & Song, Z. (2013). Support, undermining, and newcomer socialization: Fitting in during the first 90 days. *Academy of Management Journal, 56*, 1104–1124. doi:10.5465/amj.2010.0791

Kim, T., Cable, D. M., & Kim, S. (2005). Socialization tactics, employee proactivity, and person–organization fit. *Journal of Applied Psychology, 90*, 232–241.

Morrison, E. W. (1993). Longitudinal study of the effects of information seeking on newcomer socialization. *Journal of Applied Psychology, 78*, 173–183.

Van Maanen, J., & Schein, E. H. (1979). Toward a theory of organizational socialization. In B. M. Staw (Ed.), *Research in organizational behavior* (Vol. 1, pp. 209–263). Greenwich, CT: JAI.

Wanberg, C. (2012). *Oxford handbook of organizational socialization*. Oxford, UK: Oxford University Press.

ORGANIZATIONAL SOCIOLOGY

Organizational sociology examines the relationships between formal and informal organizations and their social, cultural, political, and economic environments. Broadly, organizational sociologists analyze three distinct types of organizational relationships: how society affects organizations, how organizations affect other organizations, and how organizations affect society. In answering theoretical questions arising from these three orientations, organizational sociologists acknowledge that there are many different types of organizations, such as large corporations, charities, governmental associations, police departments, and many others. Indeed, organizations consist of the coordination of work between two or more individuals sharing a common goal; therefore, both street gangs and multinational corporations are organizations. In this light, organizational sociologists analyze abstract organizational features and processes and generalize their findings to other types of organizations.

Organizational sociology moves beyond the rational systems perspective specifying that organizations exist merely to maximize profits or return on investment and instead recognizes that organizations do not operate in a social vacuum. Legal codes, social norms, and cultural expectations all influence the individuals within an organization and organizational survival. Drawing on the metatheoretical paradigms of sociology, organizational sociologists typically perceive social interaction through three lenses: symbolic interaction, structural functionalism, and conflict. Symbolic interactionist scholars study how individuals construct and understand meaning in organizations. A research question from this perspective could be, How do the characteristics of an organization activate certain status characteristics in work teams? A structural functionalist perspective examines the relationships between various organizational processes emphasizing equilibrium. A research question from this perspective asks, Why, as large organizations dominate the market, do smaller organizations proliferate in the market's periphery? Finally, a conflict perspective addresses the dynamics of power and control in organizations. A scholar from this perspective could ask, How do organizational leaders retain their power and status when going through a merger? It is important to note that these perspectives orient organizational sociologists toward particular theories or methodologies, but these perspectives do not substitute social theory.

Organizational sociology shares many linkages to almost all other subfields within sociology, such as social movement research or the sociology of education, and shares boundaries with many cognate disciplines, such as psychology, communication studies, management, human resource management, anthropology, and strategy. Topics within organizational sociology include, but are certainly not limited to, organizational culture, technology, labor, organizational environments, organizational identity, and inequality. Particularly relevant to industrial and organizational psychology, organizational sociology places the individual differences between workers, managers, and external stakeholders into the social structure of the organization, suggesting many new and exciting possibilities for innovative research.

Foundations

The origins of organizational sociology lie in a confluence of work by early scholars and practitioners in engineering, management, and psychology. During the first half of the 20th century, management theorists, such as Frederick Taylor and Henri Fayol, and mechanical engineers sought to increase the efficiency of the production process within factories through the standardization of the entire shop floor, ranging from identical tolerances for all bolts to reducing the variance of workers' motion along the assembly line. The rational systems approach to organizations tends to emphasize goal specificity and formal organizational structure as the defining characteristics of an organization and necessary requirements to maximize productivity and therefore profits. In this light, organizational performance depends on the efficient and productive coordination of both the mechanical systems of production and the people within the organization. Natural systems theorists, on the other hand, recognize that organizations are aggregations of people, each with varying, and even competing interests and goals; these theorists reject the notion that organizations operate through purely rational means. During the 1920s and 1930s, Elton Mayo and his colleagues examined work processes and aspects of human relations at the Hawthorne electrical plant, revealing the importance of informal organizational structure as a determinant of employee satisfaction and productivity. Natural systems theorists, therefore, emphasize goal complexity and informal organizational structure, acknowledging that organizations are often less than efficient and cannot be treated as machines that can merely be adjusted from time to time. The rational and natural systems perspectives of organizations, although vastly different, served as a cleft rock on which the foundation of organizational sociology was built.

The sociological study of organizations was spurred by the 1946 and 1947 translations of Max Weber's essays on bureaucracy and the 1949 translation of Robert Michels's *Political Parties*. Although efficiency and standardization were held in the utmost regard by rational systems theorists, the increasing rationalization of society was a principal concern of Weber's writings. For Weber, the bureaucratic organizational form replaces social relationships with depersonalized calculations of value in the context of market transactions. For instance, the practice of barn raising, popular in the 18th and 19th centuries, was a community event at which each contributed to building a community member's barn, absent of economic exchange; in contrast, to construct a barn in contemporary society requires a bank loan, hiring an array of construction professionals, and multiple inspections, each element occurring as a result of voluminous rules and procedures. Bureaucracies, as a function of rationality, exhibit a variety of organizational attributes: hierarchical authority structures, authority residing within the position and not the characteristics of the individual, rules prescribing interaction between incumbents, and rules prescribing jurisdictions of responsibility. Finally, Weber recognized that bureaucracy, although often slow and seemingly dysfunctional, can also be an extremely efficient organizational form.

Robert Michels, a student of Weber, took a more critical view of bureaucracy. Michels's iron law of oligarchy specifies that organizations become more bureaucratic as they grow larger, in an effort to maintain efficiency; however, through centralization, power becomes concentrated in the upper echelons of the organization. Even the most democratic organizations become oligarchies, controlled by a small cadre of powerful individuals. It is in the best interest of those at the top of the oligarchy to preserve their power, thus leading to corruption. Bureaucracies, therefore, negatively affect societal welfare and are a cause of concern. The accessibility of Weber's and Michels's work led to an outgrowth of theorizing about organizational structures and processes as abstract generalizations of organizations among American scholars, such as Robert Merton, Philip Selznick, and Peter Blau, among many others. For the first time, organizations were seen as the object of study rather than only the context of social action.

Following World War II, scientists working in diverse fields, such as biology, physics, and systems engineering, began to focus on the complexity and interactions among elements at every level of analysis within physical and social systems. For organizations, this paradigmatic shift, open systems theory, turned attention to porous organizational boundaries and the impact that multiple interests of social groups, both internal and external, have on organizations. For instance, constituent components of organizational structure are often only loosely coupled, meaning that a change in one aspect of the organization may not affect all other aspects. The open systems perspective of organizations led to an explosion of sociological theorizing of organizations and led to the contemporary framework of the field.

Organizational Ecology

Michael Hannan and John Freeman's 1977 article "The Population Ecology of Organizations" set forth a vibrant research program, analyzing organizational populations through the paradigmatic lens of Darwinian evolution and biological models of population processes. Organizational ecologists, therefore, reject the central postulate of rational systems theory that organizations freely adapt to changing environmental conditions and instead emphasize that organizational inertia leaves organizations vulnerable to environmental selection pressures, engendering substantial organizational diversity. Accordingly, organizations may be able to adapt to small environmental perturbations, but organizational death and birth accompany larger environmental changes. In this light, organizational vital rates and measures of organizational change constitute the most informative dependent variables relevant to the analysis of organizational populations.

Because of its theoretical lineage from the biological sciences, two methodological conventions underlie organizational ecology research: the inclusion of all members of an organizational population and an emphasis on organizational outcomes—mortality rate, founding rate, measures of change—as time-dependent processes. First, organizational ecologists collect data on every organization within a specific population; failure to include a full sample can obscure the true relationships between variables. For many people, organizations are large, Fortune 500 companies that make news headlines with the introduction of new product lines and have numerous multinational subsidiaries; however, the overwhelming majority of organizations are relatively small, containing fewer than 50 employees. Therefore, myopically analyzing large organizations raises concerns of validity by introducing bias through the omission of important, small organizations. Second and related, ecologists collect data on organizations over a period of time to both reduce the effects of survivor bias and examine how organizations and their environments covary temporally. For instance, organizational birth and death are daily occurrences; few organizations achieve the longevity of Kongo Gumi, the longest running family business, spanning 1,428 years, or even more than 100 years, such as Coca-Cola. It is also likely that contemporary construction companies and beverage manufacturers are different in significant aspects from their organizational ancestors. Samples of data that are drawn at a single point in time, therefore, are unable to discern the causal mechanisms underlying organizational birth, survival, or death.

Organizations compete for a set of resources, referred to as niche width. According to organizational ecologists, organizations adopt one of two strategies for survival: specialist or generalist. Specialist organizations compete over a relatively narrow range of environmental resources; examples include an artisanal bakery and a craft brewery. These organizations tend to be small and vulnerable to environmental changes. On the other hand, generalists compete over a large range of environmental resources; these organizations include big-box retail stores and mass producers of beer. Generalists tend to be larger organizations and are able to cope with environmental change better than specialists. Although niche width directly influences organizational survival, organizational ecologists have also demonstrated the explanatory power of many other variables. For instance, the "liability of smallness" and "the liability of newness" posit that organizational viability decreases for smaller and younger organizations, respectively. Finally, density dependence, or the composition of organizational forms in the population, also affects vitality rates. For example, population density increases organizational founding rates until the population's carrying capacity inhibits further growth, and organizational founding rates then decrease; the converse is true with regard to organizational mortality. Therefore, both the characteristics of organizations and the characteristics of their environments influence performance outcomes.

Niche width, although important to all organizational ecology theories, lies at the heart of resource partitioning theory. Resource partitioning theory begins with the observation of a paradox: How, as large organizations begin to dominate markets, do the founding rates and mortality rates of small specialist organizations increase and decrease, respectively? The theory posits that as generalist organizations move toward the center of the market, resources open at the periphery, a

proposition for which statistical and geometric analyses offer support. These new pockets of resources then provide sustenance for specialist organizations, thereby increasing founding rates and decreasing mortality rates for small organizations. Resource partitioning theory has been successfully applied to a variety of organizational populations, including documenting the rise of large Bulgarian newspapers and explaining the proliferation of American craft breweries since the 1990s. This theory has expanded recently to include increasingly prevalent oppositional identity movements, such as craft brewing and organic farming.

From its founding and initial growth in the 1970s, organizational ecology has become one of the most theoretically cohesive and well-developed research programs in organizational sociology.

Neoinstitutionalism

Institutional analysis in organizational sociology has a long history. Early theorists, such as Philip Selznick, acknowledged that social and cultural forces, separate from supply and demand curves, influence organizational structure and performance, breaking away from the rational systems perspectives. In this light, early institutional scholars focused on the effects of legal codes, political power, and cultural norms on organizations. However, during the late 1970s and early 1980s, institutional analysis underwent an intellectual renaissance, spurred by the publication of two seminal works: John Meyer and Brian Rowan's 1977 article "Institutionalized Organizations: Formal Structure as Myth and Ceremony" and Paul DiMaggio and Walter Powell's 1983 article "The Iron Cage Revisited: Institutional Isomorphism and Collective Rationality in Organizational Fields." These influential papers brought full attention to the cognitive foundations of institutions, complementing the earlier emphasis on the normative and regulative dimensions of institutions and presenting a novel theoretical lens through which to view organizational processes.

Neoinstitutional scholars describe institutions as rationalized myth and ceremony. Institutions specify the rules and procedures to accomplish a specific goal within a given societal context. Furthermore, the cognitive reframing of institutions emphasizes that individuals do not have to adhere to institutional beliefs themselves for institutions to exert powerful effects; instead, individuals must only believe that others adhere to institutional beliefs. In this light, individuals will act in accordance with institutional beliefs and values to achieve legitimacy. Indeed, institutional beliefs diffuse across the social landscape, becoming taken for granted among individuals. For instance, whereas rational performance metrics were scarce and underdeveloped at the turn of the 20th century, 100 years later, performance metrics are ubiquitous across every domain of social life, including nonprofit organizations and schools.

As the central premise of neoinstitutional theory, all organizations exist within an institutional environment, in which certain norms, values, and expectations become taken for granted among social actors; any opposite course of action is simply unthinkable. Indeed, if organizational ecologists ask why there are so many different types of organizations, neoinstitutional scholars ask why organizations are so similar. For example, consider that all Fortune 500 companies contain human resource departments or accounting departments (two of the numerous points of convergence); a large degree of similarity exists across organizations, regardless of industry or even nation. In this manner, legitimate organizations promote diversity and performance metrics and adorn their structures with human resource departments and boards of directors. Organizations conform to socially valued aspects of their institutional environments to attain legitimacy from external audiences. To conform to their institutional environments, organizations decouple their technical cores from their organizational structures. In this manner, organizations can maintain legitimacy without affecting their means of production.

Three mechanisms promote organizational isomorphism with the institutional environment: coercion, mimesis, and normative pressures. Governmental laws or powerful organizations can coerce other organizations to alter their structures as a condition of an ongoing relationship. For instance, the U.S. government requires federal contractors and subcontractors to be compliant with affirmative action policies. Mimesis occurs when organizations imitate highly visible organizations often during periods of uncertainty. Finally, normative pressures arise from professional groups and associations, whose members, because of their similar education and training, approach organizing in very similar ways, which constrains the diversity of organizational forms.

Resource Dependence and Networks

Amid the proliferation of macro-sociological theories of organizations arising in the late 1970s, Jeffrey Pfeffer and Gerald Salancik's 1978 book *The External Control of Organizations: A Resource Dependence Perspective* brought concepts of power and control within interorganizational networks into full focus. Briefly, the resource dependence perspective emphasizes that an organization's external environment contains other organizations, each holding various and often competing interests. Furthermore, an array of relationships, such as supplier–buyer and subsidiary–parent, ties organizations into a network of economic and social exchange relationships. Organizations, therefore, can gain power and influence by controlling other organizations' access to resources. Interestingly, resource dependence arguments are the most applicable of the three theoretical traditions in organizational sociology to the field of management. For example, Pfeffer and Salancik spend the first four chapters of their book discussing the theoretical framework of resource dependency and the remaining chapters detailing how organizations can manage and exploit resource dependencies.

The resource dependence perspective suggests various pragmatic strategies that organizational leaders can implement to alleviate external pressures from other organizations. The simplest strategy to increase organizational power is to increase firm size, relative to competitors, conferring much of the advantages of a monopoly. Another strategy is to maintain multiple interorganizational relationships that can transfer resources. Although these strategies can effectively increase organizational power and independence, organizational leaders are often unable to implement such simple tactics because of the constraints of the external environment, in which case organizations can implement various bridging strategies. First, organizations can form alliances with other organizations through the coordination of work toward common goals. Organizations can also engage in cooptation by internalizing external groups into decision-making positions. Cooptation is ubiquitous among boards of directors. Finally, mergers and acquisitions represent the most costly strategy of dependency reduction and occur through vertical integration, horizontal integration, or diversification. The final set of strategies organizations can pursue is in the form of collective action, through the formation of associations, such as trade associations, or through coordinated political action. Organizational political action—campaign contributions, lobbying, industry–government networks—has become a focus of contemporary organizational sociology, detailing how organizations have been able to influence the creation and enforcement of laws.

The central emphasis in resource dependence analysis on interorganizational linkages also relates to and enriches network analyses of organizations. For instance, the structure of the social networks surrounding alliance formation and board interlocks often reveals important organizational dynamics and connects micro-level analyses to macro-level outcomes. In addition to networks between employees, network analyses provide insight into novel forms of organizing. The network perspective of organizations describes that, as environmental complexity has increased since the 1970s, organizations have become smaller and have externalized integral components of their technical cores in an effort to enhance flexibility. An organization able to quickly adapt to turbulent, complex environments is more likely to survive. Brian Uzzi, extending the network perspective, examined firms in the New York garment industry in a series of groundbreaking papers, finding that firms embedded in rich, relational ties with other firms receive substantial economic advantages over firms with relationships exclusively characterized by arm's-length or contractual ties. Importantly, this trend reverses if an organization has too many relational ties.

Concluding Remarks

Organizational sociology considers the social and cultural environments as factors that influence organizational structure and performance. From its foundations, organizational sociology has engaged a wide audience, constructing theoretical arguments from many disciplines, particularly industrial and organizational psychology. Indeed, social and cultural environments consist of complex aggregations of attitudes, personalities, and cognitions. Therefore, although organizational sociology typically focuses on broad societal patterns, psychological processes underlie social structure and organizational phenomenon. As in the past, future research integrating psychological theories and sociological theories will greatly advance the scientific understanding of organizations and organizational phenomenon.

Daniel J. Davis

See also Institutional Theory, Organizational Structure, Changing Demographics: Implications for Organizations; Emerging Markets and Globalization; Political Polarization: Implications for Organizations

Further Readings

Adler, P. S. (Ed.). (2009). *The Oxford handbook of sociology and organization studies: Classical foundations*. Oxford, UK: Oxford University Press.

Adler, P. S., du Gay, P., Morgan, G., & Reed, M. (Eds.). (2014). *The Oxford handbook of sociology, social theory, and organization studies: Contemporary currents*. Oxford, UK: Oxford University Press.

Caroll, G. R. (1985). Concentration and specialization: Dynamics of niche width in populations of organizations. *American Journal of Sociology, 90*(6), 1262–1283.

Carroll, G. R., & Hannan, M. T. (1999). *The demography of corporations and industries*. Princeton, NJ: Princeton University Press.

DiMaggio, P. J., & Powell, W. W. (1983). The iron cage revisited: Institutional isomorphism and collective rationality in organizational fields. *American Sociological Review, 48*(2), 147–160.

Greenwood, R., Oliver, C., Suddaby, R., & Sahlin-Andersson, K. (Eds.). (2013). *The Sage handbook of organizational institutionalism*. Thousand Oaks, CA: Sage.

Hannan, M. T., & Freeman, J. (1977). The population ecology of organizations. *American Journal of Sociology, 82*(5), 929–964.

Hannan, M. T., Pólos, L., & Carroll, G. R. (2007). *Logics of organization theory: Audiences, codes, and ecologies*. Princeton, NJ: Princeton University Press.

Meyer, J. W., & Rowan, B. (1977). Institutionalized organizations: Formal structure as myth and ceremony. *American Journal of Sociology, 83*(2), 340–363.

Pfeffer, J., & Salancik, G. (1978). *The external control of organizations: A resource dependence perspective.* New York: Harper & Row.

Powell, W. W. (1990). Neither market nor hierarchy: Network forms of organization. *Research in Organizational Behavior, 12,* 295–336.

Scott, R. W., & Davis, G. F. (2007). *Organizations and organizing: Rational, natural, and open systems perspectives.* New York: Pearson Prentice Hall.

Uzzi, B. (1997). Social structure and competition in interfirm networks: The paradox of embeddedness. *Administrative Science Quarterly, 42*(1), 35–67.

ORGANIZATIONAL STRUCTURE

Organizational structure refers to the formal and informal manner in which people, job tasks, and other organizational resources are configured and coordinated. Although *structure* sounds like a singular characteristic, it is composed of a number of dimensions, because there are multiple ways in which the employees within an organization and the job tasks to be carried out can be structured. Among the most commonly studied aspects of organizational structure are *formalization, centralization,* and *complexity.*

Fundamental Elements of Organizational Structure

Formalization refers to the extent to which organizational policies, practices, and ways of completing tasks are standardized. Specifically, highly formalized organizations are those in which rules for expected behavior are clearly articulated and followed. Conversely, organizations that exhibit low levels of formalization have few standardized practices or rules. Formalization is often conveyed through formal mechanisms and documents such as job descriptions. Additionally, informal activities, such as practices that are reinforced through group norms or informal conversations with other members of the organization, serve to support the level of formalization.

Centralization refers to the distribution of decision-making authority, information, and power throughout an organization. In some organizations, all or most decisions are made by a small group of individuals, often the top management team. In highly centralized organizations, power is maintained by a select few individuals and decisions are made by a central cadre of employees. Conversely, in highly decentralized organizations, power and decision making are spread across individuals throughout the organizations. Individual employees in these organizations have the latitude and authority to make day-to-day decisions and other important decisions that affect their work. The centralization of power in an organization may be dictated and described in formal rules, policies, and job descriptions. It is also common, however, that centralization occurs informally through the behaviors and norms introduced and reinforced by those in power, such as a leader who purposefully limits access to key information.

Complexity has represented a number of different aspects of organizational structure throughout history (additional historical background is presented in a later section). Among the structural aspects that have been labeled *complexity* are *specialization, interdependency, span of control,* and *height.* Although each is somewhat unique, they all share the recognition that the organization of workers and work processes can range in design from simple to complex. *Specialization* refers to the extent to which job tasks require highly specific (i.e., specialized) work skills or, conversely, can be carried out successfully by individuals who possess more broadly available knowledge, skills, and abilities. Research- and development-based organizations are examples of organizations that are likely to be highly specialized because such activities often require unique content knowledge and skills. *Interdependency* (also called integration) refers to the integration of tasks and activities across different workers. Highly integrated organizations require the cooperation and collaboration of many different employees to get work done. Nonintegrated organizations are composed of individuals who work largely on their own and do not require assistance or products from other employees. *Span of control* refers to the number of subordinates who report to a single manager. The size of the managerial span is often associated with the varying levels of the hierarchy within an organization (height). Large spans of control are associated with flatter (i.e., horizontally configured) organizations, such as those with fewer layers between entry-level positions and top management); small spans typically correspond with tall (i.e., vertical) hierarchical organizations in which there are many levels from the bottom to the top.

Structural dimensions that have often received less attention include *departmentalization* and *physical dispersion*. *Departmentalization* refers to the existence of formal and informal divisions within an organization. These divisions are often, but not always, created by grouping subsets of jobs and often comprise similar (or related) jobs. Highly departmentalized organizations are those that have created many internal divisions, whereas highly nondepartmentalized organizations have few. *Physical dispersion* refers to the extent to which organizational members are physically distinct from one another. This term may refer to the dispersion of individuals within a single building or, in highly dispersed organizations, the spread of employees across numerous locations throughout the world. With advanced technology and globalization, physical dispersion has become a prevalent feature of organizations.

Factors Relevant to the Elements of Organizational Structure

There is convincing evidence that no one structure is best for all organizations. Because there are many factors that determine the structure most effective for any given organization, most researchers have adopted an approach called *contingency theory*. *Contingency theory* in this context refers to the idea that relevant circumstances must be considered before applying a specific organizational design. A number of contingencies determine structure; *environment, technology, strategy,* and *size* are among the most influential.

Environment is the total of the factors that occur outside of the organization but are relevant to the decision making and management of the organization. These external forces include social and cultural norms, governmental regulations, economic conditions, market competition, the relevant labor pool, the availability and nature of raw materials, and industry type.

Technology represents one aspect of the environment affecting an organization. Because of its importance historically (see the brief description of the seminal Woodward studies that follows) and strong impact on modern organizations, technology is often separated out for special consideration in its effect on organizational structure. In the 21st century, technology is often considered interchangeable with computerization, but technology, in its broadest sense, may be defined as the knowledge necessary to process raw material. Depending on the organizational product or service, the raw material might be objects or people. Furthermore, technological processes can be categorized as routine or nonroutine. Routine processes are well understood and standardized. Routine technology typically leads to more traditional organizational structure with higher levels of centralization and formalization.

When taken together, environmental factors are often categorized by their complexity. *Complexity* here refers to the heterogeneity and incompatibility of the various elements of environment enumerated earlier. Large organizations often face more complex environments because of the sometimes conflicting objectives of the various stakeholders, such as governmental regulations and resource acquisition costs. Generally, the more complex the environment, the more complex the organizational structure to accommodate that environmental complexity.

Environmental factors can also be categorized as stable or volatile on the basis of an overall assessment of the predictability of change in the environment. To meet the demands of these two types of environments, organizations may be said to use two primary approaches to structure themselves: *mechanistic* and *organic*. Mechanistic models of structure are denoted by high specialization, rigid departmentalization, strong centralization and formalization, and narrow spans of control with clear authority lines. In contrast, the organic model has decentralized authority and decision making, low standardization, and formalization with self-directed teams or work groups as the primary departmentalization strategy. It should be noted that the two classifications, mechanistic and organic, might be considered as ends of a continuum rather than definitive categories; for example, few organizations use all elements of a strictly mechanistic or organic structure but instead use some combination of the two.

To survive, an organization must have a *strategy* for providing its products or services. The strategy of an organization will differ relative to the target customer market and industry type within which the organization functions; within these constraints, an organization can select from many types of strategy, with *innovation* and *imitation* strategies representing classic types. Innovation strategies emphasize being the leader in the industry in introducing new products or services. Present-day companies such as Apple and Google serve as exemplars of innovation. Organizations that choose the imitation strategy do not produce new products or services until another organization has demonstrated that those products and services are in demand. A subtype of imitation strategy is minimizing costs in an effort to generate high profits with lowered risk. The implications of different organizational strategies, innovation or imitation, lead to structures that vary along the continuum of the mechanistic and organic models described previously. Innovation strategies are more likely to require organic types of structure, whereas imitation (and cost minimization) strategies are more apt to lead to mechanistic models of organizational structure.

The *size* of an organization is most often represented by the number of employees but may alternatively be represented by the number of plant locations or offices, net assets (manufacturing), gross sales (manufacturing or service industries), or number of units that can be produced or people who can be served. Number of employees correlates more strongly than other indicators with structural features, and the size of an organization has a strong impact on resulting structure. Large organizations have more specialization in job types, more standardization of rules and formalization of procedures, and often more decentralization of decision making.

How Modern Conceptualizations of Organizational Structure Developed

How to organize the people and the tasks of work has been of interest from the earliest of times. Although concerns for structure can be dated to the Roman legions, modern interest among management theorists stems most directly from Henri Fayol's prescriptions for management in the early 1900s. In his principles of management, Fayol recommended specialization, centralization, clear lines of authority with one superior for each employee, and unity of direction. *Unity of direction* refers to the proposal that all effort within a group be directed toward recognized organizational goals and is inherent in the hierarchical structures of many organizations.

Another pioneer in defining organizational structure was sociologist and economist Max Weber. In the early 1900s, Weber conceptualized the ideal *bureaucracy* as an organization with a hierarchical division of labor in which explicit rules were applied objectively to employees. This organizational design is widely used yet today and is characterized by high levels of specialization, strong formalization, functional departmentalization, narrow spans of control, and centralized authority and decision making. Taken together, these components follow the mechanistic model noted earlier. Since Weber's original work, the term *bureaucracy* has also come to be used as a pejorative reference to the constraints incumbent in the rules governing organizational life.

In the 1950s, Joan Woodward studied 100 manufacturing firms in England and categorized, from simple to complex, the technical complexity of their operations into three types: unit production, mass production, and continuous processing. She determined that the type of operating process an industry used determined the best structure for an organization; her findings brought to an end the search for one best structure and heralded the start of the contingency approach noted earlier. During the 1960s, Paul R. Lawrence and Jay W. Lorsch continued the study of environment–structure fit and concluded that the contingencies of the environment were critical to selecting a suitable organizational configuration. More specifically, they found that organizations with stable environments were most successful if they used traditional hierarchical (i.e., mechanistic) structures; organizations with organic structures were more successful in volatile environments.

Among the best known and longest running studies of organizational structure are those that emanated from the University of Aston group in England in the 1950s. A collection of researchers headed by Derek S. Pugh examined a wide range of organizations and codified and developed measures of such concepts as centralization, specialization, and formalization described previously.

Their work bridges the early modern era with the current era.

The Role of Structure in Organizations

A key role of organizational structure is its relationship to organizational strategy. Depending on an organization's strategy, certain structures will be more or less effective. Therefore, the alignment between structure and strategy is important. Ultimately, a recursive relationship exists whereby the effective implementation of strategy creates an appropriate matching structure that, in turn, produces outcomes and processes that support the intended strategy. For example, an organization that has *innovation* as a core strategy would likely produce a structure with low levels of formalization and high levels of decentralization, among other characteristics. Individuals who work in such a structure experience greater autonomy, freedom, and flexibility in carrying out their work tasks and, as a consequence, are likely to emerge as an innovative workforce. Thus structure and strategy reinforce each other. Mismatch between structure and strategy can lead to organizational failure.

Structure is also important because of the impact it may have on individual outcomes. A number of studies have demonstrated that organizational structure affects individual worker attitudes including job satisfaction, work alienation, role ambiguity, role conflict, perceptions of justice, motivation, and job involvement. Structure has also been shown to affect employee behaviors such as work performance, turnover, and organizational citizenship. Some relationships between structure and individual outcomes are direct (i.e., increased formalization is associated with lower levels of role ambiguity). More often, examining the interplay of individual characteristics and context are necessary to understand structure's impact on individual outcomes.

Environmental demands such as changing technology and globalization have heightened the importance of organizational flexibility in many industries. Basic structural characteristics such as centralization, formalization, and complexity directly influence an organization's capacity to respond quickly to changes in the environment. One response to the demand for flexibility has been the increased dependence on self-guided teams. Furthermore, formal hierarchical structures have become flatter, resulting in greater decentralization, generally less formalization, and, in many cases, increased departmentalization.

Practical Considerations When Structuring Organizations

Organizational leaders strive to achieve the optimal alignment between structure and strategy, but there are several structural dilemmas that should be considered when structuring or reorganizing existing roles and responsibilities. Organizations often have, as their strategies, *differentiation*, yet the work itself might require *integration*. When role structures become more complex (many people doing very different types of tasks), it becomes harder to sustain a focused and tightly integrated enterprise.

A second consideration is identifying where the structure might result in *gaps* in the work or *duplication* of tasks. If the key responsibilities are not delineated clearly within the structural configuration, important tasks can fall through the cracks. On the other hand, it is also important to evaluate employees' responsibilities to address overlap in work assignments.

The third consideration involves employee *underuse* versus *overload*. Depending on the structural configuration, one employee might be given more assignments than can be completed in a given time frame, while another employee has completed his or her tasks and is waiting for a new assignment. It is important for leaders and managers to assess employee progress on assignments to identify if the structure is contributing to underuse or overload.

Another important issue is *lack of clarity* versus *lack of creativity*. If employees are unclear about their roles, this ambiguity can lead to employees' working on tasks that fit their personal preferences. These preferences might not be aligned with systemwide goals. Conversely, when organizations are highly formalized, they may overdefine how employees are to do their work; consequently, creativity might be stifled because employees feel they should "keep to the script."

Excessive autonomy versus *excessive interdependence* is an additional consideration in organizational structure. If individual and group efforts are overly autonomous, people may feel isolated or disconnected from the organization. In contrast, if these same groups of individuals are too tightly connected, time could be wasted because of distraction, obtaining approval for decisions from the many levels in the hierarchy, and backlogs of work that affect successive steps in the work cycle. Finding a balance between autonomy and interdependence is a critical challenge for leaders and managers in creating appropriate structure.

Emergent Issues of Organizational Structure

The globalization of work and expansion of multinational firms have provided one element of the environment that has fomented changes in prevailing organizational structures. In addition, the rapid changes brought about by widespread use of computerization and information technology have especially had a large impact on the functioning of organizations. Information technology has already influenced organizational structure: Large-scale users of information technology tend to have more decentralized and less formalized structures and more flexibility in responding to the challenges of a volatile environment. Furthermore, with the globalization of work and markets, some organizations have capitalized on the advances of information technology to implement new structural forms. The *virtual organization* (also called boundaryless, network, shadow, and barrier free) may have only a small number of core employees and, in its most extreme case, no physical location beyond that needed to house a small cadre of managers or information technicians. Production or services that constitute the core of the organization's mission may be outsourced completely to sites around the globe, with information technologies serving as the primary communication links. In fact, the explosion of technologies that can be used to connect employees and managers has led to network sharing among rivals to provide a service or product. The development of virtual organizations has especially focused the attention of organizational researchers on the integration of work. Historically, when much work was done in one location by workers, integration was relatively straightforward. With the advent of newer technologies, and changes in lifestyle (e.g., more emphasis on work–family balance), systems integration has become a critical topic and one that

relates ultimately to organizational structure and its impact on employees. Additional research has begun to focus, for example, on the development of trust among employees located in disparate geographical areas, who are working together to achieve a common end, but who have never met (or will never meet) one another. Despite the constant of change, there is little doubt that the ongoing evolution in the world of work will be depicted in adaptations of organizational structure.

Summary

Organizational structure is the way people and the work to be accomplished within organizations are configured and coordinated. The primary elements of structure are centralization, formalization, and complexity. These elements are affected by forces outside the organization as well as by organizational size. Information technology and globalization are especially potent factors of organizational structures. Meaningful relationships exist between organizational structure and organizational strategy, performance, and individual attitudes and behaviors.

Janet L. Kottke and Kathie L. Pelletier

See also Emerging Markets and Globalization: Implications for Organizations; Groups; Organizational Climate; Organizational Culture; Organizational Communication, Formal; Organizational Communication, Informal; Strategy; Virtual Organizations

Further Readings

Bolman, L. G., & Deal, T. E. (2013). *Reframing organizations: Artistry, choice and leadership*. 5th ed. San Francisco, CA: Jossey-Bass.

Daft, R. (2014). *Organization theory and design*. Cincinnati, OH: South-Western College Pub.

Mintzberg, H. (1979). *The structuring of organizations*. Englewood Cliffs, NJ: Prentice Hall.

Pugh, D. S. (Ed.). (1998). *The Aston Programme, Vols. I–III: The Aston Study and its developments*. Burlington, VT: Ashgate.

Short, J. C., Payne, G. T., & Ketchen, D. J. (2008). Research on organizational configurations: Past accomplishments and future challenges. *Journal of Management*, 34(6), 1053–1079.

ORGANIZATIONAL SURVEYS

Organizational surveys are also known as employee opinion surveys or employee attitude surveys. Most experts prefer to call them organizational surveys to make it clear that the sponsor and user of such surveys is almost always an organization. Furthermore, the people asked to complete such surveys may be employees at any or all levels, including top executives. Recent estimates conclude that about 75% of all medium- to large-sized firms conduct organizational surveys, typically every year or two. Organizations in the banking, financial, health care services, and high-tech manufacturing industries are the most common users of organizational surveys. They are also used extensively within the U.S. federal government, including the armed forces.

Purpose and History

The size and content of such surveys may vary widely, reflecting the different purposes to which organizational surveys are put. Organizations generally conduct surveys for four sometimes overlapping purposes. These purposes can be placed along a continuum of defensive to offensive reasons. Starting with the most defensive, the purposes are

- to identify warning signs of trouble within an organization, such as safety problems or concerns with ethical behavior;
- to evaluate the effectiveness of specific programs, policies and initiatives;
- to gauge the organization's status as an employer of choice, as in an employee satisfaction or employee engagement survey; and
- to predict and drive organizational outcomes, including customer satisfaction, unit productivity or organizational financial results.

Regardless of purpose, surveys can be seen as tools for assessment and change. Historically, surveys have been used for assessment, much like a taking a broad-scale annual medical examination to see "how we are doing." In recent decades, the emphasis has been more on stimulating and measuring change in specific areas of strategic value, such as employee well-being, product quality, and customer satisfaction.

The survey is a popular methodology for conducting research in many areas of industrial and organizational psychology. Catherine Higgs and Steve Ashworth noted that surveys can be used for several types of research. In early stages, they can be merely *exploratory* and later move on to be fully *descriptive* of the phenomena measured. At the highest level, they can be used to test *causal* relationships. It is quite common to see journal articles reporting on studies that have used surveys to collect data. Practitioners often learn or borrow survey methodology from allied fields, such as sociology.

The typical content of organizational surveys has changed since the early popularity of employee surveys in the 1930s and 1940s. That was an era of concern for employee morale and emotional adjustment, often as desirable ends in themselves and sometimes to prevent unhappiness that might cause unionization. Typically, survey questions asked about individual employees' contentment with different aspects of work, management, and pay. They even asked about environmental issues such as parking lots, cafeterias, and lighting. Both interviews and questionnaires were used.

In the 1950s and 1960s, the emphasis shifted to the individual's job satisfaction, because of presumed links of satisfaction to better organizational productivity. Typical surveys were based on paper-and-pencil questionnaires. In the 1970s and 1980s, attempts were made to link employee satisfaction to outcomes such as turnover, absenteeism, and stress. The worker's job level and part of the organization were seen as important moderators. The technology for doing surveys also evolved to the use of self-administered standardized and scannable forms.

Since the early 1990s, an extraordinarily different view of surveys has taken hold in most organizations. Behind the change is a set of assumptions linking employee opinions and perceptions to the achievement of strategic organizational goals. In service-dominated industries, employee behaviors are now seen as directly influencing customers' reactions and loyalties and thus spilling over to bottom-line measures such as product success, market share growth, organizational profit, and stakeholder return. Set against an increasingly competitive global marketplace, the emphasis in surveys is to capture employees' views, perceptions, and reports of how their organizations work, with the aim of achieving more productive teams, better quality products and services, and more satisfied customers.

This view of surveys has led to several conceptual models, some with names like the "service–profit chain." Still others are known as "linkage research" models. They help describe to organization management just why the surveys measure the concepts they do and show how they are linked to important outcomes. Several recent studies support this way of viewing and using survey results. The relationship between employees' views and organizational outcomes, at the unit level (rather than the individual level) has proved to be more powerful than previously believed by a few meta-analytic studies, which distill the relationships found in many studies. Even more recently, large-scale studies involving hundreds of organizations have treated the overall organization as the unit of analysis and have begun to identify organizational design factors that are associated with organizational-level success.

Methodology

Survey questions may cover a wide variety of issues. Closed-ended questions are typically written as Likert-type items, to be answered on a 5-point scale of satisfaction or agreement.

- An example of the first type would be "How satisfied are you with the recognition you receive for doing a good job?" Possible answers would be very satisfied (1), satisfied (2), neither satisfied nor dissatisfied (3), dissatisfied (4), and very dissatisfied (5).
- An example of the agreement type would be "I like the kind of work I do." Possible answers would be strongly agree (1), agree (2), neither agree nor disagree (3), disagree (4), and strongly disagree (5).

Most surveys also include one or more open-ended questions, which ask respondents to write in their responses. Questions may be very general, such as "Any other comments?" Or they may be very specific, such as "What kind of training

would help you to be more effective?" To encourage frank and honest responses to all questions, strict confidentiality is almost always promised by the survey sponsor.

In the past decade, organizational surveys have been administered largely by computers, using e-mail and the Internet. This has resulted in astonishing changes in the administration, collection, and use of survey data. Surveys can now be sent electronically to eligible samples, avoiding the physical effort and expense of postal or other distribution systems. Surveys are cheaper and much more flexible once the infrastructure is available. Whereas printing a large survey might take weeks, an electronic version can be changed at the last minute (and even during a survey if a major crisis occurred). These surveys can also use "branching" techniques, so that respondents answering certain questions unfavorably can be offered more detailed follow-up items to help in diagnosis. Write-in comments are keyed in by respondents, avoiding the laborious transcription needed in paper-and-pencil surveys.

In most ways, the electronic versions of organizational surveys are quite superior to earlier versions. Careful studies show no distortion of replies compared with paper-and-pencil versions, except that write-in comments are typically twice as long. Still, computer programs make write-in comments much easier to analyze and report than in the past. In general, reporting survey data has been shortened from many weeks to a few days, and in some cases, results are immediately available. Reports to managers can also be made via computer, giving managers a chance to receive reports sooner and in more flexible formats.

Response Rates

However, electronic surveys may create problems because surveys now seem quite easy to do. One often hears of many groups within a firm launching their own internal surveys, often of dubious quality. Along with this are employee cries of "oversurveying" and a decline in response rates. In the past it was common to survey all of a firm's population, to do a census survey. Recently, many firms have shifted to doing more frequent surveys, or "pulse" surveys, often of small samples of respondents.

Typical response rates are hard to pin down with certainty. It is believed that census surveys of employees typically get response rates of anywhere from 40% to 95%, averaging about 75% to 80%. Sample surveys seem to get 10% to 15% lower response rates.

Poor response rates undermine the credibility of survey results. Some recent research, however, suggests that nonrespondents are mostly people who have other priorities and are not actively opposed to a survey or its topics. Still, it would be wise to weight any subgroups that respond at higher or lower rates than typical, in order to properly represent each subgroup in the firm. Of course, survey researchers should always compare a sample's demographics with the known population demographics to be sure the sample is representative.

Most experts believe that the size and content of a survey questionnaire will influence the response rates. Surveys with clear, well-written questions on topics that are obviously important to the individual and organization will gain more participation. Respondents will be "turned off" by surveys they think are overly long. In prior decades, it was not unusual for paper-and-pencil surveys to have more than 200 questions. Recent electronic surveys typically have 40 to 75 items and can be completed in 10 to 20 minutes. This too reflects the competitive, fast-moving business climate in many firms.

Normative Data

Managers receiving survey reports often ask how they compare with other firms. Different consortiums of companies have been born from this desire. The "granddaddy" of survey consortiums is the Mayflower Group (www.mayflowergroup.org), a group of about 40 large firms that ask the same two dozen core items in their respective surveys and share the normative data with other member firms under strict confidentiality.

Another consortium is the Information Technology Survey Group (www.itsg.org), made up of 18 high-technology firms, that operates in a similar way. The representatives of the consortium's member firms meet twice a year and share what they believe are "best practices" in doing organizational surveys. In addition, several survey vendors offer data norms based on their client data sets or on specially collected national data sets.

Other types of norm data are those that represent cultural or national differences. With many large firms now truly global organizations, some international data are available for norm comparisons. Basic advances in the social sciences are also helped through such data. Three decades ago, the European organizational scholar Geert Hofstede used international survey data from IBM to lay out several cross-cultural dimensions, such as the tendencies of people in different countries to be oriented toward the group, or collective (as in Asia), or toward the individual (as in the United States).

The use of surveys internationally has been on a steady rise. In addition to the United States, surveys are becoming increasingly popular in Australia, Brazil, Canada, China, Germany, and the United Kingdom. Across the globe, leadership teams are typically most interested in comparing the results from their organizations to country and industry normative data.

Organizational Development and Action Taking

The most important outcome of surveys is meaningful and responsive action. This is also the most elusive aspect of the organizational survey process. But experts in organizational development, working with survey researchers, have developed some excellent techniques. They recognized that survey data can be energizing and motivational. Naturally, meaningful action requires top management to be supportive and knowledgeable about the overall process. Managers must be advocates and champions of the organizational survey. Survey practitioners responsible for doing the organization's survey must educate all levels of management; they must provide the training and infrastructure for data to be collected, analyzed and reported, and then track the actions taken.

Some experts favor reporting survey data first to top management, then letting the data "cascade" down to lower levels, with top managers acting as role models for how to discuss and act on the data. Other experts prefer having the data "bubble up," with lower levels seeing it first and then reporting their findings and action plans to higher levels. Over the years, detailed protocols have been developed to "feedback" the survey results to respondents, and this is seen as a critical step to good survey practice. Recent research, however, has made it clear that action taking, not data feedback, is the critical ingredient for success. In fact, providing employees with survey data feedback and no action causes more unfavorable consequences than giving no feedback at all.

Companies that have described their experiences make it clear that the critical factor is to ensure that managers must act. It may even be best to focus on only one or two high-priority areas to work on. Many firms use survey results, and improvements or declines, as the basis for performance appraisals, incentive bonuses, and promotions. If the topics measured in the survey are truly important to the organization, then rewards and punishment for their achievement seem quite appropriate.

Organizational surveys have been used for many purposes in recent years. These include topics as different as managing the progress of mergers and acquisitions, improving a climate of diversity, reducing employee turnover, reinvigorating an organization after a business turndown, and coordinating practices in a large global organization. Surveys have also been modified to provide multiple-source feedback (360-degree reporting) for management development purposes. The organizational survey is a powerful tool for many purposes and seems destined for continuing use and influence.

Allen I. Kraut and Jack W. Wiley

See also Facilitating Survey Reponse, Online Assessment; Online Survey Data Collection Methods: Leveraging Qualtrics and SurveyMonkey; Survey Approach

Further Readings

Borg, I., & Mastroangelo, P. M. (2008). *Employee surveys in management: Theories, tools and practical applications.* Cambridge, MA: Hogrefe & Huber.

Church, A. H., & Waclawski, J. (2001). *Designing and using organizational surveys: A seven step process.* San Francisco, CA: Jossey-Bass.

Kraut, Allen I. (Ed.). (1996). *Organizational surveys: Tools for assessment and change.* San Francisco, CA: Jossey-Bass.

Kraut, Allen I. (Ed.). (2006). *Getting action from organizational surveys: New concepts, methods and applications.* San Francisco, CA: Jossey-Bass.

Wiley, Jack W. (2010). *Strategic employee surveys: Evidence-based guidelines for driving organizational success.* San Francisco, CA: Jossey-Bass.

ORIGINALITY

The production of original ideas is one of the most frequently sought after forms of performance in the modern world of work. For organizations large and small, creative solutions often form the basis of a competitive advantage in an ever-shifting business landscape. From new forms of entertainment to the latest and greatest gadget, there is clearly a thirst for novel products and processes.

Originality, however, may be more than just a new or an interesting product. Medical advances can also be traced back to individuals' or groups' pushing the envelope and searching for new ways to help their patients. Relatedly, social innovations are defined as novel solutions to complex social problems with the express intent of improving the lives of others. Military innovation, moreover, can be both defensive and offensive minded, with the conflicting aims, at times, of simultaneously impacting others and protecting one's own. Originality is, in many interesting ways, quite important.

Defining Originality, Creativity, and Innovation

As alluded to, when we imagine our favorite products or experiences, we often focus on what makes them unique, different, or original. Yet originality is only one piece of the creativity and innovation puzzle. Social scientists define creativity as the generation of ideas that are both novel and useful. Originality or novelty in isolation is better thought of as weird, funky, or strange. In contrast, very good or high-quality ideas that lack an original component are simply good ideas that, although useful, are also likely to be arrived at by most people. Thus, it is the combination of these two factors, originality and usefulness, that organizations seek most often.

Having a high-quality original idea, however, is only one of the steps toward actually seeing that idea realized. Whereas creativity is characterized as the generation of ideas, innovation is defined as the implementation of creative concepts. As many organizations have come to realize, it is one thing to have a truly original idea, but it is quite another to refine, prototype, and market that idea to others.

Inherent within the definitional discussion of originality, creativity, and innovation is that the production and implementation of novel ideas is a multistage and complex process. Several models have been developed to represent this process, but Mumford and colleagues developed the most detailed and widely used model. According to their body of work, there are eight key activities that all connect and interact to produce effective, innovative outcomes. Such activities include identifying problems to solve, generating and evaluating ideas, and monitoring solutions once they are implemented. These processes, moreover, are not linear steps but rather represent a collection of activities that often influence one another in unique ways. Consider, for example, evaluating a prototype for a new smartphone. During this phase, designers and engineers might observe that users desire a new feature not yet in the product. Thus, focus might shift back to generating ideas earlier in the innovation process. As may be surmised, original idea production and implementation is a messy proposition.

Drivers of Original and Creative Idea Production

Given that many, if not most, organizations want to be more creative and innovative, it is not surprising that researchers have spent a great deal of time thinking and studying the causes or antecedents of successful innovation. Most researchers agree that innovation and its corresponding processes are the result of the interplay between individuals and the broader context. Known as the interactionist (i.e., the interaction between a person and the environment) perspective of innovation, this approach can further break down causes into several layers or levels of analysis.

Individual Characteristics

The building block of original idea production is individual cognition. Ideas can be shaped, altered, and adjusted once they are put forth, but they must begin with people generating them. As such, there are a number of individual characteristics linked with original and creative idea production. A few notable examples include the following:

- *Personality.* Researchers have been studying personality and creativity for more than 50 years, and the role of personality in original thinking was one of the first issues addressed when creativity emerged as a scholarly topic of interest. The trait most commonly associated with creative performance has been openness to experience, from the Big Five taxonomy, a trait linked to a desire to try new and different things. This preference likely gives those high on the trait a broader range of experiences to draw from when attempting to combine previously unrelated concepts together.
- *Creative thinking ability.* Along with personality, a number of well-known scholars, such as J. P. Guilford, helped pioneer unique forms of creative thinking ability. One type of ability (also known as intellect, by Guilford and colleagues) most linked to creative outcomes as many as 40 years later is divergent thinking ability, or the capacity to generate many different solutions to a given problem.
- *Expertise.* For many years it was debated whether creativity and intelligence were in fact distinct characteristics. This debate has generally subsided, with modern scholars agreeing that the two are unique but related qualities of individuals. One way they are related is through the link between intelligence and expertise. Those with high intelligence are able to develop deep levels of expertise more rapidly and with greater ease than those with lower intelligence. With this core base of knowledge (i.e., expertise) at their disposal, individuals are able to combine concepts in new and different ways to produce original products.

Team Characteristics

The modern organization is built around group work, or collections of individuals operating in varying degrees of interdependence. As such, a growing area of study in the field of innovation is the role and impact of team characteristics and the associated social environment. Team characteristics related to successful innovation, for example, include the following:

- *Composition and diversity.* Team members who have the same backgrounds, experiences, and expertise are less likely to combine their ideas in novel ways than are more diverse individuals. A diverse collection of individuals is also able to meet shifting and changing demands as the nature of complex problems shifts over time.

- *Team climate and psychological safety.* Although diverse teams are more creative, they are also more likely to experience conflict that can hamper the sharing of truly novel ideas. As such, it is important for teams to focus on developing a strong creative climate characterized by comfort in sharing the strangest and most uncommon ideas; this form of climate is known as psychological safety.

Organization Characteristics

Individuals and teams typically operate within a broader organizational framework that also shapes original idea production and implementation. A few of these characteristics include the following:

- *Resources.* It is certainly possible for small, more nimble organizations to successfully innovate, but they are less likely do so than an organization with a large amount of resources at its disposal. Although resources can lead to bureaucracy and rigidity, resources are also linked to creative production for several reasons. Namely, resources allow organizations to acquire and reward the best talent, pursue ideas to their fullest (e.g., prototype, test, refine, repeat), and allow continuation after a radical idea fails. Smaller organizations with fewer resources, in contrast, may struggle severely when a given product is counted on for success yet comes up short in the innovation process.
- *Leadership.* There is often a bias against novel ideas in groups and organizations, with many preferring safer or less mentally taxing solutions to problems. Leaders can play a key role in overcoming this bias by encouraging employees to break from strongly held norms. Leaders can do this in a variety of ways, such as role modeling creative behavior themselves, rewarding valid attempts and producing novel products or ideas, and bringing together the right group members to solve complex problems. Leaders are truly necessary components of innovative success.

Environment Influences

Recall that creativity is defined as the generation of ideas that are both original and useful, and innovation is defined as the implementation of creative ideas. The environment can often dictate whether creative ideas move on to the later stages of the innovation process. Consider the following examples:

- *Market readiness.* Many creative ideas fail simply because they are ahead of their time. Consumers may not embrace creative ideas that are too radically different from those that came before them. Moreover, during sharp economic downturns, consumers may be resistant to take risks on products that are yet unproven.
- *Networks.* Organizations with well-tested, refined prototypes or even those experiencing small-batch success must determine a way to scale up the manufacturing of their products or processes. As such, an organization's network of suppliers and partners plays a key role in whether a novel idea can find its way to those desiring or needing it.

Conclusion

Overall, the production and implementation of original ideas is the product of a whole host of variables, including individual, team, and organizational characteristics and environmental influences. Without all of these aspects combined, original ideas may never come to fruition, and organizations may not gain the competitive advantage they often seek.

Samuel T. Hunter,
Melissa B. Gutworth,
and Jeffrey B. Lovelace

See also Creativity at Work; Group Dynamics and Processes; Innovation; Leadership and Supervision

Further Readings

Anderson, N., Potocnik, K., & Zhou, J. (2014). Innovation and creativity in organizations: A state of science review, prospective commentary, and guiding framework. *Journal of Management*, 40, 1297–1333. doi:10.1177/0149206314527128

Guilford, J. P. (1967). *The nature of human intelligence.* New York: McGraw-Hill.

Hunter, S. T., & Cushenbery, L. (2011). Leading for innovation: Direct and indirect influences. *Advances in Developing Human Resources, 13,* 248–265. doi:10.1177/1523422311424263

Ma, H. (2009). The effect size of variables associated with creativity: A meta-analysis. *Creativity Research Journal, 21,* 30–42. doi:10.1080/10400410802633400

Mueller, J. S., Melwani, S., & Goncalo, J. A. (2011). The bias against creativity: Why people desire but reject creative ideas. *Psychological Science, 23,* 13–17. doi:10.1177/0956797611421018

Mumford, M. D., Hunter, S. T., & Bedell, K. E. (2008). Research in multi-level issues: A focus on innovation. In M. D. Mumford, S. T. Hunter, & K. E. Bedell (Eds.), *Research in multi-level issues* (pp. 107–154). Oxford, UK: Elsevier. doi:10.1016/S1475-9144(07)00005-7

Mumford, M. D., Mobley, M. I., Reiter-Palmon, R., Uhlman, C. E., & Doares, L. M. (1991). Process analytic models of creative capacities. *Creativity Research Journal, 4,* 91–101. doi:10.1080/10400419109534380

Woodman, R. W., Sawyer, J. E., & Griffin, R. W. (1993). Toward a theory of organizational creativity. *Academy of Management Review, 18,* 293–321. doi:10.5465/AMR.1993.3997517

OUTSOURCING AND TEMPORARY WORK

Outsourcing is typically the domain of trade economists, whereas nonstandard work arrangements are the province of labor economists. Temporary work is one aspect of nonstandard work arrangements, just as are part-time work, contract work, and other work forms. Although there are many polemics on the positive and negative effects of outsourcing and nonstandard work on productivity and personal well-being, industrial and organizational (I-O) psychologists have paid scant attention to either. One recent change is that research on temporary workers seems to primarily come from Europe.

In the early 1980s, *outsourcing* referred to the situation in which firms expanded their purchases of products (such as automakers' buying car seat fabrics) rather than making them themselves. By 2004, outsourcing had taken on a different meaning. It referred to the arms-length or long-distance purchase of services abroad (made easier by the continuous growth of information technology). Thus, x-rays made in Boston can be read in Bombay. The argument for outsourcing was cost savings, obtained by buying products made in countries with lower wages than the United States.

Today the debate over offshoring and outsourcing debate is changing. Cheap labor is only one of many factors driving the offshoring decision. Labor costs may not be critical or even primary in the decision of whether to offshore. Wages are rising in developing countries and falling in developed countries. Companies are modifying their global supply chains, making rather than buying important parts of products or services. Companies may also find that a key to fast-paced innovation may be making rather than buying. The choice of whether to make or buy may also be determined by a complex set of governmental policies in different countries.

Outsourcing takes many forms. Some firms have partnered with competitors for decades. Among reasons for partnering with competitors are to secure sophisticated, cost-driven joint ventures, to set industry standards for product compatibility in hopes of expanding markets for everyone, and so on. Outsourcing has been done in every war the United States has fought. Other forms include out-tasking or subcontracted exportation of particular tasks or functions to a foreign enterprise, a partial exportation of a task. The foreign local subsidiary model relies on a foreign enterprise to support a foreign subsidiary of the U.S. customer, a jointly owned subsidiary to provide shared services to affiliates, and global and global multilateral outsourcing that relies on a multinational customer's enterprise to support operations in multiple countries.

Partnering and outsourcing have a number of advantages and disadvantages. Partners can teach new things, perhaps through access to best-in-class processes. Partnering competitors can learn technology secrets from one another. Where industry benefits are not well known, partnering can offer insights into a company's productivity, quality, and efficiency. Among the advantages of outsourcing are price and cost reductions, the ability to expand contract programs in short periods of time, enhanced service benefits, and finding and using new talent.

Partnering and outsourcing also have disadvantages. Lack of control is a critical disadvantage in partnering. If a U.S. oil company operating in a foreign environment partners with an in-country security organization, and the security force comes into contact with drug dealers, it can start a war the United States then must deal with. Competitors may learn from one another's operations, which may be detrimental to one or more of the organizations. The strategic aims of partners may change midstream, causing failure. When outsourcing is done from the United States to other countries, political instability may be a factor. Companies also run the risk of losing their core competencies to their outsourced partners. Unemployment backlashes may also occur.

Research on outsourcing and partnering is wanting in a number of areas. First, there are no objective metrics for evaluating outsourcing results. There is no research on the relationship between outsourcing implementation and firm value. And there is no research on the outsource contract itself.

Temporary Work

Contingent labor is one of the fastest growing industries in the United States. The temporary work revolution is not limited to the United States but is also growing in Europe. This is viewed as one of the most spectacular and important evolutions in Western societies. The term *temporary work* has many definitions. It is usually called contingent employment (in the United States and Canada); temporary, fixed-term, or nonpermanent work in Europe. Temporary employment is of limited duration and often has a fixed termination date.

The American Staffing Association (ASA; previously called the National Association of Temporary and Staffing Services) reported its demographic survey of temporary workers in 1998. This survey counted 2.8 million Americans as part-time workers. In 2013, that number was said to have jumped to 17 million people. A recent ASA survey questioned 12,000 current and past temporary or contract workers. All survey respondents said that finding permanent work was a reason to take on temporary work. Other reasons included an inability to find work from other sources, the ability to obtain work experience, and improvement of professional skills. Flexibility was also a reason

to take on temporary jobs, and many said that it would make them better employees.

The nature of temporary employment is changing. It used to be that most temps worked in clerical or administrative positions. Today temps work in many technological fields and other professions. One third work in manufacturing, but a growing number of temps work in education (both higher and lower), the legal profession, medicine, and other fields. Part of this may be because jobs are being returned to companies' home countries, and part may be due to companies' finding ways to avoid complying with the Patient Protection and Affordable Care Act.

Research on temps addresses the demographic characteristics of the workforce, how organizations use temps, individual consequences of temping, and individual responses to temping. Organizations with high variability in their product lines have increased need for temps, but they are also used when permanent employees leave their positions (e.g., vacations, long-term disability, maternity leave). Client companies reduce their training costs by hiring specialized temps. Because companies view temps as resources, temps are said to see themselves as alienated and have little or no commitment to organizations. Thus, temps may seek autonomous, mentally challenging work or control the pace of work to exert some kind of control over their environments. Or they may look for long-term assignments to counter isolation. Existing research does not explain the motivational processes in which individuals engage while temping, even though motivation is one of the most frequently researched areas in I-O psychology.

The majority of studies of the effects of temporary employment on workers are atheoretical or are grounded in theories that seem valuable in explaining attitudes, well-being, and productive behavior in permanent workers. The general findings are as follows:

- Stressors cause unfavorable attitudes, poor well-being, and undesirable behaviors.
- Temps are thought to be vulnerable to job stress because of poor job characteristics, role stress, monotonous work, and little influence over workplace decisions.
- The relationship between temporary status and job satisfaction is inconclusive.

Social comparison and social exchange theories suggest that temps compare perceptions of fairness between themselves and their permanent counterparts. Because so many of the direct relationships between psychological variables and temporary work status are inconclusive, researchers have begun to insert control variables (i.e., occupational status, weekly working hours, gender, education, etc.) into their studies. Recently researchers have looked at the positive aspects of temporary work, such as work–life balance, reduced workload, foot-in-the-door opportunities, and so on.

Temporary workers come in two types. There are those seeking permanent employment, or temporary temps, and those not seeking permanent employment, or permanent temps. About one third of each group enjoys the variety of temporary jobs and the quality of job assignments. Temporary temps are more likely than permanent temps to use temporary employment to find job leads and develop networks. Permanent temps are more likely to feel that they do not have time for permanent jobs and value the flexibility of temporary work.

Summary

Outsourcing and temporary work are both given short shrift in I-O research. Both outsourcing and temporary work are growth industries, and there are many forms of partnering that have a number of advantages and disadvantages. Existing research addresses the demography and organizational use of temps. It also addresses individual consequences and individual responses to temping. Sadly lacking is research on the motivational responses to temping and outsourcing

Karlene H. Roberts

See also Managing Talent in Global Organizations; Mergers, Acquisitions, and Strategic Alliances; Social Comparison Theory; Social Exchange Theory; Work–Life Balance

Further Readings

Hatonen, J., & Eriksson, T (2009). 30+ years of research and practice of autonomy: Exploring the past and anticipating the future. *Journal of International Management*, 15(2), 142–155.

Heineman, B. W. (2013). Why we can all stop worrying about offshoring and outsourcing. *The Atlantic*. http://www.theatlantic.com/business/archive/2013/03/why-we-can-all-stop-worrying-about-offshoring-and-outsourcing/274388/

Housman, S., & Osawa, M. (2003). *Nonstandard work in developed economies: Causes and consequences.* Kalamazoo, MI: W. E. Upjohn for Employment Research.

Jiang, B., & Quershi, A. (2006). Research on outsourcing results: Current literature and future opportunities. *Management Decision*, 44(1), 44–55.

OWENS, WILLIAM A.: FIRST RECIPIENT, SIOP DISTINGUISHED SCIENTIFIC CONTRIBUTIONS AWARD

William A. Owens, PhD, was the first recipient of the Society for Industrial and Organizational Psychology's (SIOP) Distinguished Scientific Contributions Award in 1983. He served as president of SIOP in 1969–1970. Owens held academic positions at Iowa State University, Purdue University, and the University of Georgia between 1940 and 1984, having also served in the U.S. Navy during World War II. In his academic positions, Owens supervised more than 100 theses and dissertations. He served as head of the psychology department at Iowa State University, university professor and director of the Institute for Behavioral Research at the University of Georgia, and interim provost at the University of Georgia. SIOP's Scholarly Contribution Award, for the best article in a given year, is named in his honor.

Owens, over the course of his career, published over 80 articles, books, and book chapters. Inspection of the publication record points to multiple contributions—contributions of substantive importance to many fields of applied psychology. His early work on longitudinal changes in intellectual abilities indicated that crystallized intelligence might increase through people's late 40s or early 50s. His work in developing tests for assessing creativity in machine design provided the first solid evidence pointing to the importance of conceptual combination and reorganization in creative thought. His key contribution, however, lay in his work on background data, or biodata, measures.

Background Data

Background data measures ask people to report their behavior and experiences in situations arising earlier in their lives. As a result, background data questions come in many forms. Background data questions might ask people to report the length of employment in their last job, the amount of insurance they own, whether they served in the military, how many clubs they have belonged to, how many projects they have led, and how many pull-ups they could do in high school. Indeed, self-reports of prior life experiences have been used in employment screening since the early 1900s. Typically, responses to these questions are provided in a standardized format with response options being age-group appropriate—thus, for experienced, older applicants, response options to the project leadership question might include *no projects*, *one or two projects*, *three to five projects*, *six to eight projects*, and *nine or more projects*. To develop selection measures, an empirical keying approach was employed where items were weighted and scored, based on the ability to distinguish "successful" from "unsuccessful" applicants.

Psychometric Characteristics

One theme in Owens's research focused on the substantive and psychometric characteristics of viable background data measures. His research demonstrated that (a) background data questions should have an implied or explicit situational context (e.g., "in high school," "at work"), (b) questions should be brief, (c) response options should be affectively neutral or pleasant, (d) escape options should be provided if necessary (e.g., "I have never done project work"), and (e) item response options should be presented on a continuum reflecting the frequency or intensity of behavior.

Owens's research indicated that when background data questions are written with these points in mind, they display excellent retest reliability—.80 to .90. Responses to these questions

converge with the observations of external observers—for example, friends or parents—and are not greatly influenced by either social desirability or faking. And responses to these questions reflect variables (e.g., experiential knowledge) shaping recall of prior life experience.

In another stream of research, Owens and his colleagues provided compelling evidence for the validity of background data measures. For example, this research showed well-developed background data measures typically provide criterion-related validity coefficients in the .30 range. They evidence good, cross-firm generality. They can distinguish among people following different career paths (e.g., research and development engineering, engineering sales, and general engineering), and they can be used to predict a wide variety of criteria from tenure, to job performance, to organizational citizenship.

Substantive Understanding

Owens's focus, however, was not only on the psychometric characteristics of viable background data measures. The second theme in his research was the substantive implications of background data measures. One key concern in this research was how people structure, or organize, their life histories. In a nearly 20-year effort, Owens proposed and tested a developmental–integrative model for understanding people's life histories. Essentially, this model held that people, over the course of their lives, evidence coherent patterns of life experience. In other words, he argued lifestyles give rise to responses to background data questions.

The technique used to identify these lifestyles, or patterns of life history, was cluster analysis. Cluster analysis groups together people evidencing similar life histories. In this research, broad, multidimensional background data measures were administered to people as they entered college, at the time they graduated from college, and 2 to 10 years following college graduation. Clusters, or types, of people were identified based on their responses to the background data questions presented within each of these measures including some 60 to 400 questions appropriate for each of these developmental periods.

The findings flowing from this work indicated (a) a limited number, 10 to 25, of shared patterns of life history (e.g., analytical independent, business-oriented "fraternity Joe") could be identified for both men and women in any developmental period; (b) these patterns could account for the life experiences of most (80%) of the people; (c) these patterns were stable across cohorts or new samples; (d) people's patterns of life experience could predict a wide variety of criteria, such as vocational interests, decision making, personality differences, performance on learning tasks, institutional entry, task engagement, task performance, and career success; and (e) these patterns were maintained over time, or across developmental periods. Thus, people's life history patterns provided a general system for describing and predicting their life courses.

These findings led Owens, and his colleagues, to propose people's life histories could be accounted for through an ecology model. Essentially, this model holds that people choose to enter certain situations or engage in certain tasks. Based on this experience, people develop characteristics that promote performance in, or adaptation to, this environment. Based on these developed capabilities, they, in the future, seek out, and are selected for, environments that serve to reinforce and/or further develop these characteristics. Thus, the basis for emergence of these life history styles is a systematic pattern of development and choice.

The basis for life history patterns in choice and development suggests that background data measures could be expressly developed to assess key experiences, or capabilities, giving rise to people's choices and their performance in various situations. Thus targeted, or tailored, background data questions could be written to predict entry into, and performance in, certain environments. Owens and his colleagues, over the later portion of his career, developed a set of structured procedures for writing background data questions of value for predicting different forms of performance in different settings or different jobs. In fact, these are the procedures used today in the development of virtually all sound background data, or life history, measures. And the resulting inventories have been found to evidence excellent reliability and validity while allowing people to be appraised in the context of the lives they have led.

Conclusions

Our foregoing observations indicate why William A. Owens received the first Distinguished Scientific Contributions Award. He executed a long-term systematic program of research that allowed us to understand people's life history and the background data measures we use to assess people's life history. Given the impact life history has on our future, Owens provided a framework for both understanding people's lives and predicting their future lives. It is a contribution that certainly merits recognition for distinguished science.

Michael D. Mumford
and Tristan McIntosh

See also Background Checks/Credit Checks; Practical Intelligence; Quantitative Research Approach

Further Readings

Chaney, F. B., & Owens, W. A. (1964). Life history antecedents of sales, research, and general engineering interest. *Journal of Applied Psychology, 48*, 101–105.

Mumford, M. D., & Owens, W. A. (1984). Individuality in a developmental context: Some empirical and theoretical considerations. *Human Development, 27*, 84–108.

Mumford, M. D., & Owens, W. A. (1987). Methodology review: Principles, procedures, and findings in the application of background data measures. *Applied Psychological Measurement, 11*, 1–31.

Owens, W. A. (1968). Toward one discipline of scientific psychology. *American Psychologist, 23*, 782–785.

Owens, W. A., & Schoenfeldt, L. F. (1979). Toward a classification of persons. *Journal of Applied Psychology, 64*, 569–607.

Rothstein, H. R., Schmidt, F. L., Erwin, F. W., Owens, W. A., & Sparks, C. P. (1990). Biographical data in employment selection: Can validities be made generalizable? *Journal of Applied Psychology, 75*, 175–184.

Shaffer, G. S., Saunders, V., & Owens, W. A. (1986). Additional evidence for the accuracy of biographical information: Long-term retest reliability and observer ratings. *Personnel Psychology, 39*, 791–809.

P

PART-TIME WORK

Part-time work refers to jobs in which employees work less than 30 or 35 hours per week, whereas any employees who work more than this cutoff are considered full-time. There is a wide range of types of part-time jobs and a range of how many hours a part-time employee works. Part-time work represents a multifaceted experience because of the variety of reasons people pursue this work, the types of part-time work available, voluntary or involuntary decisions to work part-time, and other aspects of such employment.

Part-time work was popularized in the United States and Europe in the 1970s, particularly in industries such as service, retail, finance, insurance, and real estate. Recent shifts in the nature and popularity of part-time work were caused by economic and legal changes. The late 20th century in the United States and Europe saw a shift in the impetus for the increase in part-time work. Previously, the number of part-time jobs had increased to meet the workforce demand for shorter hours and more accommodating jobs. In the 1990s, the shift toward part-time work began being driven by employer needs as well, such as affordable costs and flexible staffing. Part-time work can be beneficial to both employees and employers.

Today, part-time work is steadily growing in both North America and Europe, with many newly created jobs fitting the classification of part-time work. Additionally, part-time work is no longer limited to the service sector, as more employees in fields such as medicine, engineering, and business are hired as part-time workers. The growth of part-time work has been caused by economic necessity—some businesses cannot afford more full-time employees because of the added costs of full-time employment, such as benefits and insurance—as well as the trend toward flexible, nontraditional work schedules, particularly among younger workers. The number of part-time workers has historically increased during economic recessions and decreased during economic expansions when workers seek more full-time positions. In addition, part-time positions have traditionally been filled by more women.

Contingent Work

Part-time work falls under the umbrella category of contingent work, which also includes temporary work and contract work. Often these types of work are also referred to as "nonstandard" work because they do not fit the description of standard jobs (e.g., 35 or more hours per week, stable over a longer period of time, includes benefits). However, in recent years the number of contingent jobs in the American workforce (as well as other countries around the world) has steadily increased. With this rise in the contingent workforce, what was once considered "nonstandard" is fast becoming standard practice in the U.S. workforce.

Contingent work may be classified using a taxonomy developed by Daniel C. Feldman that conceptualizes contingent work along the dimensions of time, space, and the number or kinds of employees.

Although different types of contingent work differ along each of these dimensions, part-time work is specifically conceptualized as involving a smaller number of hours worked per week. Other aspects of the time, space, and number-of-employee dimensions, such as simultaneous or sequential employers and continuous employment, however, may vary from job to job. Unlike temporary work and contract work, part-time work may be continuous over time and is unlikely to involve being hired or managed by an agency or subcontractors. Nevertheless, part-time work can be temporary or seasonal and may not lead to long-term employment. The difference between part-time and other types of contingent work is that continuous employment is typically an option for part-timers; contract or temporary workers are generally employed for a defined period of time.

It is important to note that the different forms of contingent work can also overlap. For instance, an employee can be both temporary, working for a company for a set time line, and part-time, working fewer hours than a full-time, typical employee.

The Professionalization of Part-Time

Part-time professionals are a somewhat newer category of part-time work that is a reflection of lifestyle choices of the current workforce. Although part-time work is often associated with service and retail jobs held by younger workers, economic and business changes have led to an increase in the number and types of all forms of contingent work. In fact, the presence of part-time professional workers is on the rise. As employees increasingly wish for more flexible work hours, and may turn to part-time or contract work as a solution, the nature of being a working professional is being challenged. Although many workplaces may still be resistant to maintaining a large part-time workforce, which would make changes to important aspects of an organization (e.g., organizational culture, work flow management, performance) necessary, the increase of the contingent workforce in recent years is likely to perpetuate this movement in coming years.

Reasons for Working Part-Time

There are multiple reasons why someone might pursue part-time work. These reasons are often categorized as voluntary or involuntary. Both categories represent unique experiences and differing impetuses for pursing part-time work. Voluntary part-time workers are employees who do not need or want full-time employment. This category may also include minors, who are too young to hold full-time jobs but still wish to work; people who hold multiple part-time jobs; people who want greater work–life balance; people who want to supplement their spouses' incomes; and people who are moving toward retirement.

Involuntary part-time workers, however, are those employees who take part-time jobs even though that was not their original goal. Often these employees want or need full-time employment but have been unable to find it. Some people may take part-time work because of poor health or because they cannot find other jobs in their preferred fields. Involuntary workers constitute the part-time group with the highest turnover intentions; if full-time employment becomes available to them, they are likely to leave their current jobs for better opportunities.

More recently, scholars have noted that not all reasons for working part-time can be neatly classified as either voluntary or involuntary. For instance, a person may pursue part-time work because he or she is juggling multiple responsibilities. Students commonly take part-time jobs because they are able to earn money with a work schedule that can be flexible around classes and other educational obligations. Students are a group of part-time workers who, like involuntary part-time workers, have high turnover intentions, because they often seek only seasonal employment or leave their part-time work when full-time jobs become available after graduation. In addition, people may take part-time jobs to enable them to care for children or other family members. The reasons why someone works part-time can be important in predicting and understanding that person's job attitudes, as someone who wants to work part-time may be more inclined to be satisfied, committed, and unlikely to leave a job than someone who is taking the work only temporarily or as a last resort.

For young high school or college students, part-time work offers opportunities to learn about the workforce and career paths, offering early organizational socialization: the process through which people learn about work and organizations through school, family, experiences, and organizational membership. By working part-time, students not only earn money, but they can also learn important job skills, begin building their résumés, and better understand careers they may wish to pursue. For younger people, part-time work can be a fruitful opportunity.

Job Attitudes

In recent years, there have been comparisons among different types of part-time workers as well as between part-time and full-time workers in terms of job attitudes. Findings have been inconsistent, with some research indicating large differences between full- and part-time employees on organizational commitment, job satisfaction, and turnover intentions, while other findings have suggested little difference. Research that has found differences in job attitudes between full- and part-time workers has suggested that part-time workers have lower satisfaction, commitment, and engagement and higher turnover intentions than full-time workers. It is likely, though, that these results are influenced by whether people take part-time work voluntarily and whether they perceive themselves as underemployed.

The Challenges of Part-Time Work

As the number of part-time workers has increased in the past three decades, both organizations and researchers have begun paying more attention to this subsection of the workforce. Although recognition and understanding of the contingent workforce has grown, there remain challenges to be faced by workers and organizations alike.

Underemployment

Despite the recent increase in part-time work, which meets the demands of both workers and employers, challenges have also risen during the part-time boom, particularly underemployment. Underemployment may involve several facets, including involuntary part-time or temporary work, overqualification, and underpayment, and is generally classified as inadequate employment.

People often must pursue part-time work after experiencing stressful situations or setbacks

(e.g., job loss, reduced hours, spouse's job change). Workers who replace full-time with part-time work may be faced with underemployment, meaning that they have jobs, so they are not classified as unemployed, but the jobs are insufficient to support them or those they care for. Part-time work offers a supplemental or side opportunity for some, but for others, part-time work is a last resort effort to make ends meet.

Furthermore, part-time work can be an indicator of social and economic issues, such that a high level of underemployment may indicate a poor economy, high unemployment, or other national issues. Of interest to organizations, underemployment may be related to negative job attitudes, such as low commitment, low job satisfaction, and high turnover intentions, which may in turn affect performance and other organizational outcomes.

The Limits of Flexible Work Schedules

Although there have been increases in the demand and availability of part-time professional jobs, many job fields and industries do not offer part-time employment opportunities for workers who want to voluntarily decrease their workloads. For instance, employees may want to work shorter hours or limit the number of days a week they work in the years or months leading up to their retirement, yet many organizations may not be prepared to offer this form of flexible employment, or employees' roles may not be suitable to part-time scheduling (e.g., working with clients, frequent deadlines, travel). As the desire for flexibility increases among professionals, employees' opportunities for part-time work will need to be addressed in coming years.

Organizational Challenges Posed by Part-Time Workers

Like other forms of contingent workers, part-time employees offer organizations an opportunity to get the help they need without having to permanently hire and provide benefits to employees. Instead, a worker may be brought in at a part-time salary to complete work as an organization needs. The supplemental use for part-time workers enables organizations to maintain work flow and cut costs, offering a contrasting version of work as compared with part-time work in service industries. With this newer form of part-time employment, however, there are some challenges organizations must face.

As organizations bring in more contingent workers, they must decide how to hire and train these employees; many organizations struggle with how to handle these processes when dealing with nonstandard workers. Part-time employees, who may be employed at the same organization but work conflicting hours, work multiple jobs, or have other responsibilities outside of work (e.g., children, elder care) may be prevented from attending training sessions at the same time. Part-time employees often offer logistical challenges because of the nature of their work that are not issues with standard workers. Furthermore, organizations must now track more nonstandard employees than ever before. With employees coming and going with different hours, employment contracts, psychological contracts, salaries, and tenures, organizations must work harder to keep tabs on whom they are employing, when, and in what capacity. Such challenges are likely to continue growing, and organizations must adapt to this more fluid environment.

Summary

Part-time work continues to be on the rise in the U.S. workforce for economic, business, and lifestyle reasons. As a form of contingent work, part-time jobs are considered nonstandard but continue to become more common. Furthermore, part-time work, as well as other forms of contingent work, has become nuanced in recent years. Part-time work comes in many forms, and part-time workers can have numerous motivations, tenures, pay scales, attitudes, and experiences. The number of part-time workers as well as the types of part-time work that exist continue to increase in North America and Europe, raising new challenges for both workers and organizations. Nevertheless, contingent employment, including part-time employment, will likely continue to increase in popularity and frequency in the future.

Chelsea Beveridge

See also Flexible Work Schedules; Outsourcing and Temporary Work; Underemployment

Further Readings

Feldman, D. C. (1990). Reconceptualizing the nature and consequences of part-time work. *Academy of Management Review, 15*(1), 103–112.

Feldman, D. C. (2005). Toward a new taxonomy for understanding the nature and consequences of contingent employment. *Career Development International, 11*, 28–47.

Kalleberg, A. L. (2000). Nonstandard employment relations: Part-time, temporary and contract work. *Annual Review of Sociology, 26*, 341–365.

Lawrence, T. B., & Corwin, V. (2003). Being there: The acceptance and marginalization of part-time professional employees. *Journal of Organizational Behavior, 24*, 923–943.

Maynard, D., & Feldman, D. (2011). *Underemployment: Psychological, economic, and social challenges.* New York: Springer.

Thorsteinson, T. J. (2003). Job attitudes of part-time vs. full-time workers: A meta-analytic review. *Journal of Occupational and Organizational Psychology, 76*, 151–177.

PASSION AT WORK

The popular press is replete with stories emphasizing the importance of having passion for work, together with advice on how employees and their managers can develop work passion. However, systematic research on work passion did not occur until the early 2000s, when scholars built on seminal work by Robert Vallerand to examine passion in the workplace, the outcomes of work passion, and factors that drive such passion. Passion, defined as a strong inclination toward an activity that people like and find important, can extend to one's work and encompasses three elements: affective, cognitive, and behavioral. The affective element captures the strong, intense liking for and enjoyment of work, while the cognitive element captures the importance or significance of work to the individual's life, such that the work becomes internalized to one's identity and defines who the individual is. Finally, the behavioral element entails devoting significant time and effort to work. Thus, passionate workers love the work they do, view it as a significant part of their lives, and invest considerable time and energy in it.

Work passion is distinct from other seemingly related concepts, such as extrinsic and intrinsic motivation, job satisfaction, job involvement, and work engagement. Extrinsic motivation does not engender liking for or enjoyment of work that is representative of passion, while intrinsic motivation does not involve the internalization of work into one's identity. Likewise, job satisfaction, job involvement, and other similar work attitudes are different from passion in that the former either do not embody the intense positive feelings the latter encompasses or fail to capture the internalization of work into one's self-concept. Thus, work passion represents a construct in its own right and has been shown to predict various work outcomes even after accounting for the influences of other common work determinants.

Most research on work passion has adopted the dualistic model of passion, which builds from self-determination theory. The dualistic model proposes that passion can take two forms: harmonious and obsessive. Both are similar in that they entail a person's strongly enjoying and identifying with his or her work, such that the work role occupies a central part of one's identity (e.g., defining oneself as a veterinarian). However, the two are distinct in how the work is internalized. Harmonious passion involves an *autonomous* form of internalization in which individuals voluntarily and freely accept the work role as part of who they are, because of the inherent challenge and enjoyment work brings. Obsessive passion, on the other hand, involves a *controlled* form of internalization in which individuals feel compelled or pressured into defining themselves by their work. These pressures can stem from internal reasons (e.g., a sense of uncontrollable excitement when working) or external contingencies (e.g., social acceptance and esteem that comes with that work role). Consequently, whereas harmoniously passionate workers freely engage in their work and have control over when to perform work activities, their obsessively passionate counterparts are controlled by their work and cannot help but engage in work activities. Furthermore, they experience guilt, anxiety, and other negative emotions when not working.

Outcomes of Work Passion

A key reason for the emerging interest in work passion is the belief that passion shapes important work outcomes for employees and, in turn, their employers. Research supports this notion, with multiple studies demonstrating that harmonious work passion is associated with adaptive outcomes that include employees' performance and other behavioral consequences, as well as work-related attitudes and psychological consequences. Findings on outcomes ensuing from obsessive passion, however, are weaker and more equivocal, underscoring the mixed nature of obsessive passion and suggesting the presence of critical contingencies that determine whether obsessive passion will yield adaptive or maladaptive outcomes.

Behavioral Outcomes

Research shows that harmoniously passionate workers demonstrate adaptive work behaviors that include enhanced work performance and creativity, as rated by supervisors. Although such passion is also linked to higher rates of organizational citizenship behaviors (i.e., discretionary, extra-role behaviors that are not explicitly rewarded but contribute to the organization's functioning), this positive association tapers off and, in fact, becomes negative after a certain point, suggesting that too much harmonious passion may be detrimental to the performance of such behaviors. Outside the workplace, harmoniously passionate workers enjoy more positive interpersonal relationships, experience less work-family interference, and engage in more leisure-time physical activities, all of which demonstrate that the benefits of harmonious passion extend to nonwork contexts.

Although one may expect obsessive passion to predict maladaptive behaviors, research findings are mixed. In terms of predicting work performance, obsessive passion did not exhibit an effect in some studies, whereas in others, it showed a positive association only among employees whose values were aligned with the organization's, whose needs were met by the organization, and those operating in dynamic environments. Similarly, the link between obsessive passion and citizenship behaviors is multifaceted. Among employees with low collectivistic values (i.e., those who value independence and individual interests over group interests), citizenship behaviors were highest among those with very low or very high obsessive passion, whereas those with moderate levels of obsessive passion engaged in the fewest citizenship behaviors. The reverse pattern was found for employees with high collectivistic values, such that those with moderate levels of obsessive passion engaged in more citizenship behaviors than those with very high or very low obsessive passion.

Psychological Outcomes

Harmonious work passion also predicts adaptive psychological outcomes, including work attitudes (e.g., enhanced job satisfaction, career satisfaction, affective organizational commitment, occupational commitment, organizational identification, and evaluations of job demands and resources and lowered turnover intentions and burnout symptoms), cognition (e.g., flow experiences, cognitive absorption, focus), positive emotions, and improved psychological well-being. In contrast, obsessive passion is associated with more negative emotions as well as decreased psychological well-being and life satisfaction. Findings in relation to work attitudes are more equivocal. For instance, obsessive passion was positively related to job satisfaction and negatively related to burnout in some studies; in others, however, it showed no relationship. Further illustrating the complex nature of obsessive passion, a cross-national study found that obsessive passion positively predicted job satisfaction and occupational commitment among Russian employees but not among Chinese employees.

Together, these findings demonstrate that harmonious work passion contributes to success and satisfaction inside and outside of work, whereas obsessive passion operates in a nuanced fashion such that it can yield positive or negative consequences, depending on various contextual factors. This presents opportunities for future research to delve into the personal and situational contingencies that determine whether and when obsessive work passion will yield adaptive or maladaptive outcomes.

Developing Work Passion

Compared with research on the consequences of work passion, there is less work on the drivers of

passion. The few studies examining this issue suggest that people are likely to develop work passion when they have a preference for and enjoy their work; when they view it as important and meaningful to them; and when the work is aligned with, and thus can be more easily internalized to, their senses of self. In turn, such internalization is shaped by individuals' personalities and the social environment.

Individuals are likely to develop harmonious work passion when they have autonomous personality orientations, whereby they do things on the basis of personal goals, interests, and choice rather than controls and constraints. Furthermore, those with high self-esteem and emotional intelligence, and those whose work allows them to use their signature strengths are likely to experience harmonious work passion. In terms of workplace drivers, factors at the organizational level (e.g., clan culture), supervisory level (e.g., transformational leadership), and team level (e.g., team and unit autonomy support) have been found to boost employees' harmonious work passion. The determinants of obsessive passion are less clear, but preliminary evidence suggests that employees with controlled personality orientations (i.e., a tendency to do things out of pressure) and low self-esteem, as well as those working under transactional leaders and in organizations with market cultures, are likely to develop obsessive passion. More broadly, the findings suggest that enhancing employees' (a) enjoyment of what they do, (b) perceived competence at work, (c) perceived meaningfulness of work, and (d) sense of autonomy in deciding how and what to do can aid in developing harmonious work passion.

Entrepreneurial Passion

A separate but related stream of research examines passion among entrepreneurs, including passion for three entrepreneurial roles: inventor, founder, and developer. Not surprisingly, entrepreneurial passion yields higher venture growth and more funding from venture capitalists. Furthermore, passion for the inventor role is associated with more creativity, whereas passion for the founder role is linked to more creativity and persistence. Finally, passion for the developer role results in greater persistence and absorption. The dualistic model has also been used to examine entrepreneurial passion, with results replicating those on work passion. Entrepreneurs with harmonious passion tend to seek out others in their networking groups for help, report higher referral income from their networking groups, are inclined to exploit new product opportunities, and experience less burnout. In contrast, those with obsessive passion are less sought after by others in their networking groups, receive less referral income from them, experience more burnout, and are inclined to exploit new product opportunities only if they experience high nonwork excitement.

Overall, research on passion at work is at a nascent stage, with many questions and opportunities for further exploration. These include examining whether harmonious passion can exhibit a too-much-of-a-good-thing phenomenon, the contingency factors that determine when obsessive passion can yield positive or negative outcomes, and the drivers of both forms of passion.

Violet T. Ho

See also Engagement; Entrepreneurship; Intrinsic and Extrinsic Work Motivation; Self-Determination Theory; Work Motivation

Further Readings

Cardon, M. S., Wincent, J., Singh, J., & Drnovsek, M. (2009). The nature and experience of entrepreneurial passion. *Academy of Management Review, 34,* 511–532.

Chen, X.-P., Liu, D., & He, W. (2015). Does passion fuel entrepreneurship and job creativity? A review and preview of passion research. In C. E. Shalley, M. A. Hitt, & J. Zhou (Eds.), *Oxford handbook of creativity, innovation, and entrepreneurship* (pp. 159–175). New York: Oxford University Press.

Vallerand, R. J. (2010). On passion for life activities: The dualistic model of passion. In M. P. Zanna (Ed.), *Advances in experimental social psychology* (Vol. 42, pp. 97–193). New York: Academic Press.

Vallerand, R. J., Houlfort, N., & Forest, J. (2014). Passion for work: Determinants and outcomes. In M. Gagné (Ed.), *The Oxford handbook of work engagement, motivation, and self-determination theory* (pp. 85–105). Oxford, UK: Oxford University Press.

PATH–GOAL THEORY

The path–goal theory of leadership is a situational theory of leadership that is closely aligned with expectancy theory and contingency theory. Expectancy theory can be summarized as an individual's decision to act in such a manner dependent strictly on the intrinsic benefits of the results of those actions. Contingency theory contends that individuals, leaders, and companies that optimize decision making after contemplating the external and internal situations may gain efficiencies. Path–goal theory holds that the major function of a leader is to enhance subordinates' instrumentalities (i.e., perceived degree of relationship between behavior and outcome), expectancies (i.e., perceived relationship between effort and behavior), and valences (i.e., feelings regarding attractiveness of outcome) in an effort to increase subordinate force (i.e., motivational effort). Thus, although the theory is a leadership theory, it relies heavily on the work motivation literature.

Path–goal theory was originally contrived as a dyadic theory of leadership—a theory concerning relationships between appointed supervisors and subordinates—but has been expanded to include supervisor and unit relationships and more recently at the first-level individual. It is generally concerned with how formally appointed supervisors influence the motivation and attitudes of their respective subordinates. It is not concerned with organizational leadership, emergent leadership, leadership strategy, or leadership during times of organizational change; it is concerned with job task leadership. In more concrete terms, path–goal theory proposes that the primary function of a leader is to increase individual employee gains, rewards, and other positive outcomes for work goal attainment by creating a more easily traversed path to goal attainment (i.e., removing obstacles, clarifying goals, and increasing job satisfaction). Whether a leader can do so effectively depends heavily on various contextual and situational factors and subordinate characteristics. Thus, according to the theory, effective leaders are those who streamline work processes by complementing the characteristics of the environment and subordinates. If such situational affordances are present, leaders can increase subordinate motivation, job attitudes, and performance.

At an individual level, path–goal theory can be seen as the actions taken to reduce or eliminate a perceived weakness. This framework allows the identification of specific goals and the direction (path) needed for goal attainment. Perception ultimately is the determinate of the worthiness of these specific goals and the direction or path to said goals. The decision to take action toward a goal will be internally weighed by the presentiment, utility, and intricate value.

Leader Behaviors

The theory further states that a leader might display four different types of leadership styles, depending on the situation, to maximize employee effectiveness. Some researchers state that more effective leaders simultaneously incorporate all four styles because of the unique effects of each style across varying work tasks and conditions. Subordinates' acceptance of a leader's style escalates motivation, assisting in goal attainment and leading to performance gain for both subordinates and the leader. The four styles are as follows:

1. *Directive leadership.* Effective leaders should provide specific guidance of performance, set acceptable standards of performance, and provide explicit performance expectations to subordinates. Generally, this approach is best when work is unstructured and complex and/or the subordinates are inexperienced. Such an approach tends to increase subordinates' sense of security and control.

2. *Supportive leadership.* Effective leaders should be friendly to subordinates and demonstrate concern for each subordinate's well-being by considering each individual's needs. Generally, this approach is best when work is stressful, boring, and/or hazardous.

3. *Participative leadership.* An effective leader consults with subordinates by (a) soliciting ideas and suggestions from subordinates, (b) soliciting participative decision making affecting subordinates, and (c) valuing and considering subordinates' suggestions. Generally, this

approach is best when the subordinates are experts and their advice is necessary for achieving work goals.

4. *Achievement-oriented leadership.* Effective leaders set moderately difficult and challenging goals, continuously emphasize work performance improvements, and expect subordinates to achieve high levels of performance. Generally, this approach is optimal for complex work, but research suggests that it is important across all types of work.

Situational Moderators

Path–goal theory also contends that leadership effects on subordinates are moderated by two general classes of boundary conditions:

1. Environmental characteristics: task structure and demands, role ambiguity, work autonomy, task interdependence, and task scope

2. Subordinate characteristics: cognitive ability, dependence, stress, locus of control, goal orientation, and authoritarianism

Using one of the four styles of leadership described above and considering situational factors, leaders try to influence employees' perceptions and motivate them toward goal attainment by clarifying roles, expectancies, satisfaction, and performance standards.

Support for the Theory

Although path–goal theory can be classified as one of the "major triumphs" of leadership theory, empirical support for many of its mechanisms is lacking. The theoretical crux of the theory was motivation, which was posited as a mediator between leader behavior and subordinate behavior and outcomes (e.g., satisfaction, performance). However, the major pitfall of research on path–goal theory was the lack of integration of motivation into empirical assessments of the theory. Empirical assessments have focused on the direct effects of leader behavior on subordinate behavior and outcomes. This had been a major problem in most leadership and work motivation research until the early 1990s.

Additionally, empirical studies of path–goal theory were quite restrictive in the variety of leader behaviors examined, the outcomes studied, and the situational and person moderator variables examined. For example, nearly all empirical work on path–goal theory has focused on only two leader behaviors: directive leadership behavior and supportive leadership behavior. These two classes of behavior have generally been examined in light of task structure, task and job performance, and facets of satisfaction (e.g., job, intrinsic, extrinsic satisfaction), and results are mixed. Because of these shortcomings, the original theory has been recast to encourage researchers to reexamine the theory by including more leadership behaviors, motivational influences, and subordinate and work unit outcomes.

Reformulated Path–Goal Theory (1996)

The increasing use of teams and other more structurally and socially defined units in organizations has forced organizational researchers to modify their way of thinking about organizational behavior and consequently the way we conduct organizational research. This change, among others, forced path–goal theory to adapt. In 1996, the theory was recast to be more inclusive of recent theoretical advancement and more readily testable. The reformulated theory concerns work-unit leadership and is not limited to dyadic relationships. This is due partly to the transition of organizations to more team-based structures. The theory is now driven by mechanisms aimed at enhancing empowerment and motivation of all subordinates within a work unit and how such empowerment influences work unit effectiveness via motivation.

Summary

When comparing leadership theories, path–goal theory is one that has stood the test of time, even with the lack of empirical support, which is easily attributable to the lack of appropriate empirical investigations. It is a theory that has helped direct the leadership area by expanding theoretical thinking and has given rise to many important leadership theories (e.g., transformational leadership). It has done so by incorporating two important areas of industrial and organizational psychology: motivation and power. Two strengths of path–goal theory have been identified as follows: (a) It is a theoretical framework developing the understanding leadership styles as previously reviewed: directive, supportive, participative, and achievement-oriented leadership. (b) It confirms the concept that leadership can influence and motivate subordinates, and it can be seen as a practical model. Overall, and as with many other industrial and organizational psychology theories, more research is needed, especially in testing the reformulated theory. The theory is certainly worthy of future attention.

Warren Dyer and J. Craig Wallace

See also Goal Orientation; Goal-setting Theory; Self-regulation Theory; Work Motivation

Further Readings

Bass, B. (1985). *Leadership and performance beyond expectations*. New York: Free Press.

Burns, J. M. (1978). *Leadership*. New York: Harper & Row.

Evans, M. G. (1970). The effect of supervisory behavior on the path–goal relationship. *Organizational Behavior and Human Performance, 5*, 277–298

Evans, M. G. (1996). R. J. House's A path–goal theory of leader effectiveness. *Leadership Quarterly, 7*, 305–309.

Fox, R. D., & Miner, C. (1999). Motivation and the facilitation of change, learning, and participation in educational programs for health professionals. *Journal of Continuing Education in the Health Professions, 19*(3), 132–141.

Georgopoulos, B. S., Mahoney, T. M., & Jones, L. W. (1957). A path–goal approach to productivity. *Journal of Applied Psychology, 41*, 345–353.

Hackman, J. R., & Porter, L. W. (1968). Expectancy theory predictions of work expectancies. *Organizational Behavior and Human Performance, 3*, 417–426.

House, R. J. (1971). A path–goal theory of leader effectiveness. *Administrative Science Quarterly, 16*, 321–338.

House, R. J. (1996). Path–goal theory of leadership: Lessons, legacy and a reformulated theory. *Leadership Quarterly, 7*, 323–352.

Malik, S. H., Aziz, S., & Hassan, H. (2014). Leadership behavior and acceptance of leaders by subordinates: Application of path goal theory in telecom sector. *International Journal of Trade, Economics and Finance, 5*(2), 170–175. doi:10.7763/IJTEF.2014 .V5.364

Polston-Murdoch, L. (2013). An investigation of path-goal theory, relationship of leadership style, supervisor-related commitment, and gender. *Emerging Leadership Journeys, 6*, 13–44.

Wofford, J. C., & Liska, L. Z. (1993). Path–goal theories of leadership: A meta-analysis. *Journal of Management, 19*(4), 857–876.

PERCEIVED ORGANIZATIONAL SUPPORT

The term *perceived organizational support* (POS) refers to employees' perceptions of the extent to which their organization, as a whole, values their contributions and cares about their well-being. For example, employees with high POS are likely to believe that the organization they work for "has their back," shows appreciation and acknowledges their extra efforts, and would help them out if needed. On the other hand, employees with low POS are likely to feel as if their organization would not be there for them if they needed help, does not show concern for them, and does not take pride in their accomplishments.

Commonly studied predictors of POS include treatment by organizational members (e.g., supervisors), employee–organization relationship quality (e.g., fair treatment), and human resource practices (e.g., family-supportive policies). In terms of outcomes, POS has been related to a wide variety of outcomes including in-role and extra-role performance, affective commitment to the organization, and withdrawal from the organization, as well as employee well-being outcomes such as job satisfaction and positive mood. Organizational support theory (OST) is the theoretical framework helping explain why individuals are likely to form POS and to repay the organization. The three main mechanisms involved in OST are (a) the attribution process, (b) felt obligation of reciprocation, and (c) self-enhancement through fulfillment of socioemotional needs.

POS is focused on understanding employees' perspectives. That is, POS is employees' overall belief about whether the organization treats them supportively, rather than a supervisor's perspective or an organization's perspective as to whether the organization is supportive of employees. POS is a general, overall evaluation of the supportiveness of each employee's organization. POS expresses employees' evaluations of the degree of discretionary favorable treatment from the organization (e.g., fair treatment, training opportunities) and whether the organization meets their socioemotional needs (e.g., approval, esteem, affiliation, emotional support). Employees also evaluate whether the organization would provide them with future resources to do their jobs well and the organization would reward increased efforts.

POS was first introduced in 1986 by Eisenberger and colleagues. Since then, POS has seen rapid growth; more than 500 studies have examined POS in the past 30 years. POS has become a popular subject of study because it has been theoretically linked to many important organizational outcomes (e.g., performance, turnover, commitment, helping behaviors); has relevance across many organizational contexts, situations, and cultures; has a reliable measure; and has been strongly grounded in OST. In this entry, we discuss OST, predictors and outcomes of POS, and future research directions.

Organizational Support Theory

OST is a theory about employee–organization relationships and considers the development, nature, and outcomes of POS.

Personification of the Organization

A basic premise in OST is that employees tend to assign the organization humanlike characteristics; the employee tends to personify the organization. For example, an employee may think that his or her supervisor is supportive, that the organization has helpful flexible work policies, and that his or her coworkers tend to ask if they can help when the employee seems stressed. Typically, the employee will roll all of these positive evaluations into one and say something like "my organization supports me" or "my organization treats me well."

In reality, of course "the organization" itself cannot "support" or "treat" the employee a certain way; the people and the policies within the organization do that. However, because POS is a global, general assessment of how employees are treated, employees tend to assign the organization these humanlike characteristics and refer to their general view as what "the organization" does. Actions taken by agents of the organization (e.g., supervisors, coworkers, subordinates, upper management, the CEO) are also often attributed to the organization and thus comprise the employee's perception of organizational support.

Social Exchange

OST is built on the idea of social exchange. OST is an application of social-exchange theory to the employer–employee relationship such that employees will trade effort, dedication, and commitment to their organization in exchange for both tangible rewards (e.g., pay, incentives, good working conditions) and socioemotional needs (e.g., esteem, approval, and caring). Social exchange theory helps us understand why employees are willing to help the organization achieve its goals. The idea is that, for all social interactions, including those at work and with the organization, individuals develop and maintain social relationships. If individuals develop positive relationships with their organization, they are more likely to invest their own resources back into the organization on the basis of the norm of reciprocity.

Norm of Reciprocity

The norm of reciprocity is a universal norm that has been found to be influential and consistent across cultures and settings, including organizations. The norm of reciprocity is so common because individuals want to maintain their reputations and self-images and do not want to be seen as violating social norms. Individuals may also believe that by repaying their exchange partners for being treated favorably, they will also be encouraging future favorable treatment from those partners (e.g., other people or the organization). Individuals thus try to evaluate if the exchange partner (e.g., the organization) treats

them favorably or unfavorably so that the employee will know how to maintain and foster their relationship with the exchange partner in the future. These evaluations help employees make decisions about how they may be treated in the future, how they may be able to change their behavior to be treated more favorably, and how effective they have been when interacting with their organization.

Predictors and Outcomes of POS

We outline some of the well-studied predictors and outcomes of POS below. However, research involving OST has blossomed. For example, a recent meta-analysis from 2015 by Kurtessis and colleagues found that as transformational leadership, employee–organization value congruence, flexible work practices, family-supportive work policies, and job enrichment increase, POS also increases. The meta-analysis also examined a variety of outcomes and found that POS is positively related to trust in the organization, felt obligation, and organizational identification. POS is also negatively related to job stress, burnout, emotional exhaustion, and work–family conflict.

Predictors of POS

The Role of the Attribution Process in POS Perceptions: Discretionary Versus Forced Aid

When we consider predictors of POS, we must consider the role of the attribution process. Typically, aid that is attributed to the organization's discretion or control is valued more than aid that is perceived as forced or prescribed. This means that employees are keen to pay attention to discretionary treatment when evaluating the extent to which the organization is supportive. The more the employee perceives that the behavior, job condition, or policy is under the organization's control and the organization does something the employee views as favorable, the more likely POS will increase. For example, supervisors are agents of the organization and have the choice to treat their employees favorably or unfavorably because, generally, no one is forcing the supervisor to behave in a certain way.

Similarly, fair treatment from the organization is likely to be perceived as up to the discretion of the organization. Thus, it is no surprise that fair treatment and supervisor support are consistently two of the strongest predictors of POS. Below we cover the main categories of predictors of POS from the literature to date. On the basis of OST, each predictor should be more positively related to POS if perceived as discretionary rather than if forced or prescribed.

Fairness

Fairness, also known as organizational justice, has been found to have a positive relationship with POS. When employees feel as if they are being treated fairly, they are likely to think the organization cares about their well-being, listens to their thoughts and contributions, and makes decisions that are in their best interest. Examples of things employees may evaluate as fair include decisions made about formal rules and policies, giving employees accurate information in a timely manner, allowing employees to feel as if they have input into decision-making processes, treating employees with respect, and providing employees with information about how decisions are made.

Human Resource Practices and Job Conditions

Previous research has found positive relationships between human resource practices (something the organization can control) such as organizational rewards and favorable job conditions and POS. Some examples of rewards and favorable job conditions include employee recognition, increased pay and promotions, a sense of job security and autonomy, eliminating job stressors, and offering training. When employees are rewarded (e.g., recognition, pay, and promotions), they should feel as if the organization values their contributions, and thus there is a positive relationship with POS. Similarly, a feeling of job security should contribute to POS because employees should feel as if the organization wants to maintain their relationship in the future.

Supervisor Support

Supervisors often act as agents of the organization. Employees interact with them often, and they typically have control over job conditions, job

tasks, and performance evaluations and are seen as having both formal and informal status. Just as employees form general perceptions about the organization, employees form general favorable or unfavorable perceptions of their supervisors. This is commonly referred to as *perceived supervisor support*. If an employee views a supervisor as part of the organization and the supervisor treats him or her supportively (i.e., favorably, fairly, and kindly), POS is likely to increase. Similarly, employees realize that supervisors' evaluations of them are communicated to upper management, which thus makes it more likely that a supervisor's support contributes to a general view of how the organization views the employee.

Outcomes of POS

The Role of Felt Obligation and Fulfillment of Socioemotional Needs

When considering why POS relates to a wide variety of outcomes, theoretically there are two main mechanisms. The first is *felt obligation to reciprocate*. Because of the norm of reciprocity, when individuals feel as if they are treated favorably, they should feel obligated to return the favorable treatment by being committed to the organization, performing well, and helping others. Research has shown that some employees have a stronger exchange ideology than others, which means that some employees believe strongly that their efforts should depend largely on how the organization treats them, while others do not subscribe as strongly to this view. Thus, the higher the exchange ideology, the more likely employees will decide how much effort to put in on the basis of how supportively they are treated by the organization (i.e., tit for tat).

The second mechanism involved in linking POS to outcomes is self-enhancement through the *fulfillment of socioemotional needs*. Similar to support from family members and friends, POS helps employees feel as if their esteem, affiliation, and approval needs are being met. The more employees feel as if these needs are being met, the more likely they are to want to return that support and favorable treatment with higher performance, helping behaviors, and particularly affective commitment given that fulfillment of needs helps incorporate the organization into the employees' identities.

When employees have high POS, socioemotional need fulfillment from it is also likely to lead to positive employee outcomes such as reduced stress and more positive mood.

Affective Commitment

One of the most consistent relationships found in the POS literature is the positive relationship between POS and affective commitment. On the basis of the norm of reciprocity, if employees have high POS, they should have a felt obligation to return the care they receive from the organization with affective commitment (i.e., positive emotional attachment to the organization). Similarly, POS should meet employees' socioemotional needs and thus make employees feel a sense of belonging to the organization.

Performance

Organizations are always interested in ways to improve employee performance. POS has been found to increase in-role performance because employees will want to repay the organization for its support and valuing their contributions. For example, if employees feel as if the organization supports them and notices their work and that their supervisor recognizes their effort on the job, the employees will want to continue to work hard and perform well as a way to repay the organization.

Organizational Citizenship Behaviors

Organizational citizenship behaviors, also known as extra-role helping behaviors, include helping coworkers, protecting the organization, offering suggestions, and doing various tasks that are outside the employee's formal job description. POS has been positively related to organizational citizenship behaviors because employees want to put effort in on behalf of the organization and the employees should want to repay the organization with increased effort (i.e., going above and beyond their formal job tasks).

Withdrawal Behavior

Withdrawal behavior includes any behaviors that decrease active participation in the organization, including intentions to quit, lateness, absenteeism, and voluntary turnover. Because POS

increases employee's feelings of belonging to the organization as well as a felt obligation to help the organization reach its goals, helping meet employees' socioemotional needs and increasing commitment, employees are less likely to withdraw from the organization. Being on time, coming to work, and staying with the organization are all public ways of reciprocating POS.

Job-Related Affect

POS has been found to contribute to individual job satisfaction and positive mood because POS meets socioemotional needs and lets employees know that the organization cares about their well-being and values their contributions. If employees feel as if the organization values them, they should experience more positive emotional states at work, and they should have a general, overall positive attitudes toward their jobs.

Strain

Organizations are constantly searching for ways to reduce psychological reactions (i.e., strains) to stressors, or any environmental condition that causes stress (e.g., lack of resources, lack of support, lack of training). Previous research has found POS to buffer the negative effects of strain because POS fulfills socioemotional needs and gives employees the support they need when facing high demands at work. For example, if employees have a lot of work with strict deadlines, they may be feeling tired, anxious, and stressed. These negative feelings are likely to be mitigated when employees have high POS because they should feel as if the organization has their back, wants them to succeed, and will value the contributions they put forward.

Future Research

Although much is known about POS, there are still some areas in which further knowledge can be produced.

Development of POS Over Time

Although there have been some studies of changes in POS over time, more research is needed to better understand critical incidents that may positively or negatively affect POS. For example, what type of abrupt events, such as a merger, may change POS and why? Researchers should also consider using longitudinal growth modeling to better understand the life cycle of POS and at what point low levels of POS lead to turnover.

Is There Such a Thing as Too Much Support?

Most research to date has found a linear, positive relationship such that as support increases, various positive work outcomes also increase (e.g., commitment, job satisfaction, performance). However, little is known about whether there is such a thing as too much support and what happens if an employee feels too much support. Future research should consider examining nonlinear relationships between POS and various organizational outcomes.

Trickle-Down Effects of POS

Currently, empirical evidence supports the idea that an employee's own POS leads to a variety of positive work outcomes for that employee. Future research should consider evaluating and understanding how others' POS may have positive effects on a particular employee. For example, if a supervisor has high POS, how may these positive effects trickle down and have positive effects on the supervisor's employees? What happens if a supervisor has low POS and his or her employees have high POS or vice versa?

Practical Recommendations

Although POS has been linked to many important organizational and individual outcomes, little research and discussion have focused on practical recommendations for supervisors and organizations. Future research should consider providing practical recommendations that can be incorporated into supervisor training and training for upper management about messages they can send to their employees and specific policies and practices they should consider putting in place to promote POS.

*Alexandra M. Dunn and
Linda Rhoades Shanock*

See also Attitudes and Beliefs; Contextual Performance/ Prosocial Behavior/Organizational Citizenship Behavior; Engagement; Organizational Commitment; Organizational Justice; Social Exchange Theory; Social Support

Further Readings

Allen, D. G., Shore, L. M., & Griffeth, R. W. (2003). The role of perceived organizational support and supportive human resource practices in the turnover process. *Journal of Management, 29*(1), 99–118. doi:10.1177/014920630302900107

Baran, B. E., Shanock, L. R., & Miller, L. R. (2012). Advancing organizational support theory into the twenty-first century world of work. *Journal of Business and Psychology, 27*(2), 123–147. doi:10.1007/s10869-011-9236-3

Eisenberger, R., Huntington, R., Hutchison, S., & Sowa, D. (1986). Perceived organizational support. *Journal of Applied Psychology, 71*, 500–507. doi:10.1037//0021-9010.71.3.500

Eisenberger, R., & Stinglhamber, F. (2011). *Perceived organizational support: Fostering enthusiastic and productive employees.* Washington, DC: American Psychological Association Press.

Eisenberger, R., Stinglhamber, F., Vandenberghe, C., Sucharski, I., & Rhoades, L. 2002. Perceived supervisor support: Contributions to perceived organizational support and employee retention. *Journal of Applied Psychology, 87*, 565–573. doi:10.1037/0021-9010.87.3.565

Kurtessis, J. N., Eisenberger, R., Ford, M. T., Buffardi, L. C., Stewart, K. A., & Adis, C. S. (in press). Perceived organizational support: A meta-analytic evaluation of organizational support theory. *Journal of Management.* doi:10.1177/0149206315575554

Rhoades, L., & Eisenberger, R. (2002). Perceived organizational support: A review of the literature. *Journal of Applied Psychology, 87*(4), 698. doi:10.1037//0021-9010.87.4.698

Rhoades, L., Eisenberger, R., & Armeli, S. (2001). Affective commitment to the organization: The contribution of perceived organizational support. *Journal of Applied Psychology, 86*(5), 825. doi:10.1037//0021-9010.86.5.825

Wayne, S. J., Shore, L. M., & Liden, R. C. (1997). Perceived organizational support and leader-member exchange: A social exchange perspective. *Academy of Management Journal, 40*(1), 82–111. doi:10.2307/257021

PERFORMANCE APPRAISAL

Performance appraisal refers to the systematic measurement and evaluation of work behaviors, potential, or outputs (i.e., performance) as part of an organization's performance management system. These appraisals typically are conducted at the individual level of the employee but also may include formal appraisals across levels (e.g., teams, units). Performance appraisals typically focus on behaviors or performance dimensions that are required of the position, typically identified by conducting job analyses of the position. Performance appraisals focus on the primary aspects of one's job requirements and tend not to include discretionary behaviors. Reflecting social, political, and organizational changes, performance appraisal systems continue to evolve to serve many different individual and organizational purposes.

Brief History

Performance appraisals began to grow in popularity with the Industrial Revolution of the early 20th century. World War II fueled this interest as industrial psychologists were given the tasks of classifying and placing individuals in positions to increase the effectiveness of military personnel. Research on performance appraisal systems (e.g., rating formats, rating purpose, rater training, performance improvement) continued after World War II and today remains a major focus of research in industrial and organizational psychology. Performance appraisal research has gone through many phases throughout its history. The 1960s and 1970s were devoted largely to research on rating formats and the 1980s and early 1990s largely to rater cognitive processes, and this research was followed by research on 360-degree feedback or multirater systems. Research continues to investigate these topics, and more recently the issue of performance appraisals across different cultural contexts has been investigated. One constant challenge for researchers and practitioners has been the difficulty of defining and measuring job performance given its dynamic and multidimensional nature.

Variations in Approaches

Appraisals generally are classified into objective (e.g., sales volume) or subjective (e.g., supervisory ratings) measures, with the vast majority of performance appraisal systems using subjective measures of performance. Elements of the appraisal system that may differ across contexts or organizations include variations in rating purpose, rater sources, rating content and formats, and system characteristics.

Appraisal Purpose

Performance appraisals may be used for a variety of purposes, which may be classified into three categories: within-person, between-person, and system maintenance purposes. Within-person purposes involve identifying an employee's strengths or weaknesses to provide developmental feedback to the employee, set employee goals, or suggest particular training or development programs. Between-person purposes are used to make comparisons between employees and may be used to identify who should be promoted, administer merit pay increases, or decide which employees should be terminated. System maintenance purposes include using the appraisals to validate personnel selection assessments, identify organizational training needs, or document information pertaining to personnel decisions. Research indicates that organizations often use performance appraisals for multiple purposes simultaneously, and the observed ratings and attitudes of the users differ as a function of rating purpose. Appraisal purpose is an important consideration given that it directly affects how an organization's performance management system is developed, implemented, and maintained. Additionally, rating purpose affects the quality of information obtained from the evaluators, the attitudes and reactions of its users (both raters and rates), and ultimately its effectiveness in achieving its intended purpose or purposes.

Rater Source

Supervisors are the most widely used source of performance appraisal information. Recent changes in how organizations are structured and function (e.g., flatter and more decentralized, organized around team-based work) have led many organizations to collect performance information from nonsupervisory sources. These rater sources may include peers, subordinates, and customers. Research indicates that different rater sources provide different information, and a more comprehensive assessment of work behaviors may be obtained by collecting information from multiple sources. When multiple rater sources provide performance assessments of a target, the degree to which raters within a source (e.g., peers) or between sources (e.g., peers compared with subordinates) agree in their evaluations is often discussed to help the evaluated employee raise self-awareness with the intent of improving performance.

Rating Content and Format

Virtually any aspect of employee behavior, such as specific behaviors or outcomes, and any level of performance, whether individual or group, may be appraised. Early performance appraisal systems tended to focus on evaluating traits, whereas the current focus is on evaluating job-related behaviors. Performance appraisals generally evaluate past performance, but some forms may require raters to make predictions about potential or future performance. Rating formats may also differ across situations such that, for example, some formats require ratings and other formats require raters to rank-order employees.

System Characteristics

Additional features of the performance appraisal system that may differ across contexts include the frequency of appraisals; the mode by which information is collected, such as paper and pencil versus electronically; whether the raters are anonymous; whether the evaluated employee selects individuals; and whether the evaluations are confidential or public.

Summary

The evaluation of employee work behaviors continues to be an integral part of most organizations' performance management systems. Performance appraisal research has addressed myriad topics

expected to influence the effectiveness of the performance appraisal system, such as rater training programs and user attitudes. Research suggests that the effectiveness of performance appraisal systems is improved when they are based on a thorough job analysis, participants are involved in its design, and raters and ratees are trained to use the system effectively. Despite some research suggesting that the task of evaluating employee performance remains one of managers' least favorite activities, an appropriately designed and implemented system has the ability to improve individual and organizational decision making and effectiveness. To maximally achieve these objectives, recent scholars suggest that performance appraisals should not occur only once or twice a year, but the evaluation of, and feedback regarding, performance should occur daily.

Gary J. Greguras

See also Electronic Performance Monitoring; Multimodal Performance Measurement and Assessment; Performance Appraisal, Objective Indices; Performance Appraisal, Subjective Indices; 360-Degree Feedback; Performance Feedback; Rater Training

Further Readings

Day, D. V., & Greguras, G. J. (2009). Performance management in multinational companies. In J. W. Smither & M. London (Eds.), *Performance management: Putting research into practice* (pp. 271–295). San Francisco, CA: Jossey-Bass.

DeNisi, A., & Smith, C. E. (2014). Performance appraisal, performance management, and firm-level performance: A review, a proposed model, and new directions for future research. *Academy of Management Annals, 8*(1), 127–179.

Murphy, K. R., & Cleveland, J. N. (1995). *Understanding performance appraisal: Social, organizational, and goal-based perspectives.* Thousand Oaks, CA: Sage.

Murphy, K. R., & Deckert, P. J. (2013). Performance appraisal. In B. A. Bracken, J. F., Carlson, J. C. Hansen, N. Kuncel, S. Reise, & M. C. Rodriguez (Eds.), *APA handbook of testing and assessment in psychology* (Vol. 1, pp. 611–627). Washington, DC: American Psychological Association.

Pulakos, E. D., Hanson, R. M., Arad, S., & Moye, N. (2015). Performance management can be fixed: An on-the-job experiential learning approach for complex behavior change. *Industrial and Organizational Psychology, 8,* 51–76.

PERFORMANCE APPRAISAL, OBJECTIVE INDICES

Industrial and organizational psychologists (and organizational managers) are interested in knowing how well employees perform their jobs. Such information can help make administrative decisions about employees (e.g., promotions, terminations), provide feedback to employees to help them improve their performance, and evaluate human resource procedures such as selection and training. There are two general types of indices that provide information about employee performance. Subjective (or judgmental) indices are based on evaluations or judgments of others concerning employee effectiveness. Objective indices are measures of performance that are countable, or directly observable, and comparable for different employees.

Types of Objective Performance Indices

Objective performance indices are grouped in two categories: production measures and personnel data. Production measures are related to the amount of acceptable work (products or services) resulting from employee effort. Examples are production output, sales volume, and time required to complete a task. Personnel data do not directly assess an employee's work but are important to the overall performance of an employee. Personnel data are typically maintained in employee personnel files and include information related to absence, accidents, grievances, awards, disciplinary actions, and turnover.

Production Measures

Employers are concerned that their employees are productive and efficient in performing their job duties. Production measures are often considered to be the gold standard of job performance indices, because they are linked to an organization's profitability. They also usually have greater credibility than subjective performance indices, because they do not appear to rely on human judgments. The label *objective* suggests that the measures are accurate, unbiased, and reliable, but the label can be misleading.

Objective production measures exist for many jobs, especially those jobs in which tasks are well structured and frequently performed, such as the manufacture or assembly of established products or the provision of standard customer services. There are many possible production measures, some applicable to numerous jobs and others specific to a narrow range of jobs. Objective performance measures should be selected following a thorough job analysis that has identified the job's critical duties and responsibilities.

The most commonly used type of production measure is related to quantity of work, a count of the volume of work produced by employees. Specific examples are the number of lines of computer code written per hour by programmers, number of phone calls made per day by telemarketers, number of arrests per month made by police officers, percentage of standard time required to complete repairs by auto mechanics, and number of patent applications filed by research engineers.

Although also measuring work quantity, indices that assess performance in sales jobs occur frequently, and some specific examples are warranted. Most straightforward are simple indices that count for some time period the number of sales of products or services or tabulate the value of such sales. More fine-grained sales measures include number of new customers, percentage of past customers who make new purchases, number of potential customers contacted, and sales of newly introduced versus older products or services.

Another type of production index assesses quality of work. These measures count the number of errors committed or assess the number of unacceptable or damaged items produced. Specific examples include the dollar value of scrapped raw material for manufacturing employees, number of shortages and overages in cash balances for bank tellers, errors by catalog sales clerks in processing customer orders, rate of errors for data entry personnel, and cost of dishes and glassware broken by restaurant servers.

Primarily in occupations requiring employee–customer interactions using telecommunications systems, such as call center operators and telemarketers, organizations have developed automated approaches to performance measurement. These electronic performance monitoring systems can accurately measure the amount of time an employee requires to answer customer questions, process orders, or present marketing information. The frequency and amount of time that employees are not connected to the telecommunication system can also be measured. Questions have been raised about whether such performance monitoring is invasive of employee privacy or reduces employee trust in the organization. Research indicates that employees are more accepting of electronic monitoring when measured behaviors are clearly job related, employees have input into the design of the monitoring procedure, and employees have some control over when monitoring occurs. Electronic performance monitoring should increase as technological advances lead to more assessment capabilities with decreased costs.

Personnel Data

Measures of absence are the most common personnel data. The importance of absenteeism is evident: Employees cannot meet performance goals if they are absent. Although total days absent in a time period seems like a useful measure, several problems are masked by its apparent simplicity. First, employees are absent from work for many reasons, including personal illness, the illness of family members, transportation problems, and weather conditions. These varied reasons suggest that some absences are more justified than others, but decisions about absence justification may be unclear. Second, various patterns of absence result in differential impact on the organization or are linked to different causes. For example, if Mary is absent all week and Bill is absent on either Monday or Friday for 5 consecutive weeks, both are absent for a total of 5 days. Mary's absences may be caused by illness, whereas Bill's absence pattern suggests job dissatisfaction or poor work motivation. Finally, its many causes lead to inconsistent levels of absence for individual employees over time. These problems have led to the development of absence indices that attempt to account for different reasons that absence occurred. Some measure the amount of time lost because of specific causes, whereas others count the number of periods of absence (i.e., Mary's 5 consecutive days absent count as one absence period, whereas Bill's 5 days absent count as five absence periods).

Another type of personnel data measure employee accidents, usually in terms of lost work time or direct financial costs that result from the accidents. As with absence, not all accidents reflect equally on employee performance. Usually distinctions must be made in terms of the primary cause or causes of an accident and whether the accident could have been avoided if the involved one or more employees had behaved differently. Accident rates are often inconsistent unless they are based on time periods of several months or more. Research suggests that the frequency of unsafe behaviors of employees may yield more useful information than accident rates. Many unsafe behaviors do not lead to actual accidents, but reducing the amount of unsafe behavior should reduce the number of accidents. Unfortunately, it is more difficult to count unsafe work behaviors than accidents.

Turnover is another form of personnel data. Turnover can be defined as whether a particular employee is still employed by the organization at some point in time (often 1 year) after hiring. Turnover can also be defined as the percentage of employees in a job title whose employment ends during some time period (again, often 1 year). Often organizations attempt to distinguish between causes of turnover. Commonly used categories are voluntary (the employee quit) and involuntary (the employee was fired), but often these distinctions are ambiguous. Not all employees who leave an organization are equally valuable, so organizations may attempt to categorize leavers as effective or ineffective and calculate separate turnover rates for each group.

Effectiveness of Objective Performance Indices

Objective indices seem like valuable ways to measure job performance, but they also have less apparent limitations. Useful objective indices are virtually nonexistent for many jobs (especially managerial and professional) and rarely exist for all important duties and responsibilities of any job. As examples, it is difficult to measure well a manager's effectiveness with motivating employees or developing creative solutions to problems by simply counting something. A performance index that does not measure all important parts of the job is termed deficient.

Another serious limitation of many objective performance indices is that the scores are affected by situational factors not controlled by employees.

For example, assigned patrol areas affect the number of arrests made by police officers, tool quality affects the dollar value of scrapped material and products, customer questions affect the time required to process an order, and work stress from understaffing may increase employee absences. Performance measures affected by factors outside employee control are termed contaminated. Often attempts are made to minimize contamination of the index, such as by measuring officers' arrests relative to other officers in the work unit.

Another limitation of objective indices is that they often provide unhelpful performance feedback, because they assess the results of behavior and not the behavior itself. Informing an employee that too few products were sold does not provide the employee with information about what job behaviors, if any, are ineffective. Objective indices that are based on counts of specific job behaviors such as number of customers called per month and number of sales of new products may provide more useful feedback.

Although objective performance indices usually assess individual employee performance, they are often better measures of work group performance. When employees work together closely, countable measures of individual contributions are often lacking, but quantity and quality of the group's output can be assessed. Also, employees may conceal negative behaviors, such as theft or sabotage, but missing or damaged supplies and equipment can often be assessed at the group level.

Research has investigated how strongly objective and subjective measures of performance are related. The average relation can be described as moderate in strength. Although both objective and subjective indices measure job performance, it is clear that each also assesses other factors. One type is not a substitute for the other. When feasible, it is generally better to use both objective and subjective indices when overall job performance is the primary focus of the assessment.

Conclusions

Objective performance indices are not well named. Judgments are typically required when establishing these performance measures. Commonly required judgments include the time period over which performance is assessed, the breadth of behaviors or results included in the index, and adjustments to the index to account for situational factors affecting performance.

Objective indices can be useful measures of job performance when they assess behaviors that employees control and address a job's important duties. Thus, objective measures generally more useful information about the incumbents of jobs that are well structured and predictable in terms of important tasks and procedures than when they are used for jobs that require creative and adaptive responses to complex and dynamic task and situational information.

Objective measures also are better suited for use in administrative decisions about employees and evaluation of human resource programs than for providing feedback to employees. They often provide better assessments of work group performance than of individual employees when important tasks are typically performed interdependently by multiple employees.

James L. Farr

See also Job Analysis; Performance Appraisal, Subjective Indices

Further Readings

Alge, B. J., & Hansen, S. D. (2014). Workplace monitoring and surveillance research since "1984": A review and agenda. In M. D. Coovert & L. F. Thompson (Eds.), *The psychology of workplace technology* (pp. 209–237). New York: Routledge.

Bommer, W. H., Johnson, J. L., Rich, G. A., Podsakoff, P. M., & Mackenzie, S. B. (1995). On the interchangeability of objective and subjective measures of employee performance: A meta-analysis. *Personnel Psychology, 48,* 587–605. doi:10.1111/j.1744-6570.1995.tb01772.x

Borman, W. C., & Smith, T. N. (2012). The use of objective measures as criteria in I-O psychology. In N. Schmitt (Ed.), *The Oxford handbook of personnel assessment and selection* (pp. 532–542). New York: Oxford University Press.

Landy, F. J., & Conte, J. M. (2010). Performance measurement. In F. J. Landy & J. M. Conte, *Work in the 21st century: An introduction to industrial and organizational psychology* (3rd ed., Chap. 5). New York: John Wiley.

PERFORMANCE APPRAISAL, SUBJECTIVE INDICES

Work behaviors, processes, and outcomes may be measured and evaluated using a variety of different methods. Although these performance criteria may be measured with either objective (e.g., sales volume) or subjective (e.g., supervisory ratings) methods, the overwhelming majority of appraisals require raters to make subjective judgments about the performance of an employee. These subjective judgments may be either ratings or rankings and may be collected using a variety of different rating formats.

Appraisal Methods

Graphic Rating Scales

Graphic rating scales are the most widely used format for appraising performance. Graphic rating scales require raters to evaluate employee performance along a continuum of response categories or anchors that convey information about the meaningfulness of the various points along the continuum. For example, a rater may be asked to evaluate an employee's performance using a scale ranging from 1 (*fails to meet expectations*) through 5 (*exceeds expectations*). Another example requires the rater to evaluate the employee's performance by placing a checkmark on a line anchored from *poor* to *excellent*. These evaluations or ratings can easily be converted into numerical scores for the purposes of making comparisons between employees or groups or across performance dimensions. The specificity of both the anchors and the aspect of performance being evaluated varies across scales. The simplicity and ease with which graphic rating scales may be developed likely explain their widespread use. However, this simplicity is also a limitation. The anchors of the scales and the aspect of behavior being evaluated are often ambiguously defined, which may lead to inconsistencies or disagreements among raters using the same scale. It is precisely this ambiguity of the anchors and items that served as the impetus for the development of more specifically defined scales.

Behaviorally Anchored Rating Scales

Behaviorally anchored rating scales (BARSs) are a type of graphic rating scale that defines the anchors and levels of performance in specific behavioral terms. The behavioral anchors are stated in terms of expectations such as "This employee could be expected to . . . ," because it is possible that the rater may not have had the opportunity to observe the exact behavior listed on the form. This specificity in defining the behaviors and levels of performance, as well as favorable rater and ratee reactions to BARSs, likely explain much of their popularity in the 1960s and 1970s. As with any approach, BARSs have several limitations: The scale development process is time-consuming and costly, raters often disagree about the ordering of behavioral examples along the continuum, raters often have difficulty seeing the link between the behavioral example and the performance dimension being evaluated, and the scales often do not generalize from one setting to another. The research on the utility and effectiveness of BARS has produced inconsistent results, leading some to argue that the costs associated with developing BARS cannot be justified from a data quality perspective.

Mixed Standard Scales

Mixed standard scales (MSSs) are a derivation of BARSs. Consistent with BARSs, MSSs use behavioral anchors to define the type and level of performance being evaluated. However, instead of listing the behavioral anchors for a particular dimension along a continuum and requiring the rater to choose the anchor that most closely describes the ratee's performance, MSSs require raters to evaluate each behavioral example. Generally, three items are written for each performance dimension to reflect low, medium, and high levels of performance. Items from all performance dimensions are randomly mixed together and presented to the rater. The rater then indicates whether the ratee performs at, above, or below the level of performance described for each behavioral item. These judgments are then combined to produce separate scores for each performance dimension. One advantage of this approach is that several judgments are made for each performance dimension (i.e., each behavioral anchor serves as an item), and therefore internal reliability estimates may be calculated for each performance dimension. Similarly, raters who rate inconsistently can easily be identified and can be recommended to receive additional training. Likewise, items or performance dimensions that are inconsistently evaluated across raters can be identified for refinement. Because MSSs are conceptually similar to BARSs, many of the limitations noted earlier with BARSs also apply to these scales. A derivation of the MSS is the behavioral observation scale, which requires raters to report the frequency, rather than favorability, of the behaviors being evaluated.

Forced-Choice Scales

Forced-choice scales require raters to choose from among a set of statements the one that best describes the behavior, rate, or evaluated unit. Both the favorability, or social desirability, and discriminability, the degree to which the statement distinguishes between good and poor performers, of an item are considered in the development of a forced-choice scale. Statements or items are grouped so that they are relatively equal on the favorability index but differ on the discriminability index. As such, all items appear equally desirable, but only some of the items discriminate between good and poor performers. Rater responses to the items may be differentially weighted in an algorithm used to derive the overall score on a particular performance dimension, or the number of items chosen with high discriminability indices may be summated to represent the ratee's score on that particular dimension. Forced-choice scales were designed primarily to reduce rater bias by forcing raters to choose from among a list of equally desirable descriptors. Raters who wish to intentionally distort their ratings have difficulty doing so because all items appear equally favorable, and the raters likely cannot discern which items have high discriminability indices. Research suggests that rater errors such as leniency are decreased with forced-choice scales; however, some raters react negatively to the forced-choice format because it is not directly apparent to them how they are evaluating the levels of their employees. Because of the disguised nature of the scoring, raters may also react

negatively because it may be difficult for them to provide feedback to the ratees. The forced-choice rating scale is similar to the MSS in that the scale continuum or actual rating level given to the ratee is not readily apparent to the rater.

Employee Comparison Methods

All the aforementioned scales or methods require raters to make judgments about a particular target. In contrast, employee comparison methods require raters to evaluate targets relative to one another. The three most common employee comparison methods include paired comparisons, ranking, and forced distribution methods.

Paired Comparisons

In contrast to the forced-choice method, which requires raters to choose from among statements for a single target, paired comparison methods force raters to choose between two targets (i.e., ratees). With this method, the supervisor chooses the one employee in the comparison who performs at a higher level or more favorably on the aspect of performance being evaluated. Typically, all possible comparisons are made among employees such that there are $n(n - 1)/2$ total comparisons, where n is the number of employees to be evaluated. For example, if a supervisor is responsible for evaluating 10 employees, the paired comparison method would require the supervisor to make 45 paired comparisons. Once all comparisons have been completed, the rank ordering of employees may be identified by summing the number of times an employee was chosen. One limitation of this approach is that the number of comparisons required of a rater may be quite large, and the task may become time-consuming as the number of ratees and the number of rated dimensions increase. Another potential difficulty of using the paired comparison method deals with the nature of the task. Generally, raters are required to choose the employee in the pairing whose overall performance is better. Raters may have difficulty with this task because a certain employee may perform better than a different employee on one dimension but not another. To overcome this limitation, raters could evaluate specific performance dimensions, rather than overall performance. Rating performance dimensions, instead of overall performance, would increase the feedback value of the ratings to the employee but would add to the complexity (i.e., number of comparisons) of the task.

Rank Ordering

Rank ordering of ratees is another type of employee comparison method and requires raters to create a list of ratees from the best to the worst employee. This rank-ordering method is much less tedious and simpler in terms of comparisons than the paired comparison method. Although it is often easy for raters to identify individuals who should be at the top or bottom of the list, the task may become increasingly difficult in the middle of the list, where ratees may be very similar. Raters are often instructed to use an alternating ranking approach: They first select the best person in the group, then the worst person in the group, then the second-best person from the group, and so on until all ratees have been ranked. With both the paired comparison and rank-ordering methods, an ordered list of employees is created, but this listing provides no information about the absolute level of performance of any particular individual; for example, there is no way of knowing how far apart the best and worst employees are in terms of performance. Another limitation of this approach is that it is difficult to compare ratees from different lists or groups because the rankings are dependent on whom is included in each of the different groups.

Forced Distribution

The forced distribution approach requires raters to place a certain percentage of employees into various performance categories. For example, raters may be required to place 20% of the ratees in the poor performance category, 60% of the ratees in the average performance category, and 20% of the ratees in the good performance category. This method requires less detailed distinctions among ratees, because the rater is merely placing them into general categories instead of rank ordering them. One difficulty with the forced distribution approach is that the size of the performance categories that is forced on raters may not reflect the actual distribution of performance of the ratees. Although this approach may simplify the rater's task, especially when the number of ratees is large, both raters and ratees may

be less accepting of this appraisal approach if the forced distribution does not accommodate the actual level of performance among ratees.

Additional Approaches

The approaches previously reviewed represent the most commonly used techniques to appraise an employee's or a target's (e.g., team) performance. There are, however, numerous derivations and alternative techniques that could be used. For example, narrative approaches require raters to provide written statements that reflect their evaluations and descriptions of employee performance. Although this approach has several limitations, such as amount of time and the rater's ability to effectively communicate in writing, research suggests that narrative comments are effective in improving the performance of the ratees and generally are viewed quite favorably. Other examples of approaches include behavioral diaries, weighted checklists, management by objectives, critical incidents checklists, and behavioral checklists.

Summary

A variety of different performance appraisal approaches exist for measuring and evaluating employee work behaviors. Which approach is best? Comparisons of the different approaches usually involve comparing the rater errors or rating accuracy associated with the various rating approaches. Results comparing different rating formats generally have been inconsistent, and the effect sizes of rating format on rating quality have been quite small. Research has yet to produce a rating format that is clearly superior to the others. Many have suggested that rating format has little impact on data quality or appraisal effectiveness in contrast to individual, social, and organizational factors that influence performance appraisal systems. Recent research investigates the role that cultural values or individual value orientations may have on performance ratings.

Gary J. Greguras

See also Performance Appraisal; Performance Appraisal, Objective Indices; Performance Feedback; Rater Training; Rating Errors and Perceptual Biases

Further Readings

Bernardin, H. J., & Beatty, R. W. (1984). *Performance appraisal: Assessing human behavior at work.* Boston: Kent.

Landy, F. J., & Farr, J. L. (1980). Performance rating. *Psychological Bulletin, 87,* 72–107.

Murphy, K. R., & Cleveland, J. N. (1995). *Understanding performance appraisal: Social, organizational, and goal-based perspectives.* Thousand Oaks, CA: Sage.

Ng, K. Y., & Koh, C., & Ang, S., & Kennedy, J. C., & Chan, K. Y. (2011). Rating lenience and halo in multisource feedback ratings: Testing cultural assumptions of power distance and individualism-collectivism, *Journal of Applied Psychology, 96,* 1033–1044.

Smith, P. C., & Kendall, L. M. (1963). Retranslation of expectations: An approach to the construction of unambiguous anchors for rating scales. *Journal of Applied Psychology, 47,* 149–155.

Spence, J. R., & Keeping, L. (2011). Conscious rating distortion in performance appraisal: A review, commentary, and proposed framework for research. *Human Resource Management Review, 21,* 85–95.

Wong, K. F. E., & Kwong, J. Y. Y. (2007). Effects of rater goals on rating patterns: Evidence from an experimental field study. *Journal of Applied Psychology, 92,* 577–585. doi:10.1037/0021-9010.92.2.577

PERFORMANCE FEEDBACK

Feedback is a subset of the available information in the work environment that indicates how well individuals are meeting their goals. Feedback serves a variety of purposes, including guiding, motivating, and reinforcing effective behaviors while discouraging ineffective ones. Feedback is a complex stimulus entailing a process in which a sender conveys a message to a recipient regarding personal behavior at work. The presence of feedback triggers psychological processes that precede behavioral responses. Daniel R. Ilgen and colleagues outlined how psychological processes, such as recipients' perceptions of feedback, acceptance of feedback, desire to respond to feedback, and intended responses, are influenced by such factors as the recipient's own characteristics, such as individual differences; characteristics of the source, including credibility; and

characteristics of the feedback message, for example, positive or negative sign.

Feedback has three primary uses in organizations. First, it can be used for employee development. Feedback can be used to communicate information to employees regarding their performance strengths and weaknesses so that they can be recognized for what they are doing well and can focus their efforts on areas that need improvement. Relevant to employee development is the use of coaching in the feedback-seeking domain. Employee coaching can come from the manager, from an executive coach, or even from formal mentoring. Work by Paul E. Levy and Jane Brodie Gregory suggests that good coaching relationships come from individual consideration, a positive feedback environment, trust, and the demonstration of empathy. A second use of feedback is for personnel decisions. For example, data from formal feedback sessions such as performance appraisals can be used to make decisions regarding who gets promoted, fired, or laid off. Finally, feedback can be used for documentation of organizational decisions. In particular, feedback records can be used to track employees' performance patterns over time and justify organizational decision making. Feedback is considered an integral part of a newer conceptualization called performance management, which was defined by Herman Aguinis as "a continuous process of identifying, measuring, and developing the performance of individuals and teams and aligning performance with the strategic goals of the organization." The above uses for feedback can be integrated into a comprehensive performance management system, which can be used to develop, motivate, and document employee behaviors.

Although feedback has traditionally been examined within the context of how it influences individual behaviors, more dynamic approaches have been recently adopted. In the following paragraphs, we review some of these perspectives to provide a more complete understanding of feedback processes in organizations.

Feedback-Seeking Behavior

Moving beyond the view of the feedback target as a passive recipient of information, feedback has been conceptualized as an individual resource that people are motivated to actively seek. Originating in the work of Susan J. Ashford and Larry L. Cummings, this perspective portrays the workplace as an information environment in which individuals engage in feedback-seeking behavior (FSB), enacting such strategies as monitoring the environment for feedback cues or making direct inquiries of actors in the environment in an effort to obtain personally relevant information. Recent work by Frederik Anseel and colleagues also suggests that FSB should be conceptualized as an aggregate model, in which both monitoring and inquiry behaviors are important and distinct from each other.

A number of motivating factors can prompt an individual to engage in FSBs. First, feedback can reduce the uncertainty individuals experience regarding their roles or performance. Increasing role clarity can improve contextual and task performance. Feedback can also serve an error corrective function and facilitate the attainment of competence or goal achievement. Furthermore, feedback has implications for self-evaluation and impression management. Individuals' desires to bolster their egos by obtaining positive feedback or, on the contrary, protect their egos by avoiding negative feedback can drive FSB. The greater the perceived value of feedback, the more proactive individuals will be in seeking it. However, individuals with low emotional intelligence are prone to overestimate their performance, social awareness, and competency and thus will reject feedback. Moreover, age and organizational and job tenure have been found to have negative relationships with feedback seeking. Thus, considering individual differences and delivering feedback in a way that diminishes defensiveness is important.

The costs perceived to accompany FSB can also affect the frequency of feedback seeking and the manner in which individuals pursue feedback. Costs of FSB are generally construed in terms of how much effort is necessary to acquire feedback information, concerns about image or loss of face, and the degree of inference required to make sense of feedback messages. When the value is of more importance than the cost of feedback, feedback-seeking strategies are likely to be used. Monitoring the feedback environment tends to necessitate less effort and invokes fewer image concerns than direct inquiry strategies. A trade-off exists between the accuracy and clarity of feedback and the effort

and risk entailed in obtaining such feedback. Individuals desiring highly accurate feedback may forgo the safer monitoring strategy in favor of inquiry. However, because feedback interpretation can be colored by such factors as recipient motives and expectations, even clearly communicated feedback messages can be misunderstood.

Multisource Feedback

Multisource feedback, sometimes referred to as 360-degree feedback, is defined as feedback gathered about the target from two or more rating sources. These sources may include the self, supervisor, peers, direct reports, and customers. Multisource feedback can be used for a variety of purposes, including communicating performance expectations, setting developmental goals, establishing a learning culture, and tracking the effects of organizational change. In general, the benefits of a multisource as opposed to a traditional feedback system are predicated on five important assumptions:

1. Each of the rating sources can provide unique information about the target.

2. These multiple ratings will provide incremental validity over individual sources.

3. Feedback from multiple sources will increase the target's self-awareness and lead to behavioral change.

4. Feedback from multiple sources reduces idiosyncrasies of individual raters.

5. Ratees appreciate being involved in the process and tend to react favorably to this opportunity.

Research supporting the benefits of multisource feedback remains incomplete. Specifically, researchers need to clarify the aspects of multisource feedback requiring employee attention, the performance goals set by employees receiving multisource feedback, how employees react to discrepancies between multisource feedback and their performance goals, and how employees react to discrepancies between self-evaluations and multisource feedback. In addition, the individual differences and organizational conditions that determine when multisource feedback will be most beneficial are not well understood.

However, the literature has provided some suggestions for improving the effectiveness of multisource feedback. First, ratings should be made anonymously. Multisource feedback is more threatening to raters and ratees when ratings are not anonymous. Second, although multisource feedback is often used for evaluative purposes, it seems to garner the best response from employees when it is used for the purpose of employee development. However, there are benefits associated with using multisource feedback for administrative decisions; for example, multiple sources of feedback allow decisions to be based on more information. Third, it is important to note that not all individuals and organizations benefit from multisource feedback equally. Performance improvements are more likely to occur when feedback indicates that change is both vital and possible, appropriate goals are set and action is taken, and when individuals have a high receptivity to feedback (i.e., feedback orientation). Last, organizations should evaluate the effectiveness of multisource feedback programs and not simply assume that such programs are beneficial.

Implications of Feedback for Performance: Feedback Intervention Theory

A common assumption is that feedback yields consistent performance improvements. However, the literature indicates that feedback does not always result in large, across-the-board improvements in performance. In some conditions feedback improves performance, in other conditions it has no apparent effects on performance, and in certain circumstances it is actually detrimental to employee performance. To explain these inconsistencies, Avraham N. Kluger and Angelo S. DeNisi (1996) put forth the feedback intervention theory (FIT), which detailed specific conditions that help determine the effectiveness of feedback for improving employee performance.

Built largely around the notion of the feedback–standard comparison process that is the basis of control theory, FIT posits that individuals use feedback to evaluate their performance on some goal or standard. This comparison process indicates whether an individual's performance is above or below the standard, which has

implications for subsequent performance. When performance, as informed by the feedback intervention, differs from the standard, feedback recipients can either alter their efforts, abandon the standard, alter the standard, or reject the feedback message altogether.

Because feedback has serious implications for the self, FIT posits that feedback interventions regulate behavior by changing the locus of attention to either the self or the task. According to FIT, feedback that directs attention toward the self can have a detrimental effect on performance because such feedback often depletes cognitive resources and generates affective reactions. An interesting implication of this is that feedback interventions containing praise can impede task performance because such interventions likely draw attention to the self rather than the task.

On the whole FIT suggests that there are three characteristics of feedback interventions that determine the effects of feedback on performance. First, the cues of the feedback message are important because they determine whether attention is drawn to the self or the task. Feedback interventions that contain information solely regarding performance outcomes have been shown to be detrimental to performance because they likely direct attention to the self. However, this pattern has not been displayed by feedback interventions that contain process information, which draws attention to the task. Therefore, Kluger and DeNisi (1996) suggested that the effectiveness of feedback is maximized when it directs attention to task motivation and learning processes and when the solution to the problem at hand is provided. Second, the nature of the task, such as task complexity, should be considered. In particular, feedback often improves motivation. However, improved motivation does not increase the amount of cognitive resources available to complete a task. As such, motivation improves performance mostly when the task requires few cognitive resources. Finally, situational (e.g., the presence of goal-setting interventions) and personality variables (e.g., self-esteem) can moderate the effects of feedback interventions. Moreover, feedback can be further improved by reflection. According to Frederik Anseel and colleagues, when individuals are exposed to an effective feedback intervention at the task level and encouraged to step back and reflect on the feedback, they should be able to direct attention and cognitive resources to the necessary behaviors that improve performance.

Contemporary Perspectives: Person–Environment Aspects of Feedback Processes

Consistent with recent trends in industrial and organizational psychology, feedback has been described as a dynamic process involving an interaction between characteristics of the individual and situation. In particular, employees' feedback orientations and the social context in which feedback is embedded have been identified as important determinants of rater and ratee behavior and reactions to feedback. Manuel London identified these aspects of the person and the situation as important elements of what has been termed the organization's feedback culture. In particular, London suggested that organizations may create more global psychological settings—feedback-oriented cultures—by enhancing the quality of feedback given in the organization, emphasizing its importance, and supporting its use by employees. In such cultures, feedback is easily accessible and salient, and thus it is likely to influence employee beliefs and behaviors on a day-to-day basis.

Feedback orientation refers to a multidimensional quasi-trait that determines an individual's overall receptivity to feedback, guidance, and coaching. According to London, feedback orientation involves liking feedback, a behavioral propensity to seek feedback, a cognitive propensity to process feedback mindfully and deeply, sensitivity to others' views of oneself and to external propensity, a belief in the value of feedback, and feeling accountable to act on feedback. Individuals who have more favorable feedback orientations will believe that feedback is more useful, will feel accountable to use the feedback, and will be more likely to seek feedback from their work environments. Beth Linderbaum and Paul E. Levy recently developed a measure of feedback orientation called the Feedback Orientation Scale, in which four subdimensions of an individual's feedback orientation are identified: feedback utility, accountability, self-efficacy, and social awareness. In a series of studies, various researchers have linked feedback orientation to many organizational attitudes,

perceptions, and behaviors, such as satisfaction, feedback seeking, organizational citizenship behaviors, and role clarity.

Paul E. Levy and his colleagues have provided a framework for understanding the social context of feedback processes in organizations. According to this framework, distal variables such as organizational goals, legal climate, and competition; proximal process variables including organization's policies regarding feedback, feedback environment, and rater accountability; and proximal structural variables, for example, the purpose of feedback and feedback system features, are each important aspects of the organizational environment for feedback. Although all these aspects of the social context influence feedback processes, the extent to which the workplace encourages and supports the use of feedback for the purposes of improving work performance has been identified as an element of the social context, which is especially important to feedback processes in organizations. In this vein Levy and his colleagues have started to examine the feedback environment, which is defined as the contextual characteristics of organizations that support informal, day-to-day feedback processes.

The feedback environment goes beyond the formal presentation of feedback such as performance appraisal and includes information regarding how supervisors and coworkers mention and discuss feedback on a day-to-day basis. The following seven facets of the feedback environment have been identified:

1. Source credibility

2. Feedback quality

3. Feedback delivery

4. Favorable feedback

5. Unfavorable feedback

6. Source availability

7. Promotion of feedback seeking

Organizations that have more favorable feedback environments are also likely to have more effective feedback processes and communicate more information to employees that helps guide their behavior at work. It is important to determine boundary conditions for any construct. Recent work done by Allison Gabriel and colleagues indicates that aspects of the feedback environment can be disadvantageous in the wrong situation. These researchers found that individuals with a low feedback orientation were not motivated by a favorable feedback environment; in fact, this match of feedback orientation and feedback environment resulted in comparatively low levels of motivation. However, there is evidence that the feedback environment is related to a variety of positive employee outcomes, such as increased affective commitment, job satisfaction, and citizenship behaviors, as well as decreased absenteeism. Therefore, to the extent that organizations develop favorable feedback environments, they will foster positive feedback orientations from employees. These factors will serve to develop feedback-oriented cultures and maximize the effectiveness of feedback processes in organizations.

Conclusion

The early feedback literature focused on feedback in a relatively narrow context. Feedback was traditionally viewed as a stimulus to which employees respond. More recently, researchers have taken a more dynamic approach, which includes examinations of active FBS, multisource feedback, feedback's relationship to performance, and an investigation of individual and situational variables that are associated with feedback-oriented cultures. Finally, researchers have started to focus on the feedback orientation of employees and contextual aspects of the feedback process that are associated with the provision, acceptance, and use of feedback in organizations.

Paul E. Levy, Ariel Roberts, Christopher C. Rosen, and Alison L. O'Malley

See also 360-Degree Feedback; Control Theory; Feedback; Feedback Seeking; Performance Appraisal

Further Readings

Anseel, F., Beatty, A. S., Shen, W., Lievens, F., & Sackett, P. R. (2015). How are we doing after 30 years? A meta-analytic review of the antecedents and outcomes of feedback-seeking behavior. *Journal of Management*, *41*, 318–348. doi:10.1177/0149206313484521

Ashford, S. J., & Cummings, L. L. (1983). Feedback as an individual resource: Personal strategies of creating information. *Organizational Behavior and Human Performance*, *32*, 370–398. doi:10.10166/0030-5073 (83)90156-3

Ilgen, D. R., Fisher, C. D., & Taylor, M. S. (1979). Consequences of individual feedback on behavior in organizations. *Journal of Applied Psychology*, *64*, 349–371. doi:10.1037/0021-9010.64.4.349

Kluger, A. N., & DeNisi, A. (1996). The effect of feedback interventions on performance: A historical review, meta-analysis, and a preliminary feedback intervention theory. *Psychological Bulletin*, *119*, 254–284. doi:10.1037/0033-2909.119.2.254

Levy, P. E., & Williams, J. R. (2004). The social context of performance appraisal: A review and framework for the future. *Journal of Management*, *30*, 881–905. doi:10.1016/j.jm.2004.06.005

Linderbaum, B. A., & Levy, P. E. (2010). The development and validation of the Feedback Orientation Scale (FOS). *Journal of Management*, *36*(6), 1372–1405. doi:10.1177/014920631 0373145

London, M. (2003). *Job feedback: Giving, seeking, and using feedback for performance improvement* (2nd ed.). Mahwah, NJ: Erlbaum.

London, M., & Smither, J. W. (2002). Feedback orientation, feedback culture, and the longitudinal performance management process. *Human Resource Management Review*, *12*, 81–100. doi:10.1016/S1053 -4822(01)00043-2

Smither, J. W., London, M., & Reilly, R. R. (2005). Does performance improve following multisource feedback? A theoretical model, meta-analysis, and review of empirical findings. *Personnel Psychology*, *58*, 33–66. doi:10.1111/j.1744-6570.2005.514_1.x

PERSONALITY

Although many scholars have offered formal definitions of personality for almost 100 years, no consensus on any single definition has been achieved. In fact, a survey of 50 textbooks devoted to the study of personality would quite likely result in 50 distinct definitions of the term. Perhaps the chief reason for this lack of agreement is because of the broad scope encompassed by the notion of human personality. Such a broad scope is exemplified by Clyde Kluckhohn and Henry A. Murray's view that human personality can be understood at three distinct levels:

1. How we are like all other people

2. How we are like some other people

3. How we are like no other people

At the broadest level, Kluckhohn and Murray's framework suggests that there are some aspects of behavior that are common to all members of the human species. Murray, for example, in his classic taxonomy of needs, included a set of viscerogenic needs that are shared by all people. This category of needs, representing those things that humans need to survive, includes the need for air, the need for water, and the need for heat avoidance. Likewise, Abraham Maslow, in his specification of the hierarchy of needs, suggested that an individual's psychological needs could not be addressed unless the basic physiological (e.g., food, water) and safety (e.g., security, avoidance of pain) needs were met.

At the second level—the way we are like some other people—Kluckhohn and Murray suggested that, when considering specific aspects of personality, individuals will share similarities with some but not all people. Within contemporary personality psychology, this level of personality description is where the notion of personality traits resides. Traits can be defined as characteristic behaviors, thoughts, and feelings of an individual that tend to occur across diverse situations and are relatively stable over time. A trait, once identified, is something that all people possess, but to differing degrees. For example, although all people can be described in terms of their extroversion, some people are outgoing and social, whereas others tend to be more introverted and reserved. Thus, traits represent a way in which we are like some other people.

At the third level of personality description is how we are like no other people. This level of explanation includes those aspects of our personalities that make us unique individuals. As such, this level includes the experiences we have had in our own histories that have shaped the way we think, feel, and act. In his writings about this level of personality description, Daniel P. McAdams has suggested that the goal of studying personality at this level is to understand individuals in the context of their personal life stories.

Idiographic Versus Nomothetic Science

A debate has existed among personality scholars about the best approach for studying personality. Many scholars have argued that personality is best studied at the third level of Kluckhohn and Murray's framework. Science at this level is idiographic, and knowledge of personality is gained through in-depth studies of particular individuals. However, other scholars have argued that personality is best studied at Kluckhohn and Murray's second level. Science at this level is nomothetic, involving the study of general principles through the examination and comparison of many individuals. The debate over which of these approaches yields better information about the nature of human personality has, at times, been quite hostile. Although the debate has largely been argued in terms of methodological issues (i.e., the benefits and limitations of idiographic and nomothetic science), the heart of the argument is about the most appropriate level at which to understand personality. As such, the debate is in many ways pointless, because information from both levels of personality is necessary to develop a full understanding of the complexities of human personality.

Levels of Personality Description and Industrial and Organizational Psychology

All three of Kluckhohn and Murray's levels of description are important for understanding human behavior in workplace contexts. For example, if a person's basic needs are not being met, we might come to understand why the individual no longer appears to be driven for success at work. Likewise, if we were to know an individual's personal history, we might better understand the person's problems with authority from a supervisor. However, despite the applicability of the first and third levels of personality description, almost all applications of personality to industrial and organizational (I-O) psychology are associated with the second level of personality description (i.e., how we are like some other people), and more specifically, with the notion of personality traits.

What Is a Trait?

There are two perspectives on the concept of personality traits. A first perspective is that traits are internal mechanisms that cause behavior. From this perspective, agreeableness, for example, is something within an individual that causes the person to behave in an agreeable manner across a variety of situations and over time. Hans J. Eysenck's theory of extroversion is an example of this perspective. Eysenck theorized that introverts have a higher baseline level of arousal than do extroverts. When placed in a social situation with considerable stimulation, the introvert (with an already high level of arousal) would be predicted to become easily overaroused. In an attempt to reduce that overarousal, the introvert would engage in introverted behaviors, such as withdrawing from the situation. In contrast, the extrovert, with a lower level of baseline arousal, would behave in an extroverted manner to obtain stimulation from the environment, thereby increasing the level of arousal (i.e., to avoid underarousal). According to Eysenck, then, the trait of extroversion is an internal biological process that causes behavior. Data have provided support for this internal mechanism approach to personality traits. Additionally, behavior genetic research, which has found that approximately 50% of variation in many traits can be explained by genetic influences, also points to a causal mechanism behind trait-related behavior.

A second perspective, typified by the act-frequency approach, is that personality traits are nothing more than descriptive categories of behavior. As such, a trait is a label for a set of related behaviors or acts. Acts that fall into the trait of sociability include talking to a stranger on an elevator, calling friends just to say hello, talking to coworkers in the hallway, or having a conversation with a clerk at a store. There could be hundreds of acts falling within this trait classification. A person with a high standing on this trait engages in this class of acts across situations more often than do other people. This approach is completely descriptive; there is no statement about the psychological processes that lead persons to behave the way they do. Although the acts people engage in may be caused by internal causal mechanisms, the act-frequency approach does not specify the nature of those mechanisms.

The Structure of Personality Traits

Personality researchers have sought to develop a structure of personality traits for nearly 100 years. Much of this work has been based on studies of words in the English language, the so-called lexical hypothesis. The central idea of this hypothesis is that important aspects of human behavior will be encoded in the language. As such, it has been reasoned, a comprehensive understanding of personality traits can be derived from an examination of a language. The culmination of studies of the English lexicon is a structure of personality known as the Big Five. The Big Five taxonomy of personality is a hierarchical representation of the trait domain, with five broad traits representing the highest level of the classification structure. These five traits include the following:

1. **Neuroticism:** Anxious, temperamental, nervous, moody versus confident, relaxed, unexcitable

2. **Extroversion:** Sociable, energetic, active, assertive versus shy, reserved, withdrawn, unadventurous

3. **Openness:** Intellectual, innovative, artistic, complex versus unimaginative, simple, unsophisticated

4. **Agreeableness:** Trusting, trustful, helpful, generous versus cold, harsh, rude, unsympathetic

5. **Conscientiousness:** Organized, neat, thorough, systematic, efficient versus careless, undependable, haphazard, sloppy

Although some scholars have raised notable criticisms of the Big Five, and certainly other organizing structures exist, the Big Five is the dominant perspective on the organization of personality traits within contemporary personality psychology and within its applications to I-O psychology.

The term *Big Five* stems from the fact that these traits are very large, each encompassing a wide range of behavioral tendencies. It is not surprising, therefore, that scholars believe that there exist sets of more narrowly defined traits that fall within the scope of each of these Big Five traits. For example, it has been proposed that the broad trait of conscientiousness can be broken down into more narrowly defined traits of dependability and achievement striving. Likewise, it has been proposed that the broad trait of extroversion can be broken down into more narrowly defined traits of dominance and sociability. However, personality researchers are far from reaching consensus on the precise number or nature of these narrowly defined traits at the next level of the hierarchy.

Compound Traits

The determinants of behavior are clearly complex, and many behaviors, especially those relevant to I-O contexts, are not a function of any single trait. Consistent with this line of thinking, more than one trait is often found to relate to particularly important work-related behaviors. In these cases researchers have proposed the notion of compound traits, which involve the combination of fundamental personality variables into a new personality variable that is capable of predicting a particular criterion. Perhaps the best known example of a compound personality variable is that of integrity. Research has demonstrated that scores on integrity tests—designed to be predictive of counterproductive employee behaviors—are notably related to the Big Five traits of conscientiousness, agreeableness, and (negatively) neuroticism. Thus the trait of integrity can be thought of as, at least in part, the confluence of these three Big Five dimensions. Other compound personality variables include customer service orientation, managerial potential, and core self-evaluations. A unique aspect of compound personality traits is that they tend to result in criterion-related validities that are higher than those of the fundamental personality traits that compose them. Meta-analyses have shown, for example, that integrity tests tend to have greater predictive validity than do the individual traits of conscientiousness, agreeableness, or neuroticism.

Trait Personality and I-O Psychology

The role of personality within I-O psychology has had a rather tumultuous history. Today, however, personality is a topic of notable interest to both researchers and practitioners.

Research

Much of the research on personality in I-O contexts has sought to identify whether and which personality traits are related in meaningful ways to important organizationally relevant behaviors. Primary research and subsequent meta-analyses have demonstrated that personality traits are related to such organizational behaviors as task performance, contextual performance, performance in training, counterproductive work behaviors, job choice, leadership, job satisfaction, and perceptions of organizational justice, among others. This research has led to a better understanding of the personal characteristics associated with important work behaviors. For example, by developing an understanding of the relationships between personality traits and effective leadership, organizations might be better able to identify individuals with potential to be good leaders and individuals who are already leaders can be provided with information to improve their leadership skills.

Most research (and application) involving personality within I-O psychology is associated with the act-frequency approach to personality traits. A relationship between a personality trait and a criterion, as interpreted from an act-frequency perspective, suggests only that the behaviors associated with the trait classification are also important for the criterion. By way of example, an act-frequency interpretation of a relationship between extroversion and leadership would suggest that some of the acts associated with the trait of extroversion are also associated with effective leadership. Although this research is certainly useful and informative, it is descriptive in nature; there is no identification or explication of the mechanisms through which personality traits cause organizationally relevant behavior. Theory and research to identify the processes by which personality influences behavior in organizations is, however, becoming increasingly prominent.

Application

The primary application of personality in I-O contexts is the assessment of personality traits for purposes of personnel selection. The goal of preemployment testing is to make inferences about an individual's future behaviors in the workplace. Most assessments of personality traits for personnel selection are done through self-report questionnaires, but other methods can also be used to assess traits. If an applicant were to complete a self-report assessment of the trait of conscientiousness and receive a high score, an employer could surmise that this individual tends to engage in conscientious behaviors across situations and make the inference that the person will do so in the workplace as well. If the job requires behaviors that are associated with conscientious acts, this applicant could be desirable for the position. Meta-analytic research has shown that personality trait assessments can be predictive of job performance for a number of occupational groupings and across a range of performance criteria, with the strongest findings for the trait of conscientiousness.

When attempting to predict work-related behavior with personality trait assessments, care must be taken when choosing an appropriate criterion measure. The trait–situation debate taught personality researchers a great deal about what makes an appropriate criterion. The trait–situation debate arose when scholars began to argue that there was no consistency in behavior across situations. Research had shown, for example, that when children were put into various situations in which they could behave honestly or dishonestly, the children did not behave in the same ways across situations. More specifically, a child who cheated on a test in one situation might turn in a lost dollar in another. This lack of observed consistency in trait-related behaviors across situations led these scholars to argue that traits were *convenient fictions* and that situations were the stronger determinant of behavior. In further support of their point, these scholars argued that scores on personality trait assessments were not strongly related to observed behaviors. Although it took personality psychologists some time to respond to these arguments, they finally found their voice in the principle of aggregation. The principle of aggregation suggests that if behavior is considered across many situations, consistencies will emerge. These consistencies were interpreted as providing evidence in support of the existence of traits. Personality researchers argued that if behavior is aggregated across situations, scores from assessments of personality traits will be predictive of that aggregated behavior and will, in fact, account for as much variability in behavior as situations.

The lesson learned from the trait–situation debate and the resulting principle of aggregation is important for I-O psychology. Specifically, for personality to be predictive of organizationally relevant behaviors, those behaviors must be aggregated across situations. It will not be possible, for example, to predict whether an employee will be late next Tuesday on the basis of the conscientiousness score. It should be possible, however, to make a prediction regarding this person's tendency to be late over the course of a year. In short, personality does not predict specific instances of behavior well, but it can predict lawful patterns of behavior. This is a point that I-O researchers and practitioners must keep in mind. There are several cases in the published literature in which researchers have used a single instance of behavior as a criterion, and have, not surprisingly, failed to find the expected association between personality trait scores and the criterion measure.

In addition to criteria that are aggregated across observations, they should also capture what have been termed "will do" behaviors rather than "can do" behaviors. "Will do" behaviors are those behaviors that a person is likely to engage in at a typical level, whereas "can do" behaviors represent those behaviors that a person is capable of achieving when effort is maximized. For example, performing one's job under the watchful eye of a manger or under a tight deadline might best be considered "will do" behavior, as the individual is likely to exert maximal levels of effort to perform the job as proficiently as possible. How the person performs when the manager is not present or when a deadline is not pressing would represent "will do" behavior, as the level of performance is a result of internal drives and motives rather than external pressures. Research has shown that "can do" types of behaviors are better predicted by the individual's skills and abilities, whereas "will do" behaviors tend to be better predicted by elements of personality (though skills and abilities are still likely important determinants of behavior). Thus, researchers and practitioners should consider whether a criterion of interest is best understood from a "can do" or a "will do" perspective, recognizing that personality traits are likely to be better predictors of those "will do" behaviors.

Summary

Personality is a broad field within psychology that has been studied at various levels, from single individuals to groups of people to people in general. Within I-O psychology, almost all work on personality has focused on personality traits, or stable tendencies to behave in certain ways. Personality traits have been found to relate to a wide variety of employee behaviors at work. An emerging notion is that of compound traits, or broad personality dimensions that are associated with several more fundamental personality dimensions and are predictive of important work-related behaviors. The primary application of personality to I-O contexts is preemployment testing, in which scores on personality tests are used to make predictions about people's future behaviors at work. When attempting to predict behavior from personality traits, it is essential for the I-O researchers and practitioners to keep in mind the principle of aggregation and focus on "will do" behaviors.

Eric D. Heggestad

See also Big Five Taxonomy of Personality; Individual Differences; Personality Assessment

Further Readings

Buss, D. M., & Craik, K. H. (1983). The act frequency approach to personality. *Psychological Review*, *90*(2), 105–126. doi:10.1037/0033-295X.90.2.105

Guilford, J. P. (1959). *Personality*. New York: McGraw-Hill.

Hurtz, G. M., & Donovan, J. J. (2000). Personality and job performance: The Big Five revisited. *Journal of Applied Psychology*, *85*(6), 869. doi:10.1037/0021-9010.85.6.869

McAdams, D. P., & Pals, J. L. (2006). A new Big Five: Fundamental principles for an integrative science of personality. *American Psychologist*, *61*(3), 204–217. doi:10.1037/0003-066X.61.3.204

Oswald, F. L., & Hough, L. M. (2011). Personality and its assessment in organizations: Theoretical and empirical developments. In S. Zedeck (Ed.), *APA handbook of industrial and organizational psychology, Vol. 2: Selecting and developing members for the organization* (pp. 153–184). Washington, DC: American Psychological Association. doi:10.1037/12170-005

PERSONALITY ASSESSMENT

Personality assessment is the process of gathering information about an individual to make inferences about personal characteristics, including thoughts, feelings, and behaviors. Raymond B. Cattell identified three primary sources of obtaining such personality information: life data, or information collected from objective records; test data, or information obtained in constructed situations in which a person's behavior can be observed and objectively scored; and questionnaire data, or information from self-report questionnaires. Each type of data is used to make assessments of personality within contemporary industrial and organizational (I-O) psychology. Common forms of life data might include information contained in a résumé or an application blank and examinations of court, financial, or driving records in background checks. Test data would include scores on personality-based dimensions derived from the assessment center method. However, by far the most common form of personality data in I-O psychology is questionnaire data.

Self-report measures of personality can be divided into two broad categories: clinical and nonclinical. Self-report clinical measures, such as the Minnesota Multiphasic Personality Inventory, have been used for some workers, such as airline pilots and police officers, to ensure that a potential employee does not suffer from an underlying psychological disorder. These clinical measures are generally given along with an interview (life data) in the context of an individual assessment. Decisions to use these clinical evaluations for personnel selection, however, must be made carefully, because there is a notable possibility of violating the Americans with Disabilities Act.

Nonclinical self-report personality assessments, which are much more widely used in I-O contexts than are clinical assessments, are typically designed to assess personality traits. Personality traits are characteristic behaviors, thoughts, and feelings of an individual that tend to occur across diverse situations and are relatively stable over time. A trait that has been particularly important in the context of I-O psychology is conscientiousness, which captures the tendencies to be organized, thorough, systematic, and efficient. Assuming that these characteristics are desirable in an employee, a self-report questionnaire may be administered to make inferences about the conscientiousness of individuals within an applicant pool.

Content Versus Empirical Scale Development

Although there are numerous approaches to constructing a personality assessment, two broad approaches can be identified. By far the more common approach to scale development is the content approach. In this approach, items are written on the basis of a theory of the construct the set of items is intended to measure. By way of example, an item such as "I enjoy the company of others" might be written for a sociability scale. Once written, the items are then typically empirically evaluated using principles of construct validation. Because factor analysis is frequently used to evaluate items, this approach is also commonly referred to as the *factor analytic approach*.

As P. E. Meehl pointed out in 1945, however, interpreting an individual's response to such an item requires certain assumptions. For example, it must be assumed that all respondents have interpreted the item in the same way, that people are aware of and can report their own behavior, and that people are willing to tell others about their behavior. Some personality measurement theorists believed that these assumptions were untenable and suggested a different approach to personality test construction, the empirical keying approach. According to this approach, a personality item is useful to the extent that responses to it accurately differentiate two groups. For example, an item would be included on a depression scale if, and only if, depressed people responded to the item differently from nondepressed people. In the classic empirical keying approach, the content of the item is irrelevant; whether the item appears theoretically related to the construct does not matter. Because the response to the item is considered to be the behavior of interest, interpretation of scores from an empirically keyed measure does not require the assumptions associated with the content approach. Although the empirical keying approach was the basis for such well-known measures as the Minnesota Multiphasic Personality Inventory and the California Psychological Inventory, the vast majority of personality assessments in use today are based on the content approach to scale development.

Normative Versus Ipsative Assessment

Most personality assessments given in I-O contexts provide normative scores. Normative scores result when the responses to one item are independent from responses to other items. The common Likert-type rating scale, in which the respondents use the scale to place themselves along the trait continuum as represented by a single item, will result in normative scale scores. Ipsative scores, in contrast, result from response formats in which respondents choose, rank-order, or otherwise indicate preference among a set of statements presented in an item. The Myers–Briggs Type Indicator is a well-known measure that provides ipsative scores.

Normative and ipsative scores result in different inferences about a person's trait standing. Normative scores allow inferences regarding the amount of a trait that an individual possesses compared with other people. Ipsative scores, in contrast, support inferences about the amount of a trait possessed by the individual compared with the other traits assessed by the measure. Thus, a high score on a particular scale in an ipsative measure does not suggest that the respondent has a high standing on that trait but suggests rather that the respondent has a higher standing on that trait than on any of the other traits assessed by the measure. Ipsative measures, therefore, are useful for identifying a person's particular strengths and weaknesses (i.e., intraindividual differences) and may be particularly useful in vocational guidance contexts. In many I-O contexts, however, the explicit desire is to directly compare a set of people on the basis of their scores on a particular scale (i.e., interindividual differences), as in personnel selection. When comparing people is the goal, ipsative scores are inappropriate, and such measures should not be used. This statement may not necessarily be true in the coming years, however, as researchers are developing and evaluating complex item response theory models that appear to be able to produce normative scores from responses to ipsative measures.

Origins of Personality Assessment in I-O Psychology

Applications of personality assessment within I-O psychology began as early as 1915 with the creation of the Division of Applied Psychology and the Bureau of Salesmanship Research at the Carnegie Institute of Technology. In addition to developing technologies for the selection of salesmen, this group of researchers also sought to develop measures of personality (or temperament/character, as it was known at that time). Personality assessment gained further acceptance during World War I when United States military researchers developed the Woodworth Personal Data Sheet to identify individuals who might be susceptible to war neuroses. With the development of several multitrait assessment tools, the popularity of personality testing grew through the 1940s and 1950s. For example, a survey of more than 600 American companies conducted in 1953 indicated that nearly 40% of those companies used measures of personality or vocational interests in their selection systems.

Three factors led to a marked decline in the popularity of personality testing in applied contexts during the 1960s and 1970s. First, two influential literature reviews were published that suggested that there was little evidence for the criterion-related validity of personality measures for the prediction of job performance. Second, the trait–situation debate dominated personality psychology over this period of time. On the situationist side of the debate, led by Walter Mischel, it was argued that aspects of the situation, not personal characteristics, were the driving force behind behavior. Third, Title VII of the Civil Rights Act of 1964 brought increased legal responsibilities to the use of assessments in the context of personnel decisions. Largely on the basis of these factors, many organizations decided to forgo personality assessments in their selection systems, opting to avoid possible legal issues resulting from the administration of these tests.

Personality testing was given new life in applied contexts during the 1980s and early 1990s. Personality theorists finally found their voice in the trait–situation debate, effectively arguing that personal characteristics can predict behavior. The heart of the argument was the principle of aggregation, which suggests personality generally does not predict single instances of behavior well, but it does predict lawful patterns in behavior across diverse situations. But the biggest boon to personality assessment in I-O contexts was the emergence of the Big Five and subsequent meta-analyses demonstrating the criterion-related validities of some of these broad traits.

Criterion-Related Validity and the Utility of Personality Assessment

One reason for the lack of strong criterion-related validity findings for personality assessments in the 1950s was the *broadside approach* taken by researchers. This tendency to correlate every available personality test score with all available performance measures was said to have resulted in large numbers of small criterion-related validity coefficients, many of which would have been expected, on the basis of theory, to be small. With the emergence of the Big Five trait taxonomy in the 1980s, conceptual links between the traits and the criterion variables could be drawn. A result of this better predictor–criterion linkage was stronger evidence for the criterion-related validities of personality assessments. To date, numerous meta-analyses of the relationships between personality test scores and measures of work performance have resulted in positive findings. The strongest findings have been associated with the conscientiousness trait, which seems to be associated with most job-related criteria (i.e., performance, training, attendance, etc.) across almost all jobs. However, the criterion-related validities remain modest, even after the corrections typically used in meta-analytic procedures. For example, one of the most widely cited meta-analyses reported corrected criterion-related validities for conscientiousness in the range of .20 to .22 across performance criteria and occupational groups.

Many personality assessments frequently used in I-O settings have not been created explicitly for applied use. That is, the questionnaires were created to provide a general assessment of personality, and as such, the items in these measures tend to be very general and do not typically convey information about any specific situational context. When responding to such acontextual items, respondents may consider their behaviors across a wide range of social situations, such as at home with family, at a gathering with friends, at a public event, or at work. Research has found, however, that when the item content is contextualized for a work setting, for example by adding the phrase "at work" to the end of each item, the criterion-related validity of the test was higher than when acontextual items were used. Thus, by including work-based situational cues within personality items, the criterion-related validity of personality scores can be enhanced.

Most evaluations of the criterion-related validity of personality scales have been based on self-ratings, or asking a target individual to complete the assessment regarding his or her own behavior tendencies. Recent research suggests that the criterion-related validity of personality assessments might be higher if "other-ratings" are used. Other ratings involve having a person who knows a target person well—for example, a family member, spouse, close friend, or coworker—complete the personality assessment about the target person, rating the target person's behavioral tendencies. A meta-analysis by B. S. Connelly and D. S. Ones found that other ratings of personality were notably more predictive of job performance than were self-ratings. Despite the positive results associated with the contextualization of personality items and/or the use of "other" ratings, the criterion-related validity of personality assessments is lower than that of many other available selection tools, such as ability tests, assessment centers, and work samples. Despite the lower criterion-related validities, personality assessment can still be of value in selection contexts. First, the correlations between personality test scores and scores from cognitive ability tests tend to be small, suggesting that personality tests can improve prediction of performance above and beyond cognitive ability test scores. Second, personality test scores tend not to show the large mean differences between racial groups that are found with cognitive ability tests. Third, these tests can often be administered quickly and typically are relatively inexpensive.

Faking and Intentional Distortion

A major issue facing the application of personality assessment is the possibility of faking, which is also known as intentional distortion or socially desirable responding. Impression management occurs when an individual changes a response to a personality item to create a positive impression. Consider a situation in which a person would, under normal circumstances, respond to the item "I am a hard worker" with a response of *neutral* on a five-point, Likert-type scale. If that same person were presented with the same item when applying for a job and responded with *agree completely* to increase the chances of being hired, the individual would be engaging in impression management.

The precise effects of faking on the criterion-related validity of personality measures is still being debated, but it would appear that the effect is rather small. Despite the small effect on criterion-related validity, faking can have a negative influence on the quality of selection decisions, particularly when selection is done in a top-down manner. In a top-down selection context, the quality of selection decisions appears to be negatively affected by the fact that a number of low-performing people will rise to the top of the personality test distribution, increasing their chances of being selected. Fortunately, it seems that many companies tend to use personality assessments in a "screen-out" manner, whereby applicants with low scores on the assessment are eliminated from the applicant pool. Such an approach mitigates the effects of faking in that applicants with low scores are likely to have low standing on the trait and, as such, would be expected to be poorer performing employees. Thus, the decision to eliminate these applicants from consideration for the job is likely to be a good decision. Researchers are continuing to examine the precise impact of faking on selection and are working on ways to deal with faking to maintain the usefulness of personality assessments.

Summary

Personality assessment is the process of gathering information about a person to make an inference about the individual's characteristic ways of behaving. Although there are numerous methods for assessing personality, the most common form of assessment in I-O psychology is the self-report questionnaire. Meta-analyses have shown that these self-report measures can provide information that is valid for predicting various organizational outcomes. Furthermore, that criterion validity may be enhanced by writing items that are contextualized in workplace settings and/or by obtaining "other" ratings. Finally, although personality assessments can provide useful information for making personnel decisions, intentional response distortion on the part of the respondent may lessen the usefulness of those scores in applicant contexts.

Eric D. Heggestad

See also Big Five Taxonomy of Personality; Faking and Intentional Distortion; Normative Versus Ipsative Measurement; Personality; Reliability; Validity

Further Readings

Connelly, B. S., & Ones, D. S. (2010). An other perspective on personality: Meta-analytic integration of observers' accuracy and predictive validity. *Psychological Bulletin, 136*(6), 1092–1122. doi:10.1037/a0021212

Guion, R. M., & Gottier, R. F. (1965). Validity of personality measures in personnel selection. *Personnel Psychology, 18*, 135–164. doi:10.1111/j.1744-6570.1965.tb00273.x

Hurtz, G. M., & Donovan, J. J. (2000). Personality and job performance: The Big Five revisited. *Journal of Applied Psychology, 85*(6), 869. doi:10.1037/0021-9010.85.6.869

Kanfer, R., Ackerman, P. L., Murtha, T., & Goff, M. (1995). Personality and intelligence in industrial organizational psychology. In D. H. Saklofske & M. Zeidner (Eds.), *International handbook of personality and intelligence* (pp. 577–602). New York: Plenum. doi:10.1007/978-1-4757-5571-8_26

Meehl, P. E. (1945). The dynamics of structured personality tests. *Journal of Clinical Psychology, 1*, 296–303. doi:10.1002/1097-4679(194510)1:4

Mueller-Hanson, R., Heggestad, E. D., & Thornton, G. C., III. (2003). Faking and selection: Considering the use of personality from a select-in and a select-out perspective. *Journal of Applied Psychology, 88*, 348–355. doi:10.1037/0021-9010.88.2.348

Shaffer, J. A., & Postlethwaite, B. E. (2012). A matter of context: A meta-analytic investigation of the relative validity of contextualized and noncontextualized personality measures. *Personnel Psychology, 65*(3), 445–494. doi:10.1111/j.1744-6570.2012.01250.x

PERSON–ENVIRONMENT FIT

Person–environment (P-E) fit refers to the degree of compatibility between individuals and some aspect of their work environment. The concept of P-E fit is firmly rooted in the tradition of Kurt Lewin's maxim that $B = f(P,E)$, behavior is a function of person and environment. The early interactional psychologists emphasized Lewin's perspective, advocating that individuals' behaviors and attitudes are determined jointly by personal and environmental conditions. On the person side, characteristics include a wide variety of individual differences: interests; preferences; knowledge, skills, and abilities (KSAs); personality traits; working styles; values; and goals. On the environment side, characteristics similarly vary: vocational norms, job demands, job characteristics, organizational cultures and climates, team members' personalities, and company or group goals. Various synonyms have been used to describe fit, including *congruence, match, similarity, interaction,* and *correspondence*.

The basic premise of P-E fit research is that there are particular environments that are most compatible with particular individual characteristics. If a person works in those environments, positive consequences including improved work attitudes and performance, reduced stress, and lower withdrawal behaviors will result. Although the premise is straightforward, research on P-E fit is one of the most eclectic domains in organizational psychology. In part, this is due to the wide variety of conceptualizations, content dimensions, and measurement strategies used to assess or infer fit. Questions about the definition of fit, what types of fit exist and on what characteristics, and how to measure fit are addressed below.

What Is Fit?

Although terms such as congruence or match seem to imply similarity, multiple conceptualizations of P-E fit have been discussed in the literature. Two primary types of fit have been described. The first, *supplementary fit*, exists when the individual and the environment are similar on a particular characteristic. The underlying mechanism is one of similarity attraction, such that people prefer interacting with other people and with environments that are similar to themselves. The second type is *complementary fit*, which occurs when individuals' characteristics fill a gap in the current environment or the environment meets a need for that individual. Early research on stress and coping, which describes fit as adjustment, elaborated on two distinct forms of complementary fit. The first is needs–supplies fit, which exists when a person's needs are met by resources from the environment. The second is demands–abilities fit, which generally focuses on individuals' KSAs meeting environmental demands. When the focus is on fit in teams, complementary fit may include different skills or traits brought by individual team members to complete the team.

Each of these types of fit occurs at the individual level, meaning that every individual has a unique fit with his or her environment. A relatively new concept called collective fit has been introduced to describe fit at the group level. Within collective fit, *internal fit* refers to the match of individuals to each other within with the team, whereas *external fit* describes the fit of the team to the requirements of the task that they face.

Fit on What?

P-E fit research has generally concentrated on matching the individual to one of five aspects of the environment: vocation, job, organization, group, and person (i.e., supervisor, recruiter). Each of these subtypes of P-E fit has traditionally emphasized different characteristics as relevant to fit. Each type is briefly reviewed below.

Person–Vocation Fit

The broadest form of P-E fit is the fit between individuals and their vocations or occupations, labeled generally person–vocation (P-V) fit. Vocational choice theories, such as those by John L. Holland and Renee Dawis and Lofquist, fall into this category. Holland (1985) proposed the RIASEC typology, which suggests that people will be most satisfied if they pursue careers that are compatible with their interests. Fit is defined by the degree of match between an individual's interests and those of others who generally comprise his or her chosen vocation. Dawis and Lofquist's theory of work

adjustment posits that individuals and careers are compatible to the extent that a variety of personal characteristic (including skills, abilities, needs, and values) correspond with the requirements imposed by the environment, and that personal needs are simultaneously met by the environment.

Reviews of the P-V literature generally report moderate positive correlations between P-V congruence and individual measures of well-being such as job and career satisfaction, stability, and personal achievement. Correlations are higher when focusing on the congruence with specialty areas within vocations. Consistent negative relationships have been found between fit and mental distress, somatic symptoms, changing vocations, and seeking satisfaction through leisure activities unrelated to work.

Person–Job Fit

A second type of fit, person–job (P-J) fit, concerns the relationship between an individual and characteristics of a specific job. It includes the match between a person's KSAs and the demands of the job (demands–abilities fit) or the person's needs and preferences and the resources provided by the job (needs–supplies fit). Traditional notions of personnel selection, which began during World War II with the selection of soldiers into specific positions in the army, emphasized the importance of hiring people who possessed the requisite KSAs for particular jobs (demands–abilities fit), and many job satisfaction theories emphasize the meeting of personal needs by jobs (needs–supplies fit). Outcomes of P-J fit include job satisfaction and intent to hire (when evaluated by recruiters), organizational attraction, organizational commitment, satisfaction with coworkers and supervisors, and overall job performance, as well as reduced intentions to quit, strain, and turnover.

Person–Organization Fit

Person–organization (P-O) fit, defined broadly as the compatibility between people and organizational characteristics, is a third type of P-E fit. Benjamin Schneider popularized this approach to fit with the attraction–selection–attrition (ASA) model, used to explain how homogeneity naturally results from organizational recruitment and selection processes.

Although the ASA model emphasized the antecedents and consequences of homogeneity at the organizational level, Jennifer Chatman proposed a model that emphasized P-O fit from the individual's perspective. This interactive model of P-O fit emphasizes the objective fit between individuals' values and those of the organization. Many researchers have used the notion of value congruence to assess P-O fit but have followed the approach of emphasizing perceived or subjective rather than objective fit. P-O fit has also been assessed using personality traits, goals, and needs. Meta-analytic estimates demonstrate that P-O fit is most strongly associated with feelings of attachment to the organization, such as organizational commitment and intent to quit.

Person–Group Fit

A fourth type of P-E fit is the match between individuals and members of their immediate work groups. Research on demography is related to fit but generally focuses on visible demographic characteristics, whereas person–group (P-G) fit research emphasizes deeper level, less observable characteristics, such as personality traits, goals, goal orientations, working styles, and KSAs. Unlike collective fit, P-G fit focuses on the fit of an individual with the other members of the team and the team's task. In general, results have supported supplementary fit relationship, in which similarity is beneficial, in studies of P-G fit. However, for certain characteristics, such as extroversion and KSAs, complementarity has also been supported. P-G fit is an individual-level variable, which predicts individual-level outcomes, such as feelings of cohesion toward the group, satisfaction with coworkers, and contextual performance.

Person–Person Fit

The final type of P-E fit is the match between individuals and other individuals, assessed at a dyadic level. The most typically studied person is the focal person's supervisor or recruiter. Most studies of person–person (P-P) fit have emphasized personality or value similarity and demonstrate positive relationships with attitudes focused toward that other person. Satisfaction with supervisor and leader–member exchange, trust in the leader, and to a lesser degree overall performance are positively related to P-P fit with supervisor. Value similarity with recruiters has also been found to be positively related to recruiters' assessment of individuals.

How Can Fit Be Measured?

Debate over measurement has been a prominent theme in the P-E fit domain. In the *APA Handbook of Industrial and Organizational Psychology*, A. Kristof-Brown and R. Guay describe fit as ranging on a continuum of perceived general compatibility (i.e., "I feel like a good fit with my environment") to exact correspondence (i.e., calculated as equal scores on a commensurate characteristic). How fit is conceptualized, thus, determines how it should be measured. Research has demonstrated that the way fit is conceptualized and then subsequently operationalized makes a large difference in the strength of its relationship with outcomes. Perceived general compatibility almost always has a stronger relationship with outcomes, particularly attitudinal outcomes, than does exact correspondence. In a study that directly compared various measurement approaches to fit, J. R. Edwards and colleagues demonstrated that various types of fit measures are positively correlated with each other, but only weakly so.

Direct Measures

To assess general compatibility, the measurement approach is to directly ask individuals whether they believe that a good P-E fit exists. For example, people may be asked to assess how well their vocations or jobs satisfy their personal needs (P-V and P-J fit, respectively), how well their KSAs meet job requirements (P-J fit), how compatible their values are with their organizations' and supervisors' (P-O fit and P-P fit, respectively), or whether they share their coworkers' goals (P-G fit). This type of assessment captures holistic assessments of perceived fit, because the individuals are asked to mentally calculate fit using whatever internal standards they wish to apply.

Indirect Measures

To better assess fit as correspondence, indirect methods in which person and environment variables are reported separately are typically used. These could be reported by the same person (subjective fit) or from two unique sources (objective fit).

The actual calculation of fit is done by a researcher making an explicit comparison of these two descriptions. Such approaches require that the dimensions of person and environment be commensurate (i.e., using the same dimensions). Two very distinct methods for assessing fit indirectly have dominated the field: difference scores and polynomial regression.

Difference Scores

In the early 1990s, the primary means of indirect fit assessment was the use of profile similarity indices or difference scores. These methods assess the algebraic difference between person and environment variables. Despite their popularity, they have been criticized because of the inability to determine whether person and environment contribute equally to the outcome, the loss of information on the absolute level of characteristics, and the direction of differences, as well as overly restrictive statistical constraints. These limitations may result in inappropriate conclusions about the nature of the fit relationships.

Polynomial Regression

In response to the concerns over difference scores, J. R. Edwards and colleagues proposed polynomial regression as an alternative way to assess P-E fit. At its core, this approach avoids using a single term to capture fit. Instead, both person and environment, and associated higher order terms (P^2, $P \times E$, and E^2), are included as predictors in a regression. The relationship between these variables is then graphed on three-dimensional surface plots, which can be visually inspected and characteristics of the surface (i.e., slopes and curvatures) can be statistically evaluated to determine whether a fit relationship is supported. It provides a very precise depiction of the relationship between person and environment variables, but does not result in a single effect size attributable to fit.

Statistical Interactions

A final measurement strategy is to not assess fit but to infer that it exists from a statistical interaction between conceptually related person and environment variables. Studies using this approach typically demonstrate that the relationship of an environmental characteristic on an outcome is moderated by an individual characteristic, or vice versa. There is no requirement in such approaches that the dimensions of person and environment be commensurate, just that they were theoretically related. Fit is assumed to be supported if the interaction term explained significant variance in the outcomes, beyond the main effects of person and environment.

Summary

Research on P-E fit remains one of the most eclectic domains of organizational psychology. However it is conceptualized and operationalized, results consistently demonstrate that peoples' perceptions of, and objective fit with, their environment have important consequences for work-related attitudes and behaviors.

Amy L. Kristof-Brown

See also Person–Job Fit; Person–Organization Fit; Person–Vocation Fit

Further Readings

Assouline, M., & Meir, E. I. (1987). Meta-analysis of the relationship between congruence and well-being measures. *Journal of Vocational Behavior, 31*, 319–332. doi:10.1016/0001-8791(87)90046-7

Caplan, R. D., & Harrison, R. V. (1993). Person–environment fit theory: Some history, recent developments, and future directions. *Journal of Social Issues, 49*, 253–275. doi:10.1111/j.1540-4560.1993.tb01192.x

Chatman, J. A. (1989). Improving interactional organizational research: A model of person–organization fit. *Academy of Management Review, 14*, 333–349. doi:10.5465/AMR.1989.4279063

Dawis, R. V., & Lofquiest, L. H. (1984). *A psychological theory of work adjustment*. Minneapolis, MN: University of Minnesota Press.

DeRue, D. S., & Hollenbeck, J. R. (2007). The search for internal and external fit in teams. In C. Ostroff & T. A. Judge (Eds.), *Perspectives on organizational fit* (pp. 259–285). New York: Erlbaum. doi:10.4324/9780203810026

Edwards, J. R. (1991). Person–job fit: A conceptual integration, literature review, and methodological critique. In C.L.R.I.T. Cooper (Ed.), *International review of industrial and organizational psychology* (Vol. 6, pp. 283–357). Chichester, UK: Wiley.

Edwards, J. R. (1994). The study of congruence in organizational behavior research: Critique and a proposed alternative. *Organizational Behavior and Human Decision Processes*, 58, 51–100. doi:10.1006/obhd.1994.1029

Edwards, J. R., Cable, D. M., Williamson, I. O., Lambert, L. S., & Shipp, A. J. (2006). The phenomenology of fit: linking the person and environment to the subjective experience of person–environment fit. *Journal of Applied Psychology*, 91(4), 802–827. doi:10.1037/0021-9010.91.4.802.

Holland, J. E. (1985). *Making vocational choices: A theory of careers*. Englewood Cliffs, NJ: Prentice Hall.

Kristof, A. L. (1996). Person–organization fit: An integrative review of its conceptualizations, measurement, and implications. *Personnel Psychology*, 49(1), 1–49. doi:10.1111/j.1744-6570.1996.tb01790.x

Kristof-Brown, A. L., & Guay, R. P. (2011). Person–environment fit. In S. Zedeck (Ed.), *APA handbook of industrial and organizational psychology* (pp. 3–50). Washington, DC: American Psychological Association. doi:10.1037/12171-001.

Kristof-Brown, A. L., Zimmerman, R. D. & Johnson, E. C. (2005). Consequences of individuals' fit at work: A meta-analysis of person–job, person–organization, person–group, and person–supervisor fit. *Personnel Psychology*, 58, 281–342. doi:10.1114/j.1744-6570.2005.00672.x

Lewin, K. (1935). *A dynamic theory of personality*. New York: McGraw-Hill.

Rounds, J. B., Dawis, R. W., & Lofquist, L. H. (1987). Measurement of person–environment fit and prediction of satisfaction in the theory of work adjustment. *Journal of Vocational Behavior*, 31, 297–318. doi:10.1016/0001-8791(87)90045-5

Schneider, B. (1987). The people make the place. *Personnel Psychology*, 40, 437–453. doi:10.1111/j.1744-6570.1987.tb00609.x

Tsui, A., S., Egan, T. D., & O'Reilly, C. A. (1992). Being different: Relational demography and organizational attachment. *Administrative Science Quarterly*, 37, 547–579. doi:10.2307/2393472

PERSON–JOB FIT

Person–job (P-J) fit is defined as the compatibility between individuals and the jobs or tasks they perform at work. This definition includes two basic types of compatibility. The first is based on employee needs and job supplies available to meet those needs, labeled needs–supplies or supplies–values fit. The second is based on the match between job demands and employee abilities, termed demands–abilities fit. In the past, the term *P-J fit* has been used to describe fit with occupations or vocations as well, but more recently it has been distinguished from this type of fit (see the entries "Person–Environment Fit" and "Person–Vocation Fit").

Based on interactional psychology, the underlying premise of P-J fit is that characteristics of the person and the job work jointly to determine individual outcomes. There are many theories that involve joint influence of person and job characteristics, but fit is a specific domain in which commensurate measurement is generally favored. Commensurate measures assess the person and job along the same content dimensions, thus allowing an assessment of fit or match to be determined. Often the combined effects of conceptually related person and job measures (e.g., need for achievement and job complexity) are interpreted as P-J fit, even though they involve noncommensurate measures. These types of studies are based on the underlying logic of fit and are often presented as moderation effects, in which the relationship between a job characteristic and outcome is moderated by an individual characteristic, or the relationship between an individual difference and outcome is moderated by a job characteristic. Below, further discussion on the various conceptualizations of P-J fit and their consequences is presented.

Two Conceptualizations of Person–Job Fit

Needs–Supplies Fit

The correspondence between employee needs or desires and the supplies a job provides, alternately labeled needs–supplies or supplies–values fit, is traditionally the most commonly investigated form of P-J fit. However, most of the research in this category is frequently considered job satisfaction research and is based on Lyman Porter's Need Satisfaction Questionnaire, or similar measures, which ask people to describe how much their current jobs provide (actual) of a particular characteristic and also how much of that characteristic is desired (ideal). Although this research was originally considered job satisfaction work, it squarely falls within the parameters of the needs–supplies P-J definition.

The basic tenet of needs–supplies fit is that negative consequences result when job supplies fall short or exceed personal needs, whereas positive consequences are maximized when environmental supplies exactly match personal needs. The evidence is clear that when job supplies fall short of personal needs, misfit is experienced and negative personal consequences result. However, the impact of excess supplies is less clear. Research by John R. P. French, Jr., Robert Caplan, and R. Van Harrison was some of the first to explicitly examine outcomes associated with conditions of both deficiency and excess. In the mid-1990s, Jeff Edwards elaborated on areas of "misfit," suggesting four possible processes that can occur when job supplies do not correspond with individual needs. When excess supplies exist, individuals will benefit if they can either carry over these supplies to fulfill other needs or conserve the excess to fulfill a later need. Alternatively, when excess supplies hinder the future fulfillment of needs (depletion) or interfere with fulfilling other needs, individuals will suffer from greater strain. Edwards advocated for the use of polynomial regression and three-dimensional surface plot analysis to allow closer inspection of misfit and fit relationships. These techniques were specifically proposed as alternatives to the commonly used algebraic difference scores or direct measures of the discrepancy between desired and actual job attributes. Research using this approach has demonstrated that only in a small number of studies has exact correspondence produced optimal outcomes. It is most typical that higher levels of supplies (excess) create consequences equal to or even better than a perfect match between needs and supplies.

Demands–Abilities Fit

The second conceptualization of P-J fit considers fit from the perspective of the organization, rather than the individual. Demands–abilities fit occurs when the individual possesses the knowledge, skills, abilities, and other aspects (i.e., personality traits) to meet job demands. When environmental demands exceed personal abilities, strain and negative affective consequences are likely to result.

When personal abilities exceed environmental demands, the challenges of overqualification are experienced, including dissatisfaction and turnover. The concept of demands–abilities fit is the basis for traditional selection techniques that seek to find qualified applicants to fill job vacancies. Demands–abilities P-J fit is rarely, if ever, measured as fit. Instead, it is implicit in the meeting of job requirements, with additional applicant qualifications often being viewed as an advantage, rather than a misfit with the job (for an exception, see research by David Caldwell and Charles O'Reilly III that used a profile comparison process to examine the match of individual abilities to specific task requirements).

Consequences of Person–Job Fit

P-J fit has been found to have the strongest positive correlations with job satisfaction and intent to hire, followed by moderate to strong positive correlations with organizational attraction, organizational commitment, and satisfaction with coworkers and supervisors. Moderate negative correlations exist with intent to quit and strain. With regard to behaviors, P-J fit is moderately correlated with overall performance and tenure (positive) and weakly associated with turnover (negative). For all outcomes, needs–supplies fit is a better predictor than demands–abilities fit, although for strain the effects are almost equivocal. Perceived P-J fit, assessed via either a direct perception or as an explicit comparison of perceived environment and personal characteristics, generally has a stronger relationships with criteria than do measures of objective fit. This is in keeping with French and colleagues' perspective that fit between the subjective person and environment is more proximal to outcomes than fit between the objective person and environment.

Summary

Research on P-J fit has been popular since the early 1960s. In the beginning, much P-J fit research was combined with research on person–vocation fit (see the entry in this volume) and job satisfaction (see the entry in this volume) or personnel selection (see the entry in this volume) and was conducted under the rubric of need fulfillment (needs–supplies fit) or selection (demands–abilities fit). More recently the trend has been to distinguish P-J fit from other forms of fit and to focus on areas of both fit and misfit as predictors of affective, behavioral, and physiological outcomes.

Amy L. Kristof-Brown

See also Person–Environment Fit; Person–Organization Fit; Person–Vocation Fit

Further Readings

Caldwell, D. F., & O'Reilly, C. A., III. (1990). Measuring person–job fit with a profile comparison process. *Journal of Applied Psychology, 75,* 648–657. doi:10.1037//0021-9010.75.6.648

Caplan, R. D. (1987). Person–environment fit theory: Commensurate dimensions, time perspectives, and mechanisms. *Journal of Vocational Behavior, 31,* 248–267. doi:10.1016/0001-8791(87)90042-x

Edwards, J. R. (1991). Person–job fit: A conceptual integration, literature review, and methodological critique. In C. L. R. I. T. Cooper (Ed.), *International review of industrial and organizational psychology* (Vol. 6, pp. 283–357). Chichester, UK: Wiley.

Edwards, J. R. (1996). An examination of competing versions of the person–environment fit approach to stress. *Academy of Management Journal, 39*(2), 292–339. doi:10.2307/256782

Edwards, J. R., & Harrison, R. V. (1993). Job demands and worker health: Three-dimensional reexamination of the relationship between person–environment fit and strain. *Journal of Applied Psychology, 78*(4), 628–648. doi:10.37/0021-9010.78.4.628

Edwards, J. R., & Shipp, A. J. (2007). The relationship between person–environment fit and outcomes: An integrative theoretical framework. In C. Ostroff & T. A. Judge (Eds.), *Perspectives on organizational fit* (pp. 209–258). New York: Erlbaum. doi:10.4324/97 80203810026

French, J. R. P., Jr., Caplan, R. D., & Harrison, R. V. (1982). *The mechanisms of job stress and strain.* London: Wiley. doi:10.1016/0022-3999(83)90060-0

French, J. R. P., Jr., Rogers, W., & Cobb, S. (1974). Adjustment as person–environment fit. In D. A. H. G. V. Coelho & J. E. Adams (Ed.), *Coping and adaptation.* New York: Basic Books.

Kristof-Brown, A., & Guay, R. P. (2011). Person–environment fit. In S. Zedeck (Ed.), *American Psychological Association handbook of industrial and organizational psychology* (Vol. 3, pp. 1–50). Washington, DC: American Psychological Association. doi:10.1037/12171-001

Kristof-Brown, A. L., Zimmerman, R. D., & Johnson, E. C. (2005). Consequences of individuals' fit at work: A meta-analysis of person–job, person–organization, person–group, and person–supervisor fit. *Personnel Psychology, 58,* 281–342. doi:10.1114/j.1744-6570.2005.00672.x

Porter, L. W. (1961). A study of perceived job satisfactions in bottom and middle management jobs. *Journal of Applied Psychology, 45,* 1–10. doi:10.1037/h0043121

PERSONNEL PSYCHOLOGY

Personnel Psychology (*P-Psych*) publishes psychological research centered on people at work. Launched in 1948, *P-Psych* is one of the oldest and longest running applied psychology and management journals. The journal was founded to encourage and report research that applies psychological methods, understandings, techniques, and findings to the study of people at work. In their founding editorial, Erwin K. Taylor and Charles I. Mosier argued that for research findings to be meaningful, they must not only stimulate further research but also reach and be understood by those who might use them. Thus, from its inception *P-Psych* sought to publish research that was technically rigorous yet also realistic and readable. This emphasis on both rigor and relevance is something that has distinguished *P-Psych* throughout its history and has helped establish it as one of the most influential journals in the field of industrial and organizational psychology.

Journal Scope and Content

The mission of *P-Psych* is to publish psychological research centered on people at work. This broad mandate is reflected in the diversity of topics covered in the journal, spanning the full spectrum of industrial and organizational psychology, human resource management, and organizational behavior. Over the years, the journal has published highly influential articles in personnel selection, leadership, motivation and work attitudes, person–organization fit, organizational citizenship behavior, work teams, work design, job stress, organizational climate, strategic human resource management, and many other areas.

Given *P-Psych*'s emphasis on publishing research that has high levels of organizational relevance, the topics appearing in the journal have evolved over time to address the most pressing challenges facing organizations and the individuals, managers, and teams embedded within them. During the early years of the journal, there was a heavy emphasis on traditional personnel topics, such as training, job analysis, selection, evaluation, work design, and work conditions. For example, the most influential article published in the journal during the 1950s (as judged by citations) introduced the famous "faces scale" as a new type of employee attitude measure. The measure was designed to yield a better understanding of employees' opinions regarding organizational changes and current working conditions, information that hopefully could be used to promote organizational harmony and avoid serious labor trouble.

Over the years, *P-Psych* has continued to publish influential research on these topics while also expanding into new areas that reflect advances in applied psychological research, the changing nature of work and organizations, and broader societal trends. As organizations have shifted from individual to team-based work structures, for example, the journal has published a growing number of articles focused on understanding the factors that influence the effectiveness of work teams. These articles have helped establish the important role of team training, leadership, team composition, and teamwork processes, among other factors, in shaping team effectiveness. There has also been an increase in the number of articles focused on relationships at the organizational level, in particular the relationship between high-performance work systems (systems of human resources practices) and organizational effectiveness. One recent article, for example, showed that high-performance work systems enhance business unit performance in the service context by facilitating two types of organizational climate: concern for customers and concern for employees. These climates encourage employees to engage in cooperative behaviors with both customers and coworkers that are needed to achieve superior market performance. In the past few years, *P-Psych* has also published highly influential articles in areas of emerging importance, including corporate social responsibility, flexible work arrangements, the global context, and star performers.

A diverse set of approaches and perspectives is needed to investigate such a broad array of topics. Thus, *P-Psych* welcomes many different types of research, including quantitative and qualitative research as well as studies conducted in different research settings (e.g., field, laboratory) and at different levels of analysis (e.g., individual, team, organization). The journal publishes original empirical research, theory development, meta-analytic reviews, methodological developments, and narrative literature reviews. Further, the journal encourages research from authors located in different countries and on issues of international and cross-cultural significance.

Journal Editorial Process

P-Psych currently receives about 400 new article submissions each year and publishes about 30 articles annually. The journal is published quarterly, although articles are available online as soon as they are accepted. The editorial team of the journal consists of an editor-in-chief, four associate editors, and about 80 editorial board members. Each manuscript that is submitted to the journal is evaluated by two reviewers using a "double-blind" review process, in which reviewers do not know the identities of the authors, and authors do not know the identities of the reviewers. Reviewers are typically members of the editorial board, although the journal solicits reviews from a few dozen ad hoc reviewers each year. The reviewers submit their recommendations to an action editor (the editor-in-chief or one of the four associate editors), who then makes the final decision on the manuscript. The reviewers' recommendations and the action editor's publication decision are based on the article's contribution on three dimensions: (a) theoretical contribution (does the article offer new and meaningful insights or meaningfully extend existing theory?), (b) empirical contribution (does the article offer new and unique findings and are the study design, data analysis, and results rigorous and appropriate for testing the hypotheses or research questions?), and (c) practical contribution (does the article contribute to the improved management of people at work?). Before manuscripts are accepted for publication, they will typically undergo at least one, and usually several, rounds of revision and further reviews. *P-Psych* is committed to ensuring that every author has a positive experience during the review process. Specifically, the journal strives to provide authors with timely (within 60 days of submission, on average), detailed, and constructive feedback on their manuscripts.

In addition to publishing research articles, each issue of *P-Psych* includes several book reviews. Books that are submitted for review are evaluated by the book review editor to determine whether they fit within the scope of the journal and are likely to be of interest to the journal's readership. Books that meet these two criteria are reviewed by either a member of the Book Review Advisory Panel or an ad hoc reviewer. For many years, the journal also contained an "Innovations in Research-Based Practice" section, which later evolved into the "Scientist-Practitioner Forum." These sections were dedicated to addressing concerns of practitioners that might not be answered through traditional programs of research. This section of the journal was eliminated in 2011, in part because there had emerged several new outlets focused specifically on facilitating exchanges on topics of importance to scientists and practitioners in the field.

Bradford S. Bell

See also History of Industrial and Organizational Psychology in North America; Industrial and Organizational Psychology Journals; *Journal of Applied Psychology*

Further Readings

Bell, B. S. (2014). Rigor and relevance. *Personnel Psychology*, 67, 1–4.

Chuang, C-H., & Liao, H. (2010). Strategic human resource management in service context: Taking care of business by taking care of employees and customers. *Personnel Psychology*, 63, 153–196.

Kunin, T. (1955). The construction of a new type of attitude measure. *Personnel Psychology*, 8, 65–77.

LePine, J. A., Piccolo, R. F., Jackson, C. E., Mathieu, J. E., & Saul, J. R. (2008). A meta-analysis of teamwork processes: Tests of a multidimensional model and relationships with team effectiveness criteria. *Personnel Psychology*, 61, 273–307.

Morgeson, F. P. (2011). "Personnel are people!" *Personnel Psychology*, 64, 1–5.

O'Boyle, E., Jr., & Aguinis, H. (2012). The best and the rest: Revisiting the norm of normality of individual performance. *Personnel Psychology*, 65, 79–119.

Taylor, E. K., & Mosier, C. I. (1948). Personnel psychology: The methods of science applied to the problems of personnel. *Personnel Psychology*, 1, 1–6.

PERSON–ORGANIZATION FIT

Person–organization (P-O) fit is defined as the compatibility between people and organizations that occurs when at least one entity provides what the other needs, they share similar fundamental characteristics, or both. This definition includes examples of mutual need fulfillment, value congruence between individuals and organizations, personality similarity between individuals and other members of the organization, and congruence between individual and organizational goals. P-O fit has also sometimes been called person–culture fit.

Based on the interactionist perspective, in which both personal and environmental characteristics interact to predict individual outcomes, P-O fit gained greatest prominence in the early 1990s. Since that time, more than 150 studies have been conducted that emphasize the match between individuals and organizational cultures, not just the jobs within those organizations. In this entry, a brief history of the concept and its theoretical underpinnings, antecedents, and consequences are described.

A History of Person–Organization Fit

In 1958 Chris Argyris proposed that organizations were characterized by particular types of climates, which played an important role in the attraction and selection of organizational members. This view, that companies hire the "right types," suggests that there is differential compatibility of individuals and organizations. In 1987 Benjamin Schneider elaborated on these ideas, in what has become one the most respected theories of interactionist psychology: the attraction–selection–attrition (ASA) framework. At its core, the ASA framework proposes that the three aforementioned processes result in organizations characterized by homogeneous members and structures, systems, and processes that reflect the characteristics of the people who "make the place." Although principally concerned with predicting organizational level outcomes and characteristics, the ASA framework has become the theoretical cornerstone for much of the research on P-O fit.

In the late 1980s and early 1990s, P-O fit gained further prominence in the organizational psychology literature. This was in part due to the growing recognition of the importance of organizational cultures. Research by Jennifer Chatman changed the ASA model's focus on organizational-level consequences to P-O fit as it affected individuals' attitudes and behaviors at work. Her definition of P-O fit as individual–organizational value congruence became a commonly accepted definition of the concept. This was coupled with the introduction of a measurement tool, the Organizational Culture Profile (OCP), by Chatman and her colleagues Charles O'Reilly and David Caldwell, which has become the most widely used tool for operationalizing objective P-O fit. A series of articles by Jeff Edwards in the mid-1990s critiqued the use of profile similarity indices, such as the OCP, for assessing P-O fit, instead recommending that a polynomial regression be used to be better explore the precise effects of fit and misfit. Much research since that time has used the polynomial regression approach or measured P-O fit as direct perceptions of similarity. In 1993, an *Academy of Management Executive* article by David Bowen and colleagues articulated the importance of selecting applicants for P-O fit, as well as the traditional person–job (P-J) fit on the basis of skills. In 2013, *Time* magazine published an article that likened P-O fit culture matching to matchmaking in online dating. Many consulting companies are getting into the business of helping companies make these types of cultural matches, in addition to the traditional emphasis on P-J fit (see the entry "Person–Job Fit"). Kristof-Brown's review of the literature in 1996 expanded the definition of P-O fit to include a wide variety of P-O interactions such as need fulfillment, personality similarity, and goal congruence, but value congruence is still the most frequently researched type of P-O fit.

Theoretical Underpinnings of Person–Organization Fit

There are two fundamental processes underlying P-O fit. First, there is the concept of need fulfillment. As in other theories of person–environment fit (see the entry "Person–Environment Fit"), psychological need fulfillment represents a complementary perspective on fit, in which fit is determined by the extent to which a person's needs are met by the organizational environment, or an organization's needs are met by the capabilities of an individual. Theories of need fulfillment suggest

that dissatisfaction results when needs go unmet and may also be the consequence of "overfulfillment," depending on the need. The second theoretical tradition in P-O fit research is the concept of individual–organizational congruence, a supplementary approach to fit. Theoretically, congruence affects attitudes and behaviors because people are more attracted to similar others. Similarity facilitates communication, validates choices, and socially reinforces personal identities. Taken together, these mechanisms provide alternative, but not competing, explanations for why P-O fit influences individual outcomes at work. Most P-O fit studies reflect the similarity perspective, although need fulfillment is also represented, often as the interaction of an individual characteristic with an organizational system or process to predict individual-level outcomes.

Antecedents of Person–Organization Fit

Research has emphasized recruitment, selection, and socialization as antecedents to P-O fit. These processes closely mirror the three components of the ASA framework: attraction, selection, and attrition. During recruitment, organizations seek to convey particular images of themselves to applicants. In turn, job applicants draw inferences about organizational culture on the basis of all available information, including features of the compensation system, interactions with current employees, and recruitment materials. Recent research has emphasized the reliance on Web-based descriptions of company values and reward systems in applicants' P-O fit assessments. There is evidence that both job applicants and organizational recruiters consider P-O fit during selection decisions, placing it only slightly behind fit with the job in terms of importance. There is also evidence that people with experience at more companies pay greater attention to P-O fit during the organizational entry process. Socialization mechanisms are also used to convey the values and other key characteristics of the organization. Evidence suggests that time spent with organizational members prior to organizational entry, as well as social experiences with and mentoring from incumbents, is more effective at increasing newcomers P-O fit than is technical, job-related training. Together the processes before hiring and immediately after organizational entry are the strongest antecedents of P-O fit.

Consequences of Person–Organization Fit

P-O fit has been found to have the strongest positive correlations with organizational commitment and organizational satisfaction, followed by moderate positive correlations with job satisfaction, trust, and satisfaction with coworkers and supervisors and moderate negative correlations with intent to quit and strain. With regard to behaviors, P-O fit is weakly correlated with task performance (positive) and turnover (negative) but moderately correlated with contextual performance or extra-role behaviors (positive). For all outcomes accept tenure, direct measures of perceived fit (i.e., "I share my organization's values") have the strongest relationship with criteria, followed by indirect measures of the fit between personal characteristics and perceived organizational attributes, and then by indirect measures of the person and objective measures of the organization.

Summary

Research on P-O fit has proliferated since the early 1990s. Despite debates over values versus other content dimensions and how to best measure fit (see the entry "Person–Environment Fit" for a more in-depth discussion of these issues), there is compelling evidence that individuals are differentially compatible with various organizations and that this compatibility has important individual-level consequences.

Amy L. Kristof-Brown

See also Person–Environment Fit; Person–Job Fit; Person–Vocation Fit

Further Readings

Cable, D. M., & Parsons, C. K. (2001). Socialization tactics and person–organization fit. *Personnel Psychology, 54*, 1–23. doi:10.1111/j.1744-6570.2001.tb00083.x

Chatman, J. A. (1989). Improving interactional organizational research: A model of person–organization fit. *Academy of Management Review, 14*, 333–349. doi:10.5465/AMR.1989.4279063

Chatman, J. A. (1991). Matching people and organizations: Selection and socialization in public accounting firms. *Administrative Science Quarterly, 36*, 459–484. doi:10.2307/2393204

Dineen, B. R., Ash, S. R., & Noe, R. A. (2002). A web of applicant attraction: Person–organization fit in the context of Web-based recruitment. *Journal of Applied Psychology, 87*, 723–734. doi:10.1037/0021-9010.87.4.723

Dineen, B. R., & Noe, R. A. (2009). Effects of customization on application decisions and applicant pool characteristics in a Web-based recruitment context. *Journal of Applied Psychology, 94*, 224–234. doi:10.1037/90012832

Edwards, J. R. (1994). The study of congruence in organizational behavior research: Critique and a proposed alternative. *Organizational Behavior and Human Decision Processes, 58*, 51–100. doi:10.1006/obhd.1994.1029

Kristof, A. L. (1996). Person–organization fit: An integrative review of its conceptualizations, measurement, and implications. *Personnel Psychology, 49*, 1–49. doi:10.1111/j.1744-6570.1996.tb01790.x

Kristof-Brown, A. L., Zimmerman, R. D., & Johnson, E. C. (2005). Consequences of individuals' fit at work: A meta-analysis of person–job, person–organization, person–group, and person–supervisor Fit. *Personnel Psychology, 58*, 281–342. doi:10.1114/j.1744-6570.2005.00672.x

Rynes, S. L., Bretz, R. D., & Gerhart, B. (1991). The importance of recruitment in job choice: A different way of looking. *Personnel Psychology, 44*, 487–521. doi:10.1111/j.1744-6570.1991.tb02402.x

Schneider, B. (1987). The people make the place. *Personnel Psychology, 40*, 437–453. doi:10.1111/j.1744-6570.1987.tb00609.x

PERSON–VOCATION FIT

The idea that sparked person–vocation (PV) fit came from Frank Parsons, one of the earliest figures in vocational psychology, who believed that people need a clear understanding of themselves and the environment in which they work to be happy in their jobs and careers. PV fit is the relationship between individuals and their vocations or occupations. The PV literature generally has reported positive correlations between PV congruence and individual measures of well-being such as job and career satisfaction, stability, and personal achievement. In addition to having an effect on individual well-being, PV fit (or lack thereof) can have an impact on organizational commitment.

A number of theories either directly or indirectly have relevance for understanding PV fit. Some of the more prominent theories are detailed in the following text.

Holland's Theory

John Holland's theory of vocational personality types, first presented in 1959, is one of the most influential and researched theories in psychology. Holland proposed a typology that divided interests and work environments into six types. He organized the types spatially around the six points of a hexagon. The types are as follows:

1. Realistic (likes hands-on tasks)

2. Investigative (analyzes ideas)

3. Artistic (creative and original)

4. Social (helps people)

5. Enterprising (takes on leadership role)

6. Conventional (follows rules and orders)

The main premise of the theory is that individuals search for work environments that allow them to express their vocational interests and associate with other people with similar interests. Furthermore, the interaction between a person's interests and the work environment's requirements is likely to influence job satisfaction and tenure. For example, if Jane is interested in the artistic domain, she would be most likely to find satisfaction in work that has a large creative component. If, however, Jane's work environment is incongruent with her interests—say she is working in a conventional environment that does not allow her to do creative work—then she may express dissatisfaction with her job.

Holland based his theory of vocational types on empirical data derived from correlational and factor analytic studies. A plethora of research studies provide evidence of validity for the major tenets of Holland's theory for western societies. Recently, research on the evidence of validity for Holland's theory for non-western cultures has begun to appear in the literature. A benefit of Holland's theory is the ease with which the propositions and constructs can be applied to a career-counseling setting. For example, understanding how the six vocational types relate to one another helps a person match interests with the work environment. Moreover, the scale development of all major interest inventories has been influenced by Holland's theory, and instruments such as the Strong Interest Inventory and the Self-Directed Search include scales constructed to measure the six vocational types.

Theory of Work Adjustment

The theory of work adjustment (TWA) was developed at the University of Minnesota by René Dawis and Lloyd Lofquist. Like Holland's theory, TWA proposes that a person will stay in a job longer if there is congruence, or correspondence in TWA terminology, between the person and the work environment. Specifically, TWA postulates that if a person's abilities, needs, and values match the analogous workplace environment components (i.e., ability requirements and reinforcers), then job satisfaction and satisfactoriness occur. Tenure, or longevity on the job, in turn, is a result of the individual's satisfaction and satisfactoriness. In other words, the individual is satisfied if the work environment matches the person's values and needs, and the environment deems the individual satisfactory if the person's abilities or skills meet the requirements of the job. Values, an important aspect of the TWA, are grouped into six categories:

1. Achievement

2. Comfort

3. Status

4. Altruism

5. Safety

6. Autonomy

Ability also is an important consideration. In some situations, an individual's flexibility may help that person compensate for a lack of correspondence. In other words, people who are flexible can tolerate noncorrespondence more than can individuals who are inflexible.

The TWA has been applied in areas such as career counseling, career assessment, and selection. Several instruments, such as the Minnesota Importance

Questionnaire and the Minnesota Satisfaction Questionnaire, have been developed to measure TWA variables.

Social Cognitive Career Theory

The social cognitive career theory (SCCT) was derived primarily from Bandura's social cognitive theory. Bandura's theory centers on the notion that behaviors are guided by self-beliefs. Several theories spawned from the umbrella of Bandura's work, and the career domain is not an exception. The SCCT posits that person, environment, and behaviors exert overlapping influence when people develop and decide on their academic or career goals. Specifically, self-efficacy, outcome expectations, and goal representations drive career development. Below are brief definitions of these three mechanisms according to the SCCT.

1. Self-efficacy: a set of dynamic beliefs people hold about their capabilities to successfully complete tasks and reach their goals

2. Outcome expectations: how one imagines the results or consequences if a task is being performed

3. Goal representations: the decision to be involved in an activity or a future plan

The SCCT has three models that interconnect: interest, choice, and performance. The interest and choice models are often discussed in existing literature. The interest model states that both self-efficacy and outcome expectations can predict a person's interest (academic and career). People tend to focus on the development of their interests in areas in which they know they would excel and would achieve positive outcomes. According to the choice model, interest, self-efficacy, and outcome expectations are consistent with one's academic and career goal development. The performance model predicts the level of people's aspirations within the context of their interests and their choices. That is, people tend to set academic and career-related goals when (a) they know they have strong interest in this field, (b) they believe in their wherewithal to be successful in this particular field, and (c) the likelihood of achieving the goal is high.

Research on the SCCT also articulates other factors that contribute to career development. For example, gender and race/ethnicity are influential because the cultural context of people's experiences help shape their self-efficacy and outcome expectations. Values and aptitude also seem to have strong ties to the three main constructs of the SCCT.

Person–Environment Fit Theory of Stress

The person–environment (PE) fit theory of stress comes from the field of occupational health psychology. Robert Caplan, John French, and R. Van Harrison contributed to the PE fit theory of stress, which developed from the perspective of PE misfit instead of the PE correspondence view of TWA. According to the theory, PE misfit causes some disturbance in a person both psychologically and physically. The theory first makes a distinction between the person and the environment and their reciprocal relationship. Then, person and environment are divided into both objective and subjective components. *Subjective* refers to the perception of a person's characteristics or environment. *Objective* refers to the personal characteristics and physical and social environment of an individual that can be observed or assessed by others.

The theory states that if PE misfit surfaces, two sets of outcomes may occur. Psychological, physical, and behavior strains compose the first set of outcomes. These negative consequences eventually lead to poor health and unresolved PE misfit. The second set of outcomes includes coping and defensive behaviors, which are used to resolve the PE misfit. Some coping strategies, used to find ways to balance the current misfit, come from objective PE fit. One such strategy is adapting to the environment. Defensive coping strategies, such as denial, provide a means for enhancing subjective PE fit. The PE fit theory of stress also suggests that outcomes of subjective misfit can be reduced by shrinking objective misfit, and vice versa.

Attraction–Selection–Attrition Model

In the field of industrial and organizational psychology, Benjamin Schneider's attraction–selection–attrition (ASA) model looks at organizational behavior from the person-oriented side. The model proposes that an organization is defined by the *collective characteristics* of the people who work there, which are hypothesized to develop through three steps:

1. Employee attraction to the job

2. Employer selection of employees

3. Departure by employees who are not congruent with the work environment

In other words, when people are attracted to an organization by its characteristics, their personalities are implicitly congruent with the organization's characteristics. Then, the organization chooses whom to hire on the basis of whether the individual's attributes match what the organization wants. If the individual does not fit well with others in the organization, this person is asked to leave. As a result, characteristics of the employees will match the objectives of the organization; and ideally, people within the organization will get along because they are similar to one another. Some researchers, however, argue that adding diversity to an organization may bring more creativity and better problem-solving skills to the workplace than does a homogeneous working population.

The ASA model's main premise is that the attributes of people define the organization. Therefore, Schneider suggested that when changes need to occur in an organization, the process should begin with changes in personnel rather than with changes in the structure and processes of the organization itself.

Jo-Ida C. Hansen and W. Vanessa Lee

See also Attraction–Selection–Attrition Model; Careers; Person–Environment Fit; Person–Job Fit; Person–Organization Fit; Social Cognitive Theory; Theory of Work Adjustment

Further Readings

Capuzzi, D., & Stauffer, M. D. (Eds.). (2006). *Career counseling: Foundations, perspectives, and applications.* New York: Routledge.

Hansen, J. C. (2013). A person-environment fit approach to cultivating meaning. In B. J. Dik, Z. S. Byrne, & M. F. Steger (Eds.), *Purpose and meaning in the workplace.* Washington, D.C.: American Psychological Association

Leka, S., & Houdmont, J. (2010). *Occupational health psychology.* Hoboken, NJ: John Wiley.

Lent, R. W., Brown, S. D., & Hackett, G. (1994). Toward a unifying social cognitive theory of career and academic interest, choice, and performance. *Journal of Vocational Behavior, 45,* 79–122. doi:10.1006/jvbe.1994.1027

Schneider, B., Goldstein, H. W., & Smith, D. B. (1995). The ASA framework: An update. *Personnel Psychology, 48,* 747–773.

PHENOMENOLOGY

Definition and Description

Phenomenology is the study of subjective conscious experience. A concept originating in Hegel's *Phenomenology of Spirit* and driven forward by the philosophical works of Husserl, phenomenology studies consciousness from a subjective, first-person point of view. More of a way of thinking than a specific philosophical doctrine, phenomenology is primarily interested in investigating how the individual experiences events in the world, how the individual qualifies and articulates those experiences, and how they are then understood by other individuals. Phenomenology is primarily concerned with understanding and articulating what given subjective experiences are like, to gain some level of understanding about subjective experience and consciousness. Even with an awareness of another *as an other* with unique experiences, and even though one can have some understanding of what another's experiences are like, one cannot know another's experience precisely; my *awareness* of your experience is not *knowledge* of your experience, so our individual understandings of some mutual experience will be subjective and unique, as I cannot know what it is like to be you having that experience.

The particular challenge with, yet defining factor of, phenomenology is the difficulty that accompanies expressing and interpreting subjective experience. Philosophers have long confronted the problem of "qualia": individual instances of subjective experience. It is impossible to fully understand *exactly* what another person's experience is like, as we are limited by our own unique senses, perceptions, and interpretations; we can't know that our subjective experiences are the same as or even similar to another's experience of the same phenomena. This difficulty arises in articulating emotions and especially in the "meaning" of concepts, as well as sensory experiences. As a result, many qualitative psychologists have claimed phenomenological inquiry to be mainly a matter of making meaning, and should thus be addressed by interpretive approaches. Phenomenological psychology can be understood as a means of understanding subjective experience or as the application of a phenomenological method to investigate psychological phenomena, especially those dealing with consciousness and experience.

Hegel's *Phenomenology of Spirit*

Hegel attempts to outline the fundamental nature and conditions of human knowledge, asserting that the mind does not immediately grasp the objects in the world but instead relies on generating concepts of those objects. Hegel demonstrates that though concepts do in fact mediate matter, his argument of the way concepts come into being implies a certain instability or fallibility of knowledge. Hegel moves from discussion of consciousness in general to a discussion of self-consciousness: Hegel believes that consciousness of objects necessarily implies some awareness of self, as a subject, which is separate from the perceived object, but takes this idea a step further by asserting that subjects are also objects to other subjects. Self-consciousness is the awareness of another's awareness of oneself; one becomes aware of oneself by seeing oneself through another, though this conception of self-consciousness implies a certain struggle between the moment the self and the other come together, which makes self-consciousness possible, and the moment when one becomes conscious of the otherness of other selves in relation to oneself, and the otherness of oneself in relation to other selves.

Husserl and Phenomenology

Husserl's phenomenology relies on the evidence of lived experience to provide descriptions of experience and of objects experienced, rather than the more empirical focus of naturalistic inquiry. Husserl's investigations of essential structures of conscious life and experience focus on consciousness as transcendental rather than mundane, meaning that consciousness is taken not as a part of the world but as the only means of experiencing the world at all. A Husserlian approach to consciousness or subjectivity is not restricted to the mental realm alone. Instead, the phenomenological notion of embodied experience offers an alternative to Cartesian mind–body dualism: Husserl's investigations embrace both subjectivity *and* intersubjectivity, more *cogitamus* than *cogito*. Husserl also focuses on "the body as directly experienced by the embodied experiencer concerned," a major theme for phenomenological investigation.

For Husserl, phenomenology integrates psychology with a kind of logic. It develops a descriptive or analytic psychology in that it describes and analyzes types of subjective mental activity or experience. It describes and analyzes objective contents of consciousness: ideas, concepts, images, and propositions—in short, ideal meanings of various types that serve as intentional contents, or noematic meanings, of various types of experience. These contents are shareable by different acts of consciousness, and in that sense they are objective, ideal meanings. Husserl opposed any reduction of logic or mathematics or science to mere psychology, to how people happen to think. For Husserl, phenomenology would study consciousness without reducing the objective and shareable meanings that inhabit experience to merely subjective happenstances. Ideal meaning would be the engine of intentionality in acts of consciousness.

Heidegger's Further Work

Heidegger introduces his approach to phenomenology in *Being and Time* (1927). Conscious experience is the starting point of phenomenology, but phenomenology also accounts for less explicitly conscious phenomena. As Husserl and others emphasize, we are only vaguely aware of things peripheral to our attention, the rest of the world around us. Heidegger stresses that we are not explicitly conscious of our habitual patterns of action, and as psychoanalysts have stressed, much of our intentional mental activity is not even conscious at all, only becoming conscious through dedicated introspection or interrogation as one comes to realize one's thoughts or feelings.

In the text of a lecture course called *The Basic Problems of Phenomenology* (1927), Heidegger traces the question of the meaning of being from Aristotle through many other thinkers into the issues of phenomenology. Our understanding of beings and their being comes through phenomenology. Heidegger questioned the contemporary concern with technology, his writing suggesting that our scientific theories are historical artifacts used in technological practice, rather than systems of ideal truth as Husserl had asserted. Heidegger holds instead that our understanding of being comes through phenomenology.

Applications in Psychology

Phenomenological approaches to human experience have become a major element of caring professions such as counseling and nursing. Although some debate over the empirical validity of phenomenology continues, Ashworth and Chung's *Phenomenology and Psychological Science* entrenches phenomenology in the psychological tradition, tracing the evolution of phenomenological philosophy and its impact on psychological science. The authors highlight a number of overlapping themes that grew out from the roots of phenomenology into mainstream psychology, including issues of the nature of consciousness, existentialist currents in contemporary psychology, the value of qualitative methods in science-based practice, and applications of phenomenology in case conceptualization and therapy. The authors note that mainstream psychology was, in its earliest beginnings, concerned with the study of experience, engaging with topics that phenomenologists had also approached. However, the behaviorist revolution drove a wedge between most psychological sciences and the emerging phenomenological philosophy of Husserl. Husserl's philosophical purpose in founding phenomenology means, as Ashworth and Chung show, that Husserl's and other phenomenological works need to be carefully analyzed to understand their relevance to psychology.

While phenomenology has had little *direct* influence over psychology, there has certainly been *indirect* influence, such as the migration of German Gestalt psychologists to the United States in the 1930s and the definite impact of existential phenomenology engineered by Heidegger. This had an undeniable role in the establishment of humanistic psychology, counseling, and psychiatry, and so the authors espouse a view that the low impact of phenomenological thinking on psychology is regrettable. Psychology's (and psychologists') positivist slant diverted its course from that of phenomenology, though it is also true psychological science generally assumes that there is one real world with determinate characteristics, and the purpose of science is to render theories that correspond to this world. Noting this parallel line of thought, Ashworth and Chung attempt to offer contemporary applications to psychology that they believe will be of growing importance as psychologists become more and more focused on consciousness and subjective experience of consciousness. The fundamental theme of phenomenology in psychology is again the meaningfulness of lived experience.

Phenomenology has a number of interesting applications in industrial and organizational psychology, offering a lens through which one can interpret issues of diversity, organizational ethics, change management, and leadership. In each of these contexts, phenomenology draws attention to the subjective nature of experience in organizational settings, shifting away from more positivist, cause-and-effect views of industrial and organizational psychology and conceiving of the workplace as a complex interplay of numerous subjective interpretations; phenomenology applied to the organization highlights the importance of subjective experience in each of these contexts rather than ascribing a singular view of, for example, how leaders draw followers.

Phenomenological psychology is exclusively and wholly absorbed in the elucidation of experience. Conscious experience, if it is considered to be relevant, should be regarded as the lawful outcome of factors in the world such as physiological conditions and objective events. Phenomenological psychology brackets these elements of conscious experience, as Husserl's call to turn toward the things themselves is at the same time a call to turn away from the assumptions of contemporary psychological research. It would undoubtedly be possible to take the findings of a phenomenological study and subject them to the usual techniques of a quantitative psychology. Phenomenological psychology operates in terms of a world in which experience is primary and physical science is thus a derivative account.

Alexander Kello

See also After Action Reviews; Attitudes and Beliefs; Group Dynamics and Processes; High-Reliability Organizations; Identity; Organizational Culture; Personality

Further Readings

Ashworth, P., & Chung, M. C. (2007). *Phenomenology and psychological science: Historical and philosophical perspectives.* Berlin, Germany: Springer Science & Business Media.

Edwards, J. R., Cable, D. M., Williamson, I. O., Lambert, L. S., & Shipp, A. J. (2006). The phenomenology of fit: Linking the person and environment to the subjective experience of person-environment fit. *Journal of Applied Psychology, 91*(4), 802–807.

Forster, M. N. (1998). *Hegel's idea of a phenomenology of spirit.* Chicago, IL: University of Chicago Press.

Giorgi, A. (1975). An application of phenomenological method in psychology. *Duquesne Studies in Phenomenological Psychology, 2,* 82–103.

Hegel, G. W. F. (1977). *Phenomenology of spirit* (A. V. Miller, trans.). Oxford, UK: Oxford University Press. (Original work published 1807)

Heidegger, M. (1988). *The basic problems of phenomenology* (Vol. 478). Bloomington: Indiana University Press.

Heidegger, M., Emad, P., & Maly, K. (1994). *Hegel's phenomenology of spirit.* Bloomington: Indiana University Press.

Husserl, E. (2012). *Ideas: General introduction to pure phenomenology.* London, UK: Routledge.

PHYSICAL DISABILITIES AT WORK

In the United States, nearly 20 million working-age Americans have disabilities, representing approximately 10% of the population. This figure includes both physical and psychological disabilities, but physical disability is the most prominent type of disability among people of working age. Individuals with disabilities rarely experience the same access to work opportunities as do their able-bodied and comparably educated counterparts. This finding is noteworthy given that the United Nations has proposed that the full and effective participation and inclusion in society is a basic right for all and that work is an important marker of participation and inclusion. Additionally, there is legislation aimed at protecting people with disabilities, such as the Americans with Disabilities Act. Despite legislation and the social awareness it instills, it appears that individuals with disabilities still fare poorly in employment settings.

Defining Disability

Definitions of disability vary considerably. Disability is frequently defined as a physical or mental impairment that limits a person's life activities, but jurisdictional differences exist. For example, the Americans with Disabilities Act of 1990 does not list any specific impairment name (and instead focuses on the effect of the impairment on a person's life to define the disability), while the American Community Survey lists six *categories* of impairments. Even within these definitions, there are differences in terms of how they are applied. Disabilities may evolve across life spans within individuals, and their effects can fluctuate in daily (e.g., feeling worse at the end of the day), weekly (e.g., feeling less energy as the week progresses), and monthly (e.g., feeling better after treatment) cycles. Furthermore, an able-bodied individual can become disabled, and vice versa. A more encompassing perspective on disability is that of the World Health Organization's International Classification of Functioning, Disability and Health (ICF), published in 2001. The ICF takes a biopsychosocial perspective and views disability as occurring in the interaction between an individual's health conditions and the context in which he or she exists.

In applying the ICF to understand the experience of an individual with a disability, it is important to consider contextual factors, which are divided into external (the environment) and internal (personal) factors. Environmental factors are a far-reaching category and include legal frameworks, architectural aspects of one's community, home, and workplace, as well as the attitudes of their members. Personal factors include variables such as demographic characteristics, personality, education, and social background. According to the ICF, disability is best understood by taking into account functioning at different levels: specific body parts, the whole person, and the person in his or her social context. Any impairment, activity limitation, and participation restriction experienced at any of these three levels is considered a disability. At the center of the model is *activity*, which is broadly understood as the execution of a task or action by the person with the disability. Whether engagement in the activity will lead to full participation or involvement in a life situation such as work depends on the health condition and its interaction with the context (i.e., both the environment and the person).

Disability and Employment

Industrial and organizational psychologists are but one of several professional groups interested in the employment of people with disabilities. Economists, sociologists, rehabilitation therapists, and many others also research this topic. Unfortunately, each of these fields paints a somewhat bleak picture when it comes to disability and employment.

Individuals with disabilities tend to have lower employment rates, and they are more likely to work part-time or contingently than are their able-bodied peers with similar levels of education. Perhaps as a result of this employment level, workers with disabilities have lower than average salaries, are more likely to live below the poverty level, and report lower job satisfaction. Furthermore, workers with disabilities experience less career advancement (a glass ceiling) and more career stagnation and even demotions (a glass cliff), especially if the disability onset is later in their careers. Yet most people with disabilities want to work, and they exhibit very high levels of work motivation once employed. Often, work is seen as instrumental for positive identity, positive quality of life, and social integration within the community

Barriers to Employment

Much research has focused on the barriers to employment, keeping in mind that employment can mean entry as well as reentry into the workforce, career advancement, and employment retention. What matters is not just employment per se but the quality of the employment, given that individuals with disabilities are often underemployed relative to their education and skills. Furthermore, barriers can be physical (e.g., stairs) or perceptual (e.g., discrimination by a manager), and it is how a person with a disability experiences the barrier that will shape his or her behavior. Thus, we focus on the individual experience in understanding barriers that may reside within the person, within the environment, and in the interaction between the two.

We begin our classification of barriers to employment by focusing on the individual via the category of *health condition*, denoting the disability itself (e.g., multiple sclerosis, spinal cord injury) and the related *body function and structure*. The type of disability (or the combination of multiple disabilities) can act as a barrier to employment participation, depending on the job requirements. For instance, limb amputation may prevent work as a firefighter, but not as a teacher. Additionally, jobs that can be accommodated will result in greater workforce participation. For example, workers with multiple sclerosis fare better when the physical demands of their positions can be minimized. Furthermore, each disability has attendant challenges of fatigue, pain, medication schedule, and needs for rest periods that are unique to the individual. A personalized approach to accommodation and job changes is legally required unless it imposes undue hardships on the organization.

Second, the onset of the disability is an important consideration. The disability experience is different for adult-onset as compared with youth-onset or congenital disabilities, as it is for a gradual (vs. traumatic) onset. When the disability occurs in adulthood, the individual has already established a career path. The challenge then becomes reentry into the workforce or adaptation to new physical demands rather than entry. The barriers created by reentry are numerous, and the longer one is away from work, the less likely he or she is to reenter. Upon reentry, advancement opportunities may not only be limited, but individuals with disabilities may be demoted. When the onset is gradual, the challenge is when (or if) to disclose the disability, and to whom, keeping in mind that many disabilities (e.g., arthritis, multiple sclerosis) are invisible.

Youth or congenital onset means that an individual has lived with a disability prior to entering the workforce. On one hand, facing participation barriers early may have helped the worker develop useful coping skills, which could transfer to the workplace. On the other hand, the disability may have created barriers to education that subsequently limit employment prospects.

Contextual factors encompass both the environment and the person. Obvious potential barriers in the environment are architectural and mobility related. For example, relying on adapted transportation to get to work, especially when work is bound by strict schedules, can limit workforce participation. This is especially likely to be a barrier in rural areas as opposed to large urban centers, but even in the latter, adapted transportation often creates challenges. The workplace architecture can also act as a barrier if it is not accessible (e.g., small doorframes in washrooms). Both the office building and the workstations need to be accessible if barriers are to be eliminated.

In addition to these possible physical barriers, workers with disabilities may face attitudinal barriers. An oft-reported barrier is organizational leaders' legal fears. For example, managers may cite the unfounded fear of greater likelihood of accidents or injuries for workers with disabilities compared with able-bodied workers, or the difficulty of firing a worker for cause if he or she happens to have a disability. Indeed, workers with disabilities are often perceived as more litigious and more entitled than their able-bodied counterparts.

Workers with disabilities also report being subjected to stereotypes based on their disabilities. For example, managers may worry about the public image of the company if the disability has an aesthetic component. Fears of increased absenteeism, unreliability, lower task performance, and increased need of supervision are also common. Another attitudinal barrier is the misconception surrounding accommodations. Often, managers lack knowledge on how to accommodate properly or mistakenly believe that most accommodations are unaffordable. In fact, very few accommodations require major structural changes; the typical cost of an accommodation is $250, and the majority of accommodations cost less than $500. Many accommodations require no cost at all (e.g., moving a desk for easier access). At the same time, a prospective worker may not know what accommodations will be needed in a new job and may not feel comfortable disclosing a disability at the recruitment and selection stage.

Another possible source of barriers is the familial and health care network supporting the worker with disability. In addition to family demands experienced by all workers, those with disabilities often cope with additional family or partnership strains. Family members may actively discourage employment, as can members of the health network (e.g., doctors, therapists). Women and youth are especially likely to be discouraged from employment. Furthermore, some individuals with disabilities may need attendant care. Reliance on someone outside of the home for this assistance can generate financial or logistical barriers, but reliance on family members can create caregiver strain.

Finally, the personal factors aspect of the ICF model encompasses characteristics of the individual (self). First, the candidate's self-efficacy may act as a barrier, especially among younger individuals with disabilities, for whom the transition to employment may be difficult. Self-presentation skills (e.g., high interview self-efficacy) are also likely to influence workplace participation, especially in the case of visible disabilities. The knowledge, skills, and abilities acquired by the individual may also act as barriers or facilitators, and the age at the time of the disability may influence the type of training acquired (and whether retraining is necessary). Second, an important barrier to employment is the fear of losing disability benefits when one enters the workforce, especially because disability benefits may provide more income than some entry-level jobs. Furthermore, some government benefits (e.g., prescription medication, physical therapy) are not available for employed individuals, and company benefit plans may be unavailable or insufficient. Finally, because of the unpredictable nature of many disabilities, individuals may be concerned about starting a new job only to need to exit the workforce in the near future and thus be faced with the challenge of reentering the disability benefit system. A complete understanding of financial barriers must take into account jurisdictional differences, because what is a real barrier in one jurisdiction may only be a perceived one in another.

In sum, disability at work is best understood by looking at the experience of the individual as he or she interacts with his or her environment. This interactionist approach allows us to gain a deeper understanding of the barriers that he or she may face. Furthermore, it is important to think of participation in the workforce as access to work but also in terms of quality of work given the widespread underemployment experienced by workers with disabilities. Although accommodations increase participation through the activity component of the model, many employers are still unwilling or unaware of how to provide them, as shown by the number of human rights cases involving disabilities.

Silvia Bonaccio and
Catherine E. Connelly

See also Adverse Impact/Disparate Treatment/ Discrimination at Work; Americans with Disabilities Act; Bona Fide Occupational Qualifications; Diversity in the Workplace; Diversity Training; Glass Ceiling; Labor Law; Workplace Accommodations for People With Disabilities

Further Readings

Brault, M.W., (2012). Americans with disabilities: 2010. Washington, DC: U.S. Department of Commerce. http://www.census.gov/prod/2012pubs/p70-131.pdf

Bruyère, S. M., & Barrington, L. (2012). *Employment and work*. Thousand Oaks, CA: Sage.

Fabian, E. (2013). Work and disability. In D. L. Blustein (Ed.), *The Oxford handbook of the psychology of working*. Oxford, UK: Oxford University Press.

Kaye, H. S. (2001). *Disability watch, Volume 2: The status of people with disabilities in the United States*. Oakland, CA: Disability Rights Advocates.

World Health Organization. (2011). *World report on disability*. http://www.who.int/disabilities/world_ report/2011/en/index.html

PHYSICAL PERFORMANCE ASSESSMENT

Physically demanding occupations, such as manual materials handling and public safety, require the use of a variety of physical abilities to perform the job tasks. Because of the need for workers to meet the physical requirements of arduous jobs and the potential for injury, employers use physical performance tests to determine an individual's physical capabilities to meet the job requirements. The physical abilities assessed by the tests are based on the essential tasks and functions, working conditions, and ergonomic parameters associated with a job. These abilities are defined in the following text:

- Muscular strength is the ability to exert force to lift, push, pull, or hold objects. The amount of force generated by a muscle contraction is dependent on the size of the muscles (cross section) involved and muscle fiber type such as a fast twitch.
- Muscular endurance is the ability to exert force continuously over moderate to long time periods. The length of time a muscle can contract is dependent on the size of the muscles involved, the chemical composition of the muscle tissue, and the muscle fiber type such as a slow twitch.
- Aerobic capacity or cardiovascular endurance is the ability of the respiratory and cardiovascular systems to provide oxygen to the body systems for medium- to high-intensity tasks performed over a moderate time period. Aerobic tasks require continuous oxygen consumption.
- Anaerobic power is the ability to complete high-intensity, short-duration (e.g., 5- to 90-second) tasks. Anaerobic tasks are performed using stored energy in the form of adenosine triphosphate.
- Flexibility involves the range of motion at the joints including knees and shoulders to bend, stoop, rotate, and reach in all directions with the arms and legs. Flexibility at the joints is dependent on the extensibility of the ligaments, tendons, muscle, and skin.
- Equilibrium is the ability to maintain the center of gravity over the base of support such as feet. Equilibrium involves maintaining and recovering to a balanced position when outside forces, including gravity and slipping on ice, occur.

Combinations of different levels of these abilities are needed for all tasks in which muscular contraction, oxygen consumption, and energy expenditure are required. For example, low levels of muscular strength and muscular endurance in the abdominal and back muscles are required to sit in a chair. However, high levels of these two abilities are required to lift and carry 30 boxes weighing 70 pounds each. Performance of arduous job tasks typically requires all six abilities, but to different extents. Lifting 10 boxes, each 90 pounds, from a table and carrying them 100 yards to another table requires high levels of muscular strength and muscular endurance in the arms, legs, and torso, but only low levels of flexibility. The level of equilibrium needed is moderate because gravity is pulling downward as the box is carried forward. Similarly, to avoid falling over when picking up a weighted object, the base of support must be adjusted or widened, for example. This task also requires a moderate level of aerobic capacity because of the weight of the boxes, the distance they are carried, and the duration of the task. Therefore, the physical abilities interact at varying levels throughout performance of all arduous job tasks. The specificity of an ability can be determined through direct physiological measurement such as oxygen consumption, ergonomic measurement including force to torque bolts, or questionnaire data.

Physical performance tests are developed, validated, and implemented for purposes of applicant assessment, incumbent assessment and retention, and worker assessment for return to work after an injury. Physical tests are used for arduous jobs in the public (e.g., law enforcement, firefighter, emergency medical service), private (e.g., warehouse, manufacturing, longshoring, telecommunications, railroad, trades, electric, natural gas), and military sectors. Use of physical performance tests in the selection setting provides several benefits. First, individuals whose physical ability is commensurate with the demands of the job are identified. Second, physically qualified individuals have fewer injuries, which leads to lower worker compensation costs, increased productivity, and reduced turnover. Research in this area has shown reductions in injury rates of 10% to 20% for new hires who successfully completed a physical test screening when compared with individuals who did not take the test. Further, when workers were injured, those who passed the physical test had significantly lower injury costs than those who were not tested, for example, $4 million versus $12 million.

Types of Tests

Numerous physical performance tests are used by organizations to assess physical capabilities. However, these tests can be placed into one of two categories: basic ability tests and work/job simulations. Basic ability tests assess an individual's physical ability including muscular strength and flexibility. Tests such as sit-ups (muscular endurance), the step test (aerobic capacity), arm ergometry (muscular endurance), and sit and reach (flexibility) are basic ability tests. Basic ability tests measure an ability required to perform job tasks.

Work/job simulation tests include components of the job being evaluated such as dragging a hose and climbing stairs. Work simulations require individuals to perform simulated job tasks or components and may require equipment or tools used on the job. A test requiring an individual to lift boxes and place them on shelves of various heights is considered a work simulation test. Law enforcement tests that simulate pursuing and restraining a suspect are also work simulation tests.

Organizations have used basic ability, work simulation, and a combination of both test types to assess candidate and incumbent physical capabilities. Both types of test have substantial validity that ranges from 0.45 to 0.85, depending on the type of criterion measure used in the validation study. However, regardless of the type of test used, significant sex differences in performance are typically present. These differences are attributed to the physiological differences between men and women such as larger muscle mass and greater lung volume.

Development and Validation of Physical Performance Tests

Both basic ability and work simulation tests must match the job in terms of the physical abilities or the job tasks being assessed. Job analysis data provides the input to select or design basic ability tests or to identify essential tasks that can be safely simulated. Ergonomic parameters (e.g., weights of tools and objects, forces to loosen nuts and bolts, distances walked, heights) and working conditions (e.g., temperature, surface, surface incline) related to the essential job tasks should be incorporated into the test development plan. In addition, when developing or selecting physical performance tests, the safety of the examinees must be considered; their health status and fitness level is usually unknown, and their ages can range from 20 to 60 years old.

Design or selection of basic ability tests should include consideration of the tasks that require the abilities, and not just the relevant abilities. For example, if the job requires lifting 35-pound boxes to heights of 50 to 60 inches, a test of upper-body muscular strength may be more appropriate than a lower-body strength test. Similarly, if a job requires performing arduous tasks such as climbing stairs while wearing a protective nonbreathable suit with a respirator, a step test or treadmill test of aerobic capacity may be more appropriate than a bicycle test. Further, the duration of a basic ability test, such as muscular endurance, can be determined based on the time it takes to complete a physically demanding task or a series of tasks. Consideration of these parameters will result in a testing process that is more specific to the job demands.

For work simulation tests, the job's essential tasks are reviewed to determine which tasks are frequently performed and which tasks best represent the essence of the job demands. These tasks are evaluated to select which tasks can be simulated without using equipment or procedures that require on-the-job training. Use of working conditions and ergonomic parameters in the test development stage increases test fidelity. For example, a frequent and important task for firefighters is dragging a hose. This task can be safely simulated and requires no prior training, except for a demonstration of how to hold the hose. To increase the fidelity of this test component, ergonomic data such as the distances that hoses are dragged, size of the hose used, and use of assistance are evaluated to select hose size and distance parameters that are performed by one person. Other parameters related to the condition of the hose (e.g., filled with water or no water) are also examined. An example of a drag parameter that may not be included because it requires training would be opening the hose and spraying water at a target. Finally, the job analysis and working conditions information are used to ensure accurate ordering of test components, proper equipment usage, and appropriate durations for the test and its components.

The linking of job analysis and ergonomic parameters to test components provides the basis for establishing construct validity for basic ability tests and content validity for work simulations. Once the tests meet the conditions described earlier, a criterion-related validity approach can also be used to empirically establish the test validity and passing score(s).

Summary

Arduous jobs are found in numerous private (e.g., electric, telecommunications, natural gas, railroad, freight, warehousing) and public (e.g., fire, police) sector organizations. Identifying the demands of essential job tasks is paramount to development or selection of basic ability or work simulation tests. The ergonomic and working conditions parameters should be incorporated into the test development or selection to ensure that the test accurately represents the physical demands of the job. Careful attention to the details of the job task demands will ensure that the test is content or construct valid and will identify individuals who can perform arduous job tasks. Although design of physical performance tests involves different strategies than cognitive test development, most of the developmental and testing principles are similar.

Deborah L. Gebhardt and Todd A. Baker

See also Prescreening Assessment Methods for Personnel Selection

Further Readings

Gebhardt, D. L. (2000). Establishing performance standards. In S. Constable & B. Palmer (Eds.), *The process of physical fitness standards development—State of the art report*. Wright-Patterson AFB, OH: Human Systems Information Analysis Center (HSIAC-SOAR).

Jackson, A. S. (2000). Types of physical performance tests. In S. Constable & B. Palmer (Eds.), *The process of physical fitness standards development—State of the art report*. Wright-Patterson AFB, OH: Human Systems Information Analysis Center (HSIAC-SOAR).

Myers, D. C., Gebhardt, D. L., Crump, C. E., & Fleishman, E. A. (1993). The dimensions of human physical performance: Factor analyses of strength, stamina, flexibility, and body composition measures. *Human Performance, 6*(4), 309–344.

Rayson, M. P., Holliman, D., & Belyavin, A. (2000). Development of physical selection procedures for the British Army. Phase 2: Relationship between physical performance tests and criterion tasks. *Ergonomics, 43*, 73–105.

Sothmann, M. S., Gebhardt, D. L., Baker, T. A., Kastello, G. M., & Sheppard, V. A. (2004). Performance requirements of physically strenuous occupations: Validating minimum standards for muscular strength and endurance. *Ergonomics, 47*(8), 864–875.

PLACEMENT AND CLASSIFICATION

Selection is a personnel decision whereby an organization decides whether to hire individuals using each person's score on a single assessment, such as a test or interview, or a single predicted performance score based on a composite of multiple assessments. Using this single score to assign each individual to one of multiple jobs or assignments is referred to as placement. An example of placement is when colleges assign new students to a particular level of math class based on a math test score. Classification refers to the situation in which each of a number of individuals is assigned to one of multiple jobs based on their scores on multiple assessments. Classification refers to a complex set of personnel decisions and requires more explanation.

A Conceptual Example

The idea of classification can be illustrated by an example. An organization has 50 openings in four entry-level jobs: Word processor has 10 openings, administrative assistant has 12 openings, accounting clerk has 8 openings, and receptionist has 20 openings. Sixty people apply for a job at this organization and each completes three employment tests: word processing, basic accounting, and interpersonal skills.

Generally, the goal of classification is to use each applicant's predicted performance score for each job to fill all the openings and maximize the overall predicted performance across all four jobs. Linear computer programming approaches have been developed that make such assignments within the constraints of a given classification situation such as the number of jobs, openings or quotas for each job,

and applicants. Note that in the example, 50 applicants would get assigned to one of the four jobs and 10 applicants would get assigned to *not hired.*

Using past scores on the three tests and measures of performance, formulas can be developed to estimate predicted performance for each applicant in each job. The tests differ in how well they predict performance in each job. For example, the basic accounting test is fairly predictive of performance in the accounting clerk job but is less predictive of performance in the receptionist job. Additionally, the word processing test is very predictive of performance in the word processor job but is less predictive of performance in the receptionist job. This means that the equations for calculating predicted performance for each job give different weights to each test. For example, the equation for accounting clerk gives its largest weight to basic accounting test scores, whereas the receptionist equation gives its largest weight to interpersonal skill test scores and little weight to accounting test scores. Additionally, scores vary across applicants within each test and across tests within each individual. This means that each individual will have a different predicted performance score for each job.

One way to assign applicants to these jobs would be to calculate a single predicted performance score for each applicant, select all applicants who have scores above some cutoff, and randomly assign applicants to jobs within the constraints of the quotas. However, random assignment would not take advantage of the possibility that each selected applicant will not perform equally well on all available jobs. Classification takes advantage of this possibility. Classification efficiency can be viewed as the difference in overall predicted performance between this univariate (one score per applicant) strategy and the multivariate (one score per applicant per job) classification approach that uses a different equation to predict performance for each job.

A number of parameters influence the degree of classification efficiency. An important one is the extent to which predicted scores for each job are related to each other. The smaller the relationships among predicted scores across jobs, the greater the potential classification efficiency. That is, classification efficiency increases to the extent that multiple assessments capture differences in the individual characteristics that determine performance in each job.

Classification in the U.S. Military

With regard to most organizations and their personnel decisions, classification is much more of an idea than a practice. Although large organizations will apply classifications at a localized level, such as when staffing a new facility, most often an organization is considering a group of applicants who have applied for one particular job; that is, most personnel decisions are selection rather than classification. The armed services are a notable exception. Although their practice only approximates conceptual discussions of classification, the individual armed services (i.e., Army, Air Force, Navy, Marine Corps, and Coast Guard) constitute the best real-world example. On an annual basis, the services must select and assign a large number of inexperienced individuals to a large number of entry-level jobs. The situation requires use of classification principles.

Prospective armed service applicants complete a battery of tests. The tests an applicant completes are used to first determine whether the person qualifies for military service and second to assign the individual to one of many jobs. Qualification for military service is a selection decision. The methods the services use to narrow the range of jobs for selected individuals use ideas from classification.

The armed services hire approximately 180,000 new persons annually and need to fit them into roughly 800 entry-level jobs. Historically, the military was the first organization of any type to use large-scale testing for selection and job assignment, starting in about 1916. In 1976 a version of the current battery was put into use—the Armed Services Vocational Aptitude Battery (ASVAB). Although the ASVAB has gone through restructuring, renorming, and regular revision, it is the current official mental testing battery used by each service for entry and for job assignment on acceptance. The current ASVAB is a battery of nine operational tests:

1. general science (GS),

2. arithmetic reasoning (AR),

3. word knowledge (WK),

4. paragraph comprehension (PC),

5. mathematics knowledge (MK),

6. electronics information (EI),

7. auto information (AI),

8. shop information (SI), and

9. mechanical comprehension (MC).

Selection and Assignment

Before individuals are assigned to a job, they must meet minimal criteria to join the armed services. One of these is a cut score on a composite of four ASVAB tests (WK, PC, AR, and MK) referred to as the Armed Forces Qualification Test (AFQT). Other criteria include age, education, passing a physical examination, and meeting background and moral character requirements.

AFQT is used only to determine overall service eligibility and is not used to determine whether someone is qualified to be trained in a specific job. Each individual service uses the tests somewhat differently to make job assignments. The rest of this discussion tracks examples of applications used by the U.S. Army. A significant contributor to the assignment decision in the Army is the individual's score on each of nine scores of uniquely weighted composites of the ASVAB tests. Each entry-level job in the Army is associated with one of these *aptitude area composites*. The weights for each aptitude area were developed to predict training performance in Army jobs. For example, some entry-level Army jobs are assigned to the mechanical maintenance (MM) aptitude area. The weights for calculating the MM composite score emphasize the AI, SI, MC, and EI tests. Every Army job has a minimum cut score on its composite that an applicant must meet to be eligible for that job. There are many factors that determine to which job an applicant is assigned. Only one is whether the applicant's aptitude area composite score satisfies the job's minimum score. Other factors include current job openings, the Army's priorities, when applicants choose to begin their terms of service, and which jobs applicants prefer.

This job assignment process is only an approximation of the conceptual classification decision model described previously. First, the goal was not to assign applicants to jobs in a way that maximizes overall predicted performance but rather to assign applicants to jobs to

- meet minimum aptitude requirements for each job,
- fill current openings,
- satisfy applicant preferences, and
- meet other constraints.

Additionally, it is difficult to satisfy the pure version of the classification model when personnel decisions are made in real time rather than in large batches that allow classification efficiency advantages associated with optimizing assignments across a larger number of applicants. Although assignments made this way are not likely to achieve the level of classification efficiency that a model closer to the conceptual description of classification would produce, the Army application is still a substantial improvement over what would be realized by selection and unguided assignment.

The Future

Although the Army example presented is not classification in the strictest sense, it is a good large-scale approximation of classification and is frequently discussed in the literature. Nonetheless, the Army is working on potential improvements to its assignment system that would improve classification efficiency. The Army is currently considering adding applicants' actual predicted scores for each aptitude area to the decision process. That is, among other considerations, an applicant could choose or be assigned to a job for which the applicant's predicted score is higher than others among those for which the applicant meets minimum qualifications. Another consideration is the possibility of using projections of the likely scores of applicants during a time period so that the assignment takes place in the context of a large batch of applicants rather than only those applying at that particular time. Finally, the Army is actively conducting research into potential additions to the ASVAB that could increase its classification efficiency. Measures of constructs in the areas of temperament, spatial and psychomotor aptitudes, and situational judgment are being examined.

Roy C. Campbell and Christopher E. Sager

See also Army Alpha/Army Beta; Employee Selection; Project A; Selection Strategies

Further Readings

Campbell, J. P. (1991). Modeling the performance prediction problem in industrial and organizational psychology. In M. D. Dunnette & L. M. Hough (Eds.), *Handbook of industrial and organizational psychology* (pp. 687–732). Palo Alto, CA: Consulting Psychologists Press.

Rosse, R. L., Campbell, J. P., & Peterson, N. G. (2001). Personnel classification and differential job assignments: Estimating classification gains. In J. P. Campbell & D. J. Knapp (Eds.), *Exploring the limits in personnel selection and classification* (pp. 453–506). Mahwah, NJ: Erlbaum.

Waters, B. K. (1997). Army Alpha to CAT-ASVAB: Four-score years of military personnel selection and classification testing. In R. F. Dillon (Ed.), *Handbook on testing* (pp. 187–203). Westport, CT: Greenwood Press.

POLICY CAPTURING METHOD

Policy capturing has its roots in activities central to industrial/organizational (I-O) psychology. Its origins lie in the work of the Personnel Research Laboratory at Lackland Air Force Base in the 1950s, and it achieved prominence in the broader field of psychology with the publication in 1960 of Paul Hoffman's *Psychological Bulletin* paper "The Paramorphic Representation of Clinical Judgment." Although policy capturing is not derivative of Egon Brunswik's probabilistic functionalism, scholars in the Brunswikian tradition have been attracted to policy capturing as a method to address certain research questions. This attraction is based on the practice in good policy capturing research of faithfully representing the situation to which generalization is aimed. Hence, policy capturing is often loosely associated with social judgment theory, which is the contemporary manifestation of Brunswikian theory.

Tasks

Many cognitive tasks require decision makers to make inferences or decisions based on multiple, often conflicting, pieces of information. Such tasks include performance assessment and salary assignments, employment interviewing, investment decisions, medical diagnosis and prognosis, evaluation of charges of discrimination, assessment of the desirability of employment contracts, and even the selection of the most appropriate bullet for use by an urban police force—the list is endless. Such tasks abound in organizations! Policy capturing is used to investigate what factors influence the decision maker and how heavily each is weighted. Environmental outcomes are not part of the policy capturing procedure.

Data Collection

The essence of the data-gathering procedure is to have an individual respondent make a substantial number of judgments on multiattribute bundles, often paper- and-pencil or computer-presented profiles, but the judgments can be made on actual people, files, or abstracts of files or anything that can be represented by a set of quantitative variables. Typically, the attributes and the judgments are treated as interval scales, although dichotomous data such as gender are often found among quantitative variables including age, length of experience, or rating scales. The phrase *individual respondent* was not an accident, in that policy capturing entails an idiographic analysis, which may be followed by nomothetic analyses of the idiographic indexes describing the individual respondents.

Data Analysis

The appropriate data analysis depends on a number of factors, including the level of measurement of the predictors and the judgments, the function forms relating predictors to judgments, predictor intercorrelation, the presumed aggregation rule, and so forth. The common default procedure is multiple regression, but mathematical models that reflect noncompensatory rules such as conjunctive or disjunctive decision rules might also be used. Given that multiple regression is the most commonly used analytic procedure, we'll concentrate on it.

Multiple Regression

Given a sufficient number of multiattribute judgments, the investigator can use ordinary least squares regression to ascertain the degree to which each attribute accounts for variance in the judgments. Doing so requires the usual assumptions underlying regression, some of which can be violated without affecting the investigator's inferences too severely. For example, if the linear function form assumed in the regression algorithm does not correspond exactly to that used by the judge but is monotonically related thereto, the model misspecification tends to be inconsequential. Furthermore, appropriate cross-validation within subjects provides some sense of the consequences of violations of assumptions.

Performance Indexes

Standard multiple regression indexes are used to describe the judgment policy. The multiple correlation, or R_s, is crucial; if it is not substantial, the investigator cannot claim to have learned much about the judgment policy of the person without further analysis. One possible reason for a low R_s, other than the ever-present unreliability of judgment, is that the function forms relating the judgments to the attributes may be nonlinear. A second is that the judge's aggregation rule may be nonadditive, and the assumption of additivity has resulted in model misspecification. These first two possibilities can be subjected to some data snooping, such as inspecting the scatterplots for nonlinearities, fitting quadratic and multiplicative terms, and so forth.

These possibilities may be illustrated by a favorite class exercise: having the class design a policy capturing study to select a mate, serve as subjects, and analyze the data. "A malevolent deity has sentenced you to spend 10 years alone on an island. In a last-minute moment of benevolence, the deity has offered to create a mate according to your preferences as assessed via policy capturing." The students develop the attributes, but gender and age, ranging from 2 to 72 years, must be among them. Assuming linearity, the weight for age will likely be trivial, but inspection of the scatterplot of desirability on age will show radical nonlinearity and implicate an important source of judgment variance. If gender is key, the regression of desirability on, say, physical attractiveness will reveal a strange-looking array, with half the points sitting in a straight line across the bottom of the scatterplot and the other half forming a typical envelope of points.

Other reasons for a low R_s include systematic shifts in importance weights as a result of doing the task, inattention caused by fatigue, and the like. One way of obtaining information about whether the judge is systematic is including reliability profiles and assessing test-retest reliability (r_{tt}). If both R_s and r_{tt} are low, it is unlikely the judge can be modeled.

Suppose R_s is high? Then we can predict the judge's responses from the attributes, assuming linearity and additivity. We can predict a new set of judgments via cross validation of a holdout sample, mitigating concerns about capitalization on chance. But this high R_s should not be taken to mean that the judge is in fact using a linear additive model; the predictive power of the linear model is all too well known. But the weights do give us significant information about what attributes are important to the judge. Comparing the weights of different judges who have provided judgments on the same data set may reveal sources of conflict or reveal underlying sources of agreement in situations marked by conflict.

Typical Results

People are remarkably predictable in judgment tasks. If R_s is not more than .70 or so, even after taking nonlinearities and nonadditivities into account, do not place much faith in the results. It is not uncommon for expert judges in consequential tasks to have R_s values of .90 or more. An important finding is that judges often believe that they are taking many attributes into account, even though relatively few attributes control virtually all the systematic variance in the judgments.

Other Decision Models

There are many approaches to the study of multiattribute judgment, decision making, and decision aiding. Some require the decision maker to decompose the decision intuitively, such as the MAUT (multiattribute utility theoretic) model of Ward Edwards and his colleagues. Others, like policy capturing, have the decision maker make multiple holistic judgments and employ computer decomposition, such as the ANOVA approach of information integration theory. Judgment analysis is important to mention in this article because it is

often confused with policy capturing. It uses the same statistical machinery as policy capturing but refers to the situation where environmental outcomes are available, and the full power of the lens model can be brought to bear on exploring the relation between the judge and the environment.

Michael E. Doherty

See also Lens Model

Further Readings

Brehmer, A., & Brehmer, B. (1988). What have we learned about human judgment from thirty years of policy capturing? In B. Brehmer & C. R. B. Joyce (Eds.), *Human judgment: The SJT view* (pp. 75–114). Amsterdam: Elsevier Science Publishers B. V. (North-Holland).

Cooksey, R. W. (1996). *Judgment analysis: Theory, methods, and applications.* San Diego: Academic Press.

Hoffman, P. J. (1960). The paramorphic representation of clinical judgment. *Psychological Bulletin, 57,* 116–131.

Roose, J. E., & Doherty, M. E. (1978). A social judgment theoretic approach to sex discrimination in faculty salaries. *Organizational Behavior and Human Performance, 22,* 193–215.

POLITICAL POLARIZATION: IMPLICATIONS FOR ORGANIZATIONS

The concept of political polarization has become virtually synonymous with any discussion of U.S. politics in the 21st century. In its most general sense, polarization refers to the highly dichotomous relationship between the two major political parties, the Democrats and the Republicans. This dichotomy is predicated on the idea that political parties are more clearly distinguished by a fervent ideology. There is a general agreement that liberals are most closely, if not exclusively, associated with the Democratic Party and conservatives are most closely, if not exclusively, associated with the Republican Party. While such an assessment may seem obvious, the degree of homogeneity within the two parties greatly increased over the past two decades. This homogeneity is rooted in more extreme and entrenched ideological politics.

As such, an understanding of the resulting polarization is fundamental to assessing what has been described a dysfunctional federal government, one marked by gridlock, stalemate, and antipathy.

Research on political polarization in U.S. politics is extensive. Even those scholars not specifically studying the phenomenon use the concept in explaining a variety of political behaviors such as presidential–congressional relations, policymaking, voting, and public opinion. While degrees of polarized and heavily ideological parties are prevalent in other countries, this examination is limited to the United States.

The analysis of political polarization involves several key questions. First, does polarization exist, and what are the origins of polarization? Second, how should it be measured? Third, what are the consequences of a polarized political environment? The answers to all of these questions remain highly contested by scholars.

Existence and Origins of Polarization

It is indisputable that politics divide more along party lines than in past decades. Antipathy on the part of Democrats and Republicans has especially grown during the Obama administration. There is little doubt that Republicans and Democrats fundamentally disagree on the size and scope of government, but the visibility and aggressiveness of such opposition provides compelling evidence of what some would consider to be a toxic political environment. Does what is at question concern the degree to which polarization is due to the increased ideological voting, or is it more a manifestation of what have been referred as the culture wars? The second question concerning political polarization focuses on its origins. The majority of scholarship involves this question, and the answers are more ones of degree than of disagreement. Theories as to the origin of polarization include the heightened attention to divisive social issues, the country's changing demographics, the changing media environment, and more structural considerations such as partisan gerrymandering.

Divisive Social Issues

One explanation as to the origins of political polarization is the rise of issues involving morality policy such as access to abortion and same-sex marriage. The visibility of these two issues in particular has increased given other the federal and state arenas in which they are debated and legislated. At the same time, interest groups associated with access to abortion and same-sex marriage have become more active. Questions of gun control and educational reform such as the Common Core State Standards provide additional platforms for ideological identification.

Culture Wars

The theory of culture wars is an extension of the disagreement over social issues. Conventional wisdom links what is referred to as the "culture wars" to a fundamental disagreement over the moral compass of the country, particularly as reflected by an agenda of vexing social issues. Issues such as access to abortion and same-sex marriage are used to define a broader cultural divide. These differences are usually cast in a broader context as questions of religious identity and practice. While surveys reveal stark differences on morality policy, many observers feel the language of a war is overstated and potentially inflammatory. In particular, the changes in levels of religiosity speak to growingly entrenched ideological divides. Republicans are increasingly distinct from Democrats as measured by a variety of indices such as church attendance and religious affiliation. Millennial voters, in particular, are far less likely to identify with any organized religion. While not related to religion, matters concerning national security often divide along cultural lines.

Red and Blue States

Closely related to the idea of culture wars in U.S. society is the relatively recent distinction made between states as either red states or blue states. Originally determined by the margin of support for presidential candidates, these monikers have been extended to conflate cultural characteristics with electoral outcomes. States in which voting for the president has fluctuated are sometimes deemed "purple" states, but this is a variation on the general theme. Many consider these distinctions to be rather blunt tools to make generalizations on ideology and culture. Nonetheless, these red and blue state labels have become widely accepted, and as such, they are used to denote a state as either conservative or liberal. These classifications signal an ideological orientation that regardless of its veracity could have an impact on decisions by the public and businesses alike.

Changing Demographics

One of the leading explanations for increased level of ideological homogeneity involves the changing demographics of the country. Growing numbers of Hispanic/Latino and Asian American citizens are changing not only the composition of the electorate but the political agenda as well. While estimates vary, analysts suggest that by 2040, the United States will be a majority-minority population. This growing racial and ethnic diversity has not signaled an increased tolerance. Conservatives, and hence Republicans, have recently espoused an aggressive anti-immigration sentiment. Likewise, surveys reveal a growing sense that race relations have deteriorated instead of improved. According to a Pew Research Center study in August 2015, 75% of African Americans see racism as a significant problem.

Additionally, demographic trends relevant to political polarization can be found in the growing generation gap. Young people between the ages of 18 and 30 are often labeled the Millennial generation. These Millennials are more ethnically and racially diverse than previous generations. Millennials are better educated and are frequent users of social media. Millennials are far less likely than previous generations to have a religious affiliation. This generation gap is politically relevant in many ways. Millennials are more liberal in their views on gender identity, income inequality, and environmental concerns.

Changing Media Environment

Just as there is widespread agreement that a partisan media contributed to the sentiments articulated by the Tea Party movement, there is little doubt that growing presence of partisan media outlets helped accelerate political polarization. Cable television networks such as Fox and MSNBC helped spawn what analysts call an "echo chamber" where persons with strong ideological convictions listen to television and radio stations that align with their existing ideologies. The same logic extends to blogs and Web sites such as the Drudge Report and *Huffington Post*. As a consequence, these audiences become more steadfast in their beliefs as they are listening more exclusively, if not exclusively, to more partisan and ideologically biased media. If not one of the primary causes, selective exposure to more "niche" media outlets reinforces ideological homogeneity.

Partisan Gerrymandering

Redistricting of congressional districts has never been immune from partisan affiliation. The term *gerrymandering* originated in 1812 as a result of district lines drawn in Massachusetts by Governor Elbridge Gerry that were drawn in a partisan fashion so serpentine as to resemble a salamander, and hence the name *gerrymander* to describe districts designed to favor a particular party or elected official. Gerrymandered districts lead to a significant decline in competitiveness in congressional elections. As a result, the majority of seats are either safely Republican or Democrat. With electoral safety, polarization is increased and reinforced as there is little incentive to seek moderation.

Measuring Polarization

For most observers, levels of polarization in the electorate have been driven in large part by the ideological homogeneity and rigidity by legislators and party elites. Despite the widespread agreement that partisans in office have become almost exclusively ideological, a few scholars are skeptical that the intense level of elite ideological polarization has extended to the electorate. Morris Fiorina, in particular, argues that there is a "disconnect" between the issues emphasized by the elites and those of chief concern for the citizenry. Here, polarization is more of an elite phenomenon than one among the general electorate. Those more circumspect of elite-driven polarization theories look at opinion distributions and view polarization more in terms of "sorting" in which self-identified Democrats and self-identified Republicans situate themselves on the ideological spectrum. In another variation on measuring polarization, Marc Hetherington and Jonathan Weiler see measures of authoritarian disposition as valuable for explaining sorting and polarization and the visceral politics that result.

While measuring polarization by elite-driven ideologies and intractable policy divides is essential, evidence of these divides can be seen in how Americans themselves see the political environment. The most comprehensive study of political polarization in U.S. society in general is that done in June 2014 by the Pew Research Center. The Pew report assesses polarization in a variety of ways. In addition to the widely acknowledged increased ideological homogeneity in the parties, Pew looks at the antipathy toward members of the other party in the general public. Perhaps the most compelling finding is the degree to which partisans see the policies of the opposing party as a "threat" to the nation. Additionally, the findings point to a tendency for conservatives and liberals to prefer to associate with people who share their views. Respondents expressed a propensity to engage socially with persons sharing their political views. They also voiced a desire to live in a neighborhood with people holding views similar to their own. Taken as a whole, the Pew study provides unmistaken evidence that political polarization has resulted in a notable degree of personal polarization.

The same 2014 Pew Research Center study revealed that "92% of Republicans are to the right of the median Democrat in their core social, economic and political views, while 94% of Democrats are to the left of the median Republican." While political parties by their nature exist to organize differing philosophical and issue orientations, the current ideological divide is marked by an unprecedented rigidity made more disconcerting given the wider array of social and racial issues.

Consequences of Polarization

Many of the consequences of heightened political polarization are self-evident. With a precipitous decline in partisan cooperation comes an even greater increase in gridlock and stalemate. Pressing issues such as federal funding is complex and contentious. Spending for government programs and agencies has become a series of continuing resolutions in which government is funded in increments of months instead of annually. This naturally leads to heightened uncertainty in the markets and increased apprehension in the general public.

Additionally, the highly charged ideological environment has had a direct impact on political campaigns. Compounded by loosened campaign finance regulations, political action committees unaffiliated with any candidates, known as super PACs, are able to spend inordinate amounts of money opposing rather than supporting candidates. Advertisements by these super PACs are almost by definition negative and reinforce existing polarizing ideologies.

Perhaps the major consequence of polarization is the unwillingness on the part of policymakers and partisans to cooperate with those of the opposing party. This sentiment negates efforts to compromise or build consensus on complicated and pressing policy problems.

Conclusions

Regardless of the various focal points of scholars, the concept of polarization has been popularized by the media. For pundits and analysts, partisan and political polarization has become the single most significant explanation for the dynamics of U.S. politics. As surveys have shown, this negative partisanship extends to personal and professional relationships. Feelings of disaffection and alienation have a substantial impact on levels of trust in government.

As levels of political and civic civility decline, many strong partisans view persons with partisan identifications different from themselves with disdain. Polarization has broad implications for businesses and organizations as the political and social climate becomes more antagonistic and uncertain.

Susan Roberts

See also Affordable Care Act; Global Political Instability: Implications for Organizations; Immigration: Implications for Organizations; U.S. National Debt: Implications for Organizations

Further Readings

Abramowitz, A. (2012). *The polarized public: Why American government is so dysfunctional.* Upper Saddle River, NJ: Pearson.

Fiorina, M. P. (2009). *Disconnect: The breakdown of representation in American politics.* Norman: University of Oklahoma Press.

Hetherington, M. J., & Weiler, J. D. (2009). *Authoritarianism and polarization in American politics*. New York, NY: Cambridge University Press.

Hunter, J. D., & Wolfe, A. (2006). *Is there a culture war?* Washington DC: Brookings Institution and Pew Research Center.

Levendusky, M. (2009). *The partisan sort: How liberals became Democrats and conservatives became Republicans*. Chicago, IL: University of Chicago Press.

Pew Research Center. (2014, June 12). *Political polarization in the American public*. Retrieved from http://www.people-press.org/2014/06/12/political-polarization-in-the-american-public/

Pew Research Center. (2015, August 5). *Across racial lines, more say nation needs to make changes to achieve racial equality*. Retrieved from http://www.people-press.org/2015/08/05/across-racial-lines-more-say-nation-needs-to-make-changes-to-achieve-racial-equality/

POLITICAL SKILL

The word *politics* often has negative connotations for both employees and managers in organizational settings. That is, individuals may associate organizational politics with activities such as closed-room deal making or negotiations, secret pacts, the manipulation of others for one's own good, favoritism, and/or a host of other self-serving acts or behaviors. Although these activities may indeed occur under the broad umbrella of what is considered to be organizational politics, political skill itself is not inherently bad. In fact, given the nature of how work gets done in today's organizations (e.g., the interdependence and collaboration among individuals required for team and organizational success), political skill is actually a necessity and is a skill that, when used appropriately, can have a positive impact on employees, managers, and organizations alike.

The origin of the concept of political skill can be traced back to the work of Edward L. Thorndike (a famous psychologist) and Dale Carnegie (an author and entrepreneur), but it was initially written about in the literature by Jeffrey Pfeffer and Henry Mintzberg in the early 1980s. They defined political skill as the ability to influence others via tactics such as manipulation, persuasion, and negotiation. More recently, Gerald Ferris and his colleagues defined political skill as the capacity to understand people at work and then to use this information to encourage people to behave in ways that will help one achieve personal and/or work goals. For example, a leader in an organization might use his or her ability to network with others to secure valuable resources that his or her team needs in order to meet productivity goals. Or, conversely, a leader may use his or her influence or connections to secure critical, developmental job assignments for his or her direct reports (e.g., an opportunity to do job rotations in order to gain broader knowledge of the organization). In either example, these types of political skill behaviors could benefit both employees and their organizations.

Dimensions of Political Skill

Political skill is a multidimensional construct and is most commonly measured and examined in the industrial and organizational (I-O) psychology literature via Gerald Ferris and colleagues' Political Skill Inventory (PSI). The PSI is an 18-item self-report measure that evaluates one's political skill on four dimensions: social astuteness, networking ability, interpersonal influence, and apparent sincerity.

Social astuteness is the ability to keenly observe social interactions as well as to accurately interpret one's own behavior and others' behavior in social settings. It is the ability to read social situations that enables politically skilled individuals to adjust their behavior and to adapt to new environments in ways that help them successfully influence others.

Networking ability is the capacity to build connections with others, both inside and outside an organization. Politically skilled individuals often build alliances with others who have access to critical organizational resources. Given that they are generally well liked by others in their networks, politically skilled individuals can access these resources and are well positioned to take advantage of opportunities that arise.

Interpersonal influence is the ability to subtly, yet convincingly, exert influence on others. Individuals who score high on this dimension tend to be likable and know how to adapt their behavior and influence tactics to best suit the situation and the target of their influence attempts.

Apparent sincerity is whether individuals are believed to be genuine, trustworthy, and authentic. Individuals who have high levels of apparent sincerity are perceived to be transparent and to not have hidden motives. Not surprisingly, individuals with high apparent sincerity are likely to be more successful in their influence attempts.

In short, politically skilled individuals draw on one or more of the aforementioned dimensions (or skills) to influence others in an effort to achieve personal and/or work-related goals. Individuals who are the most successful at influencing others know the best dimension(s) of political skill to use for a given situation.

Correlates of Political Skill

The majority of research on this topic has been conducted using self-ratings, rather than observer ratings, of political skill. Moreover, most studies have relied on correlational research designs. Thus, although studies have linked political skill to potential antecedents and outcomes, one cannot necessarily infer that these linkages represent cause-and-effect relationships. With these caveats in mind, existing research has found relationships between individual difference variables (or potential antecedents) and the individual dimensions of political skill. For example, individuals with high self-efficacy tend to exhibit greater social astuteness, interpersonal influence, and apparent sincerity than individuals with low self-efficacy. Research has found that extroversion predicts one's social astuteness, networking ability, and interpersonal influence and that self-monitoring predicts interpersonal influence. Finally, conscientiousness is positively related to political skill.

Research has also linked political skill to important work-related outcomes. Most of these studies focused on political skill as a global construct rather than examining the individual dimensions of political skill. It has been well documented, for example, that political skill exhibits a positive correlation with overall job performance ratings. In fact, political skill correlates with performance even after controlling for variables such as self-monitoring, influence tactics, general mental ability, and personality. One study found that social astuteness was more strongly related to performance than the other three political skill dimensions. Political skill has also been found to correlate with specific dimensions of job performance, as well as two broader categories of performance known as task (essential technical job responsibilities) and contextual performance (prosocial behaviors that contribute to task and organizational success). However, meta-analytic results indicate that political skill is a stronger predictor of contextual performance than it is of task performance. Moreover, meta-analytic results reveal that political skill is a stronger predictor of task performance for employees who work in occupations that have high interpersonal and social requirements. Managerial performance has also been found to be more strongly related to political skill than other social effectiveness constructs, including emotional intelligence, self-monitoring, and leadership self-efficacy.

Political skill correlates positively with work unit performance, ratings of leaders' promotability, and ratings of leaders' effectiveness in their jobs. With regard to the latter, one study found all political skill dimensions, excluding apparent sincerity, to positively correlate with leader effectiveness ratings. This study reported interpersonal influence to be the strongest predictor of leader effectiveness. The relationship between political skill and leader effectiveness is also moderated by other variables, such as gender and organizational level. For example, apparent sincerity seems to be a good predictor of leader effectiveness ratings for female leaders but not for male leaders.

Political skill has been found to predict numerous career-related outcomes, including income, hierarchical position, reputation, career satisfaction, and career success. Interestingly, with regard to career success, one study found that political skill predicted the election success of German work councilors. Work councilors are elected officials who represent employees in German organizations by helping them negotiate and bargain with management.

There is also evidence that political skill is related to employees' perceptions of organizational support. Specifically, employees who have leaders with high political skill tend to report experiencing greater organizational support than employees who have less politically skilled leaders. Importantly, employees' perceptions of high organizational support are, in turn, associated with positive work outcomes, such as increased job satisfaction, trust, and organizational commitment.

Politically skilled individuals tend to be more effective at using influence tactics than individuals with low political skill. For example, when using ingratiation tactics, subordinates with low political skill are perceived to be more manipulative (as rated by their supervisors) than are subordinates with high political skill. Likewise, when subordinates use high levels of intimidation, ingratiation, self-promotion, supplication, or exemplification tactics at work, highly politically skilled employees receive more positive supervisor performance evaluations than employees with low political skill.

Not only is political skill associated with positive outcomes, but it mitigates negative experiences encountered by employees as well. For example, political skill reduces the adverse effects work role overload and work-related strain have on employees. In addition, social stressors are often associated with decreases in job and career satisfaction, but political skill has been found to mitigate these negative outcomes. Political skill can also diminish the adverse effects that interpersonal conflict may have on one's emotional burnout, and political skill appears to attenuate the negative impact racial dissimilarity may have on the quality of the relationships experienced in employee-supervisor dyads.

In summary, several individual difference variables (e.g., self-efficacy and extroversion) are thought to be antecedents of political skill. Political skill is also a predictor of many work-related outcomes, ranging from perceived organizational support and job stress and strain to job performance and career success. Given these latter findings, it is likely that employees and managers who possess higher levels of political skill will be more satisfied and successful in their organizations than individuals who possess lower levels of political skill. Importantly, leading scholars in the field of I-O psychology argue that political skill is distinct from general mental ability and that it is a skill that can be learned or refined through a variety of methods, such as videotaped role plays that include feedback, drama-based training, leadership training, mentoring, and behavior modeling.

Future Research Directions for Political Skill

Although quite a bit of research has been conducted on political skill to date, numerous questions remain unanswered regarding this construct. The majority of past research studies have examined political skill using a single global score (i.e., an average of participants' scores on all 18 items of the PSI), and thus, very little is known about the specific relationships between the individual political skill dimensions and potential antecedents and outcomes. More research is needed on this topic, as it is likely that the political skill dimensions will be differentially predicted by various antecedents, and that the dimensions may relate differently to various outcomes. Researchers have also called for additional studies on the relationships between political skill and variables such as interpersonal conflict and the perceived degree of similarity or dissimilarity between two individuals (e.g., subordinate and boss). Likewise, additional research is needed to explore how political skill may interact with other skills and competencies in predicting important work-related outcomes.

Although most studies have found support for the four-factor structure of political skill, a recent study conducted on a sample of organizational leaders found that the PSI included five dimensions of political skill (the original four dimensions plus "image management"). Thus, more research may be needed to determine if the five-factor structure is a better representation of the PSI than the four-factor structure. Finally, most studies to date have measured political skill via self-ratings. Given that subordinate, peer, and supervisor ratings are better predictors of outcomes than self-ratings, political skill, as indexed by observer ratings, may have a stronger relationship to various work-related criteria (e.g., performance) than what has been documented in past studies.

Phillip W. Braddy

See also Career Success; Interpersonal Skill; Organizational Politics

Further Readings

Bing, M. N., Davison, H. K., Minor, I., Novicevic, M. M., & Frink, D. D. (2011). The prediction of task and contextual performance by political skill: A meta-analysis and moderator test. *Journal of Vocational Behavior, 79,* 563–577.

Ferris, G. R., Davidson, S. L., & Perrewe, P. L. (2005). *Political skill at work: Impact on work effectiveness.* Mountain View, CA: Davies-Black.

Ferris, G. R., & Treadway, D. C. (2012). *Politics in organizations: Theory and research considerations.* New York: Routledge/Taylor & Francis.

Ferris, G. R., Treadway, D. C., Kolodinsky, R. W., Hochwarter, W. A., Kacmar, C. J., Douglas, C., & Frink, D. D. (2005). Development and validation of the political skill inventory. *Journal of Management, 31,* 126–152.

Gentry, W. A., Gilmore, D. C., Shuffler, M. L., & Leslie, J. B. (2012). Political skill as an indicator of promotability among multiple rater sources. *Journal of Organizational Behavior, 33,* 89–104.

Snell, S. J., Tonidandel, S., Braddy, P. W., & Fleenor, J. W. (2014). The relative importance of political skill dimensions for predicting managerial effectiveness. *European Journal of Work and Organizational Psychology, 23*(6), 915–929. doi:10.1080/13594 32X.2013.817557

POLYCHRONICITY

Polychronicity is a temporal orientation that reflects the extent to which an individual or a group of individuals prefers and values multitasking. Polychronicity is one of the more prominent measures of one's time sense, or how one perceives and subsequently prefers to manage time. Polychronicity is considered a continuum, whereby some people may be more polychronic, and thus prefer multitasking, and others may be more monochronic, and thus prefer working on a single task at a time. Monochronic people typically embody a more linear perception of time, whereas polychronic people embody a more cyclical, layered perception of time through which they perceive and complete tasks simultaneously rather than linearly. As a result, those who are more polychronic typically prefer to manage their time in a more unstructured and fragmented manner. Alternatively, those who are monochronic prefer to organize and segment their time in order to focus on singular tasks or activities for an elongated period of time because they are often uncomfortable switching from task to task.

Edward T. Hall first explored polychronicity as a cultural phenomenon, arguing that some cultures are more or less polychronic than others, specifically, that some countries near the Mediterranean Sea, such as southern Europe and northern Africa, were more polychronic, whereas countries in northwestern Europe, such as Germany and England, were more monochronic. Others have explored similar perspectives in different countries on the basis of cultural norms and values; for instance, Brazilian people are typically more polychronic than French or German people. Likewise, Japanese and North American people are typically more polychronic as well.

Polychronicity in Today's Work Environment

Polychronicity has seen a sharp uptick in consideration in both research and applied settings over the past few decades for a variety of reasons. First, the increased role of knowledge-based work, and subsequently autonomy, in the global economy has led to a greater focus on understanding and predicting how people consider, structure, and use time to manage their work in the absence of a predefined temporal structure derived from the work itself. Additionally, the global economy has become much more team based, requiring collaboration and integration of temporal orientations and structures to complete work. Polychronicity therefore serves as a metric by which people assess and align their work flows and can play a role in informing person–job and person–team fit.

The increased role of information technologies in the workplace has also enabled—and, some scholars would argue, forced—workers to focus on multiple activities and tasks at one time. This should theoretically benefit the engagement and satisfaction of those who are polychronic; interestingly, however, polychronicity does not necessarily benefit the performance of those who are polychronic in jobs that require multitasking. That is because polychronicity represents a preference for multitasking, not the actual behavior of multitasking. In fact, some scholars have demonstrated that polychronicity is not correlated with multitasking.

Research on Polychronicity

Although polychronicity was first described as a culture's behavioral orientation by anthropologists, organizational scholars have more recently extended the construct of polychronicity to the individual level of analysis. Some scholars have gone so far as to create individual-level measures of polychronicity (e.g., the Polychronic Attitudes Index, the Inventory of Polychronic Values), all of which have been tested for evidence of validity and reliability as psychological constructs.

Some argue that polychronicity, much like facets of the Big Five personality traits, is actually a personality trait due in part to similarity in self- and peer ratings of individual polychronicity, and just like any other personality trait, individuals can vary on the polychronicity continuum at any given time. For instance, people can flex their behavior along a continuum of polychronicity when shifting from work to leisure time. Similarly, some people can be more capable of sliding along the polychronicity continuum than others. As individuals transition from monochronicity to polychronicity, they can actually induce the experience of "flow," or the experience by which an employee experiences challenging work that stretches his or her existing skill set. Those who experience flow also intensely concentrate on the tasks at hand, lose the ability to reflect self-consciously, and experience a complete distortion of the subjective temporal experience. In other words, those who experience the shift from monochronicity to polychronicity (and subsequently flow) are intensely engaged in their work tasks, an act that is more likely for those in creative occupations, such as writers, musicians, dancers, and even rock climbers.

Polychronicity has been positively correlated with job satisfaction, various facets of the Big Five, mental ability, organizational commitment, and turnover. Polychronicity can also moderate relationships; for instance, polychronicity moderates the role between some facets of layered-task time (a temporal structure that emerges when work requires completing many tasks at the same time) and job satisfaction. Specifically, those who are more polychronic have greater job satisfaction under conditions of increased simultaneity, fragmentation, contamination, and schedule unpredictability.

There is a ripe opportunity for future research on polychronicity, particularly in two directions. First, most of the research conducted on polychronicity has focused on understanding how it relates to other individual-level variables, but less research has been conducted to understand how it

might (a) act as a moderator in affecting other relationships between individual-level variables, and (b) relate to and even interact with variables at the team or organizational level. For instance, how does polychronicity manifest at the team or group level? Or how does polychronicity interact with temporal structures that emerge from the nature of one's work and operate at the team or even organizational level to influence important outcomes like performance?

These types of explorations would help organizational scholars understand and expand on the second future direction for polychronicity research, namely, understanding how polychronicity can benefit workplace decisions in the applied sector. For instance, in what contexts should organizations use polychronicity as a predictor of new-hire performance in candidate assessments? Is it possible to build training programs that build one's polychronicity? How do we adapt work structures to ensure that employees experience the full benefits of polychronicity? These are just some of the many questions from which practitioners could benefit in better understanding, and adapting their work processes to accommodate, polychronicity.

Brett Agypt

See also Cross-Cultural Research Methods and Theory; Flow; Motivational Traits; Personality; Time Management

Further Readings

Bluedorn, A. C., Kalliath, T. J., Strube, M. J., & Martin, G. D. (1999). Polychronicity and the Inventory of Polychronic Values (IPV): The development of an instrument to measure a fundamental dimension of organizational culture. *Journal of Managerial Psychology, 14*(3), 205–231.

Conte, J. M., Rizzuto, T. E., & Steiner, D. D. (1999). A construct-oriented analysis of individual-level polychronicity. *Journal of Managerial Psychology, 14*(3), 269–288.

Hall, E. T. (1959). *The silent language.* Garden City, NY: Doubleday.

Hecht, T. D., & Allen, N. J. (2005). Exploring links between polychronicity and well-being from the perspective of person-job fit: Does it matter if you prefer to only do one thing at a time? *Organizational Behavior and Human Decision Processes, 98,* 155–178.

Kaufman-Scarborough, C., & Lindquist, J. D. (1999). Time management and polychronicity: Comparisons, contrasts, and insights for the workplace. *Journal of Managerial Psychology*, 14(3), 288–312.

Mesmer-Magnus, J., Viswesvaran, C., Bruk-Lee, V., Sanderson, K., & Sinha, N. (2014). Personality correlates of preference for multitasking in the workplace. *Journal of Organizational Psychology*, 14(1), 67–76.

PORTER, LYMAN W.: SEVENTH RECIPIENT, SIOP DISTINGUISHED SCIENTIFIC CONTRIBUTIONS AWARD

Lyman W. Porter ("Port") was a leader in the fields of industrial and organizational (I-O) psychology and organizational behavior. Despite the fact that he spent his entire career at two California universities, he described himself as "a product of a middle-class, middle-west upbringing." He was also the son of a university professor. Port graduated from Northwestern University and then pursued a PhD in experimental psychology at Yale. Toward the end of his studies at Yale, he became interested in applied psychology. Thus, he took a reading course during his final year as a PhD student and read every text in industrial psychology he could find. In the spring of 1956, Edwin Ghiselli, on the psychology department faculty at the University of California at Berkeley, wrote Carl Hovland at Yale asking if he had a finishing PhD student interested in industrial and social psychology. Hovland suggested Porter, and within a few weeks, Port was invited to apply for the position. Thus, by the fall of 1956, Port began to teach a course he had neither taken nor taught, industrial and social psychology. He was at Berkeley for the first 10 years of his career, then spent a year as a visiting professor at Yale and accepted a job as a full professor in the Graduate School of Administration (now the Paul Merage School of Business) at the two-year-old University of California at Irvine. Early in Port's career at Berkeley, he married Meredith Moeller, and by the time he left Berkeley, they had two children. The rest of this entry is devoted to Port's academic, professional–administrative, and personal achievements.

Academic Achievements

Port's first publication was a verbal learning experiment he authored with Carl Duncan, while still an undergraduate at Northwestern. He published four more papers while a graduate student, all experimental psychology studies. His first published article in industrial psychology was coauthored by Edwin Ghiselli in 1957. Port says that article helped focus his interests on managers and management as objects of research. In the following years, Port published a number of articles on the management structure of organizations and how that structure related to the kinds of people found in other parts of the organization. That interest led to an interest in how job attitudes varied across organizations.

According to Port's description of his career, it was filled with "good luck." Early in his career, he was able to find funding for an extensive study of job attitudes of a large nationwide sample of managers and executives. These data provided material for a large number of articles and a monograph published in 1964. Probably the best known of Port's early work is the extensive (for the time) cross-national survey of managerial attitudes he engaged in with Edwin Ghiselli and Mason Haire. Part of the fun of doing the study was that each of the authors lived abroad during the study. Ultimately, the authors collected attitudinal survey data from over 2,000 managers (all male) in 14 countries in Europe, Asia, and South America. The areas surveyed included attitudes and values toward work relationships, organizations, leadership, and work goals, among other variables. National groupings alone explained 28% of the variance in attitudes.

Port's next research adventure would lead to a large number of articles and a book, both coauthored with Ed Lawler. Porter and Lawler used Vroom's expectancy theory of motivation as a foundation for their work. Similar to Vroom, they stated that an individual's motivation to complete a task is affected by the reward he or she expects to secure. They categorized rewards as extrinsic and intrinsic. They also suggested that a person's view of the attractiveness and fairness of the reward affects motivation. They added that motivation is also affected by a person's ability to do the task and perception of the task.

Port's research record is enormous and was added to in the year before his death. In 1989, he received the Society for Industrial and Organizational Psychology (SIOP) Distinguished Scientific Contributions Award. He maintained his interest in motivation throughout his career but wrote about other subjects (e.g., organizational commitment, upward influence, job characteristics) as well. He says one of his favorites is a paper he did with two graduate students (Robert Allen and Harold Angle) in 1981 on the politics of upward influence in organizations. These authors conducted a survey of major textbooks in I-O psychology and management and organizational behavior, plus relevant academic journals, to find little coverage of political behavior in organizations. At the time, it was well recognized that top-down influences exist in organizations in the form of leadership. Political influences coming from the bottom up were missed. Such influences were the focus of this paper.

For 20 years, Port edited the *Annual Review of Psychology*, in which every year there were three or four articles about I-O psychology. In 2014, Port and Ben Schneider wrote an article for the first volume of the *Annual Review of Organizational Psychology and Organizational Behavior*. In it, they present a personalized view of the history, development, and current study of I-O psychology and organizational behavior (OB) that has occurred over the last 50 years. They give attention to the similarities and differences in I-O psychology and OB and conclude with suggestions for future work.

Professional and Administrative Achievements

Not only did Port largely contribute to his field through his academic research; he also contributed to change through his professional and administrative achievements. Port began his administrative activities by becoming the faculty representative to Berkeley's student government. One can only imagine his feelings as the student demonstrations of the 1960s moved into full swing.

In 1967, the Porters left Berkeley, and Port assumed the assistant deanship at the newly minted Graduate School of Administration at UC Irvine. Port created a PhD program for the school in 1969 and worked tirelessly to see the school accredited by the Association to Advance Collegiate Schools of Business (AACSB). He served as dean of the school from 1972 to 1983.

During his years at Irvine, he served several terms on the board of the AACSB. In 1988, he also coauthored with Lawrence McKibbin the first comprehensive nationwide study of management education in 25 years. That report said that business schools were too focused on analysis and gave insufficient attention to problem finding as opposed to problem solving. Port also served as UC Irvine's representative to the National Collegiate Athletic Association (NCAA) for 10 years. In 1975, Port was elected president of Division 14 (now SIOP) of the American Psychological Association. This organization denied him membership in 1959 because his work was not seen as sufficiently industrial psychological. Port was also very active in the Academy of Management (AOM). In 1971, he was appointed as the first chairman of the Organizational Behavior Division of the AOM, and in 1973, he was elected AOM president.

Personal Achievements

As well as being devoted to his family, Port was a "real" people person. He had a legion of PhD students who became his friends as well. These people populate business school faculties across the nation (Porter, 1993). At his memorial service, a number of people called him a true scholar, a gentleman, and humble. His faculty colleague at UC Irvine, Jone Pearce, noted that in the 1970s the school had the highest percentage of women faculty members of any business school in the United States and that today it has the highest percentage of women faculty members of any business school in the world. She called Port "a feminist, a classic American West pioneer feminist." She said he always wanted to hire the best talent and didn't care what that talent looked like.

Karlene H. Roberts

See also Academy of Management; Lawler, Edward E., III: Eighth Recipient, SIOP Distinguished Scientific Contributions Award; Leadership and Supervision; Society for Industrial and Organizational Psychology

Further Readings

Haire, M., Ghiselli, E. E., & Porter, L. W. (1966). *Managerial thinking: An international study.* New York, NY: Wiley.

Lawler, E. E., & Porter, L. W. (1967). The effect of performance on job satisfaction. *Industrial Relations: A Journal of Labor and Society, 7,* 20–28.

Porter, L. W. (1964). *Organizational patterns of managerial job attitudes.* New York, NY: American Foundation for Management Research.

Porter, L. W. (1993). An unmanaged pursuit of management. In A. Bedian (Ed.), *Management laureates: A collection of autobiographical essays* (pp. 1–30). Greenwich, CT: JAI Press.

Porter, L. W., Allen, R. W., & Angle, H. E. (1981). The politics of upward influence in organizations. In L. L. Cummings & B. M. Staw (Eds.), *Research in organizational behavior* (Vol. 3, pp. 109–149). Greenwich, CT: JAI Press.

Porter, L. W., & Ghiselli, E. E. (1957). The self-perceptions of top and middle management personnel. *Personnel Psychology, 10,* 397–406.

Porter, L. W., & Lawler, E. E. (1968). *Managerial attitudes and performance.* Homewood, IL: Irwin.

Porter, L. W., & McKibbin, L. E. (1988). *Management education and development: Drift or thrust into the twenty first century.* New York, NY: McGraw Hill.

POSITIVE PSYCHOLOGY APPLIED TO WORK

The roots of inquiry into what is good about human nature and optimal human functioning can be traced back to Aristotle. Indeed, the initial impetus of modern psychology was to gain an understanding of transcendent experience. This objective was echoed in humanistic psychology's interest in the self-actualizing potential of human beings. However, following World War II, psychology's emphasis shifted to a predominant attention on pathology, prevention, and human malfunctioning. In 1998, the president of the American Psychological Association, Martin Seligman, made the clarion call for a new psychological emphasis that he termed *positive psychology,* which he described as the "study of what constitutes the pleasant life, the engaged life, and the meaningful life." Such an emphasis was aimed at redirecting the focus of psychology on positive individual traits and subjective experience.

As we have moved further into the 21st century, mainstream industrial and organizational psychology has heeded Seligman's rallying cry. There has been a proliferation of research projects and books focusing on the issue. Furthermore, positive work-related constructs have grown (e.g., engagement, mindfulness, and well-being). Clearly, a paradigm shift is occurring. Essentially, positive psychology is an effort to provide a social and behavioral scientific understanding of optimal functioning that includes positive individual traits (such as optimism, courage, the capacity for love, creativity, spirituality, wisdom, and forgiveness), valued subjective experiences (such as well-being, contentment, satisfaction, flow, and happiness), and good citizenship behaviors (such as altruism, nurturance, civility, tolerance, and responsibility).

The increased emphasis on positive psychology does provide a new way of looking at old phenomena. It offers a broad conceptual framework for linking theories in several psychological fields. It is based on the assumption that happiness, goodness, and excellence are authentic states that can be analyzed by science and achieved in practice. Furthermore, they provide increased value to individual functioning and organization performance.

Positive Work

Industrial and organizational psychology has a strong history of focusing on organizational problems such as absenteeism, turnover, dissatisfaction, managing uncertainty, performance problems, justice, and achieving profitability. The influence of positive psychology can be witnessed in the recent upswing in organizational research that emphasizes optimal experience, transcendent performance, excellence, and positive deviance.

Positive work is broadly defined as work that has a beneficial impact on people's subjective well-being and increases their level of work engagement. Subjective well-being is typically measured by two variables: happiness and satisfaction. *Happiness* refers to an emotional state and indicates how people feel about their work, their life, and themselves and the extent to which they experience pleasant moods and emotions in reaction to their lives. *Satisfaction* refers to more global, evaluative, judgments about the acceptability of various aspects of work and life. As such, it is a more cognitive process. Industrial and organizational psychology has tended to focus exclusively on job satisfaction in determining worker well-being and ignored the affective component of happiness. Yet each is an important, but separate, characteristic of subjective well-being.

Good work is also defined as work that engages individuals and is intrinsically motivating. Engaged workers are energetically and affectively involved in their work activities. Engagement is defined as a positive, fulfilling, work-related state of mind that is characterized by vigor, dedication, and absorption. One of the central concepts in positive psychology is that of "flow." *Flow* was a term first coined by Mihaly Csikszentmihalyi to denote an optimal experience of intense engagement and effortless action, where personal skills match required challenges. It is also characterized by focused attention, clear goals, complete concentration, a sense of control, loss of self-consciousness, distortion of time, and intrinsic enjoyment. People seem to experience flow more often from what they do in their jobs than from leisure activities in free time. This is not surprising given that many of the precursors of flow (such as immediate feedback, commensurate challenges and skills, and clear goals) are more likely to be found in work activities. Research on the experience of flow in athletes, popularly referred to as "being in the zone," has also indicated that flow is associated with transcendent or optimal performance.

Even though the great majority of flow experiences have been reported in work, as opposed to leisure activities, relatively little research has studied flow at work. There are two reasons for this neglect. First, psychology's concern with establishing itself as a bona fide science has focused on understanding observable behavior and prohibited the discipline from understanding the subjective experience of work. Second, the tendency to reduce complex phenomena to basic, measurable skills and behaviors has prevented psychologists from understanding the complex world of work. Positive psychology has had the effect of refocusing scientific attention on the positive aspects of well-being in the workplace and in understanding the subjective experience of work.

There are several conceptual sources of flow. For example, flow is seen as a state of intrinsic motivation in which the individual is engaging in some activity for its own sake without any regard for external rewards. Flow is also a form of work involvement and engagement. Although there is no clear consensus regarding the concise meaning of job involvement, it does seem to consist of two components. First, job involvement has been defined as the extent to which an individual's self-esteem is affected by his or her performance. This aspect of job involvement implies a high level of ego involvement in that one is personally affected by the tasks one performs on the job. Intrinsic motivation is a central component of this facet of job involvement in that performance of the task affects esteem and feelings of growth. Engagement is a more interactive process at work that extends involvement by increasing individuals' enthusiasm for what they do. Job involvement, engagement, and flow, therefore, overlap to the extent that an individual is so focused on the task at hand that it produces an "autotelic" experience, one that is so enjoyable as to make one want to do it for its own sake. However, whereas job involvement and engagement implies an awareness of the impact of job performance on self-esteem, the experience of flow is described as such an acutely intense concentration on the task that the individual loses self-consciousness, and concern for the self disappears. Although engagement and flow appear to be similar, the two are treated as distinct constructs in the literature. Flow is a more acute, short-term, variable experience specifically associated with a particular task or activity, whereas engagement is a more pervasive, stable, and persistent state of mind that is associated with work in general.

Designing Positive Work

One of the aims of positive psychology is to redesign the workplace to increase worker involvement and engagement, improve individual happiness, and promote optimal performance. Research on work design and job satisfaction has identified several features of the work environment that maximize subjective well-being at work and encourage active engagement in the job. The elements associated with positive workplaces include the following:

1. **Variety/learning:** the degree to which a job requires a variety of different activities. People like to learn new skills and appreciate opportunities to challenge themselves and to personally grow.

2. **Significance:** the degree to which a job has a substantial impact on the lives or work of other people. Work from which people can derive a sense of purpose and meaning generates higher levels of satisfaction.

3. **Autonomy:** the degree to which a job provides an opportunity for control and substantial discretion in scheduling the work and in determining the procedures to be used in carrying it out. The opportunity to make decisions about the process and outcomes of one's job is associated with the development of a sense of competence.

4. **Realistic goals:** specific and difficult goals, with feedback, lead to optimal performance. Both flow and satisfaction are associated with having challenging and clear goals that provide the opportunity to use skills.

5. **Feedback:** the degree to which the activities of a job provide an individual with positive, direct, and clear information about the effectiveness of his or her performance. Positive feedback is a crucial component of engagement in learning.

6. **Social networks:** the opportunity to work in groups or teams and establish positive interpersonal contacts. Research in a variety of contexts has shown that group work is associated with better individual well-being. Social networks on the job provide the worker with companionship and social support.

7. **Transformational leadership:** a form of positive leadership that contributes to individual well-being. Transformational leadership has been shown to facilitate followers' commitment to organizational goals, enhance workers' feelings of self-efficacy, nurture personal growth, and produce superior levels of performance.

8. **Mindfulness:** opens one's eyes to reality and a new frame of reference on the job; a situation in which one can step back and experience a new set of rules and realities. Mindfulness helps us see and encounter different and new actions and outcomes.

Positive Organizational Behavior

Positive organizational research is not only interested in understanding the design and subjective experience of good work. It is also concerned with identifying individual and organizational strengths and virtues and how they enhance engagement and performance. Positive organizational scholarship studies individual and organizational characteristics, such as resilience, virtuousness, and courage, and how these are associated with extraordinary performance and high levels of organizational effectiveness. Virtuous organizations (i.e., organizations that express virtues such as compassion, forgiveness, and gratitude) have a positive effect on personal improvement and experienced meaningfulness. Work that allows the expression of positive emotions and the exercise of individual strengths is associated with knowledge creation and higher levels of organizational functioning. Positive psychology has also broadened the concept of transformational leadership to include authentic leadership. Authentic leaders transcend their own self-interest and are guided by end values that primarily benefit the interests of their constituency. They rely more on moral and ethical power than on coercion or rational persuasion. Characteristics associated with authentic leaders include optimism, integrity, honesty, high personal efficacy, future orientation, and resilience. Such leaders give priority to empowering followers and fostering positive deviance.

Summary

Positive organizational psychology is an area of scholarship and scientific study that is influenced by positive psychology's emphasis on strengths and virtues. Its aim is to identify those characteristics of individuals, organizations, and work that promote active engagement, enhance subjective well-being, and facilitate transcendent performance. Furthermore, it represents human flourishing and optimal functioning.

Clive Fullagar, Ronald Downey, Andrew Wefald, and Disha Rupayana

See also Empowerment; Engagement; Flow; Humor in the Workplace; Job Crafting; Job Satisfaction; Job Satisfaction Measurement; Mindfulness at Work; Optimism and Pessimism; Self-Leadership Theory; Work-Life Enrichment

Further Readings

Cameron, K. S., Dutton, J. E., & Quinn R. E. (Eds.). (2003). *Positive organizational scholarship: Foundations of a new discipline.* San Francisco, CA: Berret-Koehler.

Csikszentmihalyi, M. (1990). *Flow: The psychology of optimal experience.* New York: Harper & Row.

Linley, P. A., Harrington, S. & Garcea, N. (Eds.). (2013). *The Oxford handbook of positive psychology and work.* New York: Oxford University Press.

Turner, N., Barling, J., & Zacharatos, A. (2002). Positive psychology at work. In C. R. Snyder & S. L. Lopez (Eds.), *Handbook of positive psychology* (pp. 715–728). New York: Oxford University Press.

Warr, P. (1999). Well-being and the workplace. In D. Kahneman, E. Diener, & N. Schwarz (Eds.), *Well-being: The foundations of hedonic psychology* (pp. 392–412). New York: Russell Sage.

POWER NEEDS

See Achievement Needs, Power Needs, Affiliation Needs, and Goal Orientation

PRACTICAL INTELLIGENCE

The concept of practical intelligence reflects the idea that there might be some ability besides general mental abilities (*g*), some *street smarts* or *common sense* that predicts how successfully individuals handle situations in their actual lives in the form of appropriate responses, given facts and circumstances as they are discovered, and considering a person's short- and long-range goals.

This definition of practical intelligence differs from the usual conception and measurement of *g*. First, unlike tasks assessing *g*, tasks for practical intelligence are more contextualized in that they aim at an individual's own long- and short-range goals and are usually of the individual's own intrinsic interest, rather than formulated by others. Second, the task is encountered during a situation connected to the individual's ordinary experience, and, just as in ordinary life, those facts of the situation as they are discovered may

change during exposition to the problem at hand and may eventually not even suffice to make well-informed decisions. Finally, although the situation is often not well defined, there is more than one possible correct answer and more than one method of correct solution.

Sternberg argued that practical intelligence is one of three components, besides *g* and creative abilities, of successful intelligence, the ability to achieve what one seeks in life, within one's own sociocultural context, through a combination of adapting to, shaping, and selecting environments.

Approaches to Practical Intelligence

Practical intelligence has been addressed via different approaches, namely, practical know-how, practical mathematics, practical planning, practical presupposition, social judgment, and prototypes of practical intelligence.

Practical know-how refers to solving tasks such as repairing machines or navigating the ocean without *appropriate* information, such as formal education, technical manuals, or specialized tools. The most prominent form of practical know-how is tacit knowledge, practical know-how that usually is not openly expressed or stated and must be acquired by experience in the absence of direct instruction. Frequently, tacit knowledge is further classified by its focus (i.e., how to handle oneself, others, and one's task), but measures addressing these different foci usually load onto a common factor.

Practical mathematics refers to *street mathematics*, that is, mathematical calculations undertaken in everyday life that differ from the abstract mathematics formally taught in schools and that are often conducted in forms of mental shortcuts, such as when searching for the *best buys* in supermarkets or filling orders of different quantities with minimal waste.

Practical planning refers to how people organize their everyday activities and reorganize when something goes wrong. Thus, although everyone will have a routine of getting up in the morning and getting ready for work, the effectiveness of different strategies used to react to problems, such as a failed alarm clock, may differ.

Practical presupposition refers to concept learning in everyday situations that allows individuals to discover regularities in their environments, such as general ideas about the likely preferences, decisions, and actions of individuals from different groups.

Social judgment can also be treated as an aspect of practical intelligence. Given the social nature of our lives, practical intelligence may be reflected in the attainment of transactional goals and in the individuals' adaptation to their social environments, that is, their success at meeting the requirements of diverse social roles.

Prototypes of practical intelligence refers to a conceptualization introduced by Ulric Neisser, who argued that it was not possible to define intelligence as any one thing. Instead, he suggested defining practical intelligence as the extent to which an individual resembles a prototypical person who would be an ideal exemplar of the target concept.

Measurement Approaches

Given the somewhat idiosyncratic nature of practical intelligence, much research has been done in the form of case studies showing how practically intelligent individuals improvise to complete their tasks by adapting whatever resources are at hand (practical know-how), handle problems arising in their daily routines (practical planning), or solve mathematical problems easily when undertaken in a context with which they are familiar (demanding the right amount of money when selling a certain number of coconuts, each of which costs a certain amount), but not, however, when presented with the same problem in an abstract form, such as "How much is 4 times 35?"

Some of these approaches have also made use of John Flanagan's critical incident technique (CIT), which allows the identification of the strategies individuals actually use when performing specific tasks and the specific, situationally relevant aspects of this behavior. More frequent, however, is the use of simulations, which in turn are often based on CITs. These simulations differ in their level of fidelity. High-fidelity simulations, such as assessment centers, group discussions, and in-basket-like "case scenario problems" try to replicate the represented situation as realistically as possible and require individuals to respond as if they were in the actual situation. Yet most prominent, particularly

for the assessment of tacit knowledge, are low-fidelity simulations, which present a situation to individuals orally or in writing. Individuals have to either describe how they would react in the situation, as in situational interviews, or rate the quality of diverse possible reactions, as in situational judgment tests. A special kind of situational judgment test frequently used to assess tacit knowledge is the tacit knowledge inventory; these tests have been developed for diverse fields such as entrepreneurship, management, administration, sales, military leadership, college studies, and academic psychology. These inventories usually use longer and more elaborate scenario descriptions than most situational judgment tests. That said, technical advancements have allowed also situational judgment tests to gain further fidelity, for example, by presenting the scenarios in the form of video fragments, rather than in writing, and by apparently adjusting later video fragments on the basis of earlier answers. Generally, situational judgment tests are scored by giving points for answers that were more common among experts than novices, by judging the degree to which participants' responses conform to professional rules of thumb, or by computing the (often squared) difference between participants' responses and an expert prototype.

Finally, practical intelligence, particularly involving practical presuppositions, has been tested in the laboratory, such as by giving individuals descriptions of a person (e.g., a father of four vs. a student) and a target (e.g., a car with specific features) that was congruent, irrelevant, or incongruent to the person. Participants should indicate how much the person would like the target. In another study testing practical presupposition, children performed considerably worse at predicting the movement of geometric forms on a computer screen with the help of a cursor than when the same algorithm was used in a computer game in which the geometric forms were birds, bees, and butterflies and the cursor a net.

Empirical Findings

In line with Sternberg's conceptual claim that any form of intelligence can also be understood as a form of developing expertise, practical intelligence seems to increase with experience, particularly for people high in learning orientation. Practical intelligence usually shows only low correlations with measures of fluid and crystallized intelligence yet shows some validity in predicting performance in diverse real-world settings across the globe as well as participants' mental and physical health. Particularly, situational judgment tests are able to predict performance, over and above g and personality factors. This validity of a situational judgment test further increases when the test's fidelity is enhanced by choosing a video compared with a written format. Besides its own predictive validity, however, practical intelligence has also emerged as a moderator to the criterion related validity of other predictors of performance. Thus, Chan found proactive personality to show positive links to desirable job attitudes and performance, but only for participants high in practical intelligence, whereas the same effect was reversed for participants low in practical intelligence.

Concerns and Directions for Future Research

The concept of practical intelligence has not gone unchallenged. Although proponents of practical intelligence usually argue that practical intelligence is different from and superior to g, some authors, such as L. S. Gottfredson and colleagues, conceptually and empirically challenge this argument, arguing that practical intelligence and g correlate and that practical intelligence demonstrates incremental validity above g, particularly for tasks that are both simple and well learned, conditions under which the influence of g is reduced, anyway.

Other authors have argued that practical intelligence is nothing else but job knowledge. Finally, research by M. A. McDaniel and colleagues on situational judgment tests suggests that what is measured in practical intelligence may be a function of g, job knowledge, and different personality factors such as emotional stability, agreeableness, and conscientiousness.

Besides further analysis of the nomological network of practical intelligence, the use of practical intelligence in personnel selection merits further

research, both as a predictor of conceptually matching criteria—rather than assuming that practical intelligence predicts "everything"—and as a moderator to the criterion-related validity of other predictors. Also, their obvious task-relatedness may increase their face validity to applicants, hence their acceptance.

Ute-Christine Klehe

See also Assessment Center; Cognitive Abilities; Critical Incident Technique; Job Knowledge Testing; Situational Approach to Leadership

Further Readings

Baum, J. R., Bird, B. J., & Singh, S. (2011). The practical intelligence of entrepreneurs: Antecedents and a link with new venture growth. *Personnel Psychology, 64*, 397–425. doi:10.1111/j.1744-6570.2011.01214.x

Chan, D. W. (2006). Emotional intelligence and components of burnout among Chinese secondary school teachers in Hong Kong. *Teaching and Teacher Education, 22*(8), 1042–1054.

Gottfredson, L. S. (2003). Dissecting practical intelligence theory: Its claims and evidence. *Intelligence, 31*(4), 343–397. doi:10.1016/S0160-2896(02)00085-5

McDaniel, M. A., Morgeson, F. P., Finnegan, E. B., Campion, M. A., & Braverman, E. P. (2001). Predicting job performance using situational judgment tests: A clarification of the literature. *Journal of Applied Psychology, 80*(4), 730–740. doi:10.1037/0021-9010.86.4.730

Schmidt, F. L., & Hunter, J. E. (1993). Tacit knowledge, practical intelligence, general mental ability, and job knowledge. *Current Directions in Psychological Science, 2*, 8–9. doi:10.1111/1467-8721.ep10770456

Sternberg, R. J., Forsythe, G. B., Hedlund, J., Horvath, J. A., Wagner, R. K., Williams, W. M., et al. (2000). *Practical intelligence in everyday life.* New York: Cambridge University Press.

Sternberg, R. J., & Grigorenko, E. L. (2006). Cultural intelligence and successful intelligence. *Group and Organization Management, 31*, 27–39. doi:10.1177/1059601105275255

Wagner, R. K. (2011). Practical intelligence. In R. J. Sternberg, S. B. Kaufman, R. J. Sternberg, & S. B. Kaufman (Eds.), *The Cambridge handbook of intelligence* (pp. 550–563). New York: Cambridge University Press. doi:10.1017/CBO9780511977244.028

PRACTICE CAREERS IN INDUSTRIAL AND ORGANIZATIONAL PSYCHOLOGY: EXTERNAL CONSULTING ROLES

A consultant is a professional who provides professional or expert advice and support; further, an *external* consultant is someone who is employed externally on a temporary basis, usually for a fee. Consultants are uniquely situated because they are brought on to provide services but have no direct power to make changes or implement them. Industrial and organizational (I-O) psychologists typically find themselves in the role of some variation of *human capital*, *human resource*, or *talent management* consultants, all of whom focus on the people part of the client organization and aim to maximize employee performance in service of an organization's strategic objectives.

This entry focuses on the different types of external consulting roles; variations in consulting companies; and distinctions in client types that affect an external consultant's job duties, additional duties that are typically part of an external consultant's job duties, and skills needed for external consulting.

External Consulting Role Types

External consulting is a blanket term that describes many types of client engagements. For clarity, the *consultant* is the person who is being paid to provide a service or expertise to a *client* who sits in the *client organization* (or the company receiving consultation). The nature of the client engagement can vary greatly.

One primary role for external consultants is project-based strategic consulting. This engagement occurs when an organization seeks external support for a particular problem it wants to solve. As examples, agents of an organization may have identified a need to improve leadership throughout the organization, bolster employee engagement, hire more effectively, reward employees better, conduct an organizational assessment, or more effectively implement workforce planning. External consultants in a strategic project-based consulting role typically find themselves consulting on multiple projects, on varied topics, and even with multiple clients simultaneously. One challenge in this type of consulting role is time management and prioritization; balancing the needs of multiple clients simultaneously is extremely important.

Another type of client engagement is staff augmentation. With staff augmentation, the client organization needs to supplement its current workforce due to a surge in work, large organizational change, or some other environmental factor that is temporary in nature. The client organization then contracts with a consulting group to bring external consultants into the organization for a specified period of time. Frequently, with this type of client engagement, the consultants are physically colocated with the client on site at the client organization and work in conjunction with people in the client organization. External consultants in this type of role typically are dedicated solely to one client at a time, with client engagements lasting a range of time, typically six months to two years.

A consulting engagement loosely follows the seven steps below, regardless of the topic area or type of consulting role:

1. Assess the current situation and clearly identify the problem to solve

2. Assess the environment (i.e., organizational context and environmental context)

3. Develop recommendations based on research and best practices, *keeping in mind the unique organizational context*

4. Work with the client organization to review recommendations and make a plan for implementation

5. Develop tools and resources for implementation

6. Implement

7. Evaluate, and make modifications for future iterations

Successful consultation depends on the consulting team's ability to influence the client organization without direct power to do so. It is imperative that consultants take advantage of any information that is available to them about the client organization and not operate "in a vacuum." Consultants frequently must balance the desire for rigor and purity with an organization's desire for results, speed, and efficiency, and understanding organizational contexts helps greatly with that.

Characteristics of Consulting Companies

No two external consulting companies are exactly alike, but there are characteristics that vary between them that give insight into the types of work environments and services they provide. Distinctions include scope of consulting services, mission of company, and client type, among others.

Consulting firms vary in their scope of services on a range from niche to varied and expansive. For example, a consulting company could be as specialized as solely focusing on one part of the employment life cycle (i.e., performance management) for only one employee population (i.e., employees who have been identified as high potentials) within a specific organization (i.e., Department of Defense special forces). Alternatively, a consulting company can be expansive and consult on additional topics beyond human resources, such as information technology and accounting. Typically, on this end of the spectrum, the consulting company has divisions or offices that distinguish which type of consulting is delivered and operate somewhat independently, but ultimately the divisions combine to make up the entire organization and drive profits and overall company health. The scope of services provided by the consulting organization is related to the size of the organization (i.e., generally, the larger firms offer more variety in services) but not necessarily causal. There are large consulting firms with tens of thousands of employees, and conversely, there are *independent consultants* who operate as a company of one.

There are also differences in the missions of consulting companies. One major difference in mission is whether the organization is a *research-focused* organization or a *delivery-focused* organization. Primary distinctions between these two types of organizations are how the company is funded and the type of work performed within the organization. On the research-focused range of the spectrum, funding is not purely from client engagements but is also provided by research grants. In this type of organization, I-O psychologists find themselves both conducting research and applying learnings from that research to deliver science-driven solutions to organizations through consulting engagements. In a consulting agency that also focuses on research, the organization typically focuses on publishing findings and establishing itself as a leading expert on a topic or topics. On the other end of the spectrum, many organizations focus purely on client delivery and do not pursue research grants or place a large emphasis on publishing. These organizations establish themselves as experts through reputation, client reviews, referrals, and so on.

Client Type

Another characteristic of consulting organizations that may affect an external consultant's job is the consulting organization's client type. There are consulting firms that solely consult with public sector clients, firms that solely consult with private sector clients, and firms that do both. To further delineate client types, consulting firms frequently create a competitive advantage by consulting primarily with clients in a certain *sector* such as financial services, health care, defense, or hospitality. This allows the consulting agency to be an expert both in the subject matter and in the context of the client organization, which encourages efficiency in making recommendations and implementing solutions. The client type is an important consideration when someone is exploring external consulting roles. The type of client may affect flexibility in recommended solutions (i.e., public sector clients are regulated differently than private sector clients and must adhere to different laws; for example, personnel selection and performance management have different, usually more stringent, regulations in the public sector than in the private sector). This distinction holds true with client organizations that have an international presence. Typically, international employment laws differ from U.S. employment laws, so solutions presented to clients with an international presence must account for those differences by delivering flexible solutions or a one-size-fits-all solution that works within all regulations.

Additionally, one quality of client engagements that can create variations in the external consulting experience is the project team at the client organization. As can be expected, it is different to consult with a client team that is composed of other I-O psychologists as opposed to people unfamiliar with the field. When working with a team of people who have similar expertise, external consultants typically focus on production. On the other hand, if the client group has little overlapping expertise, time must be spent on education and creating buy-in (i.e., agreement to support a decision). Similarly, the extent to which the client project team has influence within the organization has a direct effect on the ability to influence change within the organization. If an external consultant's primary client is an individual contributor at the organization, the external consultant may have to spend significant time on coaching the individual contributor on ways to influence within his or her own organization and may also be brought into meetings with others in the organization to support the individual contributor in socializing solutions. Alternatively, if an external consultant's primary point of contact/client holds a leadership position in the client organization, most of the focus can be on solution development and strategy around implementation.

Beyond Consulting: Additional Job Duties

It is worth noting that external consultants frequently have job duties beyond engaging with clients. Typically, work performed by an external consultant is categorized as either *billable* or *nonbillable*. When a consultant is directly interacting with clients or performing duties in direct support of clients, his or her work is categorized in *billable hours*. These are hours for which the consulting firm can, as the name suggests, bill the client. Alternatively, if a consultant is performing other duties not directly in support of a client, his or her hours are logged as *nonbillable,* which end up falling into overhead expenses for consulting companies. Consulting firms vary in their requirements for billable hours, but consultants typically are given targets as a percentage of their total time worked, such as "90% billable," meaning if the consultant is working 40 hours a week, on average he or she is expected to spend 36 hours in direct support of clients. Many activities are expected in the nonbillable portion of a consultant's work, and they vary by consulting firm strategy, but some buckets of work include business development,

internal initiatives, and personal training and development. Business development is usually an important component of a consultant's work. Beyond building relationships with clients, demonstrating value, and gaining follow-on work from existing clients, there usually is direct business development work required. Tasks that fall under this category of work include scanning for *requests for proposal (RFPs)* or *requests for information (RFIs)* from potential client organizations and determining which are a good fit for the consulting agency. RFPs and RFIs from potential client organizations frequently require company information, an outline of the planned technical approach (in other words, the steps a company plans to take to tackle the given problem), pricing, and bios of proposed staff or proof of expertise. Unless the consulting company is organized such that it has a business development group that acts completely independently from the rest of the organization, external consultants are frequently brought in to lead proposal writing—either a portion of the proposal, or the proposal in its entirety. Other activities that fall within the nonbillable work bucket are those supporting internal company initiatives. These initiatives vary greatly, depending on the company, and can include things such as revamping the internal hiring process, delivering training within the company, or conducting a survey on organizational climate. Additionally, most companies provide training and development opportunities for consultants that fall under the nonbillable work designation.

External Consulting Skills

Multiple competencies are necessary for successful external consulting. Strong subject-matter expertise is not enough to ensure success as an external consultant. In addition to that, consultants must have interpersonal skills such as influence, listening, and communication; and consulting skills such as problem solving, project management, and decision making. Promotions within consulting companies vary depending on each company's emphasis but frequently require developing greater depth and breadth in subject-matter expertise and proven project management capability.

Katherine B. Elder

See also Assessing Organizational Culture; Benchmarking; Careers for Industrial and Organizational Psychologists; Human Capital; Human Resource Management; Managing Talent in Global Organizations; Strategic Talent Management

Further Readings

Block, P. (2000). *Flawless consulting: A guide to getting your expertise used*. San Francisco, CA: Jossey-Bass/Pfeiffer.

Lencioni, P. (2010). *Getting naked: A business fable about shedding the three fears that sabotage client loyalty*. San Francisco, CA: Jossey-Bass.

Maister, D. H., Green, C. H., & Galford, R. M. (2000). *The trusted advisor*. New York, NY: Free Press.

Mathis, R. L., & Jackson, J. H. (2003). *Human resource management*. Mason, OH: Thomson/South-western.

Schein, E. H. (1969). *Process consultation*. Reading, MA; Addison-Wesley.

Schmidt, T. (2009). *Strategic project management made simple: Practical tools for leaders and teams*. Hoboken, NJ: Wiley.

Sobel, A., & Panas, J. (2012). *Power questions: Build relationships, win new business, and influence others*. Hoboken, NJ: Wiley.

PRACTICE CAREERS IN INDUSTRIAL AND ORGANIZATIONAL PSYCHOLOGY: INTERNAL ROLES

As the complexity and speed of organizational change increases, the demand for industrial and organizational (I-O) psychology knowledge, skills, and abilities increases as well. I-O psychologists can help company leaders effectively navigate business and organizational change and are often called on to help with attracting, motivating, developing, and retaining the best and brightest talent who will generate the ideas to increase market share and thrive in change. In some instances, I-O psychology expertise is sourced through external consultants, but in many cases, organizations hire I-O psychologists to work internally. The careers that I-O psychologists hold internally for companies are typically in one of three categories: (1) technical specialist, (2) human resource (HR) center of excellence

leader, or (3) HR business partner. Each of the three types will be discussed in detail.

Technical Specialist

Perhaps one of the most common internal I-O careers, the technical specialist typically has a singular or dual focus on improving or overseeing an HR process. These processes typically entail heavy data analysis and offer the business scientific insights into workplace behavior. Roles like these typically fall into one of three different buckets: (1) selection and hiring, (2) employee engagement data, or (3) assessments. In contrast to external consultants, internal I-O specialists will often manage vendors to help with their work and/or provide technology. To understand how I-O psychologists would operate in these roles, we take a special look at their jobs and how they go about improving the lives of the employees within their organizations.

Selection and Hiring Specialists

Depending on the maturity and size of the organization, a selection and hiring specialist often works with business leaders to understand the culture and the business objectives and then determine the talent vision. Leveraging the insights of human capital research, the I-O psychology specialist will create assessments and hiring processes that ensure managers across the enterprise hire the most capable employees who fit with the company culture and have a higher likelihood of staying with the company over the long term. Often, I-O psychology specialists in these roles work very closely with talent acquisition specialists to create (a) best practice policies, (b) indicators or competencies to look for in interviews to ensure hiring managers hire quality candidates, and/or (c) assessments to select talent. These types of internal specialists will often be called on to conduct demographic and diversity analysis to ensure the company follows the appropriate laws and regulations in the countries in which it operates. I-O psychologists who enjoy data analysis and work well with legal teams will likely thrive in this type of role. The I-O psychology specialist in this role takes pride in knowing that the next generation of employees were influenced by his or her ability to effectively empower managers with the right framework, tools, and assessments to ensure the success of the organization.

Employee Engagement Data Specialists

Most organizations have evolved their business strategies to include a focus on a highly engaged workforce, but many struggle with how to measure engagement and more importantly drive engagement. I-O specialists can help leaders define the most appropriate measurement and "drivers" of engagement (factors that are highly related to engagement). I-O psychologists in these types of roles frequently create and lead the administration of surveys to measure engagement and drivers of engagement. It is often important to use advanced analysis (e.g., structural equation modeling) to find the most important areas of focus for organizations, including what most influences organizational commitment, performance, and retention. Some would say that the most difficult part of the role is helping the organization understand the advanced analysis—as a survey can lend itself to misinterpretation of data. For example, a low-scoring item on compensation may not actually be the right area to focus on based on the advanced modeling on engagement. Engagement specialists will work hand in hand with business leaders, vendors, and HR business partners to help interpret the data and put action plans together that will help the business leaders put their focus on the most important items for their workforces. Leveraging his or her understanding on individual differences and team effectiveness, the I-O psychologist can create very specific action items to increase engagement, and then recommend ways to track progress.

Assessment Specialists

Related to the hiring specialist, assessment specialists focus on the measurement of employee behavior. Most of the behavior measurement is with leaders, including leadership 360-degree feedback systems, manager effectiveness assessments, and team effectiveness assessments. I-O psychologists in these roles typically create items for these assessments, finding useful ways to score them to drive meaningful action and working with the business

and HR business partners to find ways to grow an employee's or leader's capabilities. In some instances, internal I-O psychologists are called to audit vendors' assessments. For example, if a business leader wanted to conduct an engagement activity with his or her team on emotional intelligence, the I-O psychologist would be tasked to help find a statistically valid way to measure this. I-O psychologists in this role should have a strong interest in engagement, development, and assessment.

Across all of these three roles, the common thread is that there are strong roots to the traditional skills taught within the I-O psychology curriculum: assessment, individual differences, performance, statistics, and culture. Some I-O psychology graduates will start here and spend their whole careers within this domain and become renowned experts on these topics. However, some will focus on a broader layer, which is typically within another role, the HR center of excellence leader.

HR Center of Excellence Leader

The HR center of excellence leader has a broader set of responsibilities than the specialists—although most specialists can reside on the same team as the leader. This particular role involves looking at multiple areas of employee behavior, setting vision and strategy for the area, and influencing how the pieces come together to solve a particular engagement or human capital issue.

For example, a "talent management leader" would be responsible for HR processes such as succession planning, performance ratings, and career development. In these roles, I-O psychologists tend to focus more on using research of others and applying best practices to the business—versus conducting analyses themselves. These roles have a hybrid of I-O psychology "core skills" and other skills that can be traditionally found in MBA programs, such as business acumen, project management, and business strategy.

Often, people in these roles will be asked to find "quick wins" for large cultural issues. For example, a person in this role may learn from his or her employee engagement data specialist that a driver of engagement was work–life dissatisfaction. This person may use those data along with other research on individual differences to create a very simple (but not altogether perfect) solution to drive engagement on this issue. I-Os in these roles will partner with internal and/or external "specialists" to stay up to date on best practices and research, in order to empower the last major type of role within a practice career, the HR business partner.

HR Business Partner

The final internal practice role available to a professional trained in I-O psychology is the HR business partner role. Graduate students may overlook this role because HR business partners typically have undergraduate or MBA degrees rather than I-O psychology degrees. However, I-O training can provide a unique perspective and bring insight to these roles. In addition, many large companies will require that an employee have experience as a generalist or HR business partner in order to progress to the vice president level for any HR role. If someone with I-O training wishes to lead HR practices for a company, he or she may want to consider HR business partner roles. Although in the past the HR function was considered more administrative than strategic, many organizational leaders have evolved their thinking, and many now expect their HR business partners to bring strategic advantage to their business. For example, when a company is considering entering into a new market, it may want to know how to most effectively hire, develop, and reward talent in that market. This type of thinking requires a wide mastery in skills, which someone with I-O training can bring to the business.

In HR business partner roles, someone with I-O training can become the business leader's right hand on strategic decisions because he or she can see trends in information and data, ask the hard questions about root cause analysis, and make recommendations that should have a positive impact on the organization. Those trained in I-O psychology also generally bring a thorough understanding of leadership and team development, which those with undergraduate or business training may lack. I-O training can help someone excel in the HR business partner role because those with the training bring skills that are unique and helpful to the business and often help bridge the gap between HR functions and more scientific functions or disciplines like research and development, engineering, or consumer insights.

Often, business leaders who are looking for long-term HR talent will encourage those with I-O training to spend some time in an HR business partner role. This has a variety of benefits to the organization and to the employee. One of the largest benefits is for the employee to learn more about the business and/or operations and to understand how things work in the business. If one gains this experience, he or she can then either return to a specialized role with more knowledge about how to implement tools and projects, or choose to continue as a business partner using his or her skill set working more closely with business leaders and influencing organization and talent strategy. Business leaders benefit from the unique scientific perspective someone with I-O training brings, such as seeing a trend in consumer data that others may miss based on quantitative methods training or suggesting a creative reward program based on motivation theory.

One way to understand how an I-O specialist can benefit from a business-facing HR role is to talk through an example from experience. When asked to create a 360-degree assessment to help leaders develop, it is not uncommon for an assessment specialist to create a reliable robust measure with more than 100 questions and a complicated 20-page report, describing each detail of the assessment. After working in the business and understanding the many competing priorities of business leaders, this same specialist may realize simple is better. Not only can there be more action taken from 10 very relevant questions versus 100, but a simple two-page report may have much more of an impact than a 20-page report.

Immersing him- or herself in a business can help a specialist learn to use more business-appropriate and relevant language. The HR business partner can also have much more of a direct impact on an organization through coaching and influencing business decisions. Therefore, it is highly recommended that those with I-O training consider business-facing HR positions as part of their careers, especially when working internally rather than externally.

Conclusions

The options for those with I-O psychology training are now more open and promising than ever. The differentiators between the options depend on personal preferences and strengths. Those with a keen interest in business and/or those with diverse interests and capabilities across areas of I-O psychology may benefit greatly and thrive in an internal I-O psychology career.

Angela K. Pratt and Adam J. Massman

See also Careers; Mentoring

Further Readings

Zelin, A. I., Oliver, J., Chau, S., Bynum, B., Carter, G., Poteet, M. L, & Doverspike, D. (2015, July). Identifying the competencies, critical experiences, and career paths of IO psychologists: Industry. *The Industrial-Organizational Psychologist*, 53(1), 142–151.

PREGNANCY DISCRIMINATION ACT

The Pregnancy Discrimination Act is a U.S. federal law, passed in 1978, which made it illegal to discriminate against someone for employment purposes on the basis of pregnancy. The act amended Title VII of the Civil Rights Act of 1964 to include pregnancy and related conditions in the definition of sex discrimination.

Background

Before the Pregnancy Discrimination Act was passed, the Civil Rights Act of 1964 made it illegal to discriminate against someone on the basis of race, color, religion, sex, or national origin for employment decisions. This protection did not, however, extend to pregnant women, because pregnancy was not considered to be synonymous with being female.

The legal distinction between pregnancy discrimination and sex discrimination was determined upon the ruling of *Geduldig v. Aiello*, in which the U.S. Supreme Court decided that it was lawful for an insurance company to deny disability benefits for pregnancy-related disabilities. This legal distinction was then extended to employment conditions upon the ruling of *General Electric Company v. Gilbert*, in which the Supreme Court decided that employers could legally discriminate against pregnant women on employer-sponsored health benefits.

The Supreme Court determined that neither of these cases represented sex discrimination, because some women (i.e., nonpregnant women) enjoyed the same benefits as men. Thus, pregnancy was determined to be a unique condition that was not covered under existing law at the time.

As a result, Congress proposed and voted to amend existing law via the Pregnancy Discrimination Act. The Pregnancy Discrimination Act changed one section (Title VII) of the Civil Rights Act of 1964 to include pregnancy in the definition of sex for the basis of employment discrimination. The purpose was to extend the legal definition of sex to include pregnancy, thereby making it illegal to discriminate on the basis of pregnancy and related conditions (e.g., the ability to get pregnant and medical conditions related to childbirth) for the purpose of employment.

Definitions

Pregnancy and Related Conditions

According to Supreme Court decisions and guidance from the U.S. Equal Employment Opportunity Commission, pregnancy and related conditions include current pregnancy, past pregnancy, potential or intended pregnancy, and medical conditions related to pregnancy or childbirth.

Employment-Related Purposes

The law covers any aspect of employment, including but not limited to hiring, termination, compensation, health insurance and benefits, assignment of duties, working conditions, and training.

Interpretation

Unlawful Practices

Employers cannot use pregnancy or childbirth as a reason for providing or withholding any employment-related conditions. For example, if a pregnant woman applies for a job, the employer must make a hiring decision on the basis of her qualifications alone. Such qualifications include knowledge, skills, abilities, and other characteristics that have been found (e.g., through job analysis) to be necessary to perform the job in question. Therefore, if a pregnant woman is qualified and capable of doing the job, and an employer chooses to hire someone else, the employer may face a discrimination lawsuit.

Prejudices, biases, and stereotypes about pregnant individuals are also unlawful reasons for making employment-related decisions that affect pregnant women. A prevailing stereotype, for instance, is that pregnancy indicates a woman's declining dedication to her work or career. Because this is a stereotype, and is not necessarily true of any given pregnant woman, it is unlawful to make any employment decisions on the basis of such a belief. Doing so would constitute illegal employment discrimination. In short, employers cannot make assumptions or guesses about an employee's or a candidate's qualifications on the basis of pregnancy, childbirth, or related conditions.

Lawful Employment Practices

It is permissible, and encouraged, to base employment-related decisions or conditions on merit, ability, seniority, and the quantity or quality of production, as long as these factors are not designed, intended, or used to discriminate against women affected by pregnancy, childbirth, or related conditions. For instance, if a pregnant employee has produced less work than a nonpregnant coworker, and the employer has a compensation system in place stating that pay is based on the amount of work produced, then it may be permissible for the employer to pay the pregnant employee less than the nonpregnant coworker.

Guidelines for Employers and Managers

Employers and managers should abide by the following guidelines to maintain compliance with the Pregnancy Discrimination Act:

1. Base employment-related decisions and conditions on merit and bona fide qualifications.

2. Provide equal employment opportunity (in hiring, compensation, training, etc.) to all persons, regardless of pregnancy, childbirth, or related conditions.

3. Treat women who are pregnant on the basis of their ability to work.

Related Legislation

Civil Rights Act of 1964

As noted above, this legislation made it illegal to discriminate against someone on the basis of race, color, religion, sex, or national origin. Title VII of the Civil Rights Act covers employment specifically. It is this piece of legislation that was amended by the Pregnancy Discrimination Act to include "pregnancy, childbirth, and related conditions" in the definition of sex discrimination.

Americans with Disabilities Act

This act prohibits discrimination against people who have physical or mental impairments that affect major life activities, including the ability to work. Although pregnancy alone is not a disorder or an impairment, complications from pregnancy can result in temporary impairments that affect someone's ability to work. In cases in which a pregnant woman's ability to work is in question, employers and managers should refer to the Americans with Disabilities Act in addition to the Pregnancy Discrimination Act. The Americans with Disabilities Act may require that the employer provide an accommodation to the pregnant employee if it is reasonable and enables her to carry out the work.

Family and Medical Leave Act

The Family and Medical Leave Act enables eligible employees to take up to 12 weeks of unpaid, job-protected leave from work each year for qualifying medical reasons. Childbirth, care for a newborn child, and serious health conditions (including those that result from pregnancy or childbirth) are qualifying reasons for taking leave under the act. Additional eligibility requirements include having worked for a covered employer (private-sector companies with 50 or more employees, all public agencies, and all public and private elementary or secondary schools) for at least 12 months and a minimum of 1,250 hours. In short, when an employee requests leave for pregnancy or childbirth, employers and managers should refer to guidelines in the Family and Medical Leave Act in addition to the Pregnancy Discrimination Act.

Katherine A. Frear

See also Adverse Impact/Disparate Treatment/ Discrimination at Work; Americans with Disabilities Act; Bona Fide Occupational Qualifications; Civil Rights Act of 1964, Civil Rights Act of 1991; Equal Pay Act of 1963; Family and Medical Leave Act

Further Readings

Bragger, J., Kutcher, E., Morgan, J., & Firth, P. (2002). The effects of the structured interview on reducing biases against pregnant job applicants. *Sex Roles, 46*(7–8), 215–226. doi:10.1023/A:1019967231059

Geduldig v. Aiello, 417 U.S. (1974).

General Electric Company v. Gilbert, 429 U.S. (1976).

Gueutal, H., & Taylor, E. (1991). Employee pregnancy: The impact on organizations, pregnant employees and co-workers. *Journal of Business and Psychology, 5*(4), 459–476. doi:10.1007/BF01014495

Halpert, J. A., Wilson, M. L., & Hickman, J. L. (1993). Pregnancy as a source of bias in performance appraisals. *Journal of Organizational Behavior, 14*(7), 649–663. doi:10.2307/2488227

Hebl, M. R., King, E. B., Glick, P., Singletary, S. L., & Kazama, S. (2007). Hostile and benevolent reactions toward pregnant women: Complementary interpersonal punishments and rewards that maintain traditional roles. *Journal of Applied Psychology, 92*(6), 1499–1511. doi:10.1037/0021-9010.92.6.1499

PREJUDICE

See Stereotyping

PREPARING FOR ACADEMIC CAREERS IN INDUSTRIAL AND ORGANIZATIONAL PSYCHOLOGY

Academic careers in industrial and organizational (I-O) psychology can be both challenging and rewarding. An academic career is an occupation that takes place within a college, a university, or an institute of higher education that typically involves teaching and/or conducting research, as well as engaging in service to the university and the profession. Most academic careers in I-O psychology require a graduate degree. Positions within community colleges as well as adjunct faculty positions may require only a master's degree. However, most 4-year college or university faculty positions require a PhD. Preparing for such a career involves several steps that may begin years before an actual application is submitted. These steps include determining the type of academic career that is desired, gaining relevant experience, and preparing materials for the job search.

Types of Academic Careers

Academic careers can be classified on the basis of the degree to which teaching and research are emphasized as part of one's role. Teaching-focused positions may require a professor to teach between three and five classes per academic semester. On the other hand, research-focused positions may require zero to two classes to be taught per semester. Research-focused positions will also typically require a faculty member to publish his or her research in empirical, peer-reviewed journals, and some institutions may require a faculty member to obtain external funding (i.e., grants) to support research. Between these two ends of the continuum are positions that emphasize both teaching and research (often referred to as teacher–scholar programs). In these programs, the teaching load might be about three courses per semester, and a faculty member might be expected to engage in a small amount of research that results in presentations at academic conferences articles in peer-reviewed publications. One can often determine the focus of a given position on the basis of information contained in the job advertisement or position announcement. Most programs will describe the expectations for teaching and research for a prospective faculty member, making it easy for one to assess the level of fit with the position before applying.

To determine the type of academic career to apply for, do a self-assessment and think about your interests and experiences. Are you interested in spending most days analyzing data, mentoring graduate students or postdoctoral research associates, and writing grant proposals and manuscripts? If so, a research-focused academic career might be a good fit for you. On the other hand, if you are interested in preparing and delivering lectures or discussions, designing in-class activities and exams, grading student work, and interacting with students, then a teaching-focused career might be a good fit for you. If you think you might like doing a little bit of each, then a teacher-scholar program might be the right fit. After you have considered the type of academic career that might be right for you, the next step is to make sure that you are gaining the relevant experiences to prepare you for the career of interest.

Gaining Relevant Experiences

If you are considering an academic career in I-O psychology, the first step is to enroll in a graduate program in I-O psychology, as nearly all academic careers in I-O psychology require a master's or doctoral degree. During your graduate training, it will be important to gain experience that will be relevant to the type of academic career you will be aiming for.

If you are considering a career in a research-focused position, then develop yourself as a researcher. You will need to think about what specific area of research will be your focus and what unique contributions you can make in that area. Begin by speaking with your academic adviser or other faculty members in the department about ongoing projects you can get involved in. You can then help with data collection, analysis, and manuscript writing, with the goal of publishing these efforts in peer-reviewed journals and presenting at academic conferences. In addition to this work, you will likely also be developing your own line of research, typically beginning with a master's thesis and then a doctoral dissertation. The goal for both of these projects is to publish the results in peer-reviewed journals. Even if you are considering an academic career focused on teaching, your application will be stronger if you have a few publications when you apply for the job. Therefore, publishing research in peer-reviewed journals should be a top priority while you are in graduate school.

If you are considering a teaching-focused career, then, in addition to trying to publish a few manuscripts, you should also focus on developing yourself as a teacher. You might begin by serving as a teaching assistant for a course in your department. After this experience, try to teach a few courses as the sole instructor (note that a master's degree is

typically required). Teaching your own course can often be accomplished at the same institution where you are obtaining your graduate degree, but you might also be able to obtain a position as an adjunct faculty member for one or more courses at a neighboring institution. During these teaching experiences, consider attending classes or seminars on innovative or engaging teaching techniques and give them a try while you are teaching. You can also read about innovative teaching techniques in journals that are dedicated to this subject (e.g., *Teaching of Psychology*). Because student evaluations of teaching are a key criterion during the hiring process as well as the tenure and promotion processes, focus on developing meaningful learning experiences and building student rapport so that you can obtain excellent student reviews. You might also consider asking another professor to observe a session of your class and provide you with feedback and a formal letter summarizing the teaching observation. The feedback can be used to help you develop as a teacher, and the letter can be included as part of your teaching portfolio. If you are considering a career as a teacher–scholar, you will want to obtain some experience in conducting and publishing research as well as some experience in teaching.

Internships can be another useful experience for an individual who is considering an academic career in I-O psychology (or who is unsure of whether to go into an academic or applied career). For teaching-focused positions, many job advertisements will indicate that they are looking for someone who has applied experience that they can draw upon in the classroom. For research-focused positions, an applied internship can serve as a useful source of data that can be turned into a peer-reviewed presentation or publication. If possible, try to find an internship experience that aligns with your interests and career goals. For example, individuals interested in teaching-focused careers may find it useful to complete an internship focused on training or that involves high levels of client contact. Alternatively, individuals interested in research-focused careers may find it helpful to complete an internship in an internal consulting role that focuses on research. Whichever way you go, it will be important to document the experience in your curriculum vitae and think about how this experience will help you to achieve your career goals.

Regardless of the type of institution, most universities will require faculty members to engage in service to the university and the profession. In addition, faculty search committees are often looking for indicators that an applicant is well rounded and will be a collegial member of the department. Therefore, it may also be a good idea to engage in a few relevant service-related experiences while in graduate school. For example, you could serve as a submission reviewer for the annual Society for Industrial and Organizational Psychology conference, get involved in a student organization on your campus, or engage in relevant community service (such as a résumé-writing workshop for unemployed adults). Again, whatever you choose to get involved in, think about how it can help you to reach your career goals, and be sure to document and describe the experience in your curriculum vitae.

The Job Search

The hiring process for academic careers in I-O psychology typically begins in the late summer or early fall of the year prior to the start of the position. For example, if a university is hiring for a faculty member to begin in fall 2018, it will typically advertise the position sometime between July 2017 and early spring 2018. Position announcements can be found in numerous places, including professional society online job boards (e.g., the Society for Industrial and Organizational Psychology, the Academy of Management), online academic job boards (e.g., Higher Ed Jobs, *Chronicle of Higher Education*), e-mail list servers (e.g., *Teaching of Psychology*, the Society for Occupational Health Psychology), or individual college or university human resource department Web sites. Once you find a position opening of interest, here are a few things that many colleges and universities will look for during the application process: a cover letter, curriculum vitae, letters of recommendation, a teaching and/or research statement, and a teaching portfolio (containing student reviews and syllabi) and/or writing samples (e.g., recently published or in-preparation manuscripts). Guidance on how to prepare each of these documents can easily be found by searching the Internet or by referring to the items in the "Further Readings" section below.

It is advised that you tailor your application materials to the individual institution to which you are applying. This means spending a bit of time browsing through the institution's Web site, learning about the department's faculty members, the curriculum for the programs in the department, the university's culture and mission, the student body, and the courses you would be prepared to teach in that department. Then you can talk about how you fit with the department and institution in your cover letter. Most institutions require submission of materials electronically, either through the human resource department Web site or via e-mail.

After submitting your application materials, you may be contacted by an institution for a telephone or webcam interview. The key to success for this interview is to prepare in advance. You should carefully review your curriculum vitae and think about how your experiences have prepared you for this position. Additionally, you should spend some more time researching the institution and thinking about how you fit. It is advised to prepare some notes detailing information about the institution and how you see yourself contributing to it. It is very likely that one of the questions asked during the interview will be some variation of "Why do you want to work at XYZ institution?" or "How will you be able to contribute to the program here?" Other questions asked during the interview will be related to your background in teaching or research or other information you should be able to glean from the position announcement.

If you do well during the telephone or webcam interview, you may be invited to visit the institution for an on-site interview. Most on-site visits typically last a full day, but many last several days and include a job talk; individual meetings with the department chair, faculty members, students, and members of the administration; a tour of the institution; and often meals with the members of the institution. Whereas the individual meetings are important, the key to success for the on-site visit is doing well on the job talk. The focus of the job talk will depend on the type of position you have applied for. That is, research-focused positions will typically ask you to present some of your recent research, and teaching-focused positions may ask you to teach a class. Guidance on preparing for the job talk can be found by performing a search of the Internet or by referring to the resources listed below.

Another important item to prepare prior to the on-site visit is a list of questions you can ask during the visit. You will likely want to know about the department you will be working in, the expectations for the position, the structure and culture of the institution, and the surrounding community. Carefully preparing this list of questions will help you make the most informed decision about whether to accept an offer, and it will also convey that you were prepared in advance for the visit.

Gary W. Giumetti

See also Academic Careers in Industrial and Organizational Psychology; Careers for Industrial and Organizational Psychologists; Job Choice; Job Search; Letters of Recommendation; Preparing for Careers in Industrial and Organizational Psychology Practice; Succeeding in Academic Careers in Industrial and Organizational Psychology

Further Readings

Darley, J. M., Zanna, M. P., & Roediger, H. I. (2004). *The compleat academic: A career guide* (2nd ed.). Washington, DC: American Psychological Association.

Furstenberg, F. F. (2013). *Behind the academic curtain: How to find success and happiness with a Ph.D.* Chicago: University of Chicago Press.

Kronenfeld, J. J., & Whicker, M. L. (1997). *Getting an academic job: Strategies for success.* Thousand Oaks, CA: Sage.

Lang, J. M. (2005). *Life on the tenure track: Lessons from the first year.* Baltimore, MD: Johns Hopkins University Press.

Morgan, Elizabeth M., & Landrum, R. Eric. (2012). *You've earned your doctorate in psychology . . . now what? Securing a job as an academic or professional psychologist.* Washington, DC: American Psychological Association.

Sowers-Hoag, K. M., & Harrison, D. F. (1998). *Finding an academic job.* Thousand Oaks, CA: Sage.

University of Indiana. (n.d.). *Recommended readings: Books about life in academia.* http://www.indiana.edu/~pffc/bibliography.htm

Vick, J. M., & Furlong, J. S. (2008). *Academic job search handbook* (4th ed.). Philadelphia: University of Pennsylvania Press.

PREPARING FOR CAREERS IN INDUSTRIAL AND ORGANIZATIONAL PSYCHOLOGY PRACTICE

In 2014 the Bureau of Labor Statistics identified the occupation of industrial and organizational (I-O) psychologist as the fastest growing occupation for the years 2012 to 2022. As companies continue to realize the benefits I-O psychologists bring to assist organizations and employees with workplace issues, opportunities to practice I-O psychology will continue to expand. At the same time, the growing reach of the field into new, nontraditional areas gives interested individuals a wide range of opportunities to prepare for an I-O practice career.

In preparing for a career in I-O psychology practice, individuals can direct their attention to several broad areas of development: career research and preparation, competency development, applied experience, and professional development. Within each area are specific steps, activities, and resources, but these are not presented in order of sequencing or priority. Some of these steps will be more or less important depending on whether the interested I-O practitioner (IOP) is a university or college student, an I-O psychology educator looking to enter the practice field, or a professional in another field searching for a career transition.

Career Research and Preparation

Research

Individuals can benefit from taking time to explore the field to understand the types of work that are performed and the different practice opportunities available. IOPs can work in a variety of companies and sectors, including government agencies, consulting firms, and industry organizations. Across these organizations, a practitioner can work as an internal, external, or independent consultant, and the type of work performed can vary along many subject areas of I-O psychology. Practitioners can also take different career paths, some choosing to remain as individual contributors in mainly technical positions or to take a more general managerial path that may extend their responsibilities outside of the I-O area. To help plan one's training and development, a prospective practitioner can consult professional organizations such as the Academy of Management, American Psychological Association, Society for Industrial and Organizational Psychology (SIOP), and European Association of Work and Organizational Psychology for information on graduate training programs, the types of practice careers available for I-O psychologists, the educational and experience requirements for different career paths, and examples of work performed.

Online resources such as the Occupational Information Network and the Bureau of Labor Statistics provide comprehensive information about (a) typical work activities; (b) required knowledge, skills, and abilities; (c) employment and salary trends; (d) important credentials and necessary education; and (e) typical work values and interests consistent with the work of I-O psychologists. Publications such as *TD Magazine*, *Industrial and Organizational Psychology: Perspectives on Science and Practice*, *The Industrial–Organizational Psychologist*, and *HR Magazine* are additional outlets for individuals to learn about applied work related to I-O psychology. Various online discussion groups related to specific fields can also provide valuable information about different roles, career paths, or job and internship opportunities. Conducting informational interviews with and reading profiles of I-O psychologists are excellent ways to learn about practice-based careers. These can provide firsthand accounts of what a typical day looks like for a practitioner, help identify potential paths or opportunities, and highlight potential obstacles and challenges to entering the field.

Interests, Motivations, and Values

As noted above, a wide range of practice careers exist within I-O psychology, including government agencies (e.g., federal, state, local), consulting companies (e.g., international firms, large domestic companies, small firms, independent practice), and industry (e.g., for-profit or not-for-profit companies). Also, consulting firms may vary in the degree to which they specialize in certain I-O areas, practice in a wide range of I-O areas, or provide consulting services in areas outside I-O as well. Careful analysis of one's interests,

work style, values, skills, and career goals should be conducted and factored into decisions about an individual's career path. For example, those with a strong need for collaboration, relationships, and variety may find satisfaction working as consultants within large firms, whereas individuals with strong entrepreneurial and decision-making interests may find more value working independently or running small consulting operations. Someone with strong analytical and research interests with few needs for travel may be satisfied working for a firm that offers internal research opportunities. Leveraging one's strengths and interests can help ensure a successful and satisfying career.

Preparation

Having researched and identified attractive I-O psychology practice career paths, individuals should plan and prepare for their entry into their desired practice areas. In addition to developing technical competence and gaining relevant practical experience (covered below), preparation activities include building and communicating one's professional brand (e.g., creating a LinkedIn profile, writing blogs, doing public speaking); writing and tailoring one's résumé to specific organizations, roles, and industries; practicing interviews; and creating a job search strategy and an action plan. Although few of these activities are unique to the I-O psychology profession, implemented effectively, they can help individuals direct intentional and meaningful movements toward their desired I-O psychology practice areas.

Competency Development

Prospective IOPs will benefit from developing a wide range of knowledge, skills, and competencies, such as knowledge of psychology, business and organizational acumen, and personal competencies, with consideration of any requirements for licensure and certification.

Technical Knowledge

Developing competence in I-O psychology is a prerequisite for practicing in the field, much of which is achieved through formal graduate school education. The majority of individuals interested in an I-O psychology practice career pursue master's or doctoral degrees, with a doctorate providing broader employment opportunities. Regardless of the degree pursued, knowledge often required for practicing in I-O psychology includes fields of psychology (e.g., personality, behavior, performance), ethical and legal issues, scientific research methods, statistical analysis and tools, human resources and personnel practices (e.g., training, selection, compensation, performance management, job analysis), organizational behavior (e.g., attitudes, motivation, teams, leadership) and theory, adult learning and development, career development, and organizational change and development.

Business and Organizational Acumen

As I-O psychology represents an amalgamation of the fields of business and psychology, developing practitioners can also benefit from enhancing their understanding of business and organizations. Research conducted by SIOP has identified several types of business knowledge, including financial concepts and terminology (e.g., financial statements), business development (e.g., proposal and contract development, marketing and sales), business analytics (e.g., return on investment), and organizational environments (e.g., industry and market trends). This knowledge can help IOPs build business cases for services, demonstrate their impact within the organization, and align solutions with the organization's needs and objectives while maintaining scientific rigor. Taking business elective courses while in school, reading business publications, studying companies, and seeking mentoring from business experts are ways one can obtain this knowledge.

Personal Competencies

Individuals can also benefit from the development of their personal competencies, such as the following:

- *Interpersonal skills.* Persuasion, conflict management, and team facilitation help a practitioner work collaboratively with others and influence clients, colleagues, and internal customers
- *Communication skills.* Written communication, verbal communication, and presentation skills

help a practitioner communicate services, solutions, findings, and so on, in language tailored to the client.
- *Critical thinking.* Data analysis, problem solving, creative thinking, and decision making help a practitioner research, develop, and implement solutions that meet a client's unique situation and needs.
- *Results and execution.* Setting goals, creating project plans, follow-through, work quality, and planning and organizing help a practitioner manage his or her work and ensure that projects are completed in a timely, cost-effective, and high-quality manner.

Several of these competencies are developed throughout the course of one's formal education, but interested individuals can enhance their capabilities by gaining practical experience and pursuing informal development opportunities (e.g., learning events through professional organizations).

Licensure and Certification

Obtaining licensure and/or certification may be required, recommended, or preferred by state licensing boards, organizations, or clients for practicing in some areas of I-O psychology. Many of these may require the completion of a graduate degree, achievement of a set standard of practical training and experience, and passing of certification examinations. Thus, a student or an individual seeking a career transition may not be able to obtain these in the near term. Nevertheless, understanding these requirements can help a prospective IOP plan for and obtain the necessary coursework and experience for licensure or certification.

Applied Experience

Research on leadership development has consistently noted the importance of experience as a key driver in one's development. In a similar vein, individuals interested in a practice I-O career benefit from gaining practical experience. Applied experience is important for establishing one's credentials and expertise; learning how to translate knowledge into real-world, practical solutions; building one's track record of success; identifying career paths that are aligned with one's interests and values; and reinforcing the technical knowledge and nontechnical competencies needed for success. Applied experience can come from several avenues.

Formal Internships

Sometimes required, facilitated, and/or encouraged by I-O graduate programs, these are temporary, time-defined positions that provide individuals with opportunities to gain on-the-job training and experience working within organizations. These can occur within several employment sectors and organizations described earlier and can involve both internal and external consulting roles. International internships can also be used for students wishing to work globally. Interns are often provided with mentoring and supervision by a company manager and/or one's major professor to ensure an optimal learning experience. Internships vary on the type of work they involve, so aligning the company and assignment to one's interests and goals is important.

Consulting Project Work

Prospective practitioners can also gain experience from temporary project-based consulting work. For example, students may provide assistance to colleagues or professors working on consulting projects with external clients. Or students may provide applied I-O services to other university department programs (e.g., conducting developmental assessment centers for incoming MBA students) or to local consulting firms needing short-term assistance. These activities could occur outside of the formal internship program present at the university.

Service Activities

Volunteering for I-O-related work through professional organizations or external groups also provides experience and develops skills necessary for entry into I-O practice careers. One such program is the Volunteer Program Assessment, centered at the University of North Carolina at Charlotte with several affiliate university programs. This program uses student consultants to provide free climate assessment and feedback services to nonprofit organizations. Students learn to manage projects, conduct meetings to scope out client needs and issues, administer and analyze surveys, create feedback reports, and deliver verbal feedback to organizational leaders.

Research and Teaching

Most graduate I-O psychology programs provide opportunities for students to conduct and/or lead research projects, or to teach undergraduate courses, often as part of one's assistantship. Although these experiences may, on the surface, seem to apply more directly to a career in research and academia, they are important for developing practice skills such as presenting to large groups, fielding challenging questions that require one to think quickly and leverage their expertise, handling challenging audiences, investigating and analyzing problems, formulating hypotheses and possible solutions, evaluating how well a service or product has worked, and applying evidence-based, scientific methods to address organizational issues.

Regardless of the type of experience obtained, individuals can undertake several steps to ensure a successful learning opportunity. Some best practices include showing intellectual curiosity, creating development goals to guide one's efforts, conducting regular and intentional reflection on one's experiences, documenting lessons learned, taking on challenging, new assignments that provide opportunities to learn, and seeking feedback from others.

Professional Development

Beyond formal education and applied experience, there are numerous actions an individual can take to develop additional professional capabilities critical for entry into an I-O practice role.

Professional organizations related to the field of I-O psychology, as well as those related to one's unique interests within the field, can be found at the global, domestic, regional, and local levels and offer an excellent avenue for development. Many of these organizations provide training and educational resources to help members develop the knowledge and technical expertise needed to practice successfully. For example, SIOP provides a series of webinars directed to students of I-O psychology to help them learn about and prepare for careers in the field. Through its e-learning offerings (e.g., webcasts, online courses) and resource materials (e.g., how-to guides), the Society for Human Resource Management offers a wide array of tools to increase one's understanding of human resources topics.

Many professional organizations conduct conferences that offer learning events, such as content mastery sessions, workshops on practice-based topics and techniques, and presentations of practical research. Professional organizations also publish periodicals IOPs can use to stay abreast of the latest innovations, research, and best practices. As noted earlier, another benefit of joining professional organizations is the opportunity to volunteer on committees, which can help an individual gain more experience and knowledge within a practice area. Some professional organizations, such as the European Association of Work and Organizational Psychology (http://www.eawop.org/jobs) and SIOP (http://www.siop.org/jobnet/), provide resources and services to help prospective practitioners research and pursue job opportunities.

Networking

Building a professional network with other students and practitioners is another method to prepare for a practice career. Becoming active in professional organizations is one way to grow one's network with other IOPs. Having a broad network can help one learn from others' experiences and examples. Seeking input from members of one's network can be used to broaden one's perspectives on potential issues, obstacles, and solutions to workplace problems or initiatives. Similarly, gaining "practical know-how" from experienced practitioners can help one identify ways in which to apply their knowledge in real-world workplace situations. Networks can also serve a useful function in both learning about I-O career opportunities as well as gaining access to individuals who can facilitate those career movements. Finally, as the I-O psychology community is still relatively small, building a strong network can help increase one's presence within the field.

Mentoring

Mentoring is another activity individuals can seek to enhance their professional development.

Often this occurs for students within graduate programs through one's major professor. Some programs may also facilitate senior–junior student mentoring. Mentoring can assist those seeking a career transition into I-O psychology from other areas. Some professional organizations may offer programs that provide potential practitioners, both students and nonstudents, with formal mentoring opportunities. Finding informal mentors through networking and attendance at conferences can be a valuable learning tool.

Mark L. Poteet

See also Careers for Industrial and Organizational Psychologists; Practice Careers in Industrial and Organizational Psychology: External Consulting Roles; Practice Careers in Industrial and Organizational Psychology: Internal Roles; Succeeding in Careers in Industrial and Organizational Psychology Practice; Tips for Creating a Consulting Practice; Tips for Getting an Internship

Further Readings

Ellis, A. M., Mansfield, L., & Crain, T. L. (April, 2015). *The path less traveled: Starting a career in your specialty area. Industrial–Organizational Psychologist,* 52(4), 51–56.

Hedge, J. W., & Borman, W. C. (Eds). (2008). *The I-O consultant: Advice and insights for building a successful career.* Washington, DC: American Psychological Association.

National Center for O*NET Development. (2016). Summary report for: 19-3032.00 - industrial-organizational psychologists. O*NET OnLine. http://www.onetonline.org/link/summary/19-3032.00

Society for Industrial and Organizational Psychology. (n.d.). *Psychology at work: What do I-O psychologists really do?* http://www.siop.org/psychatwork.aspx

Society for Industrial and Organizational Psychology. (n.d.). *Students are the future of I-O psychology.* http://www.siop.org/studentdefault.aspx

Society for Industrial and Organizational Psychology. (1994). *Guidelines for education and training at the master's level in industrial-organizational psychology.* http://www.siop.org/guidelines.aspx

Society for Industrial and Organizational Psychology. (1999). *Guidelines for education and training at the doctoral level in industrial/organizational psychology.* http://www.siop.org/PhDGuidelines98.aspx

PRESCREENING ASSESSMENT METHODS FOR PERSONNEL SELECTION

Given that most organizations have many more job applicants than they have job openings, employers must be able to quickly and efficiently screen out those applicants who not only fail to meet the minimum qualifications but are also unlikely to be successful on the job if hired. Prescreening assessment methods provide cost-effective ways of selecting out those applicants who are unlikely to be successful if hired. Thus, these methods take a different approach from the more detailed and involved personnel selection methods that focus on identifying the most highly qualified candidates. Technology may make the use of some prescreening assessment methods simultaneously more necessary and easier than ever to implement. Employer adoption of electronic recruitment methods combined with applicants' ability to blast résumés to hundreds of organizations with a single click can lead to unduly large applicant pools for open positions. As a result, organizational adoption of Web-based application procedures with automated prescreening of applicants may help make such large applicant pools more manageable.

Prescreening assessment methods, also referred to as *initial screenings*, *preemployment inquiries*, and *background evaluations*, encompass a wide range of popular procedures used at the beginning stages of the personnel selection process. Common prescreening assessment methods include application forms, résumés, weighted application blanks (WABs), training and experience evaluations (T&Es), reference checks, letters of recommendation, honesty and integrity testing, and drug testing. An underlying rationale across prescreening assessment methods is that past behavior is the best predictor of future behavior. Thus the assumption is that if applicants have done it in the past, they are likely to repeat it in the future. These behaviors can range from negative or deviant behaviors, such as engaging in illegal drug use or stealing from former employers, to prosocial or positive behaviors, such as taking on leadership roles or assisting coworkers with assignments before being asked.

Prescreening Assessment Methods

U.S. employers screen more than 1 billion résumés and applications each year. Application blanks most frequently assess current and historical information regarding the applicant's educational attainment and work experience. They may also be used to assess an individual's right to work in the country, as well as an applicant's willingness to engage in such undesirable work activities such as traveling extensively or working nontraditional schedules. Unfortunately, most organizations fail to use systematic procedures to evaluate the information obtained from résumés and applications, negating much of the usefulness of these prescreening methods. However, sophisticated practitioners have developed several procedures, including T&Es and WABs, to systematically evaluate and weight the various background information provided on application blanks. Because these weights are optimal for a given applicant pool, however, they must be cross-validated on a new sample to ensure that they will still be effective when used with future job applicants. WABs and T&Es have demonstrated modest relationships with later job performance and thus show some promise as efficient and effective prescreening tools, particularly when the job involves long and costly training, there is high job turnover, and the initial applicant pool is very large. More detailed methods of assessing background information, such as biographical questionnaires, however, typically go beyond mere prescreening. Thus they would be classified as substantive personnel selection, because their primary goal would then become to select the best qualified candidates into the organization, rather than selecting out the weakest candidates, which is typically done with WABs and T&Es.

Reference checks and letters of recommendation are also sometimes used as prescreening devices. Such evaluations typically cover employment and educational history, the personality or character of the applicant, and statements regarding job performance abilities. However, they can be expensive to use in the early stages of the personnel selection process when there are still many more applicants than job openings. Letters of recommendation tend to suffer from leniency bias because applicants predictably choose letter writers who provide positive evaluations. Some researchers have suggested that letters of recommendation actually reveal more about the letter writer than the applicant. In addition, there is little evidence that they are predictive of later job performance. Checking references of past employers is essential for many jobs, if only to verify the validity of past employment claims. Unfortunately, past employers are often reticent to provide additional evaluative information for fear of an accusation of defamation of character. Nevertheless, prospective employers can be sued for negligent hiring if they knowingly (or unknowingly) select a job applicant who later engages in illegal or inappropriate behavior at work. As a result, many organizations will at least attempt to contact previous employers and others who know the job applicant to verify information provided or clarify inconsistencies in the application materials.

Billions of dollars are lost each year in the retail industry because of employee theft. In addition, scores of employees are injured at work or endanger the public and their coworkers because of illegal drug use. Thus honesty and integrity tests as well as drug tests are often used as prescreening assessment methods to screen out applicants who are likely to either steal from the organization or engage in illicit drug use. Honesty tests typically take one of two forms. Overt honesty tests assess applicants' attitudes toward theft and admissions of theft. Alternatively, personality-based honesty tests evaluate counterproductive work behavior in general, of which theft is just one part. As a result, overt integrity measures are typically clear purpose tests; applicants administered personality-based integrity measures, however, rarely know what the test is assessing. Although the use of overt integrity measures may increase perceptions of invasion of privacy, such concerns may be diminished by the greater face validity of these measures. Although both forms of honesty tests have shown some promise in predicting future job performance, their effectiveness in reducing inventory loss is still largely unknown.

Meanwhile, most research on the effectiveness of drug testing has focused on the accuracy of the tests themselves (i.e., reducing false-positive or false-negative test results) or applicants' reactions to issues of invasion of privacy and procedural justice (i.e., applicants' perceptions of how the drug testing is implemented), rather than how well the tests predict job performance or reduce job-related accidents, illnesses, or sick time. As a result, the effectiveness of drug screening procedures to improve workplace performance or reduce illicit drug use among those employees who are eventually hired is still unclear.

Reducing Misinformation

Because most of the information provided on preemployment screening methods is self-report (i.e., provided directly by the job applicants themselves), embellishment, if not outright falsification, of information is common. Thus employers must take steps to make sure that the information provided by applicants is as accurate as possible. How can they best achieve this? One option is to have applicants sign a statement that all the information they provide is accurate to the best of their knowledge and that knowingly providing false information will immediately eliminate them from further consideration for the job. Additionally, using reference and background checks (as discussed earlier) can also help verify information by providing others' assessments, in addition to the job applicant's own assessment. The extent to which the organization requests verifiable and objective information, such as degrees earned or grade point average, versus unverifiable and subjective information, including how an applicant felt about the college experience, can also reduce falsification of self-reported application information. Sometimes just the written or oral threat that the organization will follow up on the information provided in the application materials is enough to significantly reduce falsifications and embellishments. Some employers have even gone so far as to include *lie scales* in their WABs and T&Es. Such scales typically include bogus job skills or experiences that would identify the applicant as lying if they report having those bogus skills or experiences.

Legal Issues

Even though prescreening assessment methods focus more on selecting out the poorly qualified candidates, as opposed to selecting in the best candidates, they are still required to meet state and federal fair employment guidelines and laws. As a result, the development and use of any prescreening assessment method should follow established professional guidelines, such as the *Uniform Guidelines on Employee Selection Procedures* and the *Principles for the Validation and Use of Personnel Selection Procedures*. This would typically entail conducting a job analysis and a study to determine the validity of using certain prescreening methods for a given job. The validity of a prescreening measure will rely not only on the type of information gathered but also on the scoring method used to examine that information. Researchers have determined, for example, that the validity of T&Es can vary widely on the basis of the scoring procedure used. Furthermore, given the job-specific nature of many prescreening measures, it is possible that the composition and validity of these measures may be less generalizable across jobs or organizations than selection methods such as structured interviews or cognitive ability tests. These unique characteristics of prescreening measures further reinforce the need for conducting thorough validation studies prior to implementation.

Failure to follow recommended validation procedures will make it difficult to defend the use of any prescreening assessment procedure that is challenged in a court of law as being discriminatory. Thus employers must determine if their prescreening devices result in adverse impact, for example, whether some protected groups are hired at a significantly lower rate than other groups because of use of a given prescreening procedure. In addition, employers should determine whether a given procedure is predictive of success on the job, can be justified as needed for business necessity, or results in an invasion of privacy. Only in doing so will employers be on solid legal footing when the need to justify and defend their use of a given prescreening assessment method is challenged in court. Unfortunately, most studies of organizational application forms find that most employers, both private and public, continue to include some illegal or inappropriate items in their prescreening measures. Among the most frequently assessed inappropriate items are inquiries into gender, race, age, disability, marital status, and arrest record.

Although receiving less research attention than other personnel selection measures, prescreening assessment methods continue to be popular because of their ease of administration, widespread acceptability by applicants, and utility for eliminating unqualified applicants. In an age in which organizations can successfully and cost-effectively boost the size of their applicant pools through use of Internet-based recruitment and application procedures, the use of prescreening selection tools may become increasingly necessary. Hence, additional research and continued monitoring of the legality, validity, and practical utility of using prescreening assessment methods is clearly warranted given both their current prominence and future potential to advance the overall selection process.

Kenneth S. Shultz and David J. Whitney

See also Biographical Data; Employee Selection; Employment Interview; Integrity Testing; Letters of Recommendation; Selection Strategies; Uniform Guidelines on Employee Selection Procedures

Further Readings

Berry, L. M. (2003). Applications and other personal history assessments. In L. M. Berry, *Employee selection* (pp. 254–287). Belmont, CA: Wadsworth/Thomson Learning.

Cascio, W. F., & Aguinis, H. (2011). Selection methods: Part 1. In W. F. Cascio & H. Aguinis, *Applied psychology in human resource management* (7th ed., pp. 255–284). Upper Saddle River, NJ: Prentice Hall.

Gatewood, R. D., Feild, H. S. & Barrick, M. (2010). Application forms and biodata assessments, training and experience evaluations, and reference checks. In R. D. Gatewood, H. S. Feild, & M. Barrick, *Human resource selection* (7th ed., pp. 337–414). Mason, OH: South Western/Cengage Learning.

Heneman, H. G., III, Judge, T. A., & Kammeyer-Mueller, J. (2014). External selection I. In H. G. Heneman III, T. A. Judge, & J. Kammeyer-Mueller, *Staffing organizations* (8th ed.). Boston: Irwin McGraw-Hill.

PRIVACY AT WORK

Defining Privacy

Privacy is a slippery concept, and its definition depends on the lens (e.g., legal, ethical, economic) used. One definition that applies to the workplace considers privacy as employees' beliefs of the degree to which they can control personal information about them that is collected, used, and disseminated by their employers. At its essence, the definition reflects concerns related to boundaries between the individual and the organization. It underlies a key reason why concerns related to workplace privacy surface: the potential conflict between legitimate organizational requirements for employee information and legitimate employee concerns of individual rights.

Organizational Requirements for Employee Information

Through the course of the employment relationship, employers require different types of information about their employees. Before the employment relationship begins, during the selection process, employers require information regarding the abilities, motivation, and backgrounds of prospective applicants. During the employment relationship, obtaining information on employee ability and motivation on an ongoing basis is also essential from the standpoint of employee training, development, performance management, and other human resource processes, including grievance procedures and termination.

Other requirements for seeking information stem from concerns associated with guarding against counterproductive (e.g., surfing Web sites, wasting time on the job, taking long breaks), unethical, and even possibly illegal behaviors (e.g., theft, substance use, compromised security of products and intellectual property) in the workplace.

Employers thus have justifiable requirements to collect, use, and disseminate employee information and do so throughout the employment relationship. For instance, to make selection decisions, employers collect employee information through interviews, personality inventories, and other selection methods. During the course of employment, organizations collect employee information by observing their inputs or their behaviors, seeking information about focal employees through colleagues, and through formal processes such as meetings and performance appraisals.

The advent of sophisticated electronic performance monitoring systems has provided employers access to greater and continuous streams of information that can be used to enhance productivity and curtail counterproductive work behaviors. Software programs can track employees' e-mail, keystrokes, and Internet use and are widely used in organizations; location-sensing technologies, widely used in the transportation industry, can track where employees are physically located at any given time; cameras, including webcams, are used for surveillance as well for assessing job performance (e.g., in protective service occupations); sociometric badges assess a range of body and voice features (e.g., tone, physical proximity) in interpersonal contexts, such as employee-customer interactions and interactions between team members.

Concomitantly, with the advent of newer Internet technologies such as social media and online social networks, employers can also access and use private information (e.g., political views, musical tastes, membership in social and religious organizations) about their current and prospective employees. For instance, employers can obtain information about prospective employees through their posts, pictures, and exchanges on social media and use this information in making selection decisions. Thus, with technological advances employers can now obtain information both through monitoring technologies that are controlled by employers and Internet technologies that are used by employees privately.

Employee Rights to Privacy

Employees expect to be treated fairly at work, and their fairness and privacy beliefs are interconnected. Employees' right to privacy is connected to their senses of self and the extent to which they wish to reveal or retain information about themselves. Privacy rights also help construct a moral boundary that permits employees to lead their lives autonomously and with respect and dignity. Put simply, employees believe that they have a right "to be left alone."

As such, if employers collect information without seeking employees' authorization or through intrusive technologies or procedures, employees consider this to be invasive and a violation of their autonomy and dignity. For instance, for selection procedures, research indicates that job applicants view interviews, application blanks, and work sample tests as less invasive compared with drug tests, background checks, lie detector tests, and medical exams for disease potential. Job applicants consider procedures to be invasive if the procedures involve examining their bodies, elicit information that could mistakenly discredit them, or insinuate that the organization does not trust them. Job applicants consider procedures to be less invasive if the procedures are frequently used, if they have prior experiences with the procedures, and if the procedures provide an avenue to present themselves favorably. Overall, if job applicants' believe that they can control the information elicited through the selection procedure, they are less likely to view it as invasive.

Furthermore, if organizations collect information that employees consider irrelevant and if this information is used in making decisions, employees view it as procedurally unfair. Research suggests that perceptions of lowered autonomy and procedural unfairness are detrimental to employee well-being. Research suggests, however, that if employees perceive that organizations collect relevant information and provide employees an opportunity to have a say in the implementation process of monitoring technologies, their privacy concerns could be assuaged. More generally, because privacy issues are intertwined with issues of fairness, they likely affect employees' job attitudes and behaviors.

Some Future Challenges for Privacy at Work

Legal, ethical, business, and technological factors are colliding to raise difficult issues regarding privacy at work, and they require more research. For instance, privacy laws differ across countries, and even across states and provinces, and thus employee expectations of privacy are protected to varying degrees on the basis of where they are located. This raises concerns regarding the use of employee information in national and multinational organizations (e.g., protection of e-mail sent across countries, obtaining information of employee misconduct across jurisdictions). Along similar lines, there are challenges related to the protection of employee data that are already collected and stored by the organization. The access and potential misuse of sensitive employee data (e.g., birthdates, background checks, health insurance records) by both internal organizational

members and unauthorized external entities can accentuate employees' privacy concerns.

Changes in technology and changes in employees' expectations of privacy are also posing complex questions to legal and organizational scholars. If employees willingly share private information through social media that can be readily accessed by virtually anyone, can they still retain expectations of privacy from employers? Is it necessary to obtain employees' consent prior to using such information? Related questions concerning diversity and employment equity are also crucial. Does employers' use of social media result in differential selection outcomes for prospective employees on the basis of their sex, age, and race?

Addressing such questions represents an important challenge for researchers and practitioners to better understand issues related to workplace privacy, especially because laws and societal norms for privacy at work are evolving. Furthermore, these considerations highlight the relevance of developing organizational privacy policies centered on employees' use of technology at work and also through social media. More research on privacy at work is necessary to help devise robust and inclusive workplace privacy policies that protect employers' interests and employees' rights.

Devasheesh P. Bhave

See also Background Checks/Credit Checks; Cyberattacks: Implications for Organizations; Cyberloafing at Work; Data Privacy; Electronic Performance Monitoring; LinkedIn

Further Readings

Acquisti, A., Taylor, C., & Wagman, L. (in press). The economics of privacy. *Journal of Economic Literature*.

Alge, B. J. (2001). Effects of computer surveillance on perceptions of privacy and procedural justice. *Journal of Applied Psychology, 86*, 797–804.

Bies, R. J. (1993). Privacy and procedural justice in organizations. *Social Justice Research, 6*, 69–86.

Determann, L., & Sprague, R. (2011). Intrusive monitoring: Employee privacy expectations are reasonable in Europe, destroyed in the United States. *Berkeley Technology Law Journal, 26*, 979–1036.

Moore, A. D. (2000). Employee monitoring and computer technology: Evaluative surveillance v. privacy. *Business Ethics Quarterly, 10*, 697–709.

Roth, P. L., Bobko, P., Van Iddekinge, C. H., & Thatcher, J. B. (2016). Social media in employee-selection-related decisions: A research agenda for uncharted territory. *Journal of Management, 42*(1), 269–298.

Stanton, J. M. (2000). Reactions to employee performance monitoring: Framework, review, and research directions. *Human Performance, 13*, 85–113.

Stone-Romero, E. F., Stone, D. L., & Hyatt, D. (2003). Personnel selection procedures and invasion of privacy. *Journal of Social Issues, 59*, 343–368.

PROACTIVE PERSONALITY

Proactive personality refers to a personal disposition toward proactive behavior or taking action to influence one's environment. People with proactive personalities scan their environments for opportunities, show initiative, and persevere until they bring about change. They attempt to exert control over their work environments and prefer to shape circumstances rather than adapt to them.

Proactive personality has received attention from researchers and practitioners for two main reasons. First, it is associated with important attitudinal and behavioral outcomes at the workplace (e.g., job performance and career success). Second, the new workplace requires proactivity in the forms of change-oriented behaviors, initiative taking, creative problem solving, and innovation in systems, structures, and relationships.

Proactive people believe that they have the power, will, and resources to change the environment; therefore, they feel less constrained by situational forces. The proactive approach is rooted in the interactionist perspective of person–environment relationship. According to this view, people not only react to the environment, but they also create their own environments. Proactive people try actively to shape their environments so they can meet their personal needs and goals, as well as the goals of their teams and organizations. In contrast, nonproactive people are passive, "go with the flow," do not look for or act on opportunities, show little initiative, and rely on others to be agents of change.

Proactive personality instigates a wide range of proactive behaviors. In Crant's model, proactive personality is one of the antecedents of proactive behavior, which influences important attitudinal and behavioral outcomes. Proactive personality is proposed to affect two types of proactive behaviors: general actions (e.g., identifying opportunities to improve things) and context-specific behaviors (e.g., feedback seeking and issue selling).

Scope and Measurement of Proactive Personality

In the nomological network of proactivity constructs, proactive personality represents the dispositional component of proactivity. It specifically focuses on one's proclivity for proactive cognition and behavior. Similar constructs that address individual differences in proactivity include personal initiative and taking charge.

Proactive personality incorporates some elements from extraversion and conscientiousness of Big Five personality dimensions. It is also associated with emotional stability, openness to experience, need for achievement, need for dominance, and optimism. Proactive people have high self-esteem, have an internal locus of control, and engage in self-monitoring. They are also high in learning goal orientation, which engages them in learning activities so they can better understand, control, and change the environment.

There is substantial evidence that proactive personality predicts individual and organizational outcomes above and beyond other personality constructs, general mental ability, and work experience. The most common measures of proactive personality are the 17-item scale developed by Bateman and Crant and the 10-item shorter version of the original scale. The proactive personality scale has good validity and reliability. It has been used in various cultural contexts and does not show socially desirable responding.

What Do Proactive People Do?

There are various mechanisms through which proactive personality affects important personal and organizational outcomes. The interactionist perspective posits that proactive people select, change, and enact on their environments. They take action to determine the courses of events in their surroundings. For example, if they need information for task accomplishment, they do not wait for information; rather, they actively seek it. If they see an opportunity for career success, they embrace it. The social capital perspective emphasizes interpersonal and social aspects of the environment. Proactive people seek and attempt to gain the support of others in their pursuits of self-directed goals. They actively manage their relationships with their supervisors. They build relationships with decision makers and engage in networking. The resources proactive people get through their relationships and networks may give them access to information, increase their influence, and help bring change to their organizations. Additionally, proactive personality is associated with motivation, role breadth self-efficacy, flexible role orientation, autonomy, and psychological empowerment.

The effect that proactive personality has on outcomes depends on the specific conditions of the environment and on the characteristics of the person. For example, stressors such as unfairness or lack of job autonomy constrain proactive people and affect their job performance more so than the performance of nonproactive people. Moreover, proactive people with high situational judgment effectiveness—that is, judging the situation and interpreting and responding to situational cues—obtain the most favorable outcomes.

Correlates and Outcomes of Proactive Personality

Proactive personality has been related to overall performance, task performance, and contextual performance. Proactive people strive to create conditions in which they are more successful at their jobs. They may construe their jobs and their environments in a way that it amplifies their strengths and optimizes performance. They monitor their surroundings and engage in instrumental behaviors such as skill development, negotiation, resource gathering, and role restructuring. They hold favorable relations with supervisors and coworkers. They build relationships and networks to get resources they need for task accomplishment, initiate action, and follow through with their ideas. Proactive people are also willing to seek opportunities to improve the conditions in their environments and to contribute to the organization in ways that extend beyond the formal requirements of their jobs. They are likely to customize their work environments in such a way that they experience greater

person–job fit and person–organization fit. They experience organizational commitment and feel more ownership of the social and organizational environment that they helped to change and shape.

Proactivity has been a prominent topic in career success literature. Proactive personality relates to both objective career success (e.g., salary and promotions) and subjective career success (e.g., career satisfaction). Proactive people select, create, and influence the situations in which they work. They also engage in career management activities such as seeking job information, obtaining sponsorship, conducting career planning, and overcoming career obstacles. Proactive people are perceived and treated as high-potential candidates for career advancement. Proactive people show more career initiative, career self-efficacy, job search self-efficacy, and career adaptation.

Proactive personality generates proactive and change-oriented behaviors, which are commonly associated with leadership. Proactive personality is associated with transformational leadership, attributes of charismatic leadership, positive leader member–exchange relationships, and leadership effectiveness. Furthermore, proactive people are more alert to their environments, so they may anticipate stressors and take action before they occur. When they experience stressors, they are more likely to use problem-focused coping strategies and rely on more psychological and social resources than nonproactive people. Other outcomes of proactive personality include entrepreneurial intent, employee creativity, proactive socialization behaviors during organizational entry, and team effectiveness.

Conclusion

Proactive personality refers to a predisposition to actively influence one's environment. Proactive people are self-starters, change oriented, and future focused. They take initiative, persevere, and bring about change. Proactive people engage in a wide range of proactive behaviors, which affect important personal and organizational outcomes (e.g., career satisfaction, job performance).

Burcu Rodopman

See also Career Success; Networking; Organizational Socialization; Personality

Further Readings

Bateman, T. S., & Crant, J. M. (1993). The proactive component of organizational behavior: A measure and correlates. *Journal of Organizational Behavior*, 14(2), 103–118.

Chan, D. (2006). Interactive effects of situational judgment effectiveness and proactive personality on work perceptions and work outcomes. *Journal of Applied Psychology*, 91(2), 475.

Crant, J. M. (2000). Proactive behavior in organizations. *Journal of Management*, 26(3), 435–462.

Fuller, B., & Marler, L. E. (2009). Change driven by nature: A meta-analytic review of the proactive personality literature. *Journal of Vocational Behavior*, 75(3), 329–345.

Grant, A. M., & Ashford, S. J. (2008). The dynamics of proactivity at work. *Research in Organizational Behavior*, 28, 3–34.

Seibert, S. E., Crant, J. M., & Kraimer, M. L. (1999). Proactive personality and career success. *Journal of Applied Psychology*, 84(3), 416.

Thomas, J. P., Whitman, D. S., & Viswesvaran, C. (2010). Employee proactivity in organizations: A comparative meta-analysis of emergent proactive constructs. *Journal of Occupational and Organizational Psychology*, 83(2), 275–300.

PROCRASTINATION

Procrastination is the behavioral tendency to voluntarily postpone or delay intended actions of personal importance or necessity, despite discomfort and the awareness of the potential negative consequences resulting from the delay. The actions that are delayed are ones intended to be completed, not all possible actions that could be completed. This delay in actions likely leads to negative consequences in health and performance.

Procrastination may occur because of task aversion (i.e., the task is unpleasant and thus avoided), temporal distance (i.e., the task is in the distant future), or individual differences (e.g., impulsiveness), as discussed in more detail below. Instead of carrying out the intended tasks, procrastinators prefer more immediate positive behaviors, such as sleeping, watching television, reading, or completing short-term tasks with immediate rewards, such as sending e-mails. When procrastination occurs, it is not because there is an external reason to delay beginning or completing these actions (e.g., waiting for more task instructions). Rather, research suggests that procrastination is an irrational delay, such that procrastinators do not entirely understand their motives for delaying tasks. Procrastinators postpone tasks despite knowing they are likely worse off for doing so.

Prevalence

Procrastination is prevalent in 15% to 25% of the population. The frequency of procrastination in academic situations, such as delaying studying for a test or writing a term paper, is much higher, with up to 80% to 90% of college students engaging in procrastination. Procrastination has been demonstrated in contexts beyond academics. Not saving for retirement is a form of procrastination, as people start saving years too late. Waiting until the day taxes are due to file results in errors because people must rush to meet the deadline. The health field encounters procrastination in that patients put off going to the doctor or seeking treatment. In the workplace, teams often exceed their deadlines, perhaps because they delay much of their work until a deadline approaches.

Measurement

Procrastination has been measured using a number of scales that rely on self-report measures. These scales include items regarding wasting time, delaying decisions or actions, or feeling guilt about not having progressed on the task as anticipated. Several studies have demonstrated that self-reported procrastination does not always relate to actual behavioral procrastination. In a study by Kathrin Krause and Alexandra Freund, students completed a self-report trait procrastination measure and then reported their planned and actual studying time over 8 weeks. There was a moderate relationship between trait procrastination (i.e., the self-report measure) and actual procrastination (i.e., the difference between planned and actual studying time); however, only trait procrastination related to negative affective well-being. These findings suggest that measuring procrastination via behaviors may not relate to the subjective discomfort that is part of the definition of procrastination.

Outcomes

As implied by the definition of procrastination, procrastinators experience discomfort with the delay. This discomfort can be expressed as negative affect, stress, guilt, or anxiety. Procrastinators may experience less stress when a task is temporally distant; however, they experience more stress than nonprocrastinators when the deadline approaches.

Procrastination has been related to negative evaluations of performance and overall poorer performance across a variety of contexts, such as lower grades, final exam scores, and health (from delayed medical treatment). The poor performance that results from procrastination may decrease self-esteem and increase depression and anxiety. These impacts on mood can in turn increase future procrastination, resulting in a reciprocal cycle. Although much research has focused on academic performance, some studies have examined procrastination in the workplace and found that procrastination on work-related tasks increases work-related stress.

Temporal Motivation Theory

A motivational perspective on procrastination views the phenomenon as an intention-action gap. An individual who procrastinates has intentions to do the work but fails to act on these intentions, and less work is actually completed. One reason for this gap may be self-regulatory failure, meaning a decrease in self-efficacy (i.e., the belief that one can successfully complete tasks) and the ability to control one's planning, organization, and actions to reach intended goals. As the deadline nears, the gap between a procrastinator's intention and action decreases and sometimes even reverses, such that right before the deadline, the procrastinator may do more work than he or she intended. The intention-action gap relates to temporal proximity. The further away a deadline or necessity of a task, the less one may be influenced to do it, and the more likely procrastination will occur.

Piers Steel and Cornelius König's temporal motivation theory incorporates the motivational and self-regulatory literature and provides a theoretical framework for procrastination that incorporates temporal proximity. The value or importance of a delayed outcome becomes increasingly greater as the outcome gets closer. As the delay decreases and the value of completing the task increases, motivation to actually complete the task increases. This can most simply be expressed in the equation:

$$\text{Utility} = (\text{Expectancy} \times \text{Value}) / (\text{Delay} \times \text{Sensitive to Delay}).$$

Utility is the desirability of a task, with the assumption that the task with the highest utility (or motivation) will be acted upon by the individual. Expectancy reflects self-efficacy, or the belief that one can complete the task. Value represents how pleasurable the task is, such that if a task is unpleasant or boring, it will have less value. Sensitivity to delay relates to an individual's impulsiveness or lack of control. Delay is the delay of rewards or punishment.

Temporal motivation theory can be applied to procrastination. For example, consider a student studying for an exam or socializing with friends. At the beginning of the period leading to the exam, socializing is more pleasant (i.e., higher value) and the reward of studying is in the future (i.e., higher delay). Thus, socializing holds more utility than studying, leading the student to socialize instead of study. When the exam date nears, studying will then hold more utility than socializing.

Procrastination and Individual Differences

Procrastination is related to several individual differences, including personality traits. Neuroticism is positively related to procrastination, as those high in neuroticism may irrationally believe that they are inadequate. Highly neurotic individuals may use procrastination as a way to self-handicap by limiting their time to complete the task and using this limited time as a potential excuse in the event of failure. Conscientiousness also shares conceptual overlap with procrastination, as conscientiousness measures the ability to be hard working and diligent. When procrastinating, there is a lack of motivation to complete the intended task, supporting the negative relationship studies have shown between conscientiousness and procrastination. Procrastination is related to impulsiveness and sensation seeking. Those who are impulsive focus more on the gratification from short-term tasks rather than long-term tasks, and those who are sensation seeking may find it enticing to delay their actions. The deliberate intention to delay an action is referred to by some researchers as active procrastination.

Active Versus Passive Procrastination

Passive procrastination can be considered procrastination in the traditional sense, such that the delay of beginning or completing an intended task is associated with negative consequences such as emotional discomfort or stress. Alternatively, active procrastination includes the deliberate decision to delay a task because one likes to work under pressure and/or feels able to complete the task in a short time before the deadline. Active procrastinators have been found to have more similarities to nonprocrastinators than traditional procrastinators, as they tend to have higher self-efficacy and better time management than passive procrastinators, who tend to have poor self-regulatory processes.

Some researchers argue that active procrastination is not a type of procrastination but rather a form of strategic delay. The consideration of active procrastination as a type of procrastination or as a strategic delay relates to how one defines procrastination. Procrastination differs from strategic delay because procrastination occurs when the delay is both irrational and accompanied by discomforts. This suggests that there is no functional form of procrastination that benefits the procrastinator. Active procrastinators are deliberately delaying the task, and thus their delay does not seem irrational. Although the mechanisms for active procrastination may differ from procrastination viewed in the traditional sense, some researchers have found that active delay is not conducive to learning as active procrastinators have high work avoidance and low motivation.

Interventions

Goal setting and goal orientation provide techniques to decrease procrastination. Setting proximal goals decreases the temporal delay of tasks, increasing motivation and reducing procrastination. Even if the intended outcome or task deadline is in the future, goals can shift the focus toward completing piecemeal actions rather than the entire task. Time management training also helps decrease procrastination by making individuals aware of their important future goals and helping them assess how they currently use their time to reach these goals. Through time management, individuals should feel in control and be better able to manage their time by maintaining focus on future outcomes. Other interventions focus on decreasing distractions that may tempt individuals because these rewards are more immediate than the task at hand. For instance, limiting the checking of e-mail or reducing the visibility of e-mail alerts could reduce the temptation to respond to e-mails and decrease procrastination on the intended task.

Jennifer P. Green

See also Goal Orientation; Goal-Setting Theory; Self-Efficacy; Self-Regulation Theory; Work Motivation

Further Readings

Ferrari, J. R., Johnson, J. L., & McCown, W. G. (1995). *Procrastination and task avoidance: Theory, research, and treatment*. New York: Springer Science & Business Media.

Klingsieck, K. B. (2015). Procrastination: When good things don't come to those who wait. *European Psychologist, 18*, 24–34.

Krause, K., & Freund, A. M. (2014). Delay or procrastination—A comparison of self-report and behavioral measures of procrastination and their impact on affective well-being. *Personality and Individual Differences, 63*, 75–80.

Steel, P. (2007). The nature of procrastination: A meta-analytic and theoretical review of quintessential self-regulatory failure. *Psychological Bulletin, 133*, 65–94.

Steel, P. (2010). Arousal, avoidant and decisional procrastinators: Do they exist? *Personality and Individual Differences, 48*, 926–934.

Van Eerde, W. (2003). Procrastination at work and time management training. *Journal of Psychology, 137*, 421–434.

PROFIT SHARING

See Gainsharing and Profit Sharing

PROGRAM EVALUATION

Historically, program evaluation has been used as a tool for assessing the merits of educational and governmental programs, where public funding demands a demonstration of accountability. The basic tenet underlying program evaluation that makes it so useful in this context is its reliance on methods that integrate science and practice to produce reliable and actionable information for decision makers. During the past decade, program evaluation has also become increasingly recognized as a useful tool for helping for-profit organizations implement and enhance human resource (HR) programs to achieve key business outcomes. Successful companies understand that survival and growth in the marketplace cannot occur without programs that are designed to improve competitive performance and productivity, engage employees in the organization's mission, and create an environment where people want to work. Recognizing the impact that HR programs have on employees and the company's bottom line, organizations need practical tools to accurately and efficiently evaluate program quality, so that they can take the necessary actions to either improve or replace them.

The field of program evaluation is based on the commonsense notion that programs should produce demonstrable benefits. Evaluation is a discipline of study that concentrates on determining the value or merit of an object. The term *program* in this entry refers to the object of the evaluation and includes such organizational functions as recruitment and staffing, compensation, performance management, succession planning, training, team building, organizational communications, and health and work–life balance.

Evaluations can help organizations identify how a program can be improved on an ongoing basis or examine its overall worth. The first approach, called *formative evaluation*, is usually conducted while the program is being formed or implemented and will generally lead to recommendations that focus on program adjustments. The specific findings might be used to identify program challenges and opportunities and provide strategies for continuous improvement. Formative evaluations seek to improve efficiency and ensure that the program is responsive to changing organizational needs.

An evaluation that is conducted to examine a program's overall worth is called a *summative evaluation* and will generally be performed when an organization is attempting to determine if the program should be replaced, rather than modified. This approach focuses on the program's outcomes and their value to the organization. The specific findings are used to address accountability or the overall merits of the program. Some decisions to replace a program or major parts of the program are easy because of major program deficiencies. However, most such decisions will be more difficult because of the need to weigh multiple strengths and weaknesses of the program as well as other considerations such as resource constraints like budget, staffing, and time.

A Six-Phase Approach to Program Evaluation

There are a variety of approaches for conducting an evaluation, but most proceed through a similar sequence of steps and decision points. We have grouped these steps and decision points into a six-phase approach for executing a successful evaluation:

1. Identifying stakeholders, evaluators, and evaluation questions

2. Planning the evaluation

3. Collecting data

4. Analyzing and interpreting the data

5. Communicating findings and insights

6. Using the results

Although other approaches and actual HR program evaluations may over- or underemphasize some steps within these phases or accomplish a step in an earlier or later phase, any evaluation will need to address the activities covered within each of the six phases. Deviations from these six phases may be related to the nature of the specific

HR program being evaluated, characteristics of the organization, composition of the evaluation team, or a variety of resource considerations.

Phase 1: Identify Stakeholders, Evaluators, and Evaluation Questions

Phase 1 requires three major sets of decisions that will have implications throughout the HR program evaluation. The identification of stakeholders is a critical first step toward ensuring that the evaluation is appropriately structured and that the results will be relevant. Stakeholders are those individuals with a direct interest in the program, because either they depend on or are directly involved in its execution in some way. An organization's leaders, the HR and legal departments, as well as other internal groups are often important stakeholders in an HR program evaluation. External stakeholders such as stockholders and customers might also need to be considered because of their potential investment in the targeted program. Accounting for stakeholders' different perspectives from the start of a program evaluation can bring two important benefits: increased buy-in to the process and decreased resistance to change. Sometimes representative groups of stakeholders also serve on an advisory panel to the evaluation team to provide guidance throughout the process and assist with needed resources.

Another decision to be made in Phase 1 involves identifying the evaluators. Although a single evaluator can conduct evaluations, we and other professionals generally recommend that a team be formed to plan and execute the evaluation process. A team approach speeds up the process and increases the likelihood that the right combination of skills is present to generate valid findings and recommendations. Using a single evaluator may limit the choice of evaluation methods to those that feel most comfortable, rather than identifying the most appropriate methods. Also, more than one explanation can often be given for a finding, and the ability to see patterns and alternative interpretations is enhanced when a team conducts an evaluation.

Identifying evaluation questions constitutes a third type of critical decision made in Phase 1. An essential ingredient to valid findings and recommendations is identifying well-focused, answerable questions at the beginning of the project that address the needs of the stakeholders. The way the evaluation questions are posed has implications for the kinds and sources of data to be collected, data analyses, and the conclusions that can be drawn. Therefore, the evaluation team must arrive at evaluation questions that not only address the needs of the stakeholders but that are also answerable within the organizational constraints that the team will face.

In many cases, stakeholder groups, evaluators, and evaluation questions will be obvious on the basis of the nature of the HR program and the events that led to its evaluation. Any number of events can precipitate a decision to conduct an HR program evaluation. These events can vary from a regularly scheduled review of a program that appears to be working properly, such as a review of the HR information system every 3 years, to the need for a program to be certified, which could be a safety inspection in a nuclear power plant, to a major revamping of a program caused by a significant or high-visibility event such as a publicized gender discrimination case.

Phase 2: Plan the Evaluation

Phase 2 focuses on designing the HR program evaluation, developing a budget, and constructing the timeline to accomplish the steps throughout the next four phases of the evaluation. A good evaluation design enhances the credibility of findings and recommendations by incorporating a sound methodological approach, minimizing time and resource requirements, and ensuring stakeholder buy-in. A well-executed evaluation requires a good deal of front-end planning to ensure that the factors likely to affect the quality of the results can be addressed. Failure to spend the time necessary to fully plan the evaluation can result in a good deal of rework, missed milestones, unmet expectations, and other problems that make findings and recommendations difficult to sell to upper management and other stakeholders.

An often overlooked aspect of the planning phase is the need to develop a realistic budget that is reviewed and approved by the sponsors of the evaluation. The evaluation team's budget should include, among other things, staffing, travel, special equipment, and space requirements. The extent of the evaluation plan will depend on the size and scope of the HR program being evaluated and the methods used in the analysis. The goal is to obtain credible answers to the evaluation questions through sound methodology and by using only those organizational resources that are absolutely required.

Phase 3: Collect Data

In most HR program evaluations, data collection will require more time than any other phase. The credibility of the evaluation's conclusions and recommendations rests largely with the quality of the data assembled, so a good deal of attention needs to be paid to *getting it right*. It is critical that this phase be carefully planned so that the data adequately answer the evaluation questions and provide the evidence needed to support decisions regarding the targeted program.

The tasks performed for this phase are concentrated on four primary sets of overlapping activities, which include

- ensuring that the proper data collection methods have been selected to properly evaluate the HR program,
- using data collection strategies that take into account organizational resource limitations,
- establishing quality control measures, and
- building efficiency into the data collection process.

A program evaluation will only be as good as the data used to evaluate its effectiveness. The ultimate goal is to deliver the most useful and accurate information to key stakeholders in the most cost-effective and realistic manner.

In general, it is wise to use multiple methods of data collection to ensure the accuracy, consistency, and quality of results. Specifically, a combination of quantitative methods such as surveys and qualitative methods such as interviews will typically result in a richer understanding of the program and more confidence in the accuracy of the results.

Phase 4: Analyze and Interpret Data

Statistical data analyses and interpretation of the results are an integral part of most HR evaluation programs. The evaluation plan and goals should dictate the types of statistical analyses to be used in interpreting the data. Many evaluation questions can be answered through the use of simple descriptive statistics, such as frequency distributions, means and medians, and cross-tabulations. Other questions may require more sophisticated analyses that highlight trends and surface important subtleties in the data. The use of advanced statistical techniques may require specialized professional knowledge unavailable among the evaluation team members. If so, the team may need to obtain outside assistance. The evaluation team is ultimately responsible for using statistical procedures that will generate practically meaningful interpretations and address the evaluation questions.

Simpler is often better in choosing statistical procedures, because the evaluation team must be able to explain the procedures, assumptions, and findings to key stakeholders who are likely to be less methodologically sophisticated than the team members. The inability to explain and defend the procedures used to generate findings—particularly those that might disagree with a key stakeholder's perspective—could lead to concerns about those findings, as well as the total program evaluation effort.

Phase 5: Communicate Findings and Insights

Phase 5 focuses on strategies for ensuring that evaluation results are meaningfully communicated. With all the information produced by an evaluation, the evaluation team must differentiate what is essential to communicate from what is simply interesting and identify the most effective medium for disseminating information to each stakeholder group. Regardless of the group, the information must be conveyed in a way that engenders ownership of the results and motivation to act on the findings.

Each stakeholder group will likely have its own set of questions and criteria for judging program effectiveness. As such, the evaluation team needs to engage these groups in discussions about how and when to best communicate the progress and findings of the evaluation. Gaining a commitment to an ongoing dialogue with stakeholders increases ownership of and motivation to act on what is learned. Nurturing this relationship throughout the project helps the evaluation team make timely and appropriate refinements to the evaluation design, questions, methods, and data interpretations.

The extent and nature of these information exchanges should be established during the planning phase of the evaluation (i.e., Phase 2). Thereafter, the agreed-on communication plan, with timelines and milestones, should be followed throughout the evaluation.

Phase 6: Use the Results

In reviewing the literature on program evaluation, the chief criticism that emerges is that evaluation reports frequently go unread and findings are rarely used. Although credible findings should be enough to drive actions, this is rarely a sufficient condition. Putting knowledge to use is probably the most important yet intransigent challenge facing program evaluators. Furthermore, the literature on both program evaluation and organizational development indicates that planned interventions and change within an organization are likely to be met with resistance. The nature and source of this resistance will depend on the program, stakeholders involved, and culture of the organization. By understanding that resistance to change is a natural state for individuals and organizations, the program evaluation team can better anticipate and address this challenge to the use of program evaluation results.

Decisions about whether to implement recommendations (e.g., to adjust, replace, or drop an HR program) will be driven by various considerations. Ideally, the nature of the stakeholder questions and the resulting findings heavily influence how recommendations are formulated. In addition, the evaluation approach, such as formative versus summative, will influence which recommendations are implemented. A primary consideration in the adjust–replace–drop decision is cost. In most cases, the short-term costs will probably favor modification of the existing program, and the long-term costs will probably favor replacement. It should be noted that replacing an HR program is almost always more disruptive than adjusting an existing system. In these situations it is not uncommon for program staff members, users, and other key stakeholders to take a short-term perspective and prefer workarounds and other program inefficiencies instead of the uncertainty that comes with a replacement program.

The Joint Committee on Standards for Educational Evaluation (founded by the American Educational Research Association, the American Psychological Association, and the National Council on Measurement in Education in 1975) published a set of standards organized around the major tasks conducted in a program evaluation. Anyone embarking on a program evaluation would benefit from a review of these standards. Other useful readings on the subject are listed below.

John C. Scott, Nambury S. Raju, and Jack E. Edwards

See also Compensation; Organizational Communication, Formal; Organizational Communication, Informal; Recruitment; Succession Planning; Team Building; Training; Work–Life Balance

Further Readings

Davidson, E. J. (2004). *Evaluation methodology basics: The nuts and bolts of sound evaluation.* Thousand Oaks, CA: Sage.

Edwards, J. E., Scott, J. C., & Raju, N. S. (Eds.). (2003). *The human resources program-evaluation handbook.* Thousand Oaks, CA: Sage.

Joint Committee on Standards for Educational Evaluation. (2011). *The program evaluation standards: How to assess evaluations of educational programs* (3rd ed.). Thousand Oaks, CA: Sage.

Morris, L. L., Fitz-Gibbon, C. T., & Freeman, M. E. (1987). *How to communicate evaluation findings.* Beverly Hills, CA: Sage.

National Science Foundation. (1993). *User-friendly handbook for project evaluation: Science, mathematics, engineering and technology education* (NSF 93-152). Arlington, VA: Author.

Patton, M. Q. (2008). *Utilization-focused evaluation* (4th ed.). Thousand Oaks, CA: Sage.

Rose, D. S., & Davidson, E. J. (2003). Overview of program evaluation. In J. E. Edwards, J. C. Scott, & N. S. Raju (Eds.), *The human resources program-evaluation handbook* (pp. 3–26). Thousand Oaks, CA: Sage.

Rossi, P. H., Lipsey, M.W., & Freeman, H. E. (2004). *Evaluation: A systematic approach* (7th ed.). Thousand Oaks, CA: Sage.

Scriven, M. (1991). *Evaluation thesaurus* (4th ed.). Beverly Hills, CA: Sage.

Wholey, J. S., Hatry, H. P., & Newcomer, K. E. (Eds.). (1994). *Handbook of practical program evaluation.* San Francisco, CA: Jossey-Bass.

PROJECT A

Project A was the name applied by the U.S. Army to its contribution to the Joint-Service Job Performance Measurement/Enlistment Standards (JPM) project, sponsored by the Department of Defense (DoD) in 1982. Lasting until 1989, Project A, which also comprises the follow-on Career Force project (examining performance during soldiers' second tours of duty and spanning 1990 through 1994), is arguably the largest selection and classification project ever conducted, involving more than 50,000 enlisted personnel in global data collections before the widespread use of computers and similar technology. Results from Project A continue to shape the way the Army selects, assigns, trains, and promotes its soldiers. Project A data remain a rich storehouse of information about individual differences and job performance. Project results and data have also had an impact on the field of industrial and organizational psychology at large, having sparked theoretical developments regarding models of job performance (contextual performance, determinants of relevant variance), a resurgence in interest regarding personality tests as selection tools, and the development of models for setting recruit enlistment standards.

The Joint-Service Job Performance Measurement/ Enlistment Standards Project

The JPM project was a congressionally mandated multimillion dollar effort that spanned 1982 through 1994. The impetus for JPM was the discovery of a scoring error that inflated the scores of lower aptitude recruits on the Armed Services Vocational Aptitude Battery (ASVAB). This miscalibration of ASVAB scores led to the enlistment of approximately 250,000 individuals who otherwise would not have qualified for entrance and increased congressional concerns about recruit quality.

In response to the miscalibration, the DoD initiated the JPM project. Two primary goals of the JPM project were to determine if the ASVAB predicted job performance and whether hands-on job performance could be measured. If so, the DoD could set enlistment standards (partly determined by scores on the ASVAB) on the basis of that job performance information. Previous standards

were tied to training success rather than job performance, and the ASVAB was validated against training performance but not against performance on the job in the field.

The DoD encouraged each branch of the armed forces to conduct its own research for JPM. The U.S. Army Research Institute for the Behavioral and Social Sciences sponsored the Army's effort. The Army's approach was ambitious, expanding the predictor and criterion domains by developing new entry-level selection and performance measures.

Study Design

Project A included both concurrent validation (CV) and longitudinal validation (LV) samples. The CV cohort included soldiers who enlisted during the 1983 and 1984 fiscal years. These soldiers completed the new selection and performance measures at the same time, approximately 2 years into their first tours of duty (CVI sample). Those soldiers who reenlisted were eligible to complete measures of second-tour (supervisory) performance (CVII sample). Soldiers in the LV cohort enlisted during the 1985 and 1986 fiscal years. They received the Experimental Battery during their first 2 days in the Army (LVP sample), measures of training performance at the end of technical training for their jobs (LVT sample), and measures of job performance once in their units approximately 2 years after enlistment (LVI) and during their second tours (LVII).

The project collected data on soldiers from 21 military occupational specialties (MOSs; i.e., jobs). The full complement of performance measures (written test of job knowledge and hands-on tests in particular) was developed for 10 of these, which were deemed Batch A MOS. They tended to be high-density jobs of central importance to Army functioning, such as infantryman, light wheel mechanic, and medical specialist. The other 11 Batch Z MOS reflected more specialized, lower density occupations, including ammunition specialist, utility helicopter repairer, and intelligence analyst; they did not have hands-on measures developed for them.

Criterion Measures

To determine whether ASVAB scores predicted job performance, the Army developed numerous performance measures to serve as criteria for its validation and performance modeling studies. Selection studies are only as meaningful as the criteria used, and Project A addressed the traditional criterion problem head-on. This approach of obtaining multiple measures of multiple job behaviors broke with conventional notions that viewed job performance as unitary, hypothesizing instead that job performance was not a single entity but was instead a complex variable to study.

Two broad categories of criterion content were considered: performance elements that are specific to a particular job (assessed by MOS-specific measures) and performance elements that are relevant to all jobs (assessed by Army-wide measures). Criteria were also categorized as *can-do* measures (assessing how well soldiers are able to perform) and *will-do* measures (assessing how well soldiers typically perform from day to day). The criteria included written tests of MOS-specific job knowledge, hands-on performance tests (also known as *work samples*), various anchored rating scales (MOS-specific performance for Batch A and performance on Army-wide dimensions for all MOS), and data from administrative files such as letters of commendation and counseling statements.

Predictor Measures

In addition to evaluating whether ASVAB scores predicted job performance, the Project A research team investigated the degree to which measures of other individual differences could increase the predictive power of this test battery. Measures of spatial ability, perceptual speed and accuracy, psychomotor ability, temperament, vocational interests, and work values, collectively denoted the Trial Battery (CV sample) and Experimental Battery (LV sample), were developed, administered to thousands of soldiers, and correlated with the various criterion measures. Results were obtained for the Army as a whole and by subgroups of interest (MOS, race/ethnicity, gender).

Major Findings

Results from Project A research and their implications for personnel psychology have filled journals and books. Some of the major findings from the project include the following:

- ASVAB is a valid predictor of performance across Army jobs and across subgroups (race/ethnicity, gender). Soldiers with higher aptitude perform better than lower aptitude soldiers on many types of performance measures.
- Measures of other ability constructs, such as spatial ability, perceptual speed and accuracy, and psychomotor ability, also predict performance across jobs but provide little incremental validity to the ASVAB.
- Performance is not unidimensional but is instead a complex multidimensional construct.
- ASVAB scores predict maximal performance (can-do criteria) better than they predict typical performance (will-do criteria).
- Measures of noncognitive constructs, such as temperament, collected under research conditions predict will-do criteria better than ASVAB, and they provide substantial incremental validity to ASVAB.
- Criterion-related validity of ASVAB scores assessed longitudinally was very similar for first-tour (LVI) and second-tour (LVII) soldiers. Noncognitive measures, however, tended to show declining correlations over time.
- The elements of performance are similar as a soldier gains experience, but leadership emerges as a performance element in the second tour.
- First-tour performance provides more incremental validity than ASVAB when predicting leadership and effort during the second tour, but it provides less incremental validity for can-do performance criteria.

Rodney A. McCloy

See also Job Performance Models; Selection Strategies; Validation Strategies; Work Samples

Further Readings

Campbell, J. P., & Knapp, D. J. (Eds.). (2001). *Exploring the limits in personnel selection and classification.* Mahwah, NJ: Erlbaum.

Project A: The U.S. Army selection and classification project. (1990). *Personnel Psychology, 43*(2).

Zook, L. M. (1996). *Soldier selection: Past, present, and future.* Alexandria, VA: U.S. Army Research Institute for the Behavioral and Social Sciences.

PROSOCIAL VALUES

Prosocial values are one category of a broader typology known as social value orientation (SVO). An individual's SVO is his or her approach to allocating resources between himself or herself and another person. SVO is predicated on the concept that individuals are not purely motivated to be self-serving; in fact, there may be individual differences with regard to one's desire to benefit others or the group relative to attempting only to maximize outcomes for oneself. Historically, SVO has had three main categories: *prosocial* (also called cooperation; i.e., being motivated to maximize outcomes for self and others), *individualism* (i.e., being motivated to maximize one's own outcomes with little or no consideration for the outcomes of others), and *competition* (i.e., being motivated to maximize one's own outcomes relative to the outcomes of others). While those espousing a prosocial orientation are often referred to as *prosocials*, taken together, individualists and cooperators are referred to as *proselfs*. More recent work has argued that the prosocial (cooperation) orientation should in fact be divided into two categories: *cooperation* (maximizing outcomes for both self and others) and *equality* (being motivated by a desire to obtain equal outcomes or to reduce the amount of difference between the outcomes obtained for oneself and those obtained for others).

The notion of prosocial values has particular relevance in today's business context as individuals and organizations strive to advance the greater good via traditional work activities. For example, the proliferation of corporate social responsibility (CSR) programs, environmental sustainability programs, and other prosocial efforts has helped create an environment in which employees are seeking jobs whereby they can actively live and promote prosocial values while they are working. In addition, understanding the impact of prosocial values on human behavior may provide additional insights into a variety of work-related issues, including but not limited to leadership development, people management, resource allocation decisions, problem solving, negotiation, and fairness perceptions.

Origins and Measurement

The concept of SVO is rooted in the study of decision making. Researchers generally believed that individuals would strongly tend to favor their own outcomes in a wide variety of decision-making tasks. However, it was uncovered that some individuals do tend to behave prosocially (i.e., by demonstrating concern for others). Early work in this area examined the choices people made in interdependent situations (i.e., situations in which joint outcomes depend on both the choice of the individual participating in the decision-making process and the beliefs that individual holds about the choices an unknown "other" would make; e.g., the prisoner's dilemma).

Research in this area evolved and led to the development of "decomposed" games that aimed to disentangle the influence of a decision maker's beliefs about the intentions of another person when understanding the choices the decision maker made. Of the three primary measures of a person's SVO in use today, the first two are decomposed games. The ring measure and the triple dominance measure require participants to allocate money or other resources to themselves and others. The third measure, known as the slider measure, is based on the decomposed game technique, but it takes the form of a questionnaire that asks participants to select their preferred resource allocations from a variety of options.

Applications

SVO and prosocial values in particular have been considered across three broad contexts within the field of industrial and organizational (I-O) psychology: individuals, organizations, and (humanitarian) causes. At the individual level, the values leaders espouse have been shown to have important relationships with leadership style, behaviors, and professional outcomes, and prosocial values in particular have been shown to be related to a wide range of variables of interest. Research questions include understanding the impact of prosocial motivations at work on outcomes such as decision making and problem solving; studies of leaders and business philosophies that have as a core objective promotion of the greater good (e.g., triple-bottom-line—people, planet, profit—approaches); deeper understanding of values-based leadership models; and studies of the relationship between prosocial leaders and organizational culture and values.

When thought of at the organizational level, prosocial values research has explored not only the more traditionally prosocial organizations, such as nonprofits, but also corporate organizations and the proliferation of CSR programs. In both for-profit and nonprofit organizations, there are clear implications for the understanding of prosocial values across a wide range of I-O–related concepts, such as understanding how to manage a diversity of workers motivated by different objectives (e.g., profitability vs. promoting the collective good), understanding the unique needs of volunteer and unpaid staff members in the nonprofit space, and considering the ideal recruiting and selection processes for prosocially oriented organizations.

Finally, work in the prosocial values space can also be applied to broader societal and humanitarian "causes," such as the provision of humanitarian aid after natural disasters and promoting the collective good by addressing macro-level global and economic issues such as poverty or the development of third world countries. Although research in these areas is in its emerging stages, it has led to the development of a growing subfield of I-O known as humanitarian work psychology.

Relationship to Other Variables of Interest

In part because decision making and resource allocation are core to the human experience, SVO and prosocial values have been examined as both antecedents and outcomes of other variables. Although some researchers have noted that a prosocial orientation can be affected by transient factors (e.g., mood, the likeability of the "other" person in a decision-making game), the construct is often treated as though it is expected to be relatively stable over time. Researchers, including those outside the field of I-O psychology, have explored the longer term impacts of factors such as cognitive and moral development, parental care, and discipline methods on the development of prosocial orientation in children and adults. Within the more traditional I-O space, variables such as job satisfaction, mood, leader fairness, and task characteristics have all been studied as possible antecedents of prosocial values.

Looking at potential outcomes of prosocial values, researchers have considered a wide range of variables. For example, increases in helping behavior, changes in motivation, performance, and job satisfaction, increases in organizational citizenship behaviors (or discretionary behaviors that promote organizational functioning), improvements in interdepartmental problem-solving behaviors, decisions around commuting preferences, increases in pro-environmental behaviors, and increases in integrative negotiation outcomes have all been linked to prosocial values.

Future Directions

The concept of prosocial values presents a unique opportunity to link together broad fields of interest (e.g., I-O psychology, humanitarian work psychology, community psychology) by making connections in a way that has not been readily enabled by other variables or concepts. In addition, it has been the genesis for research at both the individual and organizational levels and has been explored as both an independent and a dependent variable. Thus, the discovery that individuals do not always make decisions aligned solely with their own self-interest has led to a complex web of articles and studies designed to understand the causes and consequences of a prosocial value orientation.

Interest in SVO and prosocial values appears to be increasing as individuals and organizations more directly focus their time and energy on understanding how to promote the greater good and build their personal and corporate brands around positive societal change. Because prosocial values are so broadly applicable within the human context, research in this area is benefitting from a diversity of methodologies, perspectives, and approaches. However, it is already evident in the existing literature that this diversity of thought has at times created confusion over the definition of prosocial values and the difference between prosocial values and prosocial behavior. Future researchers will need to continue to be particularly sensitive to these concerns.

Christine E. Corbet

See also Contextual Performance/Prosocial Behavior/ Organizational Citizenship Behavior; Corporate Ethics; Corporate Social Responsibility; Industrial and Organizational Psychology, Poverty Reduction, and Prosocial Initiatives; Judgment and Decision-Making Process; Triple Bottom Line; Volunteer Management; Work Values

Further Readings

Eek, D., & Gärling, T. (2008). A new look at the theory of social value orientations: Prosocials neither maximize joint outcome nor minimize outcome differences but prefer equal outcomes. In A. Biel, D. Eek, T. Gärling, & M. Gustafson (Eds.), *New issues and paradigms in research on social dilemmas* (pp. 10–26). New York: Springer. doi:10.1007/978-0-387-72596-3

Grant, A. M. (2009). Putting self-interest out of business? Contributions and unanswered questions from use-inspired research on prosocial motivation. *Industrial and Organizational Psychology, 2*, 94–98. doi:10.1111/j.1754-9434.2008.01113.x

Liebrand, W. B. G., Jansen, R. W. T. L., Rijken, V. M., & Suhre, C. J. M. (1986). Might over morality: Social values and the perception of other players in experimental games. *Journal of Experimental Social Psychology, 22*, 203–215. doi:10.1016/0022-1031(86)90024-7

McClintock, C. G. (1978). Social values: Their definition, measurement, and development. *Journal of Research and Development in Education, 12*, 121–137.

Messick, D. M., & McClintock, C. G. (1968). Motivational bases of choice in experimental games. *Journal of Experimental Social Psychology, 4*, 1–25.

Van Lange, P. A. M. (1999). The pursuit of joint outcomes and equality in outcomes: An integrative model of social value orientation. *Journal of Personality and Social Psychology, 77*, 337–349. doi:10.1037/0022-3514.77.2.337

PROSPECT THEORY

Prospect theory is a psychological depiction of how people make choices between different outcomes or prospects under conditions of uncertainty and therefore risk. Since its introduction by Daniel Kahneman and Amos Tversky, prospect theory has been the leading alternative to expected utility as a theory for decision making in situations involving risk. Prospect theory posits that people think in terms of gains and losses from a set reference point as opposed to net levels of assets. In other words, relative gains and relative losses are more important than absolute gains and losses. The identified reference point is crucial in decision making because it determines the weight of the relative loss or gain.

When assigning value weights (i.e., utility) to gains and losses, more weight or value is given to losses than to an equally comparable gain. Therefore, people are generally risk averse toward gains and risk seeking toward losses. Although early work in prospect theory was conducted using choices between monetary outcomes, the majority of the findings can be generalized to other contexts of risky choices. Indeed, many phenomena examined within the field of industrial and organizational psychology involve some form or aspect of decision making. To understand how people choose between alternatives within organizations, further explanation of the value and weighting function is needed.

Value Function

When faced with a decision involving risk, people tend to think in terms of relative gains and losses rather than absolute or net levels of assets. To determine a relative gain or relative loss, people first set a reference point, which is used to anchor the alternative decision outcomes. Once the reference point is set, people then encode the decision alternatives compared with the set reference point. The encoding process is merely taking into account the deviations from the reference point. From this perspective, value (i.e., utility) is determined by the actual deviations from the reference point, rather than the resulting net asset level. Although net asset levels matter in principle, preference between prospects is not greatly affected by small to moderate changes in asset position. Typically, the reference point selected by people is derived from their current situation or their status quo. For example, when determining between risky decisions involving an investment, the reference point is typically the amount of funds in the investment account or the total amount of wealth controlled by the person. However, not all reference points are based on current situations or the status quo. People can also set a reference point on the basis of an aspirational level or some desirable level of utility. In these types of situations, people craft a conceptualization as the reference point and examine the deviations involved with decision outcomes.

A key concept that pertains to prospect theory is that the deviations from the reference point are not treated equally. First, people tend to display risk-averse behaviors with respect to gains and risk-seeking behaviors with respect to losses. To illustrate, a classic experiment found that 80% of participants preferred a certain outcome of $1,000 to an 80% chance of $2,000 and a 20% chance of nothing. If faced with the same values but experienced as a potential loss, 92% of participants preferred an 80% chance of losing $2,000 and a 20% chance of losing nothing to a certain loss of $1,000.

Prospect theory suggests that value functions are concave with respect to gains and convex with respect to losses. This depiction departs from expected utility in that value assigned to gains and losses is not considered a strictly concave or strictly convex phenomenon. Rather, this asymmetry around the reference point involves both concave and convex functions and is referred to as the reflection effect. When examining the asymmetry that is formed around the reference point, it is clear that sensitivity in the value of gains or losses decreases as one moves further from the reference point. This principal is reflected in diminishing marginal utility, in which the value of each gain or loss is considered less than the preceding gain or loss, respectively.

Second, people tend to treat losses differently than gains. Losses loom larger than gains. In other words, the value of a loss is treated more severely and upsets an individual more than the same amount gained would make someone happy. Returning to the reflection effect, the convex curve associated with gains is not symmetrically reflected in the concave function of losses. People are more sensitive to small changes in losses compared with small changes in gains. Because losses are valued higher than gains, people display loss aversion. Loss aversion is a tendency to strongly prefer avoiding losses rather than acquiring gains. Implicit to loss aversion is the assumption that what is currently possessed by an individual has more value than a comparable object not possessed. Indeed, the mere process of acquiring an object enhances the value of the object. When people ascribe more value to objects merely because they own them, they are displaying an endowment effect.

Because of loss aversion and the endowment effect, individuals often wish to sell items at higher prices than they are willing to purchase similar items. Indeed, the minimum price people desire to sell has often been found to be several times larger than the maximum price they are willing to pay.

Similarly, people tend to overweight actual losses compared with opportunity costs (nonacquired gains) regardless whether the opportunity costs are greater than the actual losses. Preferences for decision outcomes are highly contingent on whether the prospective outcomes are already considered to be currently possessed or endowed by the individual. Although both are considered to be losses, the way the losses are experienced by the individual are different because of the way the situation is framed. Situations can be presented either negatively or positively, producing framing effects.

Framing effects occur when equivalent descriptions of a decision problem lead to systematically different decisions because of the emphasis on gains (positive frame) rather than losses (negative frame). Framing effects demonstrate the flaw in rational models of human agents, who should select options that maximize utility regardless of how the decision is presented. The most famous experiment of framing effects presented participants with a choice on how to resolve a deadly disease outbreak. Participants in the positive frame were given a choice between adopting a program that would save 200 people (while 400 would die) or adopting another program in which there is a one-third chance that 600 people would be saved and a two-thirds chance that no one would be saved. Participants in the negative frame were presented with an option that if adopted would result in 400 deaths (200 saved) or an option in which there was a one-third chance that nobody would die and a two-thirds chance that 600 people would die.

Although both situations involve identical information, the way in which the situations are framed differs. Consequently, the majority of participants (72%) favored the risk-averse first option in the positive frame, whereas a similar majority of participants (78%) favored the risk-seeking second option in the negative frame. The way in which the situation is framed determines the directional shift from the reference point. In positively framed situations, there is an upward shift from the reference point, representing a gain. Conversely, in negatively framed situations, there is a downward shift from the reference point, representing a loss. Thus, the way a situation is framed has critical implications for the way an individual will decide between alternatives, regardless of mathematical equivalence.

Weighting Function

The other aspect of prospect theory that complements the value function is the weighting function. The weighting function is how people psychologically think about certainty and probabilities. Decision alternatives that involve certain outcomes are those situations in which the probability of the outcome of occurring is either 0% or 100%. Uncertain outcome are those situations in which the probability of outcome lies between 0% and 100%. Research on the weighting function suggests that people have a difficult time thinking of probabilities on a single continuum. Indeed, people tend to overweight certain outcomes relative to probable outcomes, a phenomenon termed the certainty effect. Reducing the probability by an equivalent amount has more impact when the outcome is initially certain than when the outcome is probable. A famous example to illustrate this effect is a game of Russian roulette. A person playing Russian roulette is more likely to pay far more to reduce the number of bullets from one to zero than from four to three.

Furthermore, the tendency to favor certain outcomes also has impacts on highly probable situations. When situations exhibit extremely probable outcomes, people tend to treat those outcomes as occurring with certainty. The tendency to artificially "round" up or down the uncertain probable outcome to a certain outcome is known as the pseudocertainty effect. However, when people do not artificially round the probability up or down to a certain outcome, there is a tendency to overestimate or exaggerate the small probabilities. Overweighting small probabilities can be reinforced by the availability heuristic, which is a mental shortcut that uses readily accessible examples that come to mind. The availability heuristic recalls dramatic events that influence the perception of a small probability outcome occurring. Heuristics or other motivations ultimately alter the subjective assessment of probabilities that influence decision making.

These findings of prospect theory are contrary to the expectation rule of expected-utility theory, which asserts that the utilities of risky outcomes are weighted linearly by their probabilities. Instead, people think of probabilities in three coarse categories: will happen, may happen, and will not happen.

These categories relate to high probabilities, moderate probabilities, and low probabilities, respectively. The three categories should not be thought of as existing on a linear continuum. Rather, the transition from high probabilities to moderate probabilities exhibits a large transition because of the overweighting of small probabilities and the pseudocertainty effect.

Last, there is evidence supporting that people simplify decisions between alternatives by disregarding elements of outcomes that are shared between alternatives and focusing on the differences. This phenomenon is called the isolation effect. However, alternative outcomes may be decomposed in numerous ways. Additionally, the overweighting of differences among alternatives and the simultaneous underweighting of commonalities among alternatives can lead to inconsistent preferences and therefore decisions.

Prior to 1970, research on decision making was dominated by normative theories of how people ought to make rational decisions and assumed people actually prescribed the assertions of such theories in their daily lives. Prospect theory was a notable departure from the existing theories in that it offered a descriptive theory of how people actually made risky decisions. Because of its descriptive nature, prospect theory has greatly influenced research in the fields of psychology, economics, finance, international relations, and public policy, among others. Integrating prospect theory into the field of industrial and organizational psychology yields a fruitful area of inquiry. Risky decision making is pervasive within the workplace. Many of the tenets and findings of prospect theory may offer unique contributions to research in the field of industrial and organizational psychology.

David J. Scheaf

See also Rational Decision Making Theory; Strategy

Further Readings

Arkes, H. R., & Blumer, C. (1985). The psychology of sunk cost. *Organizational Behavior and Human Decision Processes*, 35(1), 124–140.

Fiegenbaum, A., & Thomas, H. (1988). Attitudes toward risk and the risk–return paradox: prospect theory explanations. *Academy of Management Journal*, 31(1), 85–106.

Garland, H. (1990). Throwing good money after bad: The effect of sunk costs on the decision to escalate commitment to an ongoing project. *Journal of Applied Psychology, 75*(6), 728.

Kahneman, D., & Tversky, A. (1979). Prospect theory: An analysis of decision under risk. *Econometrica: Journal of the Econometric Society, 47*(2), 263–291.

Thaler, R. (1980). Toward a positive theory of consumer choice. *Journal of Economic Behavior & Organization, 1*(1), 39–60.

Tversky, A., & Kahneman, D. (1992). Advances in prospect theory: Cumulative representation of uncertainty. *Journal of Risk and Uncertainty, 5*(4), 297–323.

Wong, K. F. E., & Kwong, J. Y. (2005). Between-individual comparisons in performance evaluation: A perspective from prospect theory. *Journal of Applied Psychology, 90*(2), 284.

PROTESTANT WORK ETHIC

The notion of the *Protestant work ethic* (PWE) has its roots in Max Weber's *The Protestant Ethic and the Spirit of Capitalism*, in which he espoused the idea that the success of capitalism and economic growth throughout western Europe and North America was partly the consequence of Puritan values such as a calling to one's work and frugality with one's resources. Today, psychologists use the term *Protestant work ethic* to refer to the extent to which individuals place work at the center of their existence, abhor idleness, and value accomplishment, regardless of specific religious affiliation, if any. In fact, most research suggests few differences between religious groups on PWE endorsement, and some studies suggest that people who are non-Protestants score higher on PWE measures than do Protestants. Although there are several measures of the PWE, the most commonly used measure asks respondents the extent to which they agree or disagree (typically using a response range of 1 to 7) with statements such as the following: "The credit card is a ticket to care-less spending," "Most people who do not succeed in life are just plain lazy," and "Our society would have fewer problems if people had less leisure time."

The psychological study of the PWE has centered on two primary questions:

1. What are the antecedents of PWE endorsement?

2. What are the consequences of PWE endorsement?

Research has tended to focus more on the second of these two questions, the one more likely to be of interest to an industrial and organizational psychologist. But before examining the consequences of PWE endorsement, it is helpful to briefly examine some of its antecedents.

Antecedents of PWE Endorsement

Endorsement of the PWE is related to a general conservative ideology. Indeed, one consistent research finding is that PWE endorsement in the United States is positively correlated with extent of identification with the Republican Party. In addition, PWE endorsement is related to values such as accomplishment, salvation, obedience, and self-control. However, PWE endorsement is distinct from other forms of conservatism. For example, social dominance orientation is the belief in a societal hierarchy of groups on the basis of some group-level characteristic such as ethnic background. Right-wing authoritarianism consists of displaying high degrees of deference to established authority, acting aggressively toward societal outgroups when authorities permit such aggression, and supporting traditional values when authorities endorse those values. The PWE is related more to the notions of ambition, delay of gratification, and equitable distribution of rewards. Thus, although PWE endorsement has its roots in conservative ideology, it is distinct from general conservative orientation and other forms of conservatism.

In addition to examining its roots in general conservatism, relatively recent research has examined how PWE endorsement is a function of basic personality constructs, in particular the Big Five factors and their facets. It has been found that PWE endorsement tends to be rooted in the conscientiousness facet of achievement-striving (positive relationship), the extroversion facet of excitement-seeking (positive relationship), and the openness facet of values (negative relationship).

Consequences of PWE Endorsement

It has been reported that hiring managers placed more emphasis on a potential employee's attitude toward work than aptitude for work and that job interviews are in part intended to gain a sense of a candidate's attitude toward work. In another survey, more than half of those managers queried believed that people's attitudes toward their work were more important than even native intelligence. Thus, a number of studies have investigated the relationship between PWE endorsement (as a proxy for work attitudes) and work-related variables. In large part, these studies tend to buttress the importance of one's attitude toward work. For example, several studies indicate that PWE endorsement is positively correlated with work motivation, job-growth satisfaction, job involvement, organizational commitment, organizational citizenship behaviors, persistence in a task, and, of course, conscientiousness in performing one's duties. In addition, PWE endorsement is associated with a tendency to refrain from social loafing.

In addition to beneficial work-related outcomes, several studies have indicated that PWE endorsement is positively related to psychological well-being across different operationalizations of psychological well-being. However, two cautions of this replicated result are warranted. First, it is less clear if this finding is applicable to individuals in non-western cultures. Second and related, there is minimal evidence for why PWE endorsement is positively correlated with psychological health. It may be that because hard work is a traditional western and certainly American value; adhering to the pervasive cultural norm is the third variable responsible for this finding. Evidence for this contention comes from one study in which it was found that among overweight women, PWE endorsement was predictive of lower levels of psychological health, presumably because being overweight carries with it a stigma of being lazy. Thus, although PWE endorsement has been found to be predictive of greater psychological health, there appear to be certain boundaries on this result. Employees who endorse the PWE but are not performing up to their own or their supervisors' standards may be at risk for reduced levels of psychological well-being.

It is also important to note that PWE endorsement also appears to be related to prejudice against groups of people who violate the core value of PWE endorsement, that is, hard work. Indeed, if an employee who strongly endorses the PWE is working with fellow employees who are not pulling their weight, one might expect major impediments in such professional relationships. Likewise, for supervisors with strong PWE orientations, it might be particularly irksome to perceive that some employees are not offering their best efforts in the workplace. Even if the work itself is at least satisfactory, PWE-oriented supervisors may be biased against such employees in terms of performance appraisals and the distributions of other rewards.

What Do We Need to Know About PWE Endorsement?

Much like the constructs of *intelligence* and *extroversion*, there is wide interindividual variation in PWE endorsement. Interestingly, research strongly suggests physiological differences for why some individuals are more intelligent or more extroverted than others. Might there be a physiological disposition for PWE endorsement? The answer to this question might foster research on the PWE from investigators in a variety of disciplines. In addition, although research has attempted to understand how PWE endorsement is related to but distinct from the Big Five personality factors, additional work that disentangles PWE from the Big Five would suggest incremental utility in using PWE as a selection device. Finally, early research on PWE endorsement in the 1960s and 1970s suggested minimal concern with socially desirable responding. However, as that work is now approaching half a century in age, it would be good to revisit this important topic.

Most of this entry is based on research that has tended to treat the PWE as a unifaceted construct. However, as several researchers have demonstrated, existing measures of the PWE construct are in fact multifaceted, much as Max Weber himself conceived of the PWE. In an extensive analysis of the seven existing PWE scales, Adrian Furnham found that they tended to operationalize five different facets of the PWE. Specifically, they tapped into the importance of hard work in one's life, antileisure attitudes, religion and morality, independence from others, and asceticism. Research within personality psychology has found utility in examining smaller, more precise facets of personality as opposed to larger, more general facets of personality. Indeed, recent work on PWE endorsement has also suggested incremental value in examining PWE facets using Miller and colleagues' 65-item PWE measure. Future research in the PWE arena might benefit from continuing to address how different facets of PWE endorsement are differentially predictive of the outcomes summarized in this chapter. A relatively new measure of different PWE facets might greatly facilitate such investigations.

Andrew N. Christopher

See also Work Motivation; Work Values

Further Readings

Christopher, A. N., Furnham, A., Batey, M., Martin, G. N., Koenig, C. S., & Doty, K. (2010). Protestant ethic endorsement, personality, and general intelligence. *Learning and Individual Differences, 20*, 46–50. doi:10.1016/j.lindif.2009.10.003

Christopher, A. N., & Mull, M. S. (2006). Conservative ideology and ambivalent sexism. *Psychology of Women Quarterly, 30*, 223–230. doi:10.1111/j.1471-6402.2006.00284.x

Christopher, A. N., & Shewach, O. R. (in press). Protestant work ethic and the facets of the Big Five personality factors. *Individual Differences Research.*

Feather, N. T. (1984). Protestant ethic, conservatism, and values. *Journal of Personality and Social Psychology, 46*, 1132–1141. doi:10.1037/0022-3514.46.5.1132

Furnham, A. (1990). A content, correlational, and factor analytic study of seven questionnaire measures of the Protestant work ethic. *Human Relations, 43*, 383–399. doi:10.1177/001872679004300406

Kenrick, A. C., Shapiro, J. R., & Neuberg, S. L. (2013). Do parental bonds break anti-fat stereotyping? Parental work ethic ideology and disease concern predict bias against heavyweight children. *Social Psychological and Personality Science, 4*, 721–729. doi:10.1177/1948550613479805

Miller, M. J., Woehr, D. J., & Hudspeth, N. (2002). The meaning and measurement of work ethic: Construction and initial validation of a multidimensional inventory. *Journal of Vocational Behavior, 60*, 451–489. doi:10.1006/jvbe.2001.1838

Quinn, D. M., & Crocker, J. (1999). When ideology hurts: Effects of belief in the Protestant work ethic and feeling overweight on the psychological well-being of women. *Journal of Personality and Social Psychology, 77*, 402–414. doi:10.1037/0022-3514.77.2.402

Smrt, D. L., & Karau, S. J. (2011). Protestant work ethic moderates social loafing. *Group Dynamics: Theory, Research, and Practice, 15*, 267–274. doi:10.1037/10024484

Zulfikar, Y. F. (2012). Do Muslims believe more in Protestant work ethic than Christians? Comparison of people with difference religious background living in the U.S. *Journal of Business Ethics, 105*, 489–502. doi:10.1007/s10551-011-091-z

PSYCHOLOGICAL CONTRACT

A psychological contract is a belief based on commitments, expressed or implied, regarding an exchange agreement between two parties, as commonly used between an individual and an employer. People typically are motivated to fulfill the commitments they have made to others, consistent with their own understanding of what those commitments entail. In employment, psychological contracts can vary considerably across workers and between firms. They can be as limited to highly economic or transactional terms, such as an hourly wage for a temporary worker who ships packages over the holidays, or as complex and broad as the generous support and mutual investment characteristic of high-involvement work. Employers in turn have their own psychological contracts with individual workers.

Features of the Psychological Contract

The dynamics of the psychological contract are shaped by its defining features.

Voluntariness

Psychological contracts motivate people to fulfill their commitments because they are based on the exchange of promises in which the individual has freely participated. Commitments made voluntarily tend to be kept. A worker who agrees to work for a firm for a set time period is likely to be internally conflicted on receiving an outside offer shortly after being hired. That worker is more likely to decline the offer than a colleague who had made no such commitment to the employer.

Perceived Mutuality

An individual's psychological contract reflects the person's own understanding of the commitments made with another. Individuals act on that subjective understanding as if it were mutual, regardless of whether that is the case in reality.

Incompleteness

At the outset of employment, initial psychological contracts tend to be incomplete and need to be fleshed out over time. Neither worker nor employer can spell out all the details of an employment relationship that will last a period of time. Because of bounded rationality, neither party can recall all relevant details to be shared with another. Moreover, changing circumstances mean that not all contingencies can be foreseen. As a result, psychological contracts tend to become more elaborate and detailed over the course of the employment relationship.

Multiple Contract Makers

A variety of information sources shape how workers interpret their psychological contract with an employer. Employers are represented by several parties including the top management team; human resource representatives; and in particular, a worker's immediate superior, often the most influential agent in shaping employee psychological contracts. Informal sources such as coworkers can influence how individuals interpret the terms of their psychological contract as well as the extent to which the contract has been fulfilled. Human resource practices such as development programs and performance appraisal systems can signal promised benefits and required contributions. In particular, early experiences with an employer, from recruitment to early socialization and initial assignments to particular bosses and coworkers, can have pervasive effects over time on worker psychological contracts. When contract makers convey different messages, they erode the mutuality of the psychological contract.

Reliance Losses

When a party relies on the psychological contract as a guide to action, losses result if the other party fails to fulfill its anticipated commitments. Losses mean that benefits a party has relied on failed to materialize; and they are the basic reason why psychological contract violation and change generate adverse reactions, including anger, outrage, termination, and withdrawal of support. Efforts that both workers and employer take to manage their psychological contract with the other typically focus on fulfilling commitments as well as on managing losses when existing commitments are difficult to keep. Psychological contracts are a subset of a broader array of beliefs and expectations workers and employers may hold, where expectations that are not promise based are not relied on to the same extent as more general expectations regarding worker and employer behavior. Non–promise-based aspects of employment that workers find satisfying, such as the quality of their workspace or the camaraderie of colleagues, can eventually be viewed as part of the promised status quo—and generate negative reactions comparable to contract violations.

Automatic Processes

Once a psychological contract is formed, it creates an enduring mental model of the employment relationship. This mental model provides a stable understanding of what to expect in the future and guides efficient action without a lot of need to be refreshed or practiced. Having a psychological contract as a mental model of the employment relationship helps employer and worker function despite having incomplete information regarding the other party's intentions or expectations. Subsequent information tends to be interpreted in light of the preexisting psychological contract. For the most part, this is functional because new performance demands can be incorporated into existing understandings of a person's work role. But when existing psychological contracts are in conflict with new employment conditions, a more elaborate change process is required.

Types of Psychological Contracts

Psychological contracts can take many forms depending on the nature of the worker's job, the employer's human resource strategy, and the motives the worker has in contracting with a particular employer. Promises can be very limited in nature, as in the case of the simple economic transaction temporary work entails. Or promises workers and the employer make to each other can involve a host of relational commitments including loyalty and mutual concern. Although the myriad details of a psychological contract can be as unique as each individual, there are general patterns that differentiate how workers and employers behave toward each other.

A relational psychological contract includes such terms as *loyalty,* worker and employer commitment to meeting the needs of the other, and *stability,* an open-ended commitment to the future. Workers with relational contracts are more likely to willingly work overtime, whether paid or not, to help coworkers on the job, and to support organizational changes their employer deems necessary. Although workers with a relational contract are likely to be particularly upset when it is violated, the commitment to their employer created by such contracts often manifests in worker attempts to seek redress or remedy to maintain the relationship. Failure to remedy the situation typically leads to turnover or, should the employee remain, to reduced contributions and erosion of the employment relationship. Employers with relational contracts absorb more of the risk from economic uncertainties, often protecting workers from economic downturns. An archetypal employer with a relational contract might keep workers employed during severe economic downturns. Employers in turn offer the individual workers they particularly value more relational contracts than they do other workers who contribute less.

A transactional psychological contract includes such terms as *narrow duties* and *limited* or *short-term duration.* Workers with transactional contracts are likely to adhere to its specific terms and seek employment elsewhere when conditions change or when the employer fails to live up to the agreement. Transactional contracts characterize workers whose contributions are less critical to the firm's comparative advantage and employers operating in highly unstable markets such as entertainment and fashion. Both worker and employer are likely to immediately terminate a transactional arrangement that fails to meet their needs. Transaction contracts assign more risk to workers from the economic uncertainties the employer faces because the worker often has fewer alternatives (being less able to seek credit for future services). With transactional contracts workers tend to perform in ways consistent with the contributions they are paid to make. Employers receive a specific level of contribution and incur no future obligations to these workers. Such arrangements work well when workers are individual contributors, whose performance deliverables can be explicitly established and monitored, and where there is little need to coordinate with others. Transactional contracts are less functional when they are a by-product of violation of or poorly managed change in relational contracts where either worker or employer has lost trust in the other, resulting in a warier, arm's-length arrangement.

The emergence of a hybrid (*balanced*) form of psychological contract in recent years combines the open-ended time frame and mutual concern of relational agreements with the performance demands and renegotiation of the transactional contract. Balanced contracts state commitments on the part of the employer to develop and provide career advantage to workers, in the firm as well as in future employability elsewhere if need be, while anticipating flexible contributions and adjustment to changing economic conditions on the part of workers. Balanced contracts entail shared risk between worker and employer and anticipate renegotiation over time as economic conditions of the firm and worker interests and needs change.

Psychological contracts are related to, yet distinct from, objective conditions of work such as employment status (e.g., full-time, temporary). Part-time workers and newcomers can have highly relational agreements with an employer, and many full-timers and veterans report only limited commitments between themselves and their employers. It is necessary to drill down into the beliefs workers and managers hold and the information sources they rely on (their manager, coworkers, and events they witnessed) rather than rely on general assumptions regarding broad job categories.

Mutuality is important to the effective functioning of an employment relationship. A major feature of a psychological contract is the individual's belief that an agreement is mutual, and a common understanding exists binding the parties involved to a particular course of action. Agreement between worker and employer on what each owes the other is critical to the employment relationship's success from each party's perspective. Psychological contracts are more likely to be kept when the parties agree as to their terms. Creating mutuality is the gold standard in employment relations. When both parties agree on their joint obligations, worker attitudes and job performance are higher than where their beliefs are mismatched. Nonetheless, parties tend to have different perceptions of how well each fulfills their side of the bargain. Employers tend to rate themselves more highly on fulfilling their end of the deal than workers rate their employer. Similarly, workers rate themselves on average as having fulfilled their end of the bargain to a greater degree than their employer has. This pattern conforms to the well-established availability bias, where parties to a relationship are better able to recall their own contributions than they are those of their partners. Biases in perceptions of contributions do create problems in an important aspect of mutuality: agreement on what workers owe the employer in payback for the employer's contributions to them.

Violation where an employer or worker believes that the psychological contract has been willfully breached by the other generates a long list of dysfunctional outcomes. Anger, quitting, and lower performance, particularly in terms of discretionary contributions such as citizenship behavior, are the more overt manifestations of psychological contract violation. More subtle can be the mistrust, emotional withdrawal, and sabotage that also accompany violation, particularly in circumstances where the violated party continues in the relationship. In such cases, erstwhile relational contracts can turn transactional as the aggrieved party monitors each interaction for signs of exploitation or abuse. Although more relationally oriented employment relations may withstand threats to the psychological contract, breaches of significant important or drastic changes that are poorly managed can create a cycle of escalating violation over time. Incidents that fundamentally breach valued conditions of employment can form the basis of contract violation (e.g., where worker health and safety are affected or employers fail to support workers in providing quality care to clients or service to customers). In the aftermath of violation or poorly managed change, the process of restoring trust can require the formation of a new relationship, finding ways for veterans to begin feeling like newcomers to a new relationship.

But by far the most important aspect of the *employer's side* is the role managers play. Managers, both immediate supervisors and higher-ups, play the central role in shaping a worker's psychological contract. The presence of a supportive immediate manager can serve to amplify or downplay messages sent by the firm's HR practices regarding the nature of the employment relationship. An individual manager's own psychological contract itself influences the contracts that manager in turn creates with workers.

Actions individual workers take can influence their own psychological contracts. First, their career goals influence the kinds of commitments individuals believe they make to the employer. Second, worker personality plays a role in psychological contracts, with more conscientious workers having more relational contracts. Individual workers can negotiate special arrangements with their employers that are unavailable to their coworkers, resulting in distinct psychological contracts with the employer.

Denise M. Rousseau

See also Withdrawal Behaviors, Turnover

Further Readings

Dabos, G. E., & Rousseau, D. M. (2004). Mutuality and reciprocity in the psychological contracts of employee and employer. *Journal of Applied Psychology, 89,* 52–72.

Raja, U., Johns, G., & Ntalianis, F. (in press). The impact of personality on the psychological contract. *Academy of Management Journal.*

Robinson, S. L., & Morrison, E. W. (1995). Organizational citizenship behavior: A psychological contract perspective. *Journal of Organizational Behavior, 16,* 289–298.

Robinson, S. L., & Rousseau, D. M. (1994). Violating the psychological contract: Not the exception but the norm. *Journal of Organizational Behavior, 15,* 245–259.

Rousseau, D. M. (1990). New hire perspectives of their own and their employer's obligations: A study of psychological contracts. *Journal of Organizational Behavior, 11,* 389–400.

Rousseau, D. M. (1995). *Psychological contracts in organizations: Understanding written and unwritten agreements.* Newbury Park, CA: Sage.

Simon, H. A. (1997). *Administrative behavior* (4th ed.). New York: Free Press.

PSYCHOLOGICAL RESILIENCE

Psychological resilience is a person's capacity to maintain a relatively stable equilibrium in the face of adversity. It is the ability of a person to go through difficulties across a continuum of severity—from daily hassles to unexpected change, crises, or tragedy—and experience relatively minimal abnormal psychological functioning. People with a high level of psychological resilience are more prone to adapt positively to adverse circumstances than those who are less resilient. Because of its positive benefits, it is increasingly relevant for organizations operating in turbulent environments.

Although sometimes defined as a person's ability to bounce back from unexpected hardship, most scholars conceptualize resilience as more than recovery. Resilience involves a person's experiencing relatively minimal psychological abnormalities during and following an adverse event, whereas recovery describes the process through which a person might return to a baseline of normal functioning. For example, a person could experience the death of his or her spouse, an event largely recognized as highly stressful. The person could go through a long period of depression and negative coping behaviors such as substance abuse but then eventually regain normal psychological functioning and behavior. Such a person would have recovered, but that person did not necessarily have a high level of psychological resilience.

Instead, a person who has a high level of psychological resilience would likely react to the death of his or her spouse with an appropriate period of sadness, but he or she would neither exhibit the depth of negative emotion felt by a person with less resilience nor require as much time to return to a baseline level of functioning.

As such, psychological resilience involves the tendency to react with relative stability when an unexpected negative event occurs. It is important to note that psychological resilience differs from coping in that resilience is about how one perceives and evaluates an event whereas coping is about how one might deal with an event after the fact.

Correlates of Resilience

Research on psychological resilience is in its early stages, but a number of studies have increased understanding about what it is and what tends to correlate with it. Regarding its nature, psychological resilience is often considered to be more of a group of characteristics that a person embodies rather than a singular personality trait. Similarly, the aspects of people and their lives that tend to correlate with higher levels of psychological resilience are groups of characteristics or factors. These include cognitive, affective, and demographic and life experience factors.

Cognitive Factors

Research suggests that two factors involving cognition, or how people tend to think, influence resilience: (a) the personality characteristic of hardiness and (b) appraisal strategies. Hardiness involves the degree to which a person commits to a higher purpose or meaning in life, seeks and finds ways to control his or her environment, and views adversity as a challenging learning opportunity. Hardiness, therefore, is a mindset, a core belief system, or a worldview. This perspective allows hardy people to view adversity as less of a threat, allowing them to react in a less negative— or even positive—manner in comparison with people with less hardiness.

Appraisal strategies involve the potentially beneficial nature of people's positive biases about themselves and their situations. One way in which such a strategy may influence psychological resilience is that interpreting or reframing a negative event in a positive way, or in a way that highlights one's personal strength, may result in a person's experiencing fewer negative emotions. In a traumatic or otherwise adverse situation, such an appraisal seems to have a positive effect on people's well-being because it protects them psychologically from the dire nature of reality. It may also allow them to attach positive meaning to negative events.

For example, a resilient person experiencing rejection from a job application might cognitively reframe the situation by thinking that the job "wasn't a good fit anyway" and that the rejection "was meant to happen to allow for an even better opportunity." Such thinking often coincides with other types of positive self-talk or encouragement from others, in which people use specific phrases or mantras to endure hardship. Examples of such phrases abound, including "hang in there," "keep on trucking," and "grin and bear it." A Chinese phrase, roughly translated as "eat bitter" or "eat bitterness," refers to a similar notion of perseverance through adversity.

People who practice appraisal strategies in this manner may be more psychologically resilient than those who do not use such methods, for two general reasons. First, they may experience more resulting positive emotions and associated benefits of that positivity. Second, such strategies may help protect people's sense of worth and ability, which gives them hope for future success and allows them to continue functioning at a high level.

Affective Factors

Therefore, affect, or people's emotions and how they feel, appears to influence psychological resilience. Positive emotions, generally defined as those associated with happiness and energy, seem to be particularly important. Research suggests that positive emotions may both contribute to and result from psychological resilience.

For example, having positive emotions may allow people to adapt more easily to stressful circumstances by helping them in the coping process. Such people are more likely to use effective coping strategies such as reappraisal, meaning finding, and focusing on goals and problem solving. Such coping strategies likely allow people to withstand stress better than those who use avoidance or other less effective strategies, making these people more resilient. Highly resilient people, it follows, are more likely to use these effective coping strategies, leading to more positive emotions.

Positive emotions tend to help people deal with daily stress. These emotions, however, may play an additional role regarding psychological resilience. Namely, research suggests that one reason positive emotions may help people become more satisfied with their lives overall is that these emotions serve a resilience-building function. That is, positive emotions appear to be a psychological resource that bolsters individual resilience, which then leads to higher life satisfaction.

Given that positive emotions contribute to psychological resilience, it is important to consider how people can experience such emotions more frequently. A number of evidence-based possibilities exist, and within the context of psychological resilience, two are particularly relevant. First, the use of humor and laughter influences positive emotions, and both serve as tools for managing stress within adverse circumstances. Second, maintaining productive relationships in a social network can serve as a boost to people's emotional well-being and resilience.

Demographic and Life-Experience Factors

Research also suggests that people who are male and older tend to exhibit more psychological resilience than those who are female and younger, but understanding why this finding tends to occur requires additional study. Some studies have also found links between ethnicity and psychological resilience, but such findings have been somewhat inconsistent. More consistent and important are those findings that suggest that early life experiences play an important role in how people react to adversity.

Some early experiences tend to predict lower levels of resilience or lower abilities to deal with stress. These experiences include abusive relationships, which have been linked to increased tendencies to experience psychiatric disorders. Among animal studies, early maternal separation for long periods of time has been linked to a decreased ability to cope with stress.

Other early experiences tend to predict higher levels of psychological resilience. These typically include positive, nurturing environments during early childhood that promote a sense of safety. For example, having a healthy, close relationship with a caregiver appears to promote the ability for people to cope effectively with stress later in life.

Such positive experiences early in life need not be stressor free. In fact, additional evidence from animal studies suggests that exposure to moderate levels of stress may have a positive influence on resilience. Such exposure may help protect an organism from the negative effects of stressors later in life, with the theory being that these moderate stressors help teach resilience through the successful use of adaptive techniques and coping strategies. Additional research on human populations would provide greater insight into the influence of early life experiences on psychological resilience.

Implications and Relevance for Organizations

The topic of psychological resilience is becoming increasingly important for modern organizations for three reasons. First, some organizations whose members frequently encounter stressful circumstances have a distinct interest in developing enhanced psychological resilience among their people to improve performance. For example, members of the military often face high levels of isolation, ambiguity, boredom, and danger, among other stressors, in their work while deployed. The same types of stressors are increasingly facing civilians who work in similar circumstances, such as contracted personnel working alongside the military and civilians in global aid organizations. Branches of the U.S. military have begun in recent years to develop specific training programs with the hope of increasing resilience. For example, the U.S. Army has invested considerable resources in its Comprehensive Soldier and Family Fitness programs, which are part of its Ready and Resilient Campaign. Related work has included the concept of posttraumatic growth, in which people experience positive development in the aftermath of trauma in contrast to stress disorders.

Second, organizations today are dealing with increasingly changing environments. Such circumstances often impose unexpected demands on employees, who must then cope effectively. Having a higher level of psychological resilience among employees, therefore, could be considered a type of human capital. Just as having employees who are educated and skilled benefits an organization, having employees who can consistently respond well to the changing dynamics of modern work is an asset.

Third, scholars are beginning to theorize and explore the relationships between resilient organizational members and overall organizational resilience. From the perspective of business strategy, an organization that can weather unexpected adversity, learn from such experiences, and continue to perform at a high level is one that would likely enjoy an advantage over its competitors. To the extent that resilient employees contribute to resilient organizations, such research will prove valuable.

Research on ways to assess and develop psychological resilience among job applicants and employees is in its early stages. Specific programs intended to increase resilience among employees tend to have modest or mixed results, indicating a need for continued research. Other potentially promising avenues for developing psychological resilience may come from focusing more closely on the correlates mentioned here. Exploring the potential influence of leader behavior on resilience within groups may prove useful, for example, particularly if focused on topics such as helping team members use effective appraisal strategies and positive emotions to deal with adversity.

Benjamin E. Baran

See also Emotions; Hardiness; Individual Differences; Optimism and Pessimism; Self-Efficacy; Self-Esteem; Stress, Coping and Management

Further Readings

Bartone, P. T. (2006). Resilience under military operational stress: Can leaders influence hardiness? *Military Psychology*, 18(S), S131. doi:10.1207/s15327876mp1803s_10

Bonanno, G. A. (2004). Loss, trauma, and human resilience: Have we underestimated the human capacity to thrive after extremely aversive events? *American Psychologist*, 59(1), 20–28. doi:10.1037/0003-066X.59.1.20

Bonanno, G. A., Galea, S., Bucciarelli, A., & Vlahov, D. (2007). What predicts psychological resilience after disaster? The role of demographics, resources, and life stress. *Journal of Consulting and Clinical Psychology*, 75(5), 671–682. doi:10.1037/0022-006X.75.5.671

Cohn, M. A., Fredrickson, B. L., Brown, S. L., Mikels, J. A., & Conway, A. M. (2009). Happiness unpacked: Positive emotions increase life satisfaction by building resilience. *Emotion*, 9(3), 361–368. doi:10.1037/a0015952

Feder, A., Nestler, E. J., & Charney, D. S. (2009). Psychobiology and molecular genetics of resilience. *Nature Reviews Neuroscience*, 10(6), 446–457. doi:10.1038/nrn2649

Fletcher, D., & Sarkar, M. (2013). Psychological resilience: A review and critique of definitions, concepts, and theory. *European Psychologist*, 18(1), 12–23. doi:10.1027/1016-9040/a000124

Ong, A. D., Bergeman, C. S., Bisconti, T. L., & Wallace, K. A. (2006). Psychological resilience, positive emotions, and successful adaptation to stress in later life. *Journal of Personality and Social Psychology*, 91(4), 730–749. doi:10.1037/0022-3514.91.4.730

Tugade, M. M., & Fredrickson, B. L. (2004). Resilient individuals use positive emotions to bounce back from negative emotional experiences. *Journal of Personality and Social Psychology*, 86(2), 320–333. doi:10.1037/0022-3514.86.2.320

QUALITATIVE ANALYTIC SOFTWARE

Qualitative research is an integral part of industrial and organizational psychology, having made foundational contributions since the field gained popularity with the Hawthorne studies. Like their quantitative counterparts, researchers conducting qualitative research often support their analyses using software. Such software, collectively known as computer-assisted qualitative data analysis software (CAQDAS), is becoming increasingly popular in research in industrial and organizational psychology. It is thus important to understand qualitative analytic software in order to conduct and evaluate the studies it supports. This entry defines CAQDAS, introduces different types of software researchers may draw on, reviews the typical functionality of such software, gives a brief overview of the evolution of the software and its use in qualitative data analysis, and critiques the use of software in qualitative research.

What Is CAQDAS?

CAQDAS is software designed to support the process of categorizing, coding, and analyzing qualitative data. Software was introduced into the analytic process because the manual analysis of qualitative data is difficult and time-consuming. CAQDAS was thus designed to help simplify the process by removing many monotonous tasks (e.g., counting, searching, autocoding) from the process and enabling researchers to dedicate their

focus to the more advanced tasks, particularly interpretive coding and analysis. This software also has an important database function, whereby researchers can store and organize large volumes of data with relative ease. The software thus replaces traditional mechanisms of data storage, including filing cabinets, locked drawers, files, and storage boxes, and also seeks to improve traditional coding aids, such as whiteboards, Post-it notes, highlighters, torn-up transcripts, paper envelopes, Microsoft Word tables, and so forth. In short, by making it easier to store and retrieve data, large-scale data sets become more manageable through the use of software.

Types of CAQDAS

The increased demand for qualitative analytic software has resulted in the development of various software programs. There are now too many packages on the market to list comprehensively. However, popular proprietary software packages include NVivo, ATLAS.ti, MAXQDA, QDA Miner, and Ethnograph. Of these, NVivo and its predecessor, NUD*IST, are the programs most widely cited in the industrial and organizational psychology literature. Such software will often be referenced in the methodology sections of research papers. Cost-free alternatives to the market-leading proprietary packages include open-source software such as CATMA, CAT, ELAN, RQDA, Transana, and QCAmap. Each software package has its own advantages and disadvantages. Researchers must thus take great care to ensure that the software packages they use match the ontological and epistemological assumptions of their own work.

CAQDAS Functionality

Although the functionality available in CAQDAS was originally limited to basic tasks such as importing, categorizing and storing data, as well as engaging in some rudimentary coding, modern CAQDAS has embraced the diversity of qualitative research and responded with a multitude of functions. Thus, researchers may use qualitative analytic software for a number of tasks, including the following:

- Transcribing data
- Storing and organizing data
- Sorting and grouping data
- Coding and retrieving data
- Searching data
- Linking data
- Providing word counts
- Writing notes and annotating data
- Mapping and visualizing relationships

CAQDAS Evolution

CAQDAS packages have evolved with qualitative research in industrial and organizational psychology and consequently are now much more responsive to different types of data and file formats. Whereas software traditionally struggled with different data types, being able to work only with textual data imported in simple file formats (e.g., rich text format), most software packages nowadays allow researchers to work with a full complement of file formats. Equally important, many packages can now also facilitate the coding of audio, video, and pictorial data, at least in part. Indeed, some software has been designed specifically for this purpose (e.g., Transana was designed for use with video and audio data).

Critique of CAQDAS

There has been considerable debate within the qualitative research community about whether the introduction of software into the qualitative analytic process is appropriate and helpful. First of all, each software program provides a structural framework to use in analysis. This framework is built around certain analytical assumptions (and often designed to work with particular types of analyses, such as grounded theory). Software packages are thus inherently biased toward a particular type of qualitative analysis, and researchers must be cautious not to be blindly led by the software in directions in which they did not intend to go and which may be inappropriate given the nature of their data and their research questions.

Second, some authors argue that working with software creates an additional barrier between the researcher and the data. It creates an unnatural distance from the data that may prevent the deep contextual analysis characteristic of high-quality research. In particular, through the coding facility, software programs encourage researchers to "chunk" parts of data into separate buckets for later analysis. This may result in relationships between some of these codes and the broader context being lost, resulting in a selectiveness that leads to different interpretation and thus significantly influences findings. Such issues could create serious analytic limitations in holistic research, for instance, creating challenges to interpretive phenomenological analysis.

Third, there are some security concerns about storing data electronically. Although researchers are bound by professional codes of conduct to safeguard their data, for instance, potentially being required to place data "under lock and key" in a filing cabinet in a locked office within a secure building, it is less clear what this means in a digital context. Modern researchers will often have large volumes of data, at times sensitive in nature, digitized and easily transportable. There are questions about how secure this type of data storage is. For instance, there are queries about how secure data are on laptops and whether cloud storage is appropriate in these situations. Such questions will continue to challenge our own ethics as researchers and form an important consideration in whether and how to use qualitative analytic software.

Fourth, there continue to be serious misconceptions about qualitative analytic software. Indeed, the very notion that software can be used in the qualitative *analysis* process is often challenged. Few people would be affronted by the idea that CAQDAS may assist the analytic process by acting as a database, providing a structured framework for analysis, and offering some tools that can assist in analysis. However, there is much debate about how much actual analysis the software is capable of doing. Whereas in quantitative research, a software program may "run" a regression analysis and produce results, the same is not true in most qualitative research (even in the most formalized qualitative analysis, content analysis, there would need to be some manual coding or correction). Thus, in qualitative research, the researcher is always the analyst, and he or she must do the analysis. Software may provide tools that support the process, but software cannot take the all-important creative leap that is the hallmark of high-impact qualitative work. Some scholars thus accuse others of being opportunistic and using software in an attempt to project rigor. However, rigor in qualitative research is independent of whether a researcher uses a software program in the analytic process or not. Indeed, many high-quality studies were produced without the use of software. It is thus important to understand that software is only one of many tools that can support a strong qualitative analytic process.

Additional Resources

One of the most thorough and impressive resources for researchers wanting to better understand qualitative analytic software and its role in qualitative research is the CAQDAS Networking Project at the University of Surrey (http://www.surrey.ac.uk/sociology/research/researchcentres/caqdas/about/index.htm). The Web site provides access to a vast repository of knowledge and resources about CAQDAS.

Jane K. Lê

See also Case Study Method; Ethnography; Grounded Theory; Mixed-Methods Designs; Online Qualitative Methods; Phenomenology; Qualitative Research Approach

Further Readings

Bansal, T., & Corley, K. (2011). The coming of age for qualitative research: Embracing the diversity of qualitative methods. *Academy of Management Journal, 54*(2), 233–237.

Fielding N., & Lee, R. (1998). *Computer analysis and qualitative research*. London: Sage Ltd.

Langley, A. (1999) Strategies for theorizing from process data. *Academy of Management Review, 24*(4), 691–710.

Rynes, S. (2007). Academy of Management editors' forum on rich research: Editor's foreword. *Academy of Management Journal, 50*(1), 13.

Silver, C., & Fielding, N. (2008). Using computer packages in qualitative research. In C. Willig & W. Stainton-Rogers (Eds.), *The SAGE handbook of qualitative research in psychology*. London: Sage Ltd.

Silver, C., & Lewins, A. (2014). *Using software in qualitative research: A step-by-step guide*. London: Sage Ltd.

Qualitative Research Approach

Qualitative research is an approach to inquiry that refers to a broad umbrella domain of various research traditions and investigative and analytic practices employed by researchers in a wide range of subject disciplines. One way of understanding the variety is to understand qualitative inquiry from the perspective of three broad philosophical paradigms that represent various worldviews composed of values, beliefs, and methodological assumptions and that bring into focus different domains of study. These can be characterized as modernist, interpretive, and postmodern. Practiced from within the modernist paradigm, qualitative inquiry identifies the facts and causes of particular phenomena to test or develop theory in the context of the real world of work; for example, collecting accounts of the circumstances under which people choose to leave their jobs to theorize voluntary turnover. From the perspective of the interpretive paradigm, however, researchers are interested in understanding the relationship between people's subjective reality and their work-related behaviors—that is, what do objects and events mean to people, how do they perceive what happens to them, and how do they adapt their behavior in light of these understandings and perceptions. For example, researchers may explore people's subjective interpretation of competence at work, developing an understanding of how those subjective interpretations affect performance. From the perspective of a postmodern worldview, qualitative inquiry offers the possibility to examine and challenge the realities in which people live and work and the things they take for granted, including the assumptions of the researcher. For example, researchers may surface implicit gendering reflected in research and theorizing about leadership.

In addition to the variety generated by paradigmatic orientations, qualitative research is also practiced from many different traditions. Within these, research takes a slightly different shape and pursues different outcomes. Consider just a few. For example, researchers doing ethnographic research focus on the detailed examination of social phenomena in a small number of settings; typically, ethnography is carried out in just one social setting. Within that setting the ethnographic researcher simultaneously participates in and observes daily life to learn about its mundane and routine habits of mind and behavior. Action researchers, by comparison, aim to both provide practical advice and acquire knowledge about the dynamics of change in organizations; their research subjects are active participants in the research process. Case study researchers typically gather a variety of data, which can include both qualitative and numerical observations; and they write up a case history of the social systems studied.

Although there is considerable variety in the orientations and traditions of qualitative research, its operational practices are relatively consistent. As a set of operational practices, qualitative inquiry is distinguished by the following conditions in the practice of sampling, the practice of gathering observations, and the practice of analysis. Regardless of data-gathering modes chosen, sampling in qualitative research follows a distinct logic. Generally speaking, qualitative inquiry focuses in depth on relatively small samples that are selected purposefully. The logic and power of purposeful sampling is founded on deliberately searching out and selecting settings, people, and events that will provide rich and detailed information regarding the research question. For example, a researcher interested in understanding how ethically pioneering decisions are made might seek out research sites where such decisions are common, perhaps a biotechnology firm, and within that setting focus on the decisions surrounding the development and marketing of a new product, perhaps a genetic

profiling product, whose ethical implications are unclear. In its selective pursuit of information-rich settings and subjects, purposeful sampling is distinct from probabilistic sampling.

In terms of observation, qualitative inquiry typically takes place in natural settings where researchers are present to the social situations and phenomena they are studying. They focus their attention on ordinary situations, events, and experiences; this access to life at work as it unfolds and as it is experienced by organization members allows researchers to gain an understanding of and theorize everyday realities in the workplace. This is achieved through various data-gathering techniques, which are intensive and time-consuming.

Gathering data through participant observation, researchers enter and become a part of the actual context in which people pursue their work, learning firsthand how they accomplish their work on a daily basis; how they talk, behave, and interact; and how they understand and experience their work. Prolonged engagement with the research site is typical, because researchers often remain present for an annual cycle within the social system they are studying, spending sufficient time there to understand and learn how to conduct themselves according to the norms of the setting. Observations are logged and converted into field notes on a daily basis. Interviews provide another avenue for gaining observations, and these vary in the extent to which they are structured and formalized. For example, interviews can be organized through highly structured and standard interview protocols or semiformal conversation guides; or they can be free-flowing, informal exchanges. Interviews can be one-off events, or subjects can be interviewed multiple times to gain their stable and changing perspectives on events as they unfold. Through interviews, researchers collect people's accounts of their work lives, actions, experiences, perceptions, opinions, and feelings. As a matter of practice, interviews are usually tape-recorded and transcribed verbatim. Documents of various types, such as e-mails, memos, policy statements, reports, photographs, drawings, and audio and video materials, are also important data sources to understand how work is organized. Within any particular study, researchers often incorporate a number of data-gathering modes to gain a better understanding of the phenomena in which they are interested.

For example, although a researcher's primary data-gathering strategy may be participant observation, such as being a participant observer to an organization's product development process, they are also likely interviewing people to gain their perspective on the events observed in, say, a product development meeting, and they may collect any organizational documents relevant to that product's development.

In the act of analysis, qualitative researchers typically work with verbal language (and occasionally visual images) rather than quantitative language as indicators of the phenomenon of interest. Consistent with the outlined data gathering modes, these verbal language texts include field notes, verbatim interview transcripts, diaries, conversation records, and organizational documents of various types. It is not usual for a data set for a given study to amount to more than 1,000 pages of unstructured text to be analyzed. With the involvement of the computer in qualitative research, researchers are able to draw on a number of software packages that aid in the management and organization of their data.

Data analysis typically overlaps with data gathering, and analysis strategies roughly fall into two main groups: categorizing strategies such as coding and thematic analysis and contextualizing strategies such as narrative analysis and case studies. Coding is the main categorizing strategy; through this strategy the data set is fractured and arranged into categories so that similarities and differences between data fragments can be recognized and identified. Through these categories, data are conceptualized, and the conceptual categories are integrated into a theoretical framework. Another form of categorizing analysis progresses by sorting data into broader themes and issues. Coding categories vary in the extent to which they draw on existing theory. In contextualizing strategies, instead of fracturing the data set into discrete elements and developing categories for them, researchers attempt to understand the data in context using various procedures to identify different relationships among elements in the text. For example, through narrative analysis researchers examine the data for relationships that organize statements and events into a coherent whole. In addition, practices such as displaying data and memoing are central to and support analysis

regardless of whether researchers follow categorizing or contextualizing strategies.

A majority of qualitative studies are open-ended in their initial design, and they place minimum theoretical constraint on their data analysis and the expected outcomes of the research. This results in a research process characterized by emergence and flexibility. The term *funnel shaped* is often used to characterize this approach to design in which researchers begin with a general research question and then narrow and refine their paths of inquiry in the course of their study. This means that the activities of collecting and analyzing data, conceptualizing it, and refining research questions are in play simultaneously, influencing each other. Accordingly, data analysis is pursued in a nontheoretically constrained way; this is typical, for example, in the grounded theory approach in which data are analyzed and codes are developed by researchers through the analytic process. This process is challenging because researchers can be overwhelmed by the ambiguities and uncertainties associated with assigning meaning to hundreds of pages of words.

By contrast, some qualitative studies are more deductive in their orientation. Studies are designed and researchers pursue data collection and analysis with predetermined theoretical questions in mind and conceptual categories that they plan to elaborate and refine. For example, the form of analysis practiced in content analysis relies on existing theory to derive coding categories; these preestablished defined categories are applied to the data, and frequency counts of data fragments representing these defined categories can form the basis for quantitative analysis.

Generally speaking, qualitative inquiry results in the development of dynamic process-oriented models explaining how and why things happen as they do. Qualitative researchers' ability to be present to action as it unfolds, whether to developing work team norms or changing team behaviors, allows them to identify precisely how organization members understand their situations, the actions that flow from this understanding, what events lead to what consequences, and the underlying contextual influences on behavior and events.

Karen Locke

See also Case Study Method; Focus Groups;
Verbal Protocol Analysis

Further Readings

Krippendorf, K. (2004). Content analysis: An introduction to its methodology. Thousand Oaks, CA: Sage.

Maxwell, J. A. (2005). Qualitative research design: An interactive approach (2nd ed.). Thousand Oaks, CA: Sage.

Patton, M. Q. (2002). Qualitative research and evaluation methods (3rd ed.). Thousand Oaks, CA: Sage.

Schwandt, T. A. (2001). Dictionary of qualitative inquiry (2nd ed.). Thousand Oaks, CA: Sage.

Seale, C., Giampietro, G., Gubrium J. F., & Silverman, D. (2004). Qualitative research practice. Thousand Oaks, CA: Sage.

QUALITY OF WORK LIFE

Quality of work life (QWL) has been identified as a personal reaction to the work environment and includes perceptions of control, satisfaction, involvement, commitment, work–life balance, and well-being in relation to one's job and organization. As such, research has evolved over the years to include topics such as employee work and health outcomes, organizational processes and interventions, and work–life balance or integration. According to work by Lawler, QWL includes issues of employee job satisfaction, health, and well-being. In the 1970s and 1980s, QWL frequently referred to specific workplace interventions (e.g., team building and quality circles) that could lead to improved organizational performance. Thus, the concept of QWL has not been consistently clearly defined in the literature.

Early on, little to no responsibility was placed on the organization for facilitating or hindering QWL. As industrial and organizational researchers began to identify links between employee perceptions of QWL and important organizational-level outcomes such as absenteeism, turnover, and in some cases performance, organizational interventions began to be designed specifically to improve QWL. Thus the term was popularized in the 1970s and 1980s, because many QWL interventions at the time had a general goal of improving individuals' organizational perceptions and a secondary goal of improving productivity.

These interventions were focused on changes in the objective work environment that improve employees' overall work attitudes. QWL interventions were aimed at empowering workers by increasing control and autonomy, providing increased recognition and rewards in an effort to improve overall well-being and overall positive reactions to work. Types of interventions varied from the provision of employee counseling services to team building and quality circles in the 1970s and job design and enrichment in the late 1970s and 1980s. These interventions further evolved in the 1990s into the provision of alternative work schedules and family-friendly workplace supports such as paid family leave and dependent care support (e.g., the provision of on- or off-site child care). Thus we can see that QWL interventions are focused on organizational changes aimed at having a positive impact on individual employees' perceptions of the work environment and ultimately having an impact on enhanced job attitudes, well-being, and productivity.

Kossek discussed the QWL movement in terms of its relevance to work–life integration. Work–life research exploded in the 1980s with the publication of several key articles, such as that of Greenhaus and Beutell in the *Academy of Management Review* on the types and sources of work–family conflict and that of Felice Schwartz in the *Harvard Business Review* on the "mommy track," that broadened the attention of both academic researchers and organizational practitioners to the importance of work–life issues. Today it is clear that work and life are intimately connected and that the organization of work has a significant impact on employee health, safety, and well-being.

Outcomes of QWL

Here we discuss what we see as important outcomes of QWL. When high QWL exists, we expect to see employees who are satisfied with their jobs, feel valued by their organizations, are committed to their organizations, and have low levels of conflicts between their work and family roles and corresponding high levels of enrichment, or positive spillover, between work and family. Furthermore, in addition to positive job attitudes and possibly job behaviors, we want to extend the outcomes to general health and well-being. In fact, recent research demonstrates positive relationships between such characteristics as job control and job demands and cardiovascular disease. Other research demonstrates relationships between work–family conflict and depression. Still other research demonstrates improved overall health when employees are happy on the job. Thus, although positive job attitudes and behaviors are important, we urge researchers and practitioners not to forget about our understanding of the link between QWL and enhanced physical and psychological health.

These ideas coincide with more recent attention given to the concept of the *healthy workplace*. In fact, the American Psychological Association (APA) has begun to recognize organizations as healthy when they focus on employee well-being through the provision of supportive cultures and climates that value the importance of providing employees with low-stress work environments that contribute to employee health and well-being. The focus of the healthy workplace has moved away from the corporate bottom line toward viewing employees as the most valued resources. Furthermore, efforts by the APA and the National Institute for Occupational Safety and Health (NIOSH) have led to the development of a new interdisciplinary field that integrates occupational health disciplines and psychology and that is concerned primarily with improving QWL for employees. Specifically, occupational health psychology is focused on the prevention of stress, injury, and illness in the workplace and the promotion of safety, health, and well-being of workers. NIOSH further has taken on a new direction in the area of Total Worker Health, which is referred to as a strategy that combines traditional health and safety protection with well-being. Thus, it appears that efforts in the science and professional realm have led to further developments in understanding QWL, while the term itself has lost much of its popularity. Rather, more contemporary concepts such as healthy workplaces, health protection, health promotion, work–life balance, and organizational well-being are characteristics of what we have traditionally known as QWL.

In sum, although the term *QWL* is not commonly used today, the meaning is inherent in many aspects of organizational psychology. QWL is now more explicitly studied and discussed within the specific organizational structures and interventions that positively influence employee attitudes, health, and well-being.

*Leslie B. Hammer
and Diana Sanchez*

See also Empowerment; Job Satisfaction; Occupational Health Psychology; Stress, Consequences; Work–Life Balance

Further Readings

Greenhaus, J. H., & Beutell, N. J. (1985). Sources of conflict between work and family roles. *Academy of Management Review, 10*, 76–88.

Hammer, L. B., Demsky, C. A., Kossek, E. E., & Bray, J. W. (in press). Work–family intervention research. In T. D. Allen & L. T. Eby (Eds.), *The Oxford handbook of work and family*. New York: Oxford University Press. doi:10.1093/oxfordhb/9780199337538.013.27

Hammer, L. B., & Zimmerman, K. L. (2011). Quality of work life. In S. Zedeck (Ed.), *APA handbook of industrial and organizational psychology* (Vol. 3, pp. 399–431). Washington, DC: American Psychological Association.

Kossek, E. E. (2006). Work and family in America: Growing tensions between employment policy and a changing workforce. In E. E. Lawler & J. O'Toole (Eds.), *America at work: Choices and challenges* (pp. 53–72). New York: Palgrave Macmillan.

Lawler, E. E. (1982). Strategies for improving the quality of work life. *American Psychologist, 37*, 486–493.

QUANTITATIVE RESEARCH APPROACH

Quantitative research approaches increase knowledge by gathering data in a numerical form that then can be manipulated mathematically to reveal regularities and patterns that otherwise might be difficult to detect. This makes it possible to address a wide variety of research questions, including assessments of the meanings of psychological concepts, their levels and variability, as well as the relationships among them. Quantitative research approaches are often contrasted with qualitative approaches, which tend to collect data expressed in nonmathematical, symbolic representations and to place less focus on estimating the strength and form of relationships.

The data associated with quantitative approaches can result from simple measurement operations such as counts or categorizations or from more complex operations that may involve the creation of measurement scales that function as psychological yardsticks. For example, quantitative research approaches have allowed industrial and organizational (I-O) psychologists to develop self-report measures of a construct called job satisfaction, to determine that it has a variety of different aspects or facets (such as satisfaction with pay, supervisor, or work setting), and to study its relationships with conditions such as organizational culture or leadership that make its general level higher or lower.

In any science, researchers must collect and analyze data in a manner that can be replicated by others and is open to public inspection and criticism. I-O psychologists are no different; they rely heavily on a wide range of quantitative methods to pursue two broad endeavors. The first of these is to accurately *measure* psychological variables of interest, such as performance, personality, intellectual capacity, work attitudes, and many more aspects of the world of work. The second endeavor consists of the systematic and theory-driven *search for relationships* among variables. Often, the search for relationships involves testing theory-based hypotheses, the results of which allow scientific inferences about the presence or absence of the relationships of interest. This entry briefly describes quantitative approaches to measurement, the rationale for significance testing, and quantitative techniques for assessing relationships.

Quantitative Techniques Addressing Measurement Issues

Psychological measurement consists of developing rules that make it possible either to classify objects into meaningful categories or to identify where aspects of those objects fall on a numerical scale. Importantly, measurement is best when it is theory driven.

Two key characteristics of measures, often addressed using quantitative methods, are reliability and validity. *Reliability* may be defined in various ways; however, they all address the extent to which

the same (or equivalent) measurement procedures will yield the same results, if repeated. A variety of statistical techniques estimate reliability—including classic test theory–based procedures, such as test–retest correlation and coefficient alpha—and more recently developed methods such as generalizability theory. Closely related are indexes of agreement, which tell us the extent to which multiple observers rate the same object in the same way.

In contrast, *validity* addresses the issue of whether measures capture the true essence of the intended psychological construct. Again, various quantitative approaches can be used to assess validity. Construct validity questions are often addressed with factor analysis, which enables better understanding of the patterns of interrelatedness among measures and thus the number and nature of underlying constructs or latent variables. Exploratory factor analysis is primarily inductive, providing empirical guides to the dimensionality of a set of measures. Each separate dimension suggests the presence of a different underlying construct, and exploratory factor analysis also estimates the extent to which specific survey items or other indicators are influenced by a common underlying factor. Confirmatory factor analysis allows a more deductive approach, because the researcher can prespecify a hypothesized latent factor structure. It also permits tests of how well a given factor model fits the data and allows comparisons of alternative factor models.

Another useful quantitative approach is item response theory, which relates test item responses to levels of an underlying latent trait such as cognitive ability. This technique helps distinguish good test items that discriminate well between people high or low in a trait from poor items that do not. Item response theory also enables the development of adaptive tests, allowing researchers to assess an individual's standing on a trait without having to administer the entire measure.

Why Significance Tests Are Used

Many factors make interpreting the results of data analysis challenging. For example, psychological data often contain a lot of extraneous variability (i.e., *noise*), because measurements generally reflect not only the level of the desired variable but also other influences such as misunderstandings or impression management attempts by research participants, temporary fluctuations in mood or alertness, and other sources of systematic and random variability. In addition, many outcomes of interest in psychological research have multiple causes. Thus, a focal variable often accounts for as little as 5% to 10% of the observed variability in an outcome variable. Such small effect sizes mean that variability caused by the focal variables often is not much larger than what might be due to sampling error. Sampling error occurs because it is rarely possible to collect data from all possible members of a population of interest and so instead data are collected from only a subset of them. Unfortunately, it is not known for certain that the results found with a sample truly reflect the population values instead of occurring by chance due to sampling. Statistical significance testing provides a useful tool that helps researchers determine whether differences or associations found in the sample data should be attributed to the variables of interest or could simply be artifacts of sampling variability. Significance tests typically pit two mutually exclusive and exhaustive hypotheses against each other, with the desired result being to find evidence that leads one to reject a *null hypothesis* of no effect. However, recent trends suggest that the null hypothesis significance testing approach is often misused and misinterpreted, and alternative approaches are encouraged.

Quantitative Techniques Addressing Relationship Issues

The quantitative techniques used by I-O psychologists were developed primarily in the late 1800s, the 1900s, and into the present century. Research design and quantitative analysis were closely intertwined in their development, with different traditions arising depending on distinctions such as whether an experimental or nonexperimental research design is used. We describe some of the most commonly used techniques, which are appropriate when the dependent variable is measured at the interval level or higher. Traditionally, these techniques have relied on least squares estimation procedures and have linear and fixed-model assumptions, but easy access to computers has increased the availability of alternative estimators and made nonlinear, multilevel, and random-effects models more accessible.

The experimental method is particularly powerful because it allows causal inference. Experiments are studies in which the researcher systematically manipulates conditions in groups that have been created by random assignment and then compares the effects of those manipulations. Variations of experimental methods, called *quasi-experiments*, attempt to preserve some of the characteristics of experimental designs while acknowledging that researchers cannot always use random assignment or manipulate key variables.

The most common statistical approach for experimental data is the analysis of variance (ANOVA) model, also known as a factorial design. This type of analysis was first developed by Sir Ronald A. Fisher, who was interested in studying differences in crop yields associated with different agricultural practices. In general, ANOVA involves the comparisons of mean levels of a dependent variable across different groups created by experimental manipulations. There are many subtypes of ANOVA models, which incorporate mixed and random effects, allow analysis of incomplete design matrices, and control for covariates.

There is also a strong tradition of survey and questionnaire research in I-O psychology. Studies in this tradition do not involve manipulation of variables or random assignment of participants to groups. Although this nonexperimental approach makes causal inference more difficult, some researchers argue that this drawback is compensated for by better generalizability and construct richness. In fact, there are many interesting research questions for which experimental designs are impractical or impossible because of ethical or practical issues.

Correlation and regression analysis, as well as related but more complex path and structural equation modeling approaches, are commonly used to analyze survey and questionnaire data. Sir Francis Galton and Karl Pearson were instrumental in developing correlation and regression. Correlation indicates the extent and direction of association between two variables. For example, a positive correlation between job satisfaction and organizational commitment indicates that employees who are more satisfied with their jobs also tend to be more committed. Regression analysis is used to test whether predictor variables such as grade point average and personality linearly relate to a criterion variable such as job performance, providing estimates of the extent of the strength of the relationship and the proportion of variance in the criterion explained by the predictors. Ironically, given the sharp distinction made historically between ANOVA and regression techniques, in the 1950s, statisticians began to recognize that they were in fact subtypes of an umbrella statistical model called the general linear model, which also subsumes other important techniques such as canonical correlation, discriminant analysis, and multivariate ANOVA.

There are many important variations on the basic research designs and analytic approaches just described. For example, research designs in which data are collected at multiple times from each case or participant in the study are especially useful when researchers want to make a more persuasive case for causality or want to model change over time. Such research designs are *longitudinal* in nature and involve repeated measurements over three or more measurement periods. Like their one-shot, cross-sectional counterparts, longitudinal designs may be experimental, quasi-experimental, or nonexperimental in nature, and specialized analytic methods exist to test for relationships with longitudinal data. Similarly, many studies in organizational contexts involve the collection of quantitative data from nested units, such as supervisor-subordinate dyads, work groups and teams, and persons or larger units within organizations or industrial sectors. The collection and analysis of such *multilevel* data require careful thought and appropriate analytic techniques.

Finally, important developments in a set of quantitative techniques called meta-analysis have led to advances in many areas of study. These techniques allow researchers to cumulate the results from multiple studies of a given relationship. Meta-analysis thus more definitively addresses the question of whether a relationship is nonzero and better estimates the effect size in the population because it combines results from multiple samples.

Current Trends

Quantitative data collection via experimental, quasi-experimental, and nonexperimental designs

continues to be used extensively in studies by industrial and organizational psychologists. Analytic techniques for quantitative data are increasingly sophisticated but are simultaneously easier to implement with specialized computer software. Researchers increasingly use techniques appropriate for testing multilevel, dynamic, nonlinear, and longitudinal models; increase their use of robust or assumption-free statistics and alternative estimation methods; and critically reexamine aspects of the null hypothesis statistical testing paradigm. In addition, there has been an explosion in the use of structural equation modeling approaches, which allow the simultaneous estimation and significance testing of models that combine a measurement component (i.e., how observed measurements relate to underlying latent variables) with the analysis of structural (i.e., causal) relationships among the latent variables.

Rosalie J. Hall and Hsien-Yao Swee

See also Descriptive Statistics; Experimental Designs; Factor Analysis; Generalizability Theory; Inferential Statistics; Item Response Theory; Longitudinal Research; Measurement Scales; Multilevel Modeling; Quasi-Experimental Designs; Structural Equation Modeling

Further Readings

Bobko, P. (2001). *Correlation and regression: Applications for industrial/organizational psychology and management* (2nd ed.). Thousand Oaks, CA: Sage. doi:10.4135/9781412983815

Cumming, G. (2011). *Understanding the new statistics: Effect sizes, confidence intervals and meta-analysis.* New York: Routledge.

Gray, D. E. (2014). *Doing research in the real world* (3rd ed.). Thousand Oaks, CA: Sage.

Harlow, L. L., Mulaik, S. A., & Steiger, J. H. (1997). *What if there were no significance tests?* Mahwah, NJ: Erlbaum.

Kline, R. (2009). *Becoming a behavioral science researcher: A guide to producing research that matters.* New York: Guilford.

Nunnally, J. C., & Bernstein, I. H. (1994). *Psychometric theory* (3rd ed.). New York: McGraw-Hill.

Shadish, W. R., Cook, T. D., & Campbell, D. T. (2002). *Experimental and quasi-experimental designs for generalized causal inference.* New York: Houghton Mifflin.

QUASI-EXPERIMENTAL DESIGNS

One of the three basic experimental design types used in empirical research in industrial and organizational psychology and related disciplines is quasi-experimentation. Quasi-experimental designs are different from both randomized experimental designs and nonexperimental designs (see the relevant entries in this volume). In the process of describing the nature of quasi-experimental designs, we make reference to a number of issues having to do with the validity of inferences stemming from research. These issues are covered in the entry on experimental designs in this encyclopedia. The reader is encouraged to review that entry prior to reading this one.

Attributes of Quasi-Experimental Designs

Quasi-experimental designs have a number of features. Taken together they serve to differentiate such designs from designs of the experimental and nonexperimental varieties.

Types of Quasi-Experimental Designs

There are five major varieties of quasi-experimental designs, as was noted by Shadish, Cook, and Campbell in 2002. They differ from one another in terms of the use of comparison conditions, the use of pretests, and the degree to which they are time-series based. A *comparison condition* is used here to refer to either a no-treatment control condition or a condition that has a different level of the independent variable than the focal condition.

Single-Group Designs Without a Control Condition

In terms of single-group designs without a control condition, the weakest ones, with respect to the criterion of internal validity, have only a posttest, for example the one-group posttest-only design. Slightly stronger designs have both a pretest and a posttest, such as the one-group pretest–posttest design. Even stronger designs have multiple pretests and posttests. For designs of the latter type, internal validity can be enhanced through such means as introducing treatment at one time period and removing it at a later period, as in the removed-treatment design. This process can be repeated several times, as with the repeated-treatment design.

Designs With a Control Condition but No Pretest

A second type of quasi-experimental study uses a control condition but no pretest. One example of such a design is the posttest-only design with a nonequivalent control condition. In general, internal validity is quite problematic with studies that use this design because the researcher typically has no knowledge about any pretreatment differences on a host of variables, making it difficult, if not impossible, to attribute posttest differences to the treatment.

Designs With Control Conditions and Pretests

A third type of quasi-experimental design uses both pretests and posttests. The simplest example of this is the untreated control condition design with both pretest and posttest measures. The addition of pretests in the treatment and comparison conditions serves to improve internal validity, such as by ruling out selection as a rival explanation of posttest differences on the dependent variable.

Time-Series Designs

A fourth type of quasi-experimental design uses time-series data to assess how the introduction of a treatment affects measures of dependent variables. For time-series designs, there must be a large number of observations, such as 50 or more, of such variables before and after the introduction of a treatment. In some cases, time-series designs involve both the introduction of a treatment and its subsequent removal. Internal validity is enhanced to the degree that these changes have expected effects on the dependent variables and the changes cannot be attributed to such confounds as history-based fluctuations. In addition, internal validity can be further enhanced through the addition of a nonequivalent control condition to the basic time-series design.

Regression Discontinuity Designs

A fifth type of quasi-experimental design is the regression discontinuity design. In the most basic of such designs, the researcher uses scores on a pretest to assign individuals in a single group to treatment and control conditions. Individuals who have pretest scores at or above a given level are assigned to one condition, such as treatment, and those with scores below that level are assigned to the other condition, such as control. After the treatment, posttest scores are regressed on pretest scores. The effect of the treatment is indexed by a discontinuity in the regression lines for the treatment and control groups.

Manipulation of Variables

In quasi-experiments the values of independent variables $(X_1, X_2, \ldots X_j)$ are manipulated by the researcher. This is important in terms of the criterion of internal validity. More specifically, the fact that the manipulations precede the measurement of dependent variables serves to strengthen inferences about the effects of the manipulated variables on one or more dependent variables. However, internal validity inferences are far more problematic with quasi-experimental designs than they are with experimental designs.

The simultaneous manipulation of several independent variables is common in randomized experiments that are of the factorial variety. However, it is rare to encounter quasi-experiments with more than one independent variable. This is, at least in part, a function of the fact that most quasi-experiments are conducted in non-special-purpose settings (see the "Experimental Designs" entry for more on setting-related issues). Relative to special-purpose settings, in non-special-purpose settings, researchers typically have relatively little control over the number and nature of manipulations to which units, such as individuals or groups, are exposed. In addition, it is often difficult to deliver treatments to units in a uniform manner, reducing statistical conclusion validity. Furthermore, because individuals other than the experimenter, for example managers, have control over many features of the settings in which quasi-experiments are conducted, the same individuals may behave in ways that serve to reduce the construct validity of treatments. For example, to lessen research-related inequalities, managers may deliver desirable *treatments* of their own to units in study conditions that are scheduled to receive

less desirable research-related treatments than others. This can lead to compensatory equalization-based threats to the construct validity of the study's independent variable(s).

Nonrandom Assignment of Units to Conditions

A key characteristic that differentiates quasi-experimental designs from randomized experimental designs is that in the case of the former, there is no capacity to randomly assign units to treatment conditions. Rather than being randomly assigned to conditions by the experimenter, the units may be routed to treatment and control conditions through such means as self-selection or assignment by an administrator such as a manager. An important implication of this is that in most cases, it is difficult, if not impossible, to rule out both selection as a threat to internal validity and selection by treatment interaction as a threat to external validity.

Measurement of Dependent Variables

As is true of all other experimental design types, in quasi-experiments, dependent variables are measured. A number of techniques can be used for this purpose (see the "Experimental Designs" entry for examples). However, it should be added that because most quasi-experiments are conducted in non-special-purpose settings, the experimenter often has diminished control over the timing of measurement and the conditions under which it takes place. In addition, many quasi-experiments use data from archival records such as those of the organizations participating in a study. As a consequence, there are often problems with the construct validity of measures of dependent variables.

Control Over Confounding or Extraneous Variables

As noted above, in the case of quasi-experimental research, there is no capacity to randomly assign units to treatment conditions. As a result, there may be pretreatment differences between or among the conditions on variables that are related to the dependent variables of a study. For example, consider a hypothetical study in which a researcher tested the effects of job enrichment on job satisfaction in an organization having two geographically separate production facilities. Individuals in one facility experienced job enrichment, whereas workers in the other served as no-treatment controls. Because workers were not randomly assigned to these facilities in advance of the quasi-experimental study, they might have differed from one another at the pretreatment period on such variables as age, tenure, pay, and job satisfaction, reducing the study's internal validity.

In quasi-experimental research, assumed confounds are controlled through statistical means. For example, in a study using an untreated control condition and a pretest, a researcher might regress posttest scores on pretest scores and measures of a set of assumed confounds. Regrettably, the statistical controls used in quasi-experimental studies are typically a poor substitute for the control that can be achieved in randomized experiments. This deficiency was described by (a) Shadish, Cook, and Campbell in 2002; (b) Stone-Romero in 2002, 2009, and 2010; and (c) Stone-Romero and Rosopa in 2008, 2010, and 2011. As was explained by these authors, statistical procedures are a poor substitute for experimental design. In addition, despite what far too many researchers seem to believe, internal validity inferences are always suspect when data from studies that use quasi-experimental designs are analyzed with such methods as structural equation modeling and hierarchical regression.

Eugene F. Stone-Romero

See also Experimental Designs; Nonexperimental Designs

Further Readings

Cook, T. D., & Campbell, D. T. (1979). *Quasi-experimentation: Design and analysis issues for field settings*. Boston: Houghton Mifflin.

Shadish, W. R., Cook, T. D., & Campbell, D. T. (2002). *Experimental and quasi-experimental designs for generalized causal inference*. Boston: Houghton Mifflin.

Stone-Romero, E. F. (2002). The relative validity and usefulness of various empirical research designs. In S. G. Rogelberg (Ed.), *Handbook of research methods in industrial and organizational psychology* (pp. 77–98). Malden, MA: Blackwell.

Stone-Romero, E. F. (2009). Implications of research design options for the validity of inferences derived from organizational research. In D. Buchanan & A. Bryman (Eds.), *Handbook of organizational research methods* (pp. 302–327). London: Sage Ltd.

Stone-Romero, E. F. (2010). Research strategies in industrial and organizational psychology: Nonexperimental, quasi-experimental, and randomized experimental research in special purpose and nonspecial purpose settings. In S. Zedeck (Ed.), *Handbook of industrial and organizational psychology* (pp. 35–70). Washington, DC: American Psychological Association Press.

Stone-Romero, E. F., & Rosopa, P. J. (2008). The relative validity of inferences about mediation as a function of research design characteristics. *Organizational Research Methods, 11,* 326–352. 10.1177/1094428107300342

Stone-Romero, E. F., & Rosopa, P. (2010). Research design options for testing mediation models and their implications for facets of validity. *Journal of Managerial Psychology, 25,* 697–712.

Stone-Romero, E. F., & Rosopa, P. (2011). Experimental tests of mediation models: Prospects, problems, and some solutions. *Organizational Research Methods, 14,* 631–646. 10.1177/1094428110372673

QUEEN BEE SYNDROME

The "Queen Bee" label is given to women in leadership positions who have become successful in male-dominated work settings by trying to fit in with the masculine culture, presenting themselves in a masculine fashion, and dissociating themselves from their female colleagues. Research on this phenomenon has revealed three categories of Queen Bee behavior that senior women may show:

1. *Becoming more like men.* Because stereotypes about the characteristics of successful leaders (i.e., agentic qualities) and the gender roles of women (i.e., communal qualities) are incongruent, some women try to resolve these contradictory demands by emphasizing masculine characteristics (e.g. assertiveness, taking risks, competitiveness) and an agentic leadership style (e.g. charismatic, dominant).

2. *Emphasizing how they are different from other women.* For example, in an attempt to escape negative gender stereotypes, senior women may stress that compared to other women they are much more agentic, ambitious, and willing to make sacrifices for their careers.

3. *Endorsing and legitimizing the current gender hierarchy.* Queen Bees do this, for instance, by being very critical of junior women (more so than senior men) and by explicitly endorsing stereotypes of women as being less ambitious and less committed than men (while stressing that they are not like other women). In addition, senior women in male-dominated organizations may endorse a meritocratic ideology while denying that gender discrimination is still an issue. Finally, compared to senior men, senior women have been found to more strongly oppose affirmative action policies designed to improve opportunities for junior women, and to be less willing to act as mentors for their female subordinates.

Explanations

Whereas in the popular media the Queen Bee phenomenon is often described as a typical consequence of women's personalities and inherent competitiveness toward other women, research on the causes of the Queen Bee phenomenon has revealed that this phenomenon is a response to the hardships and gender bias women experience at work. Research to date has uncovered two routes to the Queen Bee phenomenon.

A first way by which senior women become dissociated from junior women is that their career paths and the sacrifices they have made for success in their personal lives are indeed different from the choices many other women make. Gender roles prescribe women to take primary responsibility for their families rather than pursue careers, but achieving career success requires that women prioritize their work over other life domains. As a result, senior women may feel that they have made substantial sacrifices in their personal lives, such as in relationships with their partners and friends and in their decision to have children. Recent research has revealed that this perception of having made considerable sacrifices

for one's career leads senior women to perceive themselves as very different from junior women in terms of commitment and masculine qualities. And this perception of being very different from other women in turn predicts Queen Bee responses such as a low willingness to support affirmative action policies for junior women who have not (yet) made these sacrifices. However, this research also shows that Queen Bees do not distance themselves from women in general, but more specifically dissociate from women below them who have not (yet) made the sacrifices necessary to survive in masculine organizations. As such, they do identify and associate themselves with equally successful women and support affirmative action programs that support other women at their own level to further improve their career outcomes. This finding is important because it refutes interpretations of the Queen Bee effect as stemming from general hostility and competitiveness among professional women.

Second, Queen Bee responses are triggered by male-dominated organizations in which women are underrepresented, and in which implicit and explicit forms of gender bias are present. In these organizations, women come to see their gender as a liability to career success, leading them to experience threats to their gender identity. Experimental research among senior women in the police force has shown that reminding women leaders of the gender bias they experienced in their own careers triggers Queen Bee responses, especially among women with relatively low identification with other women at work. This is explained by social identity theory, which proposes that women who encounter gender bias at work face a dilemma of promoting their personal opportunities (individual mobility) or those of women more generally (collective action). Highly gender-identified women may join other women to strive for increased gender equality. Low-gender-identified women, however, are more likely to work for their individual outcomes by distancing themselves from the negatively stereotyped group of women (as in the Queen Bee phenomenon). Attesting this analysis of the Queen Bee phenomenon as a generic response to identity threat is research showing similar "self-group distancing responses" among other marginalized groups at work (e.g., ethnic and sexual minorities who "act White" or "act straight").

Consequences

The Queen Bee dynamic can have quite negative consequences for women leaders themselves, their subordinates, and the societal position of women more broadly. To start, although Queen Bees may increase their chances to be selected for promotions—especially in masculine organizations—it is also known that women who show behavior that is in conflict with their gender role are evaluated quite negatively. As a result, Queen Bees are less likely to receive the support from their subordinates that is necessary to be an effective leader.

Furthermore, Queen Bee responses can seriously undermine opportunities for other women. First, the success of individual women is unlikely to change the female stereotype when successful women emphasize that their accomplishments are unique and atypical for women as a group. Second, although junior women benefit from having successful female role models, when senior women actively distance themselves from junior women, they are likely to demotivate rather than inspire other women. Finally, Queen Bee responses can serve to legitimize the current gender hierarchy. Negative gender stereotypes expressed and endorsed by women (e.g., a senior woman conveying negative gender-stereotypical expectancies about a female subordinate) are more influential than similar opinions expressed by men, as the former seem more credible and are less likely to be perceived as sexist.

Finally, senior women's denial that discrimination still exists and opposition to affirmative action can be used to blame women, rather than an unequal system, for women's lower outcomes. As such, Queen Bee responses are part of the societal forces that keep the gender hierarchy in its place.

Belle Derks

See also Affirmative Action; Glass Ceiling; Glass Cliff; Identity Management Strategies; Leadership and Gender; Sexual Discrimination; Stereotype Threat; Work–Life Conflict

Further Readings

Derks, B., Van Laar, C., & Ellemers, N. (in press). The Queen Bee phenomenon: Why women leaders distance themselves from junior women. *The Leadership Quarterly*.

Derks, B., Van Laar, C., Ellemers, N., & de Groot, K. (2011). Gender-bias primes elicit queen-bee responses among senior policewomen. *Psychological Science*, 22, 1243–1249.

Ellemers, N., Rink, F., Derks, B., & Ryan, M. K. (2012). Women in high places: When and why promoting women into top positions can harm them individually or as a group (and how to prevent this). *Research in Organizational Behavior*, 32, 163–187.

Ellemers, N., Van Den Heuvel, H., De Gilder, D., Maass, A., & Bonvini, A. (2004). The underrepresentation of women in science: Differential commitment or the queen bee syndrome? *British Journal of Social Psychology*, 43, 315–338.

QUESTIONNAIRES

See Survey Approach

R

RACE NORMING

Race norming is the practice of converting individual test scores to percentile or standard scores within one's racial group. In the process of race norming, an individual's percentile score is not calculated in reference to all persons who took the test; instead, an individual's percentile score is determined only in reference to others in the same racial group. After norming scores by percentile in separate racial groups, the lists are combined to make selection decisions. By norming within racial groups, the same raw score for Whites and Blacks can be converted to different percentile scores on the basis of the distribution of scores for each racial group.

For example, suppose that a White candidate and a Black candidate each earn a raw score of 74 points on a test. If the White candidate's test score is converted to a percentile only in reference to other White candidates and the Black candidate's test score is converted to a percentile only in reference to other Black candidates, the percentile scores earned by the two candidates may not be equal, even though they attained the same raw test score. Perhaps the 74-point raw score for the White candidate may be at the 60th percentile of the White distribution of scores, whereas the 74-point score for the Black candidate may be at the 65th percentile of the Black distribution of scores. When the White and Black percentile scores are combined into a common list and selection decisions are made, the candidates who scored the same 74 raw points on the test might be treated very differently. For example, if an organization decides to hire only persons who scored at the 65th percentile and above, the Black candidate would be selected and the White candidate would not. In another circumstance, the organization could decide to hire persons with the highest percentile first, which would mean that the Black candidate would be selected prior to the White candidate.

As this example demonstrates, when test scores are race normed, the score required to reach a particular percentile score for a member of one group may be different from the score required for a member of another group to reach that same percentile. In effect, the use of separate norms on the basis of race can add points to the scores of persons from a particular racial group.

In general, the adjustment of scores using within-group norming procedures or other techniques (e.g., awarding bonus points) is a common practice in work organizations. For example, many civil service exams call for bonus points to be awarded to veterans. Despite the prevalence of score adjustment, the concept of adjusting scores on the basis of race (e.g., race norming) became controversial during the 1980s. At the time, the U.S. Employment Service (USES) made extensive use of the General Aptitude Test Battery (GATB) for hiring purposes. Research has demonstrated that Whites significantly outperform Blacks and Hispanics on the GATB; therefore, the USES race-normed the data by converting test scores to percentiles within racial groups. During the mid-1980s, this practice was challenged by the

U.S. Department of Justice, and it eventually became a key issue addressed in the Civil Rights Act of 1991. The Civil Rights Act of 1991 made approaches to adjusting test scores on the basis of race illegal. More comprehensively, the act makes it unlawful to adjust or alter the scores of an employment test or to use different cutoff scores based on race, color, religion, sex, or national origin. The ramifications of this provision, both intended and unintended, have generated much discussion, and experts continue to debate how the provision should be interpreted and implemented. Furthermore, the issues surrounding race norming and related concepts continue to evolve with each subsequent interpretation that accompanies relevant Supreme Court case decisions.

Harold W. Goldstein

See also Affirmative Action; Civil Rights Act of 1964, Civil Rights Act of 1991

Further Readings

Gottfredson, L. S. (1994). The science and politics of race-norming. *American Psychologist, 49*(11), 955–963.

Gutman, A., & Dunleavy, E. M. (2013). Contemporary Title VII enforcement: The song remains the same? *Journal of Business Psychology, 28*, 487–503.

Sackett, P. R., & Wilk, S. L. (1994). Within-group norming and other forms of score adjustment in preemployment testing. *American Psychologist, 49*(11), 929–954.

RATER TRAINING

The appraisal of individual work performance occurs in some form or fashion in nearly every organization. Because these appraisals are typically used to provide feedback to employees and to make administrative decisions regarding promotions, bonuses, training, or termination, and because of the recognized importance of employees' satisfaction with the appraisal for individual and organizational outcomes, the quality of performance appraisals is an important issue in both research and practice.

A number of approaches to ensuring the high quality of performance appraisal ratings have been researched and used in practice, including different types of performance appraisal instruments, methods, and rater training programs. Many rater training programs have been developed, and we review the most common of these here. We focus on rater training developed to improve the quality of ratings and/or employee satisfaction with the appraisal process. We will summarize the effectiveness of these different approaches to rater training and relevant research and practical issues.

Here, we will explore what *frame-of-reference* (FOR) training is, how it compares with other types of rater training, its effectiveness at improving the quality of performance ratings, and research and practice issues related to FOR training.

Overview of Rater Training Programs

Rater Training for Quality

Error Reduction Programs

Rater error training programs have the explicit goal of decreasing common rater errors or biases (e.g., leniency or severity, halo, first impression, central tendency). It does this by informing raters of these sorts of common errors and how to avoid them while making ratings. *Rater variability training* is similar in intent, with an emphasis on ensuring that the variability in ratings assigned corresponds to the variability in actual performance levels.

Accuracy Increasing Programs

The early 1980s saw a shift away from training raters to avoid the types of errors just described to training based on a more proactive and direct emphasis on accuracy. This shift was partly the result of findings that suggested that training raters merely to avoid rating errors sometimes led to decreases in accuracy. Earlier forms of these training programs had included *rater accuracy training* and *behavioral observation training*, wherein much of the emphasis was on improving raters' detection, perception, observation, and recall (i.e., memory) of specific performance behaviors. These types of training programs encouraged the recording of behaviors to facilitate later recall and rating judgments. Another approach was *performance dimension training*, which relied primarily on defining the important elements of performance for the raters.

FOR Training

Another type of training that has found much empirical support in increasing rating accuracy is FOR training. FOR training provides an in-depth understanding of an organization's theory of performance, developed through interactive discussion, practice, and feedback. The main objective of FOR training is to provide raters with the knowledge and skills necessary to accurately rate performance according to an agreed-upon frame of reference. Through an interactive process, FOR training is designed to eliminate idiosyncratic standards held by raters and to replace them with a common frame of reference to be used in rating.

The FOR training process consists of four components. First, the trainees (i.e., performance raters) are familiarized with the target theory of performance through an informational presentation. This theory of performance, defined by the organization and therefore unique to the organization and to a particular job, includes the important dimensions (e.g., quality of work, taking initiative) that constitute the performance domain and their definitions. The rating scale to be used—a behaviorally anchored rating scale (BARS)—is usually presented at this time.

Second, trainees engage in a discussion of "critical incidents," or specific ratee behaviors that indicate different effectiveness levels (e.g., high, average, or low) on each performance dimension, with reference to the BARS that contains these specific critical incidents as anchors at different scale points. For example, trainees might be told that if a ratee has no defects in his or her production, that is indicative of a high performance level on the quality-of-work dimension; if a ratee always waits to be told what to do at the beginning of his or her shift, that is indicative of low performance on the taking-initiative dimension.

Third, trainees are given practice rating using this new frame of reference. Specifically, trainees usually view several videotaped vignettes of ratees and rate the practice ratees on each performance dimension discussed in the training.

Fourth and finally, trainees engage in a discussion of these practice ratings and receive feedback on the accuracy of their practice ratings (compared with expert scores).

Rater Training for Employee Satisfaction: Whole-Brain Training

The whole-brain training method, a more recent addition to rater training, starts with the acknowledgment that performance appraisals are emotional experiences for the people being evaluated. Its overall goal is increasing employee satisfaction with ratings given during the performance appraisal. One of the reasons employees give for being dissatisfied is that they believe the performance appraisal rating is a limited judgment of their abilities given that the rater is constrained by the performance dimensions in the formal appraisal process. Advocates for the whole-brain training method contend that the performance dimensions are reflective of the way the left side of the brain processes information but that the right side of the brain also needs to be activated. This would allow raters to better recall information by using both spheres of the brain and therefore make raters more effective at evaluating holistically.

The whole-brain training method consists of having managers consider their employees' performance holistically before evaluating their performance on the specific dimensions found on the performance appraisal form. To foster this holistic view of the employees, the managers are first asked to visualize their employees in different positions of the company (such as CEO) and to go so far as to imagine them in different social contexts in which they could have their whole selves represented (e.g., imagining the slogan an employee would use if running for political office). The managers are then given an opportunity to write general impressions they have of each of their subordinates and any individual performance events in the past year that stand out. Supervisors are also asked to identify their subordinates' usual moods and the intensity of these moods. Only after going through these other activities are supervisors allowed to rate their subordinates on the specific performance appraisal dimensions.

Effectiveness of Rater Training

Although the outcome most researched when evaluating the effectiveness of rater training is performance rating accuracy, several other outcomes have been studied in connection with rater training, and they include feedback and development, rater biases, and rater and ratee reactions. Several research studies have examined the effectiveness of FOR training at improving performance rating accuracy, both in its own right and compared with other rater training programs. This research revealed strong and consistent evidence that FOR training is effective in this regard and, compared with other rater training programs, results in the largest overall increase in rating accuracy.

Whole-brain training shows some promise in increasing ratees' satisfaction with the performance appraisal rating. However, more work needs to be done in this area to fully assess its effectiveness.

Other Research and Practice Related to Rater Training

FOR Training

With the effectiveness of FOR training established, research in this area primarily considers three major issues: (1) the extension of FOR training to other contexts, (2) the examination of underlying mechanisms that explain why FOR training is so effective, and (3) possible boundary conditions on the effectiveness of FOR training. Each of these areas is briefly reviewed here, along with their corresponding implications for the use of FOR training in organizations.

First, regarding the extension of FOR training to other contexts, researchers have used FOR training in assessment centers with a great deal of success. Assessment centers are an in-depth assessment technique used to evaluate candidates (often managerial candidates) for hiring or promotion. Assessors observe and then rate candidates on different performance dimensions across a number of exercises. Providing FOR training to these assessors was found to result in assessment center ratings that were more reliable, accurate, and valid than other types of assessor training.

Second, one stream of research seeks to understand why FOR training is so effective at improving rating accuracy. Proposed explanations that have received some empirical support speculate

that FOR training leads to deeper levels of processing of the material, better recall for specific performance behaviors, more accurate online impression formation, and systematic changes in the content of impressions formed of ratees (making their impressions more abstract and target referent), and that it requires raters to think seriously about the meaning of performance.

Third, although the vast majority of FOR training research supports the conclusion that it is effective at improving rating accuracy, some research has begun to recognize and examine possible boundary conditions on this effectiveness. For example, training effectiveness may depend on the extent to which a rater's performance theory is (not) at odds with the theory espoused by the organization and taught in training. Differences in theory may create cognitive interference or motivational challenges for raters in training. In addition, although most research has found that FOR training results in accuracy improvements regardless of the specific accuracy index used (e.g., elevation, differential elevation, differential accuracy, or stereotype accuracy), other researchers have found that FOR training is more (or less) effective for some accuracy components than others. Such differential effects may have important implications for the use of FOR training in practice. Finally, the examination of FOR training and evidence regarding its effectiveness has largely been contained to laboratory (experimental) settings. The politics and pragmatics surrounding the appraisal of performance in real organizations may present another boundary condition on the effectiveness of FOR training.

Whole-Brain Training

More research on whole-brain training needs to be done to determine its effectiveness for improving employee satisfaction with performance appraisal ratings over a variety of contexts and for different appraisal purposes. Although the results seem promising, in practice the time intensity of the training may pose a problem to managers who are already under tight time constraints.

Deidra J. Schleicher
and Brenda A. Barros-Rivera

See also Performance Appraisal; Performance Appraisal, Objective Indices; Performance Appraisal, Subjective Indices; Performance Feedback; Physical Performance Assessment; Rating Errors and Perceptual Biases

Further Readings

Bernardin, H. J., Buckley, M. R., Tyler, C. L., & Wiese, D. S. (2000). A reconsideration of strategies in rater training. *Research in Personnel and Human Resources Management, 18*, 221–274.

MacDonald, H. A., & Sulsky, L. M. (2009). Rating formats and rater training redux: A context-specific approach for enhancing the effectiveness of performance management. *Canadian Journal of Behavioural Science, 41*(4), 227–240. doi:10.1037/a0015165

Roch, S. G., Woehr, D. J., Mishra, V., & Kieszczynska, U. (2012). Rater training revisited: An updated meta-analytic review of frame-of-reference training. *Journal of Occupational and Organizational Psychology, 85*(2), 370–395. doi:10.1111/j.2044-8325.2011.02045.x

Schleicher, D. J., & Day, D. V. (1998). A cognitive evaluation of frame-of-reference rater training: Content and process issues. *Organizational Behavior and Human Decision Processes, 73*(1), 76–101. doi:10.1006/obhd.1998.2751

Schleicher, D. J., Day, D. V., Mayes, B. T., & Riggio, R. E. (2002). A new frame for frame-of-reference training: Enhancing the construct validity of assessment centers. *Journal of Applied Psychology, 87*(4), 735–746. doi:10.1037/0021-9010.87.4.735

Selden, S., Sherrier, T., & Wooters, R. (2012). Experimental study comparing a traditional approach to performance appraisal training to a whole-brain training method at C. B. Fleet Laboratories. *Human Resource Development Quarterly, 23*(1), 9–34. doi:10.1002/hrdq.21123

Woehr, D. J., & Huffcutt, A. I. (1994). Rater training for performance appraisal: A quantitative review. *Journal of Occupational and Organizational Psychology, 67*(3), 189–205. doi:10.1111/j.2044-8325.1994.tb00562.x

RATING ERRORS AND PERCEPTUAL BIASES

The appraisal and management of performance is an important concern in organizations. Although interest in and use of performance appraisals have increased during the past 40 years, the practice of formally evaluating employees has existed for centuries. Despite its widespread use, the performance appraisal process continues to be plagued by both technical and nontechnical problems that reduce its effectiveness. Rating errors and perceptual biases in performance ratings are two such problems.

Performance ratings—quantifiable yet subjective assessments of an individual's performance made by supervisors, peers, or others who are familiar with the employee's work behavior—are frequently used to assess work performance. However, performance ratings do not always accurately represent an employee's true level of performance. Differences between an employee's true, veridical, objective level of performance and the performance ratings he or she receives, which are believed to be caused by perceptual biases, are referred to as *rating errors*. The term *rating errors* generally refers to the unconscious and unintentional biases that influence the rating task. Biases and rating errors can be classified into several categories; the following sections describe these types of biases and errors, the contexts in which they can occur, their consequences, and possible remedies.

Types of Biases and Rating Errors

Distributional Errors

It is not uncommon to find that 80% to 90% of all employees rated by a single rater receive above-average ratings. This often indicates a *distributional error*, wherein the rater misrepresents the distribution of performance across persons they are evaluating. In other words, these errors occur when the distribution of assigned ratings differs from the (assumed) distribution of actual job performance of the group of employees being rated. Such misrepresentations can occur both in terms of the mean level and the variability of ratings provided. The three most common types of distributional errors are leniency and severity, range restriction, and central tendency errors.

Leniency and severity errors occur when the mean of the ratings of all employees rated by a particular supervisor differs substantially from the midpoint of the rating scale. For example, if the mean rating for all employees rated by a supervisor is very low, then the rater is thought to be overly severe; when the mean rating is very high, he or she is thought to be overly lenient. Recent research has shown that rating severity or leniency is a relatively stable characteristic of the rater and can be related to his or her personality. Specifically, individuals who score higher on agreeableness tend to provide more elevated ratings, whereas individuals who score higher on conscientiousness tend to provide lower ratings.

It is also possible for a rater to fail to make adequate distinctions among multiple ratees when rating their performance, an error referred to as *range restriction*. For example, consider a group of employees who vary widely in their levels of performance on one dimension, quality of work. If all of the supervisor's ratings on this dimension are erroneously clustered within a small range of scores, the variance of the supervisor's ratings will be lower than the variance of the actual performance levels of the ratees, and hence, range restriction is said to occur. Raters who commit this error fail to distinguish among ratees on individual performance dimensions, either because of a lack of opportunity to observe the employees or a conscious desire to avoid differentiating among ratees.

A *central tendency error* is a special form of the range restriction error, wherein ratings tend to cluster near the midpoint of the rating scale. This is the most common and perhaps the most harmful type of error found in organizations, as it tends to inflate the ratings of low performers and underestimate those of high performers. This type of error may be caused by a rater's unwillingness to justify high or low ratings to the organization, or to the ratee or a rater's desire to treat all employees equally and avoid hostility among ratees.

Although these distributional errors are typically assumed to reduce the accuracy of performance ratings, such a conclusion may be premature, for several reasons. First, the implicit assumption behind distributional errors is that the true underlying distribution of performance is known, which is rarely the case. Second, organizations expend considerable effort through their selection and training systems to ensure that the distribution of performance is, in fact, skewed (e.g., more high performers than low performers), in which case observed leniency or range restriction may not be an error but a reflection of the actual performance of employees. Thus, comparison of raters on the basis of such errors should be undertaken only after the relevant contextual factors affecting each group of raters and ratees have been considered.

Correlational and Halo Errors

It is not uncommon to find that raters give similar evaluations across multiple performance dimensions when evaluating one employee, even when those dimensions are clearly distinct. This is referred to as a *halo error*, and it is based on the rater's tendency to let the overall evaluation or the evaluation of one dimension color ratings on other dimensions. Consider, for example, an employee who is outstanding in his ability to convince delinquent customers to pay up but performs poorly in terms of identifying new customers and expanding his market. In such a situation, halo error would occur if his excellence in the area of delinquent accounts caused his manager to rate him highly on the other performance dimensions as well. Thus, halo errors occur when raters fail to differentiate between the different dimensions of performance. (Halo errors wherein a negative rating on one dimension adversely affects ratings on other dimensions are sometimes referred to as *horn effects*.) Halo errors are typically caused by the confirmatory biases of raters (wherein raters form initial impressions on the basis of certain performance dimensions and tend to look for confirmation rather than disconfirmation of their judgments in the evaluation of other aspects of performance), the discounting of inconsistent information, or the lack of adequate information about the ratee when making evaluations.

However, like the other errors reviewed here, the existence of halo error should be interpreted with caution. Halo effects may be a function of the actual conceptual similarity among the dimensions being rated (true halo) rather than cognitive biases and errors by raters (illusory halo). It is also possible that all of the dimensions on a performance appraisal scale relate to overall performance, so they are unlikely to be seen as completely independent by raters. In such cases, observed halo may be a reflection of actual performance rather than error.

Other Errors and Biases

Performance appraisal ratings can also be plagued by other specific errors and biases. The *similar-to-me error* refers to the tendency of some raters to rate those who resemble themselves more highly than they rate others. The *first-impression error* occurs when a rater allows early experiences with a ratee to color or distort later information when making performance judgments. *Contrast effects* refer to the tendency of a rater to evaluate ratees relative to others rather than against objective rating standards. For example, if Jane is a stellar performer and her supervisor tends to rate other employees using Jane as the comparative standard, then other employees are likely to be rated lower than they deserve.

The *recency effect* describes the tendency of minor events that have occurred recently to influence ratings more than other events that occurred during the appraisal period. Such errors typically occur when the rater does not keep formal records of performance or critical incidents involving each ratee. The tendency to attribute performance failings to factors that are under the control of the individual and performance successes to external causes is known as *attribution bias*. For example, if a supervisor attributes the successes of her subordinates to her leadership skills but their failures to their own lack of ability, her performance ratings are affected by attribution bias.

Finally, *stereotyping* refers to the tendency to generalize across groups and ignore individual differences. For example, consider William, a salesman who is quiet and reserved but whose sales record is one of the best in the company, in contrast to the stereotypical salesperson. If his supervisor has an implicit belief that extroverted, outgoing behavior is a prerequisite for being a good salesperson, she may rate William's performance lower because of that stereotype.

These errors can sometimes occur together in practice, or one error may be the cause of another observed error. For example, the contrast effect error, wherein employees are compared with one stellar employee, could result in observed severity errors.

Contextual Issues Influencing Biases and Rating Errors

Relationship Quality Between Supervisor and Subordinate

Among the contextual circumstances that could affect performance ratings is the quality of the relationship between the supervisor and the subordinate, or the leader–member exchange (LMX), a construct that can be measured both from the supervisor's and the subordinate's perspectives. Supervisors' ratings of LMX are especially influential in performance appraisal ratings and can serve as a basis for halo error.

One specific way in which LMX influences performance ratings is in supervisors' attribution of subordinates' success. When supervisors have high LMX with their subordinates, they attribute a subordinate's success to the subordinate. Conversely, when a supervisor has low LMX with a subordinate, the subordinate's success is attributed to external factors. This has implications for performance ratings because this gives rise to a different type of bias in that supervisors attribute the success of their in-group subordinates (those with high LMX) to the subordinates but that of out-group subordinates (those with low LMX) to external factors outside of the subordinates' control.

Performance Appraisal Purpose

The purpose for performance appraisals (e.g., developmental, administrative) can vary by organization, and this contextual factor also exerts a strong influence on performance ratings. When performance appraisals are conducted with the purpose of making administrative decisions, the ratings tend to be higher than when they are conducted for developmental purposes. This is consistent with leniency (vs. severity) errors. It is also possible to see more range restriction under administrative purposes than developmental purposes.

These errors can sometimes occur together in practice, or one error may be the cause of another observed error. For example, the contrast effect error, wherein employees are compared with one stellar employee, could result in observed severity errors.

Consequences of Rating Errors

Several negative consequences may befall performance appraisal and management systems characterized by the errors just described. For example, elevated ratings (i.e., the leniency error) reduce the funds available to recognize and reward stellar performance (because the funds must be shared among a larger number of employees), and therefore employees may become dissatisfied with both performance management and reward systems. Besides being a mechanism for allocating rewards, performance appraisals are also used to provide feedback. Employees whose supervisors fail to give them accurate information about performance deficiencies have little motivation (or guidance) to improve. As a result, such employees are likely to be passed over for opportunities they might have had if they had been honestly confronted with the need for change. Employees who receive inflated yet inaccurate ratings may be placed in situations they are unable to handle, causing them to experience failure. Short-term kindness on the supervisor's part may result in long-term harm to the employees.

Elevated or otherwise inaccurate ratings also make it difficult to substantiate termination decisions, not only in court (if the decision is contested) but also to the remaining employees, who may question the fairness and meaningfulness of performance ratings. Equity theory suggests that individuals are concerned not only with their own situations in an absolute sense ("How much money am I making?") but also with the way their situations compare with those of others in the organization ("How does the ratio of my input in the job to the output or reward I receive compare with that of others?"). A good performer, observing that a lackluster coworker is receiving the same appraisal ratings—and thus the same organizational rewards

for far lower contribution—perceives his or her situation as unfair. Equity theory suggests that as a result of such comparisons, the good performer will act to make the situation equitable by reducing his or her effort or even leaving the organization.

Remedial Measures

Approaches to avoiding these rating errors and perceptual biases depend on the format of the rating instrument used. Forced-choice instruments ask the rater to select one item (from a list of four or five statements) that best describes the employee's performance. Because the statements are all similar in desirability (yet differ in their relation to job performance), this format is designed to eliminate the tendency of raters to be lenient, thus minimizing bias. Forced-distribution performance appraisal systems attempt to impose a normal distribution on the ratings by forcing the rater to assign a certain percentage of employees to each performance category. Similarly, paired comparison performance rating methods force raters to make distinctions among ratees by comparing each ratee with every other one, producing an overall rank order of employees. Finally, a commonly used format is the behaviorally anchored rating scale, which specifies poor, average, and good performance levels using anchors of behavioral exemplars for each performance dimension. This format is conducive to accurate and differentiated employee performance ratings on different dimensions. Although each of these different rating formats has its advantages, each also comes with a corresponding set of disadvantages.

A more recent (and arguably more effective) approach to dealing with rating errors is to train raters in performance appraisal rating methods. For example, rater error training (RET) focuses specifically on reducing errors by making raters aware of them and their possible causes. Despite its effectiveness in reducing rater errors, research has found that RET can actually decrease the accuracy of ratings (recall that errors do not always equal inaccuracy). As a result of using RET, raters seem to replace an erroneous rating strategy (e.g., lenient or haloed ratings) with an invalid rating bias (avoid rater errors). Thus, merely avoiding rater errors does not seem to ensure accuracy.

The best-known rater training program with the goal of increasing accuracy is frame-of-reference (FOR) training. In FOR training, raters discuss the performance dimensions used in the evaluation system and the behaviors that represent different effectiveness levels on each performance dimension; they also practice making ratings and receive feedback on the accuracy of their practice ratings. Research suggests that FOR training is the single most effective training strategy for improving rater accuracy.

Deidra J. Schleicher
and Brenda A. Barros-Rivera

See also Performance Appraisal; Performance Appraisal, Objective Indices; Performance Appraisal, Subjective Indices; Performance Feedback; Rater Training

Further Readings

Borman, W. C. (1991). Job behavior, performance and effectiveness. In M. D. Dunnette & L. M. Hough (Eds.), *Handbook of industrial and organizational psychology* (2nd ed., Vol. 3, pp. 271–326). Palo Alto, CA: Consulting Psychologists Press.

Cooper, W. (1981). Ubiquitous halo. *Psychological Bulletin, 90,* 218–244.

Duarte, N., Goodson, J., & Klich, N. (1994). Effects of dyadic quality and duration on performance appraisal. *Academy of Management Journal, 37*(3), 499–521. doi:10.2307/256698

Heidemeier, H., & Moser, K. (2009). Self–other agreement in job performance ratings: A meta-analytic test of a process model. *Journal of Applied Psychology, 94*(2), 353–370. doi:10.1037/0021-9010.94.2.353

Jawahar, I. M., & Williams, C. R. (1997). Where all the children are above average: The performance appraisal purpose effect. *Personnel Psychology, 50*(4), 905–925. doi:10.1111/j.1744-6570.1997.tb01487.x

Murphy, K. R., & Cleveland, J. N. (1991). *Performance appraisal: An organizational perspective.* Boston: Allyn & Bacon.

Murphy, K. R., Cleveland, J. N., Skattebo, A. L., & Kinney, T. B. (2004). Raters who pursue different goals give different ratings. *Journal of Applied Psychology, 89*(1), 158–164. doi:10.1037/0021-9010 .89.1.158

Schleicher, D. J., & Day, D. V. (1998). A cognitive evaluation of Frame-of-Reference rater training: Content and process issues. *Organizational Behavior and Human Decision Processes, 73*(1), 76–101. doi:10 .1006/obhd.1998.2751

Smither, J. W. (1998). *Performance appraisal: State of the art in practice.* San Francisco, CA: Jossey-Bass.

RATIONAL DECISION MAKING THEORY

The so-called rational choice model of decision making does not reflect how people actually make decisions. It is nonetheless regarded as a good model for how people should make decisions, including organizationally relevant decisions. It therefore provides the basis for interventions aimed at improving decision making. Because of space constraints, the focus of this entry is on one contemporary form of the model, the weighted additive expected utility model, which arguably has the most applications to industrial and organizational psychology.

The Weighted Additive Expected Utility Model

A decision reflects a choice among several alternatives (options). In the weighted additive expected utility model, each alternative is compared along multiple attributes (dimensions or factors) in an attempt to maximize "utility." Specifically, a decision maker using this model (a) judges the importance of each attribute, (b) estimates the expected utility of each alternative across attributes, and finally, (c) chooses the alternative with the highest expected utility. *Utility* is commonly defined as the presence of pleasure and the absence of pain to the decision maker or the organization he or she represents. Consider the case of a job seeker—let us call her Minerva—who must choose among several job offers (i.e., alternatives) that vary in salary, status, and job security (i.e., attributes). If Minerva uses a weighted additive model, she would (a) determine how important salary, status, and job security are to her; (b) estimate the overall happiness potential (i.e., expected utility) associated with each job offer; and (c) choose the job offer with the highest happiness potential.

The expected utility for each alternative in this model is the importance-weighted sum of the utilities of the attributes. Mathematically,

$$\text{Expected utility} = \sum_{\substack{\text{Number of} \\ \text{possible} \\ \text{outcomes}}} \left\{ \begin{bmatrix} \text{Importance weight} \\ \text{associated with an attribute} \end{bmatrix} \times \begin{bmatrix} \text{Utility of} \\ \text{that attribute} \end{bmatrix} \right\}$$

This equation resembles expectancy-valence models of motivation and belief-value models of attitudes. The equation is also relevant to job choice decisions made by job seekers (as in the aforementioned Minerva example) and employee selection (and promotion and termination, etc.) decisions made by managers. Finally, the equation resembles a multiple regression equation (albeit without intercept and residual terms); indeed, when the expected utility scores are known, multiple regression equations can be used to generate relative importance weights empirically. The use of the term *utility* here is therefore consistent with, but broader than, its use in the context of a "utility analysis" in industrial psychology.

From Expected Value to Expected Utility: The Search for a Descriptive Rational Choice Model

Expected *utility* models such as the weighted additive model grew out of earlier expected *value* models in which utility was equated with monetary value and importance with objective probability. Both assumptions, however, were ultimately found to be erroneous. Although utility is influenced by monetary value, the relationship is nonlinear (e.g., the utility of $1,000 is higher for a poor person than a rich person). Moreover, some attributes (e.g., status and job security in Minerva's case) cannot easily be reduced to monetary value. Similarly, although importance is influenced by objective probability, subjective probabilities often differ from objective probabilities. Moreover, importance judgments are influenced by several factors other than probability (e.g., ambiguity, delay).

By embracing subjectivity, expected utility models require fewer problematic psychological assumptions than the older expected value models. Nonetheless, expected utility models retain

several assumptions. For example, the weighted additive model assumes that (a) among job offers, if Minerva prefers A to B and B to C, she must prefer A to C; (b) among a pair of job offers, Minerva must either prefer one offer or else be indifferent between the offers; (c) Minerva's preference between job offers A and B should not be influenced by the presence versus absence of job offer C; (d) Minerva's preference among job offers should not be affected by whether she views all the job offers as good or bad; and (e) Minerva's preference among job offers should be identical if she makes the decision twice (e.g., once when stressed and once when calm).

Yet even these remaining assumptions are routinely violated when people make decisions. The psychologists Kahneman and Tversky have documented numerous commonly used decision heuristics (cognitive shortcuts) that (a) violate the assumptions of expected utility models, (b) involve a complex mathematical function between monetary value and utility (concave for gains, convex for losses, and steeper for losses than gains), and (c) are frequently efficient without sacrificing effectiveness, but (d) sometimes lead to spectacularly biased (ineffective) decisions. Therefore, even the newer expected utility form of the rational choice model cannot be thought of as a descriptive theory (i.e., a theory that describes how people actually make decisions).

The Rational Choice Model as a Normative Theory

Rational choice theory is nonetheless widely viewed as a normative theory—that is, a theory of how people should make decisions. Most (though not all) psychologists continue to believe that rational decision makers should aim to maximize utility and that the aforementioned assumptions underlying the rational choice model are good approximations of the assumptions underlying rational decision making more generally. For instance, when Kahneman and Tversky argue that heuristical thinking frequently yields biased decisions, they describe "bias" as the difference between the decisions reached under heuristical thinking and those reached using the rational choice model.

The rational choice model therefore serves as a good basis for interventions intended to align actual and normative decision making. For instance, a decision aid can perform the necessary mathematical calculations (e.g., weighting and adding) required under a rational choice model, thereby sparing the decision maker from having to do so. In some cases, it may be possible to go even further by modifying the environment to actually take advantage of heuristical thinking. This strategy relies on people's tendency toward inaction, which results in them frequently choosing the default alternative. Decision making would be improved if the default alternative were provided automatically to the decision maker by a rational choice decision aid. For example, a hiring manager could be presented automatically with the job applicant who possesses the highest weighted additive score on a model that includes attributes such as a work sample test as well as measures of general mental ability and the personality trait of conscientiousness. The hiring manager could override the default alternative, but will often opt not to do so, thereby making a good decision through inertia.

Reeshad S. Dalal

See also Expectancy Theory of Work Motivation; Judgment and Decision-Making Process; Judgment and Decision-Making Process: Heuristics, Cognitive Biases, and Contextual Influences; Utility Analysis

Further Readings

Briggs, R. (2014). Normative theories of rational choice: Expected utility. In E. N. Zalta (Ed.), *The Stanford encyclopedia of philosophy* (fall 2014 ed.). http://plato.stanford.edu/archives/fall2014/entries/rationality-normative-utility

Heukelom, F. (2014). *Behavioral economics: A history.* New York: Cambridge University Press.

Kahneman, D. (2003). Maps of bounded rationality: Psychology for behavioral economics. *American Economic Review*, 93, 1449–1475.

Milkman, K. L., Chugh, D., & Bazerman, M. H. (2009). How can decision making be improved? *Perspectives on Psychological Science*, 4, 379–383.

Stevenson, M. K., Busemeyer, J. R., & Naylor, J. R. (1990). Judgment and decision-making theory. In M. D. Dunnette & L. M. Hough (Eds.), *Handbook of industrial and organizational psychology* (pp. 283–374). Palo Alto, CA: Consulting Psychologists Press.

Tversky, A. (1975). A critique of expected utility theory: Descriptive and normative considerations. *Erkenntnis*, 9, 163–173.

REALISTIC JOB PREVIEW

The *realistic job preview* (RJP) is the primary method of a realistic recruitment program. The RJP is the presentation of realistic, often quite negative, information about an organization to a job candidate. This information is given to job candidates during the selection process to help them make informed job choices, should job offers be made. Another realistic recruitment strategy is the use of certain recruitment sources (e.g., employee referrals) that communicate realistic information to job candidates while avoiding others that do not (e.g., newspaper ads). Finally, four selection methods that communicate realistic information to job candidates are briefly discussed here, because their primary intended purpose is selection rather than recruitment.

The RJP contains accurate information about job duties, which can be obtained from interviews with subject-matter experts or from a formal job analysis. The RJP also contains information about an organization's culture, which can be obtained from surveys, interviews with current employees, and exit interviews. There are four criteria for selecting information for the RJP: (a) it is important to most recruits, (b) it is not widely known outside the organization, (c) it is a reason that leads newcomers to quit, and (d) it is related to successful job performance after being hired. Because it is necessary to tailor the RJP to both the job and the organization, the RJP is not so much a specific technique but a general approach to recruitment. Furthermore, organizations may differ in the particular means used to present realistic information to job candidates; for example, organizations may use brochures, discussions during job interviews, or videos. Sometimes, a combination of these three specific techniques is used; combining the latter two is probably the best approach.

One important purpose of the RJP is to increase the degree of fit between newcomers and the organizations they seek to join. Two types of fit are affected: (a) person–job fit and (b) person–organization fit. Good person–job fit typically results in better newcomer performance and indirectly increases retention. Good person–organization fit typically results in reduced quitting and indirectly increases job performance. To the extent that an RJP affects candidates' job choices, also known as self-selection, it can improve either or both types of fit.

The information in the RJP is communicated to job applicants before they enter the organization. Realistic information disseminated after organizational entry is defined as newcomer orientation, which is different from the RJP in several ways. The most important difference is that the primary purpose of newcomer orientation is to help new hires cope with both a new job and a new organizational culture. Thus, newcomer orientation teaches solutions to common newcomer adjustment problems during organizational entry. In contrast, the RJP presents adjustment problems without solutions, as one purpose of the RJP is to discourage job candidates who are likely to be misfits with the job or organizational culture.

For a long time, the RJP was thought to affect newcomer retention more than job performance, as reported in a 1985 review by Steve Premack and John Wanous. However, a 1998 review by Jean Phillips found a stronger effect of the RJP on job performance while affirming the same effect on the retention of new hires. Unfortunately, the most recent review (2011) by Earnest, Allen, and Landis did not assess effects on job performance.

Some RJP methods are more effective than others. Specifically, the best RJP technique for hiring better performers is the video, in which recruits are shown a role model performing critical job duties successfully. Role models are an effective way to demonstrate the interpersonal and physical skills that are part of most entry-level jobs.

The best RJP method for increasing new hire retention is a two-way conversation between the job candidate and a job interviewer during the job interview. If a written RJP preceded the conversation, it is even more effective. Explaining why this is the case is more complicated. There are four hypotheses. First, the information provided in the RJP helps job candidates choose more effectively among job offers. This process of self-selection is believed to increase person–organization fit. Furthermore, research on cognitive dissonance suggests that when job candidates feel free to accept or reject a job offer, they are more likely to be committed to the choice. Second, the RJP can "vaccinate" expectations against disappointment after organizational entry because the most dissatisfying job and organizational factors have already been anticipated. Third, the information in the RJP can help newcomers cope more effectively with the stress of being in a new environment, called "the work of worry" by Irving Janis. Finally, the RJP can enhance the perceived trustworthiness or supportiveness of the organization to job candidates, increasing their initial commitment to the organization. Support for any one of these hypotheses does not necessarily mean that others are refuted, however; all are viable explanations.

Several guidelines for designing and using the RJP can be derived from the reviews of Premack and Wanous, Phillips, and Earnest et al., who used sophisticated quantitative methods. First, self-selection should be explicitly encouraged. That is, job candidates should be advised to carefully consider whether to accept or reject a job offer. This is best done during the job interview, and this may be an important reason why it is the best method for increasing new hire retention. Second, the RJP message must be credible and/or perceived by job applicants as organizational honesty in recruitment. Credibility can be achieved by using actual employees as communicators, whether in a video or a job interview. This may explain why using only a brochure is the least effective of all the methods. Third, the way typical employees feel about the organization, not just sterile facts, must be part of the RJP. Again, employee feelings are best provided in a video or a job interview. Fourth, the balance between positive and negative information should closely match the realities of the job itself. This requires careful data collection and analysis before developing the RJP. Finally, the RJP should normally be done before rather than after hiring, but not so early that the information is ignored. (An exception might be to position the RJP at the end of executive recruitment, although there is no research on executives.)

Research continues to identify the boundaries of the RJP. First, if the retention rate for new hires is very low, the job is probably so undesirable that an RJP will have no effect on job survival. For example, one study of newly hired self-service gas station attendants revealed that none of the 325 new hires lasted as long as 9 months. In fact, many quit by the end of the first month. In organizations with very high retention, the RJP may not be able to improve on that already high level. Therefore, the RJP is probably most effective when the 1-year job retention rate for newcomers is in the range of 50% to 80%. For an organization with a 50% job retention rate (for the first year after being hired), use of the RJP is estimated to increase job retention to a range of 56% to 59%, according to Premack and Wanous and confirmed by two subsequent reviews.

Second, if the labor market has relatively few job openings, the RJP will have little effect on a job candidate's job choice because the chance of obtaining multiple job offers is low. Furthermore, a very tight labor market means that new hires tend to stick with jobs even if they would prefer to leave them. Third, the RJP appears to be more effective when job candidates have some previous job knowledge or work experience because they can better understand the information that is provided. Fourth, both Phillips and Wanous found that the RJP is more effective at increasing newcomer retention in business organizations than in the military. The primary reason for the difference in job survival rates is that there are restrictions on attrition from the military.

The impact of the RJP can be translated into dollar terms (called a utility analysis) by calculating the difference between the number of new hires needed without using RJP versus the number needed when using RJP. Consider an organization that wants to hire and retain 100 new employees. If the job retention rate for the first year is 50%, the organization will need to hire 200 new employees to retain the target goal of 100. If the RJP increases job retention from 50% to 56%, the organization would have to hire only 178 people.

If the RJP increases job retention from 50% to 59%, the organization would have to hire only 169 new people. For fast food chain restaurants (e.g., McDonald's, Wendy's, Burger King, Pizza Hut) that typically hire more than 100,000 newcomers corporation-wide at a cost of $400 to $500 per hire, the dollar savings in recruitment and hiring can be in the tens of millions of dollars.

The RJP may also be relevant for other aspects of human resource management. It could easily be used to prepare managers for international assignments. Although it is intuitively appealing, there is no rigorous research on this topic—a puzzling gap, as the cost of failure in international assignments for executives is far greater than the cost of lower paying, entry-level jobs, which typify most studies of the RJP.

Realistic Recruiting Sources

Besides the RJP, there are other ways realistic information can be communicated to job candidates. One recruitment strategy is to hire from sources that have higher job retention rates and higher job performance. A rigorous review of this research by Michael Zottoli and John Wanous (2000) found that inside sources (referrals by employees and rehires) had significantly better job retention rates than those from outside sources (newspaper ads and employment agencies). Furthermore, inside sources produced better job performers, although the effect on performance was less than that on retention. However, the effects of recruitment source on retention and performance are both significant. Their usefulness in dollar terms can be estimated in the same way as the RJP. Although there are fewer recruitment source studies (25) than RJP studies (more than 50), there seems to be enough evidence that the results of recruitment source research can be taken seriously. Unfortunately, no study has yet examined organizations that combine the RJP with inside recruitment sources. Thus, the effect of combining these realistic recruitment methods is unknown at present.

Six hypotheses have been offered to explain the link between recruitment source, job survival, and job performance. First, inside recruits have more accurate information, which results in less disappointment among newcomers. Second, having accurate information enables job candidates to make better job choices. Third, inside recruits fit better with the organization because those who referred them know what it takes to succeed. Fourth, candidates from employment agencies or newspaper ads may know more about the full range of job possibilities and thus have higher turnover than candidates referred by other sources. Fifth, source differences may be the result of systematic differences in the types of candidates attracted from each source. Sixth, candidates referred by friends may be treated better by experienced employees and thus have higher retention than other new hires.

A second recruitment source strategy is to set up a company Web site that communicates realistic information to potential job candidates. Unfortunately, there is no rigorous research on real organizational Web sites as of this writing. Studies of students responding to fictitious Web sites are just now beginning to be published. However, the trustworthiness of research using college students reacting to fictitious Web sites has yet to be established.

The Web site of Texas Instruments (TI; www .ti.com) provides one example of how a Web site can be used for realistic recruitment. Job seekers are directed to a section in which a self-scored survey can be taken. The purpose of the survey is to assess both person–job fit (14 questions) and person–organization fit (18 questions), which TI refers to as "job content fit" and "work environment fit," respectively. Job seekers are asked to rate certain items on a five-point scale ranging from *strongly agree* to *strongly disagree*. After responding to the 32 items, the job seeker is then given an overall score. The score is a simple dichotomy: The candidate either fits or does not fit in at TI. In addition to overall fit, the job seeker is also shown TI's "best answer" to each of the questions. The company is careful to remind job seekers that TI's best answers are not right or wrong—rather, they indicate TI's best estimate of its typical work content and organizational culture. Unfortunately, the company does not indicate how these best answers were determined.

Realistic Selection Methods

Although RJP and recruitment sources are the two major concerns in realistic recruitment, there are four selection methods that may also communicate realistic information, complementing the use of the

RJP and inside recruitment sources. These methods are (a) probationary employment, (b) structured job interviews (i.e., the situational interview and the behavior description interview), (c) work sample tests (both verbal and motor skills tests), and (d) assessment centers. Research on these four methods has focused on job performance rather than retention. Because these techniques are primarily selection rather than recruitment methods, a detailed analysis is beyond the scope of this entry. As predictors of job performance, however, their validity and utility are both fairly well established.

John P. Wanous

See also Job Advertisements; Organizational Socialization; Recruitment; Recruitment Sources

Further Readings

Earnest, D. R., Allen, D. G., & Landis, R. S. 2011. Mechanisms linking realistic job previews with turnover: A meta-analytic path analysis. *Personnel Psychology, 64,* 865–897.

Janis, I. L. (1958). *Psychological stress: Psychoanalytic and behavioral studies of surgical patients.* New York: John Wiley.

Phillips, J. M. (1998). Effects of realistic job previews on multiple organizational outcomes: A meta-analysis. *Academy of Management Journal, 41,* 673–690.

Premack, S. L., & Wanous, J. P. (1985). A meta-analysis of realistic job preview experiments. *Journal of Applied Psychology, 70,* 706–719.

Wanous, J. P. (1992). *Organizational entry: Recruitment, selection, orientation, and socialization of newcomers* (2nd ed.). Reading, MA: Addison-Wesley.

Zottoli, M. A., & Wanous, J. P. (2000). Recruitment source research: Current status and future directions. *Human Resource Management Review, 10,* 353–382.

RECOVERY FROM WORK/ PSYCHOLOGICAL DETACHMENT

Modern-day work is demanding, especially so with increasing globalization and therefore more competition entering the workplace. As a result, employees are increasingly experiencing negative consequences associated with working, including high levels of perceived stress, conflict between work and family roles, and physical and psychological ill health. One optimal way to prevent or circumvent the negative consequences associated with demanding work is to physically, mentally, and/or emotionally recover and detach from work. Recovery from work is especially important when it is not feasible for organizations to alter stressful job characteristics (e.g., dealing with unhappy customers) or overwhelming job demands (e.g., intense time pressure).

Recovery from work is defined as the process through which an individual temporarily reduces or erases symptoms of strain (e.g., work-related exhaustion or cynicism) caused by work-related stressors (e.g., long hours or time pressure). Occupational health psychologists rely on models of work stress, such as the conservation of resources (COR) theory and the job demands–control (JDC) theory to understand the relationships between job characteristics, resources, and strain. According to COR theory, strain is a result of resource loss at work. These resources, which are depleted in an effort to meet work demands, include object resources (e.g., material goods, such as a house or a car), condition resources (e.g., role or status at work or at home), personal resources (e.g., self-efficacy or confidence), and energy resources (e.g., money and time). When an employee has too many demands relative to resources, the result is strain. Similarly, JDC theory reflects the idea that employees experience a variety of job characteristics (e.g., clarity regarding one's work role responsibilities) that are demanding on resources (e.g., personal or energy resources) as well as job characteristics that enhance their levels of control at work (e.g., control over work hours). Jobs with high levels of demand and less control are hypothesized to result in the most strain.

Both COR and JDC theories specify that excessive job demands at work relative to available resources can lead to strain, which often results in myriad negative outcomes, specifically perceived stress. To prevent stress, an individual might take time to recover from work and replenish resources depleted through working. There are several well-researched types of recovery experiences or strategies, all of which are related to a state of being psychologically detached from work. According to the *stressor-detachment model*, psychological detachment has the strongest relationships with job characteristics and job outcomes and is the most crucial of the recovery experiences for well-being outcomes. As such, organizations are beginning to recognize the significance of recovery from job-related strain and have started to provide benefits, frequently in the form of official respites from work, with the goal of facilitating psychological detachment.

Recovery Experiences

Relaxation, mastery, control, affiliation, and psychological detachment are all studied as experiences that facilitate recovery from work. *Relaxation* takes multiple different forms, including progressive muscle relaxation, in which an individual seeks awareness of muscle tension and willfully tenses and relaxes different muscle groups, and transcendental meditation, in which an individual focuses awareness on breathing and relaxation-inducing mental imagery. The goal of relaxation experiences is a state of relaxation, consisting of low arousal and high positive affect. *Mastery* experiences include learning about and accomplishing goals in nonwork hobbies (e.g., chess, rock climbing, cooking, or playing a musical instrument). Mastery experiences are characterized by activities that can increase the competence and self-efficacy of an individual, in essence building up these resources. *Control* experiences involve having a sense of control, or the ability to choose between two or more options, in areas of life besides work, such as leisure time or family activities. Control is considered an external resource that can facilitate recovery by allowing an individual to choose preferred activities that provide enhanced well-being outside of work. *Affiliation* experiences involve spending time with family and nonwork friends. Affiliation experiences give individuals the opportunity to focus on building and maintaining nonwork and nonnetworking relationships.

Relaxation, mastery, control, and affiliation recovery experiences are well studied and beneficial; however, psychological detachment has garnered the majority of attention in the recovery literature. *Psychological detachment* from work is achieved when job demands and job-related strain are both avoided and ignored when an employee is not at work. An individual who is psychologically detached has "switched off" and does not engage in work tasks after work hours. Psychological detachment is foremost a mental experience in that it takes place inside the mind by avoiding thoughts and mental imagery concerning work when the individual is physically distant from work. However, psychological detachment can also involve behaviors that promote detachment, such as not logging in to e-mail and turning off a work cell phone. These physical actions facilitate the mental "switching off" of work-related thoughts. As with most recovery experiences, psychological detachment, as a predominantly psychological experience, does not facilitate recovery from physical stressors (e.g., muscle pain due to repetitive motion).

Each aforementioned recovery experience builds up or replenishes resources differently, but by definition, relaxation, mastery, control, and affiliation experiences contribute to experiencing psychological detachment in that they may facilitate diverting thoughts away from work-related strain. For instance, if an individual spends time after work planning a family vacation, which might be both a control and an affiliative experience, the individual is thinking about the vacation destination and family activities instead of work and is therefore psychologically detaching from work.

Job Stressors and Psychological Detachment

The stressor-detachment model describes the relationships among job stressors, detachment, and outcomes by referring to the *allostatic load model* as a framework to explore the relationship between stressors and detachment. Job stressors, typically in the form of physical and psychological job characteristics, are the primary causes of employees' lack of recovering and detaching from work. The allostatic load model proposes that sustained activation of a stress response caused by strain in reaction to a stressor is both longer lasting and more influential than the initial stress response itself. Thus, the more job demands an individual experiences that result in strain and perceived stress, the longer the activated stress response will last. The long-lasting impact of certain job demands affects individuals' ability to psychologically detach outside of work.

The primary job stressors related to less psychological detachment are long work hours (i.e., >50-hour workweeks), work intensity (i.e., cognitively or physically demanding work tasks), time pressure (i.e., limited time allotted to complete work tasks), emotional and/or cognitive demands (i.e., interpersonal or mental requirements), role ambiguity (i.e., confusion or lack of clarity concerning what an individual's work role is in an organization), and role conflict (i.e., when fulfilling one role at work impedes the ability to fulfill another work role). These job characteristics are particularly demanding at work and might overtax resources. These stressors are therefore often predictive of lower levels of psychological detachment because of the perceived stress associated with the imbalance of demands and resources. There is an especially strong relationship between time pressure, which requires the use of energy resources and often results in both mental and physical fatigue, and lack of psychological detachment. When an individual arrives home from work, it may be more difficult for the individual to rebuild resources using recovery experiences, because each experience requires some modicum of energy, which has been depleted. Additionally, the sustained activation of stress caused by intense time pressure keeps the stress response elevated after the time pressure is gone. In addition to actual characteristics and demands of jobs, an employee's level of job involvement is also related to psychological detachment from work. The more an individual identifies and is involved with his or her job, the more important the job is to the individual. It follows that the more important or valued the job is to the individual, the harder it is for that individual to psychologically detach during off-work hours, because it becomes harder to stop thinking about the job during off time. However, it is possible that lack of detachment in this particular case (i.e., job involvement) is not necessarily associated with strain outcomes, because the job is central to the individual. Most of the time, however, psychological detachment is strongly related to strain outcomes.

Detachment and Strain Outcomes

Job demands and other characteristics of work relate to a lack of psychological detachment, which is subsequently related to numerous negative outcomes for both employees and organizations. When individuals do not psychologically detach from work, they are more physically and emotionally exhausted and tend to experience lower life and job satisfaction. Moreover, the lack of psychological detachment is related to psychosomatic symptoms and more direct health consequences, such as reduced sleep quality and increased anxiety.

These negative psychological and physical health outcomes also cyclically affect work outcome variables, such as job performance. For instance, physical and emotional exhaustion, outcomes of detachment, are related to less work engagement. If an employee is physically and/or emotionally burnt out, he or she may have difficulty focusing and fully engaging in task demands on the job during the day. Additionally, effects of psychological detachment on nighttime sleep indirectly affect both work outcomes and health outcomes the next day. Reduced sleep quality is related to poorer performance at work as well as heightened risk for accidents and injuries. Therefore, psychological detachment might directly affect burnout, satisfaction, and psychosomatic symptoms but also indirectly affect engagement and performance at work via these psychological and physiological pathways. Employee engagement and job performance are critical to organizational success, and industrial and organizational psychologists have developed multiple methodologies to study recovery and psychological detachment.

Studying Psychological Detachment

Researchers typically conceptualize and assess psychological detachment as how difficult it is for individuals to psychologically detach after work. That is, it might be easier or harder for certain individuals in certain situations to stop thinking about work after hours. However, psychological detachment has also been operationalized and examined more dichotomously, such that an individual's recovery experience is either psychologically detached or not. Psychological detachment and recovery are often assessed with the Recovery Experience Questionnaire, which includes questions about psychological detachment (four items), relaxation (four items), mastery (four items), and control (four items). Prior to responding to the questionnaire, individuals are asked to respond to all items with the preface "During time after work ... " on a five-point, Likert-type (1 = I do not agree at all to 5 = I fully agree) scale. Examples of psychological detachment items include "During time after work, I get a break from the demands of work" and "During time after work, I distance myself from work." In general, operationalizations of psychological detachment assume that detachment is a need for every individual, regardless of individual or job-related differences.

Research examining antecedents and outcomes associated with psychological detachment has relied on both between-person correlational and within-person across-time designs. The between-person designs have primarily focused on more objective work antecedents including work hours, overtime, and workload as primary job demands related to difficulty psychologically detaching. Within-person designs have focused more heavily on negative events, such as interpersonal conflict with supervisors or coworkers, and subsequent difficulty detaching from work.

The relationship between psychological detachment and outcomes, such as psychological and physical health and job performance, has been documented in both types of designs. Within-person longitudinal studies ranging from 1 weekend to 1 year provide evidence that psychological detachment might be more strongly related to big-picture assessments versus day-to-day affective states. For instance, multiple longitudinal studies have found that psychological detachment was more related to overall life or work satisfaction and less related to momentary positive affect.

In addition to psychological detachment's being examined solely as a predictor (e.g., lack of detachment leads to poor sleep) or an outcome (e.g., high workload leads to less psychological detachment), researchers have also explored the moderating role of psychological detachment in various relationships. As a moderator, psychological detachment has been shown to buffer the negative effects of job demands, such as workload, role conflict, and interpersonal conflict, on strain-related outcomes, including fatigue and negative affect. In the stressor-detachment model, psychological detachment acts as both a moderator and a mediator between job stressors and strain symptoms. Overall, the relationships among the three (stressors, psychological detachment, and strain and well-being outcomes) are strong.

Although theoretically included as a mediating mechanism in models linking work-based antecedents and nonwork outcomes, few studies have tested the entire pathway in a methodologically rigorous manner. Multiple cross-sectional studies have found support for partial and full mediation of psychological detachment, meaning job stressors affect outcomes such as well-being through the mechanism of psychological detachment, or the lack thereof. For instance, in one study, psychological detachment was a partial mediator between emotional exhaustion and reported need for recovery. In another study, psychological detachment fully mediated the relationship between job demands (i.e., specifically time pressure and work hours) and fatigue at work. There have been fewer studies looking at psychological detachment as a mediator using within-person or longitudinal designs. However, some have found evidence for psychological detachment as a mediator using a 6-month time lag and daily diaries.

Last, it is important to note that researchers are beginning to investigate interventions that enhance recovery experiences, such as recovery training programs. This area of inquiry is relatively new, but studies have shown positive effects of training programs on recovery experiences, recovery self-efficacy, and strains, including sleep and negative affect. This budding research area provides evidence that recovery from work can be trained, and therefore improved, for employees in jobs with high demands and low control. In addition to research-based training intervention programs, organizations are also implementing and encouraging breaks of various kinds in the workplace to facilitate psychological detachment and recovery from work more generally.

Practical Applications of Recovery From Work

Organizations are beginning to implement breaks at work, as well as encouraging certain types of breaks during off-work time, to aid individuals in recovering from work stress. In addition to traditional lunch breaks, micro breaks, which last less than 20 minutes, are increasingly being used to promote relaxation and recovery at varying intervals throughout the day. Research shows that these breaks may be effective, and employees may be able to partially recover from work stressors while still on the job. Actually psychologically

detaching from work during these breaks, however, is not beneficial, because it may be harder for employees to reengage and be productive after breaks. Instead, relaxation or mastery experiences during lunch and affiliative experiences during micro breaks, such as building and maintaining work relationships, seem to energize employees without detracting from work productivity.

Vacations are another way employers encourage psychological detachment. In part because of the 1938 Fair Labor Standards Act, the United States is the only developed nation without mandated paid vacation benefits for employees. Further complicating the situation, U.S. employees who do have paid vacation days are not using all of this critical recovery resource. On average, 3.2 days of paid vacation, per employee, went unused in 2013. Organizations are beginning to incentivize the use of vacation time, and reducing the ability to accumulate vacation days year to year, to promote recovery from work during vacation time. Overall, research supports that vacations do assist individuals in rebuilding resources for at least a short period of time following a vacation. For example, relaxation and mastery experiences on vacation were related to reduced postvacation fatigue. However, if employees experience increased job demands, such as a higher workload or more time pressure, due to needing to "make up" for the vacation days upon returning, the recovery effects from the vacation do not typically persist beyond 1 or 2 weeks. Also confounding the effectiveness of vacations is the fact that many employees do not psychologically detach from work while on vacation. For instance, many employees answer e-mails, take calls, or otherwise work during their "vacations." Some progressive organizations acknowledge these shortfalls and actually incentivize employees to take paid vacations without the ability to work (i.e., the employer shuts off access to all work-related technology).

Conclusion

Work is stressful, and recovery from work is important to reduce the ill effects of stressors on employee well-being. However, high-stress environments lead to less psychological detachment and recovery from work. Research continues to examine the antecedents and consequences of psychological detachment and other experiences promoting recovery from work, including recovery training interventions and organizationally mandated recovery activities such as micro breaks and vacations. With these continual theoretical and practical advances, employees will experience fewer negative consequences related to demanding work, and in turn, be more productive employees.

Leah R. Halper and Ryan C. Johnson

See also Emotional Burnout; Job Demands–Control Theory; Micro Breaks; Stress, Consequences; Stress, Models and Theories

Further Readings

Demerouti, E., Bakker, A. B., Geurts, S.A.E., & Taris, T. W. (2009). Daily recovery from work-related effort during non-work time. In P. L. Perrewé, D. C. Ganster, & S. Sonnentag (Eds.), *Research in organizational stress and well-being* (Vol. 7, pp. 85–123). Oxford, UK: Emerald.

Fritz, C., Ellis, A. M., Demsky, C. A., Lin, B. C., & Guros, F. (2013). Embracing work breaks: Recovering from work stress. *Organizational Dynamics, 42*(4), 274–280.

Kinnunen, U., & Feldt, T. (2013). Job characteristics, recovery experiences and occupational well-being: Testing cross-lagged relationships across 1 year. *Stress and Health, 29*(5), 369–382.

Sonnentag, S., & Fritz, C. (2007). The recovery experience questionnaire: Development and validation of a measure for assessing recuperation and unwinding from work. *Journal of Occupational Health Psychology, 12*(3), 204–221.

Sonnentag, S., & Fritz, C. (2015). Recovery from job stress: The stressor-detachment model as an integrative framework. *Journal of Organizational Behavior, 36*(S1), S72–S103.

RECRUITMENT

The term *recruitment* refers to a set of organizational activities and practices that are intended to attract potential new hires to apply to an organization and maintain that attraction through the hiring process. The goal of recruitment is to generate applicants who are qualified for employment, who will accept employment offers, and who will ultimately succeed on the job. Recruitment is an important complement to employee selection. Recruitment generates a pool of applicants from which organizations can select new employees and influences the likelihood that the most desirable candidates will accept the organization's offer of employment.

Effective recruitment that supports business strategy execution is essential to organizational success. In recent years, scholarly research and the business press have documented the importance of human capital to organizational performance. Effective recruiting is a foundation of both strategic human resource management systems and strategic execution. Because strategic execution relies on employees to transform a strategy from an idea into real services, products, markets, technologies, and prices, firms must hire people who fit the culture and have the right mix of competencies to generate sustainable competitive advantage. However, if high-potential employees are not effectively recruited, they will never apply and can never be hired. Research suggests that recruitment can have significant impact on applicant quality and the talent pool, which in turn can lead to a significant productivity advantage for the hiring organization.

Recruitment has important implications for individual job seekers as well. The hiring process is a two-way street: Employers attempt to attract qualified employees, and individuals attempt to find satisfying work. Ideally, recruitment leads individuals to make job choices that meet their personal needs and maximize person–job and person–organizational fit.

Recruitment is a process that unfolds over time. It comprises three phases. First, the organization must generate applicants. It must identify a pool of potential employees and persuade a reasonable number of individuals in that pool to apply for work in the organization. Second, it must maintain applicant interest as the candidates proceed through the organization's (sometimes lengthy) screening processes. Finally, the organization must persuade the most desirable applicants to accept job offers.

Recruitment outcomes also unfold over time. In the short run, organizations might assess what are known as *prehire outcomes*, such as the quantity, quality, and diversity of applicants or the length of time required to fill a position. In the longer term, organizations might assess long-term or *posthire outcomes*, such as the performance and longevity (retention) of the recruits. Similarly, individual job seekers initially might attend to whether or how quickly they obtained employment; later, they might focus on how satisfying the employment is. Outcomes can refer to individual outcomes (e.g., fit), group outcomes (e.g., department performance), and organizational outcomes (e.g., strategic execution).

Generating Applicants

Before beginning recruitment, organizations engage in sourcing, by identifying potential pools of applicants who would be a good fit with the position. Some have argued that the first phase of recruitment, the generation of applicants, is the most important phase. If the right individuals are not in the applicant pool to begin with, no amount of attention to maintaining applicant interest or persuading successful candidates to join the organization will result in the right hires. Certainly, this phase requires the organization to make a number of critical strategic decisions, including where to search for applicants and how to communicate with potential applicants. Fortunately, there is a reasonable body of research evidence to support these strategic decisions.

Recruiting Sources: Where to Look

One of the most frequently studied aspects of recruitment is source selection. Applicants may be sought from a variety of sources, both formal and informal. Formal sources typically involve a third-party intermediary that assists in the recruitment process, such as an employment agency, flyers in a college placement office, or a newspaper or an online job board. Informal sources typically involve direct contact between the potential employee and the employer and include such techniques as direct applications and referrals. Organizations are also increasingly recruiting through "career pages" on their own corporate Web sites. The interactive nature of corporate Web sites also allows applicants to more easily identify the extent to which specific positions in targeted organizations match their personal qualifications and needs.

Some of the newest recruiting sources are online social networking sites, including LinkedIn, Twitter, and Facebook. For example, LinkedIn is essentially a searchable online recruiting database, allowing anyone to post a professional profile, regardless of whether they are actively seeking a job. Organizations can then use LinkedIn to post jobs or to run detailed searches to find exactly the type of candidate they need and then approach these candidates directly through LinkedIn. Twitter and Facebook can be used to create organizational brands and establish relationships with people who may be interested in future jobs with the organization.

A significant body of research on recruitment source effects has accumulated over the years. The most consistent finding of this research is that informal sources (referrals in particular) tend to have positive effects on posthire outcomes. Specifically, individuals who are hired by means of referral from existing employees tend to have greater longevity and better performance in their new positions than those who are hired from other sources. Two theoretical frameworks have been proposed to explain these effects. First, it has been suggested that different recruiting sources yield individuals with different characteristics. These individual differences then translate into different posthire outcomes. Second, it has been proposed that applicants recruited from different sources have access to different information. Individuals with greater advance knowledge may be better positioned for long-term success on the job because their expectations are more realistic. Unfortunately, research testing the power of these two models has been somewhat inconclusive.

Early Recruitment Communications

Once an applicant pool has been identified or targeted, the organization must communicate with potential applicants to persuade them to apply. Quite often, this initial communication comes in the form of advertisements on employer job boards, on corporate Web sites, through recruiter contact, or on brochures in college placement offices. For each of these areas, research has investigated the role of design as well as the role of content in attracting applicants.

Design of Materials

In terms of printed and online material, research suggests that applicants are attracted to firms whose recruitment materials are informative, and both the amount and the specificity of the information seem to make a difference. In most cases, applicants seem to devalue positions about which important information is not made available. One explanation for this reaction is that the failure to provide sufficient information may be seen as a signal of undesirable organizational attributes. Firms that provide less informative materials may be seen as less concerned about applicants' (and, by attribution, employees') needs.

Recruitment materials are also more effective when they are distinctive, perceived as honest, and vivid. To attract attention, materials need to stand out from the group in some way, either through physical representation or the presentation of unusual information. For example, materials that promise uncommon benefits (such as pet insurance) may be more effective than materials that promise more conventional benefits or that seem to portray a position with accuracy, generate more attention and attraction. Applicants also prefer Web sites that provide useful information and that are easy to navigate. Job seekers are more likely to use the Internet for job hunting when the geographical scope of the job hunt is large, when they desire a large salary increase, and when a variety of types of firms (e.g., big and small) are being considered as potential employers. Use of the Internet is perceived as less effective than personal networking but superior to searching for jobs through newspaper ads or "cold calling."

Content of Materials

Research on the portrayal of specific job or organization attributes in early recruitment communication has demonstrated that applicant preferences (and reactions to specific content in ads) vary as a function of their personal characteristics. Rather than specifying absolute or universal rules about desirable attributes, studies in this area have demonstrated that applicants respond to attributes through the lens of their own values and preferences. In other words, a person–organization or person–job fit perspective prevails. For example, individual differences in demographic characteristics, values, and personality have been shown to predict attraction to job attributes such as pay system, work system (i.e., individual vs. team based), and diversity policies (affirmative action vs. equal employment opportunity). Additionally, the effectiveness of recruitment content seems to depend on corporate reputation and brand awareness.

Organizational Image

Applicants sometimes have knowledge of an organization even before the organization begins its targeted recruitment. In particular, large organizations may be familiar to many individuals. It is common for individuals to have loosely structured general impressions of a company—in other words, to hold some image of what the company is like. These general impressions or organizational images may be formed by corporate advertising, the way the firm is depicted in the media, personal experience with the company or its products, and many other factors. A number of studies have documented the impact of organizational image on applicant attraction. In particular, several studies suggest that firms that are viewed as socially responsible are attractive to potential applicants. What is less clear is whether organizations actively manipulate their images in an effort to be attractive to prospective employees and how they can best do this.

Maintaining Status

In many cases, there is a significant time lapse between a candidate's initial application and the organization's decision whether to hire that applicant. The goal of recruitment during this phase is to maintain the applicant's interest in the organization while the screening process runs its course. Every interaction between the applicant and the organization during this period can influence the applicant's interest and, as a result, has important recruitment aspects. In this section, the impact of recruiters and interviewers, as well as applicant reactions to other selection devices, are reviewed.

Recruiters

In many hiring processes, the initial application is followed by an interview. In most cases, the first interview has a dual nature: It serves as a selection device but also provides an opportunity for recruitment. Most existing research on the role of the early interview in recruitment focuses on the characteristics and qualities of the individual conducting the interview (i.e., the recruiter).

Research has consistently demonstrated that applicants prefer recruiters who are warm, informative, competent, and trustworthy and form more favorable views of the organization and are more attracted to its jobs when recruiters have these characteristics. Two theories have been proposed to explain the impact of reactions to recruiters. First, the interview is, to a great extent, an opportunity for recruiters to convey information about the organization, and warm, informative, competent, and trustworthy recruiters may simply do a better job of communicating with applicants. Second, recruiters may serve as signals for unobserved organizational characteristics. Applicants may presume that the recruiter is representative of the organization. Organizations with recruiters who are warm are perceived to be likely to have a friendly, collegial culture; organizations whose recruiters are informative are perceived to be likely to have a culture that respects employees' need for information.

Research has also attended to the demographic characteristics of recruiters, but here the results are more ambiguous. Recruiter gender, age, experience, and functional area were found to have significant effects on applicant attraction in some studies but no effects in others. Likewise, the degree of demographic similarity between the recruiter and the applicant was found to have an impact in some studies but no impact in others. Recruiter behaviors, as opposed to recruiter characteristics, seem to be the most important determinant of applicant attraction.

Applicant Reaction to Selection Devices

Because the recruitment and selection processes occur simultaneously, an organization's approach to selection will likely influence how an applicant feels about the organization and its methods, and therefore it is likely to influence whether the applicant will accept the job if one is offered. Two rationales have been offered to explain these reactions. First, applicant reactions may be a function

of privacy concerns; some selection techniques, such as drug testing and certain psychological tests, may be viewed as overly intrusive. Second, applicants may respond on the basis of their desire for and perceptions of justice; some techniques are seen as more fair, either in process or outcome, than others.

Literature in this area has focused primarily on the question of justice. Rather than identifying lists of techniques that are viewed as just or unjust, most research has focused on aspects of the selection process that may be perceived as just or unjust. The timeliness of feedback, the job-relatedness of the selection device, and the degree to which procedures are explained to applicants are examples of elements that enhance the perceived justice of selection techniques and thus are likely to lead to maintenance of applicant status. It is also clear that the context in which selection and recruitment occur can make a difference. For example, the impact of specific selection techniques on attraction to the organization can vary as a function of job type, characteristics of the organization, and applicant characteristics (in particular race).

Realism

During the maintenance phase of recruitment, organizations supplement their initial recruitment communications with additional information. Decisions regarding the nature of the information that is added are critical. One of the most frequently studied aspects of recruitment is the impact of realistic communications. Organizations can use realistic job previews (RJPs) to present a balanced and true representation of the job and the organization. Such previews are carefully designed to include both positive and negative aspects of the work. This approach can be contrasted with the more traditional sales-oriented approach, in which organizations strive to present jobs in a uniformly positive light.

Numerous theories have been developed to support the realistic approach. The first is the *met-expectations theory*, which suggests that providing realistic information prevents applicants from developing inflated expectations of what the job is like and therefore makes them less likely to suffer disappointment on the job. Second, the *ability-to-cope perspective* suggests that giving applicants advance notice of negative aspects of the job gives them time to develop coping strategies. Third, RJPs may create an atmosphere of honesty that is appreciated by applicants. Finally, RJPs may operate through self-selection: Candidates who react negatively to the unattractive aspects of the job can remove themselves from consideration.

The cumulated evidence suggests that RJPs are associated with positive posthire outcomes. In particular, applicants who receive realistic recruitment communications exhibit lower turnover and higher performance. These effects are moderated, however, by design factors such as timing (when the realistic information is provided) and medium (the method used to communicate, for example, written vs. verbal).

Closing the Deal: Influencing Job Choice

During the final phase of recruitment, an organization must persuade its most attractive applicants (those to whom job offers have been made) to join the company. This stage is critical because significant investments in both recruitment and selection processes are lost if candidates reject offers. Unlike the other two phases of recruitment, research on this final phase focuses on the thought processes of applicants as they make decisions about which job to choose. Substantially less research has focused on the activities of the organization at this final stage.

Job Choice Research: Content Issues

One of the most significant debates in the job choice literature focuses on what content is attended to during job choice—that is, which characteristics or attributes of jobs and organizations are most likely to lead to a positive job choice outcome. By and large, this debate has centered on the validity of two methods of assessing attribute preference: direct estimation and policy capturing. In the *direct estimation* technique, applicants are provided with a list of job attributes (e.g., high pay, opportunities for advancement, pleasant working conditions) and asked to rate or rank the importance of each of these factors. The underlying assumption is that more important attributes will play a greater role in job choice. However, this approach has been criticized as lacking in context. For example, it does not allow for variation in levels or for trade-offs among attributes. In addition, the direct estimation technique has been faulted for requiring more self-insight than applicants might have.

Policy capturing provides a methodological alternative to direct estimation. In policy-capturing studies, applicants are provided with a set of job descriptions across which attribute levels are systematically varied. They are then asked to rate the attractiveness of the job. Statistical regression is used to identify the degree to which specific attributes influenced attraction to the job.

It has become increasingly clear that, methodological issues aside, neither of these approaches is likely to yield a single set of universally attractive attributes. Instead, research using both techniques has identified differences in attribute preferences as a function of demographic status, individual values, and personality traits. What is known is that recruitment signals can influence applicant perceptions about their likely similarity to a prospective employer. These similarity assessments subsequently influence organizational attraction and job pursuit. Additionally, individual experience and personal values influence decision making, and these may change over time. Recent work suggests perceived justice is a key determinant of job acceptance.

Job Choice: Process Issues

Research on the job choice process offers consistent support for expectancy-based decision-making models. The expectancy perspective suggests that applicants will estimate the probability of obtaining certain outcomes if a specific job is chosen (e.g., attributes such as good benefits or pleasant coworkers), weight those probabilities by the value or attractiveness of each attribute, sum across attributes, and then select the job that obtains the highest total weighted attribute score.

Consistent findings notwithstanding, some have argued that job choice is not as rational as the expectancy model suggests. For example, some research suggests that interactions that occur during the final job offer negotiations can have an impact on job choice, above and beyond their impact on attribute levels (e.g., through their effect on perceptions of justice). However, relatively little research on this topic has been conducted.

Jean M. Phillips and Alison E. Barber

See also Job Advertisements; Job Choice; Job Search; Realistic Job Preview; Recruitment Sources

Further Readings

Barber, A. E. (1998). *Recruiting employees: Individual and organizational perspectives*. Thousand Oaks, CA: Sage.

Breaugh, J. A. (2012). Employee recruitment: Current knowledge and suggestions for future research. In N. Schmitt (Ed.), *The Oxford handbook of personnel assessment and selection* (pp. 68–87). New York: Oxford University Press.

Earnest, D. R., Allen, D. G., & Landis, R. S. (2011). Mechanisms linking realistic job previews with turnover: A meta-analytic path analysis. *Personnel Psychology, 64*(4), 865–897. doi:10.1111/j.1744-6570.2011.01230.x

Gully, S. M., Phillips, J. M., & Kim, M. S. (2014). Strategic recruitment: A multilevel perspective. In K. Y. T. Yu & D. M. Cable (Eds.), *The Oxford handbook of recruitment* (pp. 161–183). New York: Oxford University Press.

Klotz, A. C., Motta Veiga, S. P., Buckley, M. R., & Gavin, M. B. (2013). The role of trustworthiness in recruitment and selection: A review and guide for future research. *Journal of Organizational Behavior, 34*(S1), S104–S119. doi:10.1002/job.1891

Phillips, J. M. (1998). Effects of realistic job previews on multiple organizational outcomes: A meta-analysis. *Academy of Management Journal, 41*(6), 673–690. doi:10.2307/256964

Phillips, J. M., & Gully, S. M. (in press). A multilevel and strategic perspective on recruitment research: Where have we been, where can we go from here? *Journal of Management*.

Ryan, A. M., & Ployhart, R. F. (2000). Applicants' perceptions of selection procedures and decisions: A critical review and agenda for the future. *Journal of Management, 26*(3), 565–606. doi:10.1177/014920630002600308

Rynes, S. L., Reeves, C., & Darnold, T. C. (2013). The history of recruitment research. In K. Y. T. Yu & D. M. Cable (Eds.), *The Oxford handbook of recruitment* (pp. 335–360). New York: Oxford University Press. doi:10.1111/j.1744-6570.2012.01254.x

Uggerslev, K. L., Fassina, N. E., & Kraichy, D. (2012). Recruiting through the stages: a meta-analytic test of predictors of applicant attraction at different stages of the recruiting process. *Personnel Psychology, 65*, 597–660. doi:10.1111/j.1744-6570.2012.01254.x

RECRUITMENT SOURCES

Recruitment sources are among the most frequently studied aspects of employee recruitment. Recruitment sources are the avenues organizations use to reach applicants. Evidence suggests that the choice of recruitment sources is a strategic decision, in the sense that there are relationships between recruitment sources and employment outcomes. However, the exact nature and reasons for those effects remain ambiguous.

Traditional recruitment sources include employee referrals, employment agencies (including campus placement offices and executive search firms), online job boards, career pages on company Web sites, newspaper advertisements, career fairs, employee referrals, and unsolicited applications (known as walk-ins).

Recruitment sources can be either formal or informal. Formal sources typically involve a third-party intermediary that assists in the recruitment process, such as an employment agency, a college placement office, or a newspaper or online advertisement service. Informal sources typically involve direct contact between the potential employee and the employer and include such techniques as direct applications, referrals, and the rehiring of former employees.

Initial Research on Recruitment Sources

A significant body of research on recruitment source effects has accumulated over the years. Initial research was primarily descriptive in nature and explored the relationship between recruitment sources and post-hire outcomes such as employee satisfaction, retention, and absenteeism. The most consistent finding of this research is that informal sources (referrals, in particular, but also walk-ins and the rehiring of former employees) tend to have positive associations with post-hire outcomes: lower turnover and, in some cases, better work attitudes and job performance.

Recruitment scholars soon began to propose and test explanations for these findings. The two most commonly studied explanations are the *individual differences hypothesis* and the *realistic information hypothesis*.

First, regarding individual differences, it has been suggested that different recruitment sources yield individuals with different characteristics. These individual differences ultimately lead to different post-hire outcomes. For example, employee referrals might be an effective hiring source because employees choose to refer only individuals who, in their judgment, would be effective employees. This method of screening would produce a group of applicants that is superior to other groups on important job qualifications.

Second, regarding realistic information, it has been proposed that applicants recruited from different sources have access to different information. In particular, individuals recruited through informal sources may have access to more extensive, more specific, or more accurate information about the new job. Having that information might provide greater role clarity and more realistic expectations for those applicants, which, in turn, could lead to better adjustment and therefore better post-hire outcomes.

Research on the validity of these explanations has yielded mixed support. In support of the individual differences hypothesis, associations have been found between recruitment sources and individual characteristics such as age, education, experience, and physical abilities. In support of the realistic information hypothesis, informal sources have been associated with greater amounts of realistic information. However, these findings are not universal. Furthermore, relatively few studies have been able to verify that the relationship between recruitment sources and post-hire outcomes is mediated by these intervening variables. Some studies found only a modest, if any, relationship between recruitment sources and post-hire outcomes.

Contingency Perspectives on Recruitment Source Effects

The inability of the most popular explanations of recruitment source effects to fully explain the relationship between recruitment sources and employment outcomes has led to speculation about contingency factors. On the basis of a limited number of studies, there appears to be some merit to the argument that the proposed processes hold in some cases or situations but not in others. For example, one study found differences in source effects across racial and ethnic lines: Employee referrals were associated with lower turnover for White applicants, but employment agencies yielded the lowest turnover among Blacks. Another study found that the use of employee referrals in Mexico was associated with higher turnover, the opposite of the effect observed in U.S.-based research. A full range of contingency factors for recruitment source effects has not yet been specified.

Recruitment Sources and Diversity

Despite the observed advantages of informal recruiting sources, heavy reliance on these sources does raise concerns. Several studies found differences in recruitment source use by gender and by race and ethnicity, with White males more likely to use informal recruitment sources than are women or people of color. Therefore, organizations that rely on informal recruitment to reduce turnover may be trading opportunities to diversify their workforce. A complete assessment of recruiting source effectiveness should incorporate a variety of recruiting goals, something that is not always done in recruiting source research.

The Internet as a Recruitment Source

For both equal employment opportunity reporting reasons and its low cost and high speed, a recruiting source that is growing in popularity and in research attention is the Internet. Descriptive research suggests that job boards and online corporate career pages are among the most commonly used recruitment sources across a wide variety of jobs, and their use is expected to grow. Recruiters cite perceived benefits of online recruitment that include low cost and high speed. It is also possible through Web-based recruiting to provide rich, detailed information that is comparable to the information that applicants recruited through informal sources might receive.

Some of the newest recruiting sources are online social networking sites, including LinkedIn, Twitter, and Facebook. For example, LinkedIn is essentially a searchable online recruiting database, allowing anyone to post a professional profile regardless of whether they are actively seeking a job. Organizations can then use LinkedIn to post jobs or to run detailed searches to find exactly the type of candidate they need and then approach that person directly through LinkedIn. Twitter and Facebook can be used to create organizational brands and establish relationships with people who may be interested in future jobs with the organization.

Recent research suggests that Internet-based recruiting may provide a compromise between formal and informal sources. One study indicated that online recruiting yields applicants who are more diverse than those recruited through informal means (but less so than those recruited by formal means) and is more successful in recruiting qualified applicants than traditional formal methods (but less so than informal recruitment sources).

It is unlikely that any single recruiting source (e.g., employee referrals or a firm's career site) is the best for all jobs and outcomes. Understanding which recruiting sources are best for different organizational subunits and positions and for different staffing goals (including time to fill, applicant quality, cost per hire, performance, promotion, and retention) allows the talent sourcing strategy to be optimized for every staffing effort. Identifying the most effective recruiting sources and messages for active, semiactive, and passive job seekers would also help firms optimize recruiting efforts.

Jean M. Phillips and Alison E. Barber

See also Job Search; Realistic Job Preview; Recruitment

Further Readings

Barber, A. E. (1998). *Recruiting employees: Individual and organizational perspectives*. Thousand Oaks, CA: Sage.

Breaugh, J. A. (2012). Employee recruitment: Current knowledge and suggestions for future research. In N. Schmitt (Ed.), *The Oxford handbook of personnel assessment and selection* (pp. 68–87). New York: Oxford University Press.

Carlson, K. D., Connerly, M. L., & Mecham, R. L. (2002). Recruitment evaluation: The case for assessing the quality of applicants attracted. *Personnel Psychology, 55*(2), 461–490. doi:10.1111/j.1744-6570.2002.tb00118.x

Chapman, D. S., & Webster, J. (2003). The use of technologies in the recruiting, screening, and selection processes for job candidates. *International Journal of Selection and Assessment, 11*(2/3), 113–120. doi:10.1111/1468-2389.00234

Gully, S. M., Phillips, J. M., & Kim, M. S. (2014). Strategic recruitment: A multilevel perspective. In K. Y. T. Yu & D. M. Cable (Eds.), *The Oxford handbook of recruitment* (pp. 161–183). New York: Oxford University Press.

Yu, K. Y. T., & Cable, D. M. (2012). Recruitment and competitive advantage: A brand equity perspective. In S. W. J. Kozlowski (Ed.), *The Oxford handbook of industrial-organizational psychology* (pp. 197–220). New York: Oxford University Press.

REGISTERED REPORTS PUBLICATION MODEL

Concerns Regarding the Credibility of Scientific Results

Concerns are growing regarding the credibility of scientific results in both the natural and social sciences. Researchers are under increasing pressure to publish novel, positive results in order to compete for job opportunities, funding, and other resources. Academic journals are also increasingly dedicated to pursuing higher impact factors. Much of these activities occur at the expense of the pursuit of scientific truth. Furthermore, there is growing evidence that researchers are using questionable research practices (QRPs), ranging from selectively reporting results to outright data fabrication, to increase their chances of publishing their research. Consequently, there is an emerging movement that is raising concerns about credibility and calling for changes to the way in which we communicate scientific results.

Why do researchers engage in QRPs? Some have suggested that researchers do so in anticipation of bias in the peer-review process. There is emerging evidence through observational and experimental studies that suggests that editors and reviewers show a strong preference for studies with statistically significant results. For example, some experimental research has shown that reviewers rate the methodological rigor and relevance of research questions in studies more highly when results are statistically significant. When the same manuscripts were evaluated with statistically nonsignificant results, lower scores were earned, and the manuscripts were more likely to be rejected.

It is also likely that evaluations of replication studies could also be biased. For example, if a study successfully replicates past research, reviewers may perceive that no novel insight is being offered, and the replication may not be published. Conversely, if a study fails to replicate past research, reviewers may perceive that novel insight is being offered (increasing the likelihood of publication), or they may critique the methodological design of the replication study because it did not replicate the original study (decreasing the likelihood of publication). Thus, it seems that there is a potential for reviewers to be biased when reviewing the methodological rigor and the relevance of the research questions in original and replication studies.

So how do researchers engage in QRPs? For example, if an author knows that reviewers prefer statistically significant results, that author may use QRPs to improve his or her findings. Authors may selectively report results (i.e., suppress null results), they may selectively include or exclude data and control variables to turn a null result into a significant one, or they may present post hoc findings as those predicted a priori (i.e., hypothesizing after the results are known, or HARKing). In this latter case, a researcher conducts exploratory analyses in order to identify statistically significant results. Authors then proceed to report their exploratory analyses as if they were confirmatory. In addition to engaging in QRPs to address bias in the peer-review process, authors may engage in such practices out of ignorance that the practices are inappropriate or to increase the likelihood that their work will be cited as novel research by later studies.

As concerns grow about the credibility of scientific results, calls for improvement increase. Many are looking to current publishing practices as a partial solution to the credibility crisis. In the next section, we discuss how the implementation of registered reports may serve as a partial solution to the credibility crisis.

The Role of Registered Reports

The current path to publication allows for the influence of bias, which is not germane to the relevance or importance of the research, to systematically discriminate against particular research results (e.g., on the basis of effect size). To help avoid some of the bias in the review process associated with the empirical results, registered reports have been put forward as an alternative means by which to publish research that places emphasis on sound research methods and study design.

A key component of registered reports is the two-stage review process. At the first stage of the review process, potential manuscripts include only the literature review, hypotheses, and methods sections. Hypotheses are included prior to any data collection, so researchers can illustrate that their hypotheses were truly developed a priori. Additionally, the methods section includes details, such as the empirical methods and the expected sample size. Although previous research may not have uncovered precise effect size relations, it is necessary to understand the expected magnitude of the effect size in order to make sure the research is adequately powered. Researchers would receive feedback from reviewers on the methodological rigor of their study design as well as the relevance of their research questions. Thus, researchers may save valuable time and resources and improve the overall quality of their studies prior to conducting such work. Reviewers and editors are afforded the opportunity to evaluate the methodological rigor of the study as well as the relevance of the research questions (or the need for a replication study) independent of knowing the results of the study. On the basis of the aforementioned information, a journal would make a commitment to publish, or not publish, on the basis of how informative the results would be to the field and the soundness of the research design.

The second stage of the review process includes an evaluation of results as pursuant to the previously evaluated research design, not as a function of the empirical results that were found. In cases in which researchers diverged from their initial design in a meaningful way, editors and reviewers could reject the manuscript despite the preliminary acceptance. Furthermore, all manuscripts would be reviewed to ensure that the write-up follows the formats and quality expected for the journal. A hybrid version of registered reports could also be used in which a researcher submits a full manuscript, but reviewers have access only to the introduction and methods sections. Only after submitting evaluations for these two sections would reviewers gain access to the results and discussion sections.

There are several advantages of using registered reports compared with the current method of reviewing only completed manuscripts. First and foremost, registered reports change the incentive structure for researchers to focus on sound methods and analyses rather than on the outcomes. It has been noted that researchers engage in motivated reasoning where subconscious processes lead them to spend less time critically assessing confirmed or interesting results while being more critical of nonconfirmatory or uninteresting results (a bias that has been noted to extend to reviewers). Registered reports remove some of this bias because they are being evaluated on how closely the research follows the initial research design, rather than on the interestingness or novelty of the results. Second and relatedly, there is a deemphasis on the statistical significance of the empirical results. The current review process has been criticized for encouraging the publication of significant results leading to publication bias as well as "p hacking," whereby researchers engage in practices to maximize the probability of obtaining significant results. Indirectly, decreasing the emphasis on statistical significance should increase the publication of null results that have traditionally been rejected or not submitted for review. Third, because the hypotheses are known prior to data collection and analysis, researchers will not be able to engage in HARKing and will instead have to report when results are inductive in nature. In other words, registered reports do not prevent exploratory research from being conducted. Rather, authors will be able to clearly delineate between the analyses that were developed a priori and those that were post hoc. This should decrease the likelihood of dustbowl empiricism or at least make it transparent when deviations from the hypothetical–deductive scientific method have occurred. Relatedly, because theoretical justifications for hypotheses will be known and reviewed prior to results, the scientific community can be more confident that the results will replicate in future research.

Other Related Open Science Practices

As stated in the previous section, registered reports or hybrid versions of these reports may at least partially address the credibility crisis in the confidence in the scientific literatures. However, more will need to be done. In this section, we briefly review some of the other open science practices that have been proposed to add to the value of registered reports.

First, to better promote reproducibility and accelerate the progress of scientific results, journal policies could encourage researchers to share data, and study materials, such as instruments, and syntax for analysis. Individual digital object identifiers could be developed for these individual resources so as to provide intellectual credit for the original authors. Furthermore, although journals should encourage and perhaps even require sharing as a default, authors could still be allowed to appeal such policies. For example, if an author completed data collection but was unable to share the data for proprietary reasons or for fear that participant confidentiality might be violated, that researcher could submit an appeal to a journal editor upon submission and ask that the requirement to share the data be waived. Regardless, all journals should develop data-sharing policies and request authors to explicitly state in their submission letters whether they are willing to share their data.

A second open science practice that would add to the value of registered reports is the preregistration of study materials and analysis plans. The preregistration process allows researchers to document the design of their study, such as the desired number of participants, as well as a priori hypotheses. Of course, researchers could deviate from these original plans. But such changes would be documented and could be explained in the final write-up of the paper. What is more, documented evidence would exist regarding which hypotheses were truly established a priori.

A final recommendation for journals is to make more of an effort to emphasize replication studies in addition to those that offer novel results. Editors may be worried about the prestige of a journal as determined through impact factors. Hence, emphasis is placed on original study investigations at the expense of those that demonstrate that a previous study's findings were or were not replicated. Many concerns about QRPs could be mitigated if more replication research were conducted.

Remaining Issues for Present and Future

One clear direction for future efforts is to investigate the extent to which various open science practices decrease engagement in QRPs but also lead to more reproducible research and better evidence-based practices across the natural and social sciences. It is unlikely that all open science practices work equally well at accomplishing these endeavors. It is further unlikely that a particularly effective open science practice will work well universally across scientific disciplines and subdisciplines. Thus, future research needs to investigate the effectiveness of various open science practices and establish nuanced evidence that sheds light on when some practices are effective and ineffective. A second clear objective would be to then disseminate the emerging evidence of the efficacy of open scientific practices. It is necessary to provide evidence of the effectiveness of practices to encourage adoption and further customization of the practices. Hence, the promotion of open science is an ongoing process that should continue to go through iterations. The implementation of registered reports and related open science practices would be a helpful first step to improve the credibility of scientific results.

George C. Banks and
Christopher E. Whelpley

See also Ethics in Industrial and Organizational Publishing; Ethics in Industrial and Organizational Research

Further Readings

Banks, G. C., Kepes, S., & McDaniel, M. A. (2015). Publication bias: Understand the myths concerning threats to the advancement of science. In C. E. Lance & R. J. Vandenberg (Eds.), *More statistical and methodological myths and urban legends* (pp. 36–64). New York: Routledge.

Nosek, B. A., Alter, G., Banks G. C., Borsboom, D. et al. (in press). Promoting an open research culture: Author guidelines for journals to promote transparency, openness, and reproducibility. *Science.*

Nosek, B. A., & Bar-Anan, Y. (2012). Scientific utopia: I. Opening scientific communication. *Psychological Inquiry, 23,* 217–243.

Nosek, B. A., & Lakens, D. (2014). Registered reports: A method to increase the credibility of published results. *Social Psychology, 45,* 137–141.

O'Boyle, E. H., Jr., Banks, G. C., & Gonzalez-Mule, E. (in press). The chrysalis effect: How ugly data metamorphosize into beautiful articles. *Journal of Management.*

Tullett, A. M. (2015). In search of true things worth knowing: Considerations for a new article prototype. *Social and Personality Psychology Compass, 9,* 188–201.

REGRESSION TECHNIQUES

Regression analysis is a statistical procedure for estimating the direction, strength, and significance of the relationships between independent (or predictor) variables and dependent (or criterion) variables. It offers advantages over correlational analysis in that it allows analysts to derive an equation to predict a criterion variable from a (or several) predictor variable(s). This analytic technique is often used for prediction and forecasting, which is of particular interest in industrial and organizational (I-O) psychology, in which researchers and practitioners are often interested in predicting key criterion variables (e.g., employee performance and job attitudes) from important predictor variables (e.g., intelligence and personality variables). Indeed, regression techniques are some of the most commonly used statistical procedures in the field of I-O psychology. Although there are many techniques for conducting regression analysis, this entry will focus on linear, ordinary least squares (OLS) regression.

As mentioned, a chief advantage of regression analysis is that it allows analysts to derive an equation to predict criterion variables from predictor variables. The basic form of this equation when conducting simple regression is as follows: $\hat{y} = \beta X + A$, where $\hat{y}$ is the predicted value of the criterion variable, β is the estimated parameter representing the relationship between X and Y in the sample of data, X is the value of the independent variable for a given case, and A is the intercept (or constant) term (put more simply, A is the predicted value of Y when X is equal to zero). Regression analysis can compute unstandardized or standardized β values. In simple (i.e., one-predictor) regression, unstandardized β will be equal to the covariance between X and Y ($COV_{XY} = [\Sigma(X - X_{mean})(Y - Y_{mean})]/[N - 1]$, where the numerator is the sum of deviation score cross-products and the denominator is the sample size minus one) divided by the variance of X (s_X^2), whereas standardized β will be equal to the correlation between X and Y ($r_{XY} = [COV_{XY}]/[s_X s_Y]$, where the numerator is the covariance between X and Y and the denominator is the product of multiplying the standard deviations of X and Y). The appropriate way to interpret unstandardized β is as the rate of change in $\hat{y}$ per single-unit increase in X, while the appropriate way to interpret standardized β is as the number of standard deviations change in $\hat{y}$ per single–standard deviation increase in X.

OLS regression arrives at the optimal equation by minimizing errors of prediction, represented by the standard error of estimate (i.e., the standard deviation of errors made when predicting Y from X) in regression output. An easy way to visualize this is to imagine a scatterplot of the relationship between a predictor and a criterion. If plotted, the regression equation would take the form of a line that fit the data better than any other, in that the line would minimize the distance between the plotted line (which represents predicted values of Y) and the actual data points on the scatterplot. To the degree that data points are packed tightly around the line, errors of prediction will be relatively small. To the degree that data points are more dispersedly distributed around the line, errors of prediction will be relatively large.

Of course, social scientists and practitioners are often interested in forecasting a criterion variable from multiple predictor variables. In these cases, multiple regression can be used. The basic form of a multiple regression equation is as follows: $\hat{y} = \beta_1 X_1 + \beta_2 X_2 + A$, where all the equation terms carry the same meaning mentioned previously, but X_1 and X_2 represent separate predictors of the criterion variable. Importantly, the interpretation of the β values changes slightly from simple regression. In multiple regression this interpretation is as follows: β represents the rate of change in the predicted value of Y per single-unit increase in the predictor in question (e.g., X_1) while holding all other predictors (e.g., X_2) constant. In multiple (i.e., multipredictor) regression, when the predictors are completely uncorrelated (i.e., $r = .00$) with one another, unstandardized β will be equal to the

covariance between X and Y divided by the variance of the associated predictor, whereas standardized β will be equal to the correlation between X and Y. This absence of a relationship between predictors is almost never the case when studying psychological constructs and refers to the notion of multicollinearity, which is discussed further below.

Multicollinearity

Multicollinearity is a problem that occurs when two or more predictor variables are correlated with one another. This will almost always be the case to some extent when using regression analyses in the social sciences. Depending on the degree to which multicollinearity exists in one's data, this

Figure 1   The line of best fit from ordinary least squares regression analysis drawn through a relatively strong and a relatively weak relationship

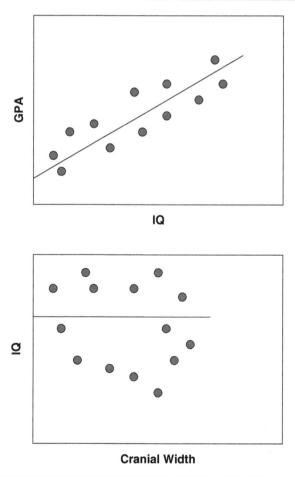

can complicate interpretation of the β weights in regression equations in addition to increasing the standard errors of those weights, making it more difficult to achieve statistical significance for a given predictor. In the worst-case scenario, perfect multicollinearity (i.e., having one predictor in the model that can be predicted with 100% accuracy by other predictors in the model) violates an assumption of OLS regression, and the analysis cannot be conducted.

It is crucial to note that when two or more predictors are highly correlated with one another and also correlated with the criterion, OLS regression handles this problem by giving the larger weight to the predictor that has the stronger correlation with the criterion. The other predictor(s) may then receive a counterintuitively small, nonsignificant weight, and the sign may even be opposite to what the researcher expects on the basis of the correlation matrix. For instance, suppose a researcher is trying to predict job performance from both job satisfaction and happiness in a multiple regression model. Job performance is correlated with both job satisfaction ($r = .53$, $p < .01$) and happiness ($r = .33$, $p < .01$). Furthermore, job satisfaction and happiness are nontrivially correlated with each other ($r = .56$, $p < .01$). The regression equation from this analysis might look as follows: predicted job performance = .51 × job satisfaction − .04 × happiness + 4.52, while the output may tell the researcher that job satisfaction is a highly significant (i.e., $p < .001$) predictor of job performance and that happiness is not (i.e., $p > .05$). Also note the counterintuitive negative sign associated with the β weight for happiness. Importantly, it would be incorrect to conclude that happiness has a negative or nonsignificant relationship with job performance. One can see that these conclusions are untrue upon examining the correlations among the variables in the equation. It is critical to remember that OLS regression does not seek to provide an equation that is easily interpretable. Rather, OLS regression seeks to minimize errors of prediction, which, especially in cases of high multicollinearity, can lead to counterintuitive weights associated with predictors that are not explaining as much unique variance (i.e., variability not explained by other predictors in the model) in the outcome of interest.

Model Evaluation

Perhaps the most common technique in regression analysis is to test the significance of individual β weights associated with predictors in the model. This is accomplished by calculating (or, more commonly, having statistical software calculate) the standard error of β, which can then be used to determine if the weight is significantly different from zero. If the 95% confidence interval (i.e., two standard errors of β in either direction) around β excludes zero, then one can conclude that predictor is a significant predictor of the criterion of interest in that model. Also of interest is examining the significance and predictive value of the model as a whole. This can be accomplished by examining the multiple correlation (R), which can be thought of as the strength of the relationship between the regression function (represented by all predictors in the model) and the criterion of interest. Although the multiple correlation coefficient is similar to the more familiar correlation coefficient, one key difference is that the multiple correlation ranges from 0 to 1, as opposed to −1 to +1, with values closer to 1 indicating stronger prediction of the criterion. This value can also be evaluated for its significance in standard regression output. The multiple correlation can also be easily converted to an effect size metric by squaring the term (i.e., R^2), which can be interpreted as the percentage of variance in the criterion that can be explained by the predictors in the model.

One problem with the multiple correlation coefficient and the corresponding R^2 effect size is that these metrics are upwardly biased, and thus an analyst may be capitalizing on chance when using them. That is, any predictor added to the equation will generally increase the magnitude of the multiple correlation coefficient. Recall that the range for the multiple correlation is 0 to 1; unlike in simple correlation, direction has no meaning for the multiple correlation, meaning that both positive and negative relationships will increase the multiple correlation. Thus, even if a predictor and a criterion are truly unrelated at the population level (i.e., $r = 0$), the predictor by chance will likely have a nonzero relationship with the criterion, thereby contributing positively to the multiple correlation. A consequence of this is that increasing the number of predictors will generally increase the multiple correlation, regardless of the true predictive value of the predictors added. This problem is referred to as shrinkage (because the multiple correlation would likely be smaller in the population when compared with the estimated multiple correlation from sample data), and there are at least two solutions to it: a statistical solution and a methodological solution. The statistical solution is to use one of a variety of corrective formulas (e.g., Wherry's adjusted R^2) that seek to remove bias from the multiple correlation by accounting for the inflation of the metric due to the number of predictors in the equation. These formulas are generally effective when sample sizes are large. When sample sizes are small and the number of predictors is relatively high, it is recommended to use the methodological solution referred to as cross-validation. When using cross-validation, an analyst first calculates empirically derived regression weights from one sample before determining the adequacy of the model if applied to another sample. That is, the analyst would use the regression equation from the first sample to calculate predicted values of the criterion ($\hat{y}$) in the other sample. Then, one can calculate a simple correlation between actual and predicted values of the criterion in the second sample. To the degree that this correlation is similar to the multiple correlation obtained in the first sample, one has support for the cross-validity of the regression equation.

Another common technique in regression analysis is to evaluate the relative contribution of predictors in a model by entering them at different steps in that model. This can be accomplished by entering one or several predictors in Step 1 of a regression analysis before entering one or several other predictors in Step 2. Then, the change in the multiple correlation coefficient (R) can be evaluated as to whether it increased significantly from Step 1 to Step 2. Additionally, the change in the squared multiple correlation (R^2) can be evaluated as to how much additional variance in the criterion is explained by the predictor (or predictors) added in the second step of the equation. This process can be repeated for as many steps as the researcher desires. There are at least two approaches analysts use to determine which predictors to enter into which step of a regression analysis: hierarchical regression and stepwise

regression. Hierarchical regression is the more theoretically sound approach, in which predictors are entered into an equation in some predetermined order on the basis of theoretical and/or practical justifications. For instance, suppose a group of practitioners are considering adding a personality test to their selection system on the basis of data they had collected within their organization. Using the hierarchical regression approach, they might enter all the predictors currently in the selection system (e.g., an intelligence test, work experience) in the first step of the analysis before evaluating the relative contribution of the new personality test in the second step of the analysis. Hierarchical regression can also be used to evaluate if an interaction term or quadratic term explains variance above and beyond the main effects in an equation, a technique that is covered more thoroughly in the moderation entry of this encyclopedia. The other approach to determine order of entry, stepwise regression, is more empirically based and basically involves continually adding predictors to an equation until the multiple correlation (R) is no longer significantly improved. For this reason, stepwise regression is useful mostly as an exploratory technique. When seeking to confirm expectations and test hypotheses, hierarchical entry is preferable. If there is no theoretical or practical order in which the predictors should be entered, they can also be included as a full set in Step 1 of the analysis.

Assumptions and Other Techniques

There are a number of assumptions about the data being analyzed by OLS regression, the most important of which will be reviewed here. These assumptions should be met in order to ensure the best linear unbiased estimates of model parameters. In other words, meeting these assumptions will yield a regression equation based on sample data that is relatively similar to the equation one would get when analyzing population data. The first assumption is that the predictors are fixed variables. Although this assumption may seem to indicate that continuous variables cannot be entered as predictors, this is not the case. Rather, this assumption simply indicates that the analyst can only make conclusions regarding levels of the predictor(s) actually present in their data. This refers to the distinction between interpolation (i.e., prediction within the range of values included in the data set) and extrapolation (i.e., prediction outside the range of values included in the data set); whereas interpolation satisfies this assumption of regression, extrapolation does not.

Another regression assumption is that the criterion is a continuous variable, or at least that it is roughly continuous. For example, if analysts are predicting job satisfaction as their criterion and measure this variable with five items on a seven-point, Likert-type scale, this would meet the continuous criterion assumption of OLS well enough so as not to cause any major problems with the analysis. This assumption is needed because $\hat{y}$ is a function of the sum of the products of regression weights and included variables as well as an intercept term, and thus $\hat{y}$ must be free to take on any of the values that might result from that equation. Violating this assumption becomes more of a problem the coarser the measurement of a criterion variable becomes, with the most serious issues resulting from using a dichotomous criterion variable (e.g., turnover coded 0 for stayers and 1 for leavers). Using a dichotomous dependent variable presents several problems for the analysis, including (a) violation of the homoscedasticity assumption (i.e., that the variance of errors of prediction across levels of the predictor variables in constant), (b) an intrinsically nonlinear model, and (c) production of predicted values of the criterion that fall outside the range of possible values for the criterion (e.g., $\hat{y}$ values could be <0 or >1, making them uninterpretable). Of course, this is not to say that dichotomous criteria such as turnover should not be analyzed at all. Rather, such outcomes should be analyzed using logistic regression, which is a direct probability model that uses an iterative maximum likelihood estimation strategy as opposed to the least squares criterion used in OLS. Although a complete overview of logistic regression is beyond the scope of this entry, this analysis strategy does share some similarities with OLS regression in that it produces significance tests for individual coefficients, provides information on the adequacy of a model an incremental improvement of that model as predictors are added to the equation, and can even produce pseudo-R^2 values that can be interpreted in a somewhat similar fashion to this effect size metric from OLS regression.

A final assumption of regression is that all predictors in the equation are interval level or dichotomous. To illustrate why this assumption is necessary, let us return to the basic interpretation of regression weights provided earlier: They tell us the rate of change in the predicted value of the criterion per single-unit increase in the predictor in question, holding all other predictors in the equation constant. Thus, the meaning of a single-unit increase in the predictor in question must maintain consistent meaning across the values of the predictor. This is the case for interval-level and dichotomous predictors, but is not the case for ordinal-level or categorical predictors. Of course, this is not to say that categorical predictors (e.g., experimental condition) are not of interest when conducting OLS regression. Rather, a coding strategy must first be used to convert the categorical variable into several dichotomous variables. Regardless of the coding strategy used, the analyst needs to construct $k - 1$ coded variables to account for the differences represented by the categorical variable, with k representing the number of categories present in the original variable. Perhaps the most common coding strategy used is dummy coding, wherein a case receives a 1 on the coded variable if its belongs to the group in question (e.g., if a participant is in Experimental Condition 1, the participant would receive a 1 on the coded variable relevant for his or her category) and a 0 on all other coded variables. This process is continued until the analyst reaches the final reference group, which receives a 0 on all coded variables. Thus, this coding strategy is best used when there is one group that is clearly a group against which all other groups should be compared, such as a control group in an experimental paradigm. Effects coding is another coding strategy that is most useful when one wishes to compare all groups with one another (i.e., the referent here is the mean of group means), while contrast coding is a coding strategy that is most useful when the analyst is interested in more specific comparisons between groups.

Alex Lindsey

See also Multilevel Modeling; Relative Importance; Structural Equation Modeling

Further Readings

Berry, W. D. (1993). *Understanding regression assumptions*. Newbury Park, CA: Sage.

Cohen, J., Cohen, P., West, S. G., & Aiken, L. S. (2013). *Applied multiple regression/correlation analysis for the behavioral sciences*. New York: Routledge.

Field, A. (2013). *Discovering statistics using IBM SPSS Statistics*. Thousand Oaks, CA: Sage.

Fox, J. (1997). *Applied regression analysis, linear models, and related methods*. Thousand Oaks, CA: Sage.

Kleinbaum, D., Kupper, L., Nizam, A., & Rosenberg, E. (2013). *Applied regression analysis and other multivariable methods*. Boston: Cengage Learning.

Menard, S. (2002). *Applied logistic regression analysis* (Vol. 106). Thousand Oaks, CA: Sage.

REINFORCEMENT THEORY OF WORK MOTIVATION

A major theory concerned with motivation at work, the operant conditioning or reinforcement theory of B. F. Skinner emphasizes the role of the environment, particularly the consequences of our behaviors. Unique in the social sciences, it categorizes events by when they occur. Antecedents such as training, goals, and company policy typically take place before the target behaviors, whereas consequences (e.g., compliments and criticism) occur afterward. Antecedents alone fail to motivate workers to do things the right way day in and day out. Instead, the drivers of our motivation are performance consequences. To motivate workers to perform at their potential, primarily positive consequences are rearranged so that they frequently and consistently follow desired performance. Reinforcement theory also sheds light on why well-meaning managers sometimes act in baffling and self-contradictory ways as well as provide the inspiration for a leadership model.

History

Although Skinner had formulated the basic principles of operant conditioning by the 1940s, they were not widely applied outside of university laboratories until the 1960s. The first settings for the use of reinforcement theory, referred to as applied behavior analysis, were the wards of institutions for the mentally retarded. Behavior analysts designed programs for patients and soon thereafter staff members. Success bred success, with settings quickly expanding from hospitals and schools in the public sector to businesses and industries in the private sector. Truck drivers and dockworkers at Emery Air Freight, after being positively reinforced, worked together more efficiently and harmoniously. During boot camp at Fort Ord, California, soldiers exchanged points for such coveted backup reinforcers as early dismissal and time off with pay. The result of the token economy program: Soldiers met rigorous standards while maintaining their morale.

By the early 1970s, industrial and organizational psychologists Lyman W. Porter and Walter R. Nord identified the behavioral approach as an innovative advance to motivation. Since then, hundreds of studies have been conducted in work settings, published in the *Journal of Applied Behavior Analysis* and the *Journal of Organizational Behavior Management*, as well as industrial and organizational journals such as the *Journal of Applied Psychology*, *Organizational Behavior and Human Decision Processes*, and the *Academy of Management Journal*. Authors work in the public and private sectors as well as in educational institutions such as the Florida Institute of Technology, the University of Western Michigan, and the University of Nevada, Reno.

Reinforcement theory has been used to improve productivity, attendance, punctuality, customer service, and occupational safety. Behavior-based approaches are widely used to reduce accidents and injuries. The Behavioral Safety Now Conference has run for 20 years. An accreditation service, set up by the Cambridge Center for Behavioral Studies, verifies that organizations comply with the principles and techniques of a fully functioning behavioral safety program.

Using Reinforcement Theory to Promote Substantial and Sustained Improvements at Work

Consequences Are Primary

Before embarking on any improvement effort, behavior analysts first ask, What happens when workers behave as desired? Do management or coworkers provide consequences, particularly positive ones, acknowledging workers? Similar queries are made about undesired behaviors. For instance, if unsafe behaviors are of concern, What happens when workers perform unsafely? Do employees regularly incur injuries? Are there penalties for acting unsafely? In short, behavior analysts concentrate on the consequences for safe and unsafe acts. If consequences are found to be sparse, rarely favorable, and at times unrelated to the desired behavior, a not atypical situation in many organizations, behavior analysts then and only then modify the situation to ensure that positive, contingent, and frequent consequences follow desired performance.

Five Types of Positive Consequences Are Often Used in Work Settings

The consequences vary from organizational and activity to social and informational:

- *Organizational.* Events indigenous to work settings such as promotions, bonuses, and special training opportunities are offered. Benefits such as free gasoline and free monthly passes on the bus system were made available as incentives for reducing accidents to workers in a regional transportation authority. The sending out of letters of recommendation was among the consequences successfully used by advisers to reinforce master's students making progress toward completing their theses.
- *Activity.* Another class of consequences is derived from the Premack principle (named after David Premack), which states that any higher frequency activity can be used as a positive consequence for a lower frequency activity. When calls to renewal customers were found to be of higher frequency than calls to new customers, the former were made contingent on the latter. Making the opportunity to sell five renewal contracts dependent on the higher frequency activity resulted in more new sales calls being made.
- *Generalized.* Generalized consequences derive their potency from the fact that they can be exchanged for backup reinforcers. Examples include cash, frequent flyer points, and coupons.

At a job training center, coupons could be traded for the opportunity to select a clerical assignment, including who, what, and where one worked.
- *Social.* Typically expressed by individuals, social consequences include commendations, compliments, criticism, reviews, and recognition for a job well done. For example, a hospital supervisor commented to a staff member, "I'm pleased to see you interacting with clients, but I'm sure Mary is even more pleased."
- *Informational.* As the label suggests, information is provided about performance. It can be conveyed in notes to employees written by supervisors, in the form of a graph of baseline and intervention levels, or by listing, as a government official did, what had been done after a hurricane: "We're feeding more people.... We're recovering more people.... We're clearing more roads.... We're building more power lines.... Every day, more victories."

Evidence of the Effectiveness of Positive Reinforcement

Reviews of the literature (e.g., by C. Merle Johnson, William K. Redmon, and Thomas C. Mawhinney, and by Alexander D. Stajkovic and Fred Luthans) attest to the efficacy of positive reinforcement. Judith L. Komaki and her colleagues examined the literature from 1969 to 1998 and found successful improvements in a variety of work settings. Of a total of 72 meticulously controlled experiments, 58 studies were in support, 10 showed mixed support, and only 4 did not show any support, for a success rate of 93%. The changes were not ephemeral; almost half of the studies lasted 26 weeks or longer, and in more than 40%, the longest intervention was at least 12 weeks. Further confirmation of the efficacy of the approach was found by Van Stelle and colleagues (2012) in a review of experiments published in the *Journal of Organizational Behavior Management* from 1998 to 2009; the authors called for further refinements in measurement (e.g., using "organizationally relevant" indices to validate the assessments used) and increases in the participation of managers, directors, and executives. But together these reviews, looking at 1969 to 1998 and 1998 to 2009, with a diverse set of authors, subjects, and settings, confirms the robustness of reinforcement theory in improving performance at work.

Antecedents Found to Play a Secondary Role

To solve performance problems at work, the most common recommendations are "to inform or exhort," both of which are antecedents. Unfortunately, the evidence for relying on antecedents alone is meager, with noticeable improvements of the performance of incumbents rare. Antecedents serve valuable educational or cuing functions, specifying expectations, clarifying relationships between behaviors and consequences, and/or signaling occasions in which consequences are likely to be applied. But only when consequences accompany antecedents do substantial and sustained improvements occur. After training, for example, performance typically increases, but only slightly. Not until consequences such as feedback are provided does performance improve markedly and do those changes last. As Aubrey Daniels said, "Antecedents get us going; consequences keep us going." Because of the essential role of consequences in motivation, the delivery of one or more often positive consequences is the mainstay of virtually all reinforcement programs.

The Explanatory Power of Reinforcement Theory

In Illuminating Why We Sometimes Do Perplexing, Often Paradoxical Things

Reinforcement theory also helps us understand why managers who purportedly believe in merit promote on seniority and why professors who profess the importance of education neglect their teaching.

Positive reinforcement can be arranged in a constructive, planned-out way. Inadvertently, however, it can produce unwanted results. The head of a public relations firm could not understand why her staff members kept postponing things. Yet the year before, when the staff was under pressure to produce an anniversary report, she gave permission to set all other work aside and to hire temporary staff members at company expense. When the report was finally completed, she gave everyone a bonus. Despite the agency head's well-meaning intentions, she may have accidentally reinforced her staff for procrastinating.

Positive reinforcement also can explain why some professors spend less time on teaching than research: because their promotion depends heavily on what appears in journals rather than in the classroom. Professors at research institutions earn tenure primarily on the basis of their publishing research in top-tier journals and procuring funding for their research. Teaching prowess, no matter how sublime, cannot compensate for a mediocre research record. Not surprisingly, even the most initially committed teachers often end up responding to the contingencies that prioritize research rather than teaching.

The principle of *negative reinforcement*, which involves escaping from or avoiding aversive consequences such as criticism or litigation as a consequence of a behavior, can explain why a normally conscientious manager would promote someone with only an adequate record rather than an exemplary employee with less seniority: to avoid complaints of favoritism or bias. The same principle provides a reason why normally ambitious lieutenants choose to remain at their rank—to avoid the increased scrutiny, responsibility, and restrictions that come with being promoted to captain—and why even the most ethically inclined people sometimes remain quiet in the face of corruption, hence avoiding censure and retaliation.

The consequences for performing as desired sometimes can be *punishing*. The head of a major research laboratory bemoaned the lack of creativity of the engineers in his group. When asked about the consequences, however, he could readily point to a host of inherently negative consequences: their time-consuming, seemingly fruitless literature searches; difficulties communicating concepts, which were, as yet, incomprehensible to their peers; and inordinate amounts of time expended before having anything to show for their efforts. All of these aversive events (punishment by application) helped explain why some engineers shunned such endeavors, preferring the tried and true.

The principle of *punishment by removal*, technically called response cost, in which a positive reinforcer is withdrawn as a consequence of a behavior, sheds light on how some preferred behaviors can be unintentionally discouraged. Even when in danger of their lives, fighter pilots often are reluctant to call for help. Such an admission, as Tom Wolfe graphically pointed out in his book *The Right Stuff*, triggered a very public chain of events: some punishing—fire trucks trundling out to the runway, incoming flights being held up, the bureaucracy gearing up to investigate, and at least one punishment by removal—the pilot's peers questioning the pilot's mettle and hence dampening the idea that the pilot had "the right stuff."

These principles often work in tandem, producing a complex yet powerful set of contingencies. Table 1 illustrates how the environment can influence even managers committed to fairness and accuracy to provide less than fair and accurate appraisals. For inaccurate appraisals, exactly the opposite of the ideal often occurs with reinforcement in abundance and punishment meted out stingingly. For instance, managers who inflate their evaluations of performance are sometimes positively reinforced by employees thankful for a break. At the same time, a manager who writes a glowing but undeserving recommendation can result in negative reinforcement in which the

manager gets to rid herself of a poor performer by foisting the troublesome employee onto another unsuspecting manager. Similarly, inaccurately deflating performance is sometimes reinforced. Exaggerating the faults of an employee is positively reinforced when a lagging but capable worker is jolted back to performing well or when the manager gets to let an unyielding worker know who wields the power. On the other hand, for accurate and fair reviews, a dearth of positive consequences exists. Unfortunately, extinction has a stultifying effect, with fewer and fewer attempts made to exert the time and energy needed to make subtle distinctions among performance levels. Moreover, some employees, disgruntled about their less than stellar reviews, may file not totally unexpected grievances. Alas, the payoffs—getting recognized by superiors, having evidence to make a case for a deserving employee—are rare or at least delayed. Hence, we can better see why even the most employee-centric managers might fail to accurately appraise their employees.

Table 1   Chart of Principles of Behavior in Tandem Suggesting Why Managers May Not Always Evaluate Employees as Accurately as They Could

Target Behavior	Consequence	Principle
Manager gives inaccurate appraisal	Infrequent reprimands Pay and raises still forthcoming	Lack of punishment by application or removal
(a) By inflating it, or	Earns gratitude from employee for not creating permanent record of poor performance	Positive reinforcement
	Promotes poor-performing employee "up and out" of department	Negative reinforcement
(b) By deflating it	Shocks lackluster employee into performing better Teaches obstreperous employee who's the real boss	Positive reinforcement
	Convinces adequately performing employee with a poor attitude to leave	Negative reinforcement
Manager gives accurate appraisal based on employee's performance	Little management recognition for accuracy Few favorable peer comments Pay, raises, and promotions not contingent on accuracy of appraisal	Extinction
	Occasional complaint/grievance More labor-intensive, time-consuming	Punishment by application
	Building documentation speeding up promotion/termination for deserving worker rare/often detained	Positive reinforcement delayed

In short, the principles of positive reinforcement, as well as negative reinforcement, punishment by application and removal, and extinction explain why people sometimes act contrary to what they espouse. Although punishment and negative reinforcement are not recommended as the primary way of changing behavior, decision makers need to be sensitive to their use of these consequences, eliminating where possible the punishing ones and redesigning the flow of the work to enable, where possible, naturally or specially arranged favorable consequences.

In Shedding Light on What Effective Leaders Do

The theory of operant conditioning has also inspired a leadership model. Not surprisingly, performance consequences played a key role. First-rate managers were predicted, in Judith L. Komaki's operant model of effective supervision, to provide more consequences than lackluster managers. Because consequences need to be related to what employees have done, Komaki hypothesized that effective leaders would inquire about performance or monitor particularly by directly sampling the work. Managers who monitor are more likely to have dependable and up-to-date information with which to provide contingent consequences. The second reason concerns the nature of the interactions between workers and leaders that monitoring facilitates. Data showed that managers' monitoring set into motion a rich set of exchanges with workers speaking up about their performance, which is followed by the manager providing a consequence or monitoring further, which leads in turn to workers' talking more about their performance. Hence, the model highlights performance consequences and monitors.

In every single one of seven field studies, Komaki and her colleagues found that the effective managers monitored, provided consequences, or did both. The consequences have been as brief as a simple "thanks," or even an "okay" said while sampling the work. Neutral consequences (e.g., "Yep. That's alright," or as an officer handed a sergeant a report, "You need a statement from the driver to complete that report") separated effective police sergeants from the lackluster ones

in a study done by Neil Brewer and his colleagues. Investment bankers, identified as exemplary in motivating others, actually thanked the bearer of bad news, acknowledging employees for bringing thorny issues to their attention. Furthermore, top-notch sailboat skippers were found to use a particular sequence during races, with monitors routinely preceding consequences in what is referred to as an AMC sequence, where A stands for an antecedent (an order or instruction), M for a monitor, and C for a consequence. And the exemplary leaders did these AMC sequences quickly. Recently, seasoned emergency medical supervisors have been taught to substantially increase their use of monitoring and especially positive consequences when receiving both good and bad news.

Besides inspiring a leadership model and providing a way of explaining why people do what they do, reinforcement theory shows how a judiciously arranged set of consequences can result in enhanced performance from day to day and season to season.

Judith L. Komaki

See also Organizational Behavior Management

Further Readings

Brewer, N., Wilson, C., & Beck, K. (1994). Supervisory behavior and team performance amongst police patrol sergeants. *Journal of Occupational and Organizational Psychology, 67,* 69–78.

Daniels, A. C. (2000). *Bringing out the best in people.* New York: McGraw-Hill.

Johnson, C. M., Redmon, W. K., & Mawhinney, T. C. (Eds.). (2001). *Handbook of organizational performance: Behavior analysis and management.* New York: Haworth.

Komaki, J. L. (1998). *Leadership from an operant perspective.* London, UK: Routledge.

Komaki, J. L., Coombs, T., Redding, T. P., Jr., & Schepman, S. (2000). A rich and rigorous examination of applied behavior analysis research in the world of work. In C. L. Cooper & I. T. Robertson (Eds.), *International Review of Industrial and Organizational Psychology 2000* (pp. 265–367). Chichester, UK: John Wiley.

Skinner, B. F. (1978). *Reflections on behaviorism and society.* Englewood Cliffs, NJ: Prentice Hall.

VanStelle, S. E., Vicars, S. M., Harr, V., Miguel, C. F., Koerber, J. L., Kazbour, R., & Austin, J. (2012). The publication history of the *Journal of Organizational Behavior Management*: An objective review and analysis: 1998–2009. *Journal of Organizational Behavior Management*, 32(2), 93–123.

Web Sites

Behavior Safety Now Conference: http://www.behavioralsafetynow.com

Cambridge Center for Behavioral Studies' behavioral safety accreditation service: http://www.behavior.org/interest.php?id=16

RELATIVE IMPORTANCE

Industrial and organizational psychologists frequently use regression to predict and explain organizational outcomes (e.g., employee job performance, team cohesion, organizational culture). However, given that most organizational phenomena are complex and multiply determined, regression models used to predict and explain these phenomena include more than one predictor. In such cases, researchers frequently want to know which of the multiple predictors in a regression model are most influential in predicting and explaining a given outcome. Relative importance analysis is designed to help researchers answer this question and allows comparing predictors in multiple regression models in terms of their contributions to explaining variance in the outcome variables.

Historically, predictor importance in regression models has been assessed using zero-order correlations between predictors and outcome variables (r), standardized regression weights (β), squared bivariate correlations (r^2), squared standardized regression weights (β^2), and product measure weights ($r \times \beta$). However, when regression models include multiple *intercorrelated* predictors that explain the overlapping portions of the outcome variance, these indices may provide misleading estimates of predictor importance. Namely, r-based indices only consider bivariate relationships between each predictor and the outcome and fail to assess each predictor's contribution in the presence of other predictors. Indices that are based on

β weights provide information regarding the incremental contribution of each predictor above and beyond other predictors and fail to assess each predictor's unique contribution to the outcome variance. Thus, using these r-based or β-based indices may lead to underestimating or overestimating the importance of predictors. Indices of relative importance address these limitations of previously used indices and provide more accurate importance estimates that take into account both unique and incremental contributions of each predictor.

What Relative Importance Is and What It Is Not

Relative importance is not to be confused with other approaches to assessing predictor importance: statistical significance, practical significance, and incremental importance. *Statistical significance* indicates the likelihood that the estimated effect of a given predictor is obtained by chance only. *Practical significance* indicates whether a given predictor has an effect large enough to produce practically meaningful changes in the outcome. The *incremental importance* of a predictor refers to the additional amount of variance a predictor explains in the outcome above and beyond variance explained by other predictors. *Relative importance* refers to the contribution of a given predictor to explaining variance in a criterion when this predictor is considered alone and in conjunction with other predictors in a regression model. Although these four approaches are different from one another, they are not mutually exclusive. On the contrary, they provide complementary information and can be used collectively to obtain a comprehensive understanding of predictor importance in regression models.

Indices of Relative Importance: Dominance Weights and Relative Weights

Two indices were proposed as measures of relative importance: dominance weights and relative weights. Both indices are similar in the sense that they allow decomposing the explained criterion variance (R^2) into portions accounted for by each predictor taken alone and in conjunction with other predictors. However, these two indices are calculated differently.

Dominance weights (proposed by David Budescu) are computed as the average contribution of each predictor to the explained outcome variance across all possible subset regressions (i.e., regressions with all possible subsets of predictors). For example, a dominance weight for predictor X_1 in a model with two correlated predictors, X_1 and X_2, is computed as the average of two R^2 values obtained in the following subset regression models: (a) R^2 in a model with X_1 as the only predictor, and (b) ΔR^2 obtained when X_1 is added to the model with X_2 as a predictor.

Relative weights (proposed by Jeff Johnson) are computed using the variable transformation approach that involves removing predictor intercorrelations before their relative importance is determined. Thus, when relative weights are calculated, the original correlated predictors are first transformed to uncorrelated predictors that are maximally related to the original predictors. This first step is important because when predictors are correlated and explain overlapping variance in the criterion, it is difficult to accurately parse out their separate contributions to criterion variance. At the second step, relative weights for the original predictors are computed as the products of two sets of scores: (a) squared standardized weights relating the original predictors to the new uncorrelated predictors, and (b) squared standardized weights relating the outcome variable to the new uncorrelated predictors.

Despite these differences in calculations, both dominance weights and relative weights are interpreted similarly (both indicate the importance of each predictor relative to other predictors in terms of their contribution to criterion variance), yield converging conclusions regarding predictor importance (provide similar relative importance estimates), and therefore can be used interchangeably. In addition, both indices can be rescaled to provide easily interpretable weights indicating the proportion of each predictor's contribution to the explained outcome variance. Rescaling is performed by dividing a dominance weight or a relative weight by the model R^2.

The choice between dominance weights and relative weights depends on the following considerations. Dominance weights allow determining patterns of dominance (complete, conditional, and general) and therefore can be preferred over relative weights when researchers are interested in examining such patterns. *Complete dominance* occurs when one predictor makes greater contribution than another predictor to each subset model that includes both of these predictors. For example, in a regression model with three predictors—X_1, X_2, and X_3,—X_1 will completely dominate X_2 if it yields higher ΔR^2 than X_2 when added to the model with no predictors and when added to the model with X_3 as a predictor. *Conditional dominance* occurs when one predictor makes greater average additional contribution than another predictor within each subset model size. For example, in a regression model with three predictors—X_1, X_2, and X_3,—X_1 will conditionally dominate X_2 if it yields a greater ΔR^2 when added to the model with no predictors, a greater average ΔR^2 when added to the model with X_2 and then to the model with X_3, and finally a greater ΔR^2 when added to the model with X_2 and X_3. *General dominance* occurs when a given predictor has a larger dominance weight than another predictor across all subset regressions.

However, dominance weights may be cumbersome to compute, as the number of all subset regressions needed to perform these computations increases with the number of predictors. For example, to compute dominance weights for a regression model with only four predictors, which is smaller than many regression models used in organizational research, 32 subset regressions are needed. Thus, relative weights are recommended for regression models with a larger number of predictors. Relative weight analysis can be performed using the user-friendly, freely available online tool RWA-Web, developed by Scott Tonidandel and James LeBreton. In addition to computing relative weights for models including but not limited to standard multiple linear regression, this tool allows conducting significance tests for relative weights and pairwise differences among them.

Extensions of Relative Importance Analysis Beyond Ordinary Least Squares Regression

Relative importance indices were originally developed for use with ordinary least squares (OLS) regression models that include continuous outcome variables. More recently, new analytic procedures were proposed to allow determining relative importance of predictors in nonlinear, multivariate, and multilevel models.

Predictor Importance in Logistic Regression Models

In logistic regression models, outcome variables are categorical (e.g., a turnover variable with two levels: left the organization vs. stayed in the organization) and predictor variables evaluate the odds of membership in one of these categories (e.g., what are the odds that an employee who has received a competitive job offer but is highly satisfied with his or her current job will leave the organization?). To determine the relative importance of predictors in such models, the traditional relative importance procedures need to be modified to account for the nonlinear relationship between predictors and categorical outcomes. This is achieved by replacing the standard OLS regression R^2 used in the traditional relative importance analysis with an R^2 analogue for logistic regression. Once this R^2 analogue is obtained, *dominance weights* can be computed as usual (i.e., as each predictor's average contribution to the R^2 analogue across all subset regressions). The same R^2 analogue can be used to derive standardized logistic regression weights that can then be used to compute *relative weights*.

Predictor Importance in Regression Models With Higher-Order Terms

When researchers want to examine interactions among predictors or nonlinear effects of predictors, they include higher-order terms (e.g., interactions, quadratic or cubic terms) in their regression models. Determining predictor importance in such higher-order models is more complicated than in simple main-effects-only models. Each higher-order term is composed of other predictors and contains information about both lower-order and higher-order effects of these predictors. As a result, the separate contributions of this higher-order term and its corresponding lower-order terms to criterion variance are difficult to single out. Thus, higher-order terms need to be residualized for the corresponding lower-order terms before their relative importance can be determined. This residualization is accomplished by regressing the higher-order term on the relevant lower-order terms and saving the residual as a separate variable that can then be used along with the main effect predictors to compute relative importance indices.

For example, to determine the relative importance of trait aggression, narcissism, and their interaction in predicting employee deviance, the interaction term is first regressed on aggression and narcissism. The obtained residual represents the pure interactive effect of aggression and narcissism and is not confounded with their main effects. This residual is then included as a predictor in a regression model along with aggression and narcissism, and relative importance weights (dominance weights or relative weights) are computed for each of these three predictors as usual.

Predictor Importance in Multivariate Models

When researchers are interested in predicting multiple correlated criteria, they use multivariate multiple regression models (e.g., a researcher might want to use trait aggression and narcissism to predict two correlated types of employees' deviant behaviors: deviance directed at other employees and deviance directed at the entire organization). Traditional relative importance analysis is designed for models with one outcome variable, and needs to be modified for models with multiple intercorrelated outcome variables. For *dominance weights*, this modification involves replacing the standard OLS regression R^2 with its multivariate analogue. Once this R^2 analogue is obtained, dominance weights can be computed as usual (i.e., as each predictor's average contribution to the R^2 analogue across all subset regression models). For *relative weights*, this modification involves removing intercorrelations among the outcome variables by transforming them to the uncorrelated outcome variables maximally related to the original outcome variables. The original outcome variables are then regressed on the transformed uncorrelated outcome variables and the resulting regression weights are used in the computations of relative weights.

Predictor Importance in Multilevel Models

Organizational researchers frequently study phenomena that reside at different levels of organizational hierarchy: at the level of individual employees, dyads, groups, organizations, and industries (e.g., a researcher might want to examine the effects of group climate and group members' openness to experience on their creativity). In such multilevel models, relative importance analysis can no longer rely on the traditional OLS regression R^2 because variance of the outcome variable is composed of multiple components (e.g., within- and between-group in a two-level model). Thus, to derive relative importance indices in multilevel models, an appropriate multilevel analogue of R^2 is needed.

The choice of the most appropriate multilevel R^2 analogue depends on whether a researcher wants to compare predictors within levels (i.e., only lower-level predictors or only higher-level predictors are compared with each other) or across levels (i.e., lower-level predictors are compared with higher-level predictors). It also depends on whether a researcher is interested in the relative contribution of predictors to outcome variance at the lower level or higher level. Once the appropriate multilevel R^2 analogue is chosen, dominance weights can be computed as usual following the traditional all subset regression approach.

To conclude, relative importance analysis is a useful supplement to regression analysis that allows comparing predictors' importance on the basis of their contribution to criterion variance. The articles provided in the list of further readings should be consulted for more information on the use of relative importance analysis in OLS regressions and more advanced models.

Dina V. Krasikova

See also Measures of Association/Correlation Coefficient; Multilevel Modeling; Regression Techniques

Further Readings

Azen, R., & Budescu, D. V. (2003). The dominance analysis approach for comparing predictors in multiple regression. *Psychological Methods, 8*, 129–148.

Azen, R., & Traxel, N. (2009). Using dominance analysis to determine predictor importance in logistic regression. *Journal of Educational and Behavioral Statistics, 34*, 319–347.

Johnson, J. W. (2000). A heuristic method for estimating the relative weight of predictor variables in multiple regression. *Multivariate Behavioral Research, 35*, 1–19.

LeBreton, J. M., & Tonidandel, S. (2008). Multivariate relative importance: Extending relative weight analysis to multivariate criterion spaces. *Journal of Applied Psychology, 93*, 329–345.

LeBreton, J. M., Tonidandel, S., & Krasikova, D. V. (2013). Residualized relative importance analysis: A technique for the comprehensive decomposition of variance in higher order regression models. *Organizational Research Methods, 16*, 449–473.

Luo, W., & Azen, R. (2013). Determining predictor importance in hierarchical linear models using dominance analysis. *Journal of Educational and Behavioral Statistics, 38*, 3–31.

Tonidandel, S., & LeBreton, J. M. (2010). Determining the relative importance of predictors in logistic regression: An extension of relative weight analysis. *Organizational Research Methods, 13*, 767–781.

Tonidandel, S., & LeBreton, J. M. (2015). RWA-Web: A free, comprehensive, web-based, and user-friendly tool for relative weight analyses. *Journal of Business and Psychology, 30*, 207–215.

RELIABILITY

Reliability can be defined as the extent to which scores of a measure are free from the effect of measurement error. Measurement error is reflected by random deviations of the scores observed on a measure from respondents' *true scores*, which are the expected values of respondents' scores if they completed the measure an infinite number of times. Mathematically, reliability is quantified as the ratio of true score variance to observed score variance or, equivalently, the square of the correlation between true scores and observed scores. On the basis of these indices, reliability can range from 0 (no true score variance) to 1 (no measurement error).

Reliability is important for both practical and theoretical purposes. Practically, it enables estimation of the standard error of measurement, an index of accuracy of a person's test score. Theoretically, reliability contributes to theory development by allowing researchers to correct for the biasing effect of measurement error on observed correlations between measures of psychological constructs and providing researchers with an assessment of whether their measurement process needs to be improved (e.g., if reliability is low).

Sources of Measurement Error

Multiple sources of measurement error can influence a person's observed score. The following sources are common in psychological measures.

Random Response Error

Random response error is caused by momentary variations in attention, mental efficiency, distractions, and so on, within a given occasion. It is specific to a moment when persons respond to an item on a measure. For example, a person might provide different answers to the same item appearing in different places on a measure.

Transient Error

Whereas random response error occurs within an occasion, transient error occurs across occasions. Transient errors are produced by temporal variations in respondents' mood and feelings across occasions. For example, any given respondent might score differently on a measure administered on two occasions. Theoretically, such temporal differences are random and thus not part of persons' true scores; they will not correlate with scores from the measure completed on other occasions (i.e., they are occasion specific).

Specific Factor Error

Specific factor error reflects idiosyncratic responses to some element of the measurement situation. For example, when responding to test items, respondents might interpret item wording differently. Theoretically, specific factors are not part of persons' true scores because they do not correlate with scores on other elements (e.g., items) of the measure.

Rater Error

Rater error arises only when a person's observed score (rating) is obtained from another person or set of persons (raters). Rater error arises from the raters' idiosyncratic perceptions of ratees' standing on the construct of interest. Theoretically, idiosyncratic rater factors are not part of persons' true scores, because they do not correlate with ratings provided by other raters (i.e., they are rater specific).

Types of Reliability Coefficients

Reliability is indexed with a reliability coefficient. There are several types of reliability coefficients. They differ with regard to the sources of observed score variance they treat as true score and error variance. Sources of variance treated as error variance in one type of coefficient may be treated as true score variance in other types.

Internal Consistency

This type of reliability coefficient is the one most frequently found in psychological research (e.g., Cronbach's alpha, split-half). Internal consistency reliability coefficients (also called coefficients of equivalence [CEs]) require only one administration of a measure and index the effects of specific factor error and random response error on observed scores. They reflect the degree of consistency between item-level scores on a measure. Because all items on a given measure are administered on the *same occasion*, they share a source of variance (i.e., transient error) that may be unrelated to the target construct of interest but nonetheless contributes to true score variance in these coefficients (because it is a shared source of variance across items).

Test-Retest Reliability

Test-retest reliability coefficients (also called coefficients of stability [CSs]) index the effects of random response error and transient error on observed scores. Test-retest coefficients reflect the degree of stability in test scores across occasions and can be thought of as the correlation between the same test administered on different occasions. Because the same test is administered on each occasion, the scores on each occasion share a source of variance (i.e., specific factor error) that may be unrelated to the target construct of interest but nonetheless contributes to true score variance in these coefficients (because it is a shared source of variance across occasions).

Coefficients of Equivalence and Stability

Coefficients of equivalence and stability (CESs) index the effects of specific factor error, transient error, and random response error on observed scores. CESs reflect the consistency of scores across items on a test and the stability of test scores across occasions and can be thought of as the correlation between two parallel forms of a measure administered on different occasions. The use of different forms enables estimation of specific factor error and random response error, and the administration on different occasions enables estimation of transient error and random response error. As such, this coefficient can be seen as the combination of the CE and the CS. Hence, the CES is the recommended reliability estimate for most self-report measures, because it appropriately accounts for all three sources of measurement error, leaving none of these sources of variance to contribute to one's estimate of true score variance.

Intrarater Reliability

Intrarater reliability coefficients, a type of internal consistency coefficient specific to ratings-based measures, index the effects of specific factor error and random response error on observed score variance. These coefficients reflect the degree of consistency between items rated by a given rater on one occasion. Because the items are rated by the *same rater* (intrarater) on the same occasion, they share two sources of variance (i.e., rater error and transient error) that may be unrelated to the construct of interest but nonetheless contribute to true score variance in these coefficients (because they are shared sources of variance across items).

Interrater Reliability

Like intrarater reliability coefficients, interrater reliability coefficients are also specific to ratings-based measures. However, unlike intrarater reliability coefficients, interrater reliability coefficients index the effect of rater error and random response error on observed score variance. They reflect the degree of consistency in ratings provided by different raters and can be thought of as the correlation between ratings from different raters using a single measure on one occasion. Because the same ratings measure is administered to *different raters* (interrater) on the same occasion, the ratings share two sources of variance (i.e., specific factor error and transient error) that may be unrelated to the target construct of interest but nonetheless contribute to

true score variance in these coefficients (because they are a shared source of variance across raters).

Estimating Reliability Coefficients

Methods for estimating the coefficients described above are made available through two psychometric theories: classical test theory (CTT) and generalizability (G) theory. Researchers adopting a CTT approach to the estimation of these coefficients often calculate Pearson correlations between various elements of the measure (e.g., items, raters, and occasions) and then use the Spearman-Brown prophecy formula to adjust the estimate as needed for the number of items, raters, or occasions across which observations on the measure were gathered. Conversely, researchers adopting a G-theory approach have focused on first estimating components of these reliability coefficients (i.e., true score variance [*universe score variance* in G-theory terms] and error variance) and then forming a ratio with these estimates to arrive at an estimated reliability coefficient (or *generalizability coefficient* in G-theory terms).

Recently, structural equation modeling (SEM) has been recommended as an alternative approach to estimate the reliability coefficients. With appropriate measurement designs, SEM can be used to estimate all types of reliability coefficients described above. Empirical evidence has shown that SEM and traditional approaches based on CTT and G theory provide very similar estimates of reliabilities.

Factors Affecting Reliability Estimates

Several factors can affect the magnitude of reliability coefficients researchers report for a measure. Their potential impact on any given estimate must be considered for an appropriate interpretation of the estimate to be made.

Measurement Design Limitations

The magnitude of a reliability coefficient depends in part on the sources of variance treated as error. Unfortunately, not all measurement designs will allow estimation of all types of reliability coefficients. Thus, even though researchers may wish to consider a source of variance in their measure as error, they may not always have the measurement design to account for it. For example, researchers cannot index the amount of transient error variance in observed scores if they did not administer their measure (or at least parts of it) on multiple occasions. In such a case, a researcher may have to report a reliability coefficient that overestimates the true reliability of their measure.

Constructs Being Measured

Items measuring different constructs may be differentially susceptible to sources of measurement error. For example, items for broader constructs (e.g., conscientiousness) are likely to be more strongly affected by specific factor error than items for narrower constructs (e.g., orderliness). Similarly, items measuring stable personality constructs (such as the Big Five) may be less susceptible to transient error than items measuring affect-related constructs.

Heterogeneity of the Sample

It is well known that range restriction attenuates correlations between variables. Because reliability coefficients can be interpreted as the square of the correlation between observed scores and true scores, they too are subject to range restriction. Reliability estimates tend to be higher when obtained from a sample of persons who vary greatly on the construct being measured and lower if the persons in the sample do not vary greatly on the construct.

Test Length

Scores on a measure are typically formed by summing or averaging responses across items. Because specific factor errors associated with items are uncorrelated, their contributions to the observed score variance when summed or averaged diminish in proportion to the number of items included in the measure. Hence, all else being equal, the more items on the measure, the higher its reliability.

Huy Le and Dan J. Putka

See also Classical Test Theory; Generalizability Theory; Validity

Further Readings

Cortina, J. M. (1993). What is coefficient alpha? An examination of theory and applications. *Journal of Applied Psychology, 78*, 98–104

Feldt, L. S., & Brennan, R. L. (1989). Reliability. In R. L. Linn (Ed.), *Educational measurement* (3rd ed., pp. 105–146). New York: American Council on Education and Macmillan.

Green, S. B., & Yang, Y. (2009). Reliability of summed item scores using structural equation modeling: An alternative to coefficient alpha. *Psychometrika, 74*, 155–167.

Le, H., Schmidt, F. L., & Putka, D. J. (2009). The multifaceted nature of measurement artifacts and its implications for estimating construct-level relationships. *Organizational Research Methods, 12*, 165–200.

Nunnally, J. C., & Bernstein, I. H. (1994). *Psychometric theory* (3rd ed.). New York: McGraw-Hill.

Schmidt, F. L., & Hunter, J. E. (1996). Measurement error in psychological research: Lessons from 26 research scenarios. *Psychological Methods, 1*, 199–223.

Schmidt, F. L., Le, H., & Ilies, R. (2003). Beyond alpha: An empirical examination of the effects of different sources of measurement error on reliability estimates for measures of individual differences constructs. *Psychological Methods, 8*, 206–224.

Traub, R. E. (1994). *Reliability for the social sciences— Theory and applications*. Thousand Oaks, CA: Sage.

RELIGIOUS DISCRIMINATION

Under Title VII of the Civil Rights Act of 1964, religion is considered a protected group. However, as the United States becomes a more diversified country in terms of its citizens' religious affiliations, there has also been a trend toward an increasing number of religious discrimination charges being filed. Although the focus on understanding religious discrimination in the workplace from a psychological perspective is limited, there is substantial evidence in terms of court cases and statistics that points to the importance of understanding how religious discrimination affects employees within their work environments.

Title VII

Employers are prohibited from discriminating against and harassing employees on the basis of their religious (or lack of religious) affiliation under Title VII. The term *religion* encompasses traditional organized religions (e.g., Christianity, Judaism, Islam, Hinduism, and Buddhism) as well as new, uncommon, informal religious affiliations and nontheistic affiliations (e.g., atheism). This concerns all employment decisions, including (but not limited to) decisions surrounding hiring, firing, recruitment, assignments, and discipline. With regard to selection and placement, Title VII prohibits the segregation of jobs on the basis of an employee's religious affiliation. That is, an employer cannot assign an employee to a particular type of job because of that employee's religious affiliation (e.g., assigning employees of a particular religious affiliation to less visible roles given the employer's perception that customers may fear those individuals).

Additionally, Title VII requires that employers provide reasonable accommodation for the religious beliefs and practices of employees and applicants. *Reasonable accommodation* means that the employer must make any adjustment to the work environment to accommodate the religious needs of the employee as long as such accommodations do not cause undue hardship to the employer with regard to the organization's functioning (e.g., an accommodation that is too costly or difficult to provide). Examples of typical accommodations employers make for religious beliefs include flexible scheduling, voluntary shift substitutions, and exceptions to company dress codes. An example of undue hardship would be if an employee's request for flexible scheduling restricts the ability of other employees to fulfill their job roles.

Finally, Title VII prohibits harassment or retaliation against employees related to religious discrimination. Harassment includes those behaviors that cause a hostile work environment that subject an employee to severe and unwelcomed ridicule, insult, or hostility. Harassment due to religious affiliation can be those behaviors directed at the employee's beliefs or the beliefs of the people with whom the employee associates. Retaliation includes those behaviors directed at an applicant or an employee who is participating in a protected activity such as filing an equal employment opportunity (EEO) charge or testifying in an EEO matter.

Title VII covers all private employers, state and local governments, and educational institutions that employ 15 or more individuals as well as private and public employment agencies, labor organizations, and labor management committees controlling apprenticeship and training. Some state-level antidiscrimination laws extend coverage to organizations with fewer than 15 people. The exceptions to Title VII coverage are that (a) religious organizations and educational institutions can show preference to employees and applicants on the basis of religious affiliation and (b) clergy members cannot file claims of federal employment discrimination because it constitutes impermissible government entanglements with church authority.

Court Cases

To combat religious discrimination in the workplace, it is important to understand how it is defined. A review of several landmark court rulings helps us understand the legal precedents that define workplace religious discrimination under Title VII. In its 1970 ruling in *Welsh v. United States*, the U.S. Supreme Court began to clarify the legal definition of "religious beliefs." One's beliefs can be adjudged "religious" when they represent in the believer's life a meaning analogous to the meaning God holds for believers of "traditional" religions. Accordingly, a "religious belief" is legally defined by (a) the sincerity with which the believer demonstrates that he or she holds the belief, and (b) whether the belief holds a position parallel to God within the believer's life. In *Brown v. Pena* (1997), the Southern Federal District Court of Florida offered a further clarifying ruling that built on this definition. The court determined that the belief must not merely be a strongly held personal preference but must have an institutional quality about it and be rooted in a theory of "man's nature of his place in the universe." In its 2000 ruling in *Swartzentruber v. Gunite Corp.*, the Northern Federal District Court of Indiana added that beliefs that are distinctly social and political in nature are not considered religious under Title VII.

The long-standing test for religious harassment was established originally in the Supreme Court's ruling in *Meritor Savings Bank, FSB, v. Vinson* (477 U.S. 57, 1986). The Court determined sexual harassment to be a specific form of sexual discrimination, and subsequent lower court cases have applied these same analyses to cases for religious harassment. Congruent with *Meritor*, religious harassment in violation of Title VII exists in workplace instances in which an employee is subject to unwelcome statements or conduct; the statements or conduct are based on religion, the conduct is severe enough for the employee to reasonably deem the environment abusive or hostile, and the employer can reasonably be held liable for these occurrences. The Supreme Court's 1993 ruling in *Harris v. Forklift Systems Inc.* further clarified that hostile work environments could be attributed not only to physical or verbal harassment but also to unwelcome religious views and practices imposed upon the employee.

In a landmark ruling, *Griggs v. Duke Power Company*, the Supreme Court specified that Title VII applies not only to overt acts of discrimination but also to practices that appear "fair in form but discriminatory in operation." This ruling established the disparate impact theory, which states that workplace policy that appears neutral on its face may be deemed discriminatory if it disproportionately affects members of protected classes. Although the often-cited disparate impact theory could also apply to religious workplace discrimination, especially regarding hiring practices (i.e., *Barrow v. Greenville Indep. Sch. Dist.*, 2007), it is rarely used in the religious context. Reasonable accommodation and undue hardship analyses are most often applied to such cases in which neutral workplace policies conflict with employees' religious practices and beliefs (see *EEOC v. Abercrombie and Fitch Store Inc.*, 2015).

Statistical Trends

Over the past 2 decades, there has been a steady increase in the percentage of discrimination charges attributed to religious discrimination made to the EEOC. In 2014, 4% of discrimination charges (3,549 charges) were religious in nature. To help put this into perspective, this has increased from the 1,546 out of 91,189 charges filed in 1994 and 2,466 out of 79,432 changes filed in 2004.

One religious group that has been frequently affected by religious discrimination in the workplace is the U.S. Muslim population. In 2011, it was estimated that although only 2% of the U.S. population identified as Muslim, 21.3% of U.S. workplace discrimination cases investigated by the federal government involved charges of discrimination against Muslims. That is, of the 4,151 discrimination charges filed in 2011, 884 of those

charges were for Muslim discrimination charges. Furthermore, a portion of national origin charges that are filed are also on the basis of the party's Muslim affiliation. For example, in 2011, 544 of the 11,833 charges filed on the basis of national origin were associated with a Muslim religious affiliation.

Trends in Research

Although there is a large body of research focused on discrimination in the workplace, the research focused specifically on religious discrimination in the workplace is extremely limited. A review article found that as of 2013, there were only seven psychology articles that were empirical in nature that looked at discrimination in the context of the Civil Rights Act. Furthermore, most of those studies focused on discrimination in terms of specific religious groups (e.g., Christians, Jews, Muslims). In an effort for shift focuses beyond discrimination in terms of the Civil Rights Act, researchers have begun to look at how religious identity and intergroup relations affect employee perceptions (e.g., perceptions of another employee's competence) and interpersonal conflict.

Christine R. Smith and C. Malik Boykin

See also Civil Rights Act of 1964, Civil Rights Act of 1991

Further Readings

Equal Employment Opportunity Commission. (2015). *Religion discrimination*. Retrieved from http://eeoc.gov/laws/types/religion.cfm

Ghumman, S., Ryan, A., Barclay, L., & Markel, K. (2013). Religious discrimination in the workplace: A review and examination of current and future trends. *Journal of Business and Psychology, 28*, 439–454.

King, J. E., McKay, P. F., & Stewart, M. M. (2014). Religious bias and stigma: Attitudes toward working with a Muslim co-worker. *Journal of Management, Spirituality and Religion, 11*(2), 98–122.

RESULTS-ONLY WORK ENVIRONMENT

The ROWE (Results-Only Work Environment) initiative was created by Cali Ressler and Jody Thompson in the human resources department of

Best Buy. One of the primary goals of ROWE is to increase employees' control over when, where, and how work is done, in order to promote creativity and productivity. The motto of ROWE is "Work whenever you want, wherever you want, as long as the work gets done."

Rather than creating one specific type of flexible work arrangement for all employees, ROWE allows each employee to be in charge of his or her own work schedule. The initiative involves a culture change that shifts the focus from the process of how work is done to work results or outcomes. Teams, rather than individuals, work together to reconceptualize work through exercises emphasizing new ways of accomplishing work. This process allows each employee to control his or her part of the work process, instead of conforming to a time, place, or method within a single work arrangement. In addition, managers are encouraged to focus on work goals instead of supervising work behaviors.

In contrast to many existing flexible work policies and practices, ROWE offers an innovative approach to work by acknowledging that there is no "one size fits all" work arrangement. Employees, rather than the organization, are allowed to decide when and where they will conduct their work as it fits their demands. In addition, teams train together in learning to use ROWE in order to identify ways to work together and implement changes that support a new organizational culture.

Changing Patterns of Work

ROWE facilitates an examination of the norms surrounding the way work is accomplished. By asking employees to identify patterns about the process of work and what is expected that might hinder their success, ROWE helps employees realize what works best for them. Common expectations of the "ideal worker" in organizations frequently include the following:

- *Working longer days or increased number of hours.* Employees are increasingly expected to work longer days, particularly those in salaried occupations, who are exempt from overtime laws. Employees may take work home with them to catch up on projects or tasks they were unable to accomplish during the standard work day. Similarly, many hourly employees are expected to be present to support salaried individuals who may or may not be required to be present in the office, limiting the control they have over their work schedules.

- *Being available to work during nonwork hours.* In addition to working longer days, employees are expected to be accessible and responsive during unexpected times, particularly nonwork time. With the increased use of technology to facilitate connections with work, employees often feel an increased pressure to be available for and respond to work demands when away from the workplace. This often creates a feeling of always "being on," such that employees are not fully able to disengage from work or recuperate from the stressors of the day.

- *Being present during work hours and appearing active.* Many supervisors perceive employees as productive if and only if they observe their work activity. Organizations with a culture of face time may expect employees to conduct work at the main worksite, even rewarding the appearance of work rather than the results.

Organizations may view these and similar behaviors as signs of productivity, focusing on how the work is accomplished over the outcomes of an employee's efforts. This can encourage a culture that suggests to employees that their outside lives are not important. Specifically, organizations may send the message that in order to succeed, employees must be willing to ignore life demands to respond to work.

ROWE presents organizations with a new way of conceptualizing work. By identifying ways in which employees can arrange work around their life demands while maintaining team and organizational goals, ROWE facilitators reframe organizational expectations about the work process. ROWE helps change the culture of the workplace through the engagement of employees in discussions about the perceptions of workplace practices and organizational norms. In particular, ROWE aims to change the patterns of work to allow employees to meet their work demands around their life demands, while maintaining productivity.

One of the important ways ROWE encourages organizations to rethink work is by creating a "counterculture" that includes a critical examination of the language used to describe employee and team behaviors. Employees are asked to identify how phrases such as "Just getting in?" may be perceived by others or may reflect subliminal organizational values of face time and long hours. These types of comments are referred to as "sludge," or comments that are intended to make a coworker feel guilty about his or her work process. To combat such obstructions to employee control, ROWE asks employees to role-play responses to sludge comments, reexamining processes that work best for each employee. Behaviors are identified that are effective in meeting the needs of the employee and the goals of the organization, rather than accommodating the existing culture.

Research on ROWE

Researchers have found that ROWE improves experiences for both employees and employers. Organizations that have implemented ROWE have experienced meaningful reductions in turnover as well as increases in productivity. Employees identify feelings of greater control over their work schedules, reduced work–family conflict, as well as improvements in health-related behaviors and well-being (e.g., more sleep). Employees also report spending less time commuting to and from work, allowing better overall fit between work and family demands.

Employees typically respond favorably to ROWE, with high engagement throughout the sessions. Women in particular find ROWE relatable and useful, often recognizing the usefulness of the program more quickly than their male colleagues. Researchers have pointed out that the links between "middle-class masculinity" and what has traditionally been valued or viewed as successful in current organizations may be threatened by the restructuring of work and reconceptualization of an organization's culture. In other words, when implementing ROWE, discussions may bring up deeper issues as to how employees who are also primary caretakers of family members are viewed by other employees or the organization as a whole. An important goal of ROWE is to help employees and organizations ask questions about the assumptions surrounding what is the "ideal" worker and how work goals are accomplished.

Current Trends and the Future of ROWE

In 2013, Best Buy made headlines when the arrival of a new CEO led to the announcement of the discontinuation of the ROWE program. Thompson and Ressler, the creators of ROWE, explained that ROWE was not the reason for Best Buy's struggles but rather a reaction to the difficult circumstances the company faced. They and others have observed how ROWE can help organizations overcome lean times by improving productivity and efficiency through the focus on outcomes rather than processes. However, some have noted that when organizations face challenges they tend to go "back to the basics."

Despite the changes at Best Buy, dozens of other organizations have implemented ROWE since its inception. Marketed to help retain talent, improve productivity, and develop accountability across personnel, the ROWE methodology is continuing to grow. Initially developed at a large, white-collar professional organization, it has moved into other occupational domains and job types (e.g., hourly workers). Although any change initiative can be challenging to implement, when implementing ROWE the literature suggests a coordinated, collective effort at all levels of the organization.

Rebecca J. Thompson

See also Flexible Work Schedules; Job Design; Telecommuting; Work–Life Conflict

Further Readings

Kelly, E. L., & Moen, P. (2007). Rethinking the clockwork of work: Why schedule control may pay off at work and at home. *Advances in Developing Human Resources*, 9, 487–506.

Moen, P., Kelly, E. L., Tranby, E., & Huang, Q. (2011). Changing work, changing health: Can real work-time flexibility promote health behaviors and well-being? *Journal of Health and Social Behavior*, 52, 404–429.

Perlow, L. A., & Kelly, E. L. (2014). Toward a model of work redesign for better work and better life. *Work and Occupations*, 41, 111–134.

Ressler, C., & Thompson, J. (2008). *Why work sucks and how to fix it*. New York: Penguin.

Ressler, C., & Thompson, J. (2013). *Why managing sucks and how to fix it*. Hoboken, NJ: John Wiley.

Results-Only Work Environment. (2015). Retrieved from http://gorowe.com

RETESTING

Retesting refers to administering or taking a test more than once. Organizations readminister tests and test takers opt to retake tests for various reasons. Regardless of the motivation, retesting is prevalent, and the practice of retesting is supported and encouraged by test publishers and governing organizations. The primary concerns associated with retesting are focused on how test scores change as a result of multiple attempts, what factors influence score change, how retesting affects validity, and the comparability of initial test and retest scores.

Rationale

There are many reasons why an organization or individual would retest, but these various reasons are captured by four broad categories: improvement, verification, administrative, and psychometric.

Retesting for improvement involves retesting for the purpose of earning a score higher than that earned on the initial test. An initial score may be improved in various ways. For example, a test taker may have experienced anxiety during the initial assessment that interfered with his or her performance and thus earn a higher retest score by taking steps to reduce anxiety on a subsequent administration. Alternatively, a test taker may have had the opportunity to improve his or her standing on the construct being assessed by the assessment, such as by studying or pursuing remedial training after an initial test, resulting in a higher score upon retesting. As a final example, a test taker may improve an initial test score by acquiring knowledge and skills that are test specific (e.g., pacing, strategy), or item specific (e.g., the answer to Item 1 is C, the answer to Item 2 is A, and so on) and apply that knowledge and skill during a retest.

A second reason why a test taker may retest is to verify a previously earned score. For example, a test taker may be asked to retest in a proctored setting after earning an initial score in an unproctored setting to prove that the test taker was able to earn that score without aid. Such procedures are becoming more common with the advent of unproctored Internet testing in selection systems.

A test taker may also retest because of administrative requirements of the testing organization. Retesting of this sort may occur for several reasons. For example, a test taker may encounter the same assessment as he or she applies for various positions. This may result when an organization uses a particular assessment as a part of the selection process across several positions (i.e., within the organization), such as when incumbents apply for internal positions and promotions. Alternatively, retesting may result when a test taker reencounters a particular assessment that is used across several organizations (i.e., between organizations). It is important to note that although an organization should be able to identify retest scores when retesting occurs within an organization, it is unlikely that an organization would be able to identify retest scores when retesting occurs between organizations (e.g., tests administered by multiple, disparate organizations). Retesting for administrative reasons may also occur when the scores on an initial test are compromised in some manner. Whether initial test scores are compromised during the conduct of the test (e.g., power failure during the test) or at some point later (e.g., initial test scores are lost), test takers may be required to retest out of administrative necessity.

A fourth reason why a test taker may encounter a retest is for psychometric purposes. Test-retest reliability estimates are an appropriate method of estimating the reliability of test scores, particularly for speeded tests. Additionally, in an attempt to establish concurrent validity, organizations may ask incumbents to retake assessments. Thus, for psychometric purposes of evaluating the reliability or validity of a selection system, a test taker might need to retest.

Prevalence

Retesting is prevalent within employment selection contexts. Estimates of external applicants who retest (e.g., those applying for positions who are not currently employed by the testing organization) range from 2% to 10%. The proportion of internal applicants who retest within an organization is even greater, with research suggesting that approximately 32% of employees retest for positions within an organization (e.g., internal promotions).

Academic selection is another environment in which retesting is prevalent. Approximately 18% of test takers retake the Graduate Management Admission Test (GMAT), 26% retake the Law School Admission Test, 30% retake the ACT or Medical College Application Test, and 50% retake the SAT I.

Support for Retesting

Retesting is sanctioned and encouraged by test publishers, professional governing organizations, and the U.S. federal government, particularly when test scores are used for selection purposes (academic or employment-related decisions). The Society for Industrial Organizational Psychology, American Psychological Association, U.S. Department of Labor, and U.S. Department of Justice have published recommendations and guidance regarding retesting. Although the recommendations and guidance are often limited in scope and detail, the rationale for retesting offered by these organizations is that retesting is a means to minimize the effect of measurement error and provides individuals an opportunity to improve their test scores.

Causes, Consequences, and Concerns of Retesting

Retest Effect

One of the primary concerns of retesting is the retest effect (also referred to as retest bias or the practice effect), the phenomenon whereby mere exposure to a test contributes to improved performance on subsequent administrations of an alternative or identical form of the test. Retest effects have been shown to be present on assessments of various constructs (e.g., abilities, knowledge, personality) and various methods (e.g., performance-based tests, situational judgement tests, interviews, self-report assessments). Meta-analytic estimates of retest score gains range between one quarter to one half of a standard deviation, although there are a number of significant moderators of the retest effect.

Moderators of Retest Performance

The magnitude of retest effects depends on many factors, including the malleability of the construct being assessed (e.g., ability vs. knowledge), the method used to assess the construct (e.g., interview vs. self-report), the time interval between the initial test and retest, test form (i.e., identical vs. alternative), and the importance of the test score (e.g., high stakes vs. low stakes). Stable constructs are, by definition, less likely to change between an initial test and a retest than unstable constructs. Test methods that require a large degree of test-specific knowledge or skill are more likely to produce higher retest scores than test methods that require a small degree of or no test-specific knowledge or skill. As the time interval between the initial test and the retest is reduced, the contaminating effect of memory on retest scores becomes greater. Therefore, test publishers and governing organizations recommend that the time interval between an initial test and a retest be sufficient enough to mitigate the effects of memory, with the length of this interval ranging widely, from as short as 30 minutes to as long as 2 years. Typical retest intervals imposed by major academic selection tests suggest a time frame of at least 1 month between attempts (e.g., ACT, 60 days; GMAT, 31 days; Graduate Record Examination, 60 days). Likewise, retest score gains are greater with an identical form versus an alternative form, because test takers are able to enhance retest scores by gaining item-specific knowledge or skills during the initial assessment. Retest score gains tend to be larger when test scores are being used to determine valued outcomes (high stakes) than outcomes that are not valued (low stakes).

Various individual differences have also been found to moderate retest effects for different predictor constructs and assessment methods. For example, cognitive ability and memory have been found to contribute to score improvement, a reinforcement of the "rich-get-richer" phenomenon or "Matthew effect," such that individuals with higher ability and memory tend to improve more when retested, especially on cognitively oriented assessments. Retest gains have also been found to be influenced by demographic differences such as race, sex, and age, although these differences are not consistent across construct and method. For example, in one study, White applicants demonstrated larger retest score gains compared with Black, Hispanic, and Asian applicants on written tests of verbal ability, knowledge, and biodata, but Black and Asian applicants improved more than

Whites on certain types of interviews. Women have been found to improve more than men on retesting for job knowledge, interviews, and assessment centers (e.g., leaderless group discussion, case analysis exercise), although these effects are not consistent across all research. Regarding the effects of age, younger applicants fare better than older applicants when retested. Additional individual differences including conscientiousness, self-efficacy, test-taking motivation, and general beliefs in tests have also been found to moderate retest gains, although these effects are typically small to moderate in size or inconsistent across settings and studies. Nonetheless, retest score change is caused by myriad individual characteristics that may be expected to contribute to retest performance.

Validity

Because no test is perfectly reliable, retest scores are likely to differ to some degree from initial scores. The varying nature of score change across the score range inevitably disrupts the rank order of test scores. Such disruptions to rank order affect relationships with other variables and therefore may reduce validity estimates. Often, concerns of validity focus on identifying which of two or more scores (e.g., initial test or retest) are most valid. Unfortunately, research has produced mixed results. In some instances, the initial scores are most valid, in others retest scores are most valid, and in yet other instances both initial test scores and retest scores are equally valid. Despite these mixed results, it is possible to identify situations or circumstances that would result in any one of these various outcomes. If the initial scores are contaminated by a construct other than the focal construct, it is likely that retest scores would produce higher validity estimates. Initial scores may be contaminated in a variety of ways (e.g., test anxiety, distractions during testing) that are unique to that administration of the test. On the other hand, it is also possible for retest scores to be contaminated by a construct other than the focal construct. Construct contamination of this sort is the primary reason why test publishers and governing organizations recommend using alternative test forms when retesting, as retest scores may be contaminated by memory (i.e., item-specific knowledge or skills) when retesting with an identical form. Of course, if the rank order of the initial test scores and retest scores is similar, so too will be the associated validity estimates.

Comparability of Test Scores

A final concern regarding retesting is the comparability of initial test scores versus retest scores. If all test takers opted to retest, then the comparability of initial test and retest scores would not be a concern. However, it is not often that all test takers opt to retest, and therefore, organizations may have no choice but to compare the initial test scores of some test takers with the retest scores of other test takers. To add further complication, it may be impossible for an organization to know whether a particular test score is an initial score or a retest score and, moreover, how many times a test taker has repeated an assessment.

Concluding Remarks

Given organizationally sanctioned opportunities for retesting, this practice is common in today's employment and education settings. The retest effect suggests that merely retaking a test will often result in score gains. There are a number of theoretical, methodological, and individual difference factors that underlie score change due to retesting, and these will serve to influence the magnitude, validity, and comparability of retest scores compared with initial test scores.

Anton J. Villado and Jason G. Randall

See also Reliability; Selection Strategies; Stereotype Threat; Test Security; Validation Strategies; Validity; Uniform Guidelines on Employee Selection Procedures

Further Readings

Hausknecht, J. P. (2010). Candidate persistence and personality test practice effects: Implications for staffing system management. *Personnel Psychology, 63,* 299–324.

Hausknecht, J. P., Halpert, J. A., Di Paolo, N. T., & Gerrard, M. O. M. (2007). Retesting in selection: A meta-analysis of coaching and practice effects for tests of cognitive ability. *Journal of Applied Psychology, 92,* 373–385.

Lievens, F., Buyse, T., & Sackett, P. R. (2005). Retest effects in operational selection settings: Development and test of a framework. *Personnel Psychology, 58,* 981–1007.

Lievens, F., Reeve, C. L., & Heggestad, E. D. (2007). An examination of psychometric bias due to retesting on cognitive ability tests in selection settings. *Journal of Applied Psychology, 92,* 1672–1682.

Schleicher, D. J., Van Iddekinge, C. H., Morgeson, F. P., & Campion, M. A. (2010). If at first you don't succeed, try, try again: Understanding race, age, and gender differences in retesting score improvement. *Journal of Applied Psychology, 95,* 603–617.

Van Iddekinge, C. H., Morgeson, F. P., Schleicher, D. J., & Campion, M. A. (2011). Can I retake it? Exploring subgroup differences and criterion-related validity in promotion retesting. *Journal of Applied Psychology, 96,* 941–955.

Villado, A. J., Randall, J. G., & Zimmer, C. U. (in press). The effect of method characteristics on retest score gains and criterion-related validity. *Journal of Business and Psychology.* doi:10.1007/s10869-015-9408-7

RETIREMENT

Retirement is a general term that has traditionally referred to older adults' disengagement from the workforce. As an area of research inquiry, it is a broad concept that has been studied by a number of disciplines, including economics, gerontology, and organizational behavior, as well as developmental and industrial and organizational psychology. Appropriately, these fields have offered many different perspectives on the concept of disengagement. Some frame it in terms of the amount of participation in the workforce (i.e., the number of hours worked), whereas others frame it in terms of the receipt of pensions as a source of income rather than paid work. Still other fields focus on disengagement as a form of commitment to and reliance on work as a source of personal identity and fulfillment. These differing viewpoints—and the theoretical perspectives that underlie them—are all valuable because each provides important insights into the concept and process of retirement. However, such divergent perspectives can make the systematic study of retirement challenging for researchers.

Retirement Trends

Increasing interest in the topic of retirement on the part of researchers, students, policymakers, organizational decision makers, and the general public has been fueled by at least three demographic trends. The first and most notable of these trends is the gradual aging of the nearly 80 million people born between 1946 and 1964, commonly known as the Baby Boomers. This group represents approximately 50% of the U.S. population in the prime working years (between ages 25 and 64). In 2010, the members of this cohort were between the ages of 46 and 64. As this cohort continues to age, the percentage of adults over the age of 65 will increase dramatically. For example, beginning in 2011, just over 10,000 Baby Boomers started turning 65 years old each day, and this rate will continue for nearly 2 decades. As a result, the vast majority of Baby Boomers will be approaching the age at which retirement is a realistic option. As they have with so many other concepts as they have moved through the life course, the Baby Boomers will no doubt redefine the concept of retirement.

The second demographic trend is the decline in workforce participation of older adults, namely men, during the second half of the 20th century. The workforce participation rate for men between the ages of 55 and 64 was 87% in 1950 but just 70% in 2012. For men over the age of 65, the workforce participation rate dropped from 46% in 1950 to a mere 23% in 2012. However, this decreasing trend appears to have leveled out somewhat since approximately 1985. For women the pattern is somewhat different. The workforce participation rate for women between the ages of 55 and 64 increased from 27% in 1950 to 60% in 2012. The workforce participation rate for women over the age of 65 also increased, from 8% in 1950 to 14% in 2012. Similar trends have been observed in most developed countries. As a result, the divergent trends for men's and women's late-life workforce participation rates will no doubt redefine the concept of retirement for generations to come.

The third demographic trend is the increasing longevity of the population in developed countries. In 1950, for example, the average 65-year-old could expect to live 13.9 more years; however, currently, that number has increased to 19 years (approximately 22% longer). Given this trend toward increased longevity, the way we define and study retirement will need to change to accommodate the fact that we may now spend upward of one third of our lives or more in retirement.

Taken together, these trends indicate that more workers will be experiencing retirement and will do so for a longer period of time than ever before. The sheer magnitude of this phenomenon raises a number of social, organizational, and individual concerns. At the societal level, the most prominent issue is the looming strain that will be placed on public (e.g., Social Security) and private pension systems by the large number of retiring workers. Thus, public policymakers will need to make many difficult yet crucial decisions in the near future about how we can best address the projected shortfalls in pension systems, particularly Social Security.

At the organizational level, both public- and private-sector employers will be faced with the loss of well-trained, highly experienced employees and, in some sectors, potential labor shortages as large numbers of workers begin to retire. Thus, employers will be faced with the decision of where and how to spend depleted resources. Should they work to retrain older workers? Provide incentives to keep older, more experienced workers from contemplating retirement? Develop mentoring programs to tap the wisdom of older workers who are quickly approaching retirement? Restructure jobs to make them more appealing and accommodating to older workers? Choosing among these options will be challenging for organizational decision makers.

Retirement and the Individual

For individuals, the questions center predominantly on deciding whether and when to retire, how to finance retirement, and how to ensure quality of life after retirement. These highly personal decisions are becoming more and more complex for those approaching retirement.

Research on decisions about whether and when to retire shows that these choices appear to be influenced by a number of factors. At the individual level, demographic variables such age, health, and wealth show some of the most consistent relationships with the decision to retire. Older workers, those whose health limits their ability to work, and those who can financially afford to stop working (because they are eligible to receive Social Security or private pension income) are more likely to retire.

Familial variables and gender are also related to retirement decisions. For example, married couples generally tend to coordinate the timing of their retirements. Those having higher quality of marital and family life appear to find retirement more attractive. Gender is also related to retirement decisions, but this relationship is more complex and likely influenced by the presence of dependents (including a spouse or aging parents) in the home. For example, women tend to retire when there are dependents in the home, presumably to engage in caregiving, whereas men tend to continue working, presumably to meet the financial demands created by having dependents in the home. In addition to these factors, lower commitment to aspects of the work role and a positive attitude toward retirement are also related to the decision to retire.

Research on quality of life after retirement suggests that, contrary to the once popular belief, most retirees do not experience retirement as a stressful crisis. Rather, most retirees adjust to retirement fairly well. Studies examining adjustment to retirement suggest that it is influenced by many of the same factors that influence the retirement decision. For example, those with better financial situations and better health tend to be more satisfied with retirement. With regard to gender, men and women with similar circumstances appear to experience retirement similarly. However, when their circumstances differ, there are often important differences between men and women. For example, women may have fewer financial resources, and therefore they are less able to afford the retirement lifestyle they prefer. Beyond these factors, people with more social contacts and social support are more likely to experience a higher quality of life in retirement.

It should come as no surprise that those who have engaged in more retirement planning also tend to have higher satisfaction with retirement. One of the most obvious issues that must be planned for is the replacement of income after one has reduced or altogether stopped working. To successfully develop and implement plans for an adequate income during retirement requires both forethought (people have to begin long before they actually retire) and a basic level of financial literacy needed to make informed financial decisions. Beyond financial matters retirement also brings with it a variety of opportunities, options, and lifestyle choices that are important to consider in advance of one's actual retirement. Among others these include how to spend one's time, how to maintain social interactions, where to live, and so on.

Evolving Conceptions of Retirement

At one point in time, retirement meant a complete disengagement from the workforce. However, recent trends suggest this definition of retirement is inaccurate. Indeed, nearly half of those who consider themselves retired indicate that they work or plan to work during their retirement. In one survey of preretiree adults over the age of 50, 72% indicated that they plan to work during retirement. This continued period of paid work during retirement is sometimes referred to as *bridge employment*, *phased retirement*, or *blurred retirement*. This transitional phase between full-time work and complete retirement allows older workers to try out retirement and determine whether it is a good fit for them. Given the trend toward increased longevity, this transition phase is likely to become more prevalent and lengthen considerably over time. However, as past research has shown, not all individuals (particularly less educated and minority workers) have equal opportunity to engage in such a transitional phase. Thus, policymakers need to consider how best to provide transitional retirement to as many individuals as possible, regardless of their means or demographic background.

Retirement is a rapidly evolving phenomenon characterized by a continuous process of preparation, transition, and adjustment. Furthermore, demographic factors are altering the way we define, view, and experience retirement. The idea that an individual can work for the same company for 30 to 40 years and then retire at age 65 with a gold watch and enjoy a life of leisure is quickly becoming extinct, if it ever really existed at all. Instead, we are seeing what scholars refer to as the "widening trajectory" of the life course. That is, we are observing a wider array of what is considered normative in terms of retirement. As a result, the study of the retirement concept and experience will continue to be a challenging endeavor.

Organizational decision makers will be faced with managing how to best meet staffing and training needs. Policymakers must also determine how best to meet the needs of the public, and individuals on the frontlines may be at a loss as to how to determine when, how, or even whether they should retire, given the increasing lack of normative standards to rely on. Only through continued diligent scholarship, study, and research will we be able to keep pace with the moving target that is known as retirement.

Gary A. Adams and Kenneth S. Shultz

See also Age Discrimination Employment Act; Career Development; Changing Demographics: Implications for Organizations; Older Worker Issues

Further Readings

Adams, G. A., & Rau, B. (2011). Putting off tomorrow to do what you want today. *American Psychologist*, 66, 180–192. doi:10.1037/a0022131

Beehr, T. A., & Bennett, M. M (2015). Working after retirement: Features of bridge employment and research directions. *Work, Aging, and Retirement, 1*, 112–128. doi:10.1093/workar/wau007

Ekerdt, D. J. (2010). Frontiers of research on work and retirement. *Journal of Gerontology: Social Sciences*, 65B, 69–80. doi:10.1093/geronb/gbp109

Shultz, K. S., & Wang, M. (2011). Psychological perspectives on the changing nature of retirement. *American Psychologist*, 66, 170–179. doi:10.1037/a0022411

Wang, M. (Ed.) (2013). *The Oxford handbook of retirement*. New York: Oxford University Press. doi:10.1093/oxfordhb/9780199746521.001.0001

Wang, M., & Shultz, K. S. (2010). Employee retirement: A review and recommendations for future investigation. *Journal of Management, 36*, 172–206. doi:10.1177/0149206309347957

RIGHTSIZING

See Downsizing

RISE OF AFRICA: IMPLICATIONS FOR ORGANIZATIONS

Since the beginning of the 21st century there has been keen interest by politicians, environmentalists, businesses, and academics in the rise of Africa. For politicians, one reason seems to be democratization. The first decade was marked by democratic processes that facilitated political stability. Environmentalists are concerned about the environmental degradation of the once pristine natural ecosystem. Businesses, typified by multinational corporations, are also interested in not only the economic progress but also the large market and natural resources of Africa. Collectively, African countries have the largest reserves of mineral deposits, some of which keep the economic wheel of the globe spinning. Africa has more than 1 billion people and a combined total gross domestic product (GDP) of about $1.6 trillion (about same as Brazil or Russia); an estimated 128 million households with discretionary income; and vibrant economies, including Botswana, Mauritius, and South Africa. On average, African countries have 4.7% annual average real GDP growth, increased spending power marked by a growing middle class indicated by the $970 billion Africans spent on goods and services in 2013. Indeed, business sectors such as agriculture, retail, banking, infrastructure, natural resources, and telecommunications abound with opportunities.

Academics, particularly in the management domain (broadly defined to encompass the macro and micro research areas such as industrial and organizational [I-O] psychology), are also beginning to show interest in Africa. In 2013, the Academy of Management (AOM) held its first ever global conference in Johannesburg, South Africa, with the purpose of bringing Africa's unique capabilities and needs to the attention of the world's organization and management scholars and at the same time providing an opportunity for interested colleagues to collaborate and work on the many interesting theoretical and practical problems presented in Africa. The AOM's effort was probably more visible because it involved a prominent global academic organization. Nonetheless, it provided a platform on which other institutions could build. Responding to these challenges and opportunities, a number of universities (e.g., Harvard, the University of Pennsylvania, Stanford, Columbia, INSEAD, Northwestern, and the Oikos Foundation) are establishing forums on African business, the purpose of which is to promote management education in Africa. Spurred on by the AOM's initiative, specialty conferences by the Strategic Management Society and Academy of International Business were also organized to focus on Africa.

Myths About Africa

To appreciate the rise of Africa that has garnered this interest, it is important to understand the myths that are held about Africa. By *myths* I mean traditional stories about Africa that have no determinable basis in fact. The first myth is that Africa is a country. It is not. Africa is a continent with about 54 countries, some of which are islands (e.g., Mauritius, Cape Verde). The second myth centers on the "Africa problem," defined as the stereotypical intractable challenge of enhancing sociocultural, economic, political, and scientific development. The extant view of the Africa problem evolved from the historical past, when Westerners were trying to figure how to effectuate colonialism. The challenges to understanding Africa then still persist today. Along with this is the third myth, that Africa is in the "stone age." This is because of the portraits of lions, hyenas, and tigers often shown in the media. There are more progressive developments in African countries that are not known because of lack of awareness or the lack of technologies to transform the capabilities. The fourth myth is that Africa is not profitable. This is just not true; Africa has enormous profit potential. Evidence of this potential is manifested in the top 30 African multinational corporations, such as Oando, Dangote, Zenith Bank, and United Bank for Africa. The fifth myth centers on the perceived low level of publications from Africa in general and specifically in the top-tier journals. What is often not known, however, is that some major theories of management emerged from Africa (e.g., Bass's transformational leadership). In addition, several Africans have published in the major journals of the field, including *Administrative Science Quarterly*, the *Academy of Management Review*, *Management Science*, and the *Journal of Applied Psychology*.

Organizations in Africa

The quest for knowledge on organizations in Africa begins with an understanding of the nature of organizations in Africa. A quick search of the Mbendi database (Mbendi.com) shows that there about 162,559 companies across multiple sectors in Africa. This seems small compared with the United States or Europe. However, all African countries are developing. In addition, African countries have both modern and traditional contexts. The modern context is associated with urban locations, which are experiencing population growth and are projected to account for about 60% of the population by 2030. The environments of modern or urban organizations rely on individual specialization and economic institutions that facilitate dyadic exchanges and industrial or manufacturing activities. Modern political systems and property rights are tradable, which facilitates commercial markets. Banking institutions tend to be the source of credit and finance, and learning is based on educational systems that are similar to Western standards. Culturally, modern contexts are open and individualistic, relying on postcolonial worldviews and nationalistic tendencies. In short, the modern contexts are represented by metropolitan centers such as Lagos, Johannesburg, Cairo, Nairobi, Accra, and Gaborone, which have features similar to Western contexts.

In contrast, the traditional contexts are represented by rural areas, which currently constitute about 60% to 70% of the population. Chieftaincy and councils of elders, an agrarian form of living, and lineage-based (rather than property rights–based) inheritance characterize such contexts. They have autarkic markets and tribal identities. Social institutions revolve around the family and communal activities, and funding for economic exchanges depends on interpersonal trust. Learning is social rather than scientific, and the human capital base is low because of a high illiteracy rate. In addition, the traditional practices of collectivism, shared values, and disproportionate interdependence are extensive in rural Africa.

These categories have implications for research and practice of management and organizations. Arguably, there is a greater need for strategic value in African organizations, because industrial productivity is critical to national development.

According to the United Nations, Africa has about 1 billion people, of whom about 50% were in the labor force between 2000 and 2011. These statistics suggest vibrant industrial activity that provides an opportunity for organizational scholars to understand the role individual, group, and organizational behaviors contribute to effectiveness of African organizations and national development.

Implications for Organizations

Africa appears poised for economic growth and prosperity as the next growth market for the global economy given rising world commodity prices, improved governance, political stability, and security. Collectively, these positive developments create opportunities for management research, education, and practice. High sustained economic growth requires, among other things, improvements in macroeconomics as well as micro-enterprise-level management for improved investment climate, global competitiveness, and innovative productive businesses that create jobs, reduce poverty, and lessen inequality among the population. As the African investment climate improves beyond resources and infrastructure, it is also beginning to attract more sophisticated foreign direct investments requiring equally sophisticated leadership, domestic organizations with the capacity to exploit positive spillovers and partners for mutual advantage, and a wide range of professional management talent. These investments come from well-established multinational corporations (i.e., Wal-Mart's $2.4 billion purchase of 51% of South Africa's Massmart) as well as corporate giants from emerging economies, such as Sonatrach of Algeria and Zain-Celtel-MTC of Kuwait.

According to the World Bank, the factors that might affect Africa's long-term development include undiversified production systems, low human capital, weak governance, state fragility, women's low levels of empowerment, high youth unemployment, climate change, and managing globalization. Indeed, there seem to be too many people in Africa who still lack access to education, clean water, and basic sanitation. There are also few well-paying jobs, low-quality housing, and major health care issues. As a result of these major challenges, the World Bank established the eight

Millennium Development Goals (MDGs) in 2000 with the aim of drastically reducing, if not eliminating, these problems by 2015. Achievement of the eight goals—eradicating extreme poverty and hunger; achieving universal primary education; promoting gender equality and empowering women; reducing child mortality rates; improving maternal health; combating HIV/AIDS, malaria, and other diseases; ensuring environmental sustainability; and developing a global partnership for development—depends primarily on central African governments as the principal agents but also secondarily on businesses, which are instrumental agents. The July 2015 MDG progress report of the World Bank showed that only 4 countries had met the MDGs, while 10 have made progress and 24 are either moderately or seriously off target. However, sub-Saharan Africa has the best record of improvement in primary education (MDG 2) of any region since the MDGs were established, having achieved a 20 percentage point increase in the net enrollment rate from 2000 to 2015, compared with a gain of 8 percentage points between 1990 and 2000. Furthermore, the annual rate of reduction of mortality among children under 5 years of age (MDG 4) was more than five times faster from 2005 to 2013 than it was from 1990 to 1995 in sub-Saharan Africa. The proportion of pregnant women who received four or more antenatal visits (MDG 5) increased from 50% to 89% between 1990 and 2014 in northern Africa. As the MDGs near their end, there is recognition of not only the failures (most of the MDGs were not achieved) but also the successes and the continued need for collective (public- and private-sector) action.

By highlighting the centrality of the private sector, the MDGs indirectly draw attention to effective management of organizations in this sector. Although management and organization in the domestic, productive, private enterprise sector is the most neglected in African countries, it is this sector in which most improvements and practical results can be achieved with significant demonstrated effects. At the same time, there are growing calls for improvement of management in the public sector, which is so critical to the delivery of basic services to Africa's population. Effective management of the public (and not-for-profit) sector can also complement that of the private sector.

Africa's business sector needs people with management expertise to analyze, streamline, reduce costs, and create value in the various local production value chains to connect and integrate them with the regional and global supply chains. Such actionable knowledge must come from the mobilization of interests and energies of management scholars to advance Africa through management knowledge, research, and practice. Given the role of management in national development, and the significance of I-O psychology to organizations, studies of I-O psychology can contribute to the development of Africa in a number of ways. First, by improving organizational productivity, I-O scholars can contribute to the strategic value of organizations in the form of competitive advantage. Second, understanding the behavior of employees in African organizations that operate in highly uncertain and unpredictable environments with relatively weak institutions might be insightful as a contrast to organizations in predictable Western environments. Highlighting such organizations will generate actionable knowledge that can advance I-O research and practice not only in Africa but also in other parts of the globe. In other words, I-O scholarship can generate actionable management knowledge born out of methodologically rigorous and relevant research.

In addition to the direct outcome of improved effectiveness of organizations, I-O research can indirectly and ultimately transform African countries by helping mobilize interests toward addressing the myriad economic, institutional, legal, and political challenges and dynamics embedded within the African context. The behaviors, attitudes, and cognitions of employees can be transferred from the workplace to communities to improve social settings and thereby transform the societies. Given that I-O psychology focuses on improving the performance, satisfaction, safety, health, and well-being of employees through research on employee behaviors and attitudes, and how these can be improved through hiring practices, training programs, feedback, and management systems, the rise of Africa has implications for I-O scholars. The implications center on what, how, and where to study organizations in Africa. With regard to what to study, topics such as motivation, selection, teams, training and development, leadership, job performance, strategic human resources, cross-cultural issues, work attitudes, entrepreneurship, affect and emotion, organizational change and development, gender and diversity, and statistics and research methodologies have organizational and national development significance. Two illustrative examples include team and organizational citizenship behavior (OCB) theories. The traditional team literature has assumptions, which, though consistent with social exchange theories, seem untenable in the African context. The assumption of hierarchy, whereby there is a controller and a controlee, and control is singularly used, is predicated on the individual as an effective agent of change. The cultural context of Africa is predicated on the group as an agent of transformation, which is more aligned with distributed task execution and self-managing units. OCBs are based on the individual agency assumption, such that voluntary behaviors that improve the context of performance are rewarded. The cultural context of Africa does not make OCBs voluntary; rather, they are obligatory. The extent to which such behaviors manifest in Africa may therefore be reexamined to generate novel insight into employee performance.

With regard to how to study, I-O psychologists are trained in the scientist–practitioner model. They can therefore contribute to an organization's success by showing how scientific outcomes improve organizational outcomes. At the moment, the use of scientific knowledge to improve organizational processes, systems, and activities seems very minimal. Along the same lines, I-O psychologists who are experts at experimental approaches can demonstrate the use of experiments in advancing organizations. In a review of the management literature, it was observed that experimental studies are lacking in Africa. Furthermore, I-O psychologists can help organizations and their employees transition among periods of change and organization development.

Current organizational forms were developed on the basis of Western, established structures. However, there is evidence that new organizational forms based on cooperation among private, public, and nongovernmental agencies are emerging in Africa. As part of the MDGs for Africa, Millennium Village Projects are being established in eastern and western Africa, with business formation as a secondary and integral phase of the project. The formation, management, and growth of those businesses are based on joint or cooperative efforts of the community, international institutions, and the respective governments. The projects in Kenya, Rwanda, Uganda, Nigeria, and Ghana are expected to be expanded across Africa. Studies of such businesses can inform not only existing theories of organizational structures but also new theories on multiagency cooperative corporate governance. I-O scholars can contribute to theory development related to these new forms of organizations. For example, they can examine the dynamics of devolved behaviors and their effects on individual, group, and organizational outcomes. Sustainability studies on green management, green organizational behaviors, and green human resource management are sorely lacking, even though environmental degradation in Africa is severe and threatening the economic, cultural, and social existence of individuals and businesses. Few, if any, sustainability studies on Africa exist in the mainstream journals, in which methodological rigor and theoretical logic tend to be strong.

Although conducting research on Africa may be intrinsically rewarding to some scholars, most researchers confront competition from other regions for their attention and increasing publication pressures. Thus, unless there is significant potential for Africa research to yield major theoretical and empirical dividends, it will continue to generate a meager level of publications. In addition, the myths may become urban legend—something accepted without question. The challenge, of course, is how to marry substantive understanding of the nuances of the African context with incisive theoretical and empirical analysis that appeals to "mainstream" journals.

In sum, I-O scholars can contribute enormously by providing a framework that can help resolve the nagging issues that have been posed by several researchers on what theories can be tested and developed in Africa given the unique contextual features of the continent. By so helping integrate Africa into the global management (and I-O) community, they can help enrich the global "scholarly conversation."

David B. Zoogah

See also Contextual Performance/Prosocial Behavior/
Organizational Citizenship Behavior; Cross-Cultural
Research Methods and Theory; Emerging Markets
and Globalization: Implications for Organizations;
History of Industrial and Organizational Psychology
in Africa

Further Readings

Adamolekun L. (2005). Re-orienting public management
in Africa: Selected issues and some country experiences.
Tunis, Tunisia: African Development Bank.

African Development Bank. (2013). Millennium
Development Goals (MDGs) report 2015—Executive
summary. Johannesburg, South Africa: African
Development Bank.

Blunt, P. (1992). East Africa strikes back—A rejoinder to
"Inside East Africa, outside the research culture."
Organization Studies, 13, 119–120.

Chironga, M., Leke, A., Lund, S., & Van Wamelen, A.
(2011, May). Cracking the next growth market:
Africa. Harvard Business Review, pp. 117–122.

Doing business in Africa. (2005, July 2). The Economist,
p. 61.

Kehl, J. R. (2007). Emerging markets in Africa. African
Journal of Political Science and International
Relations, 1(1), 1–8.

Kiggundu, M. N. (1989). Managing organizations in
development countries. West Hartford, CT: Kumarian.

McKinsey Global Institute. (2010). Lions on the move:
The progress and potential of African economies.
Retrieved from http://www.mckinsey.com/mgi

Ugwuegbu, D. C. E. (2001). The psychology of
management in African organizations. Westport,
CT: Quorum.

Van de Walle, N. (2003). The state and African
development. In N. van de Walle, N. Ball, &
V. Ramachandran (Eds.), Beyond structural adjustment:
The institutional context of African development
(pp. 1–34). New York: Palgrave Macmillan.

Zoogah, D. B., & Beugre, C. (2012). Organizational
behavior in the African context. New York:
Routledge.

RISE OF CHINA: IMPLICATIONS FOR ORGANIZATIONS

In the past 30 years, the national economy of
China has been growing rapidly, which has made
this country the world's second-largest economy.
A considerable amount of Chinese enterprises
became influential to the world. These phenomena introduce new questions in industrial and
organizational (I-O) research and practice such as
whether Western managerial theories explain the
rapid development of the Chinese economy and
whether certain characteristics of China should
be incorporated into I-O theory development and
practice. Aiming to provide insights into these
questions, this entry will deliberate on traditional
Chinese culture, the characteristics of Chinese
people, and the economic background of Chinese
enterprises.

In each section, you will see how some Western
managerial theories are applicable to the Chinese
cultural/economic background (such as collectivism, long-term orientation, and transition to
market-based economy) and how some new perspectives are induced by the unique ideas of
Chinese culture. In order to improve managerial
effectiveness, it has become more and more
important to integrate both the Western empirical
research and the Chinese managerial philosophy
for any kinds of organizations, including local
private and public firms and multinational companies running their business in China.

Traditional Cultural Ideology

Chinese culture consists of two key components:
the traditional philosophical ideas and the cultural
values.

Traditional Philosophies: Confucianism, Buddhism, Taoism, and the Art of War

The main propositions of Confucianism include
kindheartedness, justice, and discipline. Kindheartedness, defined as "loving others," is the core ethic
of Confucianism. By claiming that "he who loves
others is constantly loved by them" and that "a
kindhearted person is invincible," the Confucianists
believe that kindheartedness has significance in
social interactions. Justice, here equivalent to righteousness, is supposed to have priority over individual interest according to Confucianist values
and is considered a principle for governing a nation
or an organization. Discipline refers to regulations
of social strata and norms of social behaviors and

is believed to help safeguard social stability and supervise subordinates.

Despite originating in India, Chinese *Buddhism* has absorbed local cultural elements and become a cultural-characteristic religion. It advocates the idea of love of humanity, with an ultimate purpose of delivering all living creatures from torment.

Taoism values following the principles of nature. The Taoists believe that to achieve desirable consequences, human behaviors must follow the objective laws of nature.

Over thousands of years, the abovementioned three schools of thought have constantly interacted with one another, and thus formed the unique philosophical system of traditional Chinese culture and Chinese managerial philosophy, especially in the case of governing the country.

In addition to these three schools of thought, the *Art of War*, a treatise of military strategy and tactics attributed to Sun Tzu, has largely influenced traditional Chinese managerial philosophy. The philosophy of war maintains that it is better to conquer the heart of the people than to capture the city, whether leading troops or dealing with the enemy.

The aforementioned philosophies constitute the fundamental principles of conduct and organizational management. Chinese people value benevolence and regulation, which has much in common with the humanistic management that has emerged in Western societies during recent decades, and traditional Chinese culture advocates harmony and peace in the interaction between two parties. Instead of encouraging competition, it emphasizes maintaining harmony and avoiding conflicts, regardless of whether the interaction takes place between organizations or nations. This is essentially different from the competition principle in traditional Western culture and modern industrial civilizations such as *social Darwinism* or *law of the jungle*. As a result, maintaining the status quo is mentioned much more often than extension and development in Chinese culture. This principle of conduct seems to be beneficial to the stabilization of the organization, but may also be harmful to its innovation and expansion. However, if this is the case, there is a theoretical need to explain why and how Chinese companies have developed so quickly in the last 2 or 3 decades.

Nevertheless, during the last 20 years, with the deepening of China's reform and its opening up, the Western idea of competition and expansion has played a supplementary role in the development of China. For a foreign enterprise or organization to succeed in China, it is critical to integrate the principle of harmony and the competition principle, and to apply both in a flexible way. This is in line with Taoism's doctrine of yin–yang balance, which can be used by Western organizations that emphasize both task orientation and people orientation.

Cultural Values: Collectivism, Power Distance, Diffuseness, and Ascription

Tremendous differences in cultural values exist between Chinese culture and Western culture. Geert Hofstede extracted four dimensions of national cultural values: collectivism versus individualism, high versus low power distance, masculinity versus femininity, and uncertainty avoidance. Chinese culture demonstrates significant differences from Western culture in terms of both individualism/collectivism and power distance. The Chinese attach great importance to the collective. They consider an individual to be part of the society, and believe that individual interests should be subject to collective interests. This is obviously different from the Western individualistic cultural value. With respect to power distance, the Chinese have emphasized social classes since ancient times. The culture of discipline, which is an important component of Confucianism, restricts Chinese people from transgressing the rules that have been attached to their social roles. As a result, in Chinese management practices, creating a family-like atmosphere of caring and harmony is emphasized, as well as the hierarchical structure and the obedience of subordinates to their superiors. This emphasis is in contrast to the Western culture of equality and competition. Because of this cultural difference, interesting research and practical questions arise such as how typical Chinese companies with family-style managerial ideology could be competitive in the open world, whether Western I-O psychology principles apply to these companies, and whether these companies can still survive by keeping their traditional cultural values.

In addition to the four cultural dimensions of Hofstede, Fons Trompenaars mentioned two other dimensions that reveal cultural differences between China and the West—*specific versus diffuse* and *achievement versus ascription*. The Western culture today, largely influenced by modern industrialization, values temporal and spatial precision, which to a great extent benefits lean manufacturing and scientific management. Chinese culture, however, has its roots in East Asian agricultural tradition and exhibits diffuseness in people's temporal and spatial perception. Unlike an industrialized society, individuals in an agricultural society enjoy plenty of slack time, which may have a chronic impact on their temporal perception. Besides, consistent with the collectivist culture, their personal space highly overlaps with the public space. According to this cultural value, privacy is not regarded as important. Individuals are embedded in the collective, and contribution to the collective is highly valued, while obtaining profit from the collective is taken for granted.

Another interesting comparison is between the importance of individual achievement in Western culture and the focus of ascription in the Chinese one. In the former cultural environment, personal competence and success determine one's social status, while in the latter, consistent with the cultural value of collectivism, it is the background and interpersonal connections that determine one's social status. That means obeying the group rule rather than pursuing individual interest is more encouraged.

Due to the abovementioned differences in cultural values, plenty of foreign enterprises that failed to pay attention to those differences and lacked countermeasures for dealing with the cultural gap suffered from miserable failure. As a result, literature has suggested Western enterprises need to choose from either single proprietorship or holding controlling shares when they are entering the Chinese market. This helps Western partners to maintain the right of final decision in board meetings when conflicts with their Chinese partners arise due to the cultural differences. In fact, how multinational enterprises solve the impact of cultural value differences and conflicts on employee behaviors remains an important topic of organizational management today.

The National Character of Chinese People

A considerable body of research has demonstrated the potential effect of national character differences on organizational management styles.

Among the personality traits that exhibit Western–Chinese cultural differences, two have more influence on organizational behaviors—extroversion and locus of control.

Extroversion

Extroversion refers to the quantity and density of interpersonal interactions, the need for stimulation, and the capability of obtaining pleasure. Extroverts enjoy contact with people, are full of energy, and often experience positive emotions. They are enthusiastic, love sports, and enjoy adventure. Besides, when they are in a group, they tend to be very confident and talkative, and like to draw others' attention. Psychological research has revealed that the Chinese are significantly less extroverted than Americans. For instance, in a group meeting, rather than proactively express their own opinions, Chinese people are more likely to listen to the speech of the leader, especially when they have different opinions from the leader. One of the reasons lies in the hierarchical structure of a typical Chinese organization. Additionally, traditional Chinese culture encourages introversion, reserve, and implicity, while these characteristics are often regarded as negative in Western, especially American, culture. Being extroversively talkative is encouraged by American culture but is regarded as foolish in Chinese culture. This personality preference may lead to cultural prejudice, and thus be harmful to team leading and team construction in an organization. As for which kind of personality (i.e., introvert or extrovert) has more advantages, and under what conditions these advantages can be exerted, further research is required to make a conclusion.

Locus of Control

The theory of locus of control divides attribution tendency into two categories: internal and external. Persons with an internal locus of control consider individuals to be the decision makers and influencers of behaviors, while those with an external locus of control believe that individual behaviors are determined by exterior power. Research suggests that internal locus of control brings originality, conscientiousness, resilience, tolerance for frustration, entrepreneurship, and thus more likelihood of success. Comparatively, having been influenced by individualism, culture of competence, and industrialization, Western people are more likely to have an internal locus of control, believing that they themselves are the controllers of their behavior. On the contrary, due to the influence of traditional agricultural culture and hierarchical structure, Chinese people tend to be higher in external control, believing that their behaviors are dominated by external power, such as fate. This attribution style explains why Chinese employees tend to be less creative and are more likely to take things as they are. However, recent research has revealed that after 30 years of reform and opening up of China, although the gap still exists, Chinese people are becoming more used to internal attribution than they were. In the future, more emphasis should be placed on cultivating internal locus of control in Chinese employees, and locus of control should be implanted in the procedures of employee selection, training, assessment, the incentive system, and other I-O practices.

The Influence of Economic Transition on Organizational Management

Industrial Structure: From Labor-Intensive Manufacturing to Knowledge-Intensive High-Tech Industry

Higher education is becoming more and more prevalent in China. As is shown by recent data, the number of undergraduate students in China has reached 20 million, which is the largest in the world. The development of education is gradually changing the education structure and knowledge structure of Chinese employees, which has laid a foundation for industry transformation. However, knowledge-intensive industry is developing rapidly, and China lacks relevant research and practical experience in it. Thus, problems regarding innovation management and intellectual property management urgently need to be addressed. Whether Western experience in these problems is applicable in China still requires further study. For example, in a diffuse culture where personal space and public space highly overlap, intellectual property is not easily protected since people there tend to believe that everything should be commonly shared.

Structure of Labor Force

The labor force structure is complex in China, with three main distinctions: brainwork versus physical work, city-grown-up versus rural-grown-up, and agricultural versus industrial. An enormous amount of blue-collar workers are farming workers from rural areas, who are deeply influenced by traditional culture. They tend to be conservative rather than innovative, diffuse rather than specific, and passively waiting rather than proactively exploring, and thus are less adaptable to high-tech industries. Consequently, managing blue-collar employees in China is particularly difficult. As Western management experience may not be applicable to the national situations of China, research is urgently needed to solve this problem, especially for organizations with employees both from cities and from rural areas, whose characteristics and capacities are dissimilar, requiring a more diverse and contingent management style.

New Phenomena in Chinese Organizations

A Complex Economic System

Since its reform and opening up, China pursues a more comprehensive economic system allowing the coexistence of state-owned enterprises, private enterprises, and foreign enterprises, whose modes of operation and management exhibit stark contrast. Particularly, the contrast exists in their employment patterns, talent cultivation and promotion, salaries, group communication patterns, implementation of management by participation, and leadership styles. These differences have produced some special results, such as the flow of talent in the past several decades. At the early time when a large number of foreign companies entered China, because of the remarkably low pay level and the outdated management style of state-owned enterprises, its foreign counterparts managed to attract a mass of middle- and high-end talents with salaries much lower than those in their own countries. With the rising of China's economy, the wages of state-owned and private companies have increased sharply, which gradually weakens the comparative wage advantage of foreign companies, and thus draws talent back to local companies. Under this circumstance, to continuously attract talent, foreign enterprises have to stress other advantages, such as advanced technology and scientific management.

Another example has to do with the aging of the employees, the outdated knowledge structure, and slow personnel promotion, all of which are brought by the adherence of state-owned companies to collectivism, hierarchical structure, and lifetime employment. In addition, it would also be interesting to investigate how enterprises with different types of systems effectively compete with each other.

Decreasing Demographic Dividend and Increasing Labor Cost

Recently, China's birthrate has been declining, resulting in an increasingly aging population and the fading of the demographic dividend due to the only-child policy that has been conducted for 3.5 decades in China. That means there used to be four members of a family in the labor market for the grandparents' generation, two for the parents' generation, and only one for the only-child generation. It becomes harder to maintain the past economic mode that has relied on numerous sources of cheap labor. Some foreign companies have already left China and moved to Southeast Asia for lower labor costs. To cope with this situation, enterprises in China must change their modes of development from lowering labor costs to emphasizing efficiency, and pay attention to the mercantile rate of return, extra economic value added, per-capita production value, and per-capita profit, or they will lose vitality and competency, regardless of whether they are foreign, private, or state owned. This transition in the labor pool puts new requirements on human resource management and employee innovation.

Challenges and Opportunities Brought by Economic Rise

There are several challenges brought by the Chinese economic rise. First, the development of the high-tech industry increasingly raises the requirement of employee innovation ability, while traditional Chinese education lacks an innovative atmosphere, and is incapable of cultivating innovative talents that are able to adapt to the development of the technology industry. Influenced by the culture of discipline, traditional Chinese education requires students to respect and submit to the authority of teachers. Expressing personal opinions is not encouraged in class. Rather, students are supposed to accept the knowledge that the teacher conveys. This educational culture tends to result in slavish adherence to the rules. Students can be good learners but may not be good innovators. Meanwhile, in a Western classroom, freely expressing oneself and questioning is encouraged, which is helpful to the training of critical thinking and sense of innovation. Although it promotes the knowledge volume and the grades of students, the traditional Chinese way of education restricts students' initiative and creativity, and thus affects their performance at work. For this reason, enterprises and organizations have to take the responsibility of reeducating their employees to cultivate a spirit and habit of initiative and innovation in their employees.

Second, the market demand for high-end services is ever increasing. With the rise of the middle class, China has gradually moved into the era of experience economy, where the customers are pursuing personalized service and extremely humanized experience. This requires employees to have strong service awareness and agreeableness, and to be capable of exploring and satisfying the diverse demands of customers with enthusiasm, patience, and attentiveness. However, by now, service employees vary considerably in their education level, and their capability and attitudes are far from reaching the demand. Due to the traditional hierarchy, highly educated individuals still prefer mental labor and despise pure service-oriented jobs. Moreover, the traditional agricultural culture of China lacks the "gene" of service awareness. Therefore, in order to improve quality and competence, service firms need to break the barriers brought by traditional ideas and figure out effective ways to attract and retain highly competent service talents. How to develop employees' awareness, motivation, and quality of service has become an increasingly critical research topic.

In China, where economic development grows rapidly, the traditional Chinese culture is constantly colliding and blending with Western culture, providing new space and multiple points of penetration for the cross-cultural research of organization management. The complex economic system, industrial structure, and labor structure created diverse and complex organizational environments, which brings new potentials for examining the organization management theories of different times. Both a new Western management model and an outdated one could be revalidated in China, at this point in time. This might be the most distinctive new opportunity that the rising of China brings to the development of organization management.

Lei Wang

See also Big Five Taxonomy of Personality; Changing Demographics: Implications for Organizations; Cross-Cultural Research Methods and Theory; History of Industrial and Organizational Psychology in Asia; Human Capital; Human Resource Management; Organizational Behavior Management; Personality; *Personnel Psychology*

Further Readings

Hill, J. S. (2006). Confucianism and the art of Chinese management. *Journal of Asia Business Studies, 1*(1), 1–9.

Hofstede, G. (1984). *Culture's consequences: International differences in work-related values* (2nd ed.). Beverly Hills, CA: Sage.

Randau, H. R., & Medinskaya, O. (2015). *Chinese business 2.0: Analyze the economy, understand the society, and manage effectively*. Cham, Switzerland: Springer.

Tong, J., & Wang, L. (2006). Validation of locus of control scale in Chinese organizations. *Personality and Individual Difference, 41*, 941–950.

Trompenaars, F., & Hampden-Turner, C. (1997). *Riding the waves of culture*. New York, NY: McGraw-Hill.

ROLE AMBIGUITY

Role ambiguity—the extent to which one's work responsibilities and degree of authority are unclear—is one of the most widely studied work stressors. Because it represents a subjective perception of one's work situation, role ambiguity is typically assessed using employee self-reports.

Typical self-report role ambiguity items include "The requirements of my job aren't always clear" and "My job duties are clearly defined" (note that the second example item is reverse-scored). Some researchers refer to role ambiguity by its polar opposite, *role clarity*.

Employees who experience role ambiguity feel uncertainty about which behaviors are and are not appropriate. They may wonder, for example, whether they are engaging in inappropriate work behaviors, or they may wonder whether they are failing to engage in appropriate work behaviors. Most employees find such uncertainty to be distressing.

Research on occupational stress has given considerable attention to examining the potential effects of various work stressors on worker well-being. A *work stressor* is any aspect of the work environment that requires an employee to adapt and has the potential to cause poor health. Role ambiguity is one example of a work stressor (other examples include having a heavy workload and being bullied by a coworker). The negative health consequences produced by a stressor, such as depression, anxiety, or physical symptoms, are called *strains*.

Role theory provides the theoretical basis for the study of role ambiguity. According to role theory, each employee has a unique set of responsibilities within the organization. Formal roles are the set of official behaviors that employees perform as part of their job descriptions and are maintained by organizational policies. The formal role of a schoolteacher, for example, includes delivering lectures, grading tests, and assigning homework. Informal roles, on the other hand, develop spontaneously as part of the everyday social dynamic of the organization. Although these roles are not mandated by official policies, they are maintained by informal social interactions. An informal role of a schoolteacher, for example, might include planning and organizing staff parties. Role ambiguity is generally operationalized as uncertainty concerning one's formal roles.

Causes of Role Ambiguity

A theme common to many leadership theories is that effective leaders (a) help employees clarify their responsibilities and (b) create situations in which those responsibilities can be successfully executed. By this standard, effective leaders create work situations for their subordinates that minimize the presence of role ambiguity. When role ambiguity does arise, effective leaders work to combat it. Leadership theories also suggest that effective leaders show concern for the personal welfare of their subordinates. To the extent that supervisors care about employee well-being, they are likely to work toward reducing role ambiguity and other stressors.

Research supports the notion that effective leader behavior is associated with low levels of role ambiguity. Leader initiating structure (the extent to which leaders engage in behaviors that clarify employee responsibilities) and leader consideration (the extent to which leaders show concern for their subordinates' well-being), for example, are two leader behaviors that are associated with low role ambiguity. Furthermore, employees are likely to experience little role ambiguity when their leaders provide opportunities for employee participation and when they create a formalized work environment. In short, role ambiguity is a product of poor management practices. Indeed, many survey items measuring role ambiguity make direct reference to the respondent's supervisor.

In addition to the negative behaviors of supervisors, employees who report high levels of role ambiguity often report having generally unfavorable work environments. Some of the environmental factors associated with role ambiguity are lack of autonomy, feedback, and task identity. In other words, role ambiguity is most likely to occur in simple, unenriched jobs. Furthermore, employees who report high levels of role ambiguity also generally report high levels of role conflict.

Individual differences may predispose particular workers to experience role ambiguity. Workers who have an external locus of control, who are high in neuroticism, who are high in need for clarity, or who have low self-esteem, for example, are especially likely to report high levels of role ambiguity.

Consequences of Role Ambiguity

Perceptions of uncertainty are at the core of role ambiguity. Uncertainty, in turn, may be a mechanism by which role ambiguity results in negative health consequences. Indeed, several studies have shown that role ambiguity is related to manifestations of poor mental and physical health. For example, role ambiguity is associated with anxiety, burnout, depression, and physical illness.

In addition to negative health consequences, role ambiguity is associated with negative job attitudes and ineffective job behaviors. Role ambiguity, for example, is associated with the following job attitudes and behaviors:

- Global job dissatisfaction
- Dissatisfaction with supervision
- Poor in-role job performance
- Counterproductive work behavior
- Low levels of organizational citizenship behavior
- Low levels of organizational commitment
- Turnover intention
- Absenteeism

The correlation between role ambiguity and dissatisfaction with supervision is especially strong, suggesting that employees perceive management as the source of role ambiguity.

Important methodological issues affect the study of role ambiguity. Most of the research examining the causes and consequences of role ambiguity has used cross-sectional designs. This makes it difficult to draw strong conclusions about the causal relationships between role ambiguity and its potential causes and consequences.

Treatments for Role Ambiguity

Organizations have several options for treating role ambiguity. Because ineffective leadership is a root cause of role ambiguity, the most promising treatments are likely to target leaders. These treatments may include the following actions:

- Training managers to identify when their behaviors might lead to role ambiguity and encouraging them to modify these behaviors
- Selecting managers who are likely to engage in high levels of initiating structure and consideration
- Providing employees with extensive training aimed at clarifying their responsibilities and the scope of their authority

Given the negative consequences associated with role ambiguity, one might expect that organizations would be highly motivated to minimize the levels of role ambiguity experienced by their workers. Because organizations are often fixated on the "bottom line," however, role ambiguity and its negative effects on employees are often overlooked.

Nathan A. Bowling

See also Occupational Health Psychology; Role Conflict; Role Overload and Underload; Stress, Consequences; Stress, Coping and Management; Stress, Models and Theories

Further Readings

Eatough, E. M., Chang, C.-H., Miloslavic, S. A., & Johnson, R. E. (2011). Relationships of role stressors with organizational citizenship behavior: A meta-analysis. *Journal of Applied Psychology, 96,* 619–632. doi:10.1037/a0021887

Gilboa, S., Shirom, A., Fried, Y., & Cooper, C. (2008). A meta-analysis of work demand stressors and job performance: Examining main and moderating effects. *Personnel Psychology, 61,* 227–271. doi:10.1111/j.1744-6570.2008.00113.x

Jackson, S. E., & Schuler, R. S. (1985). A meta-analysis and conceptual critique of research on role ambiguity and role conflict in work settings. *Organizational Behavior and Human Decision Processes, 36,* 16–78. doi:10.1016/0749-5978(85)90020-2

King, L. A., & King, D. W. (1990). Role conflict and role ambiguity: A critical assessment of construct validity. *Psychological Bulletin, 107,* 48–64. doi:10.1037/0033-2909.107.1.48

Ortqvist, D., & Wincent, J. (2006). Prominent consequences of role stress: A meta-analytic review. *International Journal of Stress Management, 13,* 399–422. doi:10.1037/1072-5245.13.4.399

Role Conflict

Role conflict, which occurs when employees experience incompatible work demands, is a widely studied work stressor. A *work stressor* is any aspect of the work environment that requires an adaptive response from employees and has the potential to cause poor health. In addition to role conflict, other work stressors include role ambiguity, interpersonal mistreatment at work, and the presence of an unreasonable workload. The negative health outcomes produced by stressors—anxiety, depression, and physical symptoms, for instance—are called *strains.*

Role conflict is generally conceptualized as a type of *perception* a worker has of his or her work environment. As such, worker self-reports are typically used to assess role conflict. Prototypical role conflict items include "In my job, I often feel like different people are 'pulling me in different directions'" and "I have to deal with competing demands at work."

Role theory provides the theoretical basis for the study of role conflict. According to role theory, each employee has a unique set of work roles, and each role has its own unique responsibilities. Employees simultaneously occupy multiple roles, both within and outside the organization. A mid-level manager who is married and has children, for example, would occupy the roles of supervisor, subordinate, spouse, and parent. Role conflict is especially likely among workers who simultaneously occupy several roles.

Types of Role Conflict

Researchers have distinguished among several types of role conflict. One type of role conflict occurs when employees experience incompatibility between their values and their job responsibilities. For example, a convenience store clerk who personally objects to gambling but sells lottery tickets as part of his or her job experiences this form of conflict. A second type of role conflict involves incompatibility between employees' job responsibilities and their abilities, time, and resources. Examples of this form of conflict include having too little time to complete work tasks or lacking the training or equipment necessary to complete one's work. Similar work stressors are sometimes referred to as role overload (having too much work or having work that is too difficult) and organizational constraints (any aspect of the work environment that interferes with job performance).

Researchers often distinguish between *intrarole conflict* and *interrole conflict.* Intrarole conflict occurs when incompatibility exists within a single role, such as when one work role interferes with another work role. Interrole conflict, on the other hand, occurs when two or more roles are incompatible with each other. One form of interrole conflict occurs when workers must behave in a particular way in one role that is inconsistent with the way they must behave in another role. A prison guard, for example, is required to behave authoritatively when dealing with prisoners, but he or she would ideally behave more agreeably when interacting with family members. Most people would find it difficult to switch between these two modes of behavior.

Work–Family Conflict

Work–family conflict is a form of interrole conflict that occurs when the role requirements of work and family are incompatible with each other. Researchers have distinguished between two main types of work–family conflict: (a) work-to-family conflict and (b) family-to-work conflict. Work-to-family conflict occurs when a person's work roles interfere with the successful execution of his or her family roles. If a mother misses her son's school play because she has to attend a work meeting, for example, she experiences work-to-family conflict. Family-to-work conflict, on the other hand, occurs when a worker's family role interferes with the successful performance of his or her work role. This occurs, for example, when a father repeatedly misses work to care for an ill child. Of these two forms of conflict, work-to-family conflict is likely to produce greater health consequences.

Work–family conflict researchers also distinguish between time-based, strain-based, and behavior-based conflict. Time-based conflict occurs when the amount of time needed to satisfy the role requirements of one domain do not allow enough time to meet the role requirements of another domain. Working excessive hours, for example, can prevent employees from spending sufficient time with their families. Strain-based conflict, on the other hand, occurs when the demands of one role produce illness that interferes with performance in another role. Caring for a spouse who has a terminal illness, for example, may cause a worker to become depressed, thus undermining his or her job performance. Finally,

behavior-based conflict occurs when work roles and family roles require behaviors that are inconsistent with each other. A bill collector, for example, is expected to act aggressively at work when interacting with debtors but must act nurturing when caring for his or her children.

Work–School Conflict

People who attend school while working often experience *work–school conflict*. Work–school conflict occurs when one's work and school responsibilities are incompatible with each other. An employed student, for example, might find that work demands and school demands compete for his or her time. Researchers often make a further distinction between work-to-school conflict and school-to-work conflict. Work-to-school conflict occurs when work responsibilities interfere with school responsibilities; school-to-work conflict occurs when school responsibilities interfere with work responsibilities. Number of hours worked and course load are positively associated with work–school conflict. In addition to having negative health consequences, work–school conflict is also likely to have a negative impact on school performance.

Causes of Role Conflict

Role conflict is often the result of ineffective managerial behaviors. Leader consideration (the extent to which supervisors care about the well-being of their subordinates) and leader initiating structure (the extent to which supervisors clarify employees' roles), for example, are both negatively correlated with role conflict. Role conflict is also likely to be high when supervisors provide employees with little job autonomy.

Ineffective organizational policies are a direct cause of some forms of role conflict. Indeed, some self-reported role conflict items specifically refer to incompatible organizational guidelines. Role conflict can arise, for example, from incompatible requests from supervisors or from differing and incompatible performance standards across supervisors. Such forms of conflict are most likely to occur when organizational policies require that employees report to multiple supervisors.

Role conflict is also likely to occur within unenriched jobs (e.g., jobs that provide little feedback and are low in skill variety and task identity). Finally, role conflict is likely to occur when a person simultaneously occupies several roles. Being assigned multiple work roles, having a family, and being a student, for example, can each cause a worker to experience high levels of role conflict.

Consequences of Role Conflict

Most workplace stressors include a component of uncertainty. In the case of role conflict, employees may feel uncertain about their ability to effectively satisfy competing role demands. This uncertainty may in turn produce negative health consequences. Indeed, role conflict is associated with several indicators of mental and physical illness, such as anxiety, depression, burnout, and physical symptoms. In addition, role conflict is related to several negative job attitudes and ineffective work behaviors:

- Global job dissatisfaction
- Dissatisfaction with supervision
- Poor in-role job performance
- Counterproductive work behavior
- Low levels of organizational citizenship behavior
- Low levels of organizational commitment
- Turnover intention

However, most of the research examining the causes and consequences of role conflict has used cross-sectional designs; thus, it is difficult to draw definitive conclusions about causal relationships.

Treatments for Role Conflict

Because role conflict is often the result of ineffective leadership behaviors, many of the treatments for role conflict require the involvement of supervisors. Supervisors, for example, could be trained to identify and change supervisory behaviors that produce role conflict. Likewise, one form of role conflict occurs when employees receive incompatible demands from two or more supervisors. This type of conflict could be eliminated by having employees report to only one supervisor.

Some forms of role conflict are the direct result of organizational policies. Not having the required training or equipment to effectively satisfy one's role requirements, for example, might be the result of organizational policies. Changing such policies could therefore eliminate some instances of role conflict. Furthermore, some role conflict occurs because employees' personal values are incompatible with the role requirements of their jobs. This type of conflict speaks to the importance of hiring job applicants on the basis of their fit with job requirements.

Given that role conflict is associated with several negative outcomes, one might assume that organizational leaders would be motived to reduce the presence of role conflict. This has not been the case, however. Instead, organizations have generally given more attention to treating role conflict's symptoms than to addressing its causes.

Nathan A. Bowling

See also Occupational Health Psychology; Role Ambiguity; Role Overload and Underload; Stress, Consequences; Stress, Coping and Management; Stress, Models and Theories

Further Readings

Eatough, E. M., Chang, C.-H., Miloslavic, S. A., & Johnson, R. E. (2011). Relationships of role stressors with organizational citizenship behavior: A meta-analysis. *Journal of Applied Psychology, 96*, 619–632. doi:10.1037/a0021887

Jackson, S. E., & Schuler, R. S. (1985). A meta-analysis and conceptual critique of research on role ambiguity and role conflict in work settings. *Organizational Behavior and Human Decision Processes, 36*, 16–78. doi:10.1016/0749-5978(85)90020-2

King, L. A., & King, D. W (1990). Role conflict and role ambiguity: A critical assessment of construct validity. *Psychological Bulletin, 107*, 48–64. doi:10.1037/0033-2909.107.1.48

Michel, J. S., Kotrba, L. M., Mitchelson, J. K., Clark, M. A., & Baltes, B. B. (2011). Antecedents of work–family conflict: A meta-analytic review. *Journal of Organizational Behavior, 32*, 689–725. doi:10.1002/job.695

Ortqvist, D., & Wincent, J. (2006). Prominent consequences of role stress: A meta-analytic review. *International Journal of Stress Management, 13*, 399–422. doi:10.1037/1072-5245.13.4.399

ROLE OF THEORY IN RESEARCH

Notwithstanding the ongoing academic debate over what constitutes theory, researchers generally agree that the role of theory in research is to provide a formal and systematic explanation for a specific set of phenomena and, more specifically, the phenomena's nature and behavior. To this extent, the primary role of theory is to provide a framework for discovering and investigating explanations and predictions that help researchers to organize and navigate the complexity of the external world as we experience and observe it.

Many researchers describe theory in terms of identifying relationships among a set of *constructs* and *variables* that provide better explanations about the nature of an observed phenomenon. Constructs cannot be directly observed (e.g., cohesion), while variables can be directly observed and, therefore, measured empirically (e.g., number of interpersonal interactions). Alternatively, other scholars focus more strongly on a conceptualization of theory as a rich narrative and account of a phenomenon, where greater attention is given to its novelty and fit with the observed data.

Regardless of the specific approach to theory adopted, researchers agree that theory plays several important roles in furthering research. First, theory provides researchers with a fresh perspective or a novel lens through which to observe empirical phenomena, allowing a better understanding and prediction of the processes and outcomes under study. Second, theory has the potential to elicit interest among various academic circles and solicit further research endeavors, by turning attention to a specific set of constructs or phenomena. Third, a cross-disciplinary theory may be able to serve multiple contexts, explaining empirical phenomena in potentially different settings. Ultimately, theories should drive empirical research. Sound theory serves as the foundation for testing ideas as well as for developing new ones in every field of scientific research. This is central to the unfolding process of knowledge development.

The Process of Theorizing

Given the important role of theory in any field of research, it is important to better understand the process through which theories are generated and developed. Several scholars devote their attention to refine and further develop our understanding of the theory development process. Generally, theories emerge thorough a recursive development process (i.e., theorizing) in which researchers interpret and attempt to explain the empirical patterns observed in a set of empirical observations. To this extent, scholars agree that in generating theories, data and researchers' interpretations of data are intertwined. Ultimately, data do not generate theory independently from the researcher's interpretation of the observed patterns.

Researchers maintain that the theorizing process consists of a multitude of activities, such as abstracting, generalizing, relating, selecting, explaining, synthesizing, and idealizing. These activities contribute to the generation of various outputs (e.g., constructs, variables, models, hypotheses) that do not constitute theory in and of themselves but contribute to theory development through a cumulative process. Also, researchers recognize that theories are socially constructed in the sense that they are profoundly affected by how they are understood and applied by other researchers using them. To this extent, the quality of a theory is assessed as a function not only of its initial falsifiability and utility but also of the quality of its subsequent uses and applications. Indeed, the reception of a theory within the academic community and how it is used and further developed by other researchers deeply affect its nature and meaning. At times, theories are improved through this process of social construction, while in other situations, the original contributions are watered down, losing incisiveness and meaningfulness. For this reason, the process of theorizing can be described as resulting from and greatly affected by the cooperation between authors and readers.

Scholars agree that the theorizing process is profoundly affected by a theory's complexity. Simple theories are conceptually basic and easier to test empirically. Usually, in these kinds of theories, *propositions* (i.e., statements that at an abstract level relate constructs to one another) follow a clear and logical progression and are used to derive testable *hypotheses* (i.e., statements that at a more concrete level relate variables to one another). To this extent, a strong simple theory is internally consistent and tends to follow mostly linear logic.

On the other hand, a complex theory is more contradictory and paradoxical in nature and is characterized by nonlinearity and nonrecursiveness. These characteristics of a complex theory make the development of clear arguments, propositions, and hypotheses more challenging and less straightforward, when compared with a simple theory. Nevertheless, scholars assert that the process of theory development will greatly benefit from the combination of simple and complex theorizing.

Regardless of the theory complexity, researchers agree that the theorizing process includes two main subprocesses: theory *development* and theory *testing*. The main purpose of theory development is to generate new theoretical contributions that, over time, can solidify into what is known as a theory. Empirical research that focuses on theory development tends to follow a more inductive approach (i.e., make a broad generalization from specific observations). In this approach, researchers begin with observations of a specific set of phenomena, discern patterns, and develop a generalization from which to infer a theoretical explanation. Researchers following this approach draw from a multitude of methodologies (e.g., case study, ethnography, grounded theory). These studies typically culminate in the development of propositions that summarize the logical arguments characterizing the proposed theory. Among several approaches to theory development, an interesting and increasingly predominant one is *theory borrowing*, defined as the adoption of a theoretical framework from outside a field that can help explain phenomena of interest in a specific field. Borrowing from other disciplines is a common and important aspect of theory development in many fields of research. Two main typologies of theory borrowing have been identified in the literature. The first one is based on *analogical resonance* and consists of comparing and contrasting similar domains with a focus on elements of resemblance and similarity. The second one, in contrast, is based on *analogical dissonance*, a more complex form of blending theories that focuses on disanalogous, counterfactual, and anomalous reasoning to generate a more complex and radical theoretical statement.

The main purpose of the second subprocess, theory testing, is to falsify, validate, or refine new theories as they emerge from the theory development process. Studies aimed at theory testing tend to follow a more deductive approach (i.e., starting from a theory, predictions are developed about its consequences in the specific observed context) and use one or more theories to develop testable hypotheses. Among the studies testing multiple theories, an interesting approach in many academic fields has been *theory pitting*. This approach to theory testing sets two theories against each other in order to eliminate the weaker one in favor of the stronger one. To this extent, theory pitting is a specific process within the broader family of *theory pruning* approaches (i.e., research intended to bound and to reduce theories). Last, another fundamental, yet less valued, activity within the theory testing subprocess is empirical replication. *Empirical replication* refers to studies aimed at cross-validating the findings of previous empirical studies. Studies proposing empirical replications do not develop original concepts or relationships and, for this reason, are often considered less important than research directly aimed at theory development or original testing. Nevertheless, empirical replications are important because they allow accumulation and consolidation of knowledge, ultimately contributing to further theory refinement.

Overall, empirical articles can provide significant theoretical contributions by focusing on either theory development or theory testing, or on both. Nevertheless, being able to combine both theory development and testing within a single study is a considerably challenging task.

To conclude, theory has an important role in research. Scholars agree that theories should drive empirical research and that sound theory is the foundation of the knowledge development process in every field of scientific research.

Laura D'Oria

See also Case Study Method; Cross-Cultural Research Methods and Theory; Ethnography; Grounded Theory; What Is Theory?

Further Readings

Colquitt, J. A., & Zapata-Phelan, C. P. (2007). Trends in theory building and theory testing: A five-decade study of the *Academy of Management Journal*. *Academy of Management Journal, 50*(6), 1281–1303. doi:10.5465/AMJ.2007.28165855

DiMaggio, P. J. (1995). Comments on "What theory is not." *Administrative Science Quarterly, 40*(3), 391–397. doi:10.2307/2393790

Ferris, G. R., Hochwarter, W. A., & Buckley, M. R. (2012). Theory in the organizational sciences: How will we know it when we see it? *Organizational Psychology Review, 2*(1), 94–106. doi:10.1177/2041386611423696

Leavitt, K., Mitchell, T. R., & Peterson, J. (2010). Theory pruning: Strategies to reduce our dense theoretical landscape. *Organizational Research Methods, 13*(4), 644–667. doi:10.1177/1094428109345156

Ofori-Dankwa, J., & Julian, S. D. (2001). Complexifying organizational theory: Illustrations using time research. *Academy of Management Review, 26*(3), 415–430. doi:10.2307/259185

Oswick, C., Fleming, P., & Hanlon, G. (2011). From borrowing to blending: Rethinking the processes of organizational theory building. *Academy of Management Review, 36*(2), 318–337. doi:10.5465/AMR.2011.59330932

Sutton, R. I., & Staw, B. M. (1995). What theory is not. *Administrative Science Quarterly, 40*(3), 371–384. doi:10.2307/2393788

Weick, K. E. (1995). What theory is not, theorizing is. *Administrative Science Quarterly, 40*(3), 385–390. doi:10.2307/2393789

ROLE OVERLOAD AND UNDERLOAD

In all organizational settings, roles represent sets of behavioral expectations that are formally and informally assigned to organizational members. Roles serve the purpose of communicating expectations to employees, as well as coordinating the activities of different organizational members. In typical organizations, however, it is rarely the case that each individual employee has one clearly defined role that is recognizable and distinct from the roles of other organizational members. Rather, most organizations consist of a complex web of roles in which each employee may hold multiple roles, different roles may overlap and at times conflict, and the roles of employees may change frequently.

Because of this complex web of roles within organizations, roles can be a source of stress for employees. In fact, the most widely studied stressors

in organizations have been *role conflict* and *role ambiguity*. Because of the heavy emphasis on role conflict and role ambiguity, much less research has examined the sheer amount of role demands that an employee may face. This entry will focus on two role stressors that represent the opposite ends of a continuum representing the amount of an employee's role demands. *Role overload* occurs when employees simply have too much to do—in other words, their roles become too big. *Role underload*, on the other hand, occurs when employees have too little to do—in other words, their roles become too small.

How Do Roles Develop?

Before our discussion of role overload and underload, it is useful to discuss how roles in organizations develop. People typically enter organizations with at least a general idea of what their roles will be. A person may be hired to be an accountant, a design engineer, a grocery clerk, or a physical therapist, and on the basis of their knowledge of the job and prior training, they are likely to have a fairly good idea of what their role responsibilities will entail. In addition to these prior expectations, new employees often receive formal job descriptions and communicate with their immediate supervisors regarding role responsibilities and performance expectations. Other employees (both peers and subordinates), and perhaps even individuals outside the organization (customers), may also communicate their expectations regarding a new employee's role.

The sum total of all sources of role-related information an employee may draw upon is known as his or her *role set*. Within each employee's role set, some members are typically more important than others (e.g., immediate supervisor), but an employee still typically cannot ignore less important members of his or her role set. Given the size of a typical employee's role set, it would be ideal if the members of the role set could meet regularly to discuss the information they are conveying to the employee—this would ensure that the size of the role would be reasonable. Organizations, however, are far from ideal, so it is possible that problems in the role-sending process may occur. Our focus here will be on role demands that are too big or too small.

Role Overload:
Why Do Roles Become Too Big?

Role overload occurs when an employee's role simply becomes too demanding or too big. Role overload may occur strictly in a *quantitative* sense; that is, the number of an employee's role responsibilities is too large for the employee to handle in a reasonable amount of time. It is also possible for role overload to occur in a more *qualitative* sense. In this case, an employee may have adequate time to fulfill all of his or her role responsibilities, but some of these responsibilities may exceed his or her skills or abilities.

Perhaps the most obvious reason for role overload has to do with the role itself. Some roles are inherently "bigger" than others, regardless of the organizations in which they are found. In most organizations, roles that involve supervision of others, or regular interfacing with outside constituencies, are the most demanding and have the greatest potential for overload. It is often the case, however, that occupants of such roles are often well compensated, and organizations offer various forms of support to help cope with the high level of role demands.

If viewed from a role theory perspective, the primary cause of role overload is little or no communication between the members of a focal employee's role set. An employee's immediate supervisor, coworkers, subordinates, and in some cases customers all may make demands on an employee without knowing the demands placed on the employee by other members of the role set. This may be most likely to occur when the members of an employee's role set exist both within and outside the organization.

A second potential cause of role overload, which is separate from role theory, is simply poor job design. An organization, for example, may expect a design engineer to assume responsibility for 10 different design projects without really thinking through the consequences of such an allocation of work. In such a scenario, the employee involved will likely try to handle all of these assignments, but in all likelihood, he or she will experience at least some form of role overload.

In recent years, two workplace trends have developed that may contribute to increased role overload among employees. First, many organizations have been forced to decrease the number of employees or downsize in order to remain competitive. Although the impact of downsizing is most negative on those who are let go, survivors of layoffs may also be affected, because the role responsibilities of those laid off must be shifted elsewhere, and often this increases the role responsibilities of layoff survivors.

A second recent trend is the development of advanced forms of communication technology. Today's employees have the ability to be constantly connected to work via computers, smartphones, tablets, and other electronic devices. Although there are certainly some positives associated with this technology, one negative is that a person's work role may intrude on other aspects of his or life in a way that developers of this technology had never intended.

Consequences of Role Overload

As stated above, the vast majority of research on role stressors has focused on role conflict and role ambiguity. In fact, there is so much research on these role stressors that several meta-analyses have been done to summarize this literature. What these meta-analyses have shown is that both of these role stressors are associated with a number of psychological (e.g., job dissatisfaction, anxiety), physical (e.g., self-reported symptoms, sick days), and behavioral (e.g., decreased performance, increased absenteeism) outcomes.

To a large extent, research on role overload mirrors that done on other role stressors in that role overload is associated with a number of strains. However, compared with other role stressors, more research has focused on its health-related consequences. This is understandable, given the fact that being overloaded is often physically taxing to employees. These investigations found that reports of negative health consequences were highest in the role overload group and lowest in the matched group.

Another outcome in which the findings for role overload and other role stressors diverge somewhat is in the area of performance. Recent meta-analyses have shown that the relationship between role overload and job performance is quite mixed; that is, some studies find the relationship to be positive, whereas others have found it to be negative. The most likely reason for this is that for some individuals role overload may be viewed as a *challenge* as opposed to a stressor. This is particularly true if employees have the requisite skills and abilities to perform their jobs and are highly engaged in their work. It may also be due to the fact that the vast majority of studies have investigated quantitative, as opposed to qualitative, role overload. It is hard to imagine how having work that is too difficult could have positive motivational properties for employees. More research, however, is needed on qualitative role overload in order to address this question.

It is also important to consider that the impact of role overload may vary widely from employee to employee. People who manage their time well, those with a great deal of support from others, and those who simply do not view being overloaded as a negative probably do not respond to this stressor as negatively as others. Admittedly, though, more research needs to done on individual difference moderators on the effect of role overload and other stressors.

What About Role Underload?

While there is not a great deal of research examining role overload, even less has examined role underload. Role underload, however, is becoming more of an issue for two reasons. First, there have been recent studies suggesting high levels of boredom and disengagement among employees. This suggests that many people are understimulated by their jobs, come to work bored and disengaged regardless of the content of their work, or some combination of the two. Second, because of poor economic conditions in the past decade, many people have been forced, at least for some period of their lives, to accept work that does not fully involve their skills, abilities, and experience.

What is the impact of role underload? Although there is little research on role underload, in all likelihood the most *proximal* reaction to this stressor is a chronic feeling of boredom on the part of the employee. It is also likely that role underload leads to other negative affective reactions, such as job dissatisfaction and low organizational commitment. As with most stressors, however, responses to underload may vary considerably from employee to employee. There is some evidence, for example, that some individuals are more prone to experience boredom across situations. One would assume that such individuals would probably react more negatively to role underload compared with someone less apt to experience boredom. Much more research on role underload is needed, however, before more definitive conclusions can be drawn.

Summary and Conclusion

This entry has described two important, yet understudied, sources of stress in organizations: role overload and role underload. Both of these stressors are likely influenced by job design, yet they may also come from broader trends such as enhanced technology and stagnant economic conditions. Although responses to both of these stressors are generally negative, there may be considerable variation in how employees respond.

Steve M. Jex and Kristin A. Horan

See also Empowerment; Job Characteristics Theory; Job Satisfaction; Occupational Health Psychology; Role Ambiguity; Role Conflict; Stress, Models and Theories

Further Readings

Eatough, E. M., Chang, C. H., Miloslavic, S. A., & Johnson, R. A. (2011). Relationships of role stressors with organizational citizenship behavior: A meta-analysis. *Journal of Applied Psychology, 96,* 619–632. doi:10.1037/a0021887

Gilboa, S., Shirom, A., Fried, Y., & Cooper, C. (2008). A meta-analysis of work demand stressors and job performance: Examining main and moderating effects. *Personnel Psychology, 61,* 227–271. doi:10.1111/j.1744-6570.2008.00113.x

Jex, S. M., Swanson, N. W., & Grubb, P. (2013). Healthy workplaces. In N. S. Schmitt & S. E. Highhouse (Eds.), *Handbook of psychology* (2nd ed., Vol. 12, pp. 615–642). Hoboken, NJ: John Wiley.

Mael, F., & Jex, S. M. (2015). Workplace boredom: An integrative model of traditional and contemporary approaches. *Group & Organization Management, 40,* 131–159. doi:10.1177/1059601115575148

Morgeson, F. P., Garza, A. S., & Campion, M. A. (2013). Work design. In N. W. Schmitt, S. Highhouse, & I. B. Weiner (Eds.), *Handbook of psychology* (Vol. 12, 525–559). Hoboken, NJ: John Wiley.

Schultz, K. S., Wang, M., & Olson, D. A. (2010). Role overload and underload in relation to occupational stress and health. *Stress and Health, 26,* 99–111. doi:10.1002/smi.1268

SAFETY CLIMATE

Safety climate refers to employees' shared perceptions of an organization or group's procedures, policies, and practices with regard to safety that are rewarded, supported, and expected from employees. Consistent with other types of climate, safety climate is not an individual-level perception, but rather one that is manifest in the way that individuals agree concerning what it means to be safe in their group or organization. Furthermore, safety climate can differ as it pertains to how individuals agree in terms of the organization's support for safety versus the nature of that support within their group. Sometimes safety is an espoused value at one level, but not enacted at another level, thus creating the possibility of differences in how safety climate is experienced. Additionally, the strength of the safety climate is largely a function of the extent to which organizational members, particularly leaders, reward, support, and expect safety-related behaviors. *Rewarded* in this case refers to acknowledgement in a somewhat formal recognition process that can be directed at the individual, the group, and/or the organization. *Supported* refers to a variety of behaviors both from peers and from leaders related to encouraging the safety-related behaviors that ensure safe operations in the organization. *Expected*, in this case, refers, but is not limited, to organizational policies and procedures that ensure employees are held accountable for safety-related behaviors and the extent to which such policies are communicated. The balance of the entry includes a discussion of the challenges in operationalizing safety climate, the causes and consequences of safety climate, and future research opportunities.

Operationalizing Safety Climate

Earlier definitions of *safety climate* simply stated that it refers to the average perceptions of employees about their work environment in relation to safety. As the foregoing definition indicates, much development in terms of the specificity of the definition and how it changes across levels and context has occurred. One thing that persists from the original definitions is the emphasis on both safety behavior and the shared nature of the construct. The latter is particularly important in terms of operationalizing safety climate. In order to measure safety climate, researchers often rely on perceptions of individuals concerning their safety climate. Then, through the use of statistical processes, researchers test the extent to which the perceptions indicate adequate agreement. Specifically, researchers compare responses across a sample of individuals to see if they have adequate homogeneity in terms of their perceptions of safety climate. If they do not appear to be homogeneous (i.e., agree), then the safety climate is said to be fractured and therefore does not fit the definition of a shared understanding of what it means to be safe in that work environment.

Another more recent development in terms of the operationalization of safety climate refers to the level of analysis. As the foregoing definition indicates, safety climate refers to employees' shared perceptions of the *organization* or *group's* procedures, policies, and practices in relation to safety. The emphasis on organization *or* group acknowledges that researchers have more recently questioned the global assessment of safety climate and now encourage operationalization and measuring safety climate at the level of interest for the research question under investigation. Specifically, safety climate may differ at the group and organizational level for a given individual and his or her peers within the work environment. For example, researchers showed that individuals may have one safety climate for their immediate work group as well as for their organization. This may stem from differences in emphasis by leaders at the work group level versus those at the organization level. It may also stem from a variety of organizational and group-level factors such as organizational values, managerial efforts, group composition, work environment differences across groups within the organization, and so forth.

Another concern in terms of operationalizing and measuring safety climate is the difference between the espoused value and the actual behaviors surrounding safety climate. For example, organizations may have a series of policies, procedures, mandates, rules, handbook instructions, standard operating procedures, and so forth concerning safety within the organization. These often represent the espoused value for safety within the workplace. However, the actual behaviors of the employees may or may not reflect the espoused values, and this may be a function of cultural and leadership factors within their work group or as represented by organizational management. Thus, researchers must decide if they want to assess the espoused or the actual safety climate among the groups or organizations they are investigating.

Potential Causes and Consequences of Safety Climate

The study of safety climate emerged in 1980, and since then, a variety of outcomes and antecedents to safety climate have received attention. To start, the outcomes of safety climate probably provide a keen motivation for the overt interest over the years. Specifically, and perhaps not surprisingly, safety climate is related to safety behaviors and safety in general. Safety behaviors and safety in general are indexed and measured in a number of ways including, but not limited to, using safety equipment (e.g., hard hats), observing safety rules (e.g., keep hands out of hydraulic equipment), absence or reduction of safety reports, and reduction in accidents and deaths. Probably the most motivating from an organizational perspective is the reduction of accidents and deaths because of the dramatic toll such incidents have on individuals, families, and the organization. Although the value of life cannot be overestimated, the reality is that accidents are costly for a variety of reasons; thus, another outcome of safety climate that is used in research is the cost of accidents in organizations with increases in safety climate suggested to reduce costs. Another outcome that continues to garner interest is the detection of near misses. Near misses are those incidents that have the high potential to result in harm that have not resulted in equipment damage, injury, or death. Studies suggest that safety climate is related to the detection of near misses and subsequent learning therefrom. In sum, researchers show that as safety climate increases, safety behavior increases, detection of near misses increases, and accidents and deaths decrease.

Thus, it comes as no surprise that researchers and practitioners show a level of eagerness to identify antecedents to safety climate in order to enjoy the overt benefits previously mentioned here. Many of the studies investigating the antecedents of safety climate occurred in organizations where safety is a constant concern (e.g., military strike teams), and often the environment in which work takes place is dangerous (e.g., firefighters). These organizations, however, often work reliably in these environments with fewer accidents and mistakes than one might expect. Researchers refer to these organizations as high-reliability organizations and often study factors across management, the workforce, and the environment to discover the antecedents of safety climate.

In terms of managerial factors, research shows that organizational policies, systems and procedures, management leadership style, and management commitment to safety all impact safety climate development and maintenance in organizations. In his seminal study, Zohar identified workforce perceptions of management attitudes toward safety as a major factor in promoting safety climate, and this finding perpetuates across a variety of studies and a variety of managerial factors. Additionally, direct supervisors at lower levels in the organization appear to have an important impact on the development of a safety climate. Because of their direct interaction with those engaged in the work, their attitudes toward and support of safety-related behaviors impact employees' attitudes concerning safety climate. Recent studies show that supervisors' behaviors in safety-related meetings impact their employees' group norms concerning safety and overall group safety climate, thereby confirming previous research generally.

In terms of workforce or employee factors, research suggests that personal involvement in the establishment of safety procedures, communication about and the nature of hazards, and level of personal responsibility all influence the development of a safety climate. Additionally, given the shared nature of safety climate, group factors related to the workforce such as group-level perceptions of the supervisor have a lasting impact on group safety climate. Finally, in terms of environmental factors, research suggests that structural factors are important in developing a safety climate. These include the availability of safety training, communication about safety policies and regulations, safety-related equipment, and workplace design.

In sum, safety climate is developed by a confluence of managerial, workforce, and environmental factors, and a good safety climate promotes safety-related behaviors and safety in general, among other things.

Future Directions

Safety climate continues to receive considerable attention from researchers and practitioners, and there are many opportunities for future inquiry. As the review of antecedents and outcomes suggests, there are a variety of causes and consequences of safety climate. The nomological network for the safety climate construct, however, is not complete. For example, in a recent meta-analysis, the author observed that much of the previous work has focused on the antecedents and outcomes of safety climate without much regard to the various moderating variables that could impact those relationships. Candidates for investigation

include the nature of work groups (diversity, gender composition, personality, shared mental models, etc.), work processes (routine nature of tasks, complexity, etc.), and organizational factors (formalization, centralization, imitation, legitimation, etc.), and so on. In other words, the causes and consequences of safety climate occur in a world surrounded by people with their individual differences, inside groups with their many complexities, embedded in a variety of organizations serving a variety of needs, all surrounded by industries and societies with their unique cultures and complexities. The opportunities for theoretical, empirical, methodological, and practical expansion of the safety climate literature are numerous.

Joseph A. Allen

See also High-Reliability Organizations; Multilevel Modeling; National Institute for Occupational Safety and Health/Occupational Safety and Health Administration; Organizational Culture; Workplace Safety

Further Readings

Clarke, S. (2010). An integrative model of safety climate: Linking psychological climate and work attitudes to individual safety outcomes using meta-analysis. *Journal of Occupational and Organizational Psychology, 83*(3), 553–578. doi:10.1348/096317909X452122

Griffin, M. A., & Neal, A. (2000). Perceptions of safety at work: A framework for linking safety climate to safety performance, knowledge, and motivation. *Journal of Occupational Health Psychology, 5*(3), 347–358. doi:10.1037/1076-8998.5.3.347

Hofmann, D. A., & Stetzer, A. (1998). The role of safety climate and communication in accident interpretation: Implications for learning from negative events. *Academy of Management Journal, 41*(6), 644–657. doi:10.2307/256962

Katz-Navon, T., Naveh, E., & Stern, Z. (2005). Safety climate in health care organizations: A multidimensional approach. *Academy of Management Journal, 48*(6), 1075–1089. doi:10.5465/AMJ.2005.19573110

Zohar, D. (1980). Safety climate in industrial organizations: Theoretical and applied implications. *Journal of Applied Psychology, 65*(1), 96–102. doi:10.1037//0021-9010.65.1.96

Zohar, D. (2000). A group-level model of safety climate: Testing the effect of group climate on microaccidents in manufacturing jobs. *Journal of Applied Psychology*, 85(4), 587–596. doi:10.1037//0021-9010.85.4.587

Zohar, D., & Luria, G. (2005). A multilevel model of safety climate: Cross-level relationships between organization and group-level climates. *Journal of Applied Psychology*, 90(4), 616–628. doi:10.1037/0021-9010.90.4.616

SAMPLING TECHNIQUES

For describing or testing hypotheses about a population, sampling a small portion of the population is often preferable to taking a census of the entire population. Taking a sample is usually less expensive and less time-consuming than taking a census and more accurate because more effort and care can be spent ensuring that the right data are gathered in the right way. Data collected appropriately can be used to make inferences about the entire population.

Sampling techniques can be categorized into nonprobability samples and probability samples. A *probability sample* is selected in a way such that virtually all members of a population have a nonzero probability of being included, and that probability is known or calculable. A *nonprobability sample* is gathered in a way that does not depend on chance. This means that it is difficult or impossible to estimate the probability that a particular unit of the population will be included. Moreover, a substantial proportion of the population is typically excluded. The quality of the sample, therefore, depends on the knowledge and skill of the researcher.

In general, probability samples are preferable to nonprobability samples because results can be generalized to the entire population using statistical techniques. Such generalization is typically invalid with nonprobability samples because the exclusion of portions of the population from sampling means the results are likely to be biased. People who volunteer to participate in a study, for example, may be different from those who do not; they may differ in age, gender, occupation, motivation, or any number of other characteristics that may be related to the study. If the study concerns attitudes or opinions, volunteer participants may have different and often stronger feelings about the issues than nonparticipants.

Nonprobability samples, however, have their advantages and uses. They are relatively easy and inexpensive to assemble—for example, free-access Web surveys. They can be valuable for exploratory research or when the researcher wants to document a range or provide particular examples rather than investigate tendencies or causal processes. Moreover, techniques have been developed for obtaining unbiased results from certain kinds of nonprobability samples.

Two concepts are important to sampling in general: the target population and the sampling frame. The *target population* is the population to which the researcher wants to generalize the findings. One important characteristic of the population is the kind of entities its members are, known as the *unit of analysis*. The cases in the sample correspond to this unit of analysis. Examples of a unit of analysis are the individual, the organizational department, the organization, or some geographical unit, such as the state. The unit of analysis is characterized by a set of attributes on which the researcher gathers data. These are the variables the researcher scores for each case in the sample. For example, a researcher might explore individual characteristics such as age or years of education. Usually, the target population is circumscribed by some characteristic or combination of characteristics. It may be employees of a particular firm, or there may be a geographical limitation, such as residents of a particular city. Constraints on gender, ethnicity, age group, work status, or other characteristics may be specified as well. A target population, for example, might be permanent, full-time female employees of a particular company.

The *sampling frame* is the complete list of all units from which the sample is taken. For the target population of permanent, full-time female employees, for example, the sampling frame might be a list of permanent, full-time female employees from all of the company's locations. For telephone surveys, a list of phone numbers is a typical sampling frame, perhaps for particular area codes or in conjunction with block maps.

Probability Samples

Sample Designs

For probability samples, there are four common designs: the simple random sample, the systematic sample, the stratified sample, and the cluster sample. A *simple random sample* is drawn in such a way that every combination of units of a given size has an equal probability of being drawn. If there are n individuals in the sample and N in the population, for example, each individual's probability of being included is n/N. The simple random sample is optimal for estimating unbiased population characteristics as precisely as possible. The most commonly used statistical techniques assume and work best with simple random samples. A simple random sample can be drawn by applying a table of random numbers or pseudorandom numbers generated by a computer to the sampling frame. Unfortunately, for many target populations, it is difficult and costly to draw a simple random sample. Hence, researchers use sample designs that approximate simple random samples.

One such design is a *systematic sample*, which is drawn in such a way that every unit in the target population has the same probability of being selected, but the same is not true for every combination of units of a given size. A systematic sample might be used when the sample frame is a long, noncomputerized list. To carry it out, determine a sampling interval (I) based on the desired sample size (n): $I = N/n$. Choose at random a starting case, from the first through the Ith units in the list. Then, from that starting case, select every Ith unit. A systematic sample will approximate a simple random sample unless there is some sort of periodicity in the sampling frame, which then will lead to bias in the results.

A more controlled sampling design is the *stratified sample*, which is undertaken to ensure a specified proportional representation of different population groups in the sample. If the target population is 10% Hispanic, for example, a simple random sample drawn from the population may be more or less than 10% Hispanic. A stratified sample ensures that 10% of the sample—or some other desired proportion, say 20%—will be Hispanic. Stratified samples may be classified into proportionate and disproportionate samples. A *proportionate* stratified sample ensures that the composition of the sample mirrors the composition of the population along some variable or combination of variables. To carry it out, divide the target population into subgroups according to the desired aspect—Hispanic and non-Hispanic,

for example. Then take a simple random sample from each subgroup, with the same probability of selection for each subgroup.

In a *disproportionate* stratified sample, the proportion of different subgroups in the sample is set to differ from that in the target population. Typically, the composition of the sample overrepresents subgroups that form only a small proportion of the population. The purpose is to improve estimates for that subgroup and improve comparison between subgroups. For example, suppose the sample size is to be 500 and the target population is 5% Hispanic. A simple random sample would include about 25 Hispanic individuals, which is too small to obtain precise estimates for that subgroup. If better estimates are desired, the proportion of Hispanics in the sample can be raised, say to 20%, which will ensure that 100 Hispanic individuals are selected, thus producing more precise estimates for the subgroup and allowing Hispanic and non-Hispanic individuals to be compared more accurately. Analysis of the entire sample should be conducted using weights to adjust for the overrepresentation of some subgroups, a simple option in most major statistical packages for computers.

Cluster sampling is a common method for face-to-face data collection such as surveys. The data are gathered from a small number of usually spatially concentrated sets of units. A few departments of an organization may be sampled, for example, or a few locations if an organization has multiple locations. Cluster sampling may be chosen to reduce costs or because there is no adequate sampling frame from which a simple random sample or systematic sample can be drawn.

Sample Size

One question that commonly arises in research is how large a sample is necessary. Collecting data is costly, and it may be better to concentrate on gathering higher-quality data from a smaller sample, if possible. Several methods for estimating the necessary sample size exist. One method is simply to use sample sizes that approximate those of other studies of high quality. Some references contain tables that give appropriate sample sizes.

Two formulas may be of assistance. Let p denote the proportion of the population with a key attribute; if the proportion is unknown, $p = .5$

(which assumes maximum variability) may be used. Let e denote the sampling error or level of precision, expressed as a proportion. Thus, $e = .05$ means ± 5% precision. Finally, suppose a confidence level of 95% is desired. The sample size, n_0, may be estimated by

$$n_o = \frac{1.96p(1-p)}{e^2}.$$

If the key variable takes on more than two values, the best method may be to dichotomize it—that is, transform it into a variable that takes two values—and then estimate p. Otherwise, $p = .5$ may be used, which gives a conservative estimate of sample size. For smaller populations (in the thousands, for example), wherein population size is denoted by N, the formula

$$n_o = \frac{N}{1 + e^2 N}$$

may be used.

Other considerations may also affect the determination of the necessary sample size. If the researcher wishes to analyze subgroups of the target population separately or compare subgroups, then the sample must be large enough to represent each subgroup adequately. Another concern is nonresponse. Inevitably, not all units in the selected sample will provide usable data, often because they refuse or are unable to participate but also because of respondent error. Here, too, the sample must be large enough to accommodate nonresponses and unusable responses. Finally, money and time costs are a constraint in sampling and should be considered in planning the study so that the sampling can be completed as designed.

Nonprobability Samples

Haphazard, convenience, quota, and purposive samples are the most common kinds of nonprobability samples. *Convenience samples* comprise units that are self-selected (e.g., volunteers) or easily accessible. Examples of convenience samples are people who volunteer to participate in a study, people at a given location when the population includes more than a single location, and snowball samples. A snowball or respondent-driven sample is one in which the researcher begins with certain

respondents, called "seeds," and then obtains further respondents through previous respondents. A *quota sample* is one in which a predetermined number of units with certain characteristics are selected. For a *purposive sample*, units are selected on the basis of characteristics or attributes that are important to the evaluation. Many focus groups are samples of this kind.

Recently, advances have been made in obtaining unbiased results for populations from which probability samples cannot be drawn directly, typically because no adequate sampling frame is available. A *hypernetwork method* can be applied to a target population of objects or activities that are linked to people—for example, art objects or arts-related activities. A probability sample of the individuals can then be used to obtain a probability sample of organizations providing those objects or activities. Another method again uses the techniques of social network analysis to obtain unbiased estimates from respondent-driven samples, possibly via Web-based data collection. This method is especially helpful in estimating characteristics of hidden populations, such as the homeless or drug users in a particular location. Finally, free-access Web studies have been popular recently, which in turn has prompted research into how to adjust for the biases introduced because these are nonprobability samples.

Joseph M. Whitmeyer

See also Descriptive Statistics; Experience Sampling Technique; Experimental Designs; Focus Groups; Inferential Statistics; Longitudinal Research; Nonexperimental Designs; Quantitative Research Approach; Quasi-Experimental Designs; Statistical Power

Further Readings

Asan, Z., & Ayhan, H. O. (2013). Sampling frame coverage and domain adjustment procedures for Internet surveys. *Quality and Quantity*, 47(6), 3031–3042. doi:10.1007/s11135-012-9701-8

Cochran, W. G. (1977). *Sampling techniques*. New York, NY: Wiley.

Goel, S., & Salganik, M. (2010). Assessing respondent-driven sampling. *Proceedings of the National Academy of Sciences*, 107(15), 6743–6747. doi:10.1073/pnas.1000261107

Kish, L. (1965). *Survey sampling*. New York, NY: Wiley.

McPherson, M. (2001). Sampling strategies for the arts: A hypernetwork approach. *Poetics, 28*(4), 291–306. doi:10.1016/S0304-422X(01)80005-X

Miaoulis, G., & Michener, R. D. (1976). *An introduction to sampling*. Dubuque, IA: Kendall/Hunt.

Salganik, M. J., & Heckathorn, D. (2004). Sampling and estimation in hidden populations using respondent-driven sampling. *Sociological Methodology, 34*, 193–240. doi:10.1111/j.0081-1750.2004.00152.x

Wejnert, C., & Heckathorn, D. (2008). Web-based network sampling: Efficiency and efficacy of respondent-driven sampling for online research. *Sociological Methods & Research, 37*(1), 105–134. doi:10.1177/0049124108318333

SCALE CREATION

Scale creation is the process of developing a reliable and valid measure of a construct in order to assess an attribute of interest. Industrial and organizational research involves the measurement of organizational and psychological constructs, which present unique challenges because they are generally *unobservable* (e.g., work attitudes, perceptions, and personality traits). As opposed to observable characteristics (e.g., height, precipitation, and velocity), unobservable constructs cannot be measured directly and must be assessed through indirect means, such as self-report. Relatedly, these constructs are often very abstract (e.g., core self-evaluations), making it difficult to determine which items adequately represent them—and which ones do so reliably. Finally, these constructs are often complex and may be composed of several different components rather than being a single, solitary concept. As a result of these complexities, developing a measurement instrument can be a challenging task, and *validation* is especially important to the process of scale construction. This entry focuses on the principles and best practices of scale creation with regard to self-report scales.

Approaches to Scale Creation

There are two distinct approaches to scale creation. A *deductive* approach focuses on using theory and the already-formed conceptualization of construct to generate items within its domain. This approach is useful when the definition of the construct is known and substantial enough to generate an initial pool of items. By contrast, an *inductive* approach is useful when there is uncertainty in the definition or dimensionality of the construct. In this case, organizational incumbents are asked to provide descriptions of the concept, and a conceptualization is derived, which then forms the basis for generating items.

Construct Definition

Regardless of the approach to scale creation, in order to create a scale, a clear conceptualization of the construct is required. This entails delineating and defining the construct (i.e., stating what it *is*, and thus what it is *not*) either through a thorough literature review or through an inductive uncovering of the phenomenon. It is also important to define the level of conceptual breadth of the target construct. A construct that is very broad (e.g., attitudes about working in general) requires different types of items than one that is more specific (e.g., attitudes about performing administrative duties). Another important theoretical step is to specify the likely number of components, or *dimensions*, that make up the construct. The *dimensionality* of a construct can be understood as whether the construct is best conceived as being made up of a single variable (unidimensional) or a number of distinct subcomponents (multidimensional). For instance, job satisfaction has been conceptualized, and thus measured, as both a unidimensional and multidimensional construct. Hackman and Oldham's three-item scale is a single scale of *global* job satisfaction, whereas Smith et al.'s *Job Descriptive Index* is composed of five subscales: satisfaction with pay, the work itself, promotions, coworkers, and supervisors. Although this example shows that the same construct can be validly conceived as both unidimensional and multidimensional, properly specifying the dimensions of a construct is essential, as a distinct scale must be constructed for each one.

A key idea in construct definition is to outline the *nomological network* (i.e., how the focal construct and its specific dimensions are related to other constructs). Once the construct is defined, one can begin to specify this nomological network, which entails stating what the construct should be positively related to, negatively related to, and relatively independent of based on theory. The nomological network will be essential to the validation process, as a scale that empirically relates to other established measures in the way predicted by theory displays important types of validity evidence (convergent and divergent validity).

Purposes of Created Scale

Before discussing the specific principles of item writing, it is necessary to specify the purpose of the scale. Will the scale be used for research, selection, development, or another purpose? Is the scale intended for the general population, the population of adult workers, or another specific population? Outlining the scale's purpose and use in future contexts will allow one to identify the unique practical concerns related to the scale. This guides item creation in a number of ways, such as (1) determining an appropriate reading level for the target population; (2) identifying whether the items should refer to general or specific contexts and situations (work contexts); (3) considering differences in how respondents interpret the items (e.g., the meaning of the term *stress* in different national contexts); (4) deciding the type of scale response format and behavioral anchors, which can potentially affect scale responses; and (5) determining the applicability of reverse scoring, which may not be appropriate for positive constructs such as virtues.

Principles of Item Writing

When writing items, one aims to create an initial item pool that contains many more items than in the final scale (e.g., 3–4 times larger than in the final scale). This gives the researcher more freedom about the psychometric standard of the items that survive to the final scale. The initial redundancy and overinclusivity in the initial item pool is also desirable because it can serve to uncover subdimensions or closely related but distinct constructs. As for the actual writing of items, recommendations from a wide range of sources agree on the following principles: Items should be simple and straightforward; one should avoid slang, jargon, double negatives, ambiguous words, and overly abstract words and favor the use of specific

and concrete words; one should not use double-barreled items (i.e., two different ideas included in a single question); one should not use leading questions or statements (e.g., "Most supervisors are toxic. Please respond to how aggressive your supervisor has been to you"); and items should not be identical restatements but should seek to state the same idea in different ways. Finally, it is often helpful to provide the construct definition, relevant adjectives, and example scale items to item writers when generating items.

Scale Validation Research Design

As noted, validation is supremely important in the development of a self-report scale; in the measurement of unobservable variables, one cannot simply assume that a scale measures what it intends to. Such assumptions can lead to false scientific conclusions. Cronbach and Meehl suggest many ways in which scale validation can be conducted. Primary approaches include comparing group differences, assessing correlations with other measures, and examining the change in scale scores over repeated occasions. As mentioned, the specification of the nomological network will help a researcher determine the types of designs and measures to include. Group differences are appropriate when there is an expectation that measures should discriminate between groups (e.g., experts vs. nonexperts). On the other hand, establishing correlations with related constructs or criteria is important for assessing convergent–divergent validity and predictive validity. Furthermore, changes over time can help determine the reliability and stability of the operationalized construct. Where their use is possible, multitrait–multimethod designs are more informative than a single-method or single-trait approach to scale validation.

Regarding sampling, the preliminary sample size for examining psychometric properties of items is recommended to be 100–200, and a later confirmatory sample size should have a minimum of 300. However, this may depend on group differences and the type of analysis one seeks to conduct. Based on its theoretical and practical context, one should also seek to match the validation of the scale to its scale application. For instance, if a scale is meant for a work sample for entrepreneurs, it will be important to obtain a sample from the same subpopulation of interest. Notably, using a broader sample than the target subpopulation can artificially raise reliability of the scale. A recommended best practice is to cross-validate the scale across independent samples to show that scale properties are stable and generalizable.

Scale Psychometric Properties

After data collection, one needs to establish the reliability and validity of the scale items. At the first step, it is critical to identify a good set of items with reasonable psychometric properties. This is usually done by examining the mean, standard deviations, score range, endorsement proportions across all the options, and item–total correlation for each item. One should select items that have reasonable item–total correlations (around .20 or higher), appropriate score ranges (i.e., no ceiling or floor effects), and a utilization of different scale options.

Based on the selected items, there are different approaches for calculating reliability, but calculation of internal consistency is the most common. In general, the rule of thumb for internal consistency reliability is a minimum .70 although .90 or higher is recommended for high-stakes decisions (e.g., selection). One should also calculate the reliability of subdimensions of the construct.

It is important to distinguish reliability from dimensionality, as high reliability does not necessarily indicate unidimensionality. The number of dimensions should have been specified by theory and be confirmed by exploratory factor analysis (EFA). The number of latent factors or dimensions should equal the number of scales being developed. One may also seek to replicate the factor structures across different subpopulations to ensure the generalizability of the factor structure.

EFA loadings of items to specified dimensions should be moderate (around .4) to high (closer to 1.0), and one may choose to delete items that are inappropriately low on other dimensions or have low loadings. After theoretically based dimensionality is borne out in EFA, confirmatory factor analysis (CFA) should be conducted with a new sample, and the model should be evaluated using a number of fit indices. Although there are many fit indices that can be used, some of the most popular and useful are the comparative fit index (CFI), Tucker–Lewis index (TLI), root mean square error of approximation (RMSEA), and standardized root mean square residual (SRMR). General standards hold that the minimum standards of good fit for these metrics are CFI $\geq$ .90, TLI $\geq$ .90, RMSEA $\leq$ .08, SRMR $\leq$ .08.

After establishing reliability and factorial validity, a researcher would continue providing validation evidence by examining evidence based on the scale validation design. This may include examining group differences on scale scores or divergent and convergent validity based on other related measures. This involves examining how the new construct empirically relates to other constructs in its nomological network, and this overall process is a test of both the scale and the underlying theory driving the test.

Scale Revision

It is common to conduct several rounds of scale revision to improve on the initial items. There are several reasons for this, including poor reliability, divergence between theoretical and empirical structure, and inadequate construct representation. Revising a scale requires analyzing items with poor item–total correlations or low loadings to discern possible sources of poor item functioning. Where needed, one would also revise and write more items to tap into specific dimensions that were not adequately measured.

Louis Tay and Andrew T. Jebb

See also Construct; Factor Analysis; Measurement Scales; Nomological Networks; Reliability; Validity

Further Readings

Clark, L. A., & Watson, D. (1995). Constructing validity: Basic issues in objective scale development. *Psychological Assessment*, 7, 309–319.

Cronbach, L. J., & Meehl, P. E. (1955). Construct validity in psychological tests. *Psychological Bulletin*, 52, 281–302.

DeVellis, R. F. (2012). *Scale development: Theory and application*. Newbury Park, CA: Sage.

Drasgow, F., Nye, C. D., & Tay, L. (2010). Indicators of quality assessment. In J. C. Scott & D. H. Reynolds (Eds.), *Handbook of workplace* assessment: Evidence-based practices for selecting and developing organizational talent (pp. 27–60). San Francisco, CA: Wiley.

Hinkin, T. R. (1998). A brief tutorial on the development of measures for use in survey question questionnaires. Organizational Research Methods, 1, 104–121.

Messick, S. (1995). Validity of psychological assessment: Validation of inferences from persons' responses and performances as scientific inquiry into score meaning. American Psychologist, 50, 741–749.

Reise, S. P., Waller, N. G., & Comrey, A. L. (2000). Factor analysis and scale revision. Psychological Assessment, 12, 287–297.

Schwarz, N. (1999). Self-reports: How the questions shape the answer. American Psychologist, 54, 93–105.

Schwarz, N., Knauper, B., Hippler, H.-J., Noelle-Neumann, E., & Clark, L. (1991). Rating scales: Numeric values may change the meaning of scale labels. Public Opinion Quarterly, 55, 570–582.

Smith, G. T., & McCarthy, D. M. (1995). Methodological considerations in the refinement of clinical assessment instruments. Psychological Assessment, 7, 300–308.

SCALE DEVELOPMENT

See Scale Creation

SCIENTIFIC MANAGEMENT

Scientific management is the umbrella term for practice and research that advocates making organizations more efficient by systematically working to improve the efficiency of workers. The work of individuals associated with this movement, such as Frederick Winslow Taylor, Frank and Lillian Gilbreth, and Henry Gantt, lives on in the current management approaches of statistical process control and Total Quality Management. Because scientific management arose at the same time as the field of industrial and organizational (I-O) psychology—during the first decades of the 20th century—there was competition between the disciplines (as noted in critiques by Kurt Lewin, Charles Myers, and Morris Viteles). This entry approaches the scientific management school of thought from four points: (1) the genesis and growth of the

school, (2) the key concepts of scientific management, (3) the role of scientific management in shaping the history and trajectory of I-O psychology, and (4) the field's current status and importance in the world of work. Although Taylor's work often dominates the discussion of scientific management, the role of other researchers—especially the Gilbreths—should be acknowledged to avoid bias and to better show the linkages to I-O psychology.

Genesis and Growth of Scientific Management

Frederick Winslow Taylor is considered the founder and dominant figure in this school of thought, which is often referred to as Taylorism. Considered alongside his collaborators and contemporaries, Taylor looms large. Arthur Bedaeian and Daniel Wren, based on an order of merit ranking procedure, credited Taylor with the most influential management book of the 20th century, *Principles of Scientific Management,* although multiple books from the human relations movement make the list. Edwin Locke and others have provided flattering treatments. Taylor's treatment in his *Principles* viewed management as a systematic process and moved the field beyond the familial and craft leadership that was predominant in American industry. The scientific management approach offered stability in an era when traditional methods and assumptions were changing as a result of the confluence of progress, immigration, engineering, and education. Historian Robert Wiebe described the interval between 1877 and 1920 as a time in which many individuals and movements sought order in a country that was buffeted in a choppy sea of forces, such as industrialization and urbanization. The bureaucratic worldview coincided with a concept called *psychotechnology* in Europe.

Taylor blazed a trail as a consulting engineer and offered insights to industrialists and managers, much as Walter Dill Scott offered insights to advertising executives. After earning an engineering degree at Stevens Institute of Technology (site of the Taylor archives), he worked at the Midvale Steel Company, where he formulated his thinking. The expression of scientific management theory in *Shop Management* in 1903 and *Principles of Scientific Management* in 1911 earned Taylor widespread praise from factory owners but condemnation from trade unionists. Misunderstanding flourished on both sides. Taylor's biggest success was achieved at Bethlehem Steel, where his methods claimed to achieve a 200% increase in productivity after 2 years with only a 50% increase in wages. Careful historiographic research by Charles Wrege and his colleagues, however, shows problems with some of Taylor's claims about "Schmidt the laborer" (see Further Readings).

Key Concepts of Scientific Management

Taylor and his contemporaries advocated the study of the way workers perform tasks (most notably, time studies), collection of the informal job knowledge possessed by workers (i.e., knowledge management), and investigations aimed at improving the way tasks are performed in order to increase efficiency (defined as reductions in time). The next step is to convert the results of these studies into new methods of performing tasks with written, standardized work rules and operating procedures. Some attention is paid to the selection of workers so that they have the skills and abilities to match the needs of the task, and to training, so that workers can perform their tasks according to the established rules and procedures. Taylor also addressed the need to establish a fair or acceptable level of performance for each task and to develop a pay system that provides higher rewards for performance above the acceptable level.

Although the two approaches are often treated synonymously, Taylor's time studies were not the same as motion studies. Time studies do not include the discrete movements that the Gilbreths labeled "Therbligs" and included in their motion studies. Although there were later attempts to connect motion study to time study, Gilbreth pointed out that Taylor conducted no motion studies. The discipline of industrial engineering integrated the techniques of the early giants as codified in a 1956 handbook prepared by H. B. Maynard.

The key concepts of this paradigm include *soldiering* or restriction of output (at two levels), conducting time studies of workers to study and improve work processes, creating "functional foremen," cost accounting, and paying the person rather than the position. *Soldiering* is a term used

for workers completing no more than the amount of work that the informal work group enforces through social rules (i.e., no rate busting—rates are established and enforced by formal organizational work rules). A goal of scientific management is to find the most efficient rate and structure the work so that any and all minimally qualified workers can meet the established rate. Time-study rate systems are based on the fastest worker for each job in the organization. This worker's movements on the job are systematically examined, unnecessary movements eliminated, and a rate established for the job based on this time study. All workers are made accountable to the established rate.

The concept of the functional foremen was posited in opposition to the military management model, with supervision focusing on some aspect of work rather than the supervision (i.e., discipline) of people. Functional foremen were the forerunners of the production expediter and quality control or assurance clerk positions. Cost accounting is also known as task management, in which time clocks and time cards are the most salient feature and routing cards are used to track associated work products. Such a system allows the cost of labor per product to be tracked, archived, reported, and used for reward systems. Paying the person and not the position is the basis for pay-for-performance and per-piece rate pay systems.

Role of Scientific Management in Shaping I-O Psychology

The role of scientific management was a counterfoil to early I-O psychology, although it did provide a legacy of an objective, measurement-driven framework with an emphasis on the economic bottom line. Hugo Munsterberg, among others (such as Harold Burtt and Viteles), advocated fitting the worker to the work and focusing scientific methods on the appropriate design of each. The success of scientific management in some organizations provided the impetus in business for I-O psychologists to focus on field application versus basic laboratory science. The human relations movement and basic research findings in social psychology offered counterarguments to a strictly applied focus (e.g., scientific management principles) for the young field. Kurt Lewin's critique of Taylorism in 1920 argued that psychologists and efficiency experts should work together to make work both more productive and more satisfying. Steven Hunt's 2002 critique asked rhetorically whether organizational citizenship behaviors would detract from performance in Taylorist jobs—a question that may be countered, how many jobs are Taylorist?

Current Impact of Scientific Management

Current management disciplines, tools, and approaches influenced by the school of scientific management include statistical process control in production techniques, Total Quality Management methods, program evaluation and review technique charting methods, the critical path method, benchmarking, and business process redesign. Workforces within U.S. government entities (e.g., military, bureaucracies) continue *not* to be influenced by scientific management, and little progress in this direction is anticipated in the future.

Scott A. Davies and James T. Austin

See also Hawthorne Studies/Hawthorne Effect; History of Industrial and Organizational Psychology in North America; Human Relations Movement

Further Readings

Hunt, S. T. (2002). On the virtues of staying "inside of the box": Does organizational citizenship behavior detract from performance in Taylorist jobs? *International Journal of Selection and Assessment, 10*, 152–159.

Kanigel, R. (2005). *The one best way: Frederick Winslow Taylor and the enigma of efficiency*. Cambridge, MA: MIT Press.

Maynard, H. B. (Ed.). (1956). *Industrial engineering handbook*. New York, NY: McGraw-Hill.

Taylor, F. W. (1911). *Principles of scientific management*. New York, NY: Harper & Brothers.

Wiebe, R. (1967). *The search for order, 1877–1920* (Reprint ed.). Westport, CT: Greenwood Press.

Wrege, C. D., & Hodgetts, R. M. (2000). Frederick W. Taylor's 1899 pig iron observations: Examining fact, fiction, and lessons for the new millennium. *Academy of Management Journal, 43*, 1283–1291.

SCIENTIST–PRACTITIONER MODEL

The scientist–practitioner model casts psychologists in two separate but overlapping lights: practitioners, or working professionals who apply scientific knowledge, and scientists, or students and researchers whose professional role is to generate new scientific knowledge and refine the old. Each has a keen need and respect for the other. The scientist–practitioner model has become an aspirational goal for psychologists, and a prescription for how psychologists should be trained.

Its origins can be traced to the end of World War II, when the Veterans Administration (VA) and the United States Public Health Service (USPHS) encouraged the training of mental health professionals to work with returning veterans. At the same time, and in unprecedented numbers, students were seeking graduate education in psychology to meet this need. This put an unexpected strain on the small number of psychology departments that had been training clinical psychologists up to this point. Throughout the 1940s, small working groups within the American Association for Applied Psychology (AAAP), primarily under the direction of David Shakow, began to address these issues and develop outlines for doctorate-level training programs in clinical psychology. Early drafts recommended that students first gain a solid grounding in scientific psychology, followed later by coursework and internships in more applied practice skills. The hope was to upgrade the skills of future clinical psychologists as well as the reputation of psychology.

The AAAP later merged with the American Psychological Association (APA), and with encouragement from the VA and the USPHS, a committee was formed to address the training of psychologists, including standards for educational institutions. This committee visited doctoral training institutions to accredit those that met the standards. To address many remaining concerns, a conference was held during the summer of 1949, during which 73 psychologists and key stakeholders from the VA and USPHS gathered in Boulder, Colorado. By the end of the meeting, several resolutions had been adopted that defined psychologists as people who are trained in both scientific research and practice.

The conference had another lasting impact: Programs that adhere to the scientist–practitioner model are often identified as "Boulder model" programs. Even today, the APA accreditation standards insist that training programs reflect the principle that the practice of psychology is based on the science of psychology; in turn, the practice of psychology influences the science of psychology.

Although the Boulder conference primarily focused on clinical training, the scientist–practitioner model soon found its way into other applied areas. When the Industrial and Business Section of the AAAP became Division 14 of APA, its first two goals were to (1) ensure high standards of practice and (2) promote research and publication in the field. Many years later, when Division 14 incorporated to become the Society for Industrial and Organizational Psychology, its mission statement prominently included promoting both the science and the practice of industrial and organizational psychology. The guidelines for education and training at the doctoral level were further refined to focus on producing students who could be both generators of knowledge and consumers of knowledge. To this end, most, if not all, doctoral students in industrial and organizational psychology take coursework in research design and statistics, in addition to classes in specific industrial and organizational topics, and their program of study culminates with a significant research project, the dissertation.

The scientist–practitioner model, though pervasive, is not universally accepted as either a standard for training or a description of the activities of most psychologists. In more recent years, it has been argued that the original intention of the Boulder conferences was to provide a road map to diversifying training programs under the scientist–practitioner guideline rather than to create an expectation of conformity to a single model. After all, some graduates of psychology programs believe training overemphasizes research at the expense of practice. As a consequence, a 1973 conference in Vail, Colorado, led to the development of an alternative: the scholar–professional model. In this view, psychologists are highly trained practitioners who are consumers of research rather than generators. Programs that adopt the Vail model often grant a PsyD degree in lieu of a PhD. Future developments in the training of doctoral students may therefore yield similar divergences, such as the rise of multistrategy and interdisciplinary programs, while still incorporating the scientist–practitioner ideal as an inspiration or a basis for comparison.

Miles Moffit and William D. Siegfried

See also American Psychological Association, Association for Psychological Science; Society for Industrial and Organizational Psychology

Further Readings

Baker, D. B., & Benjamin, L. T. (2000). The affirmation of the scientist–practitioner: A look back at Boulder. *American Psychologist, 55*(2), 241–247.

Ellis, H. C. (1992). Graduate education in psychology: Past, present, and future. *American Psychologist, 47*(4), 570–576.

Society for Industrial and Organizational Psychology. (1999). *Guidelines for education and training at the doctoral level in industrial/organizational psychology.* Retrieved from http://www.siop.org/phdguidelines98.aspx

SELECTION: OCCUPATIONAL TAILORING

The most effective and appropriate selection procedures vary for different types of work and in different types of organizations. Two major considerations should guide this occupational tailoring. The first consideration is the work behavior of the people hired: What is required by the work itself, and what work-related outcomes does the organization want to achieve with the selection procedures? This consideration addresses the effectiveness of the selection procedure at bringing about desired work behaviors. The second consideration is the fit of the selection procedures with other human resource (HR) processes and systems and with the organization's culture. This consideration addresses the extent to which selection procedures complement existing HR processes and systems and are consistent with the organization's culture when it comes to the treatment of job candidates and employees.

These two considerations are often separate and independent. For example, highly technical work usually implies selection procedures that gauge acquired technical knowledge through degree and grade point average requirements and job knowledge assessment. In contrast, an organization may have a culture and recruiting strategy that emphasizes close recruiting relationships with selected technical schools and relies on faculty referrals to identify technically skilled candidates. In such a setting, a job knowledge test may be an inappropriate selection procedure even if it is the most effective procedure for ensuring that the organization hires candidates with the required level of technical skill. The tailoring of selection procedures requires a careful evaluation of both sets of considerations. (Note: This entry does not address legal risk factors because, as important as these factors are in designing selection programs, they are not usually associated with type of occupation.)

Considerations of Work Behavior

The evaluation of work behavior should begin with a consideration of the work behavior outcomes that the organization wants to achieve with the selection procedure. The organization's desired work outcomes may have a direct bearing on the information about the work that is relevant to the choice of selection procedures. Continuing the example of highly technical work, if an organization is satisfied with the technical expertise of its new hires but wants to select more loyal employees who will stay with the company, the analysis of the work would focus less on technical content and more on work context that influences employees' decisions to leave or stay.

Organizations may have any number of desired outcomes, including productivity, helpfulness, schedule adherence, retention, customer satisfaction, accountability, creativity, safety and security, and dependability. In general, the organization's desired outcomes can be organized into two major categories: work proficiency and contextual behavior. *Work proficiency* refers to the extent to which employees perform their work tasks quickly, accurately, and consistently and achieve the desired objectives of the work activity. *Contextual behavior*, on the other hand, refers to employee behavior that is valued by the organization but is not considered a specific task or element of the work itself. Examples include helping others, staying in the

organization, showing up on time, not stealing, and being accountable for results.

The distinction between an organization's interest in work proficiency and its interest in contextual behavior is important to occupational tailoring because, with few exceptions, any single selection procedure is likely to be more relevant to one type of interest than the other. To understand the relationship between selection procedures and organization interests, selection procedures may be classified into five major categories: (1) ability and aptitude; (2) personality, disposition, and temperament; (3) values, interests, and attitudes; (4) acquired skills and knowledge; and (5) work-related experience, training, and education.

Contextual Behavior

In organizations that place high value on contextual behavior, the selection procedures that are most likely to help create these outcomes assess personality, disposition, and temperament (Category 2) and values, interests, and attitudes (Category 3). The particular attributes that are most likely to create the desired outcome may be understood through an evaluation of the context surrounding the work and the organization. For example, staying in a customer service job with significant time pressure, highly repetitive volume, and rule-bound job procedures may require personality attributes associated with resilience and dependability. In contrast, staying in a sales job that requires many self-initiated customer contacts with a high percentage of negative outcomes but with significant payoffs for positive outcomes may require high levels of achievement orientation and independence. In general, with the exception of conscientiousness, the effectiveness of attributes in Categories 2 and 3 depends on the specific contextual features of the work. Conscientiousness is the personality attribute with the broadest range of positive consequences for contextual behavior across many types of work.

An important contextual consideration is the extent to which the work situation is a strong determiner of employee work behavior. When the work context is strong, there is less opportunity for personal interests, values, dispositions, and motives to influence work behavior, at least within the range of ordinarily acceptable behavior. For example, telemarketing work often requires that employees adhere to carefully worded scripts, spend closely monitored amounts of time on calls, and leave their desks at prescribed times and durations. Under such strong conditions, attributes such as creativity are unlikely to have much impact on demonstrated work behavior. In general, in order for selection procedures in Categories 2 and 3 to affect desired contextual behaviors, the work situation must be weak enough to allow the targeted attributes to influence employees' behavior. The implication for occupational tailoring is that selection procedures that influence contextual behavior are likely to be more effective in weak job situations than in strong job situations.

Work Proficiency

In organizations that emphasize the importance of work proficiency, the most effective selection procedures assess some combination of ability and aptitude (Category 1); acquired skills and knowledge (Category 4); and work-related experience, training, and education (Category 5). In this case, a thorough analysis of the work content may be necessary to identify the particular selection procedures that are most likely to be effective.

A major consideration in the maximization of work proficiency is that some relevant attributes are highly work specific, such as acquired skills and knowledge (Category 4) and physical and psychomotor abilities (a subset of Category 1), whereas the relevance of general mental ability (GMA, a subset of Category 1) is not work specific but is effective at maximizing proficiency across a wide range of types of work. One of the most well-established results in industrial and organizational psychology is that GMA is an important determiner of work proficiency across virtually all types of work. Only the cognitive complexity of the work has much influence on the effectiveness of GMA. The more complex the work, the more effectively GMA enables work proficiency.

An analysis of work content should indicate the extent to which work-specific acquired skills and knowledge are required for early work proficiency. Where early work proficiency is important, some component of the selection procedure should evaluate the important acquired skills

and knowledge. Almost always, these selection procedures should be tailored to the work. The same is true for work requirements relating to physical and psychomotor abilities. An appropriate analysis of the work content should identify the specific physical or psychomotor abilities required for work proficiency.

In the design of selection procedures intended to maximize work proficiency, a major decision point is whether GMA assessments will be used and, if so, whether tailoring the GMA assessment will have any benefit for the effectiveness of the selection procedure. To be sure, there is a wide variety of mental ability tests ranging from the most general, measuring abstract reasoning, complex problem solving, and mechanical aptitude, to the most specific, measuring arithmetic facility, clerical coding speed, and spelling and vocabulary. Whatever combination of GMA procedures is used for whatever type of work, the most effective GMA-based selection procedures assess a broader composite of mental abilities. This can be achieved by assessing one or two general abilities (such as abstract reasoning or problem solving) or by assessing three or four narrow mental abilities and relying on a composite of those narrow assessments. Often, the tailoring decision is based on the organization's interest in having the selection procedure appear reasonable and job-relevant to candidates.

Overlap Between Work Proficiency and Contextual Behavior

The overlap between considerations of contextual behavior and work proficiency should be evaluated. When successful work proficiency and desired contextual behavior have the same underlying determinants, the same selection procedure may be effective at achieving both purposes. For example, an organization's interest in minimizing turnover may be addressed by the use of a selection procedure designed to maximize work proficiency if the primary cause of turnover is poor work proficiency. However, other than the broadly beneficial effects of conscientiousness, the attributes that are most likely to affect contextual behavior tend to be different from the attributes that are most likely to affect work proficiency.

Considerations of Organization Fit

In addition to considerations of the work itself, appropriate selection procedures should be tailored to fit two aspects of the organization: (1) existing HR processes and systems and (2) the organization's culture relating to the treatment of job candidates and employees.

Existing HR Processes and Systems

Training and recruiting processes are closely connected to selection processes. A recruiting process that sources candidates only with certain attributes, such as particular degrees or grade point averages, minimizes the need for a selection process designed to assess precisely the same attributes. In general, it is unnecessarily inefficient for both recruiting processes and selection processes to target the same attributes among candidates.

New hire training processes rely on new hires having certain sets of attributes. For example, training may assume some amount of preexisting job knowledge or job experience. Selection procedures should be tailored to be consistent with the assumptions made by the new hire training process. Of course, optimal planning would consider both together and determine the most cost-effective manner for the organization to achieve the level of acquired skills and knowledge among new hires. In general, training is likely to be more expensive per new hire than selection. This tends to produce HR strategies that maximize the scope of selection to minimize the cost of training. However, organizations that have unique requirements for acquired skills and knowledge, such as a product line that is unique to the industry, may find that selection procedures are simply not cost-effective when the target skill or knowledge is rare. In this case, training may take on the role of developing the needed, but rare, skills and knowledge.

Organizational Culture

Finally, some attention should be paid to a frequently overlooked consideration in the tailoring of selection procedures. Many organizations have strong cultures relating to the treatment of employees and job candidates. The design of selection procedures should carefully consider the imperatives of the organization's culture. For example, an organization may place very high value on enabling employees to realize job progression through successful job performance. In such an environment, a selection procedure that governs employee progression and assesses the personal attributes, abilities, or skills and knowledge related to successful performance may not be consistent with a culture that values demonstrated work performance as the key to progression. Other cultures, such as highly entrepreneurial, risk-seeking environments, may have a built-in disdain for standardized practices associated with selection procedures, particularly testing. In such environments, selection procedures are sustainable only if they do not significantly inhibit the self-reliance of hiring managers. In general, professional, standardized selection procedures represent a strong subculture for making crucial people decisions. They should be tailored to match the overarching organizational culture that shapes other HR processes and systems.

Jerard F. Kehoe

See also Employee Selection; Selection Strategies

Further Readings

Campbell, W. J., & Ramos, R. A. (2010). Blue-collar selection in private sector organizations. In J. L. Farr & N. T. Tippins (Eds.), *Handbook of employee selection* (pp. 741–764). New York, NY: Routledge.

Hausknecht, J. P., & Langevin, A. M. (2010). Selection for service and sales jobs. In J. L. Farr & N. T. Tippins (Eds.), *Handbook of employee selection* (pp. 765–780). New York, NY: Routledge.

Jacobs, R., & Denning, D. L. (2010). Public sector employment. In J. L. Farr & N. T. Tippins (Eds.), *Handbook of employee selection* (pp. 705–720). New York, NY: Routledge.

Kehoe, J. F., Brown, S., & Hoffman, C. C. (2012). The life cycle of successful selection programs. In N. Schmitt (Ed.), *The Oxford handbook of personnel selection and assessment* (pp. 903–938). Oxford, UK: Oxford University Press.

Kehoe, J. F., Mol, S. T., & Anderson, N. R. (2010). Managing sustainable selection systems. In J. L. Farr & N. T. Tippins (Eds.), *Handbook of employee selection* (pp. 213–234). New York, NY: Routledge.

Tippins, N. (2002). Issues in implementing large-scale selection programs. In J. W. Hedge & E. D. Pulakos

(Eds.), *Implementing organizational interventions: Steps, processes, and best practices* (pp. 232–269). San Francisco, CA: Jossey-Bass.

Tippins, N. T., Papinchock, J. M., & Solberg, E. C. (2010). Decisions in developing and selecting selection tools. In J. L. Farr & N. T. Tippins (Eds.), *Handbook of employee selection* (pp. 363–376). New York, NY: Routledge.

SELECTION STRATEGIES

Selection and Assessment Consulting

Selection strategies differ from organization to organization in a number of ways. Some rely mostly on tests, others on interviews. Some are computer or Web based, others paper-and-pencil tests. Some automatically select candidates out, whereas others inform decisions that select candidates in—and so on. Selection strategies are the result of many design decisions, and it is safe to say that no two strategies are the same.

The purpose of this entry is to describe different selection strategies and evaluate the effectiveness of those strategies in different employment situations. These descriptions and evaluations will be limited to the manner in which information from the selection procedures is used to make selection decisions. This entry will not address strategies relating to delivery methods or types of assessment procedures. Rather, the focus will be on describing and evaluating the different strategies that organizations use to make selection decisions.

Framework

This entry is organized into two major sections. The first section will identify and describe the most common types of selection decision-making strategies. This section is primarily descriptive and highlights key differences among the strategies. The second section will evaluate these strategies based on their fit with each of several types of employment context. The employment context is defined based on three considerations: (1) employment volume (high or low), (2) mode of employment processing (continuous or episodic), and (3) the organization's culture for accountability (systems accountability or manager accountability). The decision-making strategies will be evaluated based on their fit with each of the eight combinations of volume, mode, and accountability. Although this approach is somewhat artificial—actual employment contexts are not likely to be exact combinations of volume, mode, and accountability—it has the advantage of being systematic and reveals key principles that can be applied to any employment context.

This entry will not evaluate strategies based on considerations of legal risk. Certainly, legal risk is an important consideration in the design of any selection strategy. The primary means of controlling legal risk are (a) the documentation of validation evidence and (b) various methods of minimizing adverse impact. Although legal considerations certainly influence decision-making strategies, legal risk often depends on subtle and nuanced aspects of the situation, the organization, and the particular risk, making it difficult to offer general guidelines beyond the considerations of validity, adverse impact, and consistency of application, which may be applied to any decision-making strategy.

Selection Decision-Making Strategies

Some of the strategies described here are typically mutually exclusive, such as multiple hurdles and compensatory scoring, whereas others are not, such as compensatory scoring and profile matching. The descriptions offered here summarize the relationships among the most commonly used strategies. The first two strategies, *multiple hurdles* and *compensatory scoring*, are typically viewed as mutually exclusive, although hybrid strategies are beginning to emerge. The third and fourth strategies, *cut scores* and non-cut-score-based *judgment methods*, are deliberately defined as mutually exclusive to clarify their most important differences. The fifth strategy, *banding*, is a class of methods introduced primarily to manage legal risk in certain types of situations but not equally applicable in all employment contexts.

Multiple Hurdles

A major consideration in designing a selection strategy is the cost-effective management of candidate flow. One common approach to this issue is the strategy of multiple hurdles. According to this strategy, selection procedures are administered in sequential steps. After each selection procedure is administered, it is scored. At each step, candidates whose scores fall below an established threshold are eliminated. Candidates who are not eliminated proceed to the next step, where the next selection procedure is administered and scored and additional candidates are eliminated.

Two methods of multiple hurdles can be considered. The first and most common method, the *independent method*, eliminates candidates based only on scores from the selection procedure administered at the current step in the series. The second method, the *accumulative method*, eliminates candidates at each step based on scores from all of the previously administered procedures and the current procedure. For example, consider a multiple hurdles strategy in which Step 1 is a problem-solving test, Step 2 is a work sample exercise, and Step 3 is an employment office interview. At Step 2, the independent method would eliminate candidates based solely on scores from the work sample exercise, whereas the accumulative method would eliminate candidates based on some combination of both the problem-solving score and the work sample score.

The primary advantage of the multiple hurdles strategy is that it minimizes administration cost and time by not administering additional selection procedures to candidates who performed relatively poorly on earlier procedures. Typically, this advantage is maximized by administering the selection procedures in order of cost from lowest to highest. Its primary disadvantage is that it sacrifices some amount of predictive accuracy at each decision step by considering information from only some (usually one) of the selection procedures that the organization views as relevant to the job. The accumulative method mitigates this disadvantage somewhat.

Compensatory Scoring

When organizations prefer to maximize the predictive power of each selection decision, all candidates are administered a common set of selection procedures. A composite score is then created for each candidate that combines information from the entire set of selection procedures.

This composite score is then used in some decision method to select among the candidates.

In virtually all applications of compensatory scoring, only one composite of selection procedures is used as the basis for making selection decisions. This common practice reflects an assumption that there is only one model or type of successful employee. All selection decisions seek to choose employees who fit that particular model of success. In contrast, some organizations recognize that different employees are successful and valued in different ways. Some employees may be successful because they are accurate and fast producers; others may be successful because they are able to engage others in achieving objectives. Still others may be successful because they are reliable employees who show up every day, perform well enough, and are loyal to the organization. An organization that values different models of success may prefer to use more than one composite of the same predictors and choose candidates who are predicted to be successful by at least one of the valued models. Little research has examined this possibility of simultaneous, separate composites to determine how much gain could be realized compared with the standard practice of a single, presumably optimal composite.

Compared with multiple hurdles, compensatory scoring is more expensive but has somewhat more predictive accuracy. There is no general conclusion about the actual trade-off between cost and accuracy. This trade-off depends on the actual costs and predictive validities of each of the selection procedures. However, it is common for cost differences between types of selection procedures to be very large, sometimes 500% to 1,000%, though the incremental accuracy that the second procedure adds to the first is often slight, say 10%. Of course, a 10% increase in predictive accuracy may actually have more dollar value than the cost of administering the second procedure to all candidates.

Cut Scores

The use of cut scores can be combined with any of the other strategies described here. In fact, some strategies, such as multiple hurdles and banding, invariably rely on cut scores as part of the decision-making process. However, it is useful to describe cut scores as a distinct strategy, perhaps a substrategy, and to provide information about specific methods for determining and using them.

A cut score is a particular score on a selection procedure or composite of selection procedures that serves as a threshold value for determining which candidates are excluded or included. There is no law or professional standard that requires cut scores to be either low or high. Generally, courts and professional standards acknowledge that the hiring organization may consider a variety of factors, including expected work proficiency, cost of employment, labor market conditions, and efforts to avoid discriminatory employment practices, in determining a cut score that optimizes the organization's value for its new hires.

Because many factors may influence cut scores, there are many methods for setting cut scores. Some methods rely primarily on the judgment of experts, whereas other methods rely on quantitative analyses of desired outcomes. Some methods focus on the probability that hired candidates will be successful employees, whereas other methods focus on the probability that people who will be successful employees will be hired. In any case, no cut score can be set without some form of value judgment being made on behalf of the organization. All cut scores rely on some judgment about the outcomes the organization values and desires from its selection strategy.

More than one cut score may be used to enable selection decisions. In the simplest decision process, a single cut score is used to determine that candidates who score at or above the cut score will be hired. More complex decision processes may use multiple cut scores to create ranges of scores that distinguish the most qualified candidates from the next most qualified, and so on. In all cases, a cut score defines a boundary line between candidates who are treated in different ways.

The primary advantage of cut scores is that they simplify the selection decision process. The primary disadvantage is that the use of cut scores ignores potentially useful information both above and below the cut score. For example, by relying on a single cut score set at the 75th percentile of candidate scores, the organization treats the highest-scoring candidates the same as candidates scoring at the 75th percentile. Both are hired. This process can be disadvantageous to the organization

if it only needs to hire a small percentage of the candidates. For example, suppose an organization only needs to hire 5% of the available candidates but has adopted a cut score that 25% of the candidates satisfy. In this situation, the organization is losing value from its selection strategy because the cut score does not allow it to choose just the top 5% of all candidates. Of course, in such a case, the organization may change the cut score to be closer to the 95th percentile so that it does not lose useful information.

Judgment Methods

For convenience, the term *judgment methods* is used to refer to methods of making selection decisions that are not based on cut scores to determine automatic decisions. Judgment methods include all methods for using quantitative information from the selection procedures to inform the judgment of the person making the hiring decision. Certainly, there are innumerable such methods. The two most common types of judgment methods will be described here: expectancy methods and profile-matching methods.

Expectancy methods convert the score results from the selection procedures into quantitative predictions or expectations about outcomes of interest to the organization. This conversion requires quantitative analysis that relates the scores on the selection procedures to scores on outcome measures. One method, *probability of success*, converts each selection procedure score into a probability of success. This, of course, requires the organization to define what level of outcome result corresponds to success and to provide a measure of this outcome in some study sample of employees that can be used to define the conversion. For example, suppose the organization is interested in making selection decisions to minimize the number of new hires who leave during the first 12 months. Success is defined as staying on the job for 12 months or longer. To convert scores on the selection procedure into a probability of staying for 12 months or longer, retention would need to be tracked for candidates who had taken part in the selection procedures in question. Based on an analysis of the results of such a study, for each candidate, the person making the hiring decision would be provided with a measure of the probability that the candidate will stay for 12 months or longer, as predicted by the selection procedure. The decision maker could then make an informed hiring decision based on this information and whatever other information might be available about the candidate.

Similarly, another expectancy method, *predicted performance*, provides predicted levels of performance rather than probability of success. The same types of data and analyses are required to produce this type of information, although it is no longer necessary for the organization to define success.

A second judgment method, *profile matching*, provides a different type of quantitative information to the person making the hiring decision. According to this method, the information describes the extent to which the candidate's selection procedure scores are similar to the selection procedure scores of people who have demonstrated success on the job.

Consider a sales organization, for example. Suppose this organization is implementing new selection procedures to assess achievement orientation, independence, intelligence, sociability, and integrity. As part of the study of this new process, the organization administers selection procedures to its current salespeople. Suppose that the top sellers are different from average sellers on achievement orientation, independence, and intelligence but no different on sociability and integrity. In addition, top sellers score very high on achievement orientation, moderately on independence, and moderately high on intelligence. This profile of a top seller becomes the ideal pattern of scores on these three selection procedures and distinguishes top sellers from average sellers. Each new candidate's profile of achievement orientation, independence, and intelligence scores is compared with this ideal profile. In some fashion, usually graphically or quantitatively, the decision maker is shown the extent to which each candidate's score profile is similar to the ideal profile. Like expectancy methods, the profile method provides quantitative information to decision makers as the basis for making a hiring decision but generally does not trigger any automatic decision.

Banding Methods

During the early 1990s, banding methods were introduced as a technique for selecting candidates so as to equalize the hiring rates among different groups of candidates. Although these methods were designed to minimize group selection rate differences, they also have broader applications. Banding methods all separate the full range of scores on the selection procedure of interest into several bands. The essential feature of banding is that each band of scores is defined as a range within which the organization is indifferent to the highest- and lowest-scoring candidates. Some banding methods define the indifference bands based on the reliability of differences between scores on the selection procedure; other methods define the indifference bands based on differences between predicted outcomes. Regardless of the method used to define the bands, the selection decisions are made by first considering the candidates in the top band, choosing among them, and, if any vacancies remain, moving to the next highest band and repeating the process until all vacancies are filled.

The primary advantage of banding methods is that they provide an explicit definition of the organization's indifference to the highest- and lowest-scoring candidates within a band. This enables organizations to base selection decisions on other considerations because they can be confident that candidates within bands are similarly qualified with respect to the attributes assessed by the selection procedures. The primary disadvantage of banding is that it is most effectively applied only when the whole set of candidates is known before any selection decisions are made.

Evaluation of Strategies

Eight employment contexts are listed in Table 1. For each context, the selection strategies most likely to fit with the demands of that context are shown, as well as the most significant considerations in choosing among the selection strategies. This evaluation is presented in a table format for ease of comparison and use.

The distinction between high and low volume is not based on absolute numbers of vacancies or candidates. Rather, high volume exists when the number of candidates or vacancies to be filled stretches the capacity of the existing employment process.

Mode of employment refers to the continuity of recruiting and screening processes. Continuous-mode operations manage ongoing recruiting to

Table 1 The Fit Between Employment Contexts and Selection Strategies

Employment Context			Good-Fitting Strategies
			Preferred strategies
Volume	*Mode*	*Accountability*	*Primary considerations*

High	Continuous	Systems	• Multiple hurdles
			  o Cut scores
			  o Minimized potential for high costs
			  o Rapid, automatic decisions

High	Continuous	Manager	• Compensatory scoring
			• Early-stage cut scores
			• Late-stage judgment methods
			  o Reduce volume to managers
			  o Tolerate potential for high costs
			  o Enable managers' rapid decisions and reduce workload

High	Episodic	Systems	• Banding
			• Cut scores
			• Compensatory scoring
			  o Higher risk of scrutiny
			  o Tolerance of higher costs
			  o Explicit decisions
			  o Rapid, automatic decisions
			  o Automatic control of group selection rates

High	Episodic	Manager	• Compensatory scoring
			• Early-stage cut scores
			• Late-stage judgment methods
			  o Reduce volume to managers
			  o Tolerate potential for high costs
			  o Enable managers' rapid decisions

Low	Continuous	Systems	• Compensatory scoring
			• Banding with systematized decision rules and small number of bands (two or three)
			• Cut scores at early stage, representing minimum qualifications
			  o Little potential for high cost, so maximum predictive accuracy
			  o Automated decision rules (banding) using complete information

Low	Continuous	Manager	• Compensatory scoring
			• Cut scores at early stage, representing minimum qualifications
			  o Little potential for high cost, so maximum predictive accuracy
			  o Exclude the least competitive candidates to reduce manager workload

Low	Episodic	Systems	• Cut scores
			• Compensatory scoring
			  o Automatic decisions
			  o Little potential for high cost, so maximum predictive accuracy

Low	Episodic	Manager	• Compensatory scoring
			• Judgment methods
			  o Little potential for high cost, so maximum predictive accuracy
			  o Enable manager's effective use of complete selection information

maintain an available pool of candidates to be ready when vacancies occur or to support continuous vacancies. Continuous employment processes include processes that are modulated from time to time but maintain ongoing recruiting and screening processes. A common example of continuous employment is the process used by retail sales organizations that need to maintain fully staffed sales clerk positions in the face of typically high turnover rates. In contrast, episodic employment processes stop and start over time. Typically, they start when a batch of new vacancies is to be filled or a batch of new candidates is to be recruited. Once the batch of vacancies or candidates is completed, the process stops. A common example of episodic employment is public-sector employment for police and firefighter jobs, which are frequently managed as periodic episodes of employment.

The culture for accountability is perhaps the least well-prescribed context feature. It refers to the organization's tendency to place high accountability on either its systems or its managers, especially with regard to human resource processes and systems. For example, some organizations manage annual performance management and compensation processes largely as a matter of inputting performance results into a system and then following that system's rubrics for performance assessment and compensation decisions. In contrast, other organizations rely entirely on managers to make performance management decisions and compensation decisions with little, if any, systematic structure or guidelines.

Jerard F. Kehoe

See also Employee Selection; Executive Selection; Prescreening Assessment Methods for Personnel Selection; Selection: Occupational Tailoring; Uniform Guidelines on Employee Selection

Further Readings

Aguinis, H. (Ed.). (2004). *Test score banding in human resource selection.* Westport, CT: Praeger.

Kehoe, J. F., Brown, S., & Hoffman, C. C. (2012). The life cycle of successful selection programs. In N. Schmitt (Ed.), *The Oxford handbook of personnel selection and assessment* (pp. 903–938). Oxford, UK: Oxford University Press.

Kehoe, J. F., Mol, S. T., & Anderson, N. R. (2010). Managing sustainable selection systems. In J. L. Farr & N. T. Tippins (Eds.), *Handbook of employee selection* (pp. 213–234). New York, NY: Routledge.

Kehoe, J. F., & Olson, A. (2005). Cut scores and employment discrimination litigation. In F. J. Landy (Ed.), *Employment discrimination litigation: Behavioral, quantitative, and legal perspectives* (pp. 410–449). San Francisco, CA: Jossey-Bass.

Reynolds, D. H., & Dickter, D. N. (2010). Technology and employee selection. In J. L. Farr & N. T. Tippins (Eds.), *Handbook of employee selection* (pp. 171–194). New York, NY: Routledge.

Schmitt, N., & Borman, W. C. (Eds.). (1993). *Personnel selection in organizations.* San Francisco, CA: Jossey-Bass.

Tippins, N. T. (2002). Issues in implementing large-scale selection programs. In J. W. Hedge & E. D. Pulakos (Eds.), *Implementing organizational interventions: Steps, processes, and best practices* (pp. 232–269). San Francisco, CA: Jossey-Bass.

Tippins, N. T. (2012). Implementation issues in employee selection testing. In N. Schmitt (Ed.), *The Oxford handbook of personnel selection and assessment* (pp. 881–902). Oxford, UK: Oxford University Press.

Tippins, N. T., Papinchock, J. M., & Solberg, E. C. (2010). Decisions in developing and selecting selection tools. In J. L. Farr & N. T. Tippins (Eds.), *Handbook of employee selection* (pp. 363–376). New York, NY: Routledge.

Wunder, R. S., Thomas, L. L., & Luo, Z. (2010). Administering assessments and decision-making. In J. L. Farr & N. T. Tippins (Eds.), *Handbook of employee selection* (pp. 377–398). New York, NY: Routledge.

SELF-CONCEPT THEORY OF WORK MOTIVATION

The study of work motivation centers on why employees initiate, terminate, or persist in specific work behaviors in organizations. Most traditional theories of work motivation are built on the premise that individuals act in ways that maximize the value of exchange with the organization. However, the nature of an individual's work motivation may also involve an internal, individually rooted need or motive—for example, to enhance one's self-esteem, to achieve, or to affiliate. These motives are assumed to be part of the unique, internal core of a person's self-concept.

Structure of Self-Concept

Current theories purport that the self-concept is a multidimensional knowledge structure that helps individuals organize and give meaning to memory and behavior. Indeed, psychologists have argued that attaching an object or event to the self gives it special meaning (e.g., *my* car vs. *a* car). The self-concept may be seen as consisting of attributes related to individual self-perception, including traits, competencies, and values. For example, individuals may use trait terms such as *ambitious* and *dependable* to describe their essential character or hold perceptions of the competencies they possess (e.g., "I am a good leader"). It has been argued that the self-concept is multifaceted and that the influence of specific facets depends on their activation.

Because of its size and limitations in human cognition, only a small portion of the self-concept is salient at any given moment. The term *working self-concept* (WSC) is used to reflect the highly activated, contextually sensitive portion of the self-concept that guides action and information processing on a moment-to-moment basis. The activation of the components of the self is dependent on the cues in one's current context. For example, one's self-concept may include several roles, such as being a parent, a spouse, and an employee. These alternative self-concepts are associated with different social contexts and become activated when the right social cues are present. As well, threats to the self and shifts in temporal focus can alter the activation of the self-concept.

The WSC can be viewed as consisting of three components: *self-views*, or one's perceived standing on salient attributes, and two types of comparative standards—*current goals*, which are short-term and narrowly focused, and *possible selves*, which are long-term and future focused and provide much broader comparative standards. These three components combine to create control systems that regulate motivation. Furthermore, a control system may involve any two of the three components so that one component provides the standard and the other the source of feedback. Researchers have proposed that combinations of the three components

have very different motivational consequences on work behavior.

Finally, the self-concept also has different focal levels composed of personal and social identities. Personal identity refers to self-categorization based on comparisons to others that emphasize one's own uniqueness. Social identity is based on self-definition through relations with others or through group membership, and thus it emphasizes one's similarities and connectedness. These identities are active at different times, creating a personal WSC or, alternatively, a social WSC.

Relationship Between Self-Concept and Work Motivation

The self-concept is a source of work motivation in that individuals are motivated to maintain and enhance an internalized view of the self. Specifically, the meaning that individuals attribute to information is often a function of the strength of their self-perceptions and their need to affirm their self-concept. In an organizational setting, employees make choices among behavioral alternatives, set and accept work goals, take on projects, and generally direct effort toward obtaining task and social feedback that is consistent with their self-concept. In addition, when there is conflict between the self-concept and social or task feedback, employees may engage in a number of adaptive strategies to achieve congruence between their self-concept and performance feedback (e.g., increasing effort, changing feedback).

Whether work goals are tied to current self-views or possible self-views has important implications for work motivation. When work goals are tied to current self-views, more proximal motivation mechanisms may be engaged, creating an overriding performance orientation that accentuates self-enhancement. Alternatively, when work goals are connected to possible selves, more distal motivational processes predominate that are rooted in the need for uncertainty reduction and consistency and the ability to predict and control the environment.

Possible selves normally reflect ideals toward which individuals strive, but they can also represent feared selves that individuals attempt to avoid. The contribution of these two motivational components changes with one's perceived proximity to each, with the more proximal source generally having a greater impact. For example, studies show that feared selves are powerful sources of motivation, particularly for individuals who perceive themselves to be close to the feared self. These findings have implications for work motivation: Organizational leaders may need to understand that both feared and desired selves serve as regulatory standards for employees. Consequently, for an employee who is close to the feared self, articulating a vision of an ideal may not have much motivational impact, but framing work tasks in terms of the feared self may serve as a powerful motivator. Conversely, for an individual who is close to ideal and far from the feared self, explaining how the employee can avoid the feared self may have minimal effects, but linking work activities to the ideal self may be very motivating.

Consistent with the distinction between personal identity and social identity, work motivation may also be internally or externally based. Work motivation is internally based when a personal WSC is activated by cues in the work environment. In this situation, the employee may set internal standards that become the basis of the possible self. Furthermore, the individual may tend to use fixed rather than ordinal standards of self-measurement as he or she attempts to first reinforce perceptions of competency and later achieve higher levels of competency. Employees for whom a personal WSC is chronically activated will likely have a high need for achievement and be highly motivated by task feedback. It is important to these individuals that their efforts are vital in achieving work outcomes and their ideas and actions are instrumental in performing a job well.

Work motivation is externally based when a social WSC is activated and the individual is primarily other-directed. In this case, the possible self is derived by adopting the role expectations of the reference group, leading to ordinal standards of self-evaluation. When a social WSC is chronically activated, the individual is motivated to behave in ways that meet the expectations of others and elicit social feedback that is consistent with self-concept perceptions. The individual may behave in ways that satisfy reference group members, first to gain acceptance and, after achieving that, to gain status.

Recent studies show that core self-evaluations, a concept that overlaps to a great extent with self-concept, are predictive of work motivation. Core self-evaluations refer to fundamental assessments that people make about their worthiness, competence, and capabilities. Findings suggest that individuals who choose goals that are concordant with their ideals, interests, and values are happier than those who pursue goals for other (e.g., extrinsic) reasons. Furthermore, self-concordant goals are likely to receive sustained effort over time and be more attainable and more satisfying.

In sum, the theories and findings related to self-concept and work motivation suggest that individuals are motivated to behave in ways that are consistent with their existing self-concepts. Thus, theories based on the assumption that individuals have a fundamental need to maintain or enhance their self-concept may be useful in expanding our understanding of motivated behavior in the workplace.

Heather MacDonald
and Douglas J. Brown

See also Job Involvement; Work Motivation

Further Readings

Farmer, S. M., & Van Dyne, L. (2010). The idealized self and the situated self as predictors of employee work behaviors. *Journal of Applied Psychology, 95,* 503–516.

Johnson, R. E., Venus, M., Lanaj, K., Mao, C., & Chang, C. (2012). Leader identity as an antecedent of the frequency and consistency of transformational, consideration, and abusive leadership behaviors. *Journal of Applied Psychology, 97,* 1262–1272.

Lord, R. G., & Brown, D. J. (2004). *Leadership processes and follower self-identity.* Mahwah, NJ: Erlbaum.

SELF-DETERMINATION THEORY

Introduction

Theory Overview

Self-determination theory (SDT) examines the universal human drive to grow and fulfill essential psychological needs. According to SDT, the fulfillment of these innate needs allows people to function efficiently and thrive. Furthermore, this theory discusses the interplay between these needs and external influences to differentiate between intrinsic and extrinsic sources of motivation. SDT includes a broad theory, used as a framework to study motivation and personality, and six mini-theories, which examine intrinsic and extrinsic motivation.

The theory has been applied to a variety of fields, including adolescent development, therapy, neuropsychology, health, education, goal setting, and organizational research. Within the industrial and organizational realm, research has examined many variables through the scope of SDT, including supervisor and organizational support, employee turnover, engagement, well-being, self-control, job satisfaction, prosocial behavior, burnout, compensation, job design, e-learning, goal pursuit, achievement, and organizational change.

Theory Origin

Self-determination theorists were initially concerned with an individual's internally derived choices, free from external influences. These early studies focused on intrinsic motivation, or the motivation to engage in an activity due to internal gratification and innately satisfying processes, entirely motivated by the self. However, it became apparent that these choices did not exist free of external interference. Further research investigating the role of social and environmental factors on an individual's choices led to the incorporation of extrinsic motivation, or the motivation to engage in activities to achieve externally anchored outcomes (e.g., social or tangible rewards such as prestige, promotion, or pay).

Edward L. Deci and Richard M. Ryan are largely responsible for the development and expansion of SDT. Deci and Ryan elaborated on their initial work to explain the mechanics of intrinsic motivation through basic psychological needs, individual differences in the strength of these needs, and the propensity for external sources of motivation to be internalized. In a series of studies, Deci and Ryan showed that some external rewards, like money, undermine intrinsic motivation. However, other external rewards, like verbal reinforcement and positive feedback, increase intrinsic motivation. These studies, along with subsequent research, led to the conclusion that contextual factors play a critical role in both intrinsic and extrinsic motivation.

Self-Determination Theory

Meta-Theory

SDT is an empirically based, macro theory of motivation and personality. SDT is concerned with universal psychological needs, innate growth propensities, and motivational influences that affect choices. SDT is hinged on the belief that human nature is associated with positive aspects that contribute to ideal functioning and growth, self-determined motivation, and integration of the self. The satisfaction of three innate needs (autonomy, competence, and relatedness) allows for this growth and for self-determined behaviors, or behaviors that are driven predominantly by the individual. These needs are considered inherent, existing across cultures and time.

Autonomy involves having a sense of control or free will over one's decisions and behavior, competence involves having a sense of mastery over tasks and skills, and relatedness involves having closeness and feeling mutual caring for others. The social and environmental support or thwarting of these needs affects the strength and type of motivation, which has implications for many significant consequences. For example, in the workplace, greater intrinsic motivation is related to increased task persistence and creativity, and reduced burnout and exhaustion, in employees. In contrast to many theories of motivation, SDT focuses on innate psychological needs, rather than goals and outcomes, and it has explanatory power for the potency and direction of goals.

In many situations, support for all three needs may not be provided, or there may be conflicting dynamics that undermine these needs. According to SDT, environments may enhance or disrupt psychological growth depending on the profile of needs support or obstruction. Many studies subsequent to the original research on intrinsic motivation delineated the conditions under which different types of motivation emerge. For example, what work conditions support or hinder autonomy? What situations bolster relatedness to others or a feeling of competence? With exceeding importance, how do these contexts affect self-determined motivation? When will motivation be intrinsic or extrinsic? These conditions prompted the creation of the six subtheories to explain different aspects of self-determined motivation.

Mini-Theories

The inherent psychological needs required for self-determination are closely linked to intrinsic motivation. *Cognitive evaluation theory* addresses the variability of intrinsic motivation by highlighting the role that autonomy and competence play. For example, autonomy can be undermined if employees feel controlled at work (e.g., having deadlines imposed on them or being offered extrinsic rewards), and enhanced if they are offered options. On the other hand, competence can be enhanced if they receive specific kinds of information (e.g., positive feedback regarding performance). This enhancement or undermining of needs (e.g., autonomy and competence) increases or decreases the level of intrinsic motivation felt by employees.

The influence of extrinsically motivating factors prompted the development of a second subtheory to explain their role in motivation. Extrinsic motivation can promote or hinder internalization of the regulation of tasks that individuals are obligated to engage in. According to *organismic integration theory*, fulfillment of the need for autonomy is affected by the degree of internalization (e.g., employees who adopt previously unheld values of their organization) and integration of extrinsic behavioral regulations. Autonomy is lowest when people experience external regulation—external rewards and punishments are driving compliant behaviors. When there is a slightly greater degree of internalization, they are considered to be regulating via introjection, in which case extrinsic values are adopted without ownership. There is motivation to maintain an extrinsic value for the ego's sake (i.e., to maintain self-worth). Further along the internalization spectrum, they can regulate through identification if an external value has been fully accepted as their own and is personally important. Lastly, integrated regulation occurs in conjunction with high autonomy when values have been integrated with their core values and sense of self. Although extrinsically motivated, integrated regulation shares similarities with

intrinsic motivation. The internalization of extrinsic values is also affected by relatedness (e.g., supportive managers can increase internalization of extrinsic work values) and competence (e.g., behaviors are more likely to internalize if individuals feel competent performing them).

Due to the presence of both intrinsic and extrinsic factors, research comparing their implications for well-being led to the formation of *goal contents theory*. This subtheory addresses the impact of goals on motivation by linking a focus on intrinsic goals (e.g., personal growth or close relationships) to greater psychological well-being and an emphasis on extrinsic goals (e.g., financial success or power) to lower psychological well-being. This subtheory suggests that some goals, specifically intrinsic goals, are more likely to afford the opportunity to fulfill certain psychological needs, in turn leading to increased psychological wellness. Other goals, like extrinsic goals, lack the opportunity to satisfy these innate needs, leading to a decrease in well-being.

Furthermore, *basic psychological needs theory* expands on the determination of well-being via fulfillment of the fundamental needs. In order to enjoy psychological health and positive affect, support of these needs (autonomy, competence, and relatedness) is critical. Work tasks that promote satisfaction of these needs are likely to be intrinsically motivating and to protect against burnout and exhaustion; dysfunction will result if these needs are unsatisfied.

Although all three needs are critical for self-determination, there are individual differences in motivation, such as general orientation toward the environment or the self. *Causality orientations theory* describes three different, enduring trait orientations that can coexist within individuals. This subtheory suggests that all three orientations exist in each individual to some degree, and their strength is thought to be relatively stable across time. The presence of these orientations is predictive of functioning, behavioral tendencies, and well-being. With autonomy orientation, all three needs are met, people are intrinsically motivated, and they seek fulfillment of these needs. This is positively related to self-esteem. However, with control orientation, competence and relatedness are satisfied, but not autonomy. People may be extrinsically motivated, regulating themselves through internal or external controls such as rewards, recognition, or rules. This is associated with less psychological well-being, less functional flexibility, greater defensiveness, and self-consciousness. A failure to fulfill all three needs results in an impersonal orientation, in which case behaviors are seen as beyond one's control. This orientation is associated with amotivation, poor self-regulation, feelings of incompetence, diminished persistence and effort, and ill-being.

Lastly, the fundamental need for relatedness is explicated in *relationship motivation theory*. This subtheory focuses on close personal relationships that satisfy the need for relatedness. Romantic partners, close friends, and group belongingness (e.g., work groups) are desirable and essential for well-being. The relationships that best support the need for relatedness also enhance the needs for autonomy and competence.

SDT is a theory of motivation that focuses on psychological needs (i.e., autonomy, competence, and relatedness) that are considered to be universal. The fulfillment or deficit of these needs by contextual environments, including work environments, has an impact on motivation and the strength and type of goals that individuals pursue. Whereas intrinsically motivated behaviors are an ideal representation of self-determined behavior, extrinsically motivated behaviors can also be considered self-determined depending on the level of internalization. Therefore, according to SDT, the interplay of personality, satisfaction of these universal needs, and environmental context has vast and important implications for human motivation, psychological wellness, behaviors, and performance across many life domains, including at work.

Vivian P. Chou and Alexandra Tumminia

See also Achievement Needs, Power Needs, Affiliation Needs, and Goal Orientation; Intrinsic and Extrinsic Work Motivation; Need Theories of Work Motivation; Work Motivation

Further Readings

Broeck, A., Vansteenkiste, M., Witte, H., Soenens, B., & Lens, W. (2010). Capturing autonomy, competence, and relatedness at work: Construction and initial validation of the Work-related Basic Need Satisfaction scale. *Journal of Occupational and Organizational Psychology, 83*(4), 981–1002.

Deci, E. L. (1971). Effects of externally mediated rewards on intrinsic motivation. *Journal of Personality and Social Psychology, 18*, 105–115.

Deci, E. L., & Ryan, R. M. (1985). *Intrinsic motivation and self-determination in human behavior*. New York, NY: Plenum.

Deci, E. L., & Ryan, R. M. (2000). The "what" and "why" of goal pursuits: Human needs and the self-determination of behavior. *Psychological Inquiry, 11*, 227–268.

Deci, E. D., & Ryan, R. M. (2002). *Handbook of self-determination research*. New York, NY: University of Rochester Press.

Ryan, R. M., & Deci, E. L. (2000). Self-determination theory and the facilitation of intrinsic motivation, social development, and well-being. *American Psychologist, 55*, 68–78.

Vansteenkiste, M., Niemiec, C. P., & Soenens, B. (2010). The development of the five mini-theories of self-determination theory: An historical overview, emerging trends, and future directions. In T. C. Urdan & S. A. Karabenick (Eds.), *The decade ahead: Theoretical perspectives on motivation and achievement (advances in motivation and achievement)* (pp. 105–165). Bingley, UK: Emerald Group.

SELF-EFFICACY

Self-efficacy is a person's belief in his or her capability to successfully perform a particular task or attain a targeted outcome. Together with the goals that people set and their habits, self-efficacy is one of the most powerful motivational predictors of how well a person will perform at almost any endeavor. Self-efficacy is a strong determinant of effort, persistence, and strategizing, as well as subsequent training and job performance. Besides being highly predictive, self-efficacy can be developed to harness its performance-enhancing benefits. After outlining the nature of self-efficacy and how it leads to performance, well-being, and other work-related outcomes, we will discuss the measurement and sources of self-efficacy. We then will consider whether it is possible to have too much self-efficacy and conclude by outlining a range of initiatives that managers can take to foster the development of their employees' self-efficacy.

Nature of Self-Efficacy

Because self-efficacy pertains to specific tasks, people may simultaneously have high self-efficacy for some tasks and low self-efficacy for others. For example, a manager may have high self-efficacy for the technical aspects of his or her role, such as management accounting, but low self-efficacy for other aspects, such as dealing with employees' performance problems.

Self-efficacy is more specific and circumscribed than self-confidence (i.e., a general personality trait that relates to how confidently people feel and act in most situations) or self-esteem (i.e., perceived self-worth), and therefore it is generally more readily developed than these two concepts. Furthermore, self-efficacy is a much stronger predictor of how effectively people will perform a given task than either their self-confidence or self-esteem.

How Self-Efficacy Affects Performance and Well-Being

Having high self-efficacy leads people to set difficult goals, work hard to attain them, and persist in the face of setbacks, as illustrated by many great innovators and politicians who were undeterred by repeated obstacles, ridicule, and minimal encouragement. Thomas Edison, believing that he would eventually succeed, reputedly tested at least 3,000 unsuccessful prototypes before eventually developing the first incandescent lightbulb. Abraham Lincoln exhibited high self-efficacy in response to numerous and repeated public rebukes and failures before his eventual political triumph. Research has found that self-efficacy is important for sustaining the considerable effort that is required to master skills involved in diverse activities including public speaking, losing weight, and becoming an effective manager.

When learning complex tasks, high self-efficacy prompts people to strive to improve their assumptions and strategies rather than look for excuses, such as not being interested in the task. High self-efficacy improves employees' capacity to collect relevant information, make sound decisions, and take appropriate action, particularly when they are under time pressure. Such capabilities are invaluable in jobs that involve, for example, dealing with irate customers when working in a call center or overcoming complex technical challenges in minimal

time. In contrast, low self-efficacy can lead to erratic analytical thinking that undermines the quality of problem solving—a key competency in an increasingly knowledge-based society.

In a dynamic work context wherein ongoing learning and performance improvement are needed, high self-efficacy helps individuals react less defensively when they receive negative feedback. In areas where self-efficacy is low, people often see a negative outcome as confirming the incompetence they perceive in themselves and lower their standards, thereby further reducing their self-efficacy, effort, and subsequent performance.

Among managers, those with high self-efficacy for their managerial role seek and act on improvement-oriented input from their employees. By contrast, low managerial self-efficacy leads managers to be (a) defensive about their managerial competency and (b) disinclined to encourage employees to provide improvement suggestions, as well as to (c) negatively evaluate employees who provide such suggestions and to (d) be reluctant to duly consider or implement those improvement suggestions. Over time, the adverse performance implications can be substantial.

As people often become anxious or depressed when they perceive themselves as unable to manage aversive events or achieve what they highly value, self-efficacy also predicts stress and occupational burnout. Specifically, low self-efficacy can foster a sense of helplessness and rumination on one's self-perceived limited capability to learn how to cope with the demands at hand. The relevant form of self-efficacy for managing such disruptive inner life dynamics focuses on the ability to manage one's debilitating thoughts and emotions. Applying this self-management ability can be a challenge that disrupts a person's focus and thus performance on his or her primary task.

Measurement of Self-Efficacy

Because self-efficacy is task specific, there is no single, standardized measure of self-efficacy. Rather, measures must gauge an individual's self-assessed capacity to either (a) achieve a certain outcome on a particular task (*outcome self-efficacy*), (b) engage in the behaviors likely to lead to a certain desired outcome (*process self-efficacy*), or (c) manage oneself to engage in these behaviors (*self-regulatory self-efficacy*). An outcome self-efficacy scale in the domain of job search might include items such as "I believe I can get a new job within 4 weeks" and "I believe I can get a new job with a starting salary of at least $95,000," with response anchors ranging from *not at all confident* to *extremely confident*. A process self-efficacy scale for job search would focus on items such as "I believe I can network effectively with at least six people during the next 4 weeks" and "I believe I can send out 15 résumés with tailored cover letters during the next 4 weeks," with response anchors similar to the outcome self-efficacy scale.

Self-regulatory self-efficacy often underlies process self-efficacy and involves (a) managing impediments and (b) mobilizing relevant means and resources. Self-efficacy, to maintain the process of a daily health-promoting exercise routine, for instance, tends to be a function of self-regulatory self-efficacy to handle various external (e.g., time pressures, family demands) and internal (e.g., being tired, feeling depressed) impediments to doing so. Self-regulatory self-efficacy is assessed in terms of confidence to effectively manage such potential impediments to engaging in a targeted behavior, as well as to mobilize the means and resources required to produce desired outcomes. In the domain of self-directed learning, for instance, students' self-efficacy to mobilize the required means and resources to support their learning and academic progress may be evaluated by assessing their self-efficacy to create environments that support their learning, to schedule and organize their academic activities, to master efficient study strategies, to secure help from peers and teachers when needed, and to motivate themselves to thoroughly complete their reading and assignments to the required standards and within the designated time frame. The key point is that measures of self-efficacy are most informative, predictive, and useful when they are tailored to focus on relevant, specific outcomes, tasks, and behaviors.

Sources of Self-Efficacy

There are three key sources of self-efficacy. The most powerful determinant of self-efficacy is *mastery experiences*, followed by *role-modeling* and then *verbal persuasion*.

Mastery experiences occur when people taste success at performing at least portions of a task.

It serves to convince them that they have what it takes to achieve increasingly difficult accomplishments of a similar kind. Self-mastery can be orchestrated by breaking down difficult tasks into small steps that are relatively easy in order to enable initial success. Individuals attempt progressively more difficult tasks regarding which constructive feedback is provided and accomplishments celebrated, before they attempt even more challenging tasks. Systematically building self-efficacy through mastery experiences thus entails structuring situations that enable rewarding success and avoid repeated failure. For example, a person who is learning to pilot an aircraft may be given many hours to progressively develop skill and confidence in the separate component skills before attempting to combine them by flying solo. Initial flying lessons are designed so that trainee pilots are challenged but also experience efficacy-building successes during each session. Managers can help employees to develop self-efficacy through mastery when they provide incrementally difficult challenges and adequate resources for individuals to regularly encounter and celebrate successes as they perform their work.

Role-modeling occurs when people observe others perform a task that they are attempting to learn or vividly visualize themselves performing successfully. Role-modeling can provide people with ideas about how to perform certain tasks and inspire their confidence so that they can act successfully. It can also instill insights about how to avoid the mistakes of others, as long as people have adequate self-efficacy to do so.

Effective role models approach challenging activities as an opportunity to learn and develop their knowledge, skills, and effectiveness rather than as a test of their talent. They respond to setbacks by exploring what can be done differently in the future. In short, good role models demonstrate the development of skill, persistence, and learning rather than the defensiveness and blaming that cause mistakes to recur and subsequent performance to decline.

Models are most effective at raising self-efficacy when they are personally liked and seen as having attributes (e.g., age, gender, or ethnicity) similar to the individuals who observe them. In one classic study, children developed greater arithmetic self-efficacy and performance after watching a video of another student, rather than a teacher, demonstrate some arithmetic operations. These dynamics should be considered when striving to identify an efficacy-inspiring mentor.

Verbal persuasion builds self-efficacy when people are encouraged and praised for their competence and ability to improve their effectiveness. Positive self-talk, underscoring that one can persist and achieve one's objectives, can also raise self-efficacy. Regardless of its source, verbal persuasion is most likely to increase self-efficacy when it is perceived as credible and emphasizes how success results from devoting sufficient effort to mastering acquirable skills, rather than depending on inherent talent. Efficacy-raising feedback highlights how consistent efforts have enabled improvements, as well as the progress made, rather than involving peer comparisons or making reference to how far individuals have to go until their ultimate objective is achieved. Effective verbal persuasion is reinforced with corresponding actions. For example, managers telling employees that they are capable but not assigning them any challenging tasks tends to erode both employees' self-efficacy and the manager's credibility. In contrast, having people draw up a progress chart before complimenting them on their genuine attainments can be a potent way of raising their sense of what they can achieve.

Figure 1 illustrates some managerial initiatives that can help build employees' self-efficacy via these three pathways. Table 1 provides a self-assessment of how frequently managers engage in related efficacy-building behaviors.

Undermining Self-Efficacy

These initiatives for building self-efficacy contrast with the subtle though common messages that erode self-efficacy. Such signals include consistently being assigned unchallenging tasks, receiving praise for mediocre performance, being preferentially selected based on one's membership to a protected group rather than on merit, being treated indifferently for faulty performance, or being repeatedly offered unsolicited help. Faultfinding and personal criticism, by oneself or others, are particularly destructive because they undermine motivation to explore and experiment, whereby individuals discover what they are actually able to achieve. Although encouraging messages can raise self-efficacy, attempts at building self-efficacy through verbal persuasion may easily degenerate into empty sermons unless they are supported by efficacy-affirming mastery experiences.

Too Much of a Good Thing?

While high self-efficacy is generally advantageous, extremely high self-efficacy can lead to excessive risk taking, hubris, and dysfunctional persistence. In most cases, however, the resulting setbacks and failures that people experience soon recalibrate their self-efficacy to a more realistic level. In general, the many benefits of high self-efficacy make

Figure 1   Managerial Actions That Increase Performance by Building Employees' Self-Efficacy

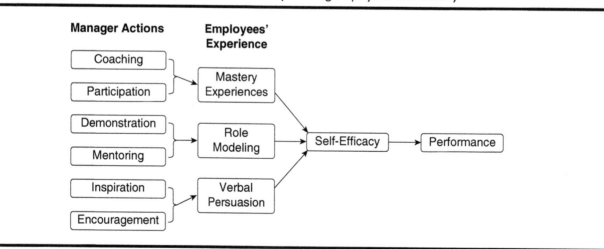

Table I   Managerial Self-Assessment: How Frequently Do You Build Employees' Self-Efficacy?[1]

Rate how often you exhibit the following behaviors, where:

1 = Never,	2 = Occasionally,	3 = Sometimes,	4 = Regularly,	5 = Almost always

Manager Actions	*To what extent do you . . .*	*Rating/5*
Coaching	• Enable employees to discern how to achieve their objectives?	
	• Help novices to break complex tasks down into components to enable them to experience initial success?	
	• Provide feedback about effective and ineffective behaviors, rather than an employee's personal style?	
	• Deal with "silly" questions or suggestions by tactfully helping employees to explore their implications?	
Participation	• Enable your employees to establish or at least participate in determining their goals?	
	• Encourage participation in decision making, where feasible?	
	• Involve employees in identifying and being assigned tasks that will develop their abilities?	
	• Seek input before making changes that will affect your employees?	
Demonstration	• Personally role-model persisting in trying different strategies in order to overcome challenges?	
	• Walk the talk—do what you ask others to do?	
	• Express enthusiasm, optimism, and not taking yourself too seriously?	
Mentoring	• Provide opportunities that may result in your employees having more experiences and expertise than you in certain areas?	
	• Inquire about the learning experiences of your employees?	
	• Make yourself available as a sounding board?	
Inspiration	• Express confidence that your employees can perform well?	
	• Establish a clear and exciting vision that your employees are inspired to strive toward?	
	• Leave your employees feeling stronger and more capable after spending time with you?	
Encouragement	• Acknowledge achievements and progress as reflecting employees' efforts and abilities?	
	• Make employees feel *safe* and supported when they have made mistakes?	
	• Applaud initiatives undertaken in order to improve performance?	

Add up your scores to estimate how much you build the self-efficacy of your employees. How would your employees rate you on these questions? Why not reevaluate yourself 1 month from now to gauge any improvement or decline in your behaviors aimed at raising the self-efficacy of your employees?

[1] This exercise is intended as a managerial self-development activity, illustrative of self-efficacy-building behaviors, rather than as a tool for assessing managers to make selection, performance appraisal, or promotion decisions.

Added from Heslin (1999).

it a worthwhile attribute to cultivate. This is best done through the simultaneous and systematic provision of mastery experiences, role-modeling, and verbal persuasion.

Peter A. Heslin, Ute-Christine Klehe,
and Lauren A. Keating

See also Social Cognitive Theory

Further Readings

Bandura, A. (1997). *Self-efficacy: The exercise of control.* New York, NY: Freeman.

Bandura, A. (2012a). On the functional properties of perceived self-efficacy revisited. *Journal of Management, 38*(1), 9–44. doi:10.1177/014920631 1410606

Bandura, A. (2012b). The role of self-efficacy in goal-based motivation. In E. A. Locke & G. P. Latham (Eds.), *New developments in goal setting and task performance* (pp. 147–157). New York, NY: Routledge.

Fast, N. J., Burris, E. R., & Bartel, C. A. (2014). Managing to stay in the dark: Managerial self-efficacy, ego defensiveness, and the aversion to employee voice. *Academy of Management Journal, 57*(4), 1013–1034. doi:10.5465/amj.2012.0393

Heslin, P. A. (1999). Boosting empowerment by developing self-efficacy. *Asia Pacific Journal of Human Resources, 37*(1), 52–64. doi:10.1177/10384111 9903700105

SELF-ESTEEM

Self-esteem (SE) is the subjective overall value that one places on oneself as a person. Few topics have received more attention in psychology than SE, and indeed, a search of the PsycINFO database in early 2015 identified more than 42,000 articles with *self-esteem* as a keyword. There are several reasons for the enduring interest in SE. First and foremost, most people are inherently curious about SE because it encompasses important information about the self, such as how worthy, competent, and well liked one is. In that sense, possessing self-knowledge necessitates understanding one's SE, and few can be indifferent to this kind of information. Second, researchers and practitioners alike have assumed

that high SE has many positive outcomes, and in fact, much of the research on SE has been focused on exploring what enhances SE. Third, SE has been shown to be related to many important variables of interest, such as subjective well-being, life satisfaction, job satisfaction, performance, competition, causal attribution, achievement, and helping. Therefore, understanding SE appears to enhance knowledge in many other areas of psychology. Because SE seems to have such major importance to researchers, practitioners, and people in general, it is not surprising that more than 150 articles are published every month on SE. Despite this proliferation of studies and decades of empirical research, the topic is not free from controversies, and there is no universal agreement about some aspects of the validity of the construct and its effects.

Theoretical and Measurement Issues

Because SE involves an evaluation of how worthy one is as a person, by definition, it seems that people with high SE should have positive self-regard and those with low SE should have negative self-regard. However, though it is true that people with high SE have positive, well-defined views of the self, people with low SE do not necessarily hold negative views of themselves. Instead, low-SE individuals tend to evaluate themselves neutrally, and their self-views tend to vary considerably from situation to situation. Indeed, recent meta-analytic evidence reveals a positive relationship between SE and SE stability ($r = .31$).

This neutrality and variability in evaluations of the self raises important theoretical questions that have not been clearly answered in the SE literature. For example, it is not completely clear why people with low SE have variable views of themselves; several incompatible theoretical explanations may account for this phenomenon. On one hand, it is possible that people with low SE lack a clear notion of who they are, and therefore they describe themselves in noncommittal, middle-of-the-road terms. Indeed, people with low SE exhibit less stability of self-evaluations and tend to give inconsistent responses to questions asking them to describe themselves (compared with those with high SE). Thus, according to the *self-concept clarity* explanation, low-SE individuals are confused and ambivalent about who they are and therefore tend to be variable and noncommittal in their self-views.

On the other hand, it is also possible that people with low SE are actually more accurate in their self-evaluations than high-SE individuals. That is, the neutrality and inconsistency of self-evaluations associated with low SE may actually represent a more accurate perception of the self that truly varies across situations and circumstances. Because we sometimes act as worthy and capable individuals and sometimes do not, people with low SE may be correct in their self-descriptions, and those with high SE may be positively biased and even detached from reality. Indeed, there is some evidence to suggest that people with high SE consistently exaggerate their positive views of the self. For example, several studies have shown that people with high SE overevaluate how much other people like them, and some researchers have even claimed that the interpersonal success of high-SE individuals exists only in their own minds.

The SE literature clearly shows that people with high SE are much less plastic in their behavior than people with low SE. For example, people with low SE are more reactive to external social cues and therefore more susceptible to negative feedback and more accepting of it than high-SE individuals. Meta-analytic evidence suggests that low-SE individuals are more likely to lower their self-expectations in response to negative feedback, whereas high-SE individuals are more likely to minimize the significance of negative information or refocus their attention on more positive self-evaluative information. Low-SE individuals are also more susceptible to attempts to influence them and more sensitive to anxiety-causing stimuli, and they are prone to be influenced by self-focus and expectancy manipulations. This tendency to be "behaviorally plastic" may be especially important in performance situations—as performance has been shown to be influenced by expectancies and self rather than task-focused manipulations.

Two underlying psychological motives may explain the behavioral plasticity pattern of low-SE individuals. On one hand, individuals want to feel good about themselves and feel that they are worthy, capable, and likable; therefore, one motive that drives people is self-enhancement. On the other hand, people also desire to be self-consistent and protect their self-conceptions from change. In other words, people are driven by the desire to predict and control important life experiences and to tell themselves a consistent story about who they are. For those with positive SE, self-consistency and self-enhancement operate in concert, but for people with negative self-views, these two drives operate in opposite directions. Low-SE people want to maintain their negative self-view in order to maintain self-consistency, but at the same time, they want to think better of themselves. Because they have contradictory motives, they look outside for cues to who they are and rely on social information to determine their future actions. For example, when people with high SE encounter negative information about themselves in the form of failure or negative feedback, they tend to reject it and do not let the information affect their expectancies or behaviors. In contrast, those with low SE often accept the information and allow it to influence their behaviors.

Causal and Relational Issues

A continuing debate within the SE literature centers on causal relations between SE and various outcomes. Because the vast majority of SE studies are correlational in nature, causal inferences are necessarily constrained, and the relationships between SE and various outcomes remain largely unknown. To establish causal inferences, researchers have historically utilized laboratory experiments and longitudinal designs. However, at least with regard to one of the most important presumed causes of low SE (i.e., social rejection), recent meta-analytic evidence reveals major inconsistencies among the results of these methods. For example, field studies consistently show that chronic rejection is associated with lower SE. Based on the results of these studies, researchers have often concluded that when individuals are rejected, not only do they feel worse, but also the rejection lowers their self-esteem. In contrast, recent meta-analysis of laboratory studies suggests that while experimental manipulations of social rejection indeed cause a slightly negative shift in emotions from positive to mildly positive or neutral, rejection has little to no effect on SE.

Research employing longitudinal designs has proven more fruitful in establishing other causal relations between SE and various outcomes of interest. For instance, a meta-analytic investigation of longitudinal data revealed that the effects of SE on depression ($\beta = -.16$) were roughly twice that of depression on SE ($\beta = -.08$)—suggesting that depression was more a consequence than a cause of SE. Furthermore, recent research using cross-lagged longitudinal design provides support to the hypothesis that SE is a cause rather than a consequence of various life outcomes such as affect and relationship satisfaction. These findings have been bolstered by recent research in quantitative genetics that suggests that approximately 40% of the between-individuals variability in SE can be attributed to genetic factors—a percentage approaching that of other personality traits. Therefore, SE could be assumed to be the cause rather than the consequence of various affective outcomes. While genetic research helped resolve some of the controversies regarding causal relationships, it also called into question the efficacy of efforts to improve individuals' overall SE. Consistent with the genetic evidence and similar to other traits, research has shown that SE is relatively stable across one's life span. However, the relative high stability of SE and the fact that SE to a large extent originates from genetic influences do not necessarily preclude that it may change over time. In fact, meta-analytic evidence suggests that SE increases from adolescence to adulthood with peak levels occurring between 50 and 60 years of age, followed by subsequent declines in old age.

High SE is most often viewed as a positive attribute to possess, but scholars have cautioned that there may be a dark side to SE—drawing similarities between high SE and narcissism. However, in fact, there is little evidence to suggest that high SE is strongly related to narcissism, and there are both theoretical and empirical reasons to suggest the constructs are conceptually distinct. From a theoretical point of view, SE refers only to the subjective evaluation of one's self-worth. Unlike narcissism, SE does not require an estimation of one's worth relative to, or vis-à-vis, others. While meta-analytic evidence shows global SE displays a small to moderate correlation with narcissism ($r = .29$), the strength of this relationship is small in comparison to the relationships between SE and other traits such as neuroticism

($r = -.50$) and extroversion ($r = .38$). Furthermore, SE has been shown to be weakly related to psychological entitlement ($r = -.04$)—an aspect of the Narcissistic Personality Inventory. While most recent evidence suggests that SE and narcissism are conceptually and empirically distinct, SE has been meta-analytically shown to exhibit strong correlations with other traits in addition to neuroticism such as locus of control and generalized self-efficacy. Researchers have empirically demonstrated these four constructs to be indicators of a single underlying construct labeled core self-evaluation.

Contributions

Despite these issues, research on SE has made some significant contributions. First, measures of SE are highly correlated with each other and generally show high reliabilities. In particular, the Rosenberg Self-Esteem Scale seems to be content- and face-valid, and it is reliable and unitary and therefore can be used with confidence. Second, meta-analytic research has shown some of the relationships between SE and important variables of interest in industrial and organizational psychology to be quite significant. For example, SE has been shown to be an important predictor of job satisfaction ($r = .26$). People with high SE actually attain more challenging jobs, and even in jobs that are not particularly complex, they see more challenges and therefore are more excited about their jobs than people with low SE. People with high SE also have higher subjective well-being ($r = .47$) and cope better with stressful situations. Self-esteem is significantly correlated with job performance ($r = .26$), and the relationship is actually stronger than the usual relationship between conscientiousness and performance, which is considered the strongest personality predictor of job performance. Another major variable of interest in the organizational literature is leadership—indeed, several studies have shown that SE is a good predictor of leadership behavior and efficacy. In addition, a recent large-scale study showed that people with high SE exhibit more "voice behavior" in organizations and therefore are less susceptible to groupthink. Overall, despite the theoretical and methodological controversies, SE has been shown to be a valuable variable of interest in industrial and organizational psychology.

Amir Erez and Andrew Woolum

See also Core Self-Evaluations

Further Readings

Baumeister, R. F., Campbell, J. D., Kruger, J. I., & Vohs, K. D. (2003). Does self-esteem cause better performance, interpersonal success, happiness, or healthier lifestyle? *Psychological Science in the Public Interest, 4*(1), 1–44. Retrieved from http://www.jstor.org/stable/40062291

Blackhart, G. C., Knowles, M. L., Nelson, B. C., & Baumeister, R. F. (2009). Rejection elicits emotional reactions but neither causes immediate distress nor lowers self-esteem: A meta-analytic review of 192 studies on social exclusion. *Personality and Social Psychology Review, 13*(4), 269–309. doi:10.1177/1088868309346065

Brockner, J. (1988). *Self-esteem at work: Research, theory, and practice.* Lexington, MA: Lexington Books.

Campbell, J. D., & Lavallee, L. F. (1993). Who am I? The role of self-concept confusion in understanding the behavior of people with low self-esteem. In R. F. Baumeister (Ed.), *Self-esteem: The puzzle of low self-regard* (pp. 3–20). New York, NY: Plenum Press. doi:10.1007/978-1-4684-8956-9_1

Donnellan, M. B., Trzesniewski, K. H., & Robins, R. W. (2011). Self-esteem: Enduring issues and controversies. In T. Chamorro-Premuzic, S. von Stumm, & A. Furnham (Eds.), *The Wiley-Blackwell handbook of individual differences* (pp. 718–746). West Sussex, UK: Blackwell.

Judge, T. A., & Bono, J. E. (2001). Relationship of core self-evaluations traits—self-esteem, generalized self-efficacy, locus of control, and emotional stability—with job satisfaction and job performance: A meta-analysis. *Journal of Applied Psychology, 86*(1), 80–92. doi:10.1037//0021-9010.86.1.80

Okada, R. (2010). A meta-analytic review of the relation between self-esteem level and self-esteem instability. *Personality and Individual Differences, 48*(2), 243–246. doi:10.1016/j.paid.2009.10.012

Orth, U., Robins, R. W., & Widaman, K. F. (2012). Life-span development of self-esteem and its effects on important life outcomes. *Journal of Personality and Social Psychology, 102*(6), 1271–1288. doi:10.1037/a0025558

Sowislo, J. F., & Orth, U. (2013). Does low self-esteem predict depression and anxiety? A meta-analysis of longitudinal studies. *Psychological Bulletin, 139*(1), 213–240. doi:10.1037/a0028931

vanDellen, M. R., Campbell, W. K., Hoyle, R. H., & Bradfield, E. K. (2011). Compensating, resisting, and breaking: A meta-analytic examination of reactions to self-esteem threat. *Personality and Social Psychology Review, 15*(1), 51–74. doi:10.1177/1088868310372950

SELF-FULFILLING PROPHECY: PYGMALION EFFECT

The *Pygmalion effect* is a special case of the self-fulfilling prophecy in which raising a manager's expectations for worker performance in fact boosts performance. The Pygmalion effect first appeared in educational psychology when psychologists experimentally raised elementary schoolteachers' expectations for a randomly selected subsample of pupils, producing significantly greater achievement gains among those pupils than among control pupils. Subsequent research has replicated this phenomenon among adult supervisors and subordinates in military, business, industrial, and service organizations and among all four cross-gender combinations—that is, both men and women lead male and female subordinates to greater success when they expect more of them. Interpersonal expectancy is inherent in most leader–follower interactions, and the Pygmalion effect undoubtedly characterizes many—if not most—manager-worker relationships.

Several theories have been proposed to explain why raising leader expectations boosts subordinate performance. Common to all explanations is a causal chain that begins with the impact of the leader's expectations on and his or her *own* behavior toward subordinates, which, in turn, arouses some motivational response on the part of the subordinates and culminates in subordinate performance that accords with the leader's expectations. Self-efficacy has emerged as the key motivational mediator in this process. Self-efficacy is an individual's belief in his or her ability to execute the behaviors needed to perform successfully. Experimental research has shown that self-efficacy is a major determinant of performance. When individuals believe they have what it takes to succeed, they try harder. Conversely, those who doubt they can succeed refrain from exerting the effort to apply the ability that they do have and end up accomplishing less than they actually could.

The *Pygmalion-at-work model* posits that having high expectations moves the leader to treat followers in a manner that augments their self-efficacy, which, in turn, motivates subordinates to expend greater effort, culminating in enhanced performance. Thus, the Pygmalion effect is a motivational phenomenon initiated by the high expectations for performance held by a leader who believes in his or her followers' capacity for success. In a largely unconscious interpersonal process, leaders with high expectations lead their followers to success by enhancing their self-efficacy.

The self-fulfilling prophecy is a double-edged sword: As high expectations boost performance, low expectations can depress performance in a negative process dubbed the *Golem effect*. The word *golem* means "oaf" or "dumbbell" in Hebrew and Yiddish slang. Managers who expect dumbbells get dumbbells. Field experiments have shown that Golem effects can be mitigated by informing supervisors that subordinates with relatively low qualifications have high potential to succeed.

Another variant of the self-fulfilling prophecy is the *Galatea effect*. Named for the statue sculpted by the mythical Pygmalion, this is an intrapersonal expectancy effect involving only the worker. Self-starters fulfill their own prophecies of success; believing in their own capacity to excel, they mobilize their internal motivational, cognitive, emotional, and physical resources to sustain the effort needed for success even without any external source (e.g., a supervisor) of high expectations. However, Galatea effects can also be Golem-like. Individuals who harbor a negative self-image expect to fail; they refrain from using their skills and abilities, thereby needlessly but unintentionally fulfilling their own gloomy prophecy.

Finally, research shows group-level expectancy effects in which a manager's high expectations for a whole group, distinct from expectations for particular individuals, culminate in the group's exceeding the performance of control groups. This is an especially important phenomenon in teamwork, which has emerged as an ubiquitous, defining feature of modern organizations, as well as in team sports.

A fascinating but elusive aspect of interpersonal self-fulfilling prophecies involves the communication of expectations. Some of this communication is verbal and conscious, but much of it is not. Managers exhibit many nonverbal behaviors by which they convey their expectations, whether high or low, to subordinates. When managers expect more, they unwittingly nod their heads affirmatively more often, draw nearer physically, maintain eye contact, speak quickly, and show greater patience toward those they are supervising. These nonverbal behaviors serve to "warm" the interpersonal relationship, create a climate of support, and foster success. Other ways in which leaders favor those whom they expect more from include providing them with more input, more feedback, and more opportunities to show what they can do, whereas those whom managers expect less of are left neglected "on the bench."

Fortunately, the high expectations that motivate enhanced performance also augment subordinate satisfaction. In every Pygmalion experiment in which satisfaction was measured, it was significantly increased. Satisfaction is not a surprising by-product. High expectations and the resulting superior performance are satisfying because, by and large, employees want to succeed, and they are more satisfied when they do. Thus, all the news is good news as far as the Pygmalion effect is concerned.

Meta-analyses have confirmed that the magnitude of the Pygmalion effect in management is medium to large. The Pygmalion research is unique in organizational psychology because it is entirely based on field experimentation, lending it extraordinary internal and external validity. Experimental design confirms the flow of causality from leader expectations to follower performance, and the field settings confirm its generalizability. What remains to be shown is the practical validity of the Pygmalion effect. Although experimental replications have produced the effect in organizations, attempts to get managers to apply it through managerial training have been less successful. Managers' prior acquaintance with subordinates appears to be a barrier to widespread application. Virtually all of the successful replications occurred among newcomers whose managers had not known them previously. Familiarity apparently crystallizes expectations because managers do not expect their subordinates to change much. Therefore, the most effective applications may be made among managers of new subordinates.

Recent extensions to additional mediators and moderators that promote or inhibit Pygmalion effects have enriched the theoretical literature. Some approaches assign a more active role to follower characteristics in the Pygmalion interpersonal process. Examples are followers' perceptions of their leaders' (a) trustworthiness, (b) ability to judge followers' ability accurately and form accurate expectations, (c) benevolence toward followers, and (d) integrity. Another extension involves naturally occurring Pygmalion effects. These are conceived as being born of leaders' "implicit followership theories," which are conceptions of followers that leaders carry around in their heads. These conceptions inform leaders' expectations regarding followers and can lead to Pygmalion or Golem effects. Furthermore, an extension of the self-efficacy mediator posits external efficacy, or "means efficacy," as an additional motivational mechanism that is a lever managers can pull to trigger positive self-fulfilling prophecy. Whereas self-efficacy refers to individuals' beliefs in their *internal* resources such as skill, knowledge, willpower, endurance, resourcefulness, and any other traits deemed useful for successful performance, external efficacy refers to beliefs about task-relevant *external* resources that may be used to facilitate performance. These external resources include tools (hence "means efficacy"), colleagues, supervisors, subordinates, the organization, and any other circumstances that the individual may believe facilitate—or hinder—successful performance. Field-experimental corroboration of the role of means efficacy in mediating the impact of expectations on performance has led leadership scholars to incorporate means efficacy into their leadership studies. Thus, we now know that the road to successful leadership involves leader action that augments followers' beliefs in their own capacity to perform successfully and in the utility of the available means to help achieve such success. Researchers have also found that high leader expectations influence quality and quantity of performance differentially. Creativity has also been shown to be associated with high expectations. Finally, questions regarding differences between men and women and between civilian and military settings in the size of the Pygmalion effect continue to attract scholars' attention.

Organizational innovations and other deviations from routine that unfreeze standard operating procedures—and expectations—are particularly conducive to Pygmalion effects. Organizational development programs or profound changes in personnel or in organizational structure or function resulting from, for example, mergers and acquisitions or managerial transitions open a window of opportunity. Savvy managers piggyback on these unsettling events and raise expectations to promote successful change and productive outcomes. In one classic industrial example, the introduction of simple job rotation and job enrichment produced significant improvements in productivity when accompanied by experimentally disseminated information that raised expectations from the new work procedures, but neither innovation improved productivity when expectations were not raised.

The practical upshot is clear: Change—any change—presents managers with an opportunity to create productive Pygmalion effects. It is incumbent on those who want to lead individuals, teams, and organizations to success to convey high expectations whenever the opportunity presents itself. Conversely, cynical expressions of doubt about reorganizations, innovations, or developmental interventions condemn them to failure. Thus, the practical agenda for managers is twofold: They must counteract any manifestations of contrary expectations, and they must implant high expectations.

The essence of the Pygmalion effect is that managers get the workers they expect. Expect more, and you will get more. However, the converse is true, too: Expect less, and you will get less. All managers should strive to play a Pygmalion role by cultivating high expectations of their subordinates' potential and by communicating those expectations to foster high self-expectations among subordinates regarding their own potential for success and regarding the productive means available to them. High expectations are too important to be left to chance or whim; they should be built into all manager–worker relationships and should be part of all managerial training and development programs.

Dov Eden

See also Leadership and Supervision; Training

Further Readings

Avolio, B. J., Reichard, R. J., Hannah, S. T., Walumbwa, F. O., & Chan, A. (2009). A meta-analytic review of leadership impact research: Experimental and quasi-experimental studies. *Leadership Quarterly,* 20(5), 764–784. doi:10.1016/j.leaqua.2009.06.006

Eden, D. (1992). Leadership and expectations: Pygmalion effects and other self-fulfilling prophecies in organizations. *Leadership Quarterly,* 3(4), 271–305. doi:10.1016/1048-9843(92)90018-B

Eden, D. (2003). Self-fulfilling prophecies in organizations. In J. Greenberg (Ed.), *Organizational behavior: The state of the science* (2nd ed., pp. 91–122). Mahwah, NJ: Erlbaum.

Eden, D. (in press). Field experiments in organizational psychology and organizational behavior. *Annual Review of Organizational Psychology and Organizational Behavior,* 2.

Eden, D., Geller, D., Gewirtz, A., Gordon-Terner, R., Inbar, I., Liberman, M., . . . Shalit, M. (2000). Implanting Pygmalion leadership style through workshop training: Seven field experiments. *Leadership Quarterly,* 11(2), 171–210. doi:10.1016/S1048-9843(00)00042-4

Eden, D., Stone-Romero, E,. & Rothstein, H. (2015). Synthesizing results of multiple randomized experiments to establish causality in mediation testing. *Human Resource Management Review,* 25(4), 342–351. doi:10.1016/j.hrmr.2015.02.001

Hannah, S. T., Avolio, B. J., Walumbwa, F. O., & Chan, A. (2012). Leader self and means efficacy: A multi-component approach. *Organizational Behavior and Human Decision Processes,* 118(2), 143–161. doi:10.1016/j.obhdp.2012.03.007

Karakowsky, L., DeGama, N., & McBey, K. (2012). Facilitating the Pygmalion effect: The overlooked role of subordinate perceptions of the leader. *Journal of Occupational and Organizational Psychology,* 85(4), 579–599. doi:10.1111/j.2044-8325.2012.02056.x

Lees-Hotton, C. A., Cullen, K. L., & Svyantek, D. J. (2014). Pygmalion expectations, leader gender, and subordinate gender influence on performance. In D. J. Svyantek & K. T. Mahoney (Eds.), *Organizational processes and received wisdom* (pp. 101–125). Charlotte, NC: Information Age.

McNatt, D. B. (2000). Ancient Pygmalion joins contemporary management: A meta-analysis of the result. *Journal of Applied Psychology,* 85(2), 314–322. doi:10.1037/0021-9010.85.2.314

Merton, R. K. (1948). The self-fulfilling prophecy. *Antioch Review,* 8(2), 193–210. doi:http://www.jstor.org/stable/4609267

Rosenthal, R. (2002). Covert communication in classrooms, clinics, courtrooms, and cubicles. *American Psychologist,* 57(11), 839–849. doi:http://dx.doi.org/10.1037/0003-066X.57.11.839

Stirin, K., Ganzach, Y., Pazy, A., & Eden, D. (2012). The effect of perceived advantage and disadvantage on performance: The role of external efficacy. *Applied Psychology: An International Review,* 61(1), 81–96. doi:10.1111/j.1464-0597.2011.00457.x

Whiteley, P., Sy, T., & Johnson, S. K. (2012). Leaders' conceptions of followers: Implications for naturally occurring Pygmalion effects. *Leadership Quarterly,* 23(5), 822–834. doi:10.1016/j.leaqua.2012.03.006

SELF-LEADERSHIP THEORY

Self-leadership is a process through which individuals use specific sets of behavioral and cognitive strategies to more effectively lead themselves in accomplishing both intrinsically motivating and not naturally motivating tasks. Critics have often argued that self-leadership theory overlaps with other classic motivation theories, but the purpose of normative theories like self-leadership are to prescribe *how* things should be done rather than explain why certain phenomena occur. Self-leadership theory specifically prescribes behavioral, natural reward, and thought strategies to help people more effectively lead themselves. *Behavior self-leadership* (BSL) strategies focus on ways individuals can increase their self-awareness to effectively manage their behaviors. *Natural self-leadership* (NSL) strategies are aimed at increasing one's intrinsic motivation to accomplish a task by either changing the task itself to be more rewarding or changing one's perceptions of the task by focusing on its more rewarding aspects. *Thought self-leadership* (TSL) strategies aim to develop and maintain more constructive patterns of thinking through identifying and challenging dysfunctional beliefs, mentally picturing success, and using constructive self-talk.

The following sections of the entry will discuss the theoretical underpinnings of self-leadership, describe the specific self-leadership strategies in more detail, review some of the more important empirical findings, and then highlight some of the main criticisms, future research directions, and practical implications on the topic.

Theoretical Background

As previously mentioned, self-leadership is a normative theory that draws on other theories, namely self-regulation theory, social cognitive theory, and cognitive evaluation theory, to explain *how* to implement self-leadership strategies and *why* they are effective. Self-regulation theory asserts that people begin to regulate their own behavior when they perceive a discrepancy between their past performance and a set standard—these standards are simply assumed to exist, and little attention is paid to how they are determined. To minimize or erase the discrepancy between their behavior and the standard, people can either (a) change their behavior by adjusting their effort or (b) cognitively reevaluate and adjust the standard to meet their level of performance. Self-regulation theory is very broad and provides a basis for understanding natural human behavior, but does not provide much direction to those who want to improve their performance. As it turns out, many people are not naturally good self-regulators.

Self-leadership theory takes self-regulation theory's broad descriptive view of human behavior and applies principles from social cognitive theory and cognitive evaluation theory to explain how we can achieve optimal performance. Social cognitive theory states that our behavior can be explained by the triadic reciprocal relationships among our thoughts, behaviors, and environment. While self-regulation theory explains performance as an act to reduce the discrepancy between our past performance and a set standard, social cognitive theory proposes a cycle of discrepancy reduction, followed by discrepancy production. Basically, after we align our performance with the set standard, we set a higher, more challenging standard—how challenging largely depends on feedback, provided through our thoughts and environment and our self-efficacy (i.e., the degree of confidence felt toward achieving a goal). Cognitive evaluation theory explains that the way to maximize our motivation toward goal attainment is to set intrinsically motivating goals (or standards), where the rewards of task performance increase feelings of competence and self-determination. Self-regulation theory in itself does not explain where the standards that people strive to achieve come from—cognitive evaluation theory explains how we can optimize our performance by setting personally meaningful and hence intrinsically motivating goals.

Self-leadership is not an alternative to self-regulation theory, but is complementary, as it provides strategies for improving our self-regulation. BSL strategies teach us to set challenging goals and to be more aware of our performance, as well as our environment (e.g., challenges, the performance of others), in order to provide ourselves with accurate feedback. NSL strategies tell us to set intrinsically motivating goals or to infuse our pursuit of externally imposed goals with inherently rewarding tasks. Lastly, TSL strategies advise us to break our irrational and dysfunctional thought patterns with more constructive self-talk and mental images, which provides us with realistic feedback and boosts our self-efficacy. By helping us to set and manage self-regulatory standards, self-leadership strategies increase our degree of internal influence and effectiveness.

Self-Leadership Strategies

BSL strategies are essentially self-management techniques that help people regulate their behavior in order to increase their performance. BSL strategies include self-observation, self-goal setting, self-reward, and self-cueing. Self-observation is engaging in a heightened state of awareness regarding one's performance and its outcomes. Goal setting is a very well-established strategy that advises people to set specific and challenging goals in order to fulfill their personal interests or their organization's interests. Self-reward strategies help to increase the effort level toward attaining a goal (e.g., purchasing a new laptop for achieving a sales record). Self-cueing involves manipulating one's environment to trigger positive behaviors or refrain from negative ones (e.g., placing sticky notes with motivational phrases in a visible place). In essence, BSL strategies comprise the fundamental techniques for how to set and attain goals.

NSL strategies help people make their tasks more intrinsically rewarding in order to energize their task-oriented behavior. The first NSL strategy is to build more naturally rewarding aspects into the task to increase the pleasure derived from task-oriented behavior (e.g., job redesign). The second NSL strategy is to concentrate on the more rewarding aspects of the task and cognitively suppress the negative ones. NSL strategies help people increase their feelings of competence and self-determination, which are invigorating and help to optimize performance.

TSL strategies instruct people to replace their dysfunctional thought patterns, mental images, and self-talk with more constructive alternatives. These strategies are rooted in cognitive-behavioral therapy, which asserts that people can change their behavior by changing their perception of reality—their thoughts. People should examine their reoccurring thought patterns and replace their irrational and dysfunctional beliefs with more constructive thought patterns. Similarly, people are advised to pay attention to their self-talk, or the internal dialogue that runs through their mind, and replace the dysfunctional self-talk that distorts their reality with more constructive dialogue that is more accurate and affirming. Lastly, the mental imagery TSL strategy instructs people to envision themselves succeeding at a task prior to actual performance. These three strategies elevate people's self-efficacy and mood, as well as provide more accurate instructions and feedback for successfully performing a task, which helps optimize their performance.

Measurement of Self-Leadership Strategies

Almost all research on self-leadership was conceptual in nature before the Revised Self-Leadership Questionnaire (RSLQ) was developed in 2002. The RSLQ is a 35-item self-report measure that consists of nine factors, which map onto the three main dimensions (or strategies) of self-leadership (i.e., BSL, NSL, and TSL). The RSLQ was developed in English, and has been translated into six different languages since, showing adequate cross-cultural validity in Afrikaans, Portuguese, Turkish, Hebrew,

and German samples. The RSLQ items had to be slightly modified from the original version to improve their validity in Chinese samples. Researchers have also developed a shortened version of the RSLQ, the Abbreviated Self-Leadership Questionnaire (ASLQ), which is a nine-item measure and consists of three factors that represent BSL, NSL, and TSL strategies.

Self-Leadership and Personality

Scholars have debated on whether or not self-leadership is distinguishable from particular personality traits. Researchers have pointed out that people with certain personality traits may naturally enact self-leadership behaviors. For instance, one study found an interaction effect between conscientiousness and self-leadership trainings on self-leadership behaviors, such that participants of self-leadership trainings who lacked conscientiousness showed a greater increase in the use of self-leadership behaviors posttraining than their highly conscientious counterparts. This supports the idea that self-leadership behaviors are learnable skills that are subject to change, not fixed and stable personality traits.

Research examining the relationships between self-leadership strategies and extroversion, emotional stability, and conscientiousness found that extroversion and conscientiousness were positively related to all three self-leadership strategies, while emotional stability was positively related to only NSL. The researchers speculated that self-leadership strategies might be behavioral manifestations of certain personality traits. Besides the Big Five personality traits, research has shown self-leadership to be positively related to narcissism, learning orientation, and internal locus of control, among other factors.

The Outcomes of Self-Leadership

Most of the literature on self-leadership is conceptual in nature, linking it to outcomes like creativity, empowerment, independence, and commitment. A quality review of all of the relationships between self-leadership and its proposed outcomes is beyond the scope of this entry—the following subsections review self-leadership's strongest empirically supported relationships.

Performance

Self-leadership is a theory that ultimately seeks to help people improve their personal effectiveness. BSL strategies, which are core self-management behaviors, can directly improve performance; however, their influence is enhanced by cognitive and motivational functions. For instance, the BSL strategy "goal setting" is a much more powerful tool for improving performance when people set personally meaningful goals and feel strongly that they can attain those goals—two mechanisms that comprise NSL and TSL strategies. A recent study supported this theory, finding that TSL and NSL strategies moderate the relationship between BSL and performance. While certain self-leadership strategies directly improve performance, self-efficacy and positive affect may mediate this relationship. The following subsections offer a brief summary on self-leadership's relationship to self-efficacy and positive affect.

Self-Efficacy

Self-efficacy is the most widely used explanatory mechanism for connecting self-leadership to performance. Self-efficacious people set higher standards and persist more in the face of adversity, which generally helps them outperform people with less self-efficacy. While studies have shown that each of the self-leadership strategies can enhance self-efficacy, TSL strategies are particularly crucial. People are less likely to correctly approach a problem and exert enough effort to overcome it if their thought patterns are irrational and dysfunctional. However, when people implement TSL strategies, they optimally shape their thought patterns over time to be more opportunity oriented through the repeated use of constructive self-talk and mental imagery. Indeed, self-leadership trainings, as well as trainings that just include TSL strategies, have demonstrated that they can improve employees' job performance by increasing their self-efficacy.

Positive Affect, Stress, and Satisfaction

Self-leadership strategies beneficially influence affect-related variables (e.g., mood, stress, and satisfaction), which are often viewed as mediators of performance and organizational outcomes (e.g., absences and turnover). Studies investigating the benefits of self-leadership trainings show that they reduce participants' strain by improving their positive affect and general self-efficacy. Employees who engage in self-leadership strategies, like not obsessing about their failures and focusing on the enjoyable aspects of work, enjoy their work and minimize stressors more than those who do not, thus experiencing less job strain. Out of the self-leadership strategies, TSL strategies may have the strongest relationships with affect-related variables—the assumption that our thoughts are strongly related to our emotions is one of the central tenets of cognitive-behavioral therapy—the most widely used therapeutic approach in clinical psychology. TSL strategies encourage employees to replace their dysfunctional thoughts (perfectionism, dependence on others, etc.) with more constructive ones. Recent research demonstrated that self-leadership strategies have indirect, beneficial effects on employees' subjective well-being and job satisfaction by lessening their dysfunctional thought patterns.

Benjamin Uhrich

See also Employee and Leader Self-Talk; Leadership Development; Positive Psychology Applied to Work; Self-Determination Theory; Self-Efficacy; Self-Regulation Theory; Social Cognitive Theory

Further Readings

Houghton, J. D., & Neck, C. P. (2002). The revised self-leadership questionnaire: Testing a hierarchical factor structure for self-leadership. *Journal of Managerial Psychology, 17*(8), 672–691.

Manz, C. C. (1986). Self-leadership: Toward an expanded theory of self-influence processes in organizations. *Academy of Management Review, 11*(3), 585–600.

Neck, C. P., & Houghton, J. D. (2006). Two decades of self-leadership theory and research: Past developments, present trends, and future possibilities. *Journal of Managerial Psychology, 21*(4), 270–295.

Neck, C. P., & Manz, C. C. (1992). Thought self-leadership: The influence of self-talk and mental imagery on performance. *Journal of Organizational Behavior, 13*(7), 681–699.

Neck, C., Manz, C., Van Belle, D. A., Mash, K., Coogan, M. D., Brettler, M. Z., . . . & Mills, R. C. (2011). *Mastering self-leadership: Empowering yourself for personal excellence.* Upper Saddle River, NJ: Prentice Hall.

SELF-REGULATION THEORY

The term *self-regulation* refers to a complex and dynamic set of processes involved in setting and pursuing goals. It is commonly used to refer to a broad set of theories that seek to describe, explain, and predict these goal-directed processes. Although many theories of self-regulation exist, each proposing some unique characteristics, researchers generally agree on several fundamental features of self-regulation.

Goals and Goal Setting

The most fundamental aspect of self-regulation theory is the idea that much of human behavior is directed toward accomplishing goals. Indeed, it is the pursuit of goals that forms the focus of much of self-regulation theory. The term *goal* takes on a fairly broad meaning in this context, referring to desired future states that individuals wish to attain.

Goals can differ from one another in many ways. For example, they may be assigned by others (e.g., by one's supervisor), they may be self-set by the individual, or they may be determined by some combination of the two (e.g., participatively set). Goals can vary in both difficulty and specificity, as well as in content. They can be near-term (proximal) goals or long-term (distal) goals. Goals can even vary in the extent to which one is consciously aware that the goal is guiding behavior. All of these characteristics have important influences on cognition, affect, and behavior.

One of the most consistent findings (although it is not without exception) is that difficult, specific goals often result in high levels of performance. Although this finding has great practical benefit by itself, self-regulation theorists seek to understand precisely how, when, and why such goal-setting effects are obtained. Thus, self-regulatory theories not only focus on goal setting, but give major emphasis to understanding the dynamic processes involved in goal striving over time. This increased understanding of goal-related processes provides valuable information about how motivational interventions can best be implemented.

Feedback and Self-Monitoring

Feedback plays a critical role in self-regulatory processes. In this context, feedback refers to information concerning an individual's progress toward attaining a goal. By comparing feedback to goals, an individual can determine the level of success he or she is having in pursuing the goal. If the feedback indicates that he or she is not making sufficient progress, then changes are often undertaken, such as investing more effort, trying different approaches to meet the goal, or even abandoning the goal altogether. In monitoring and reacting to feedback, individuals are sensitive not only to the magnitude of any discrepancies between their goals and their current state, but also to the velocity of discrepancy reduction, and even to changes in velocity (i.e., acceleration or deceleration). For example, faster progress tends to evoke more positive affective responses and more optimistic expectations for success.

Feedback need not come from outside sources (e.g., one's supervisor)—indeed, such external feedback is often unavailable. Thus, individuals often rely on *self-monitoring* to evaluate their progress toward achieving their goals. Unfortunately, individuals are notoriously flawed in making such self-evaluations, typically perceiving their progress to be better than it really is. As a result, without sufficiently frequent and specific external feedback, individuals often make poor decisions in the pursuit of their goals, such as investing less time and effort than is truly necessary for success and persisting with ineffective strategies.

Goal Hierarchies

Most theories of self-regulation propose that goals are arranged hierarchically in a series of means–ends relationships. For example, a car salesperson may have a goal to obtain a pay raise. To accomplish this goal, the individual must get a positive performance evaluation from his or her supervisor during the annual performance appraisal. To get a positive evaluation, he or she must sell at least eight new cars per month, and so on.

The importance of goals higher up in the hierarchy can determine how committed individuals are to particular goals lower in the hierarchy. For example, if a student is seeking an A grade in a psychology course because he or she sees it as a necessary step toward fulfilling a lifelong dream of getting into graduate school, his or her commitment to obtaining the grade is likely to be very high. In contrast, if an A is not seen as important for attaining other valued goals, lower commitment is likely to result.

Goal hierarchies are highly complex. Rather than having a strict one-to-one relationship between higher-level and lower-level goals, a higher-level goal, or end, can often be obtained by achieving several alternative, lower-level goals, or means (i.e., equifinality—"all roads lead to Rome"). Likewise, a given lower-level goal or means can often serve many higher-level goals or ends (i.e., multifinality—"kill two birds with one stone"). Goal hierarchies are also highly individualized. Each individual's hierarchy may be distinct and change over time. Some theorists postulate that an important determinant of individual personality is the goals that exist (or the relative importance of such goals) near the top of one's hierarchy.

Approach Versus Avoidance Goals

Up to this point, goals have been described as future states that individuals wish to attain. Such goals are often referred to as *approach goals* because individuals seek to move toward these states. However, *avoidance goals* are also powerful influences on behavior, representing undesired future states that individuals wish to avoid. For a variety of reasons, the self-regulatory processes resulting from approach and avoidance goals differ in subtle but very important ways.

One important way in which approach and avoidance goals differ is in the affect (i.e., emotions) that arises from successful and unsuccessful pursuit. In short, success at an approach goal often leads to excitement or elation, whereas success at an avoidance goal often leads to relief or relaxation. Failure at an approach goal often leads to sadness or depression, whereas failure at an avoidance goal often leads to anxiety or nervousness. Because emotions can have important influences on the way individuals perceive and react to the world around them, the distinction between approach and avoidance self-regulation is of great practical importance.

Summary

Despite the vast insights and many practical applications that have emerged from the research on self-regulation, researchers are only just beginning to understand all of the implications of this complex, dynamic, and individualized process. Nonetheless, it appears clear that the implications are many, and increased understanding in this area will likely yield further improvements in effectiveness in the workplace and beyond.

Aaron M. Schmidt

See also Feedback; Goal-Setting Theory; Path–Goal Theory

Further Readings

Carver, C. S., & Scheier, M. F. (2011). Self-regulation of action and affect. In K. D. Vohs & R. F. Baumeister (Eds.), *Handbook of self-regulation: Research, theory, and applications* (2nd ed., pp. 3–21). New York, NY: Guilford Press.

Diefendorff, J. M., & Chandler, M. M. (2011). Motivating employees. In S. Zedeck (Ed.), *APA handbook of industrial and organizational psychology: Maintaining, expanding, and contracting the organization* (Vol. 3, pp. 65–135). Washington, DC: American Psychological Association.

Locke, E. A., & Latham, G. P. (2002). Building a practically useful theory of goal setting and task motivation: A 35-year odyssey. *American Psychologist, 57*(9), 705–717. doi:10.1037/0003-066X.57.9.705

Schmidt, A. M., Beck, J. W., & Gillespie, J. Z. (2012). Motivation. In N. Schmitt & S. Highhouse (Eds.), *Handbook of psychology: Industrial and organizational psychology* (Vol. 12, 2nd ed., pp. 311–340). London, UK: Wiley.

Shah, J. Y. (2005). The automatic pursuit and management of goals. *Current Directions in Psychological Science, 14*(1), 10–13. doi:10.1111/j.0963-7214.2005.00325.x

SERVANT LEADERSHIP

Servant leadership refers to leaders who guide, motivate, instill hope, and create a humble and caring environment through establishing a high-quality relationship with their followers. Robert Greenleaf in 1977 first coined the term *servant leadership* and introduced it in the management literature. In his seminal article "The Servant as Leader," he claimed that a leader should view himself first as a servant, then as a leader. A servant leader places the subordinates' motives, values, and interests above his or her own. A servant leader's inherent desire and primary objective is to serve first, as opposed to lead. Servant leaders intend to transform their subordinates to become stronger, independent, sensible, and more likely to become servants themselves.

The concept of servant leadership puts the leader in a nonfocal position within a team where the leader's prime concern is to provide resources and support to the followers without the hope of getting praise and appreciation in return. The central assumption of servant leadership is that leaders give up their own self-interests in favor of the larger collective well-being of the organization and society.

Conceptualizing Servant Leadership

Although the term *servant leadership* originated in the late 1970s, many different explanations attempting to classify servant leadership behaviors have since emerged, resulting in various conceptualizations of servant leadership. Consequently, there have been difficulties in arriving at a precise operationalization of servant leadership. Four models of servant leadership have gained popularity—namely, the Spears, Laub, Russell and Stone, and Patterson models of servant leadership.

On the basis of Greenleaf's definition of servant leadership, Spears identified 10 attributes of servant leadership: (1) listening, or the ability to understand and focus on communication; (2) empathy, or considering others' perspectives and accepting them; (3) healing, or the capacity of curing individuals emotionally; (4) awareness, or being fully informed; (5) persuasion, or convincing others based on logic and factual evidence rather than on position; (6) conceptualization, or thinking and resolving tasks; (7) foresight, or anticipating consequences of events and utilizing intuition; (8) stewardship, or maintaining trust of others and fulfilling others' needs; (9) commitment to growth of followers, or taking care of followers' personal, career, and spiritual development; and (10) building community, or trying to find a way to create bonding among those who work in the organization.

Laub operationalized servant leadership as comprising six major traits: (1) valuing people,

(2) developing people, (3) building community, (4) displaying authenticity, (5) providing leadership, and (6) sharing leadership. Russell and Stone asserted that servant leaders encompass attributes of vision, trust, credibility, service, modeling, pioneering, appreciating others, and empowerment.

Similarly, Patterson introduced his framework of servant leadership that was an extension of the transformational leadership model. Patterson's model identified "agapao" love, humility, altruism, vision, trust, empowerment, and service as the seven key dimensions of servant leadership. Page and Wong defined servant leadership as serving followers by developing their welfare to achieve mutual goals. They developed a conceptual framework for measuring servant leadership on the basis of four dimensions: personality, task, relationships, and processes. Clearly, all these models conceptualize servant leadership with overlapping attributes and measures that intend to capture those attributes. Despite recent attempts to come up with an overall framework that fully captures all aspects of servant leadership, there remains a lack of consensus among scholars regarding a consolidated model of servant leadership. Nonetheless, Spears's model of servant leadership and its operationalization through Barbuto and Wheeler still is the most popular framework for conceptualizing and measuring servant leadership.

Servant Leadership and Other Related Leadership Constructs: Commonalities and Distinctions

The leadership literature identifies servant leadership as having a considerable overlap with some of the contemporary leadership theories, particularly transformational, ethical, authentic, spiritual, and Level 5 leadership. Although these terminologies share a lot of conceptual similarities with servant leadership, there are clear differences that make servant leadership theoretically and empirically distinct from other leadership styles.

Transformational leadership has the most overlap with servant leadership, especially the individualized consideration and intellectual stimulation dimensions of transformational leadership, which bear resemblance with several key features of servant leadership. However, consistent with the notion of service in servant leadership, servant leaders possess the key attributes of humility, honesty, and interpersonal acceptance, which are not central to transformational leaders. In addition, transformational leaders focus on the attainment of organizational goals, whereas servant leaders' prime objective is to consider followers' needs and fulfill them.

Ethical leadership is another construct that shares similarity with servant leadership. Ethical leadership emphasizes displaying appropriate conduct within organizations based on organizational norms and values. It is similar to servant leadership in the aspects of the leader being trustworthy and fair and communicating openly with followers. Although the morality and fairness component of ethical leadership strongly overlaps with servant leadership attributes, the latter is concerned with putting others first and being modest, which are not of primary concern in ethical leadership.

Authentic leadership is another comparable construct that shows commonalities with servant leadership. Authentic leadership is concerned with the leader being genuine and instilling feelings of expressing one's "true self." Authenticity is one of the key features in servant leadership; however, the latter is focused on moral love, selfless caring, and emotional healing of followers, characteristics that are notably absent from authentic leadership.

Spiritual leadership, another closely related construct, emphasizes creating a workplace that is intrinsically motivating for the follower and from which individuals can derive meaningfulness, identity, and a sense of inner bliss. Although the underlying tenets of this construct do resemble servant leadership, spiritual leadership has been operationalized in a manner where organizational culture is the focus of attention, whereas servant leadership focuses on the leader's service behaviors toward followers.

Finally, Level 5 leadership refers to a style where successful leaders possess personal humility and professional will. Level 5 leadership shows resemblance with servant leadership on traits of modesty and providing direction; however, the former has to do more with organizational success and less with developing and nurturing followers. In sum, servant leadership shows many similarities to related leadership constructs, yet it is positioned as a conceptually and empirically unique and distinct construct.

Antecedents and Consequences of Servant Leadership

The antecedents of servant leadership can be grouped into three major categories: motivational aspects, personality or individual characteristics, and cultural values. Although motivational causes of servant leadership have been researched to a lesser extent, scholars have examined the inner needs—values of truthfulness, integrity, fairness, and humility—as key determinants of servant leadership. Among the Big Five personality factors, high agreeableness and low extroversion have been strongly linked to servant leadership. In addition, individuals who are high in self-determination have the capacity to regulate their behavior, a vital factor in order to act as a servant leader. People who are at the moral cognitive stage of development, which is the highest level of ethics and morality, are also more likely to become servant leaders. Cognitive complexity is also found to be an individual characteristic that can contribute to the development of servant leadership.

Lastly, culture has been cited as a major force promoting servant leadership. The GLOBE (Global Leadership and Organizational Behavior Effectiveness) studies of leadership have identified two cultural dimensions, humane orientation and low power distance, to be strongly linked to servant leadership. Cultures that rate high on humane orientation instill values of displaying affection and kindness, accepting mistakes, and being sensitive toward others' needs, which is vital in becoming a servant leader. Similarly, cultures low in power distance are more likely to ingrain servant leaders within organizations, as there is a lesser gap between the leader and followers in terms of sharing of authority, decision making, status, and other privileges.

Strong theoretical and empirical support for a number of attitudinal, psychological, and behavioral outcomes of servant leadership exists at the individual, team, and organizational levels. Empirical studies employing cross-sectional research designs in a number of occupations across different countries have found servant leadership to promote high levels of job satisfaction, organization commitment, work engagement, and psychological empowerment and low levels of turnover intentions among followers. Servant leaders inculcate trust in their followers, foster employee loyalty, increase identification with the leader, and create a conducive work environment. Servant leaders, through their selfless actions, help build positive perceptions of procedural justice, service climate, and person–organization fit among employees.

Servant leadership has been found to be negatively related to employee burnout, stress, ego depletion, and need for recovery and fosters better psychological health over and above job stressors. In addition, servant leaders positively influence followers' job performance, organizational citizenship behavior toward other individuals and the organization, and creativity. Servant leaders' motivation to serve first and their altruistic motives prompt employees to fulfill their job responsibilities, go beyond their work duties, and contribute effectively at the workplace. Servant leadership also affects team effectiveness in the form of team performance, team potency, team- or unit-level organizational citizenship behavior, and team identification within organizations.

Moreover, servant leadership has been found to influence organizational outcomes such as corporate social responsibility, organizational performance, and sustainability. Studies indicate that servant leaders focus more on building relationships, as opposed to return on investment; show a concern for serving all stakeholders, not just shareholders; emphasize ethics; and are open-minded and caring. This in turn fosters an environment where these leaders achieve better organizational outcomes in both the short and long term.

A Way Forward for Servant Leadership

Servant leadership is an important construct in the domain of leadership, yet it is pertinent to realize that some important challenges need to be addressed. One of the major concerns with the concept of servant leadership is that it sounds too idealistic, which somewhat reduces its appeal to practitioners. Second, the bulk of the early research on servant leadership was theoretical and prescriptive in nature, which later led to emergence of many models to identify servant leadership traits. Later, several measures were developed to test these underlying servant leadership models. Unfortunately, this led to lack of convergence in terms of measurement and application of the construct.

Clearly, more theoretical and empirical research is needed to synthesize the existing frameworks and provide a consolidated theoretical understanding of servant leadership. There is a need to combine various measures to develop a better scale that conceptualizes and taps into the notion of servant leadership in a useful way. Also, efforts should be made to empirically discriminate servant leadership from other similar constructs such as authentic, ethical, and transformational leadership. Another concern is that the notion of *servant* gives it a negative connotation. The term itself might also imply someone who is passive and obedient and can forsake power. Scholars need to address this issue in their future conceptualizations of servant leadership. Critics also argue that conceptualizations of servant leadership that focus on the elements of humility, modesty, and selfless love for followers suggest that there is a probability of manipulation from followers. Relatedly, leadership that is selfless and giving to such an extent might be considered a sign of weakness, thereby increasing the chances of being exploited by selfish followers.

It is very important that as a way forward we study servant leadership in different cultures. It would be interesting to see how the concept of servant leadership is perceived in newer contexts, especially the developing and emerging economies of Asia. It is possible that a servant leader is seen as helping and supportive in one culture and weak and lacking authority in another. Therefore, research in newer contexts would help discern whether servant leadership results in beneficial or harmful consequences in different cultures.

Usman Raja and Saima Naseer

See also Charismatic Leadership Theory; Leadership and Supervision; Transformational and Transactional Leadership; Workplace Spirituality and Spiritual Leadership

Further Readings

Graham, J. W. (1991). Servant-leadership in organizations: Inspirational and moral. *The Leadership Quarterly*, 2, 105–119.

Greenleaf, R. K. (1977). *Servant leadership*. Mahwah, NJ: Paulist Press.

Hunter, E. M., Neubert, M. J., Perry, S. J., Witt, L. A., Penney, L. M., & Weinberger, E. (2013). Servant leaders inspire servant followers: Antecedents and outcomes for employees and the organization. *The Leadership Quarterly, 24*, 316–331.

Laub, J. A. (1999). *Assessing the servant organization: Development of the servant organizational leadership assessment (SOLA) instrument* (p. 00125). Boca Raton: Florida Atlantic University.

Liden, R. C., Wayne, S. J., Liao, C., & Meuser, J. D. (2014). Servant leadership and serving culture: Influence on individual and unit performance. *Academy of Management Journal, 57*, 1434–1452.

Page, D., & Wong, T. P. (2000). A conceptual framework for measuring servant leadership. *The human factor in shaping the course of history and development.* Lanham, MD: University Press of America.

Spears, L. C. (1998). *Insights on leadership: Service, stewardship, spirit, and servant-leadership.* New York, NY: Wiley.

Van Dierendonck, D. (2011). Servant leadership: A review and synthesis. *Journal of Management, 37*, 1228–1261.

SERVICE CLIMATE

Service climate is a type of organizational climate with a strategic focus on customer service and customer service quality. In research on organizational climate, there is a distinction between *molar* climate, or the general climate that employees experience in organizations, and *focused* climate, or the aspects of the environment that are related to strategic goals or specific processes in the organization. The focused approach to studying organization climate has grown substantially in recent years, and one of the most heavily researched focused climates is service climate. Service climate is defined as the shared meaning that organizational members attach to policies, practices, and procedures they experience with regard to customer service as well as the behaviors that are rewarded, supported, and expected with regard to customer service. This overview begins with a brief history of the service climate construct, followed by a summary of findings from past research and some emerging issues that are directions for future research.

The earliest work on service climate was done by Benjamin Schneider and his colleagues in the 1970s and 1980s. In several studies of bank branches, they found that customer perceptions of service quality were higher in branches where managers emphasized service, where employee efforts to deliver service quality were rewarded, and where there were active efforts to retain customers. Their work laid a foundation for the general idea that what *employees* experience in terms of their organization's policies and practices about customer service predict what *customers* experience in terms of service quality. The study of the relationship between employee perceptions of service climate and customer perceptions of service quality provided the foundation for what has come to be known as linkage research, which addresses the connection between employee perceptions of their work environment and important organizational outcomes, such as business performance or customer satisfaction. A number of outcomes of service climate have been studied over the years, including customer evaluations of satisfaction and service quality, customer retention and loyalty, individual- and group-level service performance, employee attitudes (e.g., job satisfaction, organizational commitment, and intention to stay), engagement, effort, and organization-level financial outcomes. The linkage between service climate and such outcomes has been demonstrated in a variety of environments, including bank branches, grocery store departments, health care settings, insurance agencies, restaurants, and hotels.

Research on the outcomes of service climate established the importance of establishing a service climate in customer service organizations. The question then becomes how to establish such a climate. Studies of the antecedents of service climate address that question. One of the most commonly studied antecedents of service climate is leadership. Service climates are more likely to be established when leaders are transformational, such that they are able to communicate a vision to employees and transform their values to be aligned with the values and goals of the organization. Service climates are also more likely to be found in units led by servant leaders, who are focused on serving the needs of their employees, such that those employees are then better able to serve the needs of customers. Whereas transformational and servant leadership are general leadership styles, research has also examined leaders' emphasis on customer service, or service leadership. Meta-analytic findings across a number of studies suggest that service leadership has a stronger relationship with service climate than the more general leadership styles. Thus, it seems to be the case that leaders who value service are more likely to create an environment that emphasizes service by putting into place the policies, procedures, and reward systems that communicate to employees the importance of providing high-quality service to customers.

In addition to leadership, research has shown that service climates are more likely to form when there is a strong infrastructure supporting employees and their work. This infrastructure includes personnel support, equipment or supply support, organizational culture, internal service (the extent to which customer service employees receive the support they need from other departments within the organization), and human resource management practices such as training. The logic is that in order for employees to provide the highest-quality service to customers, they need to be in the best position to be able to do so. For instance, employees need to have the knowledge and skills to be able to do their jobs, which can be addressed through effective training. They need access to certain resources and information from other departments, because without them, they cannot help their customers as effectively. They need systems that work effectively so that customers are not having to wait around due to slow or poorly functioning equipment or computers. And, more generally, employees need to feel supported and cared for by their organization so they can in turn optimally support and care for their customers.

Integrating the research above on the antecedents and outcomes of service climate, researchers have begun to examine the chain of variables through which internal organizational processes ultimately lead to financial outcomes. As one example, a study of grocery store departments in the United States found that employees' ratings of their department managers' service leadership predicted employees' ratings of their departments' service climate, which then predicted managers' ratings of the department employees' customer-focused organizational citizenship behavior (OCB). In turn, customer-focused OCB predicted customers' reports of satisfaction with the departments, which then predicted departments' quarterly sales.

As another example, a study of retail stores, hair and beauty salons, and restaurants and cafés in Taiwan found that employee reports of their stores' high-performance work practices (e.g., staffing, training, and compensation) were positively associated with employee reports of service climate. In turn, service climate was positively associated with managers' reports of the stores' service performance, which predicted managers' reports of the stores' market performance relative to competitors. Both of these studies illustrate the important role that employees' experiences within their organizations play in creating perceptions of service climate; how the impact of leadership and human resource practices can, at least in part, be explained by the service climate they help create; and the important role that service climate can play in contributing to an organization's financial performance.

As illustrated in the previous examples of research on service climate, studies of service climate often focus on organizational units. The units under consideration can be departments (as in the grocery store department study), branches (as in the studies of bank branches), or stores (as in the study of retail stores, hair and beauty salons, and restaurants and cafés). Conceptualizing variables at the unit level of analysis assumes that there is some level of agreement about how people perceive the unit, and this level of agreement can be statistically assessed. The level of agreement about a unit's service climate is referred to as the strength of the service climate. The study of climate strength has raised awareness that organizations should not only want the level of the service climate to be high, but also seek to have strong agreement about the climate, or high climate strength. In contrast, if the levels of the service climate are low, it is better to have a weak climate than a strong climate (in other words, it is better to have some individuals disagreeing that the climate is negative rather than all individuals agreeing that service is not a priority). This idea that climate strength moderates the effects of climate on outcomes is relatively new, and although it has received support in some studies, others have not found such effects. Thus, researchers are continuing to better understand the role of climate strength in understanding service climate and its effects in organizations.

In addition to climate strength, a number of other boundary conditions or moderators of climate–outcome relationships have been identified by researchers. These studies address questions about the conditions under which the relationship between service climate and service outcomes is strongest versus when it is weaker. As an example, studies have shown that the relationship between service climate and service outcomes varies depending on the frequency of customer contact. When there is a great deal of customer contact, service climate has a stronger relationship with service outcomes, because customers' perceptions of the service quality and their satisfaction will be based more on their interactions with employees, and it is when there are many such interactions that having a service climate matters most. Other research has shown that the relationship between service climate and service outcomes is strongest when the product being delivered is more tangible, when service employees are interdependent (they rely on each other to get work done), when internal service is high (employees provide good service to each other), and when the type of service is personal (vs. nonpersonal).

Service climate itself has been studied as a moderator or boundary condition as well. One such study examined how service climate impacted the relationship between individual employees' customer orientation and their actual customer-oriented behaviors. The researchers found that customer orientation was related to customer-oriented behaviors when service climate was high but not when it was low. The argument was that a service climate provides more opportunities for service workers to act on their customer orientation; in other words, they have the resources, training, and supports in place that allow them to do their jobs to the fullest. When service climate is low, those supports are not in place, and thus even though employees may have high levels of customer orientation, they are not able to provide the high-quality customer service they desire to give. In another example, a study found that service climate moderated the relationship between customer orientation and job autonomy as predicting customer-focused voice (employees speaking up about customer service issues) in a hospital context. Specifically, a service climate had a compensatory effect such that it resulted in employees speaking up more about customer service issues even when customer orientation and job autonomy were low.

A rich literature on service climate has developed over the past 4 decades, but there is certainly potential for additional understanding of the construct. Future research directions include several possible expansions of the scope of past research. Past research has been somewhat limited in terms of geographical breadth, such that cross-cultural work would be useful to test the generalizability of existing research. Additional complexity in terms of studying service climate across multiple levels simultaneously (e.g., group, department, and organization); integrating the role of higher-level leadership, including a broader range of supports from within the organization (e.g., informational technology and marketing); and studying how service climates develop and change over time would yield a more sophisticated understanding of the relationships among antecedents and outcomes of service climate.

Mark G. Ehrhart and Karen Holcombe Ehrhart

See also Customer Satisfaction and Service; Groups; Leadership and Supervision; Multilevel Modeling; Organizational Behavior; Organizational Climate; Organizational Culture

Further Readings

Bowen, D. E., & Schneider, B. (2014). A service climate synthesis and future research agenda. *Journal of Service Research, 17*, 5–22.

Ehrhart, M. G., Schneider, B., & Macey, W. H. (2014). *Organizational climate and culture: An introduction to theory, research, and practice.* New York, NY: Routledge.

Hong, Y., Liao, H., Hu, J., & Jiang, K. (2013). Missing link in the service profit chain: A meta-analytic review of the antecedents, consequences, and moderators of service climate. *Journal of Applied Psychology, 98*, 237–267.

Schneider, B., Bowen, D. E., Ehrhart, M. G., & Holcombe, K. M. (2000). The climate for service: Evolution of a construct. In N. M. Ashkanasy, C. P. M. Wilderom, & M. F. Peterson (Eds.), *Handbook of organizational culture and climate* (pp. 21–36). Thousand Oaks, CA: Sage.

Schneider, B., Macey, W. H., Lee, W., & Young, S. A. (2009). Organizational service climate drivers of the American Customer Satisfaction Index (ACSI) and financial and market performance. *Journal of Service Research, 12,* 3–14.

Schneider, B., & White, S. S. (2004). *Service quality: Research perspectives.* Thousand Oaks, CA: Sage.

Yagil, D. (2014). Service quality. In B. Schneider & K. M. Barbera (Eds.), *The Oxford handbook of organizational climate and culture* (pp. 297–316). New York, NY: Oxford University Press.

SEXUAL DISCRIMINATION

Sexual discrimination occurs when individuals are treated differently or receive different outcomes solely because they are men or women. Title VII of the Civil Rights Act of 1964 made sexual discrimination illegal in the U.S. workplace. Specifically, Title VII prohibits discrimination against any employee or applicant for employment because of his or her sex with regard to hiring, termination, promotion, compensation, job training, or any other condition or privilege of employment. Title VII prohibitions also include sexual harassment and pregnancy discrimination. Although Title VII protects both sexes, women are systematically more likely than men to be victims of sexual discrimination.

Legally, sexual discrimination is identified as manifesting itself in one of two forms: disparate treatment and disparate impact. *Disparate treatment* refers to the differential treatment of an individual intentionally and specifically because that individual is a man or a woman. This includes discrimination predicated on assumptions about the abilities, traits, or performance of individuals on the basis of sex. Examples of disparate treatment are asking men and women different questions during a job interview, offering a lower starting salary because the recruit is a woman, or exhibiting reluctance to hire a woman for a job that requires long hours and travel.

Disparate impact constitutes a broader definition of gender discrimination and is more complex. Disparate impact results when a particular group is systematically and adversely affected by a company's policy. Although the policy may not have been created with the intent of discrimination, it may nonetheless disproportionately exclude individuals on the basis of sex for reasons that are not job related. For example, requiring applicants to take a selection test that involves lifting 100 pounds, even though 30 pounds is the maximum a person would need to lift on the job, might unnecessarily screen out qualified female applicants.

Evidence of Sexual Discrimination

Women have made substantial gains in the last several decades in the work domain: They now compose nearly half the U.S. labor market and had a labor force participation rate of 46.16% in 2013. In addition, women are closing the education gap, earning more bachelor's and master's degrees than men and increasing their representation in business, law, and medical schools. Given the strides that women have made, coupled with the illegality of sexual discrimination, is sexual discrimination really a problem in the modern workplace? If so, what is its prevalence?

According to many sources of data, it is clear that sexual discrimination remains a concern in the work domain. One piece of direct evidence is the sheer number of sexual discrimination charges filed with the Equal Employment Opportunity Commission (EEOC), a key federal agency responsible for the enforcement of Title VII. In 2014, the EEOC received 26,027 charges of sex-based discrimination, a number that has been on the rise in the past 15 years. Moreover, these data are unlikely to capture the whole picture. Many women do not challenge the discriminatory practices they encounter in the workplace for fear of losing their jobs, and others are deterred by the personal and financial costs associated with submitting a claim.

Examining the general topography of the U.S. workforce and the way women fit into it, a clearer picture of gender inequity emerges. For example, although women make up nearly half of the U.S. workforce, they continue to be concentrated in occupations that are traditionally considered female—often support roles that are low in status and pay. In 2003, the top five occupations held by women were administrative assistant (96.3% female); registered nurse (90.2%); nursing, psychiatric, and home health aide (89%); elementary and middle school teacher (80.6%); and cashier

(75.5%). Meanwhile, women remain decidedly underrepresented in roles that are traditionally considered male—roles that are often highest in authority, responsibility, and prestige in organizations.

This seemingly impenetrable barrier to women's entrance into the highest echelons of organizations is often referred to as the *glass ceiling*. Indeed, the higher up the organizational hierarchy, the more scarce women become. For example, in 2015, 45% of the Fortune 500 labor force was made up of women, yet only 25.1% of executive officials and 19.2% of board members were women. Twenty-three (4.6%) women were CEOs. Not surprisingly, in light of these figures, only 8.1% of the Fortune 500 top earners were women.

Gender inequities are also evident in the way women are compensated; women continue to be paid less than men. In 2013, among full-time workers, women were paid 78% of what men were paid; this wage gap has remained virtually stagnant over the past decade. Differences in the jobs and occupations held by men contribute somewhat to this discrepancy; however, even after controlling for factors such as education, job training, work experience, and occupation, more than half of the gap in earnings remains unexplained. Indeed, economists often attribute approximately 40% of the pay gap to discrimination (i.e., factors other than characteristics of workers or their jobs).

Despite the significant advances that women have made over the past few decades, sexual discrimination continues to be a problem in organizational life. Women are consistently employed in lower-status jobs and earn less than men. This begs the question, why? In considering the causes of sexual discrimination in the workplace, gender stereotypes frequently are designated as the culprit.

Antecedents of Sexual Discrimination

Gender Stereotypes

The belief that women and men are different is widely shared in our culture; in fact, research suggests that men and women are often viewed as polar opposites. Men are thought to be rational, independent, decisive, and assertive, whereas women are described as illogical, dependent, indecisive, and passive. Men and women are also described differently with respect to the qualities of warmth and expressiveness, with women rated more favorably. Yet the traits associated with men and women are not only different but valued differently. Although each sex is credited with desirable traits, it is generally argued that male traits are more highly valued in Western culture than those associated with women. That is, achievement-oriented traits typically ascribed to men have been shown to be more highly valued than nurturing and affiliation-oriented traits typically ascribed to women; this is particularly true with respect to the work domain.

How do these stereotypes translate into discrimination in the workplace? The answer to this question lies not only in the stereotypes about women but also in conceptions of what is required to effectively handle jobs that are considered to be male. Taken together, these elements determine performance expectations—expectations that ultimately become the precursor to sexual discrimination.

Expectations about how successful or unsuccessful an individual will be when working at a particular job are determined by the fit between the perceived attributes of the individual and the perceived attributes required for success at that particular job. If the fit is good, then success will be expected; if the fit is poor, then failure will be expected. These fit-derived performance expectations, whether positive or negative, play a key role in evaluation processes because individuals have a tendency to perpetuate and confirm them. Once an expectation has been formed, it becomes a lens through which information is filtered, including what is attended to, how it is interpreted, and whether it is remembered and recalled when making critical decisions.

Applying this reasoning to women in organizations, the lack of fit between the stereotype-based perceptions of women's attributes and the perceptions of many job requirements leads hiring managers to conclude that women are ill equipped to handle certain types of work—namely, work that is considered to be male sex-typed—and the expectation that women are unlikely to succeed in traditionally male roles. These performance expectations are powerful in their impact: They create a tenacious predisposition to view women in a way that is consistent with the expectation, thereby detrimentally affecting the way they are regarded and the way their work is evaluated. The behavioral consequence is sexual discrimination.

From Expectations to Discrimination

Research has demonstrated that negative performance expectations often permeate the entire process of women's careers. In personnel selection, there is a tendency for men to be preferred over women of similar qualifications when the job is one traditionally held by men. For example, researchers have found that for managerial positions, the *same* résumé is rated more favorably when it is believed to belong to a man rather than a woman. Women are also placed in positions that seem more appropriate for their attributes—ones in which the fit seems good. Thus, women tend to be placed in staff rather than line jobs, where they can provide support and assistance, something they are thought to be well equipped to do.

When women do attain jobs that are considered to be male sex-typed, the effects of negative expectations persist. Men and women producing identical work are often evaluated differently, with women's work regarded as inferior. Even when a woman's successful performance is indisputable, evaluators may attribute it to some factor other than the woman herself, be it another person (if she has worked in a group), the ease of the task, or some transient factor such as luck. If it is impossible to dismiss her role in her success and she is acknowledged as competent in a male sex-typed role, then she is likely to face a different type of discrimination—she seems to be disliked and suffers interpersonal consequences. There are many "shoulds" and "should nots" attached to gender stereotypes that, when violated, have negative consequences. Thus, the *same* assertive behavior that is seen as tough and decisive (and appropriate) when acted out by a man may be seen as "bitchy" (and inappropriate) when enacted by a woman.

These findings have obvious implications not only for entry-level access to organizations but also for advancement opportunities such as training programs, promotions, and career trajectories in organizations. These individual processes, at an aggregate level, account for macro-level discrimination: the discrepancies in the types of roles women occupy, the roles they don't, and the compensation they receive for their work.

Summary

Despite being made illegal by the Civil Rights Act of 1964, discrimination on the basis of sex continues to be a problem in today's work organizations. At the root of this problem are gender stereotypes and the expectations they produce, which ultimately result in the differential treatment of men and women on the basis of their sex.

Michelle C. Haynes
and Madeline E. Heilman

See also Adverse Impact/Disparate Treatment/ Discrimination at Work; Civil Rights Act of 1964; Civil Rights Act of 1991; Glass Ceiling; Sexual Harassment; Stereotyping

Further Readings

Eagly, A. H., & Carli, L. L. (2007). *Through the labyrinth: The truth about how women become leaders.* Cambridge, MA: Harvard Business Press.

Heilman, M. E. (2012). Gender stereotypes and workplace bias. *Research in Organizational Behavior, 32,* 113–135. doi:10.1016/j.riob.2012.11.003

Heilman, M. E., & Haynes, M. C. (2008). Subjectivity in the appraisal process: A facilitator of gender bias in work settings. In E. Borgida & S. T. Fiske (Eds.), *Beyond common sense: Psychological science in court* (pp. 127–155). Oxford, UK: Blackwell.

Sexual Harassment

Sexual harassment at work is generally described by psychologists in terms of offensive, degrading, and/or harmful verbal or nonverbal behaviors that are of a sexual or gender-targeted nature. Various behaviors can be viewed as constituting sexual harassment. Examples include repeated requests for a romantic date despite rejection, belittling a person on the basis of his or her gender, and violent behaviors such as attempted or completed rape. While women are the more common victims of sexual harassment, men are occasionally harassed. In the cases of both female and male victims, men tend to be the most common perpetrators.

Sexual harassment is often viewed as a significant source of stress for victims. Indeed, victims can experience various psychological, physical, and/or behavioral problems, many of which can be problematic for organizations. Sexual harassment has received a considerable amount of attention in numerous countries by the media, by lawmakers, and by organizational researchers. Many organizations have instituted policies and practices intended to prevent such harassment and to provide support for their victims.

To better understand workplace sexual harassment, the following passages provide an overview of (a) various forms of sexual harassment and how they are commonly measured by organizational researchers; (b) sexual harassment and the law; (c) causes of sexual harassment; (d) consequences of sexual harassment; and (e) how sexual harassment compares to other types of aggression in the workplace.

Forms of Sexual Harassment and Their Measurement

Louise F. Fitzgerald and her colleagues have played a pivotal role in advancing our knowledge of the various behavioral manifestations of sexual harassment and how they can be measured. They have described three forms of sexual harassment: gender harassment, unwanted sexual attention, and sexual coercion.

Gender Harassment

Gender harassment refers to verbal and nonverbal behaviors not aimed at sexual cooperation but that convey insulting, hostile, and degrading attitudes toward a person's gender. Put otherwise, this form of sexual harassment constitutes putting someone down on the basis of his or her gender. Examples of such behaviors include making crude sexual remarks, displaying or distributing sexually offensive material, and making sexist comments.

Unwanted Sexual Attention

This form of sexual harassment denotes verbal and nonverbal behavior that is offensive, unwanted, and unreciprocated. Unwanted sexual attention is distinguishable from gender harassment in that it indicates an inappropriate and unwelcome come-on as opposed to a put-down.

Behaviors that may constitute unwanted sexual attention include attempts to discuss sex, leering, and repeated requests for drinks and/or dinner despite rejection, as well as physical behaviors such as touching someone in a way that makes him or her feel uncomfortable and attempting to stroke or fondle someone. Attempted or completed rape can be viewed as an extreme form of unwanted sexual attention.

Sexual Coercion

Sexual coercion is the extortion of sexual cooperation in return for job-related considerations, such as job security, promotions, and compensation (e.g., salary, bonuses). Behaviors exemplifying this form of sexual harassment include making subtle bribes, making subtle threats, and making a person afraid of poor job-related treatment if he or she does not agree to provide a sexual favor.

While gender harassment, unwanted sexual attention, and sexual coercion have been proposed as conceptually distinct forms of sexual harassment, they tend to be highly correlated because they often co-occur in the same organizational contexts. For example, victims of sexual coercion virtually always report having also experienced unwanted sexual attention and gender harassment in the same context.

Measuring Sexual Harassment

Fitzgerald and her colleagues have developed a questionnaire intended to measure how frequently employees believe they have been the target or victim of each of the three forms of sexual harassment described above. This questionnaire is titled the Sexual Experiences Questionnaire, or SEQ. When completing the questionnaire, individuals are presented with a series of statements (items) describing behaviors denoting each of the three forms of sexual harassment and are asked to rate the frequency with which they have been the target of such behaviors over a given time period. While the SEQ is arguably the most widely known and studied measure of sexual harassment, some have made efforts to refine it. For example, Jennifer Berdahl and Celia Moore's measure also asks respondents to evaluate their experiences in order to determine whether they were harassing and to what degree. This was done to ensure the measurement is more in keeping with the subjective conceptualization of sexual harassment as behavior that is judged as threatening and bothersome to the recipient.

Sexual Harassment and the Law

Various countries have laws in place intended to curb the occurrence of sexual harassment. For example, the United States, Canada, Australia, Denmark, Ireland, New Zealand, Sweden, and the United Kingdom have equal opportunity laws that address sexual harassment. As one illustration of the legal perspective on sexual harassment, the United States considers sexual harassment as a form of sex discrimination that violates Title VII of the Civil Rights Act of 1964. The legal definition of sexual harassment entails two types of sexual harassment, including quid pro quo and hostile work environment. Quid pro quo is equivalent to the notion of sexual coercion described above. Hostile work environment involves sex-related conduct that is frequent or severe enough to unreasonably interfere with a person's work performance or create an intimidating, hostile, or offensive work environment. A person is considered to have experienced sexual harassment if the sex-related behavior meets the requirements for either quid pro quo or hostile work environment. Legally defined as such, there is the potential for all three forms of sexual harassment described by Fitzgerald and colleagues to be legally recognized as unlawful sexual harassment.

According to the Equal Employment Opportunity Commission (EEOC), sexual harassment can occur in a variety of circumstances, including but not limited to the following: (a) The victim as well as the harasser may be a woman or a man. The victim does not have to be of the opposite sex; (b) the harasser can be the victim's supervisor, an agent of the employer, a supervisor in another area, a coworker, or a nonemployee; (c) the victim does not have to be the person harassed but could be anyone affected by the offensive conduct; (d) unlawful sexual harassment may occur without economic injury to or discharge of the victim; and (e) the harasser's conduct must be unwelcome. The EEOC also notes that it is helpful for the victim to inform the offender that the conduct is unwelcome and must stop. The victim should use any employer complaint mechanism or grievance system available.

When investigating allegations of sexual harassment, the EEOC considers the circumstances, such as the nature of the sexual advances, and the context in which the alleged incidents occurred. A determination on the allegations is made from the facts on a case-by-case basis. Unfortunately, it is often very difficult to prove that sexual harassment has taken place, especially if no objective evidence is provided. Moreover, many victims feel that making a formal complaint could be worse than saying nothing at all. Not surprisingly, many victims choose not to make formal accusations. Considering the challenges associated with the legal pursuit of sexual harassers, as well as the interests of potential victims and of their employing organization (the organization can suffer financially from a tarnished reputation, poor employee morale, and having to pay damages), it is clearly desirable to prevent the occurrence of sexual harassment. Knowing the likely causes of sexual harassment provides a road map for such prevention.

Causes of Sexual Harassment

Situational Causes

Many organizations have implemented policies or practices intended to curb the occurrence of sexual harassment. Some research suggests that these policies may be beneficial. For instance, female as well as male employees are more likely to experience sexual harassment when they perceive their organization as more tolerant of sexual harassment. Clearly communicating and applying policies against sexual offenders would likely give people the impression that sexual harassment is not tolerated. Also, male employees are less likely to sexually harass women when they believe that such behavior would be punished by their organization.

Another situational factor that has been studied is the extent to which the workplace is dominated by one gender. For example, some research shows that female employees are more likely to report having been sexually harassed in work contexts that are male dominated.

Harasser Characteristics

Research on harasser characteristics has focused largely on male harassers. For example, some work has investigated men's likelihood to sexually harass (LSH), which refers to their readiness to use social power for sexually exploitative purposes. High LSH men seem to have a particular profile, such as being prone to sexual violence (e.g., expressing a likelihood to rape), cognitively linking social dominance with sexuality, subscribing to traditional male sex-role stereotypes, having negative and hostile attitudes toward women, and having highly authoritarian personalities. There is some evidence showing that high (vs. low) LSH men are more likely to engage in different forms of sexually harassing behavior. There is also evidence suggesting that men are more likely to sexually harass women when they have had more sexual experience, have been the victims of childhood sexual abuse, and hold beliefs regarding the sexual harassment of women that tend to blame the victim.

Harasser Goals

Some work has cast doubt over the notion that sexual harassment is fundamentally driven by sexual desire. Instead, such behavior seems to be at least partially driven by the goal to protect one's social identity or status. As an illustration, men seem more likely to engage in sexually coercive behavior with a woman who threatens their masculinity. Similarly, women with relatively more masculine personalities (assertive, dominant, and independent) seem to be more frequently sexually harassed than women with personality traits more in keeping with feminine ideals.

Consequences of Sexual Harassment

Sexual harassment has often been conceptualized by psychologists as a significant source of stress for targets. Thus, much of the research investigating potential consequences of sexual harassment has tested whether targets of sexual harassment experience greater psychological, physical, and behavioral manifestations of stress, many of which can be problematic for the effective functioning of organizations.

Psychological Consequences

Studies show that the more people report having experienced sexual harassment, the more they are likely to report reduced job satisfaction (a commonly measured work attitude), reduced commitment to the organization, reduced satisfaction with life in general, and increased psychological distress (e.g., anxiety, depression, fear, and hopelessness about the future). It is also possible for victims to psychologically avoid feelings of stress by denying (to themselves and to others) that harassment ever took place.

Physical Consequences

Research suggests that the more people report having been sexually harassed at work, the more they are likely to complain of physical ailments such as severe headaches, shortness of breath, and feeling exhausted for no apparent reason. Such ailments are likely a response to the stress experienced by being harassed.

Behavioral Consequences

Employees who have experienced sexual harassment are more likely to neglect their job tasks, be absent from work, and feel a desire to quit their job. These types of behaviors and behavioral intentions potentially exemplify how some targets of sexual harassment choose to avoid the context in which the stressful event occurred, namely their job and/or organization. Other behavioral responses to sexual harassment can be exhibited by victims, such as confronting the offender directly (relatively rare), socially coping (i.e., getting support from colleagues, friends, and/or family members), and advocacy seeking (i.e., bringing the alleged harassment to the attention of organizational authorities). Unfortunately, few victims ever seek such advocacy out of fear of individual or organizational retaliation, which may explain why organizational policies intended to reduce sexual harassment are not always very effective.

Consequences for the Observers of Sexual Harassment

Some research suggests that observing (but not being the direct target of) sexual harassment can be harmful. For example, observing someone else in the work group being the target of sexual harassment seems to increase symptoms of occupational stress and the desire to withdraw from the organization. Moreover, such indirect exposure to sexual harassment seems to exacerbate the negative effects of being directly subjected to sexual harassment.

Sexual Harassment and Other Types of Aggression at Work

Much of the research on workplace sexual harassment has progressed independently from research on other types of aggressive behavior at work, such as general incivility or nonsexual bullying. Some scholars have recently argued that sexual harassment is but one among many types of workplace aggression. Despite their conceptual similarities, relatively little is known about how sexual and nonsexual types of workplace aggression differ in terms of their causes or consequences. Reviews of studies investigating nonviolent forms of workplace aggression revealed that nonsexual aggression more often than not shares a stronger relationship with various indicators of stress than does sexual harassment. There are various possible reasons why the negative outcomes of nonsexual aggression seem stronger in magnitude than those of sexual harassment. One of them may be because victims of sexual harassment seem more likely than victims of nonsexual workplace aggression to depersonalize their mistreatment and attribute blame to the perpetrator or to the perpetrator's attitudes toward their gender.

Laurent M. Lapierre

See also Abusive Supervision; Counterproductive Work Behaviors; Sexual Discrimination

Further Readings

Berdahl, J. L., & Moore, C. (2006). Workplace harassment: Double jeopardy for minority women. *Journal of Applied Psychology*, 91(2), 426–436.

Dekker, I., & Barling, J. (1998). Personal and organizational predictors of workplace sexual harassment of women by men. *Journal of Occupational Health Psychology*, 3(1), 7–18.

Fitzgerald, L. F., Drasgow, F., Hulin, C. L., Gelfand, M. J., & Magley, V. J. (1997). Antecedents and consequences of sexual harassment in organizations: A test of an integrated model. *Journal of Applied Psychology*, 82(4), 578–589.

Fitzgerald, L. F., Gelfand, M. J., & Drasgow, F. (1995). Measuring sexual harassment: Theoretical and psychometric advances. *Basic and Applied Social Psychology*, 17(4), 425–445.

Lapierre, L. M., Spector, P. E., & Leck, J. D. (2005). Sexual versus non-sexual workplace aggression and victims' overall job satisfaction: A meta-analysis. *Journal of Occupational Health Psychology*, 10(2), 155–169.

Maas, A., Cadinu, M., Guarnieri, G., & Grasselli, A. (2003). Sexual harassment under identity threat: The computer harassment paradigm. *Journal of Personality and Social Psychology*, 85(5), 853–870.

O'Leary-Kelly, A. M., Bowes-Sperry, L., Bates, C. A., & Lean, E. R. (2009). Sexual harassment at work: A decade (plus) of progress. *Journal of Management*, 35(3), 503–536.

Willness, C. R., Steel, P., & Lee, K. (2007). A meta-analysis of the antecedents and consequences of workplace sexual harassment. *Personnel Psychology*, 60(1), 127–162.

SHARED LEADERSHIP

Shared team leadership represents a mutual influence process carried out by members of a team where they lead each other toward the achievement of goals. It is characterized as collective team leadership by team members and involves collaborative decision making and shared responsibility for outcomes. Shared leadership is viewed as an emergent leadership process that can be contrasted with the traditional hierarchical, or vertical, approach to leading teams. Typically, hierarchical leadership is a top-down process that is engaged by a formally designated team leader who is ultimately responsible for decision making and accountable for team outcomes. In contrast, shared leadership describes an informal influence process that develops over time among the members of a team who take it upon themselves to lead each other, to contribute to decision making, and to be accountable for team outcomes.

A number of similar terms have been used to refer to the phenomenon of "shared leadership," such as *peer leadership*, *collective leadership*, *co-leadership*, *distributive* or *distributed leadership*, and *collaborative leadership*. Typically, these terms have been used interchangeably; all refer to a collective form of leadership influence involving multiple individuals, within or across different individuals or organizational units. As such, leadership can be shared among the members of a group (within-group leadership) or exceeding the boundaries of a work group or team (between-group leadership).

The idea of shared leadership was first mentioned in 1924 by Mary Parker Follett, who stated that leadership could arise from particular individuals with the most relevant skills in a particular situation. In the 1950s, during an era when the notion of teams and teamwork in organizations was growing in importance, shared leadership was seen as a collective leadership phenomenon. Since that time, shared leadership has been recognized in most of the major epochs of leadership research. For example, some of the early group research found that in contrast to the norm of hierarchical leadership, two or more informal leaders often emerge in leaderless groups, such as one focused on the group task and one concentrating on relational issues.

Shared Leadership as a Group Process

Shared leadership describes a collective team leadership phenomenon, where multiple individuals lead themselves and others toward the accomplishment of one or more team goals. Shared leadership and its application to team-based work structures has received increased attention over the past decade due to, in large part, the widespread adoption of team-based work structures in organizations. The leadership of teams, in contrast to the management of traditional and individual work arrangements, has presented new challenges to management. This is particularly true regarding virtual teams composed of highly skilled employees and knowledge workers, whose tasks are complex and highly interdependent, and who are able to engage in high levels of coordination and required to integrate and share their knowledge

and expertise. Shared leadership requires all team members to be capable of, and willing to engage in, leadership functions and leadership roles.

Various conceptualizations have been proposed for shared leadership, but there are a few consistent themes. A common notion is that this leadership approach represents a group or team process. For example, shared leadership is defined as an emergent team property that results across multiple team members and that can significantly impact team and organizational performance. In addition, shared leadership is generally characterized by the spreading or natural dissemination of leadership to all team members, rather than to only a few of the members. Shared leadership thus describes a team process where leadership is carried out by the team as a whole, rather than solely performed by a single designated individual. Beyond this, shared leadership can occur across different levels of the organization—that is, between and within units—and it could be shared among different team leaders or among the leaders and members of a team. While shared leadership usually takes place within the boundaries of a team or work group, it is possible that it exceeds the boundaries of a team and is shared across teams and work groups, within and beyond the boundaries of an organization. In the latter scenario, shared leadership is more frequently referred to as dispersed leadership.

Shared Leadership Versus Hierarchical (Vertical) Leadership

Shared leadership is different from classical hierarchical or vertical leadership. In hierarchical leadership, one individual is designated by the organization as a leader (such as of a project team), and he or she influences followers toward accomplishing goals. While a collective form of leadership, shared leadership is not mutually exclusive to other leadership forms and behaviors, but can be engaged in simultaneously with other approaches such as vertical leadership. Scholars have indicated that shared leadership is possible among team members, even when there also is a single designated leader. Multiple leadership actors and activities can occur at the same time—that is, simultaneously, sequentially, or reciprocally, and in dynamic interdependence—and leadership is not exclusive to vertical leadership behaviors. Furthermore, shared leadership does not mean that the distribution of leadership or influence among team members is necessarily equal among team members, in terms of leading their team, but that there is participation among team members rather than leadership solely from a single team leader.

Measuring Shared Leadership: Network Approach Versus Collective Leadership Behaviors

There is no "one best way" to measure shared leadership. Instead, it is important to note that different measurement approaches have been used to measure shared leadership. Some researchers have used a network-based approach and have investigated the distribution or "networks" of influence. That is, they assessed the distribution of leadership among team members, with the objective of understanding the role of influence among certain individuals in teams toward each other, the structure of networks (e.g., having more leaders is not always better), and the centrality of certain team members within the team. This approach assesses distributions of influence, or the rotating shift of different leadership roles, as well as simultaneous and sequential engagement of team members in team leadership behaviors. In this respect, different team members may engage in leadership behaviors, and their leadership may work together simultaneously or sequentially, in an additive or compensatory way, across the different stages of a project or the team life cycle.

Other researchers have addressed the collective engagement in traditional "vertical" team leadership behaviors. That is, they assess specific leadership behaviors that are performed collectively by the team. Shared leadership behaviors studied in this approach comprise a wide range of leadership behaviors, ranging from task- and person-oriented leadership (consideration and initiating structure) to transformational and transactional, empowering, and visionary leadership. Researchers using this approach typically have used questionnaires and surveys to assess collectively performed forms of vertical leadership. Some have argued that shared leadership is to be enacted in parallel with hierarchical leadership (i.e., using the same behavior as leaders).

Others have stated that team members do not need to perform the *same* kind of leadership behaviors as their supervisors. Instead, their leadership should build on, substitute, augment, or even complement hierarchical team leaders' leadership. Thus, multiple ways of measuring shared leadership are prevalent in the literature. Together, these various approaches allow for assessing different aspects of the shared leadership process.

Antecedents of Shared Leadership

Scholars have identified different categories of antecedents of shared leadership. One group of antecedents includes structural support factors that represent mechanisms an organization can implement to encourage the engagement of shared leadership behaviors in teams. Examples include reward systems (e.g., team-based rewards) and information management that promotes sharing of information needed to make decisions and provide feedback.

A second category of antecedents is vertical leadership behaviors, through which a formally designated team leader encourages the team members to engage in shared leadership. Scholars have noted certain hierarchical leadership behaviors that contributed to the development of shared leadership. For example, transformational leadership has a positive influence on shared leadership development through the development of a shared vision and shared goals as well as inspiring members to engage in extra-role behaviors, including shared leadership. Scholars also have found empowering leadership to encourage team members' shared leadership. Also, participative leadership is an important predictor of shared leadership, because it increases commitment to the team and team goals through proactive involvement by members in developing and defining their own team goals.

A third category of antecedents comprises team member characteristics. Understandably, personality traits, qualities, or characteristics of team members affect team members' willingness to engage in shared leadership. Scholars have found that team members are more prone to share leadership when they are higher in trust propensity, more collectivistic, and higher in self-management, all of which promote the willingness to share information, take the lead, and influence, which are important aspects of successful shared leadership. Furthermore, shared leadership is more likely to emerge in teams with more agreeable and conscientious members, and in teams with higher levels of emotional stability and extroversion. Finally, the capability, motivation, and willingness of members to share leadership roles are also included in this antecedent category.

Moderators and Boundary Conditions of Shared Leadership

There are several boundary conditions to the effectiveness of shared leadership. For example, scholars have found that shared leadership is more effective in tasks that are more complex and dynamic, and when tasks are more difficult. Task interdependence has been documented to further intensify the effectiveness of shared leadership, assumedly due to the increased need to collectively evaluate and exchange information, and to make complex decisions. Shared leadership also has been shown to be more effective in highly diverse teams, in its relationship to high levels of performance. Furthermore, shared leadership has been found to be particularly applicable and relevant in virtual or geographically dispersed teams and to compensate for vertical leadership challenges faced by those teams.

Outcomes of Shared Leadership

According to the input–process–output approach to teams, shared leadership is likely to influence outcomes. Scholars have documented that shared leadership is positively related to attitudinal, behavioral processes and emergent states, as well as subjective and objective performance outcomes. Furthermore, shared leadership has been found to lead to increases in the perception of team effectiveness by team managers, team members, and customers. It has been found to have positive effects on new venture, sales team, and complex software development team performance. Shared leadership has also been shown to be positively related to performance among U.S. Army light infantry platoons and in unionized production and manufacturing settings. Furthermore, scholars have documented that shared leadership has the capacity to positively impact outcomes at multiple levels of organizations, including organization-, team-, and individual-level outcomes, in various types of team and organization settings.

Conclusion

Shared leadership describes a collective influence process among team members that is directed toward the accomplishment of team goals. The use of team-based work forms has become widespread in today's organizations, and shared leadership has been viewed as a viable leadership form in team and group settings. A shared leadership approach holds the promise of addressing challenges related to the complexity and dynamic nature of these work arrangements, because of the limitations that exist from only having a solo, hierarchical leader. As more and more organizations adopt flatter and more team-based organizational structures, it is vital to understand the complex nature of the shared leadership process and how it enhances the effectiveness of organizational teams.

Julia E. Hoch

See also Group Development; Group Dynamics and Processes; Groups; Leadership and Supervision

Further Readings

Carson, J. B., Tesluk, P. E., & Marrone, J. A. (2007). Shared leadership in teams: An investigation of antecedent conditions and performance. *Academy of Management Journal, 50,* 1217–1234.

D'Innocenzo, L. D., Mathieu, J. E., & Kukenberger, M. R. (2014, March 10). A meta-analysis of different forms of shared leadership–team performance relations. *Journal of Management* [Published online before print]. doi:10.1177/0149206314525205

Gibb, C. A. (Ed.). (1954). *Leadership* (Vol. 2). Reading, MA: Addison-Wesley.

Hoch, J. E. (2013). Shared leadership and innovation: The role of vertical leadership and employee integrity. *Journal of Business and Psychology, 28,* 159–174.

Hoch, J. E., & Dulebohn, J. H. (2013). Shared leadership in enterprise resource planning and human resource management systems implementation. *Human Resource Management Review, 23,* 114–125.

Hoch, J. E., & Kozlowski, S. W. J. (2014). Leading virtual teams: Hierarchical leadership, structural supports, and shared team leadership. *Journal of Applied Psychology, 99,* 390–403.

Pearce, C. L., & Conger, J. A. (2003). *Shared leadership: Reframing the how's and why's of leadership.* Thousand Oaks, CA: Sage.

Van Nicolaides, C., LaPort, K. A., Chen, T. R., Tomassetti, A. J., Weis, E. J., Zaccaro, S. J., & Cortina, J. M. (2014). The shared leadership of teams: A meta-analysis of proximal, distal, and moderating relationships. *Leadership Quarterly, 25,* 923–942.

Wang, D., Waldman, D. A., & Zhang, Z. (2014). A meta-analysis of shared leadership and team effectiveness. *Journal of Applied Psychology, 99,* 181–198.

SHIFT WORK

Shift work is a term used to describe an arrangement of working hours that differs from the standard daylight working hours (i.e., 8:00 a.m. to 5:00 p.m.). Organizations that adopt shift work schedules extend their normal working hours beyond the traditional 8-hour shifts by using successive teams of workers. Notable examples of organizations that adopt shift work schedules include hospitals, fire stations, and police stations. However, forces such as industrialization, new technologies, and the increasing global economy have contributed to the creation of a society that operates 24 hours a day. This 24-hour society has led to an increase in the need for shift work. In fact, it is currently estimated that 15% to 30% of all workers in industrialized societies are involved in some type of shift work. Although shift work remains more common in certain occupations (e.g., process-control industries, emergency services, and transport), the growth of shift work systems is expected to continue at a rapid pace.

The types of shift work systems that organizations adopt differ on a wide array of characteristics, such as the number and length of shifts. For example, one organization may adopt two 12-hour shifts, whereas another may adopt three 8-hour shifts. Shift work systems can also differ in the direction and speed of shift rotation. Shift systems that rotate employee schedules from morning shifts to evening shifts to night shifts have a forward rotation, whereas shifts that rotate counterclockwise (i.e., night to evening to morning) have a backward rotation. With regard to the speed of rotation, shift systems fall into three major categories: (1) permanent shift systems (e.g., permanent night shift); (2) slowly rotating shift systems (e.g., weekly rotating); and (3) rapidly rotating shift systems (e.g., an employee works the morning shift on Monday, the evening shift on Tuesday and Wednesday, and the night shift on Thursday and Friday).

A recent review of shift systems produced five general recommendations regarding the design of shift work systems. First, it seems that night work should be reduced as much as possible; however, if this is not possible, an organization should adopt a rapidly rotating system. Second, long shifts (e.g., 9 to 12 hours) should be avoided. Third, flexible work arrangements should be integrated with shift systems. Fourth, shift changes within the same day should be avoided, and the number of consecutive days worked should be limited. The final recommendation suggests that forward rotation is most preferable.

Although shift systems remain highly popular with employees on the front end because they seem to provide a degree of flexibility, research investigating shift work has found that such schedules have primarily negative effects for both individuals and organizations. The problems associated with shift systems fall into three broad categories: disturbance of circadian rhythms, physical and psychological ill health, and social and domestic disruption.

Disturbance of Circadian Rhythms

A great deal of research has investigated the impact of shift work on individual circadian rhythms. In general, humans have evolved over thousands of years as a species that habitually sleeps during the night and is awake during the day. The rotation of the Earth around the sun creates a 24-hour cycle of light and dark, which is internalized by humans and forms a natural internal body clock. All human circadian rhythms normally show a fixed-phase relationship. For example, body temperature peaks around 8:00 p.m., and all other circadian rhythms reach their maximum at the appropriate time, allowing us to eventually fall asleep at night.

Problems occur for shift workers as a result of the mismatch between environmental time cues and the internal timing system. Although the natural light–dark cycle, the clock time, and other social cues may remain the same, the timing of shift workers' work and sleep is delayed. Evidence suggests that adjustments to the shift workers' body clock are slow, if they occur at all. This mismatch between the environment and the internal body clock has been linked to negative outcomes such as sleep deprivation.

Psychological and Physical Ill Health

Most of the early work on the psychological outcomes of shift work focused on the exploration of shift workers' attitudes, such as job satisfaction. This research suggests that, in general, although workers welcome the idea of shift systems up front, they are typically less satisfied with their work than non–shift workers and thus have higher turnover.

Additionally, the research generally shows that psychological and emotional distress accompanies shift work; however, these results are mixed. Although some studies failed to find any psychological differences between shift workers and non–shift workers, one recent study found that shift work influenced depression through work-to-family conflict. Thus, in general, though evidence suggests that shift workers are generally less satisfied with their jobs, the results with respect to other emotional and psychological outcomes, such as depression, are inconclusive.

Much more research has explored the physical consequences of shift work. Research has found sleep to be extremely disrupted by shift work. In general, many bodily functions are at their highest level of activity during the day. Thus, it is often difficult for individuals to sleep during the day because they are attempting to sleep at a time that is not natural for their circadian rhythm. The most prominent outcome of this lack of quality sleep is chronic fatigue.

Chronic fatigue is linked with greater incidence of physical injury. In general, a greater number of serious job-related injuries occur among employees who work night shifts. Additionally, night shift workers are more likely to be involved in automobile accidents on the drive home from work than day shift workers. Thus, the increased risk of injury seems clear. However, several potential confounds must be considered—for example, night

shift workers are often less experienced and work with less supervision.

By far, the most prevalent health complaint associated with shift work is gastrointestinal problems. According to a recent study, 20% to 75% of night and shift workers complain of gastrointestinal problems such as irregular bowel movements and constipation, compared with 10% to 25% of non–shift workers. Although some research has found no difference between day and shift workers in gastrointestinal disease, the consensus is that these types of disorders are more prevalent in shift- and night-working populations. One explanation for the increase is that shift workers have less regular eating schedules and may have less access to healthful foods.

The relationship between cardiovascular disease and shift work has also been explored. Though there has been much debate, recent studies all seem to support a relationship between shift work and cardiovascular disease. Many characteristics of shift workers are considered predictors of cardiovascular disease (e.g., poor eating habits, gastrointestinal disorders, sleeping disorders, and less favorable working conditions). Thus, the risk of cardiovascular disease should be a concern for shift workers.

Aside from chronic fatigue, injury, digestive disorders, and cardiovascular disease, shift work has additionally been shown to have negative effects on the reproductive cycle of women (e.g., increased menstrual pain and lower rates of pregnancy) and to influence drug activity and effectiveness. The latter point suggests that persistent shift or night work may be incompatible with the efficacious treatment of disease.

Social and Domestic Disruption

In addition to the psychological and physical effects, shift work is related to several social and domestic variables. For example, although organizations may believe that it is advantageous to operate on a 24-hour schedule, estimates place the cost of shift work among U.S. companies at $70 billion per year. Research has shown higher rates of absenteeism and turnover among shift-working populations. Thus, the $70 billion cost results in part from lost productivity because of absenteeism and higher medical bills because of increased injury and accidents. Not only are many of these job-related accidents harmful to the company and dangerous for the worker, but also these careless accidents can have detrimental societal consequences. Additionally, shift work is associated with a decreased ability to balance work and non-work responsibilities. In fact, divorce rates for shift workers are up to 60% higher than those for day workers.

Individual Differences and Social Support

Several individual difference variables have been shown to be important to the relationship between shift work schedules and outcomes. Several of these individual difference variables involve individual circadian types. For example, morningness, or a preference for going to bed early and rising early in the morning, is moderately associated with difficulty adjusting to night work. Additionally, sleep flexibility (i.e., the ability to sleep at unusual times) and vigor (i.e., the ability to overcome drowsiness) predict an individual's level of tolerance for shift work.

In addition to differences in circadian type, age and personality are frequently investigated individual differences. With regard to age, the older an employee is, the less tolerance he or she will have for shift work. Over the age of 50, it becomes increasingly difficult for individuals to alter their sleep–wake cycles. In addition, many physical ailments increase with advancing age, and this increase in physical problems affects older individuals' ability to adjust to shift work. In general, it is recommended that shift work be voluntary after the age of 40. With regard to personality, it has been found that introverts are generally more morning oriented than extroverts, making it more difficult for them to adjust to shift work. Neuroticism has also been linked to lower levels of shift work tolerance. However, some evidence suggests that neuroticism is an outcome of prolonged shift work exposure. Thus, the exact role that neuroticism plays in shift work tolerance is not yet understood.

Another individual difference variable that has been explored is the amount of social support an individual experiences. In general, results suggest that supervisor support is extremely important in buffering the negative effects of work stress, and the positive effects of support seem to be particularly important for shift workers. Thus, it is extremely important to encourage supervisors to take an active interest in the well-being of their shift workers.

Summary

Research suggests that shift work has negative effects for individuals, organizations, and society. These effects are many and serious. However, this does not mean that shift work should be abandoned. For many organizations, shift work is a necessity. These organizations need to understand not only how individual differences affect shift work tolerance but also, perhaps more importantly, how to design a shift work system that is minimally detrimental to employees. Although some research has been conducted, researchers should focus their attention on designing optimal shift work systems.

Boris B. Baltes and Kevin Wynne

See also Flexible Work Schedules

Further Readings

Costa, G. (1996). The impact of shift and night work on health. *Applied Ergonomics*, 27(1), 9–16. doi:10.1016/0003-6870(95)00047-X

Haines, V. Y., Marchand, A., Rousseau, V., & Demers, A. (2008). The mediating role of work-to-family conflict in the relationship between shiftwork and depression. *Work & Stress: An International Journal of Work, Health & Organizations*, 22(4), 341–356. doi:10.1080/02678370802564272

Knauth, P. (1996). Designing better shift systems. *Applied Ergonomics*, 27(1), 39–44. doi:10.1016/0003-6870(95)00044-5

Martin, J. E., Sinclair, R. R., Lelchook, A. M., Wittmer, J., & Charles, K. E. (2012). Non-standard work schedules and retention in the entry-level hourly workforce. *Journal of Occupational and Organizational Psychology*, 85(1), 1–22. doi:10.1348/096317910X526803

Parkes, K. R. (2003). Shiftwork and environment as interactive predictors of work perceptions. *Journal of Occupational Health Psychology*, 8(4), 266–281. doi:10.1037/1076-8998.8.4.266

Schmieder, R. A., & Smith, C. S. (1996). Moderating effects of social support in shiftworking and non-shiftworking nurses. *Work and Stress, 10*(2), 128–140. doi:10.1080/02678379608256792

Smith, C. S., Folkard, S., & Fuller, J. A. (2003). *Shiftwork and working hours.* In J. C. Quick & L. E. Tetrick (Eds.), *Handbook of occupational health psychology* (pp. 163–183). Washington, DC: American Psychological Association.

Sparks, K., Cooper, C., Fried, Y., & Shirom, A. (1997). The effects of hours of work on health: A meta-analytic review. *Journal of Occupational Health Psychology, 70*(4), 391–408. doi:10.1111/j.2044-8325.1997.tb00656.x

Taylor, E., Briner, R. B., & Folkard, S. (1997). Models of shiftwork and health: An examination of the influence of stress on shiftwork theory. *Human Factors, 39*(1), 67–82. doi:10.1518/001872097778940713

SIMULATION, COMPUTER APPROACH

The word *simulation* refers to any procedure that is meant to imitate a real-life system. Simulations are especially useful in examining situations that are too complex, too difficult, or too costly to explore in the real world. The computer is often used for this purpose because it is able to efficiently model systems and process data. The phrase *computer simulation* is a broad rubric for a range of different types of methodologies; the following are their general forms.

Monte Carlo Simulation

In a Monte Carlo simulation, values for uncertain variables are generated by the computer to reproduce information found in the real world. Named for the city of Monte Carlo, Monaco (where the primary attractions are games of chance at gambling casinos), a Monte Carlo simulation generates data pseudorandomly to explore hypothesized models. Much like the random behavior in games of chance, a Monte Carlo simulation selects values at random to simulate a variable. For example, when you roll a die, you know that a number from *1* to *6* will come up, but you don't know what number will come up for any particular roll. In much the same way, a Monte Carlo simulation works by first defining the possible values that simulated data can take as the same values found

in the real world and then using that definition to generate random numbers. In this way, any number of variables that have a known range of values but an uncertain value for any particular time or event (e.g., interest rates, staffing needs, stock prices, inventory, or phone calls per minute) can be generated and used to test hypothetical models or relationships. In a typical Monte Carlo simulation, behavioral processes are entirely simulated by the computer.

Microworld Simulation

Microworld simulations have a higher level of realism. Microworld simulations are complex, computer-generated situations used in controlled experiments that are designed to study decision making. Microworld simulations represent a compromise between experimental control and realism and enable researchers to conduct experimental research within a dynamic, complex decision-making situation. In a typical microworld simulation, the situation is generated with a moderate degree of fidelity, and behavioral processes are examined as humans navigate through it. The simulation is typically only unidimensional—that is, participants are instructed to make decisions that are cognitively complex but that do not invoke a range of senses (e.g., visual, aural, olfactory, tactile, and proprioceptive).

Virtual Reality Simulation

At the most realistic level, a virtual reality (VR) simulation is defined as a computer-simulated, multisensory environment in which a perceiver—the user of the VR computer technology—experiences *telepresence.* Telepresence is defined as feeling present in an environment that is generated by a communication medium such as a computer. In the context of VR, telepresence occurs when the VR user loses awareness of being present at the site of the human–computer interface and instead feels present or fully immersed in the VR environment. Thus, a successful VR simulation reproduces the experience of reality with a high degree of accuracy so that behavioral processes can be examined as humans navigate through the simulated environment. The simulation is typically multidimensional—that is, the best VR simulations attempt to invoke the full range of participants' senses (i.e., visual, aural, olfactory, tactile, and proprioceptive).

Simulation Games

Traci Sitzmann in 2011 coined the term *simulation games* to mean "instruction delivered via personal computer that immerses trainees in a decision-making exercise in an artificial environment in order to learn the consequences of their decisions" (p. 490). Simulation games and microworlds are similar in that they attempt to model reality with a similar degree of moderate fidelity. The two forms of computer-based simulation differ in their purpose. Specifically, microworlds are primarily designed to study decision-making processes; simulation games are designed to instruct individuals on how to make optimal decisions. Other key features of simulation games are that they are competitive, interactive, engaging, goal focused, and rule governed.

Examples From the Literature

Computer simulations have been used to explore a multitude of real-world situations. What follows are a number of examples, broken down by simulation type, that may help to make the exposition more concrete.

Monte Carlo Simulations

Monte Carlo simulations have been used to investigate such phenomena as faking on personality inventories, the effect of forced distribution rating systems on workforce potential, adverse impact in selection, statistical properties of various indices, and withdrawal behaviors, to name just a few.

Microworld Simulations

Microworld simulations have been used to study a number of situations, including a sugar production factory, a fire chief's job, a beer game, and a water production plant. These microworlds vary along four dimensions: (1) dynamics—that is, the system's state at time t depends on the state of the system at time $t - 1$; (2) complexity, or the degree to which the parts interconnect, making it difficult to understand or predict system behavior;

(3) opaqueness, or the invisibility of some parts of the system; and (4) dynamic complexity, or the effect of feedback structures on a decision maker's ability to control a dynamic system.

VR Simulations

VR simulations have been used to create virtual environments to assess large-scale spatial abilities, to model responses to a fire, and to prepare trainees for job experiences that normally would have high costs (e.g., flying an airplane), the risk of costly damage to equipment (e.g., landing a plane on an aircraft carrier), or the potential for injuries to the trainee (e.g., training in a race car).

Simulation Games

Simulation games have been used to instruct players on how to run a hotel kitchen, serve customers in an ice cream shop, better understand corporate benefit plans, teach copy machine repairs, and run a human resource department, to name just a few.

Advantages and Disadvantages of Computer Simulations

There are trade-offs with any methodology. The major advantage of computer simulations is that they are particularly well adapted for situations in which it would be difficult, because of cost, safety, or validity, to examine a particular phenomenon in a real-life situation. With a computer simulation, any one of a number of naturally occurring parameters can be manipulated in a controlled laboratory setting many times without endangering participants, spending large sums of money, or resorting to correction formulas for participants who drop out.

The major disadvantage of computer simulations is their lack of external generalizability—that is, the degree to which the results of the computer simulation apply to actual situations and behavior in real life. However, external generalizability can be enhanced in several ways:

- When conducting Monte Carlo studies and designing microworlds, choose parameter estimates sensibly (e.g., from prior empirical studies).

- When conducting VR simulations, ensure that VR environments invoke maximal vividness and interactivity.
- When designing simulation games, ensure that the rules governing the game and the consequences resulting from player choices model the real world as accurately as possible.

Chet Robie and Shawn Komar

See also Human–Computer Interaction; Judgment and Decision-Making Process; Quasi-Experimental Designs; Virtual Organizations; Virtual Teams

Further Readings

Gamberini, L., Cottone, P., Spagnolli, A., Varotto, D., & Mantovani, G. (2003). Responding to a fire emergency in a virtual environment: Different pattern of actions for different situations. *Ergonomics, 46*(8), 842–858. doi:10.1080/0014013031000111266

Gonzalez, C., Vanyukov, P., & Martin, M. K. (2005). The use of microworlds to study dynamic decision making. *Computers in Human Behavior, 21*(2), 273–286. doi:10.1016/j.chb.2004.02.014

Scullen, S. E., Bergey, P. K., & Aiman-Smith, L. (2005). Forced distribution rating systems and the improvement of workforce potential: A baseline simulation. *Personnel Psychology, 58*(1), 1–32. doi:10.1111/j.1744-6570.2005.00361.x

Seitz, S. T., Hulin, C. L., & Hanisch, K. A. (2000). Simulating withdrawal behaviors in work organizations: An example of a virtual society. *Nonlinear Dynamics, Psychology, and Life Sciences, 4*(1), 33–65. doi:10.1023/A:1009515928602

Sitzmann, T. (2011). A meta-analytic examination of computer-based simulation games. *Personnel Psychology, 64*(2), 489–528. doi:10.1111/j.1744-6570.2011.01190.x

Waller, D. (2005). The WALKABOUT: Using virtual environments to assess large-scale spatial abilities. *Computers in Human Behavior, 21*(2), 243–253. doi:10.1016/j.chb.2004.02.022

SITUATIONAL APPROACH TO LEADERSHIP

The situational approach to leadership asserts that there is no one best way to lead others and emphasizes that the style and behavior of the leader should depend on the characteristics of followers. Specifically, the situational approach to leadership model provides leaders with insight regarding the most effective leadership style to demonstrate based on the readiness of the followers. This approach contends that a leader will elicit maximum performance from followers when the leader's behaviors are tailored to the followers' ability, willingness, and level of confidence.

Known previously as the life cycle of leadership theory and situational leadership theory, the situational approach to leadership has been revised several times, and the terminology has been modified with each revision.

Research examining the behavioral approach to leadership has demonstrated that leaders engage in both directive and supportive behaviors (also recognized as task and relationship behaviors):

- *Directive behavior.* One-way communication clearly explaining each needed detail to the follower to ensure the completion of the task
- *Supportive behavior.* Two-way communication with an interpersonal focus, which demonstrates the leaders' desire to build and maintain relationships

The situational approach to leadership suggests that effective leaders practice both directive and supportive behaviors, yet their use depends on the developmental level of their followers (previously termed maturity).

Follower Development Level

There are two follower factors, which comprise the follower development level. The first is competence. It asks the question, "Do you have the skills and knowledge to successfully complete the task?" The second determinant, commitment, asks, "Does the follower possess the motivation and self-assurance to successfully complete the task?"

- *Competence.* Learned job-related abilities, knowledge, and skills gained from education and/or experience (earlier versions of the model referred to this as job maturity)
- *Commitment.* Motivation and self-confidence (earlier versions of the model referred to this as psychological maturity)

The combination of competence and commitment is divided into four categories, indicating the four levels of development (D1–D4) the follower possesses:

D1. Not committed and not competent; not developed or developing

D2. Committed but not competent; low to moderate development

D3. Not committed but competent; moderate to high development

D4. Committed and competent; developed

When the follower's developmental level is determined, an appropriate leadership style can be identified. The four leadership styles include directing, coaching, supporting, and delegating.

Leadership Styles

Directing (Telling)

The directing leadership style (S1), previously referred to as telling, is utilized when the lowest development level (D1) is representative of the follower's development level. The directing style of leadership involves relaying information to the follower in a very clear, specific manner. The directing style primarily consists of one-way, top-down communication. The follower's roles and assigned tasks are explicitly and specifically stated so that the follower is clear about how, where, and when to do the tasks. In the directing style, the leader solves the problems and makes the decisions.

For example, the directing leadership style is appropriate when a new engineering graduate (follower) walks into the office on her first day. The new employee has a foundation of engineering principles from the classroom setting, but she is unaware of the practices and principles under which her new employer operates. If her boss (leader) directs her on what to work on and when, her performance will increase because she has the requisite skills to do the tasks, but she probably does not know what needs to be done.

The directing style is also appropriate in extreme situations requiring rapid decision making and action. For instance, a leader of an electrical power line maintenance crew who sees lightning nearby is likely to tell his crew to descend from the electrical poles immediately and without question.

Coaching (Selling)

The coaching leadership style (S2), previously referred to as selling, is linked with the second level of development (D2). Within this leadership style, the leader's supportive behavior increases to a higher level, allowing two-way communication, and directive behaviors remain high. The leader still provides much of the direction for the follower, but the leader listens to the follower and allows the follower to grasp and understand the explanations and reasoning behind the leader's decisions. In the S2 leadership style, final decisions are still made by the leader.

For example, a track coach (leader) provides detailed instruction to a novice hurdle jumper (follower). The coach explains how to jump hurdles and provides encouragement to the jumper. The jumper begins running down the track and clears three out of five hurdles. The coach praises the jumper for jumping the three hurdles, and the jumper asks the coach for further guidance on how to improve (i.e., clear all five hurdles). The jumper is developing both the competence and commitment to jump and improve her abilities. Her performance will increase as the coach continues to encourage and support her efforts, while providing guidance and direction on how to perform the task more effectively.

Supporting (Participating)

The supporting leadership style (S3), previously referred to as participating, is practiced when the third phase of development (D3) is reached. The leadership style is low directive behavior, but the supportive behaviors remain high. In this stage, the leader and follower engage in two-way communication and joint decision making. The leader's words and actions need to be encouraging and convey support for the follower's decisions to help facilitate confidence and motivation in the follower.

Take, for instance, a skilled and well-trained nurse (follower) with years of experience. The nurse understands what tasks and duties need to be performed on a daily basis, and stays abreast of current medicines and treatments. The nursing supervisor (leader) does not need to tell the nurse what to do in a step-by-step manner; in fact, such actions would likely be perceived negatively by the nurse. However, as the nurse completes his daily activities, the nurse will need to inform his supervisor of the patients he has seen and their ailments. The nurse will also need the supervisor's input on decisions and the supervisor's support. The nurse has the skills and training to perform the job, but may at times feel unsure of the decisions he is making to treat his patients. Therefore, the nurse's performance will increase if the leader actively listens to the nurse, while encouraging and praising the nurse's work.

Delegating

The final leadership style, delegating (S4), is adopted when the follower is both committed and competent (D4). Within the delegating style, leaders remove themselves even further, which results in low directive behaviors and low supportive behaviors. The follower is now at a developmental stage that enables autonomy and requires only general supervision from the leader. The leader has little need to provide support because the follower is confident and motivated to take on the responsibility of the assigned tasks. This leadership style is appropriate for "peak performers."

An illustration of the appropriate use of the delegating leadership style is a follower who has worked in the marketing field for over 20 years and has continually landed projects leading to substantial profits for the company. She does not need a leader who tells her what to do; she already knows the processes and required tasks. She has the skills and abilities to do the job. She possesses the willingness and confidence to take initiative. Supporting behaviors from her boss (leader) may not decrease her performance on the job, but she requires only minimal support. Her performance will increase if her boss delegates projects to her, while keeping her apprised of organizational goals and the big picture. Her boss should be available for consultation and should praise and reward her successes.

Extensions and Applications of the Model

The situational approach to leadership offers some general suggestions relating to a leader's span of control (the number of followers the leader is responsible for supervising). Specifically, the model advises that the number of direct reports a leader can effectively lead is a function of the development level of the individual followers. That is, the span of control of a leader who is supervising followers at the D4 level can be larger than a leader who is managing a group of people who are all at the D1 level.

In the 1980s, Blanchard founded Blanchard Training and Development and proposed a revised model, Situational Leadership II (SL2). While many of the changes appear to be cosmetic, SL2 did redefine follower readiness levels 1 (high on commitment and low on competence) and 2 (some competence but low commitment). The model has also been extended and applied to the leadership of work groups and teams. In this application, the readiness of the group or team is determined by the alignment of the followers toward a common goal. A group in the forming stage is at the D1 level, a group in the storming stage is at the D2 level, a group at the norming stage is at the D3 level, and a group at the performing stage is at the D4 level. The leadership styles (S1—defining, S2—clarifying, S3—involving, and S4—empowering) in this group-level adaptation of the model are analogous to those previously described.

Measures and Uses

The situational leadership model is a training model intended to enhance leader–follower communications. The training provides the leader with the information needed to adapt to various situations leaders and their followers may encounter. Research has offered limited support for the original model and no support for SL2; thus, while the model generally lacks empirical evidence, it is one of the most frequently used training models for leadership in corporate America. The most current instruments used to measure competence and commitment (the *manager rating scale* and the *staff rating scale*) originated from the Center for Leadership Studies; however, Blanchard and colleagues offer alternative measures for the SL2 model.

Mark C. Frame and Michael B. Hein

See also Leadership Development; Situational Approach to Leadership; Situational Leadership Theory

Further Readings

Blanchard, K. H., Zigarmi, D., & Nelson, R. B. (1993). Situational leadership after 25 years: A retrospective. *The Journal of Leadership Studies*, 1(1), 22–36.

Blanchard, K. H., Zigarmi, P., & Zigarmi, D. (1985). *Leadership and the one minute manager: Increasing effectiveness through situational leadership*. New York, NY: Morrow.

Graeff, C. L. (1997). Evolution of situational theory: A critical review. *Leadership Quarterly*, 8(2), 153–170.

Hersey, P., & Blanchard, K. H. (1982). *Management of organizational behavior: Utilizing human resources* (3rd ed.). Englewood Cliffs, NJ: Prentice Hall.

Hersey, P., & Blanchard, K. H. (1996). *Management of organization behavior: Utilizing human resources* (7th ed.). Upper Saddle River, NJ: Prentice Hall.

Thompson, G., & Glaso, L. (2015). Situational leadership theory: A test from three perspectives. *Leadership and Organizational Development Journal*, 36(5), 527–544.

Thompson, G., & Vecchio, R. P. (2009). Situational leadership theory: A test of three versions. *The Leadership Quarterly*, 20, 837–848.

Vecchio, R. P. (1987). Situational leadership theory: An examination of a perspective theory. *Journal of Applied Psychology*, 72(3), 444–451.

SITUATIONAL JUDGMENT TESTS

Many work situations require the job incumbent to make a judgment about aspects of the situation and respond to the practical situational demands. An effective response to the practical demands of a situation may require the appropriate use of some combination of one's abilities and other personal attributes. Situational judgment tests (SJTs) are psychometric tests that are specifically designed to assess individual differences in this overall ability to make effective judgments or responses to a wide variety of situations.

SJTs are typically administered in a paper-and-pencil mode, although they may be implemented in other modes, such as video-based items and interview questions. The SJT is made up of several situations, each presenting a hypothetical but realistic critical incident and several possible courses of action in response to the situation. The instructional and response format is dependent on the specific SJT. In many SJTs, respondents are required to rate each possible course of action on a 5-point effectiveness scale or indicate the best and worst action among the alternatives provided. In other SJTs, respondents are asked to rate each possible action in terms of the likelihood that they would adopt it or indicate their most likely and least likely actions among the possible actions provided.

Unlike many established cognitive ability and personality measures, which may be acquired "off-the-shelf" for valid use in many job settings, the SJT to be used in a personnel selection or employee development context typically has to be tailor-made for the job or work situation in question. This is partly because the SJT is defined by its test method rather than test content. This is opposite to cognitive ability and personality measures, which are tests defined by their test content representing specific a priori intended test constructs (i.e., cognitive ability or personality traits).

Development of SJTs

Most modern versions of SJTs derive from the work of Stephen Motowidlo and his colleagues, which builds on Robert Sternberg's concept of *tacit knowledge* (i.e., job-relevant knowledge needed to accomplish everyday tasks that are usually not openly stated or part of any formal instruction) and improves the measurement of the concept by using job analyses to identify the types of judgments made on a specific job and to improve their content and face validity. The development process usually involves the identification of a set of work-related constructs that are targeted in an SJT. Job incumbents are asked to generate critical incidents or situations that require ability or expertise related to these constructs. Other job incumbents provide a set of possible actions that could be taken to resolve or improve the situations, and a third group, usually subject-matter experts, provides effectiveness ratings of each solution and judgments about the best and worst of the solutions. These ratings and judgments are analyzed and used to develop a final item and scoring key that is applied to the items. (Detailed examples of the SJT development process are provided in the references listed in Further Readings.)

Probably as a result of the job-relevant features of the test development process, studies have shown that respondents tend to have more favorable perceptions of SJTs compared with other types of employment tests, such as cognitive ability and personality measures, because they believe the tests are relevant to work situations and valid in predicting job performance. In addition to the evidence on the face validity of SJTs, there is increasing evidence that SJTs can produce substantial zero-order and incremental criterion-related validities. Although the literature and database on SJTs are not as extensive as those available on cognitive ability and personality measures, the empirical evidence on SJTs has been steadily increasing. However, the theoretical or conceptual underpinnings of SJTs remain much less understood as compared to cognitive ability and personality measures.

Criterion-Related Validity of SJTs

In a meta-analysis of the criterion-related validities of SJTs, Michael McDaniel and his colleagues found that the average observed validity of 102 validity coefficients was .26, a figure that increased to .34 when it was corrected for criterion unreliability. However, there was substantial unexplained variability (55%) in coefficients around this population value, suggesting that the validity of an SJT is likely to be moderated by many variables. Moderator analyses indicated that measures developed as the result of job analyses yield larger validity coefficients than those that are not based on job analyses, but the results of other moderator analyses were inconclusive because of the small number of studies or small total sample size in one or more of the groups of studies formed by the moderator variable.

Several primary studies involving employees in a wide variety of jobs conducted since Motowidlo et al. revived interest in the SJT method have produced validities similar to the averages reported by McDaniel et al. In addition, several studies found that SJTs produce validity increments (in predicting job performance) over cognitive ability, personality, job knowledge, and experience measures.

The criterion-related validity of SJTs in predicting performance seems well established. Although SJTs appear to be related to cognitive ability and, in some studies, to personality measures as well, incremental validity of SJTs over and above personality and cognitive ability has been reported in multiple studies. The substantial variability in correlations may result because different constructs are being measured depending on the types of situations included on the SJT. When the situations require cognitive-based constructs such as planning, organizational ability, and analytical problem solving, SJT scores correlate highly with cognitive ability test scores compared with situations that require constructs associated with interpersonal or leadership skills, for example, which are more personality based.

SJTs tend to have lower adverse impact by gender and ethnicity, as compared to cognitive ability tests. However, the level of adverse impact may vary considerably depending on the nature of the test content in the specific SJT and even the mode (e.g., paper-and-pencil vs. video-based) in which the SJT is administered.

Construct Validity of SJTs

In contrast to the emerging evidence on the criterion-related validity of SJTs, there is much less research on the construct validity of SJTs. The bulk of the studies on SJTs are not explicitly designed to examine the nature of the constructs assessed by SJTs, and therefore the construct validity evidence available to date is indirect, at best. The constructs underlying SJTs are likely related to the concepts of adaptability, contextual job knowledge, and practical intelligence, but the precise nature of the test constructs is inextricably tied to the specific content of the SJT items.

Efforts to conduct factor analysis on SJT items typically produce little support for a priori factors that researchers have tried to incorporate into their items. The first factor in these analyses usually accounts for two to three times the variance of the second factor, but unless the scale comprises a large number of items, internal consistency (coefficient alpha) reliabilities are typically low. One explanation for these results is that responses to a single SJT item with its varied options may be the result of a variety of individual difference constructs, including both ability and motivational or personality constructs. This is consistent with empirical findings indicating that SJTs are correlated with a variety of variables, including cognitive ability and personality traits.

Given the nature of SJTs and the extant research findings, it is unlikely that SJTs measure any single unidimensional construct, even though it may be legitimate to use an overall SJT score to represent the composite (multifaceted) ability or effectiveness in situational judgment. Like interviews and many paper-and-pencil tests, SJTs may be better construed as a method of measurement that can be adapted to measure a variety of job-related constructs in different situations. However, some types of situational judgment constructs are almost inherently assessed in typical SJTs. That is, SJTs may be construed as a method of testing that constrains the range of constructs measured.

Like the interview, SJTs have dominant constructs (although they are different in nature from those in the interview method) that are readily or almost inherently assessed. Primary dominant constructs include *adaptability constructs*, which are likely a function of both individual difference traits and acquisition through previous experiences, and *contextual knowledge constructs*, which may be gained through experience in real-world contexts. Collectively, these SJT-dominant constructs can be represented by the global construct called *practical intelligence*. However, unlike the interview, SJT-dominant constructs are not associated with the structural format of the SJT (i.e., candidates are presented with a problem situation followed by the requirement to generate, endorse, or rate a series of response options). Instead, the dominant constructs are associated with the core characteristics of the test content of typical SJTs.

The details of these construct validity issues are beyond the scope of this entry. Interested readers may refer to works by David Chan and Neal Schmitt, which elaborate on three distinct but interrelated core characteristics of SJT content (i.e., practical situational demands, multidimensionality of situational response, and criterion-correspondent sampling of situations and response options in test content development) and relate them to SJT performance as well as job performance (including both the "can do" and "will do" aspects of performance). Chan also provided construct validity evidence for SJTs as measures of practical intelligence constructs by demonstrating that higher levels of proactive personality and tolerance for contradiction are adaptive when SJT scores are high but maladaptive when SJT scores are low.

There is emerging evidence on the face validity and criterion-related validity of SJTs, but studies that directly address the fundamental issue of construct validity are lacking. Research on the construct validity of SJTs could help to identify the boundary conditions for the criterion-related validity of SJTs. Such research would also clarify the SJT constructs and increase our understanding of the nature of SJT responses and their relationship to job performance and other work-relevant variables. Finally, the increased conceptual clarity would increase the scientific defensibility of the increasing use of SJTs in personnel selection and employee development.

David Chan

See also Critical Incident Technique; Practical Intelligence; Selection Strategies; Validity

Further Readings

Chan, D. (2004). Individual differences in tolerance for contradiction. *Human Performance*, 17(3), 297–325. doi:10.1207/s15327043hup1703_3

Chan, D. (2006). Interactive effects of situational judgment effectiveness and proactive personality on work perceptions and work outcomes. *Journal of Applied Psychology*, 91(2), 475–481. doi:10.1037/0021-9010.91.2.475

Chan, D. (2014). Emerging themes in adaptability research. In D. Chan (Ed.), *Individual adaptability to changes at work: New directions in research* (pp. 177–192). New York, NY: Routledge.

Chan, D., & Schmitt, N. (1997). Video-based versus paper-and-pencil method of assessment in situational judgment tests: Subgroup differences in test performance and face validity perceptions. *Journal of Applied Psychology*, 82(1), 143–159. doi:10.1037/0021-9010.82.1.143

Chan, D., & Schmitt, N. (2002). Situational judgment and job performance. *Human Performance*, 15(3), 233–254. doi:10.1207/s15327043hup1503_01

Chan, D., & Schmitt, N. (2005). Situational judgment tests. In A. Evers, O. Smit-Voskuijl, & N. Anderson (Eds.), *Handbook of personnel selection* (pp. 219–242). Oxford, UK: Blackwell.

Libbrecht, N., & Lievens, F. (2012). Validity evidence for the situational judgment paradigm in emotional intelligence measurement. *International Journal of Psychology*, 47(6), 438–447. doi:10.1080/00207594.2012.682063

Lievens, F., & Chan, D. (2010). Practical intelligence, emotional intelligence, and social intelligence. In J. L. Farr & N. T. Tippins (Eds.), *Handbook of employee selection* (pp. 339–355). New York, NY: Routledge.

Lievens, F., Peeters, H., & Schollaert, E. (2008). Situational judgment tests: A review of recent research. *Personnel Review*, 37(4), 426–441. doi:10.1108/00483480810877598

McDaniel, M. A., Morgeson, F. P., Finnegan, E. B., Campion, M. A., & Braverman, E. P. (2001). Use of situational judgment tests to predict job performance: A clarification of the literature. *Journal of Applied Psychology*, 86(4), 730–740. doi:10.1037/0021-9010.86.4.730

Motowidlo, S. J., Dunnette, M. D., & Carter, G. W. (1990). An alternative selection procedure: The low-fidelity simulation. *Journal of Applied Psychology*, 75(6), 640–647. doi:10.1037/0021-9010.75.6.640

Schmitt, N., & Chan, D. (2014). Adapting to rapid changes at work: Definitions, measures, and research. In D. Chan (Ed.), *Individual adaptability to changes at work: New directions in research* (pp. 3–17). New York, NY: Routledge.

Weekley, J. A., & Jones, C. (1999). Further studies of situational tests. *Personnel Psychology*, 52(3), 679–700. doi:10.1111/j.1744-6570.1999.tb00176.x

SITUATIONAL LEADERSHIP THEORY

The situational leadership (SL) theory, developed by Paul Hersey and Ken Blanchard, is one of the most widely known frameworks for explaining managerial effectiveness. Although the framework is particularly popular among practicing managers and professional trainers, it has not enjoyed comparable attention from the academic community of industrial and organizational researchers. Nonetheless, the theory is recognized among researchers for its intuitive appeal, though it is not considered a clearly valid or robust framework for the prescription of leader behavior.

Situational leadership theory continues to tie in with other contemporary views of what makes for effective supervision. For example, three contemporary workplace perspectives are completely in accord with SL's essential principles: (1) Self-directed work teams (a popular performance-enhancement technique) advocate that supervision should be minimal when employees are sufficiently capable of being self-directed; (2) employee competence and dedication or professionalism can be viewed as potent substitutes for leadership; and (3) leaders need to be both socially intelligent and flexible in their behavior.

In relation to other perspectives on leadership, SL theory is often viewed as one of several situational models that arose during the 1960s and 1970s. As part of a trend toward incorporating situational elements into explanations of leader effectiveness, the theory's appeal was driven by dissatisfaction with earlier paradigmatic approaches that emphasized leader traits and leader behaviors to the exclusion of situational attributes. This theory also builds on earlier behavioral (or stylistic) approaches in that it includes a prevalent perspective wherein leadership is conceptualized along two independent dimensions: leader consideration and leader initiation of structure. The theory is novel, however, in its attempt to specify which combination of leader behaviors along these two dimensions is optimal in light of follower maturity. Within this theory, follower maturity is most often defined as a combination of the ability to perform a task and the willingness (or commitment and motivation) to accomplish a task.

SL theory was first introduced in 1969 as the "life cycle theory of leadership." In the revised later version, Hersey and Blanchard provided a thorough description of the theoretical foundation for the original version of their model. This version presented SL theory's principles for dealing with newer employees with greater directiveness, and then substituting directiveness with supportiveness as employee seniority increased. At the highest levels of follower maturity, the need for both leader structuring and social supportiveness declines further, such that at the highest levels of follower maturity, leader structuring and consideration are irrelevant to follower performance. Based partly on feedback from managers and critiques of SL theory from researchers, SL theory has emerged most recently as a restated set of prescriptive principles. In this newer version of SL theory, termed *situational leadership theory II* (SLT II), Blanchard has modified the interaction between directive and supportive leader behavior and follower competence and commitment. Specifically, four levels of follower development and their corresponding alternative optimal styles of leadership are outlined: (1) Followers, low on competence but high on commitment, will benefit from directing behavior, which is low leader consideration combined with high leader structuring. (2) Followers, low on competence to having some competence in combination with low commitment, will benefit from coaching behavior, which is high leader consideration combined with high leader structuring. (3) Followers, who are moderate to high on competence but show variable commitment, will benefit from supportive behavior, which is high leader consideration combined with low leader structuring. (4) Followers, high on both competence and commitment, will benefit from delegating behavior, which is low leader consideration combined with low leader structuring. This transitioning of prescribed leader style can be summarized as moving from directing to coaching, to supporting, and, ultimately, to delegating (along a prescriptive curve).

The theory's intuitive appeal lies in its simplicity, as well as the self-evident correctness that is attendant to human (especially child) development. Consider that one would not attempt to handle a class of first graders in the same fashion as one would attempt to handle eighth graders, high school students, or college students. Clearly, one would be engaging in more telling at the lowest level of maturity and, ideally, far more delegating at the college (especially the graduate) level. The model is also appealing to military leadership training because raw recruits undergo a transformation as they gain ability and commitment. Because we all vary our own behaviors based on circumstances and expect to be treated differently based on self-perceived efficacy, the model's proposed dynamic is inherently enticing. The model is broadly attractive because it focuses on managerial dynamics rather than true leadership, which can be vested in any group member and typically refers to some form of incremental influence beyond one's nominal position or headship. Hence, the model offers practical guidance to people who find themselves in positions of responsibility (who may have little interest in the subtleties of a variety of alternative models of leadership that are long on evidence of aggregate correlational associations but short on specific advice as to how to relate to individual employees).

An empirical demonstration of the validity of the model's core tenet (the value of leader adaptability)

is desirable. However, a variety of obstacles have impeded progress in studying the model in a rigorous fashion. First, the model is embedded in a training package that includes (along with training videos, worksheets, puzzles, games, and practice activities) a preferred instrument for assessing leader style. Although theoretical ties to the Ohio State University measures of consideration and initiating structure are evident, the instruments that are recommended for assessing a leader's personal style may not possess comparable psychometric merit. Additionally, the definition and measurement of employee maturity, a key construct, requires further development.

Despite these problems, empirical studies of SL theory's most essential social dynamic have been attempted, yielding a mixed pattern of results. One study of 303 teachers in 14 high schools found support for the model's predictions for low-maturity subordinates (i.e., followers who were low in competence and commitment performed better with supervisors who were high on structuring but low on consideration) and for moderate-maturity subordinates (i.e., moderate structuring combined with higher considerateness was optimal). However, no support was found for high-maturity subordinates. In a replication of this study with a sample of nurses, similar directional (but nonsignificant) support was found for the earlier findings. In a further replication and extension of this line of research, 332 university employees and 32 supervisors were studied. The authors tested the suggestion that the model may be valid from an across-jobs perspective (in which norms govern how subordinates expect to be treated by a supervisor based on their competency and commitment) rather than a within-jobs perspective. Yet the results continue to suggest that the original model has limited descriptive utility. However, further analyses have indicated that supervisory monitoring and consideration interact with job level such that monitoring has a positive impact for lower-level employees, whereas considerateness has a more positive impact for higher-level employees. This suggests that the model's most central and intuitively appealing aspect may be correct, whereas specific predictions based on follower maturity may be incorrect. In a related study of 1,137 employees across three organizations, it was found that employees with higher levels of education and greater levels of job tenure express less preference for supervisory structuring.

This suggests that an understanding of employee expectations of supervisor behavior may be valuable in optimizing the level and nature of supervisory involvement with subordinates.

Although more than 4 decades have passed since the exposition of SL theory, evidence of the theory's descriptive accuracy is sparse. Particularly, assessment of follower competence and commitment poses several problems for testing the validity of SL theory mainly due to ambiguity surrounding the conceptual definition of follower competence and commitment. Previous studies have used peer rating, self-appraisals, or supervisor rating of followers' development level. In addition, objective indices and follower job level have been suggested as surrogates of development level without obtaining strong support for SL theory. However, recently conducted studies on SLT II, where leaders and followers from various business settings participated, have applied a leader–follower congruence approach (measuring the degree of agreement between leader ratings of follower competence and commitment and follower self-ratings), which has proven to be a promising avenue for future research. It seems SLT II's predictions are more likely to hold when leader assessment and follower self-assessment of competence and commitment are congruent. This finding may change the approach for testing the validity of the theory. A leader–follower congruence approach may constitute a future avenue for research on SLT II, and suggest that SL theory continues to be a promising approach to understanding leadership.

Robert P. Vecchio and Geir Thompson

See also Leadership and Supervision; Situational Approach to Leadership

Further Readings

Blanchard, K. H. (2010). *Leading at a higher level.* Upper Saddle River, NJ: Prentice Hall.

Blanchard, K. H., Zigarmi, D., & Nelson, R. B. (1993). Situational leadership after 23 years: A retrospective. *Journal of Leadership Studies, 1,* 22–36.

Fernandez, C. F., & Vecchio, R. P. (1997). Situational leadership theory revisited: A test of an across-jobs perspective. *Leadership Quarterly, 8,* 67–84.

Hersey, P., & Blanchard, K. (1969). Life-cycle theory of leadership. *Training and Development Journal, 23,* 26–34.

Hersey, P., Blanchard, K., & Johnson, D. E. (2001). *Management of organizational behavior: Leading human resources* (8th ed.). Englewood Cliffs, NJ: Prentice Hall.

Norris, W. R., & Vecchio, R. P. (1992). Situational leadership theory: A replication. *Group and Organization Management, 17,* 331–342.

Thompson, G., & Glasø, L. (2015). Situational leadership theory: A test from three perspectives. *Journal of Leadership and Organizational Studies, 36,* 527–544.

Thompson, G., & Vecchio, R. P. (2009). Situational leadership theory: A test of three versions. *Leadership Quarterly, 20,* 837–848.

Vecchio, R. P., & Boatwright, K. J. (2002). Preferences for idealized styles of supervision. *Leadership Quarterly, 13,* 327–342.

SMITH, PATRICIA C.: SECOND RECIPIENT, SIOP DISTINGUISHED SCIENTIFIC CONTRIBUTIONS AWARD

Patricia Cain Smith was born in Minneapolis, Minnesota, on October 28, 1917, moving with her family to Nebraska shortly thereafter. She persevered through a difficult childhood, including many relocations because of her father's (often failing) business ventures, being ostracized for her family's liberal/socialist leanings, and the suicide of the father she adored when she was 15. And perhaps because of these challenges, Smith focused on her studies in school (graduating as valedictorian of her small graduating class) and at home (learning about gambling odds and how to perform "lightning calculations"). Her unorthodox parents provided vocational programming that would guide her career: a keen interest in both numbers and people, the values of hard work and accountability, and the uncanny ability to seize opportunities in any situation.

Smith entered the University of Nebraska in 1935, graduating with a degree in mathematics and psychology in 1939. She began her graduate studies in experimental psychology at Northwestern University and transferred to Bryn Mawr College. Although she thoroughly enjoyed the insights that came from psychological experimentation, her interests shifted from basic psychology to applied psychology when she moved to Cornell University to work under T. A. Ryan in the area of industrial and business psychology. She completed her PhD at Cornell in 1942 with a major in industrial psychology and a minor in experimental psychology and neurology, completing her dissertation on the topic of industrial monotony and boredom (which would become her first publication in 1953). In that same year she married a fellow graduate student, Olin Smith. As her husband headed off to the Army, Smith headed off to work in industry. She received three encouraging replies to more than 250 letters of inquiry and accepted an 18-month internship with Aetna Life and Affiliated Companies. There, under the direction of industrial and organizational (I-O) psychologist Marion Bills, she learned personnel psychology and the professional skills for women to work successfully with senior management. Smith then went to work at Kurt Salmon Associates, where she was given almost unlimited opportunity to market and apply the principles and practices of industrial psychology in the areas of selection, placement, and training as well as her beginning interest in job attitudes. In the next 4 years, Smith supervised the implementation of nearly 100 new personnel departments throughout the country (in 1 year, she traveled more than 100,000 air miles; First Lady Eleanor Roosevelt was the only woman who flew more miles that year).

Her husband's discharge from the military and the exhausting lifestyle of full-time national consulting led Smith to explore—and only very briefly—a more traditional role as homemaker while continuing as part-time research director at Salmon and Associates. As her husband resumed his doctoral studies at Cornell University, Smith quickly accepted opportunities to teach part-time at Ithaca College and Wells College, which led to a summer appointment at Cornell University that turned into an academic year appointment as assistant professor. In Smith's own words, "My period of attempted domesticity was terminated" (Smith, 1988, p. 143). Smith was promoted to associate professor in 1954 and full professor in 1963. Smith would later learn that she was the first woman to be granted tenure in the endowed schools at Cornell, the first woman to be accepted as a graduate faculty member in those schools, and the first woman to be promoted to full professor. In 1966, Smith left to join the growing doctoral program in I-O psychology at Bowling Green State University,

a coup for the director of that program, Robert Guion, who was on his way to becoming an exceptionally accomplished I-O psychologist. Smith retired from Bowling Green in 1980 but remained active in research until her death in 2007.

The Career of Patricia Cain Smith

Smith's academic background and professional experiences resulted in several unifying beliefs that guided her significant contributions to I-O psychology. First, replicable and generalizable research demanded accurate measurement. Second, research must be grounded in theory and be relevant, applying general psychology, individual differences, psychophysics, scaling, measurement, and research methods to solve practical issues that employees and employers face. Third, researchers should identify the areas of research they wish to pursue, and be ready and flexible to pursue them whenever the opportunity arises. Smith's seminal contributions in the areas of monotony, job satisfaction, and behaviorally anchored rating scales flowed naturally from her strategy: "Rather than following a grand research plan, I merely bore in mind several problems needing research and watched for opportunities to study them" (Smith, 1988, p. 145). Olin Smith, her then fiancé, introduced Smith to the owner of a garment factory, who allowed her to closely observe work and interview the workers to gather both objective and perceptual data on short-cycled work tasks. Smith published the first studies in monotony, identifying the importance of individually set goals in determining output and that subjective feelings of monotony, although not common, were a function of both the individual and the situation. Subsequent opportunities arose in which Smith and her student were able to experimentally manipulate batch size and demonstrate the more general finding that task design has a major impact on employee job attitudes.

Smith and her team of students at Cornell (including Chuck Hulin and Ed Locke, who would themselves have distinguished careers) were ready when Smith took on a consulting project to study the impact of retirement age policy, including the attitudes of retirees and future retirees (i.e., current employees). The carefully designed studies with careful measurement and scaling and examining multiple factors including individual differences, task characteristics, and the context of the work resulted in the development of the Job Descriptive Index and accompanying national norms, which became the gold standard for the measurement of job satisfaction around the world. Her 1969 book *The Measurement of Satisfaction in Work and Retirement* became a critically acclaimed model for conducting field research in applied psychology, and Smith and her colleagues published numerous articles and chapters that further developed additional measurement instruments and advanced the field's understanding of the causes, consequences, and measurement of job attitudes.

Smith's consulting project with the National League for Nursing to evaluate different programs for improving nursing practices provided the opportunity to follow up on concerns that both job performance and selection interview ratings were unreliable and invalid because of global first impressions. Her 1963 article with Lorne Kendall describing the development of what came to be known as Behaviorally Anchored Rating Scales provided helpful guidance on scale construction (including the practical educational benefit of rater participation in identifying and scaling work behaviors) and greatly influenced scale development efforts in I-O psychology. This remains a frequently cited article, and the technique continues to be used in applied settings for research as well as job performance.

In addition to these three research efforts, which had a significant impact on shaping further research efforts and best practices in workplace psychology, Smith also influenced the field in her 1954 book with T. A. Ryan *Principles of Industrial Psychology*, her 1968 *Annual Review of Psychology* chapter with C. J. Cranny "The Psychology of Men at Work," and her 1976 chapter in the *Handbook of Industrial and Organizational Psychology*, "Behaviors, Results, and Organizational Effectiveness: The Problem of Criteria." Several other publications were particular points of pride for Smith. These include her 1986 "guidelines" for cleaning research data to avoid common mistakes, which were developed over years of experience; her 1992 chapter in which she presented her ongoing understanding of the construct of job satisfaction; and her 1998 article with Stanton that synthesizes her insights from more than 50 years of research and consulting on job attitudes into very practical themes and recommendations for

integrating research results into theory and practice. Smith received the 1984 Distinguished Scientific Contributions Award from the Society of Industrial and Organizational Psychology for her career's work on the study and practice of psychology in the workplace.

Patricia Cain Smith was a devoted scholar, teacher, mentor, and friend. All of her pursuits were done with insight, thoroughness, and humor. To use her own words, "Remember that psychology can be great fun.... The joy is particularly great if it can be shared."

William K. Balzer and Bonnie A. Sandman

See also Boredom at Work; Criterion Theory; Job Satisfaction Measurement; Rating Errors and Perceptual Biases

Further Readings

Ryan, T. A., & Smith, P. C. (1954). *Principles of industrial psychology*. New York: Ronald Press.

Smith, P. C. (1976). Behavior, results, and organizational effectiveness: The problem of criteria. In M. Dunnette (Ed.), *Handbook of industrial and organizational psychology*. Chicago: Rand McNally.

Smith, P. C. (1988). Patricia Cain Smith. In A. N. O'Connell & N. F. Russo (Eds.), *Models of achievement: Reflections of eminent women in psychology*. Hillsdale, NJ: Lawrence Erlbaum.

Smith, P. C. (1992). Why study general job satisfaction? In C. J. Cranny, P. C. Smith, & E. F. Stone (Eds.), *Job satisfaction: How people feel about their jobs and how it affects their performance*. New York: Lexington.

Smith, P. C., Budzeika, K. A., Edwards, N. A., Johnson, S. M., & Bearse, L. N. (1986). Guidelines for clean data: Detection of common mistakes. *Journal of Applied Psychology, 71,* 457–460.

Smith, P. C., & Cranny, C. J. (1968). The psychology of men at work. *Annual Review of Psychology, 19,* 467–497.

Smith, P. C., & Kendall, L. M. (1963). Retranslation of expectations: An approach to the construction of unambiguous anchors for rating scales. *Journal of Applied Psychology, 47,* 149–155.

Smith, P. C., Kendall, L. M., & Hulin, C. L. (1969). *The measurement of satisfaction in work and retirement*. Chicago: Rand McNally.

Smith, P. C., & Stanton, J. M. (1998). Perspectives on the measurement of job attitudes: The long view. *Human Resources Management Review, 8,* 367–386.